Public Policy Toward Retailing

An International Symposium

Edited by

J. J. BODDEWYN
Graduate School of Business Administration
New York University

and

STANLEY C. HOLLANDER
Graduate School of Business Administration
Michigan State University

Lexington Books
D.C. Heath and Company
Lexington, Massachusetts
Toronto   London

309
B666p

Library of Congress Cataloging in Publication Data

Boddewyn, Jean J.
  Public policy toward retailing.

  Includes bibliographical references.
  1. Retail trade—Addresses, essays, lectures. 2. Retail trade—Law and legislation—Addresses, essays, lectures. 3. Commercial policy—Addresses, essays, lectures. I. Hollander, Stanley C., 1919-   joint author. II. Title.
HF5429.B57   309   72-5330
ISBN 0-669-73296-6

Published simultaneously in Canada.

Printed in the United States of America.

International Standard Book Number: 0-669-73296-6

Library of Congress Catalog Card Number: 72-5330

Contents

List of Tables

Public Policy Toward Retailing:
An International Symposium

1 Introduction

J. J. BODDEWYN AND STANLEY C. HOLLANDER

There is something paradoxical about public policy toward retailing as found around the world. On the one hand, most national economic plans give little or no attention to the retail trades, or for that matter, to other significant elements of marketing,[1] and few public officials would claim that their countries have a specific policy regarding retailing. On the other, all governments are inevitably concerned with many aspects of retailing and have developed more or less explicit, coherent, and consistent policies toward the retail trades.

This paradox helps explain why the retailing-public policy interface has not been studied in anywhere near the degree that is needed. A number of excellent studies are available, but most of these are primarily one-country analyses, and many concentrate upon relatively narrow segments of policy and/or retailing.[2] Besides, studies undertaken in other languages are more or less inaccessible to English-speaking scholars. Hence, this volume attempts to convey an idea of the range of policies toward retailing in some twenty countries, of the major environmental and institutional variables accounting for these variations, and of their ultimate results.

Conceptual Framework

"Public policy" refers to deliberate action taken by the various parts of a government in pursuit of certain *objectives*. This action takes the form of particular *instruments* which have definite *effects* in the face of current *forces*.[3] Hence, the study of public policy deals not only with its contents, but also with its making and application.

"Retailing" concerns the selling and physical distribution of goods and services to ultimate consumers. It can be analyzed in terms of *actors* connected in relationship *structures*, and interacting in activity *processes* (buying and selling, promoting, pricing, storing, etc.) that result in various economic and non-economic *functions* or contributions. Retailing systems are found in various *environments*, that is, in countries at different stages of economic development, with different types of political regimes and social structures, and under different value systems.[4]

Public policy may or may not deal with these various interrelated dimensions of the retailing systems. However, the following outline provides a fairly comprehensive analytical framework of the retail features affected in whole or in part by public policy.

1

I. *Actors*

    A. Areas of retailing (commodities, locations, etc.) reserved to the state or public authority, and areas available to private enterprise

    B. Other restrictions on entry and stay

        1. Limits on number of entrants and practitioners, including limits on total number of licenses, mandatory spatial separation between similar outlets, etc.

        2. Personal requirements for entry and stay

            a. Nationality, birth, or ethnic requirements
            b. Education, apprenticeship, experiential or examination requirements
            c. Other requirements: character references, sponsorship, minimum capitalization, military service, etc.

        3. Organizational requirements or limitations on entry and stay, e.g., restrictions on corporations

        4. Mandatory reservation of shopping centers or other retail space for particular types of retailers, e.g., for small merchants

    C. Encouragement of entry and stay

        1. Publicly-provided education and training

        2. Subsidization

            a. Low-cost land sales or rentals
            b. Tax relief
            c. Import privileges
            d. Low-cost or guaranteed financing
            e. Other forms

    D. Restrictions on growth

II. *Structure*

    A. Enforced atomism and competition

        1. Anti-trust and anti-cartel legislation

        2. Restrictions on store and firm size

B. Control or encouragement of horizontal ties among retailers

1. Statutory trade associations

2. Mandatory and permitted cartels

C. Control or encouragement of vertical relationships (cf. III E 3)

1. Prohibition, control, or encouragement of vertical integration

2. Regulations affecting "dual distribution" marketing programs, i.e., programs in which manufacturers (or wholesalers) who own some retail outlets compete with their own independent retailer customers in selling to ultimate consumers

3. Control of relationships with non-consuming participants in the final-purchase decision-process (e.g., control of relationships between pharmacists and physicians)

D. Control or modification or relationships between retailer-types (i.e., Palamountain's "intertype competition": the rival relationships of retailers of different size, operating method, or original commodity allegiance)

Note: Intertype competition is often controlled by regulation of actors (category I above) or of process (category III below). However, as is well known, this type of competition is often a primary source of friction and thus deserves special attention.

E. Control or encouragement of inter-sectorial relationships

1. Retailer representation and influence in statutory industrial, economic, planning, and consultative bodies

2. Encouragement or discouragement of factor-utilization in retailing vis-à-vis other sectors (e.g., encouragement or restraints upon employment in retail trades)

3. Mandatory or encouraged relationships with consumer groups

III. *Process*

A. Prohibition, restriction, or encouragement of particular operating methods (or types of business) such as mail-order sales, canvassing (house-to-house selling), and street vending

B. Location

1. Zoning and land-use ordinances

2. Shopping precinct development

3. Legislation or common-law precedents giving merchants vested interest in current locations

C. Plant and facilities

   1. Public provision of store buildings, parking facilities, access roads, etc.

   2. Requirements concerning facilities and equipment

D. Operations

   1. Hours legislation, including both mandatory closing hours, and Sunday (or similar) closing requirements

   2. Employee training

   3. Labor relations

   4. Permitted or prohibited actions for protection against shoplifting and other theft

E. Merchandising (selection and purchase of goods for resale)

   1. Mandatory merchandise lines

   2. Prohibited merchandise combinations

   3. Control of vendor relations

      a. Acts permitted or prohibited to retailers, e.g., solicitation of discriminatory prices or allowances
      b. Acts permitted or prohibited to vendors, e.g., arbitrary termination of dealer franchises

   4. Labeling

   5. Display requirements and restrictions

   6. Rationing arrangements, including restriction of rationed commodities to certain types of outlets, and plans that require consumers to register with particular or specified stores to obtain rationed items

7.   Controls over sales dates (freshness of products) and food ingredients

F.   Promotion

    1.   Limitations of competitive promotion, price advertising, etc.

    2.   Retailer access to government-controlled advertising media

G.   Pricing controls

    1.   Mandatory maximum or minimum prices

    2.   Resale price maintenance (individual and collective)

    3.   Prohibited price discriminations

    4.   Price-posting laws

    5.   Trading stamp, prize, and premium legislation

H.   Bookkeeping, finance, and taxation

    1.   Mandatory language for books of account and records (sometimes used as an ethnic control)

    2.   Restrictions on credit practices (minimum down-payment, maximum interest rates, number of installments, etc.)

    3.   Taxation

I.   Post-transactional services

    1.   Required warranty and repair services

    2.   Mandatory customer options for merchandise return or for cancellation of purchase contract

J.   Market and operational research

    1.   Census studies

    2.   Accumulation and dissemination of retail operating statistics such as operating-cost averages

    3.   Technical studies

4. Government-operated or subsidized management consulting services for retailers

IV. *Functions* (Anticipated and/or Real Contributions of Retailing)

A. Fulfillment of private consumption demands

1. Preservation and satisfaction of present consumption patterns

2. Improvement or change in private consumption patterns

B. Maintaining and/or improving the utilization and allocation of productive factors

1. Providing a desirable level and pattern of labor utilization

   a. Retail employment under conditions of over- and under-employment
   b. Retailing's function as a training ground for entrepreneurship
   c. Ethnic-group employment functions

2. Providing desirable levels and patterns of utilization for other factors, including land-use patterns

3. Stimulating and/or providing outlets for increased production

C. Other macro-economic functions that may be ascribed (in part) to retailing

1. Helping to stabilize or change price levels

2. Helping to balance international payments

D. Socio-cultural and miscellaneous functions

1. Contributions to socio-cultural development, analagous to the role of merchants in community-building in the American West

2. Provision of recreational and advisory services for consumers, particularly to the extent that shopping is a congenial rather than an instrumental activity in a given environment

3. Miscellaneous governmental or public tasks, such as postal or tax-collection duties, that may be assigned to the retail sector

Format, Scope, and Limitations

The following original essays were especially written for this volume by various specialists in the fields of education, government, business, and trade associations. Most essays provide comprehensive country studies. While the general body of laws affecting commercial transactions is relevant, the chapters emphasize more particularly those laws and regulations that *explicitly* affect retailing, although they also include any necessary discussion of significant implicit policy (including the lack of overt action) and of general economic and social policy.

Obviously, policy may not be uniform across all commodity branches of retailing, or across all national, geographic, and political subdivisions. Thus, pharmaceutical retailing or gasoline distribution may be subject to special control or support; and there may be variations in state, provincial, and municipal regulations. In such cases, the chapters deal with the major or most significant variations.

In the same vein, it is evident that those essays presenting an overall analysis of public policy in a particular country, cannot possibly deal with all explicit facets of that policy, but have to focus on the significant elements without which the situation cannot truly be understood. Particular emphasis is given to the last forty years since the current domestic trade policies in many countries seem to be either positively or negatively related to social and economic measures that were introduced during the Great Depression of the 1930s.

National variations exist both in the degree of demarcation between the various branches of retailing and in the extent to which retailing itself is separated from wholesaling and craft-manufacturing. While some of the chapters consider the way in which the presence or lack of such differentiation has influenced and/or resulted from public policy, retailers are here considered as those actors who primarily sell and distribute goods to ultimate consumers. Minor statistical and census classification differences (such as whether lumber-yards and restaurants are considered as part of retailing or of some other sector) are handled on an ad hoc basis.

The selection of countries reflects two major criteria: (1) providing a spectrum of public policies toward retailing, and (2) finding experts. The first and main criterion was satisfied through the selection of countries that vary greatly in terms of the sophistication of the retailing sector, of physical-economic-political-social-cultural environments, and of stage of development of public policy. Unfortunately, experts were not readily available for certain countries, and all of the essays leave many questions unanswered. The editors hope, however, that the publication of this volume will lead to further studies and, possibly, to a second volume of complementary essays.

In general, the essays do not provide extensive analyses of the retailing systems in the countries under discussion, partly because of a shortage of space, and partly because information on that score is fairly readily available. However, more is said on this count in the case of lesser-known countries and when the state itself plays a major role in running the retailing system, since the condition of the latter is a much more direct product of public policy.

The concluding chapter (Conclusions) provides an overall analysis in terms of:

(1) the factors and forces that have contributed to the development of public policy toward retailing; (2) the evolution of policy in terms of objectives, instruments, and effects; (3) the making and application of policy; and (4) recommendations for future policy.

Notes

1. For a discussion of the lack of attention to marketing in many development plans, see: J. C. Abbott, "Marketing Issues in Agricultural Development Planning," in R. Moyer and S. C. Hollander, eds., *Markets and Marketing in Developing Economies* (Homewood, Ill.: R. D. Irwin, 1969), 87-116.

2. For titles of major studies dealing in whole or in part with public policy toward retailing, see the partial bibliography at the end of this chapter.

3. For an excellent analysis of the concept of public policy, see: E. S. Kirschen et al., *Economic Policy in Our Time* (Chicago, Ill.: Rand McNally, 1964), Vol. I, *General Theory*.

4. This conceptual framework is developed in Chapter 3 of J. Boddewyn, *Comparative Management and Marketing* (Glenview, Ill.: Scott, Foresman & Co., 1969), and in the Introduction to J. J. Boddewyn, *Belgian Public Policy Toward Retailing Since 1789* (East Lansing, Mich.: Division of Research, Graduate School of Business Administration, Michigan State University, 1971). See also S. C. Hollander, *Restraints on Retail Competition* (East Lansing, Mich.: Division of Research, Graduate School of Business Administration, Michigan State University, 1965).

Partial Bibliography

Assael, Henry. "The Political Role of Trade Associations in Distributive Conflict Resolution." *Journal of Marketing* 32 (April 1968): 21-28.

Boddewyn, J. J. *Belgian Public Policy Toward Retailing since 1789.* East Lansing, Mich.: Division of Research, Graduate School of Business Administration, Michigan State University, 1971.

———. *Comparative Management and Marketing.* Glenview, Ill.: Scott, Foresman & Co., 1969.

Carson, David. "Legal Barriers to Effective Distribution." *Proceedings of the 1957 Boston Conference on Distribution.* Boston, Mass., 1957: 47-50.

Chambre de Commerce Internationale. *Réglementations et liberté de la distribution.* Paris, France: International Chamber of Commerce, 1953.

Collins, N. R., and Holton, R. H. "Programming Changes in Marketing in Planned Economic Development." *Kyklos* 16 (1/1963).

Fletcher, F. M. *Market Restraints in the Retail Drug Industry.* Philadelphia, Pa.: University of Pennsylvania Press, 1967.

Grether, E. T. *Marketing and Public Policy.* Englewood Cliffs, N. J.: Prentice-Hall, 1966.

Grether, E. T. *Price Control under Fair Trade Legislation.* New York: Oxford University Press, 1937.

Hollander, S. C. *Restraints on Retail Competition.* East Lansing, Mich.: Division of Research, Graduate School of Business Administration, Michigan State University, 1965.

Jefferys, J. B.; Hausberger, Simon; and Lindblad, Göran. *La productivité dans la distribution en Europe; Commerce de gros et détail.* Paris, France: Organisation Européenne de Coopération Economique, September 1954 (Chapter VIII: "Lois et institutions ayant une incidence sur les activités distributives").

Kirschen, E. S., and others. *Economic Policy in Our Time.* Vol. I, *Theory.* Chicago, Ill.: Rand McNally, 1964.

Palamountain, J. C. *The Politics of Distribution.* Cambridge, Mass.: Harvard University Press, 1955.

Preston, Lee E. "Market Control in Developing Economies." *The Journal of Development Studies* 4 (July 1968): 481-96.

Thompson, Donald N. *Franchise Operations and Antitrust.* Lexington, Mass.: Heath-Lexington Books, 1971.

Yamey, B. S. *Resale Price Maintenance.* Chicago, Ill.: Aldine, 1966.

2 Australia

DONALD F. DIXON

The Australian colonies were federated into a commonwealth in 1900.[1] The Commonwealth Constitution, which limits the federal government's authority to specifically designated powers, gives the six states primary control over their internal affairs. Although the Federal Parliament has the power to legislate with respect to foreign and interstate trade and commerce, the state parliaments retain the right to legislate with respect to intrastate trade.

The major forms of retailing–government interaction, even in the case of large chains with interstate operations, thus come at the state and local levels. The emphasis in this chapter therefore will be upon state policy toward retailing. Attention will be focused upon public policy in the three eastern states, New South Wales, Victoria, and Queensland, which together contain about 80 percent of the commonwealth population. An effort is made to detect trends in activities among the several states; minor differences in policy arising from the separate acts of each state will not be considered.

Australia is highly urbanized. The two dominant cities, Sydney (N.S.W.) and Melbourne (Vict.) are each slightly larger than Philadelphia, and together with the other capital cities account for one-half of the commonwealth's approximately 11 million population. Consequently the municipal ordinances of the largest cities are also of special importance for retailing.

The Australian political economy has been essentially a laissez-faire one, at least insofar as retailing is concerned. However, the relevant governments have intervened in retailing in several limited respects: (a) to control entry (the actors) and some aspects of operations (process) in selected trades that appear to have special characteristics of public interest; (b) to control operations (process) in several ways for the purposes (function) of protecting, variously, consumers, employees, small competitors, and suppliers; and (c) very tentatively to curb some manifestations or potential sources of monopoly power (structure). The major such interventions are outlined below.

The Regulation of Particular Types of Retailing

Early policy was concerned with direct regulation of the operation of particular types of retailers, and was aimed at the protection of the public as well as the interests of those in the trade. Pawnbrokers, pharmacists, and innkeepers were

11

licensed as early as the mid-nineteenth century. The Pharmacy Act 1876 (Victoria) provided for the registration of druggists by a Board of Pharmacy. Licensing requirements could be very restrictive. Under local option rules liquor acts provided for a limitation of the number of inns and grocers who sold liquor. In New South Wales, for example, the Liquor Act of 1912 fixed the number of licenses at that which had existed on January 1, 1906. Similar provisions appeared in Victorian licensing acts.

Another form of retailing subject to control in the nineteenth century was the non-store retailer. Hawkers and Pedlars Acts imposing licensing requirements began to appear as early as 1849.[2] Further control was exercised by other types of legislation; the Police Offences Act of 1900 (Victoria) prohibited sellers from "lingering or loitering in the street," while the Metropolitan Traffic Act of 1900 (N.S.W.) prohibited solicitation for the sale of goods in a public street.[3] There was special attention paid to particular product categories. Victoria, in 1896, provided that milk was not to be "cried out" or delivered after noon on Sunday, although there was no prohibition against sales in shops. Similarly, the delivery of meat on Sunday was prohibited. A Hawkers Act of 1904 prohibited the sale of spirits or any sales between sunset and sunrise by hawkers in Tasmania.[4]

The Victorian Hawkers and Pedlars Act (1958), consolidating earlier legislation, indicates that general social disdain of non-store retailing has not abated during the century. Applicants for Hawkers licenses must produce "a certificate of good character from at least two known and respectable persons." Furthermore, a hawker is subject to search by police without a warrant, and if found carrying liquor, the sale of which is forbidden, the burden of proving that the liquors were not for resale "shall be cast upon the party carrying them."

The states are also specifically concerned with retailers of used, second-hand, and waste merchandise. The earliest acts were designed to prevent the resale of stolen goods. Victoria undertook the regulation of collectors and dealers in marine stores (second-hand merchandise) in 1890. Such businesses were to be licensed by the police and were required to keep goods in unaltered condition for four days after purchase. In 1906 New South Wales and Western Australia passed Second Hand Dealer Acts that imposed licensing requirements and provided that all purchases were to be recorded. In New South Wales, any goods thought to be stolen were to be produced to the police. The Western Australian act further prohibited purchases from persons "apparently under the age of sixteen years" or from any intoxicated person.

Subsequent legislation became concerned with controlling the "nuisance" aspects of trade in waste and scrap. The Health Act (Victoria, 1915), designed to curb "noxious and offensive trades," required dealers in marine stores to obtain the written consent of the relevant municipal government. This provision was really intended to deal with the purchase, rendering, and sale of old bones and waste fats, an activity that had also come to be embraced within the term "marine stores." However, in Hendy and Rider (1919) the courts failed to distinguish between the various meanings of the term.[5] Hendy, a retailer of bottles and old metal whose business included none of the noxious aspects of rendering fat and who was licensed as a dealer in special wares under the Victorian Marine Stores and Old Metals Act, was held to be a marine stores merchant and convicted of failure to obtain the Health Act permit.

Various other forms of retailing are also subject to licensing requirements. The Victorian Tobacco Sellers Act (1915) required the registration of all sellers of tobacco and snuff. Under the Local Government Act 1919 (New South Wales) the Manly Council required a license for fish retailers.[6] The restrictive effects of licensing were apparent in gasoline retailing during the 1920s when gasoline began to be sold in bulk, rather than in cans. Previously garages were subject to licensing under such legislation as the Inflammable Liquids Act, 1915 (N.S.W.), which specified methods of storage, but seems not to have restricted the number of retailers. However, with bulk distribution, the gasoline pumps themselves began to be subject to licensing restrictions by municipalities. Generally, licenses were issued sparingly, because of a fear of traffic congestion, and this produced some local monopoly power. Furthermore, in Melbourne, the City Council permitted a garage to have only two pumps, and this meant that only the two leading brands were sold in the city, with smaller sellers essentially excluded from the market.[7] This form of restriction lost its effect only when retail establishments began to take the form of drive-in stations rather than garages with curbside pumps.

Sellers of milk are licensed under the various states' milk marketing legislation for the regulation of collecting, treating, and distributing milk, to eliminate unhygienic, wasteful, or unnecessary agencies, and to fix minimum prices to be charged by milk vendors to the public. Sellers are required to register with Milk Boards, and in at least one instance, a Milk Board has the authority to allocate trading areas to retailers.[8]

Most of this early licensing legislation remains in force today without substantial change. In Victoria, for example, a series of acts in 1958, consolidating earlier legislation, specify that licenses are required for retailers of liquor, tobacco, and milk, and for second-hand dealers, hawkers, pawnbrokers, and money lenders.

Some retailers, such as pharmacists, who require special qualifications, are also subject to restrictions imposed by the Health Act. Generally speaking, a pharmacy must be self-contained, even if operated as part of a larger establishment, by being walled off and having no means of access from the rest of the establishment. This requirement has sanitary and health implications, but it also has obvious economic implications for attempts to operate pharmacies as parts of, for example, department stores. Victoria, New South Wales, and Queensland prohibit the operation of more than three pharmacies under a single ownership. Some of these current controls over retail pharmacies are essentially the same as those imposed early in the century, but at least one report indicates that part of the regulations were added in the 1940s when rumors circulated that Boots Pure Drugs, Ltd., the giant British cut-price chain, was planning to expand to Australia.[9]

Another area of government restriction, involving rather strict censorship of commercial media, also has a peripheral effect upon retailing. The impact of this form of restriction may be suggested by a recent case under the Questionable Literature Act 1954 (Queensland). The Literature Board of Review prohibited the distribution of "Playboy" magazine, and the court held, on appeal, that the magazine was objectionable under the act in that it unduly emphasized matters of sex, "there being a palpable over presentment of such matters."[10]

Conditions of Employment and Shop Hours

Prior to the twentieth century Australian social legislation was not significant, in part because early public policy was derived from English law. For example, retail shops were generally closed on Sunday because of the English Sunday Observance Act (1677), which applied to tradesmen as well as others who were not engaged in "work of necessity." By 1833 the N.S.W. Police Act prohibited trading or dealing on Sunday, with certain exceptions for butchers, bakers, fishmongers, greengrocers, bakers, and apothecaries. Sunday trading prohibitions were reinforced by the Victorian Public Health Act of 1888, various municipal by-laws, the Police Offenses Act 1901 (N.S.W.), and specific state legislation, such as the Tasmanian Sunday Observance Act of 1908.

During the century both public attitudes and marketing innovations have brought changes in Sunday trading limitations. In 1914 the High Court held that cigarettes sold from "penny-in-the-slot" machines were not included in the prohibition of Sunday trading.[11] More recently, this type of problem arose in connection with coin-operated gasoline pumps. In 1952 the Industrial Court of Queensland prohibited Sunday trading by gasoline stations, but the High Court ruled that there was no authority for the issuance of such a prohibition.[12]

The first Australian Factories and Shops Act, passed by the State of Victoria in 1873, forbade the employment of any female in a factory for more than eight hours in a day. The 1890 Victorian Act provided for a weekly half holiday; an amendment in 1896 required "a sitting accommodation" for shop assistants in the proportion of one seat for each three persons employed. By 1898 provisions for trading hours for shops began to appear. The Western Australia Early Closing Act required every shop to be closed daily at 6:00 P.M., except Wednesday and Saturday, with certain classes of trade exempted.[13] Delivery men were separately treated; in the New South Wales Early Closing Act (1899) "Every person employed by a butcher or milk vendor in delivering meat or milk is to have a half holiday one weekday in each week, and every baker's man delivering bread is to have a holiday on one weekday each month." The problem of "scrambled merchandising" was recognized in an amendment in 1900 which provided that a shop "in which the mixed business of a fancy goods seller and news agent is carried on, must close at the hour fixed for fancy goods shops." Shopkeepers who were required to close were protected by legislation prohibiting the hawking during closing hours of goods to which the closing rules applied.

There has been a good deal of subsequent legislation dealing with trading hours, much of which has been concerned with inconsequential adjustments of regulations. For example, a report of the Western Australia Early Closing Act of 1912 included the comment that it was "mainly for the purpose of settling the vexed question whether the day on which shops must be closed at one o'clock shall be Saturday or Wednesday."[14] The general pattern of permitted store hours has not changed substantially during the century, and all except certain specifically-designated types of merchants are generally required to close by six o'clock in the evening.

One of the main activities of retail associations has been lobbying for shorter trading hours and the strict enforcement of existing legislation. These efforts have had only mixed success, however, partly because of the growth in intertype competition between different types of retailers who sell similar product lines, but who are subject to different mandatory closing hours. One estimate in the early 1930s was that one-fifth of all grocery sales in N.S.W. were made after the supposed closing hours. The grocers' association blamed this condition on lax enforcement and "inefficient" housewives, that is those whose requirements did not coincide with the traders' desires.[15] The N.S.W. Traders Protective Association supplied the names of the offending grocers to the appropriate agency, but the number of prosecutions was insufficient to curtail after-hours trading. Despite subsequent legislature that required the registration of shopkeepers, after-hours trading continued, partly due to the continued growth of "mixed" shops that sold groceries together with other products. These shops were permitted longer hours, but were only to sell non-grocery items after the legal hours for grocery stores. The enforcement of such a requirement was virtually impossible. After-hours trading has become a problem in gasoline retailing as the oil companies have introduced exclusive dealing contracts. Retailers contend that the companies have utilized their increased bargaining power to induce operations beyond the permitted hours.[16]

Consumer Protection

Australia has remained essentially a common law country, following English precedent much more faithfully than American courts. Generally, Australian legislation has followed the English pattern as well. Terms of sale are controlled by each state's Sale of Goods Acts, initially passed in 1895 and 1896, which are patterned very closely upon the English Act of 1893. One of the most important aspects of these Acts is the retailer's responsibility for the implied quality of the product sold. In ordinary situations, if the buyer discloses the purpose for which the good is used, so that he is relying upon the seller's skill or judgment, then there is an implied condition that the goods will be reasonably fit for such purpose. One case that is of interest here went to the Privy Council on Appeal from the High Court of Australia. The plaintiff developed dermatitis from woolen underwear. It was held that the goods were sold with the implication that they were reasonably fit for the purpose for which they were purchased.[17]

A number of Public Health Acts passed by the states in the late nineteenth century were concerned with the quality of food as well as the maintenance of clean premises, and included such issues as the display of meat in butcher shops. Moreover, some of these Acts prohibited the sale of adulterated food or drug products. In some instances particular products received special attention, as in the Victorian Bakers and Millers Statute of 1890. A series of subsequent acts, consolidated in the 1958 Bakers and Millers Act, requires that bread "shall always be well made" as well as specifying the ingredients used and providing that shops may be searched for evidence of the prohibited ingredients. The Adulteration of Food Act 1879 (N.S.W.) attacked the entire problem more directly. Much of the litigation arising from this act centered upon the adulteration of milk, especially by watering; however, the watering of gin seems also to have been a problem.

Packaging was also regulated very early in the century. Various state Weights and Measures Acts, based upon the English Act of 1852, were sufficient when the retailer's main function was breaking bulk. Special cases, such as the weight of loaves of bread, were handled by various State Bread Acts, as early as 1835, and some of the Health Acts included provisions concerning quantities sold.

With the growth of packaging there arose codes of marking and packaging, some of which were enacted by local governments. For example, the Municipal Corporations Amendment Act 1903 (South Australia) authorized municipal governments to make bylaws to compel branding of foodstuffs with the gross or net weight. Earlier legislation, the Trade Marks Act 1892 (South Australia) had provided that every seller who chose to state the weight of a package was compelled to make a true statement. However, he was not compelled to indicate the weight if he did not choose to do so. The managing partner of a retail grocery firm unsuccessfully attacked a bylaw of Port Adelaide compelling the branding of specified food products with the weight.[18]

The Pure Food Act 1908 (N.S.W.) prohibited the sale of adulterated or falsely described foods, and provided that packages of food were to be labeled with the description and weight of their contents. False description did not extend to "puffing" however, for an early decision held that a statement as to the efficiency of a drug was merely a statement of opinion and did not come under the Act. In the same year the Victorian Health Act required that every package of food show a description, the weight or volume of contents, the identity of the seller or maker, the place of manufacture, and the proportion of other substances used for preservation, coloring, or flavoring. The Goods Act, also of 1915, required a trade description to be attached to goods that were not regulated under the Public Health Act.

Other legislation has been concerned with the problem of sellers passing off inferior products. The Victorian Footwear Regulation Act of 1916 made it an offense to sell boots and shoes with soles other than entirely leather, unless conspicuously stamped with the name of the other material used. In 1944 several states passed acts to ensure that synthetic fiber would not be passed off as wool; labeling procedures were specified, and particular descriptive terms that might be misleading were prohibited. In 1934 South Australia and Victoria passed acts to protect the butter and cheese industry from the competition of margarine. Not only was the manufacture of margarine restricted, but any restaurant serving margarine was required to post notices on its walls announcing that margarine was being served.

Thus, each state developed its own set of regulations regarding standards, packaging, labeling, and the sanitary handling of foods. As a result of increased interstate trade arising from improved transportation, especially following the Second World War, the lack of consistency among the regulations of the several states became a serious problem. Previous efforts at greater uniformity had been undertaken, but were abandoned in 1927.[19] These efforts were resumed in 1952, and uniform packaging acts were passed by most states in 1967. These mainly imposed restrictions and requirements on those who "prepack," but also imposed obligations upon retailers to ensure that the package meets the requirements of the legislation. Specifically, certain expressions were proscribed, to avoid misleading the buyer; statements implying that the article is for sale at a price less than its customary price are prohibited; using packages that may be deceptively larger than the goods in them is regulated; the actual weights or measures used can be prescribed; an approved brand or the name of the maker or seller must be indicated on the package, and the package must be marked with its true weight.

A more direct attack on the problem of consumer protection was undertaken in the form of Consumer Protection Acts passed by several states in the 1960s. The Victorian Act (1964), for example, established a Consumer Affairs Council with power to investigate and recommend the desirability of legislative or administrative action in the interests of consumers. The New South Wales Act (1969) provides for the appointment of a Commissioner for Consumer Affairs and the establishment of a bureau to advise individuals, to deal with complaints by consumers, and to conduct research, as well as to undertake educational work in matters affecting the interests of consumers.

Regulation of Promotional Efforts

Some early legislation subjected advertising to control in the public interest. Under Local Governmental Acts passed by many states in the early 1900s, municipal councils were given the power to regulate advertising (billboards or signs on buildings, fences, cliffs, rocks, trees, etc.) near footways and roadways, and impose license fees for such signs. Prohibitions might be imposed, and existing signs ordered removed, where they were thought to "disfigure the natural beauty of the landscape."[20] In 1916 South Australia passed the Control of Advertising Act that extended control beyond municipalities, restricting advertising visible from any public road, sea beach, or navigable waterway, which spoiled the enjoyment of the scenery or disfigured the natural beauty.

Particular types of advertising were prohibited as early as 1892, when Victoria passed an Indecent Advertisements Act. Other states subsequently passed similar legislation prohibiting the publication of matter of an indecent, immoral, or obscene nature, or which related to venereal or contagious diseases affecting the generative organs or functions, or to any complaint arising from "the relation of the sexes, pregnancy, or any diseases peculiar to women." Such legislation was sufficient to prohibit the distribution of advertising pamphlets containing descriptions of various ailments and suggesting the use of the advertiser's proprietary medicine for treatment.[21]

False and misleading advertising has also been the subject of legislative control. In 1934 Victoria prohibited promotional statements which to the knowledge of the person publishing them were false in any material particular. In other instances, the advertising of particular products has been the subject of regulation. An amendment to the Food and Drug Laws of South Australia in 1943 provided for regulations to prescribe the form of advertising for food and drugs. The New South Wales Factories, Shops and Industries Act (1962) also contains prohibitions against false trade descriptions and advertising that is false and misleading in any material particular.

Misleading advertising was also attacked in the Prices Amendment Act 1963

(South Australia), because of a particular type of problem found in retailing: "It has been found that, although goods are advertised . . . at the opening of the store on the day when the advertisement appears the goods have not been there. Further, the goods cannot be shown, nor can a satisfactory account be given of what has happened to them, if they ever existed.[22] The Act prohibits advertisements that give a false impression concerning the quantity of goods the retailer has available for sale at the specified price.

One of the earliest merchandising techniques to be prohibited by legislation was the use of trading stamps. The Victorian Trading Stamps Act (1901) provided that "No person shall on the sale of any goods issue any trading stamps." The first case reported under this Act involved a manufacturer of laundry starch who enclosed coupons in the packages of his product offering a wringer in return for a stated number of coupons. Action was brought against a retailer handling the starch, but he was found not to have issued stamps within the meaning of the Act.[23] This decision was based upon a distinction between two- and three-party trading stamps. Two-party trading stamps and gift coupons are those manufacturers and retailers issue and redeem on their own, while three-party stamps are those issued by trading stamp companies. One trade association described the three-party stamp as one "circulated by parasitical companies not engaged in industry, but profiting by the activities of traders. . . . it represents the exploitation of both the trading and buying community."[24]

In Moran & Cato the court held that the Victorian Act was intended to prevent the issue of stamps by trading stamp companies: "It was intended expressly to allow traders and manufacturers *bona fide* to issue coupons payable to themselves."[25] Such stamps, issued by the sellers, sometimes described as "gift coupons," were also objectionable to retailers because they were often issued by manufacturers whose lines did not carry the customary margin. Furthermore, "The manufacturer uses the customer as the fulcrum to exert pressure upon the retail grocer to stock products because of their coupon appeal, without regard to their intrinsic value; and this unwarrantable influence and interference in the conduct of his business is humiliating and embarrassing to the grocer."[26]

Other states passed trading stamps acts similar to that of Victoria. Trading Stamps Abolition Acts were enacted by Tasmania in 1900 and Western Australia in 1902, but no cases involving these acts seem to have been reported. Queensland passed a prohibition against trading stamps in 1912, but this act apparently was not especially effective until an amendment, passed in 1947, overcame the evasion of the earlier law by the redemption of stamps in another state. Western Australia also passed a new trading stamp act in 1948.

South Australia prohibited trading stamps in 1904, with the explicit exception that stamps were permitted if redeemable at the issuing establishment. A new act was passed in 1924 extending the definition of trading stamps to those "entitling the holder to free admittance to any theater or race course; travel by rail, tram, or boat, or to obtain or receive any valuable consideration or benefit or advantage of any kind whatsoever." Despite this obvious attempt to fill legislative loopholes, "The contest between the legislature and the coupon-trading system was evidently not decided in favour of the legislature . . . and accordingly the Act of 1935 was passed."[27] Here the issue at hand again becomes the distinction between two- and three-party stamps. The legislature was opposed to both forms: "The real object of the Act is to suppress unfair dealing . . . articles are procured by consuming so much of the commodity. It is a discount on purchases."[28]

The 1935 statute directly attacked not the issue of trading stamps, but the exchange transaction by which stamps or coupons were handed over in return for some goods. The legislature "thought it advisable to suppress all encouragement to the consumer to commence saving up stamps or counters with the object of exchanging them and obtaining his reward."[29]

The South Australian Act (1924-35) was not especially important until 1962 when the Supreme Court of South Australia extended the meaning of "trading stamp" to another type of transaction. It was held an offense for a company to insert an advertisement in a daily newspaper representing that any person buying a particular item would be able to buy in addition any one of four listed articles at a price that was much lower than the market value of those articles. The Court held that this advertisement "was designed and intended to accomplish the same result as a trading stamp and that it was thus within the scope of the Act."[30]

Hire Purchase Transactions

Under the sale of goods legislation, installment purchases are possible by means of a contract of sale that provides for immediate possession by a buyer who agrees to pay by installments. But in Australian law, a purchaser who is in possession of a good can transfer title to a third party, so that an installment sale provides no security for the original seller. If the buyer is required to pledge the goods back to the seller for security a "conditional bill of sale" is required, and this must be registered. Registration, and the annual renewal of this registration, is not only annoying but also means that the contract is open to public inspection. Not only might such inspection be embarrassing to the purchaser, but it also provides an opportunity for a creditor of the purchaser to intervene and prevent the transaction.

As a result of such difficulties in installment and conditional sales there evolved hire purchase agreements in which the seller "lends" the goods to the purchaser while at the same time granting an option to buy. The last rental payment exercises this purchase option. Many such agreements also have involved a further complication. The buyer signs a contract not with the retailer but with a finance company with which the retailer has a permanent contractual arrangement, under which the finance company purchases the goods from the retailer and in turn "hires" them to the purchaser. The agreement provides that the company may repossess on the breach of the contract.

Under these circumstances the purchaser faces several difficulties if the goods prove to be unsatisfactory. His warranty is limited because his contract is with the finance company rather than with the retailer. Furthermore, if he attempts to return the goods he may be subject to "penalty" payments; often upon repossession buyers have lost all benefit of any payments made. The agreements became exceedingly complex and buyers were usually in a very weak position because sellers virtually defined their own terms of contract with the result that there were opportunities for deception as well as unfortunate purchase decisions by gullible members of the public.

The courts generally regarded hire purchase agreements from the traditional laissez-faire viewpoint, considering such arrangements as a matter of contract law, with some special features, and hence left the parties to work out the provisions of such agreements without intervention. This meant that justice was especially inadequate during the depression of the early 1930s, so that several states passed Hire-Purchase Agreement Acts during the decade.

Generally these acts regulated the conditions under which the seller could proceed against the goods; i.e., the provisions generally were aimed at protecting the unsuspecting purchaser. In particular, sellers were prevented from profiting from the act of repossession.

A model Hire Purchase Act was adopted at a conference of state and federal officials in 1959, and the main provisions of this Act have been adopted by all states, although there are some differences in detail. The seller is made responsible for his representations concerning the goods, and some implied warranties are established, including fitness for purpose. Furthermore, when the goods are returned or repossessed, the seller is only entitled to the return of his capital investment and the interest and other charges for the time which the purchaser held the goods.

However, the law remains exceedingly complicated. Some sellers contend that an undesirable feature of the acts is that they create many potential offenses on the part of the sellers because the provisions permit unwitting breaches.

In Victoria, Queensland, and Western Australia, Door-to-Door (Sales) Acts (1964) require that some credit sales and hire-purchase transactions made by door-to-door salesmen must be in writing and that the purchaser can repudiate the agreement by written notice to the headquarters of the firm. Salesmen are prohibited from delivering the goods until after a cooling-off period and are also prohibited from trying to influence the buyer during this period. Again there are substantial differences among the three acts. Furthermore, in South Australia a Book Purchasers Protection Act concerns the sale of books and pictures made at the place of residence or employment of purchasers.

Statutory Marketing and Price Controls

Collective marketing and pooling arrangements at the primary producer level tend to have ultimate effects upon food retailer supplies and purchase prices. Moreover, as will be noted below, some of these marketing plans have more direct retail implications. Compulsory pooling arrangements for primary products were established by the Commonwealth Government under the (First World War) War Precautions Act. Many of them were continued after the war, through various Federal Export Control Boards, as a means of avoiding wide variations in the income of the producers. State pooling legislation was also enacted during the war, and much of this too was continued after hostilities had ended.[31] Although some federal acts relating to dried fruit, dairy products, and wheat were declared invalid by the Privy Council (the country's highest appellate body) in 1936, these products were subsequently controlled by a joint arrangement between the federal and state governments.

The various wartime acts essentially provided for the expropriation of specified products, the government being given very wide discretion as to the prices offered. After the war, "Compulsory Cooperation" schemes were developed by the states to replace direct government control. The first of such programs was the Agricultural Organization Scheme established by Queensland in 1922. Under this legislation the government might announce its intention to provide for the controlled marketing of most agricultural products. If a poll of the relevant producers showed that 60 percent were in favor of the program, a board was authorized to undertake the marketing of the whole of the product. By 1931, fifteen of the principal agricultural products of Queensland, representing over three-quarters of the annual value of the agricultural production of the state, were marketed under such schemes.[32] Similar acts were passed by New South Wales in 1927 and Victoria in 1935, and this legislation is still in effect.

Statutory marketing controls mainly have indirect effects upon retailers. However, some types of "orderly marketing" arrangements, such as the Dried Fruits Act, 1924 (South Australia), have a more direct impact. The Dried Fruits Board has the power to fix both the retail and wholesale prices, as well as to determine the amount to be marketed. The Queensland Butter Marketing Board, established in 1925, has the right to be the sole seller of "pat" butter in the Brisbane area. The objectives of this provision are to obtain additional profit for the producers, as well as to replace the numerous brands in the market with one product of uniform quality.

Another example of the impact of compulsory marketing schemes can be seen in the actions of the Egg Board of Victoria. Under the Victorian Marketing of Primary Products Act, 1953-56, the Egg Board required that a sign be placed near eggs displayed at retail showing the place of origin, and if the eggs were obtained from the board, the words "Board Eggs" were to be shown. This regulation was declared void by the High Court.[33] Subsequently, an amendment to the Act, the Marketing of Primary Products Act (Egg Marketing) 1965 (Victoria) provided that all eggs sold by retail in the state were to be graded and tested for quality as well as marked and stamped by the Board. This was viewed as a matter for consumer protection, but the regulation effectively limits the retailer's source of supply. If he acquires out-of-state eggs, he is required to deliver them to the Egg Board for grading and marking, as well as paying the costs of this process.[34]

Dairy products are also subject to price control. In 1926 a voluntary scheme of price stabilization for milk producers was introduced in Western Australia, and this was followed by a Dairy Product Marketing Act. The Milk Board of Western Australia, established in 1932, maintains statutory supervision over the supply and sale of milk in most of the state, including the establishment of minimum prices that may be charged to the public. Similar legislation was passed by New South Wales in 1929, Victoria in 1933, and other states in the following decade.

During the Second World War the Commonwealth Government received emergency powers, under the National Security Regulations of 1939-40, which permitted a broad expansion of marketing controls and the regulation of prices. Commonwealth price control ended in 1948, when a referendum seeking authority for permanent powers over rents and prices was rejected. At that time the states continued price control for a small number of products. In Queensland, for example, price controls were continued for flour, bread, milk, cream, and gasoline. In 1961 the price fixing authority for dairy products was transferred to the Milk Board, and in 1967 control over flour, bread, and gasoline was removed. It is interesting to note that the Profiteering Prevention Act 1948, under which price control was exercised, was not repealed, so that price control could be imposed once again without legislative action.

The major vestige of wartime price control today is in gasoline retailing. In 1955, the year that premium gasoline was reintroduced after the war, South Australia, New South Wales, and Queensland still retained price control. New South Wales relinquished control in that year, but reimposed retail price control in 1959 after a lapse of four years, in response to an increase in the retail margin that had been established by the retailer association. Queensland ceased the control of prices in 1967, so that today only South Australia and New South Wales continue to exercise control over prices. The control of the retail price in New South Wales appears to be nominal. On the other hand, control in South Australia is very comprehensive, involving both grades of gasoline, the kerosene fuels, automotive distillate, diesel and furnace oil. Furthermore, in the case of gasoline, both the wholesale price and retail margin is controlled, for both grades.

Price control in South Australia is tantamount to national control of petroleum prices, because the decisions of the Prices Commissioner in South Australia are accepted by the industry as determining maximum wholesale prices for most of the controlled products in the Commonwealth. Thus prices are generally the same in the capital cities and main distribution areas throughout Australia.

Although the same wholesale price for premium gasoline is found in all states, except Tasmania, retail prices vary among the states. Reseller margins are now controlled only in South Australia and New South Wales; in the other states margins are established by the local reseller associations. There is a wide variation in retail margins. In 1969 the Western Australian margin was the equivalent of 7d., while that in Victoria was 9d. Changes in retail margins since the reintroduction of the premium grade in 1955 also have varied from state to state. In South Australia, where the retail price is controlled, the retail margin has been increased by 4d., an amount exceeding that of any other state. On the other hand, the New South Wales retail margin, where the retail price is also controlled, has risen only 2½d.

Determinations by the South Australia Prices Commissioner are based upon intensive investigation into the operation of the companies, as was the case during wartime control. All companies submit Australia-wide data indicating the landed costs of refined products and distribution costs. The landed cost, termed import parity value, is calculated from the average value of three months' stocks. Distribution costs from ocean terminals, including overhead, transport, storage, and marketing expenses, also are submitted by each company, and a weighted average calculated. These costs include administrative expense, storage and handling, marketing and transportation costs. Political considerations also enter into the price which is established, but, in essence, the price formula means that refined products sell for the prices at which they could be imported. The mechanism of the formula is not especially valid for integrated companies, and it has become increasingly irrelevant as the proportion of imported products has declined with the growth of home refining.

The basic price of gasoline is quoted for "free delivery areas," which are geographic areas within which no additional transport charge is made to the customers. Historically the "free delivery areas" were the capital cities where the companies had their ocean terminals, but with the development of domestic refining the grographic price structure has changed.

As new ocean terminals have been constructed, prices in the vicinity of these terminals have been reduced, and this in turn has led to lower prices in the surrounding areas. For some time after a terminal is constructed the companies are permitted to charge a differential rate to permit a rapid amortization of the terminal's capital cost. It is understood, however, that in each instance terminals are to become "free delivery areas" within a few years.

Outside the "free delivery areas" price differentials are established to recover the additional expenses that are incurred. The companies contend that these differentials permit the recovery of freight costs, but not the additional cost of marketing in the country areas. Nevertheless, differentials have been a matter of public concern throughout the history of the industry.

These differentials not only have been a matter of public controversy, but also of concern to the government in its effort to stimulate the development of the country regions of the Commonwealth. As early as 1955 the question of a uniform price for petrol throughout Victoria has been discussed, although no decision was reached.[35] In 1957 a Western Australia Parliamentary Select Committee on Uniform Price of Petrol investigated such a possibility, but concluded that it would be impractical. It was calculated that the companies would be required to raise the metropolitan price from four to six pence to subsidize the country prices. The committee suggested the alternatives of reducing rail rates for petrol or permitting the use of truck transportation, but concluded that "It is extremely doubtful if either of these proposals would ever be contemplated."[36] The issue here is the government's effort to support rail transport. In Queensland, New South Wales, and Western Australia, government regulations designed to protect the railway systems from competition prohibit the use of road transport in some instances. Thus rail transport is typically utilized between seaboard bulk installations and country depots, even though it is more expensive than road transport.

Despite the economic argument against a subsidy scheme, the issue was successfully pressed by the Country Party Leader, Mr. J. McEwen, so that it became an issue in the 1963 election campaign. In his policy speech for the elections Sir Robert Menzies promised that the government would "bring about a change in the price of petroleum products so that nowhere in Australia will the normal price be more than four pence a gallon above the level of capital city prices."[37] The scheme, which went into effect on September 16, 1965, provided that the oil companies were to be paid subsidies for petrol, power kerosene, automotive distillate, and aviation fuels, at selling points where the differentials above capital city prices exceeded four pence a gallon on December 31, 1964.[38]

Controlling Monopoly Power

Australia provides an unusual opportunity to observe the effects of restrictive practices, for the country has never seen any sustained effort at protecting the economy from the effects of market power. Until recently it was one of the few industrial nations in the world where a laissez-faire policy toward restrictive trade practices had survived.

Many basic industries are controlled by single firm monopolies, and many of the leading manufacturing firms are either monopolists or dominant members of highly concentrated industries. Trade association restrictions are also exceptionally widespread. Australian retailing is highly concentrated, especially in view of significant merger activity following the Second World War. It has been estimated that in 1961-62 the six organizations that dominate general merchandise sales accounted for more than 10 percent of total retail sales in the Commonwealth.[39]

By opening up new markets for new firms and new products, the rapid rate of economic growth helped somewhat to mitigate the effects of a restrictive business climate, but it has generally failed to establish workable competition in Australia.

There has been little public concern over the growth of monopoly power. Partly this is because private economic power has never had quite the freedom of action that was observed during the late nineteenth century in the United States, for example. From the start most of the railways were state owned, so that a railroad trust never emerged. Nevertheless, there has been some concern over monopoly power in interstate waterways. In 1937 one commentator argued that anti-trust laws should be enacted to protect the public from combinations of producers, middlemen, and shipowners.[40] There was particular concern expressed over shipowners because interstate trade was so heavily dependent upon water transport. Shipowners thus had the potential "by arrangement for mutually exclusive dealing in a particular trade with producers or middlemen, to oppress competitors and possibly gain a monopoly."[41] Another reason for a lack of concern over monopoly power was that most Australian secondary industries were not firmly established until the twentieth century, by which time the labor movement was an important countervailing force in the political arena.

Furthermore, the conventional arguments in favor of monopoly seem to have been generally accepted without critical evaluation. The economies of scale argument for monopoly has not been widely questioned, and the possibility that technological developments create opportunities for efficient small-scale production has not been examined. Finally, the prevailing view that free competition is a luxury for larger economies that might hamper the growth of a developing economy has not been exposed to the more basic issue as to whether efficient resource allocation is less important in a young country than an advanced one.

The policy of tariff protection also is an important element in the lack of control of monopoly power. Both major political parties maintain that the tariff should be used to protect domestic industries from competition from abroad. An industry is accorded protection by the Tariff Board if that industry is "efficient"; the standard of efficiency is usually whether the cost structure is comparable to that in the United States. By narrowing the buyer's choice of goods to Australian manufacture the tariff has helped many producers to positions of considerable economic power.

The business climate has tended to support the development of restrictive practices. During the depression of the 1930s firms joined together in restrictive agreements to assure themselves a minimum price and some sales. This represented an element of security to a business community haunted by uncertainty. Once established, restrictive practices took on a life of their own; cooperation between competitors became a habit and competition seemed abnormal. The Second World War accentuated this pattern further. Each trader found that much of his planning was done by the government—he was allocated a market, told what to produce, and in what quantities. In return, he was guaranteed a price that afforded a "reasonable return" on his investment. This type of arrangement was convenient, and the vacuum left by the repeal of wartime regulation felt uncomfortable. The private restrictive practices that developed to fill this vacuum owed a great deal to the wartime controls, for "They materially assisted the establishment of a tradition of consultation about prices and other matters between both firms and industries and state authorities. The secretaries of some associations still regularly use the price formulas devised by the wartime Commonwealth Prices Commissioner to recommend prices and margins to their members."[42]

An early suggestion for dealing with the effect of monopoly power was limited to the exercise of the Commonwealth's power over customs duties. In 1902 the minister of customs introduced an amendment to the Customs Act which provided that if the sale of any good was restrained so that the advantage of the seller was promoted at the expense of consumers, these goods would be admitted free of duty. Such a reduction in duty was to give to the public "the benefit of reasonable competition."[43] This provision does not seem to have had any significant effect.

The first attempt made by the Commonwealth to control monopoly power directly was the Australian Industries Preservation Act of 1906, which was modeled in part on the Sherman Act. But the Commonwealth Act was rendered ineffective by the failure of the first important prosecution; the High Court declared two sections unconstitutional and this judgment was upheld in the Privy Council.[44] The major problems were the difficulty of interpretation and of proving an intent to cause detriment to the public. The Privy Council interpretation was that the statute was designed to promote and protect the welfare of industries; the Act was entitled "An act for the preservation of Australian Industries and for the repression of destructive monopolies." Thus the welfare of the producers, and to a lesser extent the workers, in a particular industry was the major consideration, not the welfare of the consumers as in the United States. On the assumption that what was not in the producers' and workers' interest was not in the public interest, monopolies that did not raise prices unduly were not subject to the charge of monopolizing. Thus the preservation of competition has not been sought because of its beneficial result to the consumer. This apathy toward competition "lies at the heart of the failure to control monopoly in Australia."[45]

The problem inherent in applying the Act is illustrated in a Victorian case. An association of Victorian electrical appliance retailers met with two large manufacturers to determine a policy to meet the competition of discount houses. The retailers agreed to boycott any manufacturer who sold to discount houses. One of the blacklisted discount houses brought action under s. 4 (1) of the Australian Industries Preservation Act which refers to "Any person who . . . engages in any combination . . . in restraint of or with intent to restrain trade or commerce . . ." The Court held that interstate trade was not involved, even though the manufacturers obtained supplies from out-of-state factories, so that the Act was not relevant. The connection was held to be "too remote." Moreover, the Court held that the defendant's action was beneficial, rather than injurious, to the public interest, because by reducing the rate of transition from "orthodox" retailing toward price competition it prevented "a serious dislocation to a section of the economy with loss and hardship to large numbers of retailers and employees."[46]

Another, more direct means of exercising control over private monopoly power has been by government ownership of business either to replace private monopolies or to increase the number of rivals in an industry.[47] The Labor party, in its role as a reform party, has created most government enterprise during its term in office. However, the Liberal and Country parties have been reluctant to discard these elements of control. Australia's railways have been government owned since the nineteenth century, in most states power generation and public transport have been operated by the state government, and the federal government has established banking, airline, and shipping companies to compete directly with private enterprise. This pattern of government ownership has not been extended to retailing. In the early 1920s the New South Wales government operated a bakery and automobile garage, but these mainly served other government departments.[48]

State Attempts at Control of Monopoly

The shortcomings of federal activity has led to some state efforts at control. The first attempt to deal with restrictive practices in New South Wales was in the Industrial Disputes (Amendment) Act of 1909, which was mainly concerned with strikes and lockouts. However, the Act also included many of the provisions of the Australian Industries Preservation Act. Later these provisions were included in the Industrial Arbitration Act of 1912.

The next relevant legislation was related to price control in the First World War. At the outset of the war the Commonwealth Government apparently felt that it lacked price control powers, for the prime minister requested that the premiers of the various states undertake price control measures. The parliaments of all states except Tasmania passed control regulations, and appropriate administrative bodies were in existence within two months of the outbreak of war. However, the legislation passed in the various states was not consistent, and there was an almost complete absence of coordination in the operations of the administrative bodies in the various states.

In 1916 a Commonwealth Prices Adjustment Board was established under the Federal War Precautions Act, with the power to fix maximum prices. After the lapse of the federal legislation several states reenacted state price control.

In New South Wales the Profiteering Prevention Act (1920) established a mechanism for investigating monopolies and combinations in restraint of trade. The Victorian "Fair Profits Commission," also established in 1920, had control over the prices of "Necessary Commodities." The Commission further had the power to inquire into the existence of trusts or trade combinations. In Queensland, the Profiteering Prevention Act of 1920, although essentially concerned with establishing maximum prices for necessities in a period of rapidly rising prices, contained five sections dealing with combines. It was an offense to offer concessions on condition that the recipient deal exclusively, to refuse to supply because a person would not comply with the directions of a commercial trust, to monopolize or conspire to monopolize the supply or demand for any commodity in the state, or to sell at prices fixed by a commercial trust or association. One example of the application of the Act was its use in the late 1930s to defeat a horizontal price fixing agreement among members of a Queensland gasoline retailers trade association.[49] This agreement, made in 1938, provided that retailers not selling at specified retail prices would be subject to a substantial fine, which was calculated to offset any profits that the retailer might enjoy from price cutting.

The New South Wales Profiteering Prevention Act was replaced in 1923 with the Monopolies Act, containing provisions similar to those in the Commonwealth Act. However, inquiries under the Industrial Commission have been ineffective and litigation under the Monopolies Act both exceedingly rare and ineffective.

South Australia passed a Fair Prices Act in 1924 directed against trade combines by reason of the existence of which prices are "fixed or increased to the detriment of the public." The Act provided for inquiries by the Board of Industry into the existence of any alleged combine. The Board might fix the price of any article in which it found a combine to exist. This legislation also was ineffective; only one case has been reported under the Act.

A more recent effort to control restrictive practices was the Western Australian Unfair Trading and Profit Control Act (1956). This Act established a director of investigation who, having reason to believe that a person is guilty of unfair trading, may bring charges before the Unfair Trading Control Commissioner. The commissioner determines the validity of the charges and may accept an undertaking from the person that the unfair trading will cease. Alternatively, the commissioner, in conjunction with an advisory council, may issue an order to comply with specified prices or trading practices. In the first case under the Act the commissioner charged that Cockburn Cement had "monopolized" the production and sale of Portland cement in Western Australia as a result of agreements with the only other producer. The commissioner's findings were put aside by a Justice of the Western Australia Supreme Court because it had not been shown that Cockburn had possessed monopoly power; and even if it were shown, it would not be an illegal possession of such power.[50] Subsequently a Liberal-Country Party Coalition replaced the Act by the Trade Association Registration Act of 1959, which requires registration, but makes no attempt at control by injunction, prosecution, or otherwise. The concern here with trade associations is especially relevant to retailing. The Report of a Western Australian Royal Commission in 1958 indicated that trade association activity was an important form of restrictive practices. There seemed to be a standard pattern of restrictive practices through exclusive dealing, price fixing agreements, and collusive tendering.[51]

The South Australian Parliament passed a Prices Act Amendment in 1963 containing new provisions aimed at controlling retail trade, with special emphasis upon protecting small business against more powerful rivals. Section 33c responds to the problem of disproportionate discounts obtained from suppliers, which may result in forcing smaller retailers out of business, by providing that "A retail trader shall not by any threat, promise or intimidation induce or procure or attempt to induce or procure a manufacturer or wholesale trader to sell to him ... under terms or conditions ... more favorable than those upon which that manufacturer or wholesaler is selling or offering for sale ... to other retail traders."

Price cutting that was alleged to be engaged in mainly by some larger selling organizations to the detriment of smaller rivals, whose finances do not permit them to match this form of competition, is dealt with in s. 33a, which provides that it is an offense for a retailer to place a limit on the quantity of goods that may be purchased at a particular price or for a retailer to refuse to supply a quantity of goods demanded by an intending purchaser.

The Trade Practices Act–1965

A renewed effort toward federal control was taken with the Trade Practices Act of 1965: "An Act to preserve competition in Australian trade and commerce to the extent required by the public interest." The regulations under the Act became effective on September 1, 1967, and the repeal of the Australian Industries Preservation Act was effective at the same time.

The Trade Practices Act prohibits collusive bidding; otherwise trade practices which are agreed to by firms that would otherwise be competitors are "examinable." Trade agreements are to be registered with the Commissioner of Trade Agreements, who decides if proceedings are to be instituted. A Trade Practices Tribunal, which examines agreements brought forward by the commissioner, may make cease and desist orders.

Examinable practices include a buyer inducing a discriminatory advantage, a supplier forcing another person's goods as a condition of selling his own, a trade association inducing a business to refuse to deal with a third party, a dominant seller (who has at least one-third of the market) who utilizes his power to refuse to deal, engages in predatory price cutting, or imposes terms that could not otherwise be imposed if it were not for his dominant position. In considering whether a practice is contrary to the public interest, the Tribunal must take as the basis of its consideration the principle that the preservation and encouragement of competition are desirable in the public interest.

The potential impact of the Act upon retailing may be significant. The first report of the commissioner indicates that the number of horizontal agreements involving retailers that were registered is relatively small, but, since no analysis is offered, the actual extent or nature of these agreements is not known.[52] However, there are nearly 6,000 vertical distribution agreements between manufacturers or wholesalers and retailers. If a distribution agreement contains restrictions, as on prices or outlets, and if the manufacturer engages in direct sales, in competition with retailers, then the arrangement comes within the Act. Many retailers are involved because one registration by a supplier may involve large numbers of retailers.

A number of complaints have arisen under the Act, and these are viewed by the commissioner as a useful means of focusing attention; a number of major cases being studied began in this way. The practice of collective inducement to refuse to deal seems presently the most likely practice to lead to proceedings. The complainants have been largely retailers, and those complained of have been manufacturers or wholesalers or else the trade associations the complainant desires to join. At the retail level most effect seems to come from distribution agreements, particularly in regard to exclusive dealing and price maintenance on manufacturers' brand lines.

Many vertical agreements complement horizontal ones. The most common restriction is upon price competition, but also very common is a limitation upon distribution channels, and often the two restrictions run together. The agreements seek to protect those within the structure, other sellers cannot obtain the particular goods at prices that would permit them to compete effectively. Resale price maintenance is widespread, both on producer and consumer goods. It is sometimes a part of a horizontal agreement, but more often is a feature of vertical agreements, often coupled with exclusive dealing.

Both exclusive dealing and resale price maintenance have been common in Australian marketing throughout the century. As early as 1901 Standard Oil obtained a market position in Australia by offering retailers a rebate if they sold American kerosene exclusively.[53] Exclusive dealing contracts between manufacturers or wholesalers and retailers have been upheld as valid restraints of trade because "In the case of contracts in restraint of trade, made between parties at arms' length, the court is slow to hold a restriction, which they themselves have agreed upon, to be unreasonable."[54] In the late 1800s a brewer advanced money for the purchase of a public house, in return for a mortgage and a covenant that as long as the premises was licensed the mortgagor and all successive occupiers would deal exclusively with the brewer. The Court held the covenant was valid as long as the sum that had been advanced was not repaid.[55] More recently, in *Peters* v. *Patricia's,* a five-year agreement provided that so long as the seller supplied ice cream at the agreed prices the retailer was bound not to sell ice cream other than that supplied by the seller. The Court held that this restraint was reasonable as between the parties; the issue as to whether the restraint was injurious to the public was not raised.[56]

Resale price maintenance has also been prevalent in Australian retailing. As early as 1915 some retail prices were maintained in the grocery trade by suppliers who advertised both retail and whosesale prices.[57] Contractual price maintenance also existed in the early part of the century. For example, the Palmolive Company required agreements to be signed by grocers in which it was promised that Palmolive soap would be sold at the price established by the company.[58] Refusal to deal has also been a means of maintaining retail prices. In a case under the Queensland Profiteering Prevention Act of 1920 the court held that the intention of the Act was not to prevent "even a monopolistic company from refusing to sell unless the buyer enters into some agreement . . . to resell the commodity on terms imposed."[59]

The High Court has also permitted the enforcement of price maintenance when a retailer does not obtain the product directly from the supplier. Grocers and other retailers selling "Persil," a soap powder, were required to sell at a fixed price. A cash and carry store offered its customers a discount "toward cartage costs" when two packets of Persil were included in an order. Subsequently the manufacturer refused to continue supplies, but the retailer obtained the product from another source. The supplier took legal action on the basis of the contract's provision that the restriction applied even if the product was obtained otherwise than directly from the manufacturer.[60]

It would seem that the Trade Practices Act has potential impact upon resale price maintenance because its provisions are so extensive.[61] The common practice of agreement among sellers as to a price, together with agreements to take punitive action against retailers, or refusal to deal or withdraw discounts, come within the Act. Furthermore, when a seller employs direct distribution as well as selling through independent distributors, he is imposing a restriction upon competitors when he requires a distributor to charge a stipulated price.

The position of exclusive dealing is less clear. In 1951 the major oil companies undertook a program of converting the existing system of multi-brand retailers to exclusive dealers. The agreements that were introduced provided for not only exclusive dealing, but also a number of other restrictive provisions. An early form of such agreements was upheld in *Ampol* v. *Mutton,*[62] where the Court followed the decision in *Peters* v. *Patricia's* and earlier cases.

However, an English case—*Petrofina (Gt. Britain) Ltd.* v. *Martin* (1965) 2 W.L.R. 1299—held that an exclusive agreement was an unreasonable restraint of trade. The Court of Appeal affirmed this decision, and thus an exclusive dealing agreement may be unenforceable unless incorporated in a transfer of real estate or similar property, and then only if it is no more restrictive than necessary to protect the mortgagee's interest as to the value of his loan.

This type of agreement would not be illegal in Australia, but an attempt to protect such agreements from being considered by the Trade Practices Tribunal was made by the attorney general at the second reading stage of the Trade Practices Act. Section 39 (2B) was introduced to excuse a tying practice undertaken to secure a lease or a loan of money. This subsection and the one following it were not accepted by Parliament.[63] This type of vertical arrangement involving retailers is not clearly beyond the scope of potential regulation.

Regulation of Foreign Retailing

In addition to state regulations, foreign goods imported into Australia are subject to the provisions of the Federal Commerce (Trade Description) Act 1905-1966. This Act requires that there be applied to imported goods appropriate "trade descriptions" indicating accurately the quantity and composition, country of origin, seller's name, and other information. The effect of this Act was evident as early as 1908 when a shipment of patent medicine from the United States was detained by Australian customs authorities "on account of extravagant claims." The U.S. Consul examined the goods and reported that the wrappers claimed that the product would cure forty types of illness, and "had the medicine been a cure for thirty-nine less maladies it would have had a better chance to get through."[64] A further warning to American exporters came in 1916, when it was reported that the enforcement of the Act was "becoming more rigid."[65] The amendment of the Act in 1966 also suggests that it is still considered an important element in the Commonwealth's trade regulation scheme.

The means of marketing American goods early in the century was largely by local agents or salesmen from the United States.[66] At that time no restrictions were placed upon salesmen from abroad, either in the form of licenses or other fees.[67] By the 1920s some American companies had opened sales branches in the larger capital cities, but this tended to result in numerous difficulties concerning taxation. More typically, business was conducted by local companies, registered under the appropriate State Company Acts. There were no important restrictions upon foreign companies marketing in this manner.[68] Today, distributing through an Australian subsidiary is common, where the sales volume is relatively large, and especially where the parent company wishes to retain control over distribution.

Most of the American and other foreign firms doing business in Australia, either directly or through Australian subsidiaries, have, of course, concentrated upon industrial or wholesale sales. However, some direct selling companies, such as Singer, have operated in the Australian market for a number of years and British capital has played a role in some long-established department store firms. Safeway and Kresge are two more recent American entrants into Australian retailing.

Foreign nationals are generally permitted to own property and carry on business in Australia on the same basis as Australian citizens, and foreign companies are free to participate in nearly all areas of business, subject to compliance with domestic regulations. Furthermore, Australia has always provided a favorable climate for foreign business interests; successive governments of varying political persuasions have welcomed investment from abroad as an important means of maintaining economic growth. No special approval of investment from abroad is required, for there is no specific legislation dealing directly with such investment. However, some areas of business, particularly communication and mining, are reserved to Australian controlled firms. There are no legal provisions requiring local participation in the equity or management of companies established by foreign interests. However, there is a growing public sentiment that opportunities should be provided for local participation in businesses established by foreign investors.

In the application of laws and regulations, foreign-owned enterprises receive substantially the same treatment as does an Australian enterprise. Indeed, in Australia, a "foreign" company is one incorporated under the laws of any state or nation other than the state in which the business is located. Each such foreign company is required to register in the state, but generally no annual or license fee is charged.

Concluding Comments

There is neither a national policy, nor a consistent set of state policies, toward retailing in Australia. The lack of national policy derives in part from the constitutional and judicial limitations upon the powers of the federal government. State policy has not been broadly conceived because of an attitude of indifference toward retailing, as well as marketing in general. The regulations that do exist have evolved haphazardly throughout the century, mainly as offshoots from other interests, such as public health and labor conditions. Facts about retailing problems and practices, upon which regulatory activities might be based, do not exist; even fundamental census data for business has not been compiled consistently. Finally, there is little professional interest in retailing, or its regulation.

Government regulation of business has never had popular support; individualism and competitive activity are not accepted social norms, and the concept of "public interest" is vague. Furthermore, both labor and large business exercise considerable power in the Commonwealth. Even in the area of restrictive practices, legislation has not been designed to protect the interests of the consumer so much as those of labor and business itself. There is no mechanism for developing an informed public. The almost impenetrable veil of secrecy that surrounds Australian business has been protected under the new Trade Practices Act. In Britain, details of agreements that have been registered are available for public inspection; in Australia the register is secret. Moreover, it is significant in light of the fragmented nature of state regulation that no central agency has been established to maintain contact among the states to coordinate regulatory activity.

Given the nature of the Australian political system, and a social environment dominated by an attitude of "live and let live," it is unlikely that a coordinated public policy toward retailing will emerge in the foreseeable future.

June 1970

Notes

1. Prior to the adoption of the Federal Constitution the several states had been British Crown Colonies with varying degrees of self-government under separate constitutions granted by the Imperial Parliament.

2. Until 1918, a hawker in Victoria was required to have a separate license for each municipality in which he traded.

3. Hawkers who did not hold a license could be charged under vagrancy acts.

4. An N.S.W. Act of 1918 made it an offense for a hawker to have spiritous liquor in his possession, whether for sale or otherwise.

5. Hendy and Rider (1919) 26 C.L.R. 5.

6. *Manly Municipal Council* v. *Kalajzich* (1964) 10 L.G.R.A. 98.

7. City of Melbourne, Proceedings of Council, 1926-27, p. 642.

8. *Lowe* v. *Cant* (1962) S.A.S.R. 78.

9. H. Daniel and M. Bell, *Australia: The New Customer* (New York: The Ronald Press Co., 1946), pp. 88-89.

10. *Literature Board of Review* v. *H.M.H. Publishing Company* (1964) Qld.R.261.

11. *Spence* v. *Ravenscroft* (1914) 18 C.L.R. 349.

12. *Attorney General of Queensland* v. *Wilkinson* (1958) 100 C.L.R. 422.

13. Similar legislation was passed in Queensland and South Australia in 1900. The lists of trades exempted in South Australia were long: chemists, milkmen, eating houses, restaurants, ham, fish, fruit, tobacconists', hairdressers', and confectioners' shops, railway news-stalls, undertakers, public-houses, and wine-shops. Subsequently, in 1902, shops were exempted if they were operated by a shopkeeper who employed only members of his family.

14. *Journal of Comparative Legislation,* Vol. 14 (1914), p. 149.

15. G.A.J. Simpson-Lee, "New South Wales Traders' Protection Association, 1923-1944," *The Economic Record* 29 (1953), p. 241.

16. Annual Report, Service Station Division, Australian Automobile Chamber of Commerce, 1966-67.

17. *Grant* v. *Australian Knitting Mills* (1933) 50 C.L.R. 387.

18. Groom and the City of Port Adelaide (1922) 31 C.L.R. 109.

19. F. H. Reuter, "National Problems of Pure Food and Pure Food Legislation – Australia," *Food, Drug and Cosmetic Law Journal* 15 (1960), p. 728.

20. Local Government Act of Victoria, 1915.

21. *Howe* v. *Cassidy,* 1907 St.R.Qld.

22. Alex C. Castles, "State Control of Unfair Trading Practices in Australia," *The Australian Law Journal* 38 (1964), p. 167.

23. *Moran & Cato Pty Ltd.* v. *Cantlon* (1914) 18 C.L.R. 578.

24. G. A. J. Simpson-Lee, "New South Wales Traders' Protection Association, 1923-44," *The Economic Record* 29 (November 1953), p. 242.

25. *Moran & Cato Pty Ltd.* v. *Cantlon* (1914) 18 C.L.R. 578 at 585.

26. Simpson-Lee, *The Economic Record* 29 (November 1953), p. 242.

27. Home Benefits Proprietary Limited and Crafter (1938-39) 61 C.L.R. 701 at 708.

28. Ibid., p. 705.

29. Ibid., p. 725.

30. *Goodwin (Adelaide) Ltd.* v. *Brebner* (1962) S.A.S.R. 78 at 81.

31. F. R. Beasley, "Produce Pools in Australia," *Journal of Comparative Legislation* 10 (1928), pp. 74-81, 259-273.

32. A. G. Whitlam, "Marketing Organization," *The Annals of the American Academy of Political and Social Science* 158 (1931), p. 117.

33. *Peppers Self Service Stores* v. *Scott* (1958) 98 C.L.R. 606.

34. This regulation was sustained in *Harper* v. *The State of Victoria* (1966-67) 40 A.L.J.R. 49.

35. *Annual Report,* Victorian Automobile Chamber of Commerce, 1955-56.

36. *Australian Automobile Trade Journal,* March 1, 1957, p. 44.

37. *The Australian,* September 16, 1964.

38. States Grants (Petroleum Products) October 1965, No. 27 of 1965 9D.

39. P. H. Karmel and Maureen Brunt, *The Structure of the Australian Economy* (Melbourne: F. W. Cheshire, 1963), p. 73.

40. "Comparative Study of the Antitrust Laws of British Dominions and of their Administration," *Journal of Comparative Legislation,* 1937, pp. 68-69.

41. Ibid., p. 68.

42. J. Hutton, "Restrictive Trade Practices Legislation, Trade Associations and Orderly Marketing Schemes in Western Australia," *The Economic Record* 40 (1964), pp. 193-4.

43. U.S. Department of Commerce and Labor, Consular Reports, August 1902 (No. 263), pp. 672-73.

44. *Huddart Perker* v. *Moorhead* (1909) 8 C.L.R. 330. Several attempts by federal governments to extend power in this field by referendum failed.

45. D. J. Stalley, "Federal Control of Monopoly in Australia," *The University of Queensland Law Journal* 3 (1959), p. 280.

46. *Bourke Appliances Pty. Ltd.* v. *Wonder* (1965) V.R. 511 at 520-21.

47. One writer suggests that the effect upon monopoly power was mainly indirect, for in an analysis of government enterprises in New South Wales, it is concluded that "The practical motive behind nearly all the enterprises was nothing more than . . . reducing government costs." R. S. Parker, "Public Enterprise in New South Wales," *Australian Journal of Politics and History* 4 (1958), p. 212.

48. U.S. Department of Commerce, *Commerce Reports,* January 22, 1923, p. 254.

49. *Garage and Service Stations Association of Queensland Inc.* v. *Stellmach* (1940) St. R. Qd 60.

50. *Cockburn Cement Pty. Ltd.* v. *Wallwerk* (1958) 59 W.A.L.R. 75.

51. Report of the Honorary Royal Commission on Restrictive Trade Practices and Legislation, 1958, pp. 12-13.

52. Commissioner of Trade Practices, *First Annual Report* (Canberra: Commonwealth Government Printer, 1968).

53. *Australasian Hardware and Machinery,* June 2, 1902, p. 226; *The Grocer of Australasia,* August 27, 1904, p. 1.

54. *Cooper* v. *Cooper* (1941) 65 C.L.R. 162 at 184.

55. *Tooth* v. *Parkes* (1900) L.R. (N.S.W.) Eq. 173.

56. *Peters* v. *Patricia's* (1947) 77 C.L.R. 574.

57. *Southern Grocer,* May 20, 1915, p. 35.

58. This form of agreement was upheld in *Palmolive C. (Australasia) Ltd.* v. *McCaskie* (1925) 26 S.R. (N.S.W.) 212.

59. *Smith* v. *Shell Co. of Australia Ltd.* (1934), S.R.Qd at p. 10.

60. J. Kitchen & Sons and Stewart's Cash and Carry Stores (1942) 66 C.L.R. 116.

61. J. G. Collinge, "Resale Price Maintenance and the Trade Practices Act," *Law Institute Journal* 41 (1967), p. 482.

62. *Ampol* v. *Mutton* (1953) 53 S.R. (N.S.W.) 1.

63. R. Baxt, "Restraint of Trade at Common Law – The Tied 'House' or Oil Station," *The Australian Lawyer* 7 (1967), p. 87.

64. U.S. Department of Commerce and Labor Monthly Consular and Trade Reports, July 1908 (No. 334), pp. 169-70.

65. *Exporting to Australia,* U.S. Department of Commerce, Misc. Series No. 45, 1916, p. 12.

66. *Marketing Goods in Foreign Countries,* U.S. Department of Commerce and Labor, Special Consular Reports, Vol 34 (1905), pp. 160-64.

67. *Commercial Travellers in Foreign Countries,* U.S. Department of Commerce and Labor, Special Consular Reports, Vol. 28 (1904), pp. 37-38.

68. *Australia, A Commercial and Industrial Handbook,* U.S. Department of Commerce, Special Agents Series, 1922.

3 Belgium

J. J. BODDEWYN

Basic Principles

Belgian public policy towards retailing is a mixture of three fundamental approaches to organizing economic life. *First,* there is the principle of *liberté du commerce,* that is, the freedom to start and operate a business. However, this laissez-faire principle was embodied in an old French-Revolution decree of 1791 which added that commerce can be reasonably regulated in the public interest by national and/or local authorities.

Sparsely used during the nineteenth century and until World War I, this qualification received fuller expression when the Great Depression of the 1930s definitely fostered the *second* principle that government should intervene "whenever freedom oppresses, and regulation liberates."[1] However, interventionism also came to take the form of promoting and assisting certain groups and practices.

Third, the corporative principle of self-regulation, which harks back to the pre-Revolutionary guild system, was quiescent until the turn of this century when small business (the "middle classes"[2]) began to agitate for greater professional control over commercial entry and practices. This later development is particularly evident in the role granted to professional associations in the regulation of licensure and weekly-closing, and in the halting of unfair competitive practices.

Major Forces

The emergence and interweaving of these liberal, interventionist, and corporative principles reflect general ideological currents found in other parts of Belgium's economy and society, but also the evolution of retailing itself and of other forces as well.

Evolving Retailing

The core of Belgian retailing is the small sedentary merchant who has been increasingly threatened by other types. In the first half of the nineteenth century, the threat came from itinerant traders; it continued with the advent of

37

department stores, which pitched large stores against smaller ones after 1860; and it went on with the "five-and-tens" of around 1930 which redemocratized ratailing, as did the supermarkets and discount houses of the 1950s and 1960s. These new types of retailers repeatedly introduced new competitive policies and practices usually centered on prices, but also on promotion and assortment. Besides, periods of inflation (after World War I) and unemployment (during the 1930s) swelled the ranks of small retailers, often with marginal stores.

Belgian retailing came in fact to be divided into three main groups: (1) traditional, sedentary, full-time, small and medium retailers, now down to about three-fourths of the stores and shops; (2) large stores (department stores, chain stores, consumer cooperatives), relatively minute in number, but with a growing share of the market (about 15 percent in the late sixties); and (3) a marginal group of intermittent (e.g., in public markets), itinerant (e.g., door-to-door) accessory (e.g., the wife's side business, or the moonlighter), and artificial (e.g., the company store) retailers who used to represent as much as one-third of Belgian retailing, but who are progressively being squeezed out on account of better employment opportunities, taxes (including social-security contributions), registration, and licensing requirements. Of the first group, about one-eighth is presently "semi-integrated" through voluntary chains and other forms of association. Large-scale retailing is increasingly dominated by foreign owners that have acquired Belgian firms, and this new factor may well affect public policy in the future.

The Middle-Classes Movement

The nineteenth century had seen the industrial sector bloom, and the working classes stake their basic claims for decent economic and social treatment. Similarly, the middle classes came of age around the turn of the century when they requested public help in the matters of credit, education, and association, and protection against unfair competitive practices. Above all, they wanted public recognition of their unique economic contribution of skill, ubiquity, service, and entrepreneurship, and of their social usefulness as an intermediary group—both buffer and gateway between high bourgeoisie and proletariat, and between Left and Right. In this respect, they felt neglected or ignored rather than abused. However, adverse economic developments in the 1920s and the 1930s—inflation, depression, discriminatory fiscal measures, as well as new aggressive or marginal retailers—added injury to insult. Economic facts were thus endangering a social movement, but they also helped the middle classes acquire greater consciousness, identity, and unity; and this facilitated recourse to political action.

The Common Market

The European Economic Community (1957) has affected retailing by generating a climate more favorable to growth and modernization, in contrast to the

Malthusian atmostphere that had prevailed since the Great Depression. Besides, it has necessitated new regulations in such matters as taxation (the tax-on-value-added system), professional licensing (foreigners from member countries can no longer be discriminated against), and competition. As the Common Market moves slowly toward the alignment of national legislations, its impact on Belgian public policy is likely to increase—not the least in the matter of consumer protection (e.g., food ingredients and labeling). Some Benelux agreements (e.g., about trademark registration) are also relevant in Belgian public policy.

The Consumer Movement

In Belgium as elsewhere, consumers are getting better organized and are becoming more vocal. Besides, government sees in "consumerism" an issue much less controversial than the rivalry between small and large retailers. These new pressure and interest are increasingly affecting the development of public policy toward retailing.

Emerging Public Policy

Objectives

Until the 1930s, there was really no sectoral policy toward retailing because public policy largely amounted to letting a slightly constrained market system achieve desirable economic goals. The few regulatory measures were largely conceived as marginal improvements of the free enterprise system (e.g., in the matters of fraud and health).

After World War I and its difficult aftermath, and particularly during the depression of the 1930s, the government became involved in expliciting economic and social goals, and responsible for insuring their achievement. This new involvement of the state immediately involved retailing in the goals of price stabilization, full employment, and higher productivity. However, during the poor 1930s, public policy dealt mostly with the protection of the commercial middle classes in order to achieve some equilibrium among competing forms of distribution and between economic change and social stability—really an attempt to provide better social integration in Belgian society.

The more prosperous post-World War II years allowed the elaboration of a comprehensive and positive program for the middle classes in replacement of a fragmentary and protectionist one. This period also permitted the beginning of a public policy toward the whole of retailing that incorporates the following goals which have not always been clearly stated and which have at times conflicted:

1. Maintain the small and medium independent retailer for the economic, political, social, and cultural contributions he makes, by insuring equal chances and fair remuneration for all retailers.
2. Improve general economic development (expansion of production and im-

provement in the allocation of factors of production) and assist price stability through greater productivity in retailing.
3. Ameliorate the pattern of private consumption by protecting consumers against dubious commercial practices and abuses of economic power.

An emerging goal is optimal land use and environmental protection, which is likely to assume greater absolute and relative importance in coming years.

Instruments

To achieve these goals, government has enacted a vast array of laws and decrees. The latter set not only the general rules of the game, which are still, in principle, rules of freedom of entry and competition, but they also provide many measures of direct control over marketing activities—from relations with suppliers, land-lords, and licensors, to pricing, product, promotion, and land-use practices. Besides, the executive government does now enter into contractual agreements with private firms in such matters as prices (law of 23 December 1969).

Government is also increasingly in a position to promote or demote a certain sector, subsector, or practice. Various monetary measures, such as the granting of cheaper and more abundant small-business credit, figure prominently here, while such assistance has been denied to large retailers and itinerant traders.

In another vein, the new tax-on-value-added system (1971) is likely to have some structural effect on retailing since—unlike the previous business transaction tax—it is neutral as to the amount of vertical integration in the system. Further-more, public expenditures on commercial education, research and statistics, and on the administration of various programs, are much larger. Additionally, there are now more public institutions to group and represent retailers through consultative bodies.

This expanded set of tools allows government a large freedom of maneuver, as it can simultaneously encourage entry into retailing through education and credit programs for newcomers, but also restrict it through: (1) licensing; (2) various legal incapacities (e.g., for minors) and incompatibilities (e.g., for public officials); (3) the discretionary restriction of the number of itinerant traders and non-EEC businessmen; (4) court decisions imposing closure as a penalty; (5) land-use controls; and (6) its rarely-used power to reserve the exercise of economic activities to designated persons and firms.[3] Moreover, the powers of investigation and enforcement attached to a particular measure are multiplied by the fact that the pervasiveness of the interventionist network allows the Executive to use or withhold many instruments to warn, bother, bully, or coerce whoever does not obey a particular law or does not cooperate with government.

Still, it is being increasingly recognized that there are practical limits to public intervention as government cannot know and do everything, and as the benefits of competition and innovation have again been acknowledged in the postwar period. Hence, there is greater willingness to give play to market forces (*vide* the

1960 law against abuses of monopoly power, and the Common Market directives on freedom of establishment), and to have the government "help do" rather than "do," in an increasingly corporative framework.

This last tendency reflects the recognition that economic participants are better equipped to consider what is "fair" and "unfair" than the government which, in this view, should limit itself to combat what is "illegal," that is, contrary to the public order. This view also mirrors a relative disaffection with atomistic competition, and the growing demand by interested parties throughout society for participation in the making and application of the policies that affect them.

Structure

The Economic Affairs Ministry supervises the application of most commercial regulation, sometimes in collaboration with, or for other ministries (e.g., Public Health, Finance, Labor, Public Works, Education). It is more particularly responsible for supervising the development of large-scale retailing. On the other hand, the middle classes (including small and medium-sized retailers and craftsmen) obtained their own ministry in 1954. This Ministry of the Middle Classes[4] has handled mainly those special regulations and programs affecting firms below a certain size (e.g., twenty employees in the case of commercial firms), but also all itinerant traders and foreign businessmen; and it would like to extend its jurisdiction over the entire services sector, irrespective of size. The Ministry of Public Works is likely to become more important on account of its land-use planning responsibilities.

The following sections analyze major regulations bearing on retailing. The focus is on national laws, which are enacted by Parliament, and applied by the Executive. The latter issues royal and ministerial decrees as well as directives to implement the laws; and it applies them all. Adjudication is mostly performed by the Judiciary, although there are a few administrative courts in such matters as licensure, work permits for foreign businessmen, and abuses of economic power. Needless to say, the volume of regulations to apply, the limited resources of the various authorities, doubts about the validity of certain regulations, and the clogging of court calendars have frequently restricted enforcement.

Cities now play a smaller role in regulating commercial practices and in taxing retailers. However, they are associated with the application of the laws on licensing and weekly closing of stores; and the recent legislation of land-use planning and urban renewal has given them greater powers in what promises to become a major aspect of public policy toward retailing.

Belgium being a statutory-law country, jurisprudence does not play a major role in the application of economic laws, but is more important in the application of civil and commercial law (e.g., regarding contracts). Customs are considered in such matters as unfair competitive practices.

Regulating Retailing Actors

Few Closed Fields

Outside of public utilities, which monopolize the retailing of water, gas, and electricity (and sometimes sell appliances), private enterprise conducts practically all retail activities. Only in the "company store" area are private firms statutorily curtailed in order to prevent the exploitations of employees (the first motive after 1887) and to reduce "unfair competition" against established retailers (the more recent motive of the law of 15 May 1956). Company stores are now largely restricted to the sale of meals, health and social services, work clothing and equipment, and of the firm's own products and services. Autonomous personnel cooperatives are authorized only if they have their own premises and are not run by employees during their regular working hours; and company subsidies are only allowed if they come out of net profits.

There are restrictions on civil servants holding business positions; and foreigners must obtain a permit to start and operate a business, but the latter restrictions have been largely eliminated as far as businessmen from other Common Market countries are concerned.

Barriers of Entry

Outside of the pharmacy[5] and itinerant trade fields, there is no legal limit on the number and spacing of stores. However, trade associations informally control minimum distance between stores in such areas as newspapers and photographic equipment. Besides, licensure laws have certainly complicated entry, while the development of land-use planning increasingly restricts the location of stores. There is also a 1935 royal decree which allows (under certain stringent conditions) the members of an industry to restrict its expansion in case of overcapacity, but it has not received any application in retailing.

Itinerant Trade. Non-sedentary merchants have been the object of fiscal discrimination since 1819, and of curtailments since 1935, in order to shield consumers against fly-by-night operators and to reduce tax evasion, but also to protect established retailers. There is now in fact an informal *numerus clausus* applied by the Ministry of the Middle Classes, limiting itinerant trade in public markets, on the street, and from door to door, to somewhat less than 40,000 practitioners. In view of the greater respectability of this field where major consumer firms are now active (e.g., Tupperware and Avon), relaxation is likely. Common Market directives are working in the same direction.

Licensure. The law of 24 December 1958 allows conditions to be laid down for the exercise of a profession in the crafts, small and medium trades, and in small-scale industry, provided: (1) licensure is requested by the most representative professional federation, which also drafts the entry requirements; (2) this request is seconded by the officially representative High Council of the Middle

Classes, which scrutinizes it and may propose modifications; and (3) the executive government agrees to embody the seconded proposal into a decree. Requirements center on education, apprenticeship, and (until recently) equipment, but not on capitalization and reputation (honorability). Established practitioners and heirs (among others) are automatically granted a license when access to a profession is newly regulated.

This legislation certainly has a corporative tone since the initiative is left to professional interest groups, although: (1) their request is scrutinized by other bodies; (2) they do not pass on an applicant's request for certification, once access to a particular profession has been regulated; and (3) no one has to be a member of a professional association to make such an application.

Licensure is a key feature of the middle-classes program because it makes professional education practically compulsory for new entrants; it boosts the role of, and encourages membership in, professional associations; and it facilitates "notoriety" (honorability) credit granted on the basis of one's good business reputation. An important psychological factor militating in favor of licensing was the advent of the European Economic Community (1957-1958), which, under the principle of "freedom of establishment," allows foreign businessmen from member countries to enter Belgium freely. Belgian tradesmen were afraid that this would lead to an invasion of foreigners denied access in their own countries.

While a score of professions are now regulated, the bulk of non-craft-related retailing has remained unaffected for lack of any easy way of organizing and representing this very amorphous field. It has also been very difficult to amend existing regulations. Hence, the law was revised on 15 December 1970 to authorize several professional federations to initiate the regulation of a particular field. Besides, the executive government, after consultation of the High Council, can require evidence of "managerial knowledge" *(connaissances de gestion)* from those running retail and wholesale firms—in fact, nothing more than various forms of secondary or commercial education or of experience will be required. Entry requirements have also been simplified for all professions, with greater emphasis being put on broad commercial and managerial skills acquired through education or experience, rather than on purely technical ones.

Encouragement of Entry and Expansion

The middle classes have been the main beneficiaries of public programs designed to encourage entry and expansion through training and credit facilities (see below). On the other hand, large-scale distribution has been practically excluded from the benefits of the 1950 and 1966 economic expansion laws although, in principle, this was changed under the 1970 revision of these laws. Taxes have played a less obvious role in this matter.

Credit for the Middle Classes. There had long been numerous obstacles to the development of middle-classes credit, but two stood out particularly: (1) the requirement by credit institutions of *real* (e.g., buildings, equipment, stock, personal fortune) rather than *personal* guarantees (e.g., ability and potential) when granting loans; and (2) the relatively high cost of such credit on account of the smallness and occasional riskiness of loans. Many remedies were proposed, and quite a few private initiatives were taken, including credit unions where small businessmen pooled their savings, and mutual-guarantee societies where they vouched for each other. However, they met with little success for lack of support, resources, and good business practices.

The government started to intervene after 1913; but even the 1929 creation of a subsidized Small Professional Credit Fund (and other institutions) authorized to borrow on the market with the state's guarantee, to make short-term loans to approved credit institutions, and to discount various negotiable instruments, was not sufficient. For one thing, public institutions remained as cautious in their lending as traditional banks.

Finally, the Vanden Boeynants law of 24 May 1959 provided a firm basis for "notoriety" loans through the creation of a Guaranty Fund and the further encouragement of mutual-guarantee societies; and it authorized interest subsidies for certain types of loan. This law has proved very successful; and the government now spends about $4 million a year on this program (versus less than $.2 million in 1957). Other subsidies are available in the context of government attempts to revitalize declining regions through "economic expansion" laws (1959, 1966, 1970).[6]

Professional Education for the Middle Classes. Apprenticeship programs for craft-related activities have been supervised by government since around the turn of the century; and commercial education is available in subsidized public and private schools. In 1947, the government set up a National Committee for Professional Education and Development designed to program and coordinate various initiatives emanating from middle-classes associations, but largely financed by the state. The aim here is not only to provide pre- and continuing education, but also to foster a small-and-independent business ideology, something not done by regular commercial schools. The bulk of the Middle-Classes Ministry budget is now devoted to professional education.

The emphasis is increasingly on the concentration of programs in multi-professional centers throughout Belgium; and on the acquisition of management, entrepreneurship, and marketing skills rather than on purely technical training and ideological indoctrination. These programs have received a major boost from the licensing law which requires evidence of adequate preparation and/or experience (e.g., through apprenticeship); but they need to be better related to the future opportunities outlined in economic forecasts and plans.

Tax-Relief. Consumer cooperatives have long benefited from minor tax exemptions. Controversy, however, has tended to focus on the respective tax burdens of large incorporated retail firms and of their small unincorporated competitors. Small retailers have complained that unincorporated firms pay relatively more taxes, and that the business-transaction tax did bear more heavily on non-integrated firms, thereby favoring larger stores.[7] The latter have retorted that tax evasion is much more prevalent among small stores, and that the single levying of the business-transaction tax, and ultimately the adoption of a tax-on-value-added (TVA) system in 1971, have eliminated any fiscal discrimination.

This discussion has been largely inconclusive, and there is no major public policy in this respect. However, the TVA system started on 1 January 1971 is neutral as far as vertical integration is concerned, although it provides an optional simplified system for small firms. Besides, in the matter of direct taxation, small businessmen can be taxed on their presumed rather than actual business income. Municipalities tax firms on the basis of the motive power installed and the size of the workforce, but no discrimination is intended here against large stores.

Restrictions on Growth

At first, department stores (dating from around 1860) were penalized by some municipalities through taxes based on various measures of physical size. Ultimately, the expansion of large stores (defined at one time as any store employing more than five employees in more than three branches of trade) was severely restricted outside of the fifteen cities with more than 50,000 inhabitants, through several "padlock" laws from 1936 to 1961, following the advent of five-and-ten stores during the depression. The modernization of Belgian retailing was definitely delayed by these laws.

In a subtler way, land-use planning as well as the proposed and ultimately inevitable regulation of closing hours (see below) are likely to hamper the relative growth of large stores.

Regulating Retailing's Structure

Obviously, many rules bearing on entry and growth have been enacted and applied for structural reasons—largely in order to protect the small, traditional, sedentary retailer's share of the market. The government, however, has also encouraged collective action and representation; and it is now paying greater attention to the modernization of retailing, thereby looking favorably at progressive firms of all sizes.

Atomism and Competition

In the European context, freedom of trade includes the right to enter into agreement with one's competitors, provided other major public goals (such as limiting inflation) are not jeopardized. Hence, cartels are legal in Belgium, but they do not seem to have been significant in retailing, if only because suppliers can impose some common behavior on their distributors through resale price maintenance and refusal to sell.

Horizontal Ties

Professional Membership and Cooperation. There are no statutory trade associations in Belgium, but the government has encouraged membership in professional and interprofessional[8] associations by: (1) providing legal forms for their incorporation as "professional unions" or "non-profit associations"; (2) subsidizing many of their educational programs; and (3) enacting laws on licensure and weekly-closing which gives them some co-regulatory power (see above and below). Cooperation among small retailers through buying groups, cooperatives, and voluntary chains has been applauded by government, but it has received only minor tax relief. Cooperative department stores organized by small retailers have recently been encouraged through the granting of public credit.

Vertical Relationships

There is no requirement that intercompany agreements be officially reported, or that they be put in writing. Distributors can grant different discounts to customers; and resale price maintenance (RPM) is condoned and readily enforceable on grounds of breach of contract (if there is one) or of unfair competition (if there is none, as the non-signer's clause is not applicable in Belgium). Besides, refusal-to-sell is not only permissible, but widely practiced. For certain products, such as bicycles, records, tires, and watches, wholesalers cannot be bypassed on account of private agreements to that effect; and exclusive dealership agreements are also legal and common, resulting sometimes in denying the sale of branded products to large stores.

However, refusal-to-sell is illegal if it is intended to harm a competitor and to create scarcity conditions for speculative reasons, and/or if it results in the abuse of one's economic power.[9] Besides, it is now forbidden when it jeopardizes the execution of a "program-contract" whereby a firm commits itself vis-à-vis the government to hold down certain prices [law of 23 December 1969]. Moreover, a firm can be prosecuted if its RPM prices are "abnormal" [law-decree of 22 January 1945]; and the government can always fix a maximum price below the presently imposed one. Additionally, the EEC's antitrust regulations have weakened exclusive dealerships that restrict cross-border trade, particularly following the Grundig-Consten case (but there has been some more recent relaxation in the Kodak and Omega cases). It is likely that resale price maintenance and refusal-to-sell will be further restricted in Belgium if only because neighboring countries have done it, but also because such a restriction makes sense in the context of curtailing inflation. (There is already an agreement between major brand manufacturers of consumer products and large retailers, whereby discounting is allowed under certain conditions.)

The law of 27 July 1961 severely restricts the freedom of the grantor of an exclusive dealership of unlimited duration, since he must in most cases give sufficient notice of cancellation, *and* pay an indemnity to compensate the grantee for the clientele he created and for certain expenses he incurred. The law of 13 April 1971 has extended these obligations to "quasi exclusive" dealerships,

to those of great importance to the grantee, and even to those of limited
duration if renewed twice. Besides, preliminary notice must be given before
cancelling a limited-duration dealership. The intent here is to protect small
distributors, but it also reflects the growing tendency to recognize "intellectual
rights" to the fruits of one's work (as with the right to renew one's commercial
lease).

Intertype Competition

Established retailers of any size tend to view new marketing types as "disorganiz-
ing the market"; and the government has frequently sided with them in this
matter. Several of the enactments bearing on entry and growth (see above) were
motivated by such considerations. There is also a growing concern for ensuring
"fair" competition, which has frequently resulted in regulations of marketing
practices designed to restrict intertype competition (see below). Still, it is being
acknowledged that the survival and growth of the commercial middle class
require specializing in what they can do best, and doing it well. This spells out
focusing on products and services where novelty, care, taste, and other advantages can surpass or complement mass distribution. It also means professionali-
zation through private and public forms of education, cooperation and licensure,
as well as state subsidies for modernization and for alleviating the social problems created by the need for continuous adaptation and restructuration.

Hence, the future of small and medium-sized retailers is no longer visualized
as a stark choice between "natural disappearance" à la laissez-faire and "artificial
survival" through protectionism. Instead, it is now seen as resulting from the
combination of the self-efforts of the better practitioners and of a positive
public program. The overall philosophy can be summarized as: "Let the best
survive and prosper, but let's make sure that independent retailers have a real
chance to start, survive, and prosper." Public policy is thus increasingly expected
to focus on those small firms that are "in transit" to a larger size or remain small
because it suits their function; while a third group of firms that are "too small"
would receive "social" help to facilitate their transition to other occupations or
even into early retirement.

Intersectorial Relationships

Interest in growth has spurred economic planning (started in 1959) which is
paying much more attention to the tertiary sector in the third 1971-1975 plan.
This is in contrast to the traditional emphasis on industry in Belgian public
policy because distribution has long been thought to be inefficient, to drain
manpower needed elsewhere, to contribute to inflationary demand, and to
generate unnecessary needs. It is now perceived that the tertiary sector is less
vulnerable to economic fluctuations and can thus contribute more steadily and
predictably to the growth of the Gross National Product and of full employ-

ment. Besides, modern forms of retailing can help keep prices down in inflationary times.

Professional associations (including the one grouping large stores) received a definite boost from the post-World War II development of consultative bodies (mainly, the Central Economic Council and the High Council of the Middle Classes) where they are usually represented, and whose advice is often solicited by government. Retailing also sits on the National Committee for Economic Expansion, a small but highly influential advisory body; and it is represented on other public bodies such as the Economic Planning Bureau. While such bodies have not eliminated other lobbying channels, they are important media for informing and influencing government, and for educating opponents. However, retailing lacks a strong unified voice because of the abiding (although slowly declining) hostility between small and large firms, and because there has not been any major issue to unite all retailers against government and other interest groups.

On the other hand, there is now greater rapport between distribution and consumer groups. The advisory Consumers Council, however, does not formally include representatives (only "experts") from distribution, largely because it is difficult to find an acceptable way of balancing the representation of small- and large-scale retailing—a problem also encountered within the Central Economic Council, where there is only a special Distribution Commission rather than a full-fledged professional council to represent that sector.

Regulating Retailing Processes

Regulation has been variously motivated by the desire to protect traditional retailers, to enhance fair competition, to shield consumers against unscrupulous practices and some of their own tendencies, and to provide efficient and harmonious use of the land.

Location

Zoning and Land-Use Planning. Municipalities have long been empowered to restrict land use for commercial purposes, through zoning. Following the laws of 29 March 1962 and 22 December 1970, much of this power has shifted to the provincial and the national authorities who are in the process of developing more comprehensive plans. Since distribution has not yet been sufficiently drawn into that kind of planning, large retailers worry about the likely restriction of shopping centers, while small retailers are quite concerned about finding space anywhere. Shopping-center promoters must often pay for access roads and utilities lines; and since 1970, builders must provide adequate parking on their premises or nearby, or contribute to a special parking fund. On the other hand, urban renewal is under way in a number of cities where better access roads and subways are being developed with public money.

Vested Interest in Location. The holders of commercial leases were favored by the law of 30 April 1951 which: (1) sets a minimum nine-year duration to these leases, with a triennial revision of rents; and (2) allows them to have their nine-year leases renewed twice (three times since the law of 27 March 1970), or to obtain compensation when their lease is not renewed for legitimate reasons.

Labor Relations and Social Security Benefits

After 1905, Sunday employment was restricted (with various exceptions for the tertiary sector); and the law of 15 July 1964 regulates the minimum and maximum number of hours (with exceptions for family members) and how late employees can work (with exceptions for "successive teams" in the case of stores opening late at night).

The social security laws have been used to squeeze out marginal retailers by imposing minimum contributions to pension, family-allowances, and medical care funds, irrespective of size. On the other hand, the middle classes have obtained various subsidies (particularly in the matter of pensions) because independent businessmen cannot readily bear the full cost of social-security taxes, whose burden is normally split between employers and employees.

Operations

In order to protect retailers, the state has been increasingly inclined to oppose unbridled competition. Of course, the notion of "fair" practices has always been present in commercial law. Thus, the Belgian businessmen sitting on commercial courts have long had to settle cases according to current notions of fairness. Besides, fraudulent and misleading practices have been forbidden by various articles of the Penal Code, and by international conventions regarding the protection of industrial property (e.g., the Paris Convention of 1883 and its subsequent amendments).

However, since the 1930s, businessmen and their trade associations can request cease-and-desist injunctions against acts contrary to fair commercial practices which injure or tend to injure their professional interests (Art. 1 of royal decree No. 55 of 23 December 1934). The novelty was that businessmen no longer had to wait for someone to *actually* injure them before they could sue. Now, they can ask commercial courts to restrain whoever has engaged in acts "contrary to fair usages" and *likely* to hurt their reputation, business, or capacity to compete.

Besides, "consumerism" is becoming a big issue in Belgium as consumers get better organized and represented in public advisory bodies, and because the Ministry of Economic Affairs sees in consumer protection an issue much less controversial than arbitrating the rivalry between small and large retailers. Yet, laws and regulations dealing with consumer *protection* are not new as the inspection of weights and measures was first introduced in 1855. In 1890, the government was authorized to control food ingredients and to prohibit food adulteration and misleading statements (this last law was strengthened on 20 June 1964). Consumer *information* received its first boost in 1923 when price posting was required for all non-luxury products, and it was reinforced by the ministerial decree of 30 April 1948. More in the vein of *protecting consumers against themselves,* were the 1957 and 1965 restrictive regulations of installment credit, which require minimum down-payments and impose a maximum number of installments, but also include "truth-in-lending" provisions as well as limits on charges. There is now also a cooling-off period when credit sales have been made in the home (law of 8 July 1970).

Commercial Practices. The double interest in fair competition and honest service to customers is evident in the new regulations affecting commercial practices (law of 14 July 1971). Broadly supported by established retailers, these revised and expanded rules reveal concern with purging retailing of undesirable elements such as marginal operators (e.g., mobile "hole-in-the-wall" tradesmen), specula- tors (e.g., promoters of "chain" sales; senders of unsolicited merchandise; and those that issue trading stamps and coupons in the hope that many will not be redeemed), and fakers of liquidations, clearances, and special sales.

Besides, the new law expands consumer protection by: (1) requiring more and better information as to the price, size, nature, and denomination of products; and (2) forbidding misleading and/or confusing indications and state- ments, particularly in the matter of price comparison. For the first time, consumer associations are authorized to institute proceedings against those who violate the new rules. The greater restriction of combined offers is partially inspired by the same desire to better inform the consumer, since it is felt that they prevent proper price comparison.

Another goal is that of improving the customer's purchasing patterns by: (1) further discouraging premiums which are thought to prevent prices from declin- ing or give the customer things he does not need or hardly needs; and (2) further attempts to drive out shady operators who sell shoddy or unserviceable goods. Also evident is the objective of protecting the customer against himself, as is apparent in the prohibition or restriction of practices that tempt, shame, or bully the consumer into buying more things than he originally contemplated or needs, through combined offers, unsolicited sales, liquidations, auctions, clear- ances, and "special" sales. Large stores, however, were not too happy with the new restrictions on the latter two since price competition is one of their favorite marketing tools.

Table 3.1 highlights the new regulations of commercial practices. There are, of course, many additional qualifications and exemptions.

"Depenalizing" Economic Regulation. The fast cease-and-desist injunction be- fore a commercial court, previously reserved for unfair practices, can now be requested by interested parties (including consumer and professional associa- tions) for any infraction of the above regulations about commercial information and practices. Such an injunction can be appealed before a higher court. Penal action in regular courts remains possible with a variety of sanctions (fine, prison term, publicizing of the judgment, etc.), particularly in cases of bad faith, violation of an injunction, and repetition. However, it was deemed essential to

Table 3-1

Highlights of the Law of 14 July 1971 on Commercial Practices

I. Commercial Information

A. *Price Publicity*
- Prices must be posted in an apparent and unequivocal manner, and in writing.
- Whoever posts slashed prices must explicitly refer to the prices he previously and habitually (i.e., for at least one month, outside of food products) charged for identical products and services in the same store. The starting date of this price decrease must be posted as long as it lasts.
- It is permissible to reduce prices without making reference to previous prices, and to refer to a regulated or fixed (RPM) price; but comparing one's price to those of someone else is forbidden.

B. *Quantity Indications*
- Containers, tags, or invoices must indicate the net weight, volume, length, or number in legal (usually metric) units.
- The executive government is authorized to further regulate such matters as sizes and permissible discrepancies between the indicated and real quantities.

C. *Product Make-up, Quality and Denomination*
- The executive government can (and does) regulate these matters.
- Misleading signs and indications of origin are forbidden, the latter to be supervised by the Ministry of the Middle Classes.

D. *Commercial Publicity*
  Are forbidden: (1) publicity likely to confuse or mislead the public as to the identity of the firm, and the nature, make-up, origin, quantity, or quality of the product; (2) the publicity of forbidden practices; and (3) misleading, disparaging and/or individual comparisons. However, simple exaggerations and the unavoidable identification of a competitor are not forbidden per se.

II. On Certain Commercial Practices

A. *Selling Below Cost*
- Profitless sales, (that is, below purchase or replacement cost, or with an exceptionally low profit margin) are forbidden with the exception of liquidation and clearance sales, or unless they are necessary in order to dispose of obsolete or deteriorating products, or to meet competition.
- Suppliers cannot forbid such sales when legally permitted, provided they have been offered the opportunity to repurchase the remaining stock.

B. *Liquidation Sales*
- Such sales (possibly below purchase or replacement cost) can take place only if they result from: court decisions; the settling of an estate; the liquidation of the stock of the previous owner; going out of business or dropping certain lines; eliminating or transferring a branch; major remodeling of the store; serious damage to the inventory; and other major causes. In addition, no new merchandise can be acquired for liquidation purpose; the Ministry of Economic Affairs must be notified in advance; no similar going out of business or dropping of certain lines can have taken place during the past three years; the liquidation sale normally has to be held on the firm's regular premises; and price reductions have to be real if such is suggested.

C. *Clearance Sales*
- These sales are limited to out-of-fashion, out-of-season, and shopworn goods habitually sold by the retailer, held when the clearance starts, and not sold at reduced prices during the preceding month.
- Prices must really be reduced and lower than those habitually charged.
- The use of the term "clearance" *(soldes)* is restricted to this type of special sale.
- Clearance sales must be held on the premises where the cleared goods have been habitually sold.

Table 3-1 (continued)

- The executive government determines after consultation with the Central Economic Council and the High Council of the Middle Classes, the periods when such sales can be held (different periods may apply to resort areas; and exceptions probably will be made for border areas where Belgian retailers have to compete with foreign ones.)

D. *Selling at Reduced Prices*
- Announced price reductions have to be real.
- If a price reduction is announced as limited in duration, the seller must have a sufficient stock (or deliver later), and the sale cannot last less than one day. This does not apply to deteriorating products. (The terms "clearance" and "liquidation" cannot be applied to such sales at reduced prices, but it is permissible to announce a special sale "while the supply lasts.")

E. *Public Auctions*
- Auctions of new manufactured products are forbidden unless they are necessitated by the bankruptcy, death, or retirement of the owner, or by a court order. In general, only second-hand products or art objects can be auctioned off at retail. Various measures regulate the publicizing, location, operation, and control of such auctions, now exclusively under the jurisdiction of the Ministry of Economic Affairs (rather than the municipalities, as in the past).

F. *Chain Sales*
- It is forbidden to organize chain sales (*ventes en chaine*) and to participate in such schemes. As an example of this system, a firm sells coupons to a buyer who, after reselling them at cost, receives from this firm and for free a product whose value corresponds to that of the coupons sold. The sales thus build up geometrically until either subsequent coupon-holders quit (the usual occurrence) or the firm goes bankrupt. Until now, this scheme was not regulated per se, but successful prosecutions have been based on charges of fraud and/or unfair competition.

G. *Itinerant Sales*
- Unless a special authorization has been granted, all displays, offers, and sales conducted in places other than a firm's official premises (as recorded in the Trade Registry) are forbidden. This measure, however, does not apply to business conducted at commercial fairs. While itinerant trade already is regulated strictly in public markets, on the street, and from door to door, its regulation did not apply to those who move their business frequently from one premise to another or conduct sales outside of their official premises.)

H. *Forced (Unsolicited) Purchases*
- It is forbidden to send to someone who did not request it any product accompanied, preceded, or followed by a notice to the effect that this product can be acquired for a certain price or sent back to the original sender, even at no cost. The recipient of such an unsolicited item does not have to return it nor pay for it, even if the notice implies that keeping the product amounts to its tacit purchase. (This measure also applies to unsolicited products sent on a trial basis.) An exception can be made for philanthropic purposes (for example, Christmas seals). This is a new regulation but previously, the sender of an unsolicited item did find it hard to force payment for it because of the lack of explicit consent on the part of the consignee (Article 1108 of the Civil Code).

I. *Combined Offers* (Premiums)
- The general principle is maintained of forbidding any transaction conditional upon another, apart from a few considered as reasonable and customary. It applies to combined offers of good and services as well as of coupons or stamps allowing one to acquire goods and/or services.
- The new law is much more restrictive since it only authorizes the combined offer of related objects making up a set (*ensemble*) and of identical products and services, provided that they can be acquired separately at their habitual price and that the overall

price reduction does not exceed one-third (the principle of "Three for the price of two").
- The law also allows the giving away of normal accessories and services; the provision of normal containers commensurate with the value of the products; small samples; publicity items if branded and not exceeding 5 percent in value; chromos of minimal value; lottery tickets; and titles to participate in games and contests, provided that most people cannot win significant prizes.
- Other items that can be given away freely are: (1) coupons to acquire an identical product or service, provided the potential saving does not exceed one-third of the regular price; (2) trading stamps redeemable in cash; and (3) coupons or stamps (not exceeding one-third of the original expenditure) allowing one to acquire an identical or similar product or service for free or at a reduced price, provided they can be obtained from the same retailer.
- The executive government also can exclude certain products or services, limit the value of premiums, and restrict combined offers to products or services sold by the same retailer for at least one year, after consulting with the Central Economic, Middle Classes, and Consumers Councils.
- Finally, firms issuing stamps and coupons must present certain guarantees, and they come under various controls which have been reinforced.

III. On Unfair Competitive Practices

"Are forbidden all acts contrary to fair commercial practices whereby a businessman injures or attempts to injure the professional interest of one or more other businessmen." The previous text read: "When, by an act contrary to fair commercial or industrial practices, [a businessman] takes away or attempts to take away from his competitors (or one of them) part of their clientele, or harms or attempts to harm their reputation, or more generally injures or attempts to injure their competitive capacity . . . " (Article I, royal decree no. 55, 23 December 1934).

"depenalize" the application of most commercial regulations because many violators act in good faith, and because businessmen are loath to drag competitors before regular courts where procedures are costlier and slower.

Government agencies have been granted broader powers to investigate all possible infractions. On the other hand, an ongoing restructuring of commercial courts, where one jurist and two businessmen now serve as judges, could result in more judgments favoring traditional retailers, because business judges tend to come from smaller firms and from middle-classes professional associations.

Problems of Law-Making. Combined offers provide a good illustration of the problems encountered by government in reconciling various interests through legislation. Specialized retailers have objected strongly to premiums (whether granted directly through joint purchases or indirectly through coupons and stamps) since these allow a variety of merchandise (small appliances, blankets, suitcases, toys, etc.) to be acquired from "abnormal" channels. They even consider them as an instrument of unfair competition because premiums allow the public to obtain certain items at prices which a specialized firm cannot regularly offer. Besides, consumer associations oppose premiums because they confuse the consumer and detract his attention from what should be his main concern, namely, price and quality.

On the other hand, some small retailers opposed the further restriction of premiums because: (1) stamps provide them with a competitive weapon against large retailers who do not use them; and (2) trading stamps are convenient for those retailers who sell items whose low value does not lend itself to the immediate granting of a premium (stamps are still authorized in the new law).

Opposition to stricter regulations also came from those who offer coupons that allow consumers to acquire other more or less related products at discounted prices (e.g., gasoline companies selling small appliances; and cooking-oil firms selling deepfryers). It would, of course, be difficult to eradicate this practice which at best only amounts to diversification, and at worst can still be conducted by abandoning coupons and simply distributing catalogs or opening discount stores next to a service station (some firms started doing this in anticipation of the law). Yet, only by imposing "normal" margins could the government even attempt to deal with discounting.

On their part, large retailers have not been too concerned about combined offers, but they are particularly excited about the additional conditions set for conducting clearances sales, for selling at reduced prices or below cost, and for claiming price reductions, since price competition and its publicizing constitute some of their major weapons.

Closing Days and Hours. According to procedures similar to those for licensure, professional associations can request that stores be closed for a twenty-four-hour period each week. About two-thirds of small retailers are already covered by the law of 22 June 1960, which also applies to large retailers who remain closed on Sunday anyway although there is increasing talk of opening on that day. Sunday opening is not prohibited per se, but the obligation of weekly closing and labor laws which restrict Sunday employment do in fact prevent it.

Regarding closing hours, many small retailers have long remained open late (mainly for the sale of convenience goods) while large stores and smaller shopping- and luxury-goods stores closed at 6 P.M. However, after 1961, downtown department stores began to stay open one night a week until 9 P.M., while some supermarkets and suburban branches are now open every weeknight.

This development has disturbed a sizable number of small retailers who have thus lost a competitive advantage, while others have had to start opening at night to remain competitive. The problem is complicated by moral considerations, as unions insist that workers should not have to work too often at night (in fact, a special part-time workforce is mostly used); while petty traders claim that they are entitled to free time at night for leisure, continuing education, and family life. Consumers have only partially been heard on this matter; and a major study is now under way under the sponsorship of the Central Economic Council. Several bills have already been considered, and some curtailment seems likely before the 1970s are over.

Product Lines. Outside of the pharmaceutical field, there is no restriction on merchandise lines apart from the fact that retailers have to satisfy licensure requirements whenever they exist, and thus may be hampered in adding another line if its trading is licensed. However, the new regulation of combined offers may restrict the type of premiums that a manufacturer or retailer can grant to goods related to his normal assortment.

Rationing was largely eliminated in the late forties, and stores are not obliged to maintain minimum stocks. In times of war and shortage (e.g., the Suez Crisis), the government has occasionally favored large retailers considered less likely to divert scarce supplies to the black market.

There are many controls on the quality of products, but no requirements yet that the latter be dated for freshness (apart from milk). The retailing of alcoholic beverages has its own special regulation.

Pricing. Prices began to be regulated during World War I and its immediate aftermath of inflation; and price regulation received its final consecration with the law-decree of 22 January 1945 and its subsequent amendments designed to control undue price increases.

The basic regimen is that of the "normal" price based on operating costs and reflecting market conditions, as appreciated by the courts; and no "abnormal" profit may be realized. The law's teeth, however, lie in the government's power to fix maximum prices and margins, as has been repeatedly done for important goods and services (some twenty of them, currently) figuring on the Consumer Prices Index.

Besides, since 1950 (particularly, following the ministerial decree of 8 October 1959), price increases by the manufacturer or importer must be notified in advance to the government which can now ask that they be postponed for up to sixty days. Distributors (including retailers) can increase their prices only to the extent necessary to reflect the increases legally allowed to their suppliers, but without increasing their percentage margin (ministerial decrees of 8 October 1959 and 2 September 1966).

Besides, firms and associations can enter into "program contracts" with government (law of 23 December 1969), which free them from other price regulations (e.g., prior notification of price increases), provided they agree to hold or reduce certain prices.

In all these price matters, the government generally consults the advisory Prices Regulation Commission on which sit representatives from business, labor, and consumer associations.

Various inflationary pressures linked to strong labor demands, the introduction of the tax-on-value-added system, and international monetary problems, have recently led to even stricter controls (law of 30 July 1971). The government has now been granted the power to: (1) impose maximum prices (for up to six months) for a *single firm* rather than simply for a *type of product;* (2) obtain all the necessary information about that firm's revenues and costs whose recording can be standardized by the government, except for small and medium firms; and (3) to order the closing down of a delinquent firm for up to five days (but salaries would still have to be paid to the employees). However, the government has to consult the Prices Regulation Commission before fixing maximum prices; appeals for such administrative acts are possible; and firms can obtain the removal of the sanctions, after paying an administrative fine. (This law again applies only to manufacturers and importers, but distributors are indirectly affected by it since their own price increases can only reflect the former's.)

On the other hand, intercompany price agreements (and other types of agreements) need not be reported to the government; firms can extend different discounts to different customers; and resale price maintenance (RPM) is condoned although refusal to sell has now begun to be regulated.

Consumer Credit. The law of 9 July 1957 is both economic and moral in intent. It aims at protecting consumers against overcharges, high-pressure salesmanship, and arbitrary behavior on the part of lenders. Besides, the government and the National Bank want to exercise control over credit sales believed to accentuate the ups and downs of the economy and to contribute to inflation through the generation of additional bank credit. However, this law also reveals a desire to curb what is thought to be the lower classes' inability to resist the lure of credit buying; and it provides a means of affecting consumption patterns by facilitating or discouraging the sales of certain products (e.g., cars).

The law applies not only to credit sales of consumer goods and services, but also to personal loans designed to finance such purchases (law of 5 March 1965). Sales between $60 and $3,000-4,000 are covered if they involve at least four maturities. A minimum down-payment (15-25 percent) is required, and the government does regulate the maximum charges allowed as well as the duration of the contract (it varies by product).

The cancellation of a contract by the seller or lender is considerably restricted; while the clauses providing for the penalization of delinquent customers are left to the appreciation of the courts. Many infractions on the part of the seller or lender allow the customer to pay only the cash value of his purchase, while retaining the advantage of installment payments. All litigations have to take place close to where the customer resides; and only part of his salary can be garnished. Contracts must mention the cash and credit prices of the purchase, as well as the monthly charge. Lending firms must be licensed, while retailers referring customers to lending institutions have to be registered. A seven-day "reflection period", during which people sold goods at home can cancel the contract they signed, was imposed by the law of 8 July 1970.

The growth of consumer credit has probably been slowed down on account of these measures since it represents only about 5 percent of private consumption amenable to installment sale. However, credit cards and charge accounts have recently been introduced, although their legal status is still uncertain.

Promotion. Belgium is one of the few European countries where the state radio and television networks do not broadcast any commercial advertising. However, there are regular consumer-oriented programs about best buys and product tests, although no brands are mentioned. Outdoor advertising is regulated, mostly for aesthetic reasons.

Bookkeeping. While the law has long specified which books and records must be kept and in what manner, this requirement is seldom enforced in the case of smaller businessmen who may lack thereby the proper evidence when litigating various commercial and fiscal matters. The new tax-on-value-added and—hope-fully—the licensing laws and their educational requirements, are expected to lead to some gradual improvement in this matter.

Registration. All business firms have been required since 1927-1929 to obtain a numbered listing in the Trade Registry, and to display this number on their premises, stationery, advertisements, and vehicles. This requirement, now tightened up since 1956, not only is intended to provide better information to creditors and current statistics about business occupations, but also to clamp down on marginal operators who avoid various taxes and thus compete unfairly.

There are also various registration requirements for those who provide and/or finance credit sales and loans, and for those who issue stamps and coupons.

Facilities and Equipment Following the 1967 disastrous fire at the Innovation department store, safety requirements (sprinklers, number of exits, etc.) were tightened. For quite a while now, stores have been required to provide various facilities such as chairs and cafeterias for their employees. The food trades are, of course, regulated in numerous hygiene matters.

Research, Information, and Advising

There are many gaps in the knowledge needed to regulate, monitor, and plan the development of retailing, but the Belgian government, apart from conducting various rather unsophisticated censuses (the latest was made as of 31 December 1970), as well as more regular surveys of retail sales, has encouraged and subsidized the study of distribution and of the commercial middle classes. This study is now carried out by such consultative bodies as the Special Distribution Commission (within the Central Economic Council) and the High Council of the Middle Classes, and by such research-and-training oriented organizations as the Belgian Productivity Agency, the Economic and Social Institute of the Middle Classes (1946), and the Belgian Distribution Committee (1955). All of these bodies are subsidized by the state; and the last two collaborate on training small-business consultants, and they diffuse their research findings through publications and development programs. Professional associations are also active in these areas.

Effectiveness

Measuring the effectiveness of public policy is notoriously difficult because clear-cut goals and before-and-after benchmarks are often missing, and because many symbolic purposes and dysfunctional effects are frequently present.[10]

Yet, in terms of the objectives mentioned at the outset of this chapter, the Belgian government has largely succeeded in boosting the small retailer's chances of survival if he chooses to avail himself of the many forms of help available in such matters as education, training, and cooperative action. Many petty retailers have already disappeared in a country long famous for its plethora of small stores, but this evolution has been rather orderly if only because general economic conditions have been good.

However, some of the measure taken to help the commercial middle class have definitely conflicted with the other goal of improving the efficiency of retailing. This is particularly evident in the padlock laws (1935-1961) which restricted the expansion of large stores, and thereby postponed the development of supermarkets, shopping centers, and discount houses.

Similarly, protecting the consumer has occasionally been conceived in a narrow and negative sense of restricting distributive types (such as itinerant traders) and practices (such as special sales) that bother the traditional retailer. Much less has been done to enhance the convenience, efficiency, and satisfaction of his shopping. The ongoing discussion of closing hours illustrates this tendency to consider the retailer or the retail clerks unions rather than the customer, and to moralize about the latter's shopping habits.

Still, the general tone of government action has become more positive as the need for modernization has been acknowledged since the end of the 1950s; and consumers are better protected than before. On the other hand, the pursuit of price stability is beginning to hurt retailing more and more as the government extends its control over prices and margins. This last development could well finally unite retailers of all stripes at the same time that consumers begin to be heard. The forces affecting the making and application of public policy could thus well change in the near future.

The Unfinished Task

There are still many ambiguities and shortcomings in Belgian public policy which has often failed to recognize the positive contributions of retailing while typically stressing such negative elements as "too many intermediaries," "parasitism," and "hidden persuasion." Mentalities and institutions are fortunately changing, although they will certainly require better information to appraise retailing's contributions and shortcomings.

Besides, the multiplication of laws and regulations, and of public bodies charged with their implementation, dictates greater coordination and therefore better structures at the policymaking and application stages. In particular, the existence of the two separate Ministries of the Middle Classes and of Economic Affairs does not facilitate a coordinated view, especially since Economic Affairs has traditionally been more concerned about industry than commerce. In fact, other ministries are involved in regulating retailing, and this further complicates the making and application of public policy in this area. The increasing role of the Public Works Ministry in the matter of land-use planning is likely to further complicate coordination.

Furthermore, the government does not always consider retailing in the making and application of other policies (e.g., taxation, social security, and land-use planning); and many regulations affecting retailing have been devised in the context of something else, such as inflation fighting or consumer protection.

Public policy is also too discriminatory, or discriminatory in the wrong place. Thus, the best firms of any size must be encouraged—the best small firms as well as the best large firms, and those that already exist as well as those of the future. In this context, commercial education is one area where the entirety of retailing, not just small retailers, must be considered because greater efficiency requires better-prepared personnel for all kinds of firms. Moreover, retraining and relocation needs are no longer limited to small retailing but are now found in large firms that close down superfluous or inefficient branches, following the opening of larger units and mergers among firms. Hence, social programs to help displaced people will have to be extended to include everyone.

Additionally, subsidized credit ought no longer to be restricted to large-scale industry and the middle classes, because large retailers also contribute to the achievement of various public goals such as full employment and price stability. It is not necessarily a matter of making more credit available, but of channeling it where it will be most useful, and of removing various obstacles to its improved distribution—from regulations that discriminate against retailing in general and large retailers in particular, to traditional ways of lending money that must be changed.[11]

Finally, the new policy must resolutely favor competition and innovation instead of still trying to shield established retailers against newcomers, marginal operators, aggressive marketers, and those that diversify their assortments. Here, it will be necessary to watch the growing concentration of power among large retailers as these merge.

Yet, there is still room for a separate policy for the commercial middle classes. In fact, it would be better to conceive it in terms of "equal chances" for the smaller, viable, useful firm which is needed as a source of new talent, as a complement to the mass merchandiser, as an outlet for non-bureaucratic temperaments, as a counterbalance to great economic power, as a step on the social ladder, and as a necessary socio-political element in a pluralistic society. Similarly, this "small-and-medium firms" policy would provide the social measures needed to help those who want out (e.g., early retirement, as is already offered in the Netherlands).

The Likely Future Policy

Reality is bound to differ from this model, irrespective of its merits. After all, "politics is the art of the possible," and Belgium is a country of half-measures where nothing is ever settled. Besides, even the best policies take time to develop as vested interests must be phased out, and new mentalities created. Still, change is likely along the following lines.

Actors

a. The requirement of minimum education and/or experience qualifications for all entrants, in application of the revised licensure law.

b. The extension and improvement of educational (including retraining) programs for retailers and would-be retailers.
c. The facilitation of credit (some of it subsidized) for more retailers of all sizes.

Structure

a. The further encouragement of cooperation among retailers.
b. The further restriction (but not the banning) of resale-price-maintenance and of refusal-to-sell, although the former may largely disappear on its own.

Process

a. Further restrictions on retail locations through land-use planning.
b. Restrictions of evening opening hours, while Sunday openings may be partially authorized.
c. Simpler but better-enforced bookkeeping requirements for small retailers.
d. More and better statistics; greater support of research and of the diffusion of its findings; and more advising services to small retailers.
e. Greater use of public radio and television to educate and inform consumers; and the introduction of limited commercial advertising.

These measures will further restrict the basic principle of freedom of trade, but retailers will also be in a better position to shape and affect government intervention which is now more attuned to, and equipped for, developing public policy toward retailing. Besides, retailers will further participate in the making and application of laws and regulations as the corporative principle of self-regulation regains part of its former importance.

Notes

1. Another justification for regulation has been that in statutory-law countries such as Belgium, the lack of regulation of a commercial practice may hamper its use. Thus, some middle-classes credit organizations refused for a while to lend money to the members of voluntary chains because the legislation was not clear on that count.

2. In the French language, this group is always identified in the plural form *(classes moyennes)*—hence, middle-class*es*. The limits of this group are hard to define as it includes not only small and medium retailers (including craft-related ones such as bakers), but also other craftsmen and small industrialists, the liberal professions, and even white-collar employees, and farmers—up to one-fourth of the Belgian population when their families are included.

3. There are prison and fine penalties, but also administrative sanctions

(e.g., canceling of licenses and registrations) and moral ones (e.g., publicizing condemnations). Private parties can also request cease-and-desist injunctions from the commercial courts.

4. The Belgian cabinet of January 1972 included a Secretariat for the Middle Classes within a Ministry of Agriculture and Middle Classes.

5. Pharmacies are limited in number in each city and neighborhood. There are many other restrictions, but they will not be considered here. The pricing of pharmaceutical products is also strictly regulated on account of the huge expenses incurred by the mandatory health-insurance system.

6. Independent businessmen are now largely covered by a variety of social security benefits such as family allowances (1937), health insurance (1963), and pensions (1954). However, these benefits are still lower than for salaried employees, if only because there is no employer to pick up part of the cost, although the government is subsidizing this system.

7. Business-transaction taxes *(taxes de transmission)* originally taxed the full value of each transaction, apart from the ultimate sale to the consumer. A vertically integrated firm could thus skip one or more of these taxes whose rate increased from 1 percent to 7 percent between 1921 and 1970. After World War II, this repetitive tax *(taxe en cascade)* came to be largely levied only once *(taxe forfaitaire)*—at double the rate. The tax-on-value-added (TVA) now includes four rates (6-25 percent) depending on the "necessity" character of the good or service. Essentially, it taxes the gross margin taken by each link in the distribution channel.

8. "Interprofessional" federations group professional associations along national, regional, and local lines; but they remain somewhat divided along religious and political lines, although decreasingly so.

9. The law of 27 May 1960 forbids (unspecified) abuses of economic power, but it has not found any application in retailing yet.

10. A more elaborate discussion of the effectiveness of Belgian public policy is provided in J. J. Boddewyn, *Belgian Public Policy Toward Retailing Since 1789* (East Lansing, Mich.: Division of Research, Graduate School of Business Administration, Michigan State University, 1971), 227-29.

11. Credit-granting practices in Belgium are still very conservative, even for large firms, as lending agencies stress real guarantees rather than the potential of an investment on the basis of such factors as "flow-of-incomes."

Supplementary Bibliography

1. A full-length treatment of this topic can be found in J. J. Boddewyn, *Belgian Public Policy Toward Retailing Since 1789* (East Lansing, Michigan: Division of Research, Graduate School of Business Administration, Michigan State University, 1971).

2. Two studies fairly close in coverage to this one are: "Problèmes et politique

de distribution," *Documents-CEPESS,* I, 5(1962); and Marcel Wullaerts, "Parlement en Middenstand," in *500 jaar parlementair leven in Belgie, 1464-1964,* Vol. 2, *Parlement* (Leuven, Belgium: Uitgeverij Nauwelaerts, 1966), 171-221.

4 Brazil

POLIA LERNER HAMBURGER

Trying to present an overall view of Brazilian public policy towards retailing is a complex task. The retail structure itself is highly complex, and includes a wide variety of firms ranging from the rural general store to the sophisticated boutique; from the old corner grocery store to the modern, shining supermarket. The retail structure also varies considerably from region to region. This diversity can be explained in part by the different cultural, social, demographic, and physical environments in the numerous regions of Brazil. But most of the current diversity is due to the regional imbalance or inequalities in degrees of economic development (gradations of underdevelopment) in the various portions of the country.

The basic system of jurisprudence (Civil Law, Commercial Code, and Criminal Law) also presents complexities and will seem strange to the reader who is more accustomed to Anglo-American common law. Under Brazilian law, a new type of business or other organization tends to have little or no legal standing until its operating methods are explicitly recognized, by statute, as a "characteristic institution." Thus the emerging modern types of retailers, including super-markets, were disadvantaged until their operations were explicitly legalized by the appropriate legislative bodies, as we will discuss later in this chapter. This disadvantage has not yet been removed for all new types of retailing in all parts of the country.

Moreover, government policy towards retailing changes from time to time. Public policy towards the *feiras* (street fairs) and *mercados* (public markets) has particularly been subject to evolution, as noted below in our discussion of retail process. Attempts at controlling the drastic inflationary tendencies of the 1950s and 1960s also produced many fiscal measures with significant and complicated implications for the retail sector. Finally, avowed policies of social reform, particularly in relation to labor questions, tend to influence the relative competitive capabilities of large and small retail enterprises. As will be noted, entry into the market is largely unrestricted but governmental policy can tend to favor or handicap the various entrants.

Actors

Retailing in Brazil is mainly a private enterprise area. Except for a few attempts to stabilize supply of essential goods in times of shortage and to keep prices in line through SUNAB's agencies, the government has not participated in the retail distribution of goods. SUNAB–Superintendencia Nacional do Abastecimento (National Supply Agency)–was created in 1962, initially as a semi-autonomous agency of the federal executive, and later subordinated to the Ministry of Agriculture. SUNAB was established with comprehensive powers to regulate and perform activities in the marketing sector. Its general authority includes:

1. preparation and execution of a national plan for the supply of essential products;
2. maintenance of a national system of storage and refrigeration facilities;
3. establishment of import and export quotas for essential products;
4. "intervention" in the private sector to ensure the unhindered distribution of essential goods and services;
5. maintenance of stocks for the purpose of supply and price regulation;
6. establishment of information systems regarding production, distribution, and consumption, with the right to requisition data from whatever source necessary;
7. regulation of transportation and distribution services;
8. establishment of norms and execution of measures designed to regulate and improve marketing conditions;
9. establishment and regulation of prices;
10. examination of the stocks and written records of any marketing firm;
11. performance of all other acts necessary in carrying out its responsibilities.[1]

As part of its efforts to keep prices down, SUNAB distributes basic food products through a system of "mixed economy" (partially public and partially private ownership) outlets known as COBAL. COBAL establishments were tax exempt until mid-1967, when this advantage was taken away. But the volume of goods distributed through COBAL has never been a very significant share of the total of goods distributed. Lacking the necessary warehousing facilities, COBAL cannot satisfactorily perform its role as a price stabilizer.

Outside of the normal requirements of registering, licensing, and complying with federal, state, and local ordinances, there are no restrictions on entry. There are no limits on the number of entrants and no mandatory spatial separation between similar outlets. One exception is the case of feiras, or public markets, where the number of licenses for merchants is limited by the local authorities, generally through the Prefeitura's Secretaria de Abastecimento (Municipal Bureau of Supply).

The right of entry, if the special conditions specified by law are met, is assured by the Constitution.[2] The requisites for entry in retailing are the same as in any other kind of business,[3] and are specified in the Commercial Code.[4] Articles 1 to 31 define a merchant as any person who is legally eligible to engage in commerce and who does engage in such activities, in his individual name or a firm name, as his customary occupation. The act of commerce can be practiced individually by the merchant (natural person) or collectively (juridical person– the commercial firm).

Of course, anyone entering trade must also satisfy the normal civil law requirement for competency to engage in legal acts. Thus, the 1916 Civil Code (Article 5) establishes the norms for eligibility to engage in commerce.

Civil service employees (county, state, and federal), the military, the bankrupt (until they have fulfilled all of their obligations under the Bankruptcy Laws),[5] and those who have committed crimes against property are ineligible to engage in commerce. The law also defines the conditions under which emancipated minors and married women may become merchants in their own right.[6] Resident foreigners may enter trade under the same general conditions as Brazilian nationals, since the Constitution assures them the same rights as Brazilian citizens.[7] The foreigners, however, must prove their legitimate entry and status in the country, in addition to all other requirements for registration and licensure.[8]

Foreign capital, be it money or assets or both, may freely enter retailing, provided an authorization has been granted by the Central Bank. (This is forbidden in certain other sectors such as electric power, petroleum, and all communication media). The foreign capital might be brought in under several alternatives: (1) foreign headquarter–Brazilian branch relationship; (2) Brazilian firm with majority of foreign capital; and (3) joint-venture–Brazilian and foreign capital equally represented.

In the first case, several requisites have to be met that explain why there are very few firms in this category:

1. A decree of the executive power, granting permission to operate for a given period of time, is required. Before this period expires, the firm has to ask for this permission to be renewed.
2. The firm has to present the statutes under which it was organized, with stated objectives and form of operation, in accordance with the laws of the country of origin, translated into Portuguese, and then verified that they do not conflict with the Brazilian legislation.
3. The firm has to have a representative in Brazil with full powers to act.
4. The Brazilian branch has to be registered in the Junta Commercial.
5. The firm has to add "do Brazil" to its original name. Ex: Company XYZ do Brazil.

In the alternatives 2 and 3, the firms abide by the Brazilian Lei das Sociedades Anónimas (Corporation Laws).[9]

In all the three cases, when the foreign capital is brought in it has to be approved and registered by the Central Bank. This registered capital is the basis for the remittance of profits to the foreign country.10 Up to now, the criterion used by the Central Bank to approve the entry of foreign capital relates to the existing balance of payments. It is to be expected that this control will be extended to include a selectivity criterion: type of industry, importance for the Brazilian economy, etc.[11]

There are no barriers to entry, in the retailer's case, but neither is there encouragement of entry. Tax exemptions such as enjoyed by COBAL establishments and cooperatives have been removed. The existing feiras enjoyed some advantages, but they have been subject to constant debate and it is unlikely that their number will be allowed to grow. There are no special facilities for financing, either. On the contrary, although there are plans to encourage location of industries in certain areas, plans to help small and medium industries, etc., no such plans exist for retailers. Most independent retailers are, to a large extent, self-financing. But the larger retail chains and the firms that are increasing their installment sales volume have had to resort to financing companies. Some large chains formed their own financing company. Observations made by Slater and others regarding the difficulties of financing for retailers in Recife[12] may be generalized, in our opinion. Exceptions to the above remarks are some plans, recently, for financing supermarkets by SUDENE (Superintendencia de Desenvolvimento do Nordeste—Superintendency for the Development of the Northeast) and Caixa Economica Federal, of São Paulo (Governmental Saving and Loans Association).[13] Other exceptions are two cities in the state of São Paulo that recently offered a free site each for construction of a supermarket abiding by their specifications of selling area, product lines offered for sale, etc.

On the other hand, there is incentive to expand Brazilian retailing êntrepreneurship to foreign countries (at least one supermarket chain is doing it already). Profit obtained by the Brazilian branch in the foreign country is not subject to Brazilian income tax. Besides, the Brazilian products exported to these branches are exempted from the product-and-value-added taxes discussed later in this chapter. Very often the cost of transporting from Brazil to the branch located in the foreign country is less than the total of tax exemptions.

Structure

Encouragement of Ties Between Retailers

Retailers are not required to join the "retailers' union," but are required to pay a union tax. Any benefits that the union might obtain will extend to all in the trade, qualification being granted by the payment of the tax, not by being a member of the union.

Moreover, most retailers generally voluntarily join the local Associação Comercial (Chamber of Commerce) and Clube dos Lojistas (Retailers' Club). The former is broader in scope and action. Its members include bankers and industrialists, as well as retailers, and so it has been less effective in defending specific interests of retailers. The latter have been specially active in cooperative promotion activities.

The supermarkets have formed a National Association of Supermarkets (ABRAS) and this association is gaining importance both in the diffusion of the supermarket concept and in the defense of the supermarkets' interests.

Enforced Atomism and Competition

There are no restrictions on growth or vertical integration. Vertically integrated firms enjoyed a tax advantage under the old IVC-turnover tax system, since the vertical integration eliminated what would have otherwise been a taxable trans-action between two independent firms. The replacement of the turnover tax in 1965 by the ICM-value-added tax eliminated this advantage.[14]

Both the Constitution and a special law contain provisions concerning growth and concentration of economic power. The 1969 Constitution forbids abuse of power, characterized by dominance of markets, elimination of competition, and arbitrary increase in profits.[15] There have not been de facto serious problems in these respects. There are no restrictions on store and firm size. Some retailers and some chains have experienced extraordinary growth, lately, but with no stronger reactions than the smaller retailers' complaints that "we cannot compete with them anymore"—but it has resulted in no restrictive measures, insofar.

The general legal provisions are the same for all retailers. There might be some feeling that feira merchants and small atomistic retailers do not pay as much taxes as they should; but specially in the latter case, the fact arises not so much from protective factors but rather from the difficulty of controlling and enforc-ing the existing regulations.

There is some evidence that established retailers (and also the Association of Supermarkets) exerted pressure against the tax exemptions that were granted to cooperatives and that they have been very vocal in their criticisms against the feiras (but, in our opinion, have not yet mobilized political pressure comparable to the feira merchants' strength). Also, in our opinion, retailer representation through trade associations and retailer influence in statutory industrial, econom-ic, planning, and consultative bodies have tended to be less than proportional to the sector's relevance to the economy.

There are practically no restrictions on vertical ties between manufacturers and retailers, although the courts would not enforce a contract that is considered excessively onerous to one of the parties. Exclusive dealerships are permitted, private brands are allowed, and manufacturers may own retail stores.

Process

Supermarkets, consumer cooperatives, and fairs (feiras), because of their special characteristics of operation, have been the object of special ordinances. The supermarkets were introduced in 1953 and had, initially, a slow development, due to legal factors (they were not recognized everywhere as a characteristic institution) and to social-economic factors, related to buying power and habits and to conditions of operation (high rent, taxes, etc.). In order to operate under different conditions than the other retailers, as far as hours were concerned, they had to be characterized at law as a special kind of institution. The supermarkets themselves were interested also in being clearly denoted as a distinct retailing institution, the intent being, from the beginning, to obtain some special advan-tages for their operation.

In 1957 the supermarket was *legally defined* in the state of Guanabara as a "self-service store selling food products and products for house cleaning and maintenance, with an area of, at least, 500 m^2."[16] In 1968 the supermarket was legally defined for the city of Sao Paulo as "a retail establishment, operated by a single natural person or juridical person, adopting self-service and displaying and selling in the same location, permanently, food and other products for the household."[17]

The conditions for characterization as a supermarket required the establishment to keep at least the following departments: meat and seafood, vegetables, fruits, and dairy, and that the *selling area for the food products be at least 2/3 of the total selling area.* (The ABRAS—Brazilian Association of Supermarkets—is trying to change the *underlined* restriction, due to the plans of the larger chains to introduce the "hypermarket": a combination of discount-house and super-market.) In the last years, the development of supermarkets has gained momentum.[18]

Consumer cooperatives are voluntary, non-profit organizations that buy products to sell to their associates. They can be sponsored by both private companies and the government, or both, for the benefit of their employees, or by associations for the benefit of their members. Defined and controlled by a general special law that covers the entire cooperative system,[19] they benefited from tax exemption and had a great development between 1955-1960[20] selling food, household maintenance products, and even in some instances clothing and durable goods. (This expansion provoked a reaction among other retailers who had to pay all taxes, and who complained that the cooperatives enjoyed an unfair advantage.) Due to these reactions some of the cooperatives' tax advantages were discontinued, which led to a decline in their activities.

Feiras (street fairs) are "open-air, non-continuous (non-daily) markets made up of small private businesses selling only one class of products."[21] They are licensed by local government. The feiras were created during World War I, specially for the distribution of food products. But over time, they changed and today have specific operating characteristics that include mobility of the feira from one place to another (the stalls are set up on public streets or parking lots); operation on a fixed day in the week (sometimes twice a week), in the morning hours; and a wide variety of products offered for sale. Since the merchants do not have rent, water, and light costs; are exempt from certain taxes; and enjoy reductions in others (and have more possibility of evading taxes), the feiras can be a distribution system with relatively low costs. They offer the advantages of mobility—"they come close to the consumer"—periodicity, large availability of product lines and wide assortment within each line, the possibility of easy comparison of products and prices, and more flexibility in pricing (reduced prices for perishables at the end of the selling period). Going to the feira became an established habit for most Brazilian families, since all the advantages mentioned above were intensified by the lack of transportation in large cities (this is changing lately) and by middle and upper income families' habit of taking along or sending their servants to do the shopping.

But the feiras present problems too and have been criticized on the grounds of lack of hygiene, adulteration of weights and measures, difficulties for street cleaning, and the noise and transit difficulties they create for the neighborhoods where they locate. They are specially resented by established retailers, who see them as a low-cost (and in some sense subsidized) competitive threat. The existence of the feira has been a controversial issue in recent years, especially in the large cities, but because of the several interests involved a definite solution has not been found yet. Feira merchants are, in most cases, atomistic retailers; but together, because of their large number, they can exert political power. Besides, they have on their side quite a number of housewives for whom the feiras are still a satisfactory place to shop, especially for perishable fruits and vegetables. The feiras seem to be decreasing in number in Rio, and more recently also in São Paulo, but are still important in the distribution structure.

In some towns and cities we also find markets (mercados), generally "public markets," in the sense that the city government owns and operates the fixed market structure—the buildings and facilities where private merchants, selling one class of products, congregate.

Location, Plant, and Facilities

The zoning ordinances establish where retailing establishments can or cannot be located. These zoning ordinances are a part of the Código de Obras (Building Ordinance) for every town or city.

Over time repeated attempts have been made to give retailers who occupy rented premises vested interests in their locations.[22] Some legislation has been enacted for this purpose, but it has not proven to be very effective. Landlords who have desirable property to rent can insist upon leasing contracts that include provisions which weaken the tenants' rights to renewal and that make enforcement of those rights complicated and expensive.

Generally there is no public provision for store buildings or special off-street parking facilities (except for public markets that are city-owned). Generally, no adequate planning provisions for commercial areas are made (except in the case of Brazilia, the new capital, an entirely planned city). Despire the Código de Obras ordinances, some streets and areas gradually change from residential to commercial because of the growth of towns and cities. Slowly, at first, then more rapidly, service shops and then disguised retail stores appear, and from these to open commerce is only a minor step.

There are no specific requirements for parking space, though in larger cities, where the prrblem is very acute, some retailers in a neighborhood join together to rent empty sites that their customers can use as parking places. The parking problem will become more and more serious, since those empty sites are destined to be occupied by new buildings in the future, and since the number of cars in circulation is increasing. Most supermarkets do have parking space (and so do the few existing shopping centers), but it is not a requisite of their legal characterization. There are legal restrictions on parking, and loading and unloading hours, in most towns and cities. As transit and parking problems increase, defying transit authorities' ingenuity to solve them, towns and cities are subject to frequent changes in transit directions that have strong impact on retail stores in the areas affected. An example where strong political forces have been exerted on this score, over time, is Rua Augusta, the fashion street of São Paulo, Brazil's greatest city, where transit authorities' ordinances forbidding parking provoked strong reaction from the retailers.

In addition to the general building requirements, such as the building ordinance provisions concerning fire protection in new structures and the labor law provisions concerning employee comfort facilities, special hygienic requirements exist for certain types of business,[23] e.g., food stores, pharmacies, hairdressers, and barbers.

There are also requirements concerning weights and measurements equipment. In 1962 the INPM (Instituto Nacional de Pesos e Medidas — National Institute of Weights and Measurements) was created, under the Ministry of Industry and Commerce, to control statements of quantities in packaged goods and control weights and measurements norms in general. Because of its highly centralized nature, the Institute was, at best, only partially successful in performing its control activities. Consequently, responsibility for specific control functions was subsequently delegated to state institutes that were to be created for that purpose, while INPM retained responsibility for establishing basic standards and other related central functions.[24]

Pursuant to this arrangement, the State of São Paulo, for example, created its institute, IPEM-SP, whose objectives include consumer protection, equipment and instrument checking and validation, and the diffusion of nationally-established technical standards throughout the state. IPEM-SP controls weights and measurements of packaged merchandise, checks gas pumps both as to quantity and quality of gas stated in the gas stations, checks the weight of the bottled gas, and checks also scales of stores and feiras.

Operations

Hour legislation, including both mandatory and maximum hours, Sunday closing, and local holidays, is established locally (except for national and state holidays, when closing is mandatory by either federal or state regulation. Pharmacies are required to stay open—by a rotating system ("plantão")—on holidays, Saturday afternoon, and Sundays (when other commerce is closed). Supermarkets were allowed, when recognized in the legislation, to keep open until 8:00 P.M. three nights a week, including Saturday evening and on the day before holidays. (In São Paulo, one supermarket chain has obtained special license for one of its stores to stay open "24 hours a day, seven days a week" as is advertised.) In December stores generally stay open every night until 10:00 P.M. and also on Saturday afternoons until 6:00 P.M., by special license. The night opening of stores in São Paulo, for a long time a topic of discussion, finally was authorized in 1970, despite the strong opposition of small retailers and the employees' union (Sindicato dos Comerciários). Selling hours can also be extended on Saturdays before special promotion dates (Mother's Day, Father's Day, St. Valentine's Day, etc).

Labor Relations

Social legislation is oriented, in its general lines, by the Constitution. Article 166 of the Constitution assures the freedom of both professional and trade union association.

The basic legislation concerning labor relations is contained in the CLT-Consolidation of the Labor Laws (Consolidação das Leis do Trabalho) decree—Law No. 5452 of May 1, 1943, and amended several times since. This comprehensive body of labor legislation is one of the most progressive and protective in the world. This extensive codified work containing 922 articles subsumed under eleven major titles regulates all aspects of labor relations. Compliance with the extensive body of labor legislation entails complex legal and bureaucratic tasks for each firm, and, of course, expenses that amount to a significant percentage of the total payroll. This leads large retailers to complain that they are much more severely affected than the smaller retailers who do not have any, or only a few, employees.

Certain provisions with regard to nationalization of labor are taken care of by the two-thirds rule: an employer who operates a concession or who is engaged in a commercial or industrial enterprise, whenever he hires three or more employees, is required to maintain a proportion of two-thirds Brazilian nationals in his personnel. (Foreigners who have resided in the country for more than ten years and have a Brazilian spouse or child are considered as Brazilians for the purpose of the law.) The ratio must be maintained not only in relation to the number of employees, but also in regard to total wages paid. In addition, a Brazilian employee may not receive lower wages than a foreigner for similar work. Exceptions are made for certain career employees with greater seniority than the Brazilian employees in the same positions, or when the remuneration is in the form of commission or for piecework, related to greater production.

All foreign employees must have a special identification card and their nationality recorded in the employment registry. Control of these laws is enacted through the requirement that each employer must submit, annually, a list of all employees to the Ministry of Labor.

Other important aspects of labor legislation refer to the payment of severance and retirement allowances,[25] weekly rest,[26] Christmas bonus,[27] and social security contributions. They also establish rules for protection of minors employed and for apprenticeship. Although the C.L.T. (section IV–Art. 429) specifically mentions apprenticeship development for minors employed in industry, but not in commerce, it is obvious that both sectors are affected, since the Constitutional provision is clear: Commercial and industrial firms are obliged to provide apprenticeship conditions for their minor workers, and to promote the training of their qualified personnel.[28] This apprenticeship training is delegated to SENAC (Servico Nacional de Aprendizagem Commercial – National Service of Commercial Apprenticeship), subordinated to the National Confederation of Commerce, and funded by a contribution of the commercial firms (1 percent of the total payroll except in the case of firms that keep their own courses of commerce, considered adequate by SENAC).[29]

The commercial firms that have more than nine employees have to employ and enroll in the SENAC schools a number of minors as apprentices, the number to be determined by SENAC National Council, which later delegated this decision to the Regional Councils.[30] This number requisite has not been enforced. SENAC could not with its present facilities enroll all eligible individuals if the provision were rigorously enforced.[31] A document from the Ministry of Labor, Industry, and Commerce lists the commercial functions that demand specific apprenticeship (thirty-two functions) as well as the ones that do not, and the maximum time limit for "in job" training.[32] Retail trade is one of the thirty-two listed functions.

Retailing establishments, of course, have to comply with all labor law requisites that are general for all firms, but they have a few specific problems of their own. A common cause of labor dispute that usually ends in the Labor Courts is the amount that salesclerks who are compensated under a commission plan are to receive for the weekly rest day. The law is not clear in this point.[33] The jurisprudence decision has been to pay the sales clerks according to an average of the commissions they earned in the week days actually worked.

Problem might arise, also, if the retailer is not careful in setting the arrangements for changes or extension of working shifts in special cases, as mentioned in the section above (promotional occasions, night openings, etc.). For instance, in São Paulo, the unions have agreed that if there is extension of working time, the overtime rate to which the commission-earning salesclerk is entitled shall be calculated on the basis of the hourly average of commissions in the last twelve months, plus specified premiums.[34]

Merchandising

Merchandising controls are relatively limited. There are no rationing arrangements for any goods, or requirements for the consumers to register with particular or specified stores to obtain rationed items. In cases of shortage of essential goods, SUNAB may assume control of inventories and redistribute them through COBAL's or regular retailers' outlets.

Price advertising is allowed. There is no special advertising code, but the Criminal Code forbids the following practices, among others, as unfair methods of competition: publishing advertisements containing false statements to the detriment of a competitor for the purpose of taking undue advantage; supplying or spreading false information that may be damaging to a competitor for the purpose of profit; employing fraudulent means to divert customers from others; producing, importing, exporting, storing, or selling merchandise with a false indication of origin; designating merchandise as being similar to another seller's goods; placing one's name on someone else's merchandise without consent; using someone else's commercial name; claiming rewards for honors that were not received; and selling falsified or spoiled merchandise in other vendors' containers.

Brands, commercial names, trademarks, signs, or symbols of advertising are extensively dealt with, in regards to concept, registration, and protection, both in the Commercial Code and Lei da Propriedade Industrial (Law of Industrial Property).[35] Promotional practices involving contests, lotteries, etc., require special registration (carta-patente) to insure that they are fair and honest.

Pricing Controls

Guaranteed minimum prices, if and when they exist, are generally for the protection of the producer, not the retailer. CFP (Production Financing

Commission) conducts programs of minimum price supports at the producer level for selected agricultural commodities. Some manufacturers use resale price maintenance as part of their distribution and pricing policies.

Successive attempts have been made to enact price control, either by SUNAB action, through CONEP (Comissão Naçional de Estímulo para Estabilização de Precos—National Commission on Incentives for Price Stability) and by tax incentives for firms that would stabilize their prices. This policy was initiated in 1965,[36] and because many of the laws and decrees involved were inconsistent or contradictory, the policy was not successful. Similarly, an income tax reduction of 20 percent was offered in 1966 to firms that kept their price increases down to 30 percent or less of the general price index increase during the period from October 1, 1960 to December 31, 1967.[37]

In 1968, a new approach to price regulation was introduced, with extinction of CONEP and creation of CIP (Comissão Interministerial de Precos — Interministerial Committee on Prices) to determine and implement the measures necessary to regulate prices within the general orientation of the economic policy of the federal government. The members of the Interministerial Committee on Prices are the Ministers of Finance, Industry and Commerce, Agriculture and Planning and General Coordination, under the presidency of the Minister of Industry and Commerce. The CIP has a Consultive Committee with representation of: the National Confederation of Industry, National Confederation of Commerce, National Confederation of Agriculture, National Confederation of Workers in Industry, National Confederation of Workers in Commerce, and National Confederation of Workers in Agriculture.

A variety of price control techniques are used at the producer and industrial supply level. The major control at the retail level is a margin limitation: the firm cannot increase its percentage gross margin more than 10 percent over the average of the last two years. In addition, specific maximum retail prices are established for some products, such as carbonated beverages, beer, sugar, and coffee. A specific retail margin is fixed for beef. All these attempts to control and regulate prices reflect a concern over prices as a part of the overall effort to curb inflation—a major goal for the government.

Bookkeeping, Accounting, and Finance

Complex requirements of records and bookkeeping to comply with the licensing, registering, tax, labor laws, and price control complicate both the businessmen's task and the possibility of adequate control and enforcement by the competent authorities. Also the administrative cost is great because the taxpayer has to withhold income tax, social security contributions for his employees, etc. The firm has to create special services to handle these matters. Very small merchants (capital and sales volume are the criteria for smallness) do not have to maintain accounting records. Their taxes are assessed by estimate.

Legal restrictions are imposed on interest rates for credit transactions,[38] but these restrictions provide no real control since various unregulated service fees, etc., may be added to the basic interest charges, accounting for the difference between "quoted" and "real" interest rates.

Taxes

Present policies concentrate a large share of the revenues in the hands of the federal government, which then assumes a redistributive role, so as to decrease the inequalities among the several regions. The Tax Reform[39] was based on two premises:[40] (a) the consolidation of taxes of similar nature, with a clear definition of the economic base for each group, and (b) integration of the tax systems within a national economic and juridic plan, replacing the use of three autonomous systems—federal, state, and municipal. To express the first premise, all taxes were classed in four groups:

a.   taxes on foreign commerce;
b.   taxes on property and income;
c.   taxes on production and circulation of goods;
d.   special taxes that because of their technical characteristic or extraordinary character do not fit any of the three previous groups.

Export taxes were transferred from state to federal government, in view of the fact that these taxes are part of the foreign commerce policy, an area of federal government jurisdiction.

Although other taxes, including the IPI—an excise tax on manufactured products—enter into the final costs and prices of consumer goods, the turnover and value added taxes have been the most significant from the retailer's viewpoint. In 1934 the IVC—turnover-tax was transferred from the federal government to the states, becoming non-uniform, with rates varying from state to state. It was also cumulative—"a tax in cascade"—charged several times from the buying of raw materials until final sales to the final consumer. These characteristics created some problems: inadequate development of inter-regional commerce and exports and vertical integration (the tendency to circumvent the wholesaler) mainly for tax avoidance purposes.

The IVC was replaced by the ICM (Imposto de Circulação de Mercadorias — value added tax). It is still of multiple incidence (paid every time a transaction occurs), but not cumulative anymore, being now charged on value added. Practically the system operates by crediting ICM for entries and debiting for outgoing merchandise, the balance reflecting the tax assessed to the firm. Although recognized by most as a progress over the old IVC, the practical interpretation and application has involved some problems, a fact demonstrated by the large number of amendments to the original provisions. Some examples of these problems: if a firm uses imported goods in its production process or buys them to resell, it places itself out of the dual credit-debit system explained before, and thus operates only on the debit side. Fiscal authorities have accepted the credits in the case of imported machinery or equipment, but the difficulty still applies to all the other imports.[41]

Moreover, all states do not have the same ICM rates, and these are different from the interstate rate (now fixed at 15 percent). Consequently, a seller who charges the same price to two buyers, one in the same state, the other in another state, will have a better net result in the interstate sale. He similarly will be better off if he buys in his own state for productions or resale.[42]

These problems led the Federation of Industry in the state of Guanabara (Rio de Janeiro) to petition the government for an equalization of the ICM rates for the whole country. But in the project submitted to the Senate in August 1970, for progressive reduction for ICM rates, the interstate rate remained fixed at 15 percent, even though the intrastate rates were to be progressively decreased from 1971 to 1974, and the difference between the state rates were to be retained.

There are also numerous technical problems of interpreting the law. One of the most interesting concerns the exact definition (and determination of exact time and place) of a transaction leading to tax liability. Most authors emphasize that only a change in ownership, rather than physical movement of the goods, is necessary to create a tax liability. While the practical implications of this interpretation have not always been clear-cut, it is evident that it will affect the prices retailers pay and charge.

There have been several attempts to study the effect of ICM on final retail prices, as compared to retail prices under the previous IVC. A very detailed study concluded,[43] in 1967, that "with a markup of 30% to 50% in all stages (of the channels of distribution), there are some points where the new system is more favorable than the previous one. But, for a markup higher than 60%—not extraordinary—the ICM presents disadvantages for the final consumer, in relation to the old system." We assume that, as of today even after the several changes and amendment to the ICM system, these conclusions still would hold.

The old "tax of industries and professions"—a local tax, initially with the characteristic of a licensing tax, gradually lost this characteristic and became a disguised local sales tax, with the same problems of cumulative charges. It was eliminated in the tax reform, and the local government receives instead a participation in the state ICM tax.

A large number of amendments, laws, and regulations have been enacted, to amend, explicate, or add to the general provisions of the Tax Reform. The retailer has some problems in understanding and correctly applying this extensive body of legislation. This is especially true in the case of the ICM tax.

Functions

The paucity of available statistics hampers a complete evaluation of retailing's function in the Brazilian economy. Basic statistics for retailing are available in the Censo Comercial (Commercial Census) taken by the IBGE (Instituto Brasileiro de Geografia e Estatistica). Census are taken every ten years, the shortcomings of the process being in the delay to publish the data and in the publication of periodical estimated re-evaluations. There are no statistics available, on a regular basis, for real operating costs, average stock turnovers per line of merchandise, etc. There is also a lack of technical studies and of specialized management consulting services for retailers.

The Brazilian retailers, as their counterparts all over the world, perform the basic functions related to their role as liason between the producer (via or without wholesaler) and the final consumer. Some have had effects on manufacturing, through designs and specifications for products marketed under own brands (for example, the Sears stores, some supermarket chains).

Retailing has also made some evident contributions to the economy, not only by the employment of people in the trade, but also by providing a field of easy entry for the small capitalist. Also, by fostering installment selling, retailers have helped create a mass market for durable goods, have provided conditions for expansion in the durable goods industries, and have contributed to a better standard of living.

General Conclusions

Although this chapter does not attempt to give a detailed presentation of all laws and regulations in matters affecting retail business (a task that would require several books, at least), one can draw some conclusions, even from this brief and general exposition.

1. An analysis of the major, basic codes of legislation, the Commercial Code, the Consolidation of Labor Laws and also the Tax Reform, does not disclose enough specific retailing provisions to indicate specific or special policies towards retailing. This apparently is due to a lack of concern with this important sector of the economy. Only recently has government been aware that retailing can also be "big business."
2. Because of the retailers' close proximity to consumers (and so, to public opinion), there have been sporadic rigorous "checks" on retailing practices. At the time they occur, there investigations of obedience to laws and regulations seem to indicate a policy of great concern over what is happening in the retail sector. In our opinion, the fact that those checks are sporadic corroborates our first conclusion of a lack of special policy toward retailing.
3. The large number of complementary regulations issued by a large number of governmental agencies, all of which the retailer has to know and comply with, becomes an additional problem in his daily activities.[44]

    This extensive and fluid body of legislation that complements the basic codes and consolidation of laws complicates the businessmen's ability to understand and correctly comply with the legal requisites. It also complicates our task of presenting an overall view of the status quo. This conclusion can be credited or debited to (according to one's opinion) the liberal character of the Brazilian Commercial Laws.
4. This complexity and these difficulties give rise to the paradoxical "perceived unfair competition" of large and small firms against each other—the large claiming that by necessity of their own internal control, they have to keep detailed records, pay all taxes, as the small do not—and these claiming that they cannot, like the large concerns, afford all the specialized services (bureaucratic services, accountants, lawyers) to help them understand and act in accordance with the complex regulatory requirements.
5. Finally, it should be stressed that in a highly dynamic country in process of development, like Brazil, changes occur often in all sectors, including

retailing, and statements and analyses like the ones presented in this chapter are necessarily subject to constant revision.

January 1971

Notes

1. Brazil — Superintendencia Nacional do Abastecimento, Antecendentes, Organização Legislaçao Correlata, Documento No. 1 da SUNAB (Rio de Janeiro, SUNAB, 1963), pp. 21-22 in Charles Slater and others. "Market Processes in the Recife Area of Northeast Brazil," Research Report No. 2, Latin American Studies Center, Michigan State University, 1969, p. 53.

2. Brazilian Constitution, October 17, 1969, art. 153, paragraph 23.

3. Personal requirements for entry are made in respect to pharmacies, where each establishment must have a professionally qualified pharmacist. Also, hair-dressers and barbers, to obtain their "Carteira Profisional" (Worker's identify card), have to exhibit a certificate showing professional ability issued by schools maintained by the respective unions (The Consolidation of Brazilian Labor Laws, May 1, 1943, art. 1872).

4. The Brazilian Commercial Code dates back to June 25, 1850, and is closely based on the French, Spanish, Portuguese and Dutch Codes, that all emphasized the "merchant." From 1850 on, an extensive list of laws and decrees was added to the Brazilian Commercial Legislation.

5. Theophilo de Azeredo Santos, "Manual de Direito Comercial," Forense-Rio, 2nd. edition, 1965, p. 67.

6. Law 4. 121, August 27, 1962, establishes the juridical situation of the married woman, changing art. 147 of the Civil Code.

7. Brazilian Constitution, 1969, art. 153.

8. Theophilo de Azeredo Santos, op. cit., p. 68.

9. Decree — Law 2627, September 26, 1940.

10. This remittance is regulated by the Lei de Remessa de Lucros (Law of Remittance of Profits), Law 4131, September 3, 1962, modified by Law 4390, August 29, 1964, as implemented by decree No. 55,762, February 17, 1965.

11. Detailed requisites can only be obtained from close examination of updated Central Bank's rules. The Bank keeps a loose-leaf system of control that facilitates this examination.

12. C. Slater and others, op. cit., pp. 2-33 and 6-17.

13. The regulation of financing for building and buying of real estate for the operation of supermarkets was published in the São Paulo Diário Oficial of March 19, 1969, year LXXIX, No. 53, pp. 47-48. But nobody has made use of it yet, due to the prevailing specified rate of interest considered high by super-market entrepreneurs.

14. We will discuss the meaning of these taxes later on this paper, under the heading of *taxes.*

15. 1969 Constitution, art. 160, item V; thus confirming the statement of art. 148 of the 1946 Constitution; art. 157, item VI of the 1967 Constitution and the Law No. 4137, September 10, 1962: Regulation on the Abuse of Economic Power.

16. Law No. 894, August 22, 1957 and Decree No. 14-147, November 6, 1958, State of Guanabara.

17. City Law No. 7208, November 13, 1968, São Paulo.

18. Almost 500 owners of supermarkets of fourteen states participated in the 5th National Convention of Supermarkets in São Paulo, in 1970.

19. Waldomiro Bulgarelli, "Regime Jurídico das Sociedades Cooperativas." Biblioteca Pioneira de Estudos Cooperativos, Livraria Pioneira Editora, 1955, "Conclusões," p. 88.

20. CNCE, "Eléments sur les Circuits de Distribution dos Produits de Consommation au Brésil," Centre National du Commerce Extérieur, Paris, 1968, pp. 61-62

21. Charles Slater and others, op. cit., p. 53.

22. Law No. 24. 150, 1934 ("Lei de Luvas") is the basic document on the subject.

23. Specifications are set and controlled by the state's Secretary of Hygiene.

24. Decree Law No. 240, February 28, 1967.

25. Law 5, 107, September 13, 1966, implemented by Law 59.820, December 20, 1966.

26. Law 605, January 5, 1949, implemented by Decree No. 27.048, August 12, 1949.

27. Law 4. 090, July 13, 1962 and Law 4.749, August 12, 1965 and Decree No. 57.155, November 8, 1965.

28. 1969 Constitution, art. 178, paragraph one.

29. Decree Law No. 8.621, January 10, 1946.

30. Decree Law No. 8.622, January 10, 1946.

31. A circumstance already foreseen in decree-law No. 31.546, October 6, 1952, that proposes the concept of apprentice employee, art. 2°, paragraph 2°.

32. M.T.I.C. No. 28, February 4, 1958.

33. See note 26.

34. Inter-union agreement, Proc. No. TRT/SP 262/1968 – A – Clause VII – letter "c."

35. Commercial Code, Title II, and Decree-Law 245, of 1967.

36. Portaria Interministerial G.B. 71, February 23, 1965; followed by Law No. 4.663, June 3, 1965; decrees 57.271 of November 1965, and 57. 618 of January 10, 1966, and Law No. 4.862 of November 29, 1965.

37. Art. 2 of Decree-Law No. 38 of November 18, 1966, Art. 10 of Decree-Law No. 156 of February 10, 1967, Decree No. 60205 of February 10, 1967. Decree No. 60,720 of May 12, 1967 as cited in "Brazilian System of

Fiscal Incentives," *A Economia Brasileira e suas Perspectivas (Estudos APEC,* Vol. VIII). Rio de Janeiro: APEC Editora S.A., 1969, pp. 277, 281.

38. Usury Law, modified by a Resolution of the Central Bank.

39. Constitutional Amendment No. 18 of December 1, 1965, and Law No. 5172 of October 25, 1966.

40. For a detailed exposition of the Tax Reform, see *Aspectos da Tributária (Série Monográfica – Instrumentos Administrativos de Implementação Economica – Fundação Getúlio Vargas & Banco Interamericano de Desenvolvimento,* No. 4). Rio de Janeiro: Escola Interamericana de Administração Pública, 1967.

41. "O ICM na Formação dos Precos," *Conjuntura Economica* (Fundação Gétulio Vargas), February 1969, pp. 98-99.

42. Ibid., p. 101.

43. Meyer Stillman and Mitsuo Matsunaga, "ICM e a Politica de Precos das Empresas," *O Estado de São Paulo,* January 8, 1967.

44. As an example, one of the speakers at the 5th Convention of the ABRAS (Associação Brasileira de Supermercados – Brazilian Association of Supermarkets) quoted over thirty agencies (federal, state, and local) by which a supermarket in Guanabara can be checked, controlled (and fined, if not complying with all of the different regulations emanating from them).

5 Canada

ROBERT G. WYCKHAM AND MAX D. STEWART

Introduction

Retail decision making in Canada is affected in almost every instance by government legislation, regulation, and control. Public policy at the federal, provincial, and municipal levels influences retail structure and strategy. At the federal level legislation controlling price discrimination has the effect of regulating the potential power of the retailer to obtain price concessions from his suppliers. Indirectly, federal excise taxes and tariffs modify the array of products available to the retailer for sale. The availability of federal funds for capital loans to retailers has the potential to change the retail structure in the competition of large against small, specialist against generalist, and independent against chain. At the provincial level, consumer protection legislation forces the retailer to disclose certain information about his credit programs to consumers. Provincial labor legislation causes the retail manager to design his staffing to conform with the law and still maintain effective utilization of personnel. At the municipal level, zoning laws dictate where the retailer may locate, and what size and shape his buildings may take. Store hours and days of opening may also be regulated by the local community through its elected representatives.

Canadian retailers may even be affected by foreign governments in making decisions about their operations in this country. American anti-trust legislation can influence merger decisions of U.S. subsidiaries in Canada; U.K. regulations on balance of payments can influence investment by British retail subsidiaries operating in Canada. Present tendencies suggest more direct federal influence on foreign-owned enterprises doing business in Canada. Whatever new policies might develop in this area will have little effect on the total retail scene that is predominantly Canadian-owned.

The system of Canadian government, as enacted under the British North America Act of 1867,[1] is comprised of a federal government and a number of provincial governments (presently ten). To the federal government are entrusted matters essential to the development, unity, and permanence of the country. These include the regulation of trade and commerce, taxation, postal service, currency, banking, weights and measures, interest rates, bankruptcy, and criminal law (within which are contained laws relating to monopoly and unfair trade practices), all of which affect the retail decision maker. The provincial governments are responsible for a specific set of local matters including direct taxation,

81

property and civil rights, provincial incorporation of companies, licensing of retail concerns, and control of municipalities. Provincial governments delegate certain of their powers and duties to the municipal governments, for example, local taxation, licensing and regulation of retailers, inspection of the sale of natural products, and land zoning.

In view of the widespread effects of public policy on retailing, it is surprising to find a dearth of published material on this subject in Canada. Reading the accounts of the development of retailing in Canada, both by historians and participants, one is struck by the almost total lack of any indication that public policy had anything to do with assisting, retarding, or maintaining retail trade. It is also surprising to see how little attention governments have paid to retailing, with the exception of regulation. The report of the Royal Commission on Canada's Economic Prospects in 1958 allocated three out of 509 pages to retailing and wholesaling. When the economy of an area turns down, the government gives its attention to aiding farmers and manufacturers, but not retailers. And yet, retailing is a major facet of the Canadian economy. It is estimated that 52 percent of the consumer's dollar represents the costs of marketing activities and that retailing accounts for 53 percent of the costs of marketing. In 1961 approximately 12 percent of Canada's labor force was engaged in retailing.

Among the myriad of government departments and regulatory agencies, retail corporate bodies, and retailing associations, only a few appear to stand out in the public policy interface between the regulator and the regulated. On the government side the major structure is the Department of Consumer and Corporate Affairs. The Retail Merchants Association and the Retail Council of Canada are the two most important retailing associations.

Department of Consumer and Corporate Affairs

Under various legislative responsibilities assigned to it by the British North America Act, the government of Canada carries on policies and activities that concern consumer affairs and hence affect retailing. Until recently, federal activities that influenced the retailing field were scattered across at least a dozen different departments.[2] The prospects for coordination were slight; the likelihood that both consumers and businessmen would be confused and find difficult the obtaining of needed information was great.

Significant milestones in that regard were passed in 1966 and 1967. First, the establishment of the Department of Registrar General marked a beginning of a continuing process of bringing together a number of heretofore uncoordinated activities, namely administering the following:

Bankruptcy Act,
Canada Corporation Act,
Combines Investigation Act,
Copyright Act,
Industrial Design and Union Label Act,
Patent Act, and
Trade Mark Act.

Second, a Department of Consumer and Corporate Affairs was established in

1967, following closely upon the recommendations of the Economic Council of Canada. Except where assigned by law to another department, the duties, powers, and functions of the Minister of Consumer and Corporate Affairs extend to all matters relating to consumer affairs; standards of identity and performance in relation to consumer goods; legal weights and measures; and the areas previously under the Registrar General. All matters are of course confined to areas of federal jurisdiction. The Act calls for coordination of relevant programs of the government of Canada; cooperation with provincial agencies and other interested parties; improved consumer information and necessary inspection services for the protection of the Canadian consumer. The minister is also expected to initiate appropriate consumer programs.

In addition to the duties of the Registrar General of Canada, as indicated above, the powers, duties, and functions of other statutes that affect consumers and retailing have been transferred to the Minister of Consumer and Corporate Affairs. These include several transferred from the Department of Trade and Commerce:

Electrical and Photometric Units Act,
Electricity Inspection Act,
Gas Inspection Act,
National Trade Mark and True Labelling Act,
Precious Metals Marking Act, and
Weights and Measures Act.

The department also participates together with other departments in the administration of the following statutes:

Canada Agricultural Products Standards Act,
Canada Dairy Products Act,
Fish Inspection Act,
Food and Drugs Act, and
Maple Products Industry Act.

They embrace quite extensive regulations prescribing in detail contents, grades, standards, and labels.

Two recently enacted statutes, Hazardous Products Act (June, 1969) and Textile Labelling Act (March 1970),[3] providing similar kinds of regulations, are administered by the Department of Consumer and Corporate Affairs. The Minister of National Health and Welfare is also concerned with some aspects of hazardous products regulations.

It seems reasonable to suggest that the establishment of the Department of Consumer and Corporate Affairs and the assignment to it of a general coordinating function represents a significant shift in emphasis. Matters affecting consumers, and hence directly or indirectly the retail industry, have been made a major responsibility of a single cabinet minister. To the older attitude of "let the buyer beware" has been added something of the philosophy of "let the seller take care." That subtle but discernible change in public policy is illustrated by the opening in April 1968 of Box 99, Ottawa, to provide a medium of communication with consumers. Since its inception, there has been a steady and growing flow of complaints and inquiries from the public. In addition to aiding consumers in their quest for satisfactory retail products, Box 99 is a source of useful information to the department as to current problem areas.

Structure

Organizations of Retailers

There are two major organizations to which Canadian retailers belong. The largest, with a membership of 10,000, is the Retail Merchants Association which is composed mainly of small independent retailers (although Woodwards, a major west coast department store chain, is a member of the British Columbia division). This organization was originally conceived of as a pressure group to further the interests of independent retailers. Over the seventy-five-year history of the organization, it has been involved in attempts to curb trading stamps, arrest the growth of chains, eliminate phoney closing-out sales, stop price wars through resale price maintenance, and limit store opening hours. The second group is the Retail Council of Canada, whose membership includes the major retailers of the nation. This national organization is a well-financed and politically strong pressure group. The Retail Council participates in the financing of research of general interest to its members.

Firm Structure and Control

Public policy influences retail firm structure in terms of the types of legal organization available, the amount and character of integration (vertical and horizontal) allowed, and the degree of exclusiveness of distribution permitted.

Retailing in Canada may be carried on as a proprietorship, a partnership, a private corporation,[4] a public corporation, or a cooperative. Numerically, the most popular of the legal forms for retailers is the proprietorship. In 1961, 71.5 percent of all retail stores were proprietorships and they did 30.9 percent of total retail sales. Partnerships accounted for 8.8 percent of total stores and 6.8 percent of total sales in 1961. Both the proportion of total stores and total sales for proprietorships and partnerships have been declining over the years. Corporations, both private and public, made the largest percentage of retail sales, 57.9 percent in 1961, and the proportion is growing, with only 18.2 percent of the number of stores. The cooperative is the least popular form of structure with .8 percent of total stores and 1.3 percent of total retail sales in 1961.[5]

The corporate form of ownership appears to be directly related to ease of growth, and hence size (because of limited liability, access to professional skills, and ease of raising capital) and so to a growing dominance of the retail sector. Only 2.9 percent of all stores had sales over one-half million dollars in 1961 and yet they made 41.5 percent of retail sales.[6]

The battle between the independent retailer and the chains is of long standing in Canada. The Hudson's Bay Company is said to have been the first chain-type retail operation in Canada, establishing a series of trading posts across the nation after 1670.[7] It was not until the decade of the 1920s, however, that chains became a major factor in the retail field with 7 percent of total sales.[8] No anti-chain store legislation was enacted to deter their growth (although provincial minimum loss acts were implemented without success and some municipalities placed higher taxes and licensing fees on chains) so that by the mid-1960s about 20 percent of all retail sales were carried out by chains. (This proportion does not include department stores, who tend to operate as chains, and have 8.6 percent of retail sales.) Public policy, which did not hinder chain growth, also allowed the development of combinations of wholesalers and independent retailers to compete with chains. Individual chains grew by internal expansion and by purchasing competitors (Eatons took over Spencers in 1948; Hudson's Bay bought out Morgans in 1960). It does not appear that the anti-combines laws have slowed this development, although considerable political heat was generated in the past.[9]

Integration. Vertical integration by retailers began with the larger operators (Eatons, Simpsons) taking over the functions of the powerful wholesaler-importers in the 1870s. Eatons integrated into production in the late 1880s[10] and set up an independent wholesale business in 1892.[11] Although vertical integration was a topic of interest to the Royal Commission on price spreads in 1935, there is no evidence of subsequent anti-trust activity. In the 1960s, vertical integration was common in grocery, drug, department, gasoline, shoe, clothing, and drug retailing.

Horizontal integration of diverse types of stores is less common. When this has been done it generally has been accomplished through a holding company structure; for example the Weston group of companies includes firms retailing bakery goods, groceries, and drugs. No attempt has been made by anti-combines authorities to limit this development.

Exclusive distribution is not illegal under federal law. Manufacturers, distributors, and retailers are permitted to establish exclusive distribution arrangements with territorial protection.

Foreign Ownership. Of 25,869 corporations in the retail trade in 1967, there were 4,544 reporting under the Corporations and Labour Unions Return Act; of these, 259 had 50 percent or more of their voting shares held by non-residents.[12]

A superficial examination of department store ownership indicates that the large majority of control is held in Canada.[13] The discount store sector appears to have a large measure of ownership outside of Canada, principally in the United States. Of the major chain grocery merchants, only two seem to be owned outside the country. The two largest chains of variety stores are wholly owned U.S. subsidiaries.

Increasing pressure from various quarters has resulted in some changes in the foreign ownership-management situation.[14] The Hudson's Bay Company, which has had its headquarters in London, England for 300 years, has moved its offices to Winnipeg. Principal reasons for the move were said to be weaknesses related to foreign exchange and taxation risks. The company hopes to increase the number of Canadian shareholders.

Government Support for Small Retailing

The federal government has had a direct influence on retail size and structure through making capital loans available. For a number of years the Retail

Merchants' Association and other retail organizations agitated for a capital loan fund to assist independent retailers.[15] Presently small business loans are available to retailers at chartered banks at advantageous rates under the Small Business Loans Act. The federally-operated Industrial Development Bank will also make capital loans to retailers.

Government-Owned Retailing

The government controls the sale of alcoholic beverages in all provinces. In most provinces beer, wine, and liquor are sold in government-operated stores. These products are not available to other retailers in the Maritimes. In the western provinces, packaged beer may also be purchased in beer parlors. Beer may be sold in stores operated at breweries in Alberta, Ontario, and Manitoba. Ontario allows wine manufacturers to sell their products in company-owned outlets. Only Quebec permits the sale of beer in non-chain grocery stores. Government control of the retail sale of alcoholic beverages includes product availability, package shapes and sizes, prices, and all phases of promotion.

Prior to World War II some provincial governments were involved in the sale of electric and gas appliances through state-owned utilities. This gave them some measure of influence with respect to the availability, pricing, and promotion of these products. It would appear that this practice terminated with the war. Some public utilities are indirectly involved in the retailing of appliances through services to appliance retailers. For example, the British Columbia Hydro offers a sales training program to appliance salesmen and collects and distributes to retailers statistics on the sales of various products.

Managerial Strategies

The retail manager is regulated in the development and execution of operating strategy by public policy. In this section the most important government influences concerning product control, pricing, promotion, personnel, location, store opening, firm structure, consumer protection, and credit will be considered.

Product Control

Governmental control over products and product availability takes a number of forms. There is public regulation of the characteristics of goods available for sale in terms of quality and in terms of particular specifications for factor inputs or product performance. There is regulation as to channels of distribution and pricing of natural products (through government-sanctioned monopolies such as marketing boards) and direct control over the sale of alcoholic beverages and indirect control over such products as drugs and tobacco. There is also legislation governing the sale of products deemed dangerous, as, for example, fire arms.

The federal government influences the array of products available to the retailer by its policies relating to imports and the development of "infant" or "necessary" industries. Through the use of tariffs and import regulations and via the price mechanism certain classes and types of products from various sources are made more or less difficult for the retailer to obtain and sell. In some cases the import duty policies reflect the government's concern for encouraging the growth of particular industries or skills in the domestic market.

Resale price maintenance sections of the Combine Investigation Act give the government of Canada additional control over the availability of products at retail. Suppliers may not refuse to supply a retailer with products for the purpose of enforcing a price maintenance policy (although there are loss-leader exceptions). However, this does not outlaw selective or exclusive dealership arrangements, provided this is not done in collusion with other suppliers and provided the seller is not a monopolist. "The Eddy Match Company was convicted on this basis, and Canadian Industries Ltd. was 'persuaded' to ease their distribution policy in the Ammunition case."[16]

Products Under Special Controls. Product availability and product characteristics are also controlled by a number of federal statutes including:
Agricultural Product Standards Act,
Dairy Products Act,
Fish Inspection Act,
Food and Drugs Act,
Maple Products Industry Act,
Hazardous Product Act, and the
Textile Labelling Act.
Each of these seven statutes provides, in varying degree, for analysis, inspection, search, seizure, and forfeiture as well as direct penalties for violation. There are some items that are banned; that is, they cannot legally be advertised, sold, or imported. "Regulated" products can be advertised, sold, and imported only if the contents, packaging, and labeling comply with the detailed requirements of the law. Because these regulations are under continuing enforcement, review, and revision, the most up-to-date provisions are controlling. Although they do concern more directly importation and manufacture, a good many of the rules affect retailing of the products involved.

The National Department of Health and Welfare has been conducting a research and information program on tobacco products. By comparing the tar and nicotine content of various brands and communicating this data along with medical information on the dangers of smoking, the government has influenced the amount of tobacco products sold and the mix of these products.

The tendency toward more activity regarding product liability makes at least a brief reference to two recent judgments worthwhile. In a case arising from an eye injury to a shopper from an exploding soft drink bottle on a store shelf, the Supreme Court of Ontario gave judgment against the manufacturer (bottler), but dismissed the action against the retailers.[17] The Court held, however, that because the injured party was justified in bringing the retailer to court, he will be entitled to add to his claim against Coca-Cola Ltd. the amount he was required to pay the retailer as reimbursement of trial costs. In a case concerning a car that proved faulty, the British Columbia Supreme Court found against a car dealer in favor of the buyer.[18] The Court held that the car was so faulty as to mean a fundamental breach of contract, thereby denying the seller any protection from an exempting clause, which limited the vendor's liability.

Provincial legislation with respect to "natural products" specifies grade standards, stipulates inspection of quality and for disease, requires certain processes such as pasteurization, sets conditions of sale such as package sizes for dairy products, makes rules for marking and branding. Physical conditions under which natural products may be processed and stored, and the setting up and regulating of marketing boards to distribute natural products are also governed by provincial laws. Marketing boards have been set up for natural products under the National Products Marketing Act and provincial legislation. By controlling supply, setting quotas and prices, and regulating the flow of these products to the retail level, they constrain the retailer's decision-making role. Most provinces have had legislation banning the sale of margarine, but its sale is now allowed under certain conditions. Imitation dairy products are specifically outlawed in some provinces. In most cases the provincial legislation relating to natural products makes the retailer as well as the producer or processor liable for penalties.

Control of the sale of drugs at the provincial level takes the form of regulating who may operate a pharmacy and offer drugs for sale. In addition, an act on drug substitution is in force in Alberta and is in the development stages in British Columbia. This legislation allows the pharmacist to substitute a generic product, with the same chemical properties, if a physician prescribes a brand-name drug and does not prohibit substitution. Control by the provinces of tobacco distribution is carried out through licensing of sellers and a minimum age for purchasers.

Fireworks are also regulated at the provincial level. They are banned in some provinces and in some communities where the Municipal Act gives to the cities the right to control this product. In other provinces and cities the sale of fireworks is limited to particular times of the year (British Columbia) or to sale for public display only (New Brunswick). Federal legislation on the sale of firearms requires that retailers of guns keep records of each transaction. Most provinces have laws allowing only persons of a certain age to buy or possess firearms.

Pricing

For the most part public policy influences on pricing come at the federal level, but there are also some important provincial controls.

Federal Regulations. The Combines Investigation Act (Section 33A) makes certain pricing practices indictable offences.[19] First, it is illegal for a business to grant "any discount, rebate, allowance, price concession or other advantage" to one purchaser that is not made available to competitors of that purchaser "in respect of a sale of articles of like quality and quantity." Although this is a restraint to some extent on a retailer attempting to obtain a special concession from his suppliers, it would seem to pose no problem regarding his own selling prices. It is unlikely that final consumers would be held to be "competitors" in terms of the Act. Secondly, it is illegal to follow a policy of selling at lower prices in one part of Canada than in another, where that policy has the effect or tendency of substantially lessening competition. Although this seems to dictate to some degree a one-price policy, it is not a rigidly universal requirement across the entire nation. There is no mention of the possibility of varying costs being associated with the same price in different areas. Thirdly, a policy of "unreasonable low" prices is illegal. It is uncertain how effective that provision might be in cases of alleged loss-leaders.

Section 34 makes it an offence for any manufacturer or supplier to attempt to induce any other person to resell at a specified price or not below a specified minimum. That is, there must be no effort made toward resale price maintenance and refusal to supply because of a customer declining to resell at a specified price is illegal. There are saving clauses (sub-section 5) to the effect that a dealer may refuse to sell to a person who makes a practice of using the articles as loss-leaders (not for the purpose of making a profit thereon) or who fails to provide the level of servicing that might reasonably be expected. The combination of the ban on resale price maintenance and the saving clauses create considerable uncertainty with respect to specific application of the law.

Provincial Regulations. Provincial laws, taxes, and policies affect pricing in a number of ways. Legislation to curb below-cost selling, credit disclosure sections of consumer protection acts, and closing-out sales laws all play a role in retail price decisions. The prices of all goods at retail are adjusted by retail sales taxes. Special provincial taxes on such items as tobacco and gasoline have a direct influence on the prices of these products. All provinces directly control the prices of beer, wine, and liquor.

As a response to chain store pricing, a number of provinces enacted minimum loss acts or below-cost selling acts (Manitoba, British Columbia). These were designed to assist the independent grocery retailer to counteract the low price and loss leader activities of chain supermarkets. These laws have been generally ineffective because "if the retailer accused proves that the total price charged for the combination (of grocery products) is not less than the aggregate of the prices at which each of such grocery product might lawfully be sold, the sale is not deemed to be a violation."[20] The Commodities Retail Sales Act of British Columbia gives the right to wholesalers and producers to set retail prices. Both minimum loss acts and provincial resale price maintenance laws appear to overlap federal legislation. If this is so it is likely that Dominion jurisdiction would prevail and the provincial law would be inoperative.[21]

Consumer protection legislation has an influence on pricing in a special way. Prior to the establishment of these laws retailers could present a product for sale and advertise it in such a way as to make the price appear lower than it was. This is now much more difficult to achieve. The fire sale, liquidator's sale type of promotion also presented opportunities for the retailer to price goods so that they seemed like bargains. Licensing and inspection appears to have curbed this practice.

Retail sales taxes are levied in nine of the ten provinces. The tax rates range from a low of 5 percent in British Columbia, Manitoba, Saskatchewan, and Ontario (Alberta has no sales tax), to a high of 8 percent in Quebec (a portion of which is a municipal tax) and New Brunswick, with the remainder of the provinces at 7 percent.[22] Some products are exempted (children's clothing and furniture, educational supplies) from the tax in some provinces. It is difficult to ascertain the influence of this tax on retail prices of individual commodities, although it has been noted that some prices have been designed so that the price plus the tax result in an even dollar figure. Because the tax is added on to the advertised price, it is unlikely to have had any influence on the setting of so-called psychological prices. It is obvious that such taxes, by cutting the level of real disposable income, have an effect on total retail sales.

It seems clear that provincial authorities have set special taxes on tobacco and gasoline believing that the demand for these products is relatively price inelastic in an upward direction. Taxes on these commodities have risen steadily over the years. In most provinces the tax on cigarettes (not including retail sales tax) amounts to about 18 percent of the retail price. Taxes on tobacco products may have a significant influence on the sales and profits of retailers specializing in this commodity. About one-third of the price of gasoline is made up of provincial taxes. Whether more retail gas sales would be made at lower prices is debatable.

Promotion

Public policy set at all levels of government influences retail decisions about various aspects of promotion. Under this title we will consider mass media advertising, store signs, mail and telephone order catalogues, and closing-out sales.

Federal proscription of deceptive advertising is provided in the Combines Investigation Act. One Section, 33C, makes misleading representation as to the price at which like articles "have been, are, or will be, ordinarily sold," an offence punishable on summary conviction.[23] Section 33D, brought into the Combines Investigation Act in 1969, makes it an offence punishable on summary conviction to publish statements regarding the performance of a product without a prior adequate and proper test. More severe penalties are provided in the case of other forms of misleading representation. An increasing number of cases against retail concerns are being brought to trial, which is consistent with statements of the Minister of Consumer and Corporate Affairs that the limits of legislative provisions will be tested in court. It seems clear that revisions of the law are likely to be introduced where protection against misleading advertising would otherwise prove ineffective.

Municipalities govern the distribution and posting of bills, placards, and circulars. Retailers using this form of advertising are constrained in using this device by licensing fees (Halifax), and by regulations as to the content of the advertisement, the location of its posting, and the process of distribution to potential customers.

Municipal procedures governing store signs vary from city to city. In Fredericton, the City Council decides on each application for a retail sign on its merits, but no general rules are in force. In Montreal the sign by-law is almost forty pages in length. Among other types of signs it regulates those on the buildings and vehicles of retailers. It covers the size (area), placing, location, over-street projection, and illumination of all signs.

Although other factors were vastly more important in the success of mail-order catalogues in the promotion of goods in Canada, public policy has played a role. "The government's need for cash for tax purposes put cash in circulation; banks sprouted branches, miles of toll-free road were built, improvements in parcel post, post office and bank drafts, and railway express meant a bright future for a cash only mail order business."[24] Without favorable mail rates (Eatons paid the postage on large orders to rural areas beginning in the 1880s),[25] the distribution of catalogues and the delivery of goods to customers would have been seriously hampered. Federal regulations on misleading advertising may have helped to protect the consumer and encourage confidence in catalogues, although as part of the Criminal Code they were rarely enforced. Despite the attempts by local retailers to have municipal laws enacted to ban the hated catalogues, millions are distributed each year. Government regulation as it applies to over-the-counter sales also controls sales by catalogue.

A retail promotional device of considerable influence that is now closely controlled at the provincial and municipal level is the closing-out sale. Strong pressure by retail groups was brought to bear on this problem in the mid-1950s, to curb abuses in the use of this type of sale. Municipal ordinances and provincial regulations set out standards and fees for licensing of sales ranging from going-out-of-business to creditor's sales. Rules cover the condition of the goods for sale and forbid the sale of goods brought in especially for this type of sale.

Trading Stamps

Trading stamps have had a varied life in Canada. At the turn of the twentieth century, a number of stamp systems flourished. Federal legislation in 1905 was designed to wipe out these schemes, but allowed "manufacturers' coupons to be used in exchange for gifts."[26] Amendment of the Criminal Code of Canada in 1954 led to a vigorous revival of the use of trading stamps by retailers. Stamp companies quickly spread their programs across the country. Provincial and municipal legislation in some areas have tended to retard the use of this promotional device. For example, in British Columbia, trading stamps must have a redeemable value of at least ten cents before they can be issued. Legislation in Alberta and Saskatchewan prohibits the use of stamps, while in Manitoba the Municipal Act gives the right to regulate the use of stamps to the municipalities. In the late 1960s major grocery retailers began to drop the use of stamps (because of rising costs, consumer disinterest, political pressure, opposition in the trade) until only a few stamp companies still operate. There is no stamp activity west of the Saskatchewan border and little in Manitoba and Ontario. Trading stamps still flourish in the major centers of Quebec and the Maritimes.[27] Steinberg's subsidiary, Pinkys Stamps Ltd., provides stamps for distri-

bution through the company's supermarkets and department stores in Quebec. Recent activity by the Department of Consumer and Corporate Affairs serves to indicate that new legislation governing trading stamps may be put forward. At present, it appears that stamps are legal if they are redeemed:
1. by the vendor, or
2. in goods that are at least partly his property,
3. in the premises where the goods are purchased, and if
4. each stamp shows legibly on its face the address of the store and the merchantable value of the stamp, and finally,
5. if the stamps may be redeemed on demand at any time, no matter how small the number of stamps presented for redemption.[28]

Labeling

Government regulation of labeling is found at both the federal and provincial levels. Under Section 33D of the Combine's Investigation Act, Canada has a measure of control over labels that might be seen as misleading advertising. A number of acts administered by the national Department of Consumer and Corporate Affairs relating to natural products, textiles, and hazardous products contain provisions governing labels. The Food and Drug Act requires that food labels contain the brand name, the common name, a declaration of the net contents of the package in terms of weight or measure, a list of the ingredients, a list of preservatives, food coloring or artificial flavoring, and the name and address of the manufacturer. Drug label requirements are similar to the above, with the addition of the dosage for patent drugs and directions for use.

It is interesting to note the part played by retailers in the establishment of credible labeling. Apparently, before the turn of the present century, retailers replaced manufacturers' labels with more prestigious marks, attached false labels such as "imported" and "pure wool." Large retailers like Eatons refused to follow this practice and influenced others to stop.[29] Today many retailers operate laboratories that analyze the quality and characteristics of products from suppliers, thus ensuring more accurate labeling.

The language on labels is under provincial jurisdiction. For example, Ontario requires that all food products sold in the province contain labels printed in English. Quebec has recently extended its French labeling requirements on food packages.

Personnel[30]

The personnel strategies of retailers are affected by public policy at all levels. Three main types of legislation are important: laws allowing unions and union activity, labor standards laws, and workmen's compensation laws. In addition, government expenditures on education influence retail staffing. Originally all union and labor standards law was enacted at the federal level. At present, federal legislation in these areas covers only employees of federally-chartered companies in such activities as banking and communication. Provincial laws cover all other employees. Since 1949 all provinces have had schemes of collective liability and compulsory insurance for workmen's compensation.[31]

The federal Trades Union Act of 1872 allowed the growth and development of unionism in Canada. Under the conditions of this act unions per se were not illegal and union activity was not viewed as restraint of trade. A 1925 Privy Council decision held that the provincial governments, as well as the federal parliament, had the authority to enact labor relations laws. However, it was not until after the second world war that most provinces became active in labor legislation.

Unionism in the retail trades is not extensive, with less than 10 percent of employees members.[32] Union membership among employees of the major department stores is very low. The ability of unions to influence retail management, however, is great because key trades such as butchers, plumbers, and truck drivers are unionized. The largest unions of sales personnel are the Retail Clerks International Association with 21,000 members and the Retail, Wholesale and Department Store Union with about 20,000 members.[33]

The right to make laws concerning labor standards is vested in both the federal and the provincial governments. Legislation in this area includes: minimum wages, equal pay (for both sexes), hours of work, weekly rest-days, annual vacations with pay, public holidays, fair employment practices, notice of termination of employment, and workmen's compensation.[34] A number of provinces (Ontario, Quebec, Newfoundland) have different minimum wages by age and by sex, which seems to fly in the face of their equal pay and fair employment provisions. The lower minimum wage for women is obviously favorable to retailers. Legislation that retailers claim discriminates against them concerns daily guarantee of hours. For example, in British Columbia an employer who calls in an employee must pay that person for a minimum of four hours. Retailers argue that this makes it much more expensive to effectively allocate staff to the various peak load hours.

Government expenditures on education have an effect on the employment and training practices of retailers. The general upgrading of the education standards of citizens means a better pool of potential candidates for retailers to hire and also results in a more sophisticated consumer who demands more capable retail employees. The offering of retailing and marketing courses in high schools, institutes of technology, community colleges and universities influences career choices as well as prepares students for positions in retailing.

Location

Retail policy decisions on location become more complex with each new piece of zoning legislation and each new planning commission. General observation would lead one to believe that public planning has led to a rationalization of retail location. There appears to be less strip development on city streets and rural highways and an increasing trend to shopping centers (both neighborhood and regional, suburban and downtown). Whether this discriminates against the independent in favor of the chain is open to question. The daily press is a ready source of evidence that the processes provided for in municipal zoning laws have added a political characteristic to the economic and technical aspects of the location decision. Parking regulations affect retail location decisions in terms of influence on customer traffic generation and the economics of providing off-street parking in relation to available selling space. Location decisions are also influenced by differing business taxes, business licenses, and building and fire regulations in various communities.

Municipal zoning rules and the regulatory bodies designed to administer them are set up by the community under the authority of the provincial municipal acts and, in some cases, community planning acts (Saskatchewan). Regional or metropolitan planning is carried on in a number of areas (Toronto, Winnipeg, Vancouver) in an attempt to coordinate land use in communities that are physically together, but politically separate. The purpose of planning legislation and regulation is to ensure appropriate land use "to conserve adequate open spaces for light and air; to reduce fire hazard; to prevent undue concentration of population; to avoid congestion on the streets and to promote the health, safety and general welfare of the inhabitants . . ."[35] That the interpretation of what is favorable to general welfare is controversial can be seen from the briefs presented to zoning boards by retail groups, real estate developers, and citizens' organizations.

Zoning takes two general forms. The first is control over land use, that is, the specific purpose for which a particular piece of land may be used (residential, commercial). The second is regulation of the characteristics of the building to be constructed on the property (placement on land, height, size, and shape of building, type of facade, off-street parking, and loading space). Regulation of the characteristics of structures in some municipalities extends to aesthetics in terms of building design, materials, and landscaping. Land-use zoning usually does not distinguish between retailing and other forms of enterprise, with the exceptions of service stations and shopping centers (for example, the Oakridge property in Vancouver, sold by the Canadian Pacific Railway in 1955, could only be developed as a shopping center as part of the Comprehensive Development District).[36] Zoning laws may be used to control the level of competition of particular types of retailing within a community.

Business taxes, business licenses, and building and fire regulations are an interactive set from the point of view of the retail manager. In order to obtain and retain a license to do business within a municipality the retailer must conform to all the by-laws of the community, which means paying the business tax and maintaining his property in accordance with the building codes. Some municipalities require one license to operate a retail establishment (Winnipeg); others require a series of licenses based on the types of commodities sold or service performed (Montreal). Business taxes vary from city to city in terms of amount and the method of calculating the amount. Businesses in cities in Nova Scotia pay not more than $200 per year, while the maximum in Quebec is $5,000. The maximum in British Columbia runs from $200 to $1,500 depending on the size of the community. Most tax calculation systems are based on the appraised annual rental value of the property occupied. In Vancouver the business tax is 8 percent of the rental value, but in Winnipeg the tax rate rises from 6 percent to 20 percent of the rental value, depending on the amount of the assessment and the type of business.

Hours of Retail Operation

Hours of store opening are governed by the municipal governments in all provinces except Quebec, where province-wide rules apply. Retail practice in hours of operation varies from strict adherence to municipal regulation (West Vancouver) to flagrant disobedience with fines considered a cost of doing business (Toronto), to no regulation of opening hours (Edmonton, Fredricton). The first attempt to influence retail hours appears to have come from Canada's largest retailer, Eatons. In Toronto in 1881, Timothy Eaton began a campaign to restrict his hours of opening and gain adherence from his competitors.[37] It is interesting to note that in recent years, this same company has been in the forefront of efforts to expand store hours in various centers across the nation.

In most municipalities a wide variety of retailers are not governed by store hours, or at least not by the strict rules covering other merchandisers. These include retailers whose principal business is in the sale of tobacco, newspapers, books, drugs, confectionary, fresh fruit and flowers, bread, milk, gasoline, and automobiles.

There is a general trend to the extension of store hours with evening openings on Thursdays and Fridays. A growing battle appears to be developing between the small retailer and the department stores and chains, with the latter groups agitating for longer hours. Most communities have extended hours in the pre-Christmas period.

The majority of cities regulate the days of opening or the number of days of operation per week. One day closed in seven is the general rule. For the most part, retailers must close on officially designated holidays. An exception to this is Edmonton, where the holiday closing by-law was repealed in 1969. In Quebec the days of opening of commercial establishments is governed by a provincial statute.

Exceptions to the hours and days of opening are special shopping areas like Yorkville in Toronto and Gastown in Vancouver, where extended hours and Sunday openings are the rule. The retailers in these unique districts deal mainly in antiques, works of art, and handicrafts.

Credit

Public policy on consumer credit has influenced retailing. The growth and speed of growth of retail sales (and hence retail structures) has been affected by Canadian government policy on consumer credit. This can be seen in such things as the changing of the Bank Act in 1954 to permit chartered banks to make personal loans and the moral suasion and manipulation of the interest rate by the Bank of Canada in 1969 to cut down on the flow of consumer credit.

Consumer Protection

During the 1960s provincial legislation was enacted to give the consumer relief from a number of retail sales practices that were believed to be detrimental to public welfare. Generally these laws covered: cost of credit disclosure, advertising of credit provisions, proportionate rebates for early repayment, relief from unfair collection practices, "cooling-off" periods on itinerant sales, and relief from harsh contracts. Provincial consumer bureaus have also been set up to give advice and information to consumers and to investigate complaints.

For the retailer, these laws have affected his charge account and other credit-granting procedures in that the methods of reporting interest charges to customers have had to be changed. In some cases advertising practices have had to be adjusted to disclose the actual price of the goods, the amount of downpayment, the amount and number of installments, and the cost of credit expressed in dollars and as an annual percentage rate.

A federal bill, still to be approved by Parliament, amending the Bills of Exchange Act, will attempt to provide the consumer with protection when the retailer sells the purchaser's promissory note to a third party. Under present law, when a dealer sells finance paper to a third party, the consumer effectively has no legal right of recourse and is obliged to pay the debt whether the vendor lives up to delivery or service agreements.

Miscellaneous Retail Strategies

Two types of retailing strategies and the public policy influences on them will be considered here: door-to-door selling and automatic vending. In most provinces there are two pieces of provincial legislation governing direct selling. First there are provincial laws (or enabling legislation to allow municipalities to pass by-laws) licensing and controlling the activities of transient traders, that is, persons without residence in the community, and residents who sell from vehicles rather than fixed places of business. Special by-laws are in force in some cities (Halifax) covering the sale of subscriptions for books and magazines. License fees in force in many communities appear to be designed to limit the sale of goods by direct means. Door-to-door sellers are also regulated under consumer protection legislation (see above) by allowing purchasers to cancel contracts within a certain period, requiring delivery of a true copy of any sales contract, and limiting the rights of repossession by the seller.

Cities regulate automatic merchandising or vending machines through licensing, restrictions as to placement (only on private property—Vancouver), and control of characteristics of vending machinery (food vending, fuel oil vending—Montreal). It may be expected that additional legislation will be enacted as automatic vending grows in amount (.39 percent of total retail sales in 1965),[38] and as more and different types of products are sold by machines.

Conclusion

Although retail structures and managerial strategies of retailers in Canada are influenced by a vast number of public policies, there does not seem to be an overall public policy for retailing in the country. No coordinated policy of legislation and regulation is evident among federal, provincial, and municipal authorities. In fact it might be argued that governments have tended to ignore distribution institutions. Legislation and publicity have tended to be oriented toward protection of consumers, regulation of products, and control of manufacturers. It appears as if the fact that much of this legislation becomes operative at the retail level has not been of great concern to the law makers.

Perhaps the organizations representing retail owners and employees have played a part in the lack of a retailing policy for Canada. There does not seem to be a continuing visibility of retailing organizations. It is only at crisis points, when new laws are about to be enacted or regulations changed, that the merchants' organizations and the employees' unions attempt to make their influence felt.

It is important to note that Canada has taken a more passive role than other countries in the control of the growth of retail institutions. This is in line with the lack of rigorous anti-combines regulation applied to all corporations. No doubt in the future changes will occur, specifically with regard to vertical integration and foreign ownership.

Pricing and promotion are two strategic areas where there is a trend toward more public policy activity. The pricing of some sensitive products such as drugs, the revelation of large margins in some instances, and accusations of higher prices in lower socioeconomic neighborhoods, has made pricing a political football. Because retail advertising is all pervasive in the community, there has been a tendency for governmental authorities to attack misleading promotion violations at the retail level. No doubt these tendencies will continue.

September 1970

Notes

1. 30 Victoria, Chapter 3 (UK).

2. Economic Council of Canada, *Interim Report on Consumer Affairs and the Department of Registrar General,* July 1967, 13.

3. Canada, *Office Consolidation of the Criminal Code* (Ottawa: Queen's Printer, 1963), 33.

4. The private corporation has been a favorite type of legal structure for Canadian business. The main advantage is that a private company is not required to publicly disclose information on its affairs. Canada's largest retailer, Eatons, with sales variously estimated around one billion dollars, is a private company.

In recent years, there has been growing pressure for change in the laws on public disclosures of information from private corporations. A 1970 federal law requires all federally incorporated private companies to publish certain financial statements annually.

5. M. S. Moyer and G. Snyder, *Trends in Canadian Marketing,* Dominion Bureau of Statistics (Ottawa: Queen's Printer, 1967), pp. 85 and 87. It is likely that the small amount of sales generated by cooperatives has dampened the enthusiasm of those who would like the law to treat cooperatives as corporations for tax purposes.

6. Ibid., pp. 90, 91.

7. Clifford Henry Cheasley, *The Chain Store Movement in Canada* (Orillia, Ontario: Packet-Times Press Ltd., [undated]), p. 57.

8. Moyer and Snyder, op. cit., p. 126.

9. See for example the *Report of The Royal Commission on Price Spreads* (Ottawa: King's Printer, 1935).

10. Mary-Etta Macpherson, *Shopkeepers to a Nation: The Eatons* (Toronto: McClelland and Stewart, Ltd., 1963), p. 26.

11. William Stephenson, *The Store that Timothy Built* (Toronto: McClelland and Stewart, 1969), p. 43.

12. Dominion Bureau of Statistics, *Corporations and Labour Unions Return Act, Annual Report for 1967,* Part 1, Corporations, (9802-503) December 1969, Table 130.

13. Only very tentative conclusions can be obtained because the data only shows the percentage ownership of the major holding company by country of residence. Canada, *Inter-Corporate Ownership, 1967,* Dominion Bureau of Statistics (Ottawa: Queen's Printer, 1969).

14. See for example, Melville H. Watkins, *Foreign Ownership and the Structure of Canadian Industry,* Report of the Task Force on the Structure of Canadian Industry (Ottawa: Queen's Printer, 1968).

15. *Financial Post,* January 16, 1954. Report on a brief by the Retail Merchants' Association of Canada.

16. Bruce Mallen, "The Combines Investigation Act: Canada's Major Marketing Statute," *M.S.U. Business Topics,* (Spring 1970), 72.

17. *William Hart* v. *Dominion Stores Ltd. and Coca-Cola Ltd.* (1968) 1 O.R. 775.

18. *Thomas G. Lightburn* v. *Ritchie Mercury Sales* in Canadian Sales and Credit Law Guide, par. 21-020, 1969, CCH Canadian Limited.

19. An indictable offence roughly corresponds to a felonious offense as used in the United Kingdom and the United States.

20. British Columbia, Commodities Minimum Loss Act, 572.

21. Personal communication with Mr. Joseph Christian Stark and Company, Vancouver, British Columbia.

22. John F. Due, *Provincial Sales Taxes,* Canadian Tax Papers #37 (Toronto: Canadian Tax Foundation, 1964), p. 1.

99

23. *Combines Investigation Act,* Revised Statutes of Canada, 1952, c. 314, as amended, 1960, c. 45, Section 33C, s-s (1). A summary conviction offense roughly corresponds to a misdimeanour as used in the United Kingdom and the United States.

24. Stephenson, op. cit., p. 47.

25. Ibid., pp. 44-45.

26. *Trading Stamps: The Social, Economic and Legal Aspects of Stamp Schemes in Canada and Why They Should be Eliminated* (Toronto: Retail Merchants Association of Canada, 1961), p. 20.

27. Personal communication from D. W. Rolling, General Manager, Retail Merchants Association of Canada, August 6, 1970.

28. *Trading Stamps,* op. cit., p. 23.

29. Stephenson, op. cit., p. 15.

30. Thanks are due to Professor Robert Rogow, Simon Fraser University, for his wise counsel on this section.

31. Canada, *Workmen's Compensation in Canada,* Legislation Branch, Canada Department of Labor (Ottawa: Queen's Printer, 1969), p. 3.

32. *Incomplete Agenda – The Unorganized* (Montreal: Industrial Relations Center, McGill University, 1968), p. 6.

33. Canada, *Labor Organizations in Canada,* Economics and Research Branch, Canada Department of Labor (Ottawa: Queen's Printer, 1968), p. 111.

34. Canada, *Labor Standards in Canada,* Canada Department of Labor (Ottawa: Queen's Printer, 1965).

35. City of Regina, Zoning Bylaw Number 4306, 1.

36. Douglas E. Harker, *The City and the Store* (Vancouver: Woodward Stores Ltd., 1958), no paging.

37. Macpherson, op. cit., p. 22.

38. Moyer and Snyder, op. cit., p. 203.

6 East Germany

CLAUDE LEBÉDEL

The German Democratic Republic (GDR), like other "socialist" countries of Eastern Europe, has a planned economy of the "imperative" rather than "indicative" (as in France) type. A particular feature of the GDR system is that is was modernized as early as July 1963. The new system, resembling that advocated by Liberman in the USSR, has generally tended to insist on qualitative criteria rather than on the quantitative ones only used until then to determine the objectives and processes of a planned economy.[1]

This early reform in East Germany can certainly be explained by its very industrial character. The more diversified an economy, the greater is the role of intensive factors (e.g., productivity and profitability) compared to that of extensive factors (e.g., increase in the size of workforce through the absorption of unemployed workers and of workers released from agriculture). In a diversified economy, the Soviet-type of planning dating from the 1920s also becomes inadequate in view of the evolution of science and technology. The GDR had certainly reached this stage when the Berlin Wall was set up in 1961, and the reform was introduced in 1963.

The figures in Table 6.1 help characterize the level of economic development in East Germany, and of domestic trade within it. They show that the GDR is highly industrialized, and that trade is becoming more important.

Table 6–1
Some Characteristics of the East German Economy

	Share of National Income*		Economically Active Population	
	1950	1969	1950	1969
Industry	47.0%	60.7%	–	–
Domestic Trade	10.1%	12.5%	–	–
Total Economy	100.0%	100.0%	7,196,000	7,746,000*
			(40% women)	(48% women)
Commercial Sector (Domestic and Foreign Trade)			674,000	868,000

Sources: Annual Statistical Directories.

*At the end of 1969, the total population numbered a little over 17 million people.

101

The following sections analyze the general framework within which domestic trade takes place, the mechanisms of its planning, and its results and problems.[3]

The General Framework

The GDR's domestic trade fits into a general framework characterized by two complementary traits: (1) private property plays a reduced role, compared to those of the state and cooperative sectors; and (2) commerce is planned like other economic sectors, in a predominately centralized manner.

Ownership Types

There are three forms of property in domestic trade: (1) the socialist sector composed of a state sector *(Handelsorganisation,* H.O.), and of a cooperative sector *(Verband Deutscher Konsum,* V.D.K., German Union of Consumer Co-operatives); (2) the private sector; and (3) the mixed sector *(Kommissionshandel).*

Table 6.2 reveals the dominant role of the socialist sector in 1967 since the state and cooperative stores represented more than half of the total number of stores, and made about 5/6 of retail sales. On the other hand, the private sector with some 40 percent of the stores only rang up a little more than 10 percent of the sales.

The Private Sector. The number of private stores has kept shrinking since 1950, although it seems to have stabilized recently. Actually, there are three legal types of private stores: (1) "family" stores employing only relatives or less than six employees; (2) "small commercial production" stores with six to ten employees; and (3) "capitalist" stores with more than ten employees. These three types operate freely; they find their own supplies and customers; they can be sold or inherited; and they must obey all current regulations in such matters as salaries and taxes. Relatively little is known about their functioning, although it is apparent that:

1. From 1953 to 1958 some concentration has taken place, since the number and relative importance of *large* private stores had increased within that sector;[4]
2. In 1958 when the mixed sector (see below) began to develop, the age of private retailers was already high, what with more than two-thirds of them being over fifty years of age; and
3. In 1967, the private sector was represented in all branches of trade, apart from the selling of miscellaneous industrial products, and from diversified stores (e.g., department stores). (See Table 6.3)

Table 6-2

Distribution of Retail Stores and Sales According to Ownership Types

	1952		1960		1967	
	Number of Stores	Sales (million DM)*	Number of Stores	Sales (million DM)*	Number of Stores	Sales (million DM)*
State Sector	20,426 }	15,794	43,249 }	34,691	41,855 }	49,055
Cooperative Sector	18,907 }		36,654 }		35,930 }	
Mixed Sector	—	—	11,554	2,915	13,258	5,723
Private Sector	156,588	9,222	94,608	7,351	58,787	6,616
Total	195,921	25,016	186,065	44,957	149,830	61,394

Source:

*One East German Mark (DM) equals about 30¢

Table 6-3

Importance of Private Stores in Various Commercial Branches (1967)

Branch	Total Number of Retail Stores	Number of Private Stores	Number of Self-service Stores
Food	75,379	23,282	15,556
Shoes & Leathergoods	4,853	1,895	287
Textiles & Clothing	12,109	4,066	470
Furniture, office & sports goods	12,879	6,647	353
Household goods	8,022	3,965	1,043
Mechanical goods, optical goods, vehicles	8,077	5,364	90
Hygiene goods & household goods	24,355	13,315	333
Miscellaneous industrial products	2,513	143	365
Diversified stores	1,443	110	861
Total	149,830	48,787	19,358

The Mixed Sector. In 1959, the GDR authorities issued various measures to facilitate the creation of a mixed sector where private and state capital would join and collaborate: the *Kommissionshandel,* or "commissioned trade." This is a rather significant sector representing about 10 percent of the number and sales of retail stores, and an innovation in "socialist" countries.

The mixed sector includes formerly private firms that have signed a "commission contract" *(Kommissionsvertrag)* with a District Council *(Kreistag,* an administrative authority at the local level). The major features of this contract are as follows:

1. An assortment is assigned to the store which cannot sell any other type of product;
2. The merchandise remains state property until it is sold;
3. The private merchant deposits a sum (in cash or state bonds) equal to 33 percent of the value of the planned stock, in a frozen interest-bearing account in the State Savings Bank;
4. The merchant receives a commission (hence the name of the system) calculated as a percentage of his sales. This commission, ranging from 5.0 to 13.2 percent, must at least equal the revenue which he use to derive from his store, according to his tax returns of the last three years; and
5. The state pays the fixed expenses (rent, depreciation, lighting, heating, etc.), while the retailer pays with his commission the variable expenses (e.g., telephone) and the salaries of his employees (if any).

The Socialist Sector. This sector is made up of two parts:

1. The *State Sector* created after 1948 following the expropriation of firms belonging to former Nazis, or after nationalizing firms of particular economic importance. This sector has been developed almost exclusively in urban areas; and
2. The *Cooperative Sector* which has existed since the middle of the nineteenth century when the first consumer cooperatives were created. There are now more than 700 cooperative societies grouping some 4.1 million members in urban and rural areas. The state has granted the monopoly of creating new stores in rural areas to this cooperative sector in order to assist the development of cooperation in agriculture where private property has practically disappeared.[5]

Anyone can shop in the 35,930 consumer-cooperative stores, but in order to collect the annual rebate (3 percent maximum) determined annually by the general assembly of the cooperative, one has to be a member of it.

This cooperative sector also owns more than 1,500 factories, two-thirds of which are industrial bakeries. Lately, the cooperative sector has increasingly developed its own supply sources for food (e.g., canned goods) and non-food (e.g., furniture) products. Besides, the Consumer Cooperative Union has opened a series of department stores and a mail-order center—as the state sector had done for quite a while.

Planning and Organization of Domestic Trade

The "socialization of productive relations," that is, the collectivization of the factors of production, has been considered necessary in order to design and implement an economic development plan. In this context, domestic trade has not been singled out since it is treated just like industry or communications.

The Organization of Domestic Trade.[6] All problems pertaining to domestic trade are handled by the Ministry of Domestic Trade *(Ministerium für Binnehandel)*. It supervises directly: (1) the state enterprise (H.O.) in Wismut (1951), which groups all the special stores for mineworkers; (2) the state mail-order enterprise in Leipzig (1956); and (3) the special retail stores for Soviet residents in East Germany, and those for foreigners who must buy there and pay in such convertible currencies as dollars, pounds, and francs.

Wholesale trade is handled by joint ventures equally owned by the state and the Union of Consumer Cooperatives (there is no private capital in wholesaling). There are six such joint ventures at the national level; five or six in each *Bezirk* (there are fifteen administrative regions of the sort); and two or three in each *Kreis* (there are 222 such districts). Each wholesale society has a spatial monopoly, and specializes in a certain type of products (e.g., textiles, foods, household goods). All retail stores, whatever their ownership type, buy from these wholesaling units.

Retail trade is far less homogeneous since private stores are independent apart from the matter of prices (see below); mixed-sector stores are controlled by the local administrative district *(Kreis)* with which a commission-contract has been signed; the cooperative stores are supervised by their Consumer Cooperative Union; while the state stores (with very few exceptions) come under the Ministry of Domestic Trade.

Planning Principles in Domestic Trade. In preparing either the annual or five-year plan, the fundamental index for domestic trade is that of retail sales. From an organizational viewpoint, the essential instrument in assuring the achievement of this target is that of the *contract system.* Often overlooked by Western scholars, this system provides the fundamental legal structure for insuring that planning works.

Through contracts, a firm commits itself to supply another one with a definite quantity of a product of a particular quality, and/or is guaranteed that another firm will supply it. A planned economy thus rests on a dense and variegated network of contractual relationships among firms, on an extremely precise nomenclature of products, and on a judicial system (Contract Tribunal) charged with arbitrating conflicts about interpretation and execution. All contracts provide for indemnities in case of non-execution.

In principle, these contracts must be entered into several months before the starting date of the annual plan, since each firm director wants to insure the obtaining of his inputs and the marketing of his outputs. With prices being fixed by the state (see below), the flexibility left to the firm is rather limited, of course.

In the case of domestic trade, the situation is even simpler, since retail stores depend on a limited number of wholesalers for their supplies. The contracts between the private or "socialist" store and the wholesaling unit are usually made every six months, although for food products they are on a monthly basis, and on a yearly basis for less frequently bought and sold goods.

Planning Mechanisms

This section examines the manner in which global equilibrium is determined, the role of prices, and techniques of market analysis.

The Global Supply-Demand Equilibrium[7]

In order to match total supply and demand, the authorities use two instruments: (1) the population's purchasing power; and (2) the stocks of merchandise.

On the Demand Side. The equilibrium technique constitutes one of the oldest mechanisms in "socialist" planning. It consists of matching the sources and uses of a particular element.[8] As far as consumer purchasing is concerned, the planning authorities use the date obtained from other analyses of the "balances" from agricultural revenues, work revenues, crafts revenues, etc.:

1. On the *sources* side, the purchasing power of the population rests on:

   a. The revenues of workers, employees, members of cooperatives, and of professionals
   b. transfer payments by the state
   c. net funds withdrawn from State Savings Banks[9]
   d. net amount of credit sales (over repayments).

2. On the *uses* side:

   a. purchases of goods
   b. purchases of services
   c. payments for cultural and social services
   d. other expenses (e.g., housing construction)
   e. payments to the state (taxes)
   f. savings.

These broad categories are, of course, detailed. Such a balance is prepared annually for the entire country and the fifteen regions, although those with heavy seasonal migrations (e.g., along the Baltic Sea) are corrected in order to account for the presence of vacationers during certain periods of the year.

The item "purchases of goods" (also called "purchasing fund of the population") is particularly relevant for this analysis since it corresponds to what the population will have available (according to the planners) for buying merchandise in retail stores.

On the Supply Side. Potential supply must include not only consumer demand, but also two other elements of unequal but significant importance: (1) purchases by foreign tourists and members of the diplomatic corps (as estimated); and (2) retail purchases by business firms (e.g., of office supplies). It is possible, thereby, to determine the fund or stock of merchandise (locally produced or imported) required for consumption by the population, and to be distributed through the retail trade. Such an analysis leaves out: (1) agricultural auto-consumption; and (2) the so-called "social" consumption by boarding schools, hospitals, industrial cafeterias, army barracks, and prisons. The first one is only nominally included in statistical computations, while the second is only included in computing the balance for wholesaling.

On the basis of a nomenclature or master-list, some 5,000 product-balances are calculated for each region on a quarterly basis:

1. *Sources:*
   initial stock
   local production
   deliveries from other regions

2. *Uses:*
   stock
   exceptional demand
   exports
   deliveries to other regions
   extra reserves
   losses

The Role of Prices

In a capitalistic system, the total equilibrium between supply and demand is achieved through the price mechanism, and motivated by profit considerations. In a planned economy, on the other hand, the law of supply and demand no longer plays this regulatory role since the state controls all prices and can therefore affect demand directly.

Fixing Retail Prices. These prices are fixed by the state in the context of the national economic plan. Each price is the same throughout the country, and must be applied by all retailers, whatever their status (private or "socialist"). However, for certain foods such as eggs and potatoes, there is a summer and a winter price.

The 1963 economic reform in East Germany included a fundamental reform of wholesale prices. They are not usually published, but they were modified to correspond as closely as possible to their "real" costs of production. In particular, depreciation costs were included (they are called "fixed capital" in socialist economies in contrast to such "variable capital" as salaries and raw materials). Previously, this fixed capital had been constantly understated, thereby resulting in some waste of production potential.

However, this revision of wholesale prices was not accompanied by one of retail prices.[10] This means that the state now knows better what the production costs are, but that it subsidizes through the budget (if necessary) the spread between these costs and retail prices. Each retail price is thus the sum of a certain number of elements, all centrally controlled:

1. *The initial wholesale price,* to the extent that together with the other elements it does not exceed the retail price. If it does, the state subsidizes the difference, even though the authorities attempt to make wholesale prices reflect desired production costs, and to lower the latter through better productivity. However, all firms do not have optimum production costs;
2. *The wholesale gross margin,*[11] designed to cover the physical distribution of merchandise; and
3. *The retail gross margin,* determined either on an absolute (per unit) or a percentage basis.

Retail Store Profit. The store's gross profit equals the difference between the purchase price (wholesale price plus wholesale margin) and the selling price. From this profit are deducted operating costs and the turnover tax (1.5 percent on food products, and 3.5 percent on manufactured goods) in order to obtain the net profit.

In the "socialist" sector, this net profit is distributed among: (1) a premium fund rewarding the the achievement or overachievement of the plan; (2) a cultural and social fund to finance the vacations and excursions of the personnel; and (3) the technical expansion fund (e.g., to help finance the introduction of self-service in the store). On the other hand, the owner uses his profit as he sees fit, in the private and mixed sectors.

Credit Sales. The fact that credit sales exist in Eastern European countries is often ignored. They were introduced in East Germany in 1956 for two apparent reasons: (1) to accelerate the sales of certain types of products; and (2) to help certain segments of the population acquire manufactured goods more rapidly.

The government lists those products that can be purchased on credit, and a semi-annual consumer-credit plan is prepared on a geographical basis. However, it is the State Savings Bank and not the store which grants the credit and reimburses the retailer. The installment and the interest due (about 5 to 6 percent) are generally deducted from the borrower's paycheck.

Market Analysis [12]

The balances of consumer purchasing power and of merchandise stocks allow the state to determine the overall equilibrium that can be influenced rather significantly by the government's price policy. Still, the problem of satisfying consumer demand remains present.

The Ministry of Domestic Trade includes a Market Analysis Institute (Leipzig), which makes demand studies in collaboration with the Central Statistical Office, since the early 1960s. This Institute uses family budgets and it direct surveys to determine consumption functions and to prepare mathematical consumption models.

Family Budgets. The analysis of family budgets focuses on the level and structure of expenditures by households in the most important social and economic groups, and it relates them to these households' revenues, in order to detect and analyze differences and changes. Each year, 5,100 households are studied (3,500 in the non-agricultural sector; 600 in the state agricultural sector; and 1,000 in the cooperative agricultural sector). They must detail many of their characteristics (e.g., profession), their income, and their expenditures by quantity and price for various types of products (food, manufactured goods, services, etc.). The survey also inquires into the quality obtained and about unsatisfied needs.

Direct Surveys. [13] Since family budgets lump too many things together, they are complemented by consumer surveys—particularly since the new planning system supposes that productive firms know consumer reactions to their output. There have been quite a few consumer surveys since 1963 in such areas as heating system used in the house, ownership of household goods, types of food consumed during the evening meal, and Saturday afternoon closing hours for stores (since the five-day workweek has been introduced). Not all survey findings are published, however.

Consumption Functions[14] **and Mathematical Models.** Basing themselves on family budgets and consumer surveys, planners have calculated consumption functions for about a hundred products in order to prepare the 1964-1970 plan. Since prices are fixed by the government, this analysis has focused on income elasticity in order to ascertain what changes in demand would result from an increase in income for various types of products and incomes. Besides, various matrix models have been prepared on the same bases.

Results and Problems

This last section considers patterns of consumption, the distribution network, and some marketing techniques.

Consumption Patterns

Tables 6.4 and 6.5 provide some information about the consumption of certain food items, and household-equipment ownership. Of course, these data do not completely reflect the evolution of the level of living since they do not include publicly provided goods, nor information about the quality and availability of goods.

From Tables 6.4 and 6.5 one can see that manufactured goods have progressed faster than food products:

1. In particular, the ownership of manufactured goods has progressed in a spectacular way; with rates doubling in five years for cars (starting quite low, of course), refrigerators and washing machines, while increasing by 50 percent for TV sets.

2. For food products, the traditional consumption of pork has not increased as fast as that of beef and veal. Still, coupled with the relative decline of potato consumption, this seems to indicate an improvement in consumption.

3. On the other hand, much less progress is evident as far as fruits are concerned, since their rate of consumption decreased although that of exotic fruits definitely increased.

The East German press often echoes consumer complaints about the quality

Table 6–4

Per Capita Consumption of Selected Food Items
(Kilos per inhabitant)*

	1955	1965	1969
Pork meat (bones included)	30.7	36.2	39.5
Beef and veal meat (bones included)	10.9	18.5	20.7
Poultry (bones included)	3.4	4.0	4.8
Butter, margarine, vegetable and animal fats	28.5	33.7	33.3
(of which margarine)	(8.3)	(9.5)	(8.7)
Potatoes	174.6	156.5	150.0(1968)
Fresh vegetables	48.0(1960)	47.9	48.7
Canned vegetables	12.7(1960)	15.9	17.8
Fruits: fresh, canned, and exotic	80.1(1960)	46.5	51.1
(of which, exotic fruits)	(7.1)	(7.8)	(12.4)
Sugar	19.4	18.1	18.0
Beer (in liters)*	68.5	80.6	92.0

*A kilo equals about 2.2 pounds; and a liter approximates one quart.

Table 6–5

Household Ownership of Certain Manufactured Goods (percent of households)

	1964	1967	1969
Passenger cars	7.1%	11.0%	13.9%
Radios	86.7	89.3	91.5
Television sets	42.2	60.0	66.3
Electric Refrigerators	20.4	37.7	48.3
Electric Washing Machines	22.4	38.1	47.7

and availability of certain products, but it still would seem that an improvement
has taken place.

The Distribution Network[15]

Planning has definitely attempted to improve the physical spread of retail stores.
The basic unit here is such that consumers should not have to walk more than
eight to ten minutes in densely populated areas, and from fifteen to twenty
minutes in less dense areas, in order to buy daily purchased goods. Thus, a city
of 45,000 inhabitants typically includes some sixteen basic retail units, each
serving from 800 to 11,000 people; while in new residential quarters, there is a

basic retail unit for every 12,000 people. In the country, each small town represents one basic unit.

The key concept is that of a concentric system of stores, depending on the type of demand. *At the first level* are those stores selling goods demanded daily (food, supplies, notions, hygienic goods, etc.). They must be located in close proximity to customers. *At the second level* are those stores that sell products with a fairly regular, "periodical" demand (e.g., clothing, textiles, shoes, sports goods, small tools, stationery and office supplies, etc.). Such stores serve several basic units. Finally, *at the third level* are those stores whose merchandise is sold on a non-periodical basis (e.g., furniture, musical instruments, tools, cameras, cars, etc.). They serve an entire city or major borough.*

Thus, in a rural zone with 7,450 people living in seven villages (with a respective population of 300, 400, 500, 600, 750, and 4,500 people), each village will have a store selling daily demanded goods, while the largest one will also have a fish store and additional departments for periodically demanded goods. In the major city of a district *(Kreisstadt),* with some 20,000 inhabitants living in seven basic units with a population ranging from 1,500 to 4,500 people, each unit will have a store selling daily demanded goods; two units will have a fish store; and one unit will have a store for periodically demanded goods, and another for non-periodical goods.

This approach is complemented by the planning of the optimal selling area needed on the basis of the turnover per square meter and per employee, but also depending on the location (large town, industrial area, agricultural area), and even per type of store (department stores are handled differently). Table 6.6 illustrates these size criteria for three types of product.

Such planning, of course, requires a lot of statistical data collected on the basis of a master list allowing the allocation of sales among the three types of demand (daily, periodical, non-periodical).

Some Marketing Techniques

Together with Czechoslovakia, East Germany is the "socialist" country where self-service developed most rapidly. Self-service stores were introduced in 1958, and their number has grown very fast (see Table 6.7).

As Table 6.2 indicated, some 80 percent of these self-service stores are found in the food sector.

Conclusion

One of the most interesting aspects of the technical discussions following the economic reform of 1963 has centered on the role of consumption and distribution in productive processes.[16] Traditionally, socialist planners have considered

---

*This distinction corresponds roughly to the one among stores selling convenience, shopping, and luxury goods. [Translator's note]

Table 6-6

Size Criteria for Retail Stores

	Turnover in millions of D.M.	
	Per square Meter of selling area	Per Employee
Fruits, vegetables, potatoes		
1. Department stores	–	–
2. Large cities	12.0	160
3. Industrial zones	12.0	160
4. Agricultural zones	9.0	130
Other food products		
1. Department stores	18.0	200
2. Large cities	18.0	200
3. Industrial zones	18.0	200
4. Agricultural zones	12.5	165
Radio and Television sets, musical instruments, records		
1. Department stores	50.0	1,000
2. Large cities	30.0	850
3. Industrial zones	24.0	450
4. Agricultural zones	20.0	400

Table 6-7

Number of Self-Service Stores

1958	174
1959	4,096
1960	13,032
1961	15,049
1962	16,732
1967	19,358

commerce as non-productive (that is, as not creating value) although wholesaling has been considered as productive in national accounts. Undoubtedly, this restrictive way of looking at commercial phenomena helps explain negative feelings towards advertising and market analyses. Shortages, of course, reinforced this tendency. On the other hand, the improvement of the level of living and, particularly, the increased purchasing power of the population have brought about a change in attitudes. Thus, the notion of a "socialist market system" has appeared even though its meaning has not been deeply analyzed yet. Still, following certain ideas of the Russian professor Liberman, East German planners now underscore the interest presented by a situation where supply exceeds demand in a socialist economy.

June 1971

Notes

1.   Active discussions continue about the application of the 1963 reform in such matters as the determination of net profit rates in industrial and commercial firms, of gross-profit rates, and of the optimal size of firms.

2.   The concept of "national income" is not the same in capitalist and socialist economies. In the latter, it does not include all services, as it does not rest on the notion of "commercial exchange" but of "productive sector." Yet, in this respect, the German Democratic Republic (GDR) considers domestic commerce as a productive sector while other socialist countries do not. As in all Eastern European socialist countries, foreign trade is a state monopoly.

3.   In order to follow these developments and debates, the following sources are particularly useful: *Neues Deutschland* (daily), *Die Wirtschaft* (weekly), *Der Handel* (monthly), and *Einheit* (monthly).

4.   Heinrich Rössler, *Privater Einzelhandel und socialistische Entwicklung* (Berlin, DDR: Verlag Die Wirtschaft, 1960).

5.   This refers to private ownership of the means of production, while private ownership of consumer goods, houses, and—within certain limits—of small pieces of land and a few heads of cattle remains.

6.   See Wolfgang Heinrichs, *Oekonomik des Binnenhandels in der DDR* (Berlin, DDR: Verlag Die Wirtschaft, 1962, and later editions); and his *Der Einzelhandelumsatz und seine Planung* (Berlin, DDR: Verlag Die Wirtschaft, 1959).

7.   See Gunter Manz et al., *Bilanzierung der Warenzirkulation* (Berlin, DDR: Verlag Die Wirtschaft, 1969); and Albert Keck, *Die Bilanz der Geldeinnahmen und -ausgaben der Bevölkerung* (Berlin, DDR: Verlag Die Wirtschaft, 1968).

8.   This simple procedure requires multiple iterative calculations if one wants to modify the equilibrium, and if no relation can be established among the elements on the basis of a common unit of calculation (e.g., a monetary unit). Intersectoral tables are faster to handle since computers allow the matrix to be inverted.

9.   Individuals cannot have a checking account or a savings account within the banking system which is reserved to the industrial, commercial, and agricultural sectors. However, they can have such accounts with the savings banks.

10.   The Czech and Polish reforms have resulted in substantial retail price increases so that the Polish government had to backtrack.

11.   See Wolfgang Heinrichs, *Die Handelsspanne und die Planung der Erlöse im sozialistischen Einzelhandel* (Berlin, DDR: Verlag Die Wirtschaft, 1959).

12.   For more details, see the bibliography in this author's "L'étude de la demande des biens de consommation en économie planifiée," *Consommation* (1964/2). See also: Albert Dietrich and Olaf Schmutzler, *Statistische Methoden in der Marktforschung* (Berlin: DDR: Verlag Die Wirtschaft, 1968). The Market Research Institute in Leipzig publishes its journal *Marktforschung* quarterly.

13.   See Hans Fischer and Herbert Köppert, *Konsumentenfragung in der*

sozialistischen Marktforschung (Berlin, DDR: Verlag Die Wirtschaft, 1967), and Helmut Merker, *Betriebliche Marktforschung* (Berlin, DDR: Verlag Die Wirtschaft, 1967).

14. See I. A. Schwyrkow, *Die Elastizitätskoëffizienten der Konsumtion und die Methodik ihrer Berechnung* (Berlin, DDR: Verlag Die Wirtschaft, 1963), *Die laufenden und perspektivischen Modelle von Nachfrage und Bedarf* (Berlin, DDR: Verlag Die Wirtschaft, 1968), and *Die Oekonosmisch-mathematische Analyse der gegenseitigen Abhängigkeiten von Verbrauchsfunktionen* (Berlin, DDR: Verlag Die Wirtschaft, 1970).

15. See Herbert Karsten et al., *Die Planung und Organisation des Verkaufsstellennetzes* (Berlin, DDR: Verlag Die Wirtschaft, 1964).

16. Heinrich Rössler, *Die Konsumtion im Reproduktionsprozesss* (Halle, DDR: Martin Luther University, 1967).

7 France

PIERRE CORTESSE

The lack of an appropriate legal distinction between wholesale and retail trade, and the heterogeneous character of many concerns, often make it impossible to distinguish clearly the questions which relate specifically to the retail trade. However, the much larger number of enterprises, their role in the price-fixing process, and the economic and social difficulties which many of them face, give retailing a particular importance.

The French commercial system, undergoing profound and lasting transformations, has for some years been in a state of structural and social crisis which has affected it all the more strongly because it has remained sheltered from change for such a long time. This crisis is not yet completely under control, even though the indispensable modernization of structures and channels is far from being completed.

Still, the principles and general direction of French public policy toward retailing are rather clear, and the measures taken in the past decade are in keeping with the country's general economic policy which stresses the pursuit of a well-balanced growth, and participation in international competition.

The French Commercial System

The most recent survey of the commercial system made by the National Institute of Statistics and Economic Research (I.N.S.E.E.) for 1966, and its updating on the basis of various statistics and surveys, do not give an entirely satisfactory idea of the recent evolution of the commercial system.

The Place of Commerce Within the Economy

The number of commercial enterprises (including service-performing firms related to commerce, with the exception of banks, insurance companies, transportation, and construction companies) was evaluated at about 950,000 for 1970. Some 275,000 of them were retail food supply concerns; 273,000 retail concerns handled goods other than foodstuffs; there were 368,000 hotels, bars, restaurants, and other service-performing concerns; and 80,000 were wholesale businesses.

The total gross product yielded by these firms in 1966, estimated at roughly

117

102 billion francs[1] ($20.4 billion) as against 245 billion for industry. While this amount has rapidly increased since 1966, the number of businesses has slightly diminished (17,000 less), from 1966 to 1970, thereby expressing a two-fold change: (1) a sizable decrease in the number of food-supply concerns (about 20,000), and (2) a very slight increase in those dealing in other products.

In terms of the population, in 1970 there was one retail business for every 92 inhabitants—a density approximating that of West Germany and Great Britain. Retail firms, in the strict sense, numbered 505,000 in 1966, of which only 11 percent were incorporated.

Active Employment in Commerce

In 1966, the number of gainfully employed persons in commerce (including service firms) was about 3,500,000 (two-thirds of which were salaried employees). The growth of employment in this sector averaged about 2.2 percent per year—a rate higher than that of industry, and an increase exclusively due to the growing number of salaried employees at the annual rate of about 3.7 percent during the past ten years. On the other hand, the number of business owners and managers diminished by about 100,000 between 1954 and 1968, that is, 15 percent less in fifteen years' time. In the same period of time, the average number of salaried employees per establishment rose from 1.2 to 2.4. Nevertheless, over one-third of the businesses still have no salaried employees, and only 5 percent of them employ over ten persons. Besides, the average age of the business owners and managers is rather high:

under 35 years of age	13.7%
35 to 54	46.8%
over 55	36.0%
not stated	3.5%
	100.0%

Distribution of Firms by Sectors and Products

Total retail sales in 1969 amounted to about 261 billion francs ($52 billion), of which 108 billion francs ($21.6 billion) was in foodstuffs. "Independent" unincorporated retailers made about 75 percent of the sales, although new marketing forms (mail-order, discount, self-service, and the large suburban stores) have recently been growing fast. None of these new techniques seems likely to alter appreciably the predominance of in-store sales (94 percent), which is more and more often done in self-service and in large or medium-sized stores.

Through the evolution of sales methods and distribution channels, French retailing has undergone a significant change which gathered momentum after 1965. However, this transformation affects sectors and regions very unevenly. It is rapid and often ruthless in the newly-urbanized areas (with the exception of the Paris suburban area), but remains hardly perceptible in some areas. Although fairly advanced in manufactured foodstuffs and drinks, the evolution has hardly affected such other sectors as luxury goods or fresh-food products.

The Various Forms of Commerce

One can distinguish four categories of commerce:

1. *Traditional commerce,* generally specialized, is composed of small and medium-sized enterprises, predominantly family run, with few salaried employees and mostly located in city centers. An important proportion of the heads of businesses in this category have remained attached to established positions and to economic protectionism, and they are either opposed to or reluctant to undertake the transformations necessitated by economic evolution.

   Whether he had resigned himself to an evolution which he did not really understand, or took the initiative in commercial change, this kind of tradesman in the sixties was faced with problems of a nature and extent hitherto unknown. Protected for a long time by demographic stagnation and by the immobility of the urban structure, he is now faced with growing insecurity. Even when he is not in direct competition with a supermarket or a discount store, he still knows that he can be affected at any moment by the construction of a freeway, an urban renewal program, the creation of a new city center, or the transfer of an industry.

2. *Adjunct or Accessory Commerce* is performed by persons who also have other sources of income (e.g., salaries, old-age pensions, agricultural incomes). In 1966, 38.7 percent of the heads of businesses declared that they received income from other sources than their businesses, while 13.4 percent considered the income they derived from their businesses as a secondary income. Such firms are generally located in farming areas and deal in non-specialized lines often connected with some kind of service. They are usually classified as "multiservice stores," are often operated by elderly people, and are mostly located in areas with a declining population.

3. *Associated Retailing* includes voluntary chains of wholesalers and retailers, together with buying groups and retail cooperatives. Some of these associations have reached a form of organization which makes them similar to chain stores, while others are but loose groupings; and their operations and available services are extremely diverse. There are probably at present about 70,000 such associated businesses, 60 percent of which deal in foodstuffs.

4. *Large-scale Commerce* (department stores, "popular" five-and-ten stores, consumer cooperatives, chain stores, mail-order houses, and discount stores) includes few concerns (about 1,600), employs 250,000 wage-earners, and produces 25 percent of the annual retail trade turnover (1969). Mostly an

outcome of traditional commerce, it is characterized by the predominance of family-run enterprises, but some important mergers and acquisitions have recently taken place.

The Image of Commerce

For the man in the street, commerce often appears much more as a necessary evil than as a wealth-producing activity. The "black market" of wartime has left in the popular mind lasting memories which are revived by the sometimes excessive price increases that occur in periods of inflation or shortage. Tradesmen are aware of being, as some of their representatives are fond of repeating, the "nation's unloved ones." Often belonging to a lower-middle class that has only recently risen from the lower classes, and very much attached to stability, they are always ready to resort to extreme measures as soon as they feel that their position is being jeopardized. In the middle fifties and again in the sixties, France witnessed the rise of a strong opposition movement inspired by conservative and Malthusian views which originated among the small businessmen and the socio-professional classes close to them.

Such uneasy relations between the retail trade and the rest of the community are not altogether new, as commerce has never been highly esteemed in France. An activity long considered as unworthy of the ruling classes, until a short time ago it was still held as a last resort and a refuge for the mediocre. Few college graduates, even of the business schools, took up this occupation. This situation is changing gradually as the function of commerce within the economy becomes better understood. For the over-simplified picture of the businessman as a costly intermediary for the community, a more objective and varied image is now being progressively substituted.

The Objectives of Retail-Trade Policy

During the 1960s, after a quarter of a century characterized by a complete immobility of structures, the retail trade underwent a real transformation. Brought about by the development of supermarkets (in the fifties) and of even larger "hypermarkets" (around 1960), the development of modern commercial techniques (discount and self-service stores), and the extension of the tax on value added (TVA) to the retail trade, this transformation affected a very large number of businesses of all sizes, and challenged the whole economic, social, and political balance of this sector.

It was on account of such phenomena that a true retail trade policy was progressively elaborated in France by the Minister of Economy and Finance, assisted by the Under-Secretary for Domestic Commerce and by the Domestic Trade and Prices Bureau (D.G.C.I.P. in French) who set forth a number of objectives and brought together in a unified program the means of action, real or projected. The fact that the bureau in charge of domestic commerce was merged in 1965 with the Prices Bureau, one of the most important bureaus within the

Ministry, shows clearly that retail trade policy was dominated by a major concern for a balance between prices and incomes.

The Lowering of Distribution Costs

Until the early sixties, the public authorities, dealing with a commercial body that was little inclined to modernization and was protected from competition through its privileged connections with industry and through the slow changes in economic structures, applied themselves to checking the multiplying effect of inflationary tensions produced by the retail trade. They did it by acting or trying to act through a regulation of retail price levels and margins, in a rather short-term perspective.

Later on, when modern management methods and new merchandising techniques became more widespread, the modernization of commerce appeared as the only way to achieve a durable lowering of distribution costs. Hence, the encouragement of such modernization, which largely came about spontaneously, was progressively substituted for the regulation of prices and margins. However, strong inflationary pressures in 1963, 1968, 1969, and 1971 made it impossible for the authorities to give up entirely a direct action on retail prices, since the increase in competition and the effect of the modernization of commerce on prices are still very uneven and vary according to sectors and products.

The Problems of Small and Medium-sized Firms

Continued price controls, sharper competition, and heavier social security charges and taxes have brought, for many retailers, an insufficient increase in income, or even a stagnation or deterioration of their business.

After a long period of stagnation, the commercial equipment on the outskirts of the large cities underwent a very rapid development, particularly after 1968, owing mainly to the generalization of the TVA tax (which favors the low-margin stores) and the success of the first supermarkets and hypermarkets. Meanwhile, some of the smaller "independent" tradesmen, chiefly those handling foodstuffs and those located in rural areas, had already been affected by regional migrations and the process of urbanization, and were handicapped by obsolete equipment and management. They now found themselves in great difficulty as a result of the multiplication of large-surface stores. Hence, businesses in which savings had been invested with a view toward retirement, or as a protection against currency depreciation, were now depreciated to a point where, in many cases, they lost their entire value.

There are now quite a few older businessmen who cannot find buyers for their businesses, and are reduced to living on an old-age pension which is all the smaller because of their continued reluctance to put a sufficient sum into a retirement plan. Among the younger ones, there are many who have borrowed money to buy a business or to equip a shop, with the prospect of a stable and sheltered situation, who have suddenly found themselves engaged in unexpected and fierce competition for which they were not prepared. Still others, whose businesses have remained prosperous, face the future with misgivings as their advantages are being threatened or are very likely to be in the near future. Out of this situation has arisen an intense dissatisfaction with the public authorities for having raised taxes and social security dues. This led to protests and demonstrations which gained in violence and determination between 1967 and 1970.

The general uneasiness among small and medium-sized tradesmen was often aggravated by the occasionally abusive practices of some large-scale firms. The increase in competition in some lines (e.g., groceries, beverages, household electrical appliances) has led them to resort more and more frequently to rather unfair practices in their dealings with both their suppliers and customers. Besides, an often rash and reckless investment race has been started, which contributes to independent businessmen's worries. A large increase in advertising competition and extreme price-cutting made possible by extremely advantageous purchasing conditions obtained from suppliers who cannot resist the pressure put upon them by important purchasers, have also had a bad effect on small firms. Such a situation, of which the favorable impact on price levels is not to be denied, soon appeared not only unacceptable on the social—and therefore political—level, but also dangerous in the long run, on the economic level. The risks of monopolization or of agreements between major firms came quickly to the fore, all the more so as the rush for the creation of large-surface stores tended to slow down of its own accord as a result of the difficulties met by a few firms, and as a result of the doubts expressed by bankers and financiers as to the profitability of certain schemes.

Slowing-Down Commercial Modernization

The public authorities, aware of the necessity of setting limits on the functioning of the market, and conscious that it is impossible to get the majority of small businessmen to accept too rapid an evolution of structures and too sudden an upheaval in their working conditions, have directed their efforts towards a slowing down of commercial modernization, so as to ward off its excesses and to steady its evolution.

First of all, in order to avoid the development of a sense of frustration and to ensure the maintenance of a desirable balance between the various forms of commerce from the point of view of the government's policy in matters of prices and competition, it appeared that the modernization of businesses should be made possible for *all* businessmen, provided they were prepared to make a sufficient effort. A double line of action was decided upon: (1) to curb the excesses of competition and slow down the spread of large-surface stores; and (2) to provide small and medium-sized enterprises with the intellectual and material means indispensable for a transformation of their firm and management.

Secondly, in view of the rapid development of large-surface stores and the risks of reckless urbanization engendered by hasty construction decided upon only by the promoters' considerations of profit-making capacity, the government decided that the granting of building permits for such large establishments should be subject to precise considerations of the demands of commercial urbanization.

Thirdly, the rapid expansion and concentration of commercial concerns and the development of buying groups had, during the sixties, transformed the relationship between suppliers and businessmen, and in many instances had placed industrial concerns in an inferior position. Concern with an industrial policy thus led the administration to interfere in the relationships between manufacturers and businessmen in a sense favorable to the interest of industry, and by the same token, of small independent business.

Therefore, two groups of apparently contradictory, but in fact complementary, objectives (as stated above) have been set out for retail-trade policy: (1) to modernize commerce as quickly as possible in order to lower the cost of distribution; and (2) to prevent the rate of modernization from exceeding a rhythm which is socially, economically, and politically tolerable. The public authorities have therefore directed their efforts to the maintenance of a difficult balance. The evolution of legislation and regulations in the last few years clearly reflects this concern.

The Main Features of Retail-Trade Policy

The principal measures taken in the past ten years can be grouped under three main headings: (1) the role of commerce as an economic sector in the context of price, competition, and urbanization policies; (2) the specific problems of commercial enterprises in such matters as business property, taxation, and financing; and (3) "people" problems in terms of professional and continuing training, and of social welfare.

The Role of Commerce in the Economy

We have seen that the measures adopted to favor the stability of retail prices rest on two complementary objectives: (1) a system of direct action on retail prices and commercial margins; and (2) the control of competition.

Direct Action on Prices. A more or less strict regulation of prices and margins inherited from war and postwar shortages, and based on the ordinance of 30 June 1945, is still applied to large sections of the retail trade, especially in foodstuffs. It is especially in the case of farm produces sold with little or no processing (meat, milk, butter, bread, fruits, vegetables) that the regulation has been the most stringent because of: (1) the real and psychological importance of their prices; and (2) the successive raising of producer prices granted to satisfy French farmers and then those of the Common Market, and because of temporary shortages due to climatic conditions.

This regulation is accompanied by various forms of inspection and, in cases of violations, by a number of administrative or penal sanctions. The inspections made either directly by the agents of the Domestic Trade and Prices Bureau or under their control by the services of the economic police, the Customs Office, or the national police *(Gendarmerie),* contributed—particularly because of the presence of men in uniform—to the creation of tensions between the administration and retail tradesmen.

However, the removal of the regulations on retail prices and margins which still remains a long-term objective is possible only when all danger of price increases has disappeared, that is, when supplies are sufficient and competition effective. Such a situation seemed to have been achieved by the end of 1968 for goods other than foodstuffs; and these products, with the exception of home furniture, are no longer subject to regulation. The businessmen must nevertheless justify their profit margins to the administration, for instance, by showing relevant purchase invoices. On the other hand, all foodstuffs and especially farm products which undergo little processing, are still subject to regulation or at least to a system of direct supervision (see below). At the same time, the policy of regulation has been progressively replaced by a policy of price discipline, negotiated with professional commercial organizations.

Joint-Action Programs. Between 1962 and 1968, the administration sponsored several experiments of joint action among businessmen. In 1963, an informal, nation-wide group called the "Action and Liaison Committee for One Hundred Thousand Sales Units" (C.A.L.) was constituted, bringing together the larger organizations dealing in foodstuffs (chain, department, and discount stores, voluntary chains, and cooperatives) in order to set up joint sales promotions, and to abide by maximum selling prices on a number of imported goods. In counterpart, quotas of imported goods were attributed, by priority, to members of the C.A.L. group in pursuance of the decree of 19 October 1966. Another group of the same type, called "Quality - Service - Prices" (Q.S.P.), for the handling of goods other than foodstuffs, was set up in 1967 to promote collective action and promotional sales.

A similar plan was carried out as early as 1962 with a number of independent retailers, butchers, delicatessen-owners *(charcutiers),* dairymen, fish sellers, and bakers. They entered "Pilot Associations" at the urging of the administration, and pledged themselves to offer for sale every week a number of articles at prices lower than official or current prices. On its part, the administration publicized the action of the participating shopkeepers through TV advertising in the state network's program for consumers.

These three joint-action experiments between businessmen and the administration undeniably assisted price policy until 1969, especially in periods of tension when the play of competition alone—still imperfect at that time—could not contain price increases within acceptable limits.

TVA Information Program. Another program was carried out at the time of the extension to retailing of the value-added tax (end of 1967) and the later modifications in this tax on 1 December 1968 and 1 January 1970. A systematic information campaign for the businessmen was launched by the Internal Revenue Service and the Domestic Commerce and Prices Bureau, with the collaboration of professional commercial organizations. On the whole, it succeeded in limiting the impact of these fiscal changes on retail prices.

Contractual Programs. After 1968, the regulations existing at the time on most staple commodities, were replaced whenever possible, by a "contractual price system" negotiated with the profession *(régime conventionnel des prix).* This system, based on the representative professional organizations' voluntary adherence to a "professional contract," sets forth a number of obligations concerning the conditions of sale and the prices of some products. The contract is afterwards approved by a decree of the Ministry of Economy and Finance (or of the Prefect[2] when it is a contract established at the level of an administrative region), and it is binding on each business that signs it individually. Those firms which do not accept this contract are subjected to a regulatory system of taxation or price-freezing, which is more stringent than the contractual system. Most foodstuffs, with the exception of bread, milk, and butter, still subject to some price regulation, have come under this contractual system since 1968 or 1969.

Freedom of trade, therefore, has not yet been extended to all retail prices and margins. While authoritarian and repressive measures are less tolerated by trades-men, the former have been progressively replaced by contractual agreements between the government and business firms. Besides, government has kept a control and surveillance system for fresh and manufactured food products, allowing it to react promptly to excessive price fluctuations. Thus, on 15 September 1971, the French government introduced for a six-month period, and with the agreement of the French Manufacturers' Association *(Patronat),* a new and very strict price-control system, while tradesmen committed themselves to maintaining stable percentage margins during that same period.

Strong inflationary tendencies in the Western world since the beginning of 1971, market disequilibria due to either structural (e.g., in the case of beef) or climatic (e.g., for fruits) reasons, as well as the still archaic structure of certain segments of French distribution, do not preclude the reintroduction of selective coercive price-control measures—as was illustrated by the conflict between the government and French butchers in May 1972.

The Control of Competition. The survival of a supervised or contractual system of prices should not obscure the fact that an essential goal of the public authorities is to achieve satisfactory conditions of competition.

Freedom of Establishment. Freedom to establish a business remains one of the fundamental principles of commercial activity in France (Le Chapelier Act of 2 and 17 March 1791). There are no particular prerequisites for the setting up of a business except that the businessman must be over 21 years of age and a French national or citizen of one of the member-countries of the Common Market or of a country having a reciprocity agreement with France. For the nationals of other countries, setting up a business is subject to delivery by the administration of a foreign businessman's permit, after a character check.

The legal exceptions to the principle of free establishment are for the retail trade quite limited in number. They concern mainly pharmacies, tobacco stores (because of the state's tobacco monopoly and the tobacco dealers' fiscal role), beverage sales (for reasons of public health), and the sale of firearms (for security reasons). As for public markets, all regulations are within the province of the mayor of the town, and market dealers are subjected to no particular formalities save the payment of a license fee *(patente)*.

Business Hours. Likewise, the regulations concerning the business hours of large stores are, theoretically, very liberal. Only labor legislation constitutes a de facto limitation of business hours, since the law requires the presence of two shifts of employees where the working day goes beyond a certain prescribed limit, and obliges employers to give their employees a weekly time-off period of at least a day and a half or two consecutive days, including Sunday. A waiver may be granted to some businesses, chiefly food stores, but prefects can prohibit the opening of some categories of stores on Sunday. A number of decrees to this effect have been passed under the combined pressure of independent small businesses and employees' unions; and since the middle of 1969, a control procedure on the installation of large-surface stores has been enforced (see section on commercial land-use planning).

Apart from these restrictions, freedom of establishment remains the foundation of the legislative and regulatory mechanism organizing competition, set up gradually from 1945 on.

Free Competition. The basic ordinance of 30 June 1945 concerning prices established the fundamental principles whereby free competition is to be ensured: (1) persons are forbidden to impose and maintain a minimum level on the prices of goods, services, or commercial margins; (2) refusal-to-sell is prohibited; and (3) discriminatory conditions of sale or increases in price are prohibited.

These three rules were interpreted by the Fontanet circular[3] of 31 March 1960 in the context of the new 1959 economic policy favoring the development of competition. This interpretation of the principles set forth in the 1945 ordinance has never been called into question by the Supreme Court of Appeals, and it remains the main conceptual and legal document in the matters of competition.

Fair Methods of Competition. Additionally, several measures: (1) have prohibited misleading and false publicity (law of 2 July 1963; decree of 29 July 1966); (2) have forbidden sales at a loss (law of 2 July 1963, further developed in the circular of 30 May 1970), that is, below actual purchase prices; (3) have regulated the offer and granting of premiums (law of 20 March 1951, and decree of 5 April 1961); (4) have banned "chain" sales[4] (law of 5 November 1963) and unsolicited sales (decree of 9 February 1961); and (5) have regulated improvised sales on the street or in temporary quarters, as well as the labeling of articles.

Besides, the ordinance of 29 September 1967 empowers the Minister of Economy and Finance to: (1) regulate conditions of sale whenever they are intended to achieve, or result in, differential prices for the same article; (2) limit the resulting differentials in prices; and (3) prohibit any indication by the producer, wholesaler, or importer of "suggested prices" for retail selling.

The Working of the Market. This series of measures has oriented the working of the market in a liberal direction. It is in large part owing to this legal interpretation that discount stores and large-surface suburban stores were able to make such progress in the 1960s.

During this same decade, important parallel changes occurred in power relationships between commerce and industry. In the years immediately following the war, manufacturing concerns predominated over distributing firms, and industry could impose its rule on a commercial sector divided into a great number of small isolated enterprises. This situation entirely changed after the late fifties as the increasing concentration of businesses and the more and more important role of central buying offices have progressively reversed this power ratio.

On the one hand, bargaining on sales terms has led producers to grant, often quite recklessly, important rebates and discounts, not only to the large organized firms, but also to the more traditional types of specialized retailers who were facing severe competition from the new forms of commerce. At the retail level, the rebates granted on artificially inflated "suggested prices," reached, by the end of the sixties, very high levels which were generally irrelevant. The public authorities have therefore attempted to eliminate such competitive excesses.

More Restrictive Measures. After extensive consultations with representative businessmen's organizations, the Minister of Economy and Finance published, on 30 May 1970, a circular providing a new interpretation of three essential points.

1. *Profitless Sales.*—The law of 2 July 1963 prohibited the sale of new articles below their purchase price. However, administrative practice led to a very loose interpretation of this text, accepting, for instance, as the purchase price, the price stated on the invoice, less any end-of-year "fidelity" rebates and quantity discounts. This justified very low purchase prices by playing on the allocation of rebates, and made very difficult the immediate determination of the purchase price of an article. The circular of 30 May 1970 put an end to this tolerance and imposed as the purchase price, the net price calculated by taking into account only the rebates or discounts mentioned on the invoice.

   In May 1972, the government, yielding to the demands of traditional tradesmen, for the first time imposed a minimum markup (3.75 percent) above purchase price for the sale of alcoholic beverages, without satisfying this group disappointed by the low margin imposed.

2. *Special Prices (prix d'appel).*—On account of various excesses by modern forms of commerce, this circular also states that systematic recourse to low sale prices on an article or a limited number of products of well-known brands can lead one to question a retailer's good faith. Such a systematic practice now authorizes a supplier to refuse to sell to this retailer.

3. *Publicizing Reduced Prices.*—This practice has been regulated by the decree of 29 July 1966, and again by the circular of 30 May 1970, which provides further protection for the consumer. Many business concerns had more and more frequently taken to announcing important discounts that were mostly

fictitious, and therefore confusing to the consumer. The 1966 decree provided that the reference price explicitly or implicitly stated by the retailer should be either the officially fixed price, the price suggested by the producer, or any "reconstructed" price equal to the purchase cost and the margin usually practiced in that line of business. The memorandum of 30 May 1970 now prohibits any reference to such reconstituted prices and obliges the businessman to state clearly the net price charged to the consumer.

More recently, new measures designed to insure fair competition were taken: (1) a decree of 7 April 1971 (applicable after 14 October 1971) reinforces the prohibition against premiums; and (2) a decree *(arrêté)* of 16 September 1971 about price marking, tagging, and posting obliges tradesmen to indicate very clearly the prices of goods offered for sale.

The Role of the Consumer. Tighter regulations cannot insure that competition will always be fair because the large number of businessmen, the changability of commercial practices, and the inventiveness of advertising men are as many obstacles to effective control. Nothing can actually replace the consumer's own watchfulness.

In view of the insufficient action of consumers' associations, and in order to develop the consumers' role in matters of competition and to make them assume an effective part in the working of the market, the government set up a public agency that has become the technical instrument of a consumer policy. Created by the law of 22 December 1966, and organized by the decree of 5 December 1967, the state-financed National Consumers Institute was given the tasks of protecting and informing the consumer, of undertaking a number of technical experiments, and of studying the problems of improving the quality of goods and services. After a difficult start, this Institute, which publishes a monthly magazine (200,000 copies in the spring of 1972) and puts out regularly the results of product tests and comparisons, is beginning to have an impact. Following this first success, consumer organization, participation, and influence may well increase in the economy.

Direct Intervention of the Public Authorities. In a number of instances, however, the severe tensions caused by excesses in competition (e.g., the retail prices charged by some discount stores were at times lower than wholesale prices) led the government to intervene directly in order to limit the effects of competition.

1. Discount sales of gasoline developed considerably in 1968 and 1969, following the advent of hypermarkets. Thanks to the large rebates granted by oil companies, their discount stations were able in some cases to lower the selling price of high-octane (super) gasoline to consumers, by more than 10 percent and as much as 13 centimes (about 2.6 U.S. cents) per liter. Such a policy of low sale prices aroused violent protest from retail station owners, particularly the independent managers of gas stations for the big oil companies. To avoid creating an uncontrollable situation, the representatives of the discount stations, at the urgent request of the administration, agreed, in accordance with the terms of a contract renewable every six months, to limit the discount on high-octane

gasoline to 5 centimes (about 1 U.S. cent) per liter. This agreement, which was generally effective until the fall of 1971, was then broken by some discounters who took advantage of the government's new price-control campaign. In the face of unhappy traditional distributors, the government in late April 1972 issued a decree limiting discounts to 6 centimes (about 1.2 U.S. cents) per liter until 31 December 1972.

2. The introduction of television advertising for various brand names did not come about until the autumn of 1968 and was reserved for a certain number of sectors selected according to a number of economic criteria. The most widely distributed brand names were finally allowed on TV, but distributing firms as such were refused access to the television screen so that any difficulties with small and medium-sized business might be avoided.

These two examples illustrate the very strong pressure constantly exerted by small business on the public authorities. The essential objective, therefore, of a balance between prices and incomes which served to justify the introduction of a liberal policy toward competition, though not completely lost sight of, no longer constitutes an exclusive goal. Instead, the straightening out of business practices has come to be the most immediate concern for government. This is the price that has had to be paid for turning down the most Malthusian demands of some business groups, although some of them have succeeded in retaining their supporters and spokesmen in Parliament.

Commercial City Planning. The circular of 24 August 1961, signed by the Minister of Construction and the Under-Secretary of Commerce, laid down first general directives in the matter of commercial urbanism. This text was meant to insure that a minimum of commercial equipment be provided in newly con-structed districts by opposing the tendency of promoters and city planners to neglect or underrate the role and importance of commercial facilities in their plans and programs.

According to this circular, the required commercial facilities were divided into three categories: (1) secondary shopping centers that were to offer within a radius of 1,000 feet the basic articles for everyday use; (2) primary shopping centers including all kinds of stores; and (3) public market-places. This concep-tion constituted a significant progress, but it was the result of studies which had not sufficiently taken into account the foreseeable evolution of commerce, the problems of competition, and especially the revolution introduced by new sales techniques. Thus, the number of supermarkets went from about 500 in 1965 to 1,833 in 1970; and hypermarkets increased in number from three in 1966 to 115 in 1970. Within a few years' time, the nature of the problem had completely changed.

The administration undertook a revision of its conceptions and established a new doctrine of commercial city-planning, based on the idea of the necessary coexistence of all forms of commerce, considered from the point of view of a satisfactory working of competition and of the satisfaction of consumer needs. On the other hand, it became obvious that the stiff competition between large-surface stores and the traditional forms of commerce, insofar as it tended to weaken some independent businesses, especially food and grocery stores, was likely, in some instances, to bring about the eventual decline of city-centers. The idea of a necessary equilibrium between the city-center and the outlying shopping centers (largely inspired by foreign examples) had thus come to the fore.

Political considerations, especially those touching on the financial situation of cities, have not been totally absent from the solutions decided upon because the establishment of large-surface stores, at the periphery of urban centers or even in outlying suburban areas, deprive the city centers of their resources. Yet, it is the core of the metropolitan area that bears the burden of investments which benefit the whole of the structure.

A triple objective was therefore fixed for commercial city-planning: (1) to ensure a balanced development of urban districts at the least possible cost to the community; (2) to take into account the strong hostility of small businessmen toward large-surface stores; and (3) to take into consideration the financial position of the core cities and, if need be, the political forces present.

This new policy on commercial city-planning was defined by a circular from the Minister of Equipment and the Under-Secretary of Commerce, of 27 July 1969, as modified by a law of 31 December 1969, and by a circular from the Prime Minister of 30 June 1970. Although asserting that freedom of establishment and modernization of commerce are indispensable, these three texts refer to principles of organization for urban districts and to a necessary balance between the various forms of commerce. They try to define a line of action that would fall half-way between complete liberty and a system that would subordinate the opening of new businesses to the authorization of the administration.

The main provision of the new system is the creation of a Commercial Urban Planning Commission in each administrative region. Presided over by the Prefect and staffed with representatives from the administration and from all the commercial forms, its job is to comment on the studies, guidelines, programs, and urbanistic plans. It is also to give its opinion on all projected stores with a selling area of over 30,000 square feet. Besides, the circular of 30 June 1970 provides that whenever there are too many competing projects for the same city, the administration is to take the initiative of bringing the promoters together to compare and adjust their plans; it also provides that priority be given to projects that include both large-surface stores and traditional businesses.

A central board composed only of officials from the Ministry of Equipment and the Ministry of Economy and Finance coordinates the activities of the regional commissions and gives its opinion on the projects for which no agreement or decision can be reached at the regional level. However, the Minister of Equipment or the Prefect remains ultimately the final authority which can decide whether to give or to refuse a building permit, which is required for all sizable construction, whatever its purpose.

Strictly speaking, the building permit, which emanates from an entirely separate legislation, can be refused only for motives related to city-planning (traffic, sites, thoroughfares, etc.). Yet, the existence of the commissions and the fact that in several instances they have given negative opinions for motives having nothing to do with city-planning have influenced the decisions of the Prefects and the Minister of Equipment and led to cancellation or postponement of a number of projects. There is no doubt, therefore, that through the expedient of a purely consultative procedure, freedom of establishment, at least in the case of large-surface stores, has been in practice, subjected to a number of restrictions, often based on doubtful local considerations. Conversely, there are good reasons for considering that the reckless race to build commercial installations has been checked, and that from the viewpoint of collective interests, useless or superfluous investments can and have been avoided.

In most instances, the promoters readily agreed to negotiate, and on the whole they have understood and accepted the restraints imposed by the new regulations. Small business, for its part, is entirely opposed to the establishment of large-surface stores and, taking a negative and Malthusian stand, demands more and more the total prohibition of new large-surface stores. The Chambers of Commerce and Industry and the city councils, considering their immediate interests, have often echoed such demands.

Looking beyond short-term economic considerations, one may well ask how relevant this regulation will have been in the end. At the stage of surveys and overall guidelines for which the commissions have rarely been consulted, the information provided to tradesmen and their opinion about the desirability of new commercial installations can only facilitate the decision-making process. This is a fruitful area which has not yet been fully explored. On the other hand, on the individual project level, intervention raises delicate questions of choice or preference, which are far from being solved.

In general, priority has been given to shopping centers combining small and large stores, modern and traditional. While this situation is not a panacea, large firms have come to accept it because it satisfies the concern of city-planners as well as the more enlightened and active independent businessmen.

Ownership, Taxation, and Financing

Commercial Ownership. This legal concept *(propriété commerciale)* refers to the right of a leaseholder who operates a business on rented premises to secure on the expiration of the lease, its renewal or the payment by the proprietor of a compensation called an eviction indemnity, equal to the value of the business (stock-in-trade or goodwill) plus the costs of moving and re-establishment.[5] The right to a renewal of the lease was established by a law of 20 June 1926 to control the practice of taking back the commercial premises on the expiration of the lease, either for the proprietor's own use or to lease them over to new tenants at a higher price, because of the improvements made by the former tenant. This legislation was therefore originally initiated to protect commercial leaseholders, chiefly retailers operating small shops.

Between 1938 and 1953, because of difficulties arising from the war and post-war conditions, various extensions were granted to leaseholders. A decree of 30 December 1953 put an end to this system of lease extension and instituted new regulations for commercial leases which, in the main, codified the previous system. Since 1953, the movement for the protection of tenants' rights has been confirmed, especially by the law of 12 March 1965.

At present, commercial leases, set at a minimum duration of nine years, are revisable every three years, when the rents are fixed according to the quarterly index of construction costs published by the administration, unless the commercial value of the business has varied by more than 10 percent. On the other hand, at the expiration of the nine-year lease, the renewal is handled on the basis of free discussion between lessor and lessee, although it must be remembered that if the lease is not renewed, the former lessee must be compensated. Besides, if the parties cannot agree on the price of the lease, the courts decide.

In practice, this system has frequently resulted in a distortion of the laws of the market because past rent freezes and the tri-annual indexing based on construction costs have, in many instances, led to rent levels much lower than those that would have resulted from the free play of the market. This artificial lowering of rents gives the business a high value, not only on account of its traditional components (clientele, reputation, signs, tools, fittings, etc.)., but also by the lessee's right to a renewed lease. The renewal of leases thus often brings about increases which are all the greater because the rents had remained at a low level for a long time. However, the spokesmen of independent business, basing their argument on a few instances of sharp increases in rents in the select central districts of major cities, have already asked legislators to restrict the owners' liberty on this point.

Such a situation also affects the establishment and management of a business since it requires a large initial capital outlay to purchase a lease, which remains tied down and cannot be fiscally amortized. The situation is further aggravated by the extreme complexity of this legislation and the innumerable difficulties encountered in putting it into effect.

In the same intention of protecting tradesmen, the legislation (principally the law of 20 March 1956) on free management *(gérance libre)* allows the owner of a business *(fonds de commerce)* to lease it if he has personally operated a business for seven years and held the stock-in-trade himself for at least two years. This provision, designed to keep possible speculators out of the business market, is a source of additional rigidity which can no longer be completely justified. Finally, the law of 16 July 1971 on "despecializing commercial leases" has authorized tenants to exercise commercial activities different from those specified in the lease.

Altogether, with the appearance of new marketing types and techniques and the parallel depreciation of a number of businesses, the rights and obligations deriving from "commercial ownership" appear to present a rather illusory protection for tradesmen since very often a stock-in-trade bought at a high price has lost its value a few years later. In fact, the banks that nearly always require the pledging of the stock-in-trade as security for loans on equipment consider only its real value. Tradesmen have gained some new rights, but carrying conditions, the provision of rent increases, and the obligation to renegotiate new leases do not always favor them. Only the best or the most prestigious locations in the urban centers, and especially in the major cities, still have a high value, because of the strong pressure exercised by the demands of leading international companies, airlines, banks, and travel agencies. Moreover, real estate promoters have given up selling the right to a lease in their new construction projects, preferring to set the rents at a higher level. This is the system that seems to prevail in the new shopping centers.

France, of all the Common Market countries, is the one whose legislation on this point is most extensive and complex. This is why there is no doubt that sooner or later this legislation will have to be revised. However, for a few more years, no reform seems possible because of the attachment of small business to the present system.

Taxation. The businessman's allergy to taxation has, at most times, been the determining factor in the relationship between his group and the public authorities. As early as 1953, the activity of "fiscal brigades" trained to control the collection of all types of taxation (direct and indirect taxes, registration fees, etc.) to which a firm is liable, with the consequent increase of the tax base, gave rise to a movement of opposition to fiscal control, called *Poujadisme,* which in 1956 sent nearly fifty deputies (out of about 500) to the National Assembly.

Since that time, fiscal policy in the field of retail trade has been guided by a number of considerations: (1) alleviation of the pressure of taxation; (2) neutrality of taxation as regards the various commercial channels and the different situations (particularly geographical); (3) equality of taxation for the different forms of commerce; and (4) simplifying the taxation of small businessmen, especially its bases and collection. There have been many problems, however.

1. The demands of financial policy have not always made it possible to achieve tax reductions. Independent businessmen, therefore, have expressed considerable dissatisfaction and have strongly supported protest movements that have brought their fiscal demands to the fore.

2. As concerns the income tax, measures of tax relief favoring the non-wage-earning "independent" classes were passed in 1970. The government has initiated a policy of tax alignment for non-salaried and salaried groups, the former being at present much more heavily taxed than the latter (up to two or three times more, for some family and income situations) for an equal known income, although this known income cannot be established with much certainty. Measures were taken to that effect in connection with the 1971 and 1972 budgets: elimination of the supplementary income tax, and extension to low-income independent (non-salaried) workers of the 5 percentage-points income-tax reduction which until then applied only to salaried workers.

At the same time, the government has declared its intention to undertake serious action against tax evasion, which, on the businessmen's own admission, is rife within the commercial sector—particularly among small, family firms—and constitutes an appreciable factor in the distortion of competition.

Besides, a simplified system is available for commercial enterprises whose present sales are below 500,000 francs (about $90,000), that is, for the very small businesses.[6] They are subjected to a contractual *(forfaitaire)* system of taxation, negotiated with the Internal Revenue Service on the basis of elementary accounting data. A simplified system was also established in 1970 for businesses with a turnover between 500,000 francs ($90,000) and one million francs ($180,000).

3. The commercial license *(patente)* which is paid to the townships, and to which nearly all economic activities are subject, is a form of taxation based on the "contributive capacity" or potential of the firm. Its complex and antiquated collection have led progressively to appreciable differences in the treatment of

operating enterprises, particularly according to their geographical location. Thus, the rates of two neighboring towns may entail very noticeable differences in the fiscal charges of two rival firms. Such situations are frequent because of the great number of towns and the multiplicity of urban divisions within metropolitan centers. However, in the last ten years, especially between 1965 and 1970, in order to achieve the objectives set by the Fifth Modernization and Equipment Plan, the towns found themselves under the obligation of financing a large part of their collective equipment, and of relying more on the commercial license tax to increase their resources. For this reason, the revenues from this license tax increased from 1.6 to 6.8 billion francs between 1959 and 1969.

While waiting for a thorough reform of this business tax, the government has taken two measures favoring retail trade: (1) it eliminated the exceptions after 1971-1972 benefiting certain types of organizations (e.g., state savings banks, farm credit institutions, farmer cooperatives), thereby lightening the burden on other business taxpayers; and (2) it reduced the business taxes paid by small retailers by 12 percent in 1971 and 15 percent in 1972. Still, it can be predicted that the business license tax will remain a source of dissatisfaction for small and medium-sized business firms for a few more years.

4. The most important element of fiscal policy toward retailing in the last twenty-five years has been the extension of the value added tax (TVA) to all its branches, on 1 January 1968. The desire to improve conditions of competition and to encourage the modernization of commerce resulted in a triple objective: (1) to put an end to the cases of double taxation that existed in some sectors; (2) to encourage the modernization of commercial enterprises by allowing them, as in the case of industrial enterprises, to deduct the amount of the tax paid on their investments from the amount of the same tax due on sales; and (3) to put a stop to the distortions created by differences in the systems of taxation applicable to the various commercial channels.

Putting the value added tax into general use has indeed acted as an efficient incentive for commercial investments and as a means for speeding up the modernization of commerce. On the other hand, for the less dynamic business-men, it has constituted a handicap in their competition with modern forms of commerce since larger gross margins result in more taxes; and older businessmen have often had difficulty adapting themselves to this new system of taxation.

A multiplicity of rates (five in all), and the changes introduced each year since 1968 either in the rates themselves or in the classification of goods and services subject to the various rates, have contributed to the irritation of small retailers. The prospect of a reduction in the number of rates and in the rates themselves, and the ongoing reclassification of similar products, have helped appease them. Nevertheless, the de facto advantage for large businesses consti-tuted by quicker refunds of the tax paid on investments than is possible for small and medium-sized businesses is still frequently attacked by the representa-tives of traditional commerce.

On the whole, the series of post-1968 measures reducing fiscal and admini-strative burdens has created a better atmosphere, but traditional tradesmen continue to attack both: (1) the overall management of the financial system, which is still presented (although without evidence) as working to the detriment of small business, and (2) the commercial license tax, which is still resented as excessively heavy.

The Financing of Commercial Investments. Small and medium-sized enterprises can now benefit from more advantageous interest rates, longer loans, and better conditions of repayment than those of the market, thanks to the government's efforts in this field.

1. The Central Fund for Hotel, Industrial and Commercial Credit (C.H.C.I. is a cooperative credit union, but the appointment of its president is subject to the government's approval) helps small and middle-sized enterprises in acquiring fixed assets and other assets, as well as working capital. The amount of the loans it grants cannot exceed one million francs ($180,000). Repayment terms of up to twenty years are allowed, with the possibility of deferred repayments.

2. The Central Fund for Cooperative Credit (a union of cooperative organizations, with a variable capital, whose chairman and general manager are appointed by the government) may grant loans to consumers' cooperatives as well as to retailers' cooperatives and their members. These loans can be utilized for financing fixed assets and working capital, the purchase of land, or of a stock-in-trade.

3. The National Credit Bank (a private corporation whose chairman and two managing directors are appointed by the government) may act under the same conditions as the Central Fund for Hotel, Industrial and Commercial Credit, but with no limit set on its loans. In practice, it does not finance small concerns as its clientele is chiefly made up of medium or large businesses.

4. The mutual-guarantee societies *(sociétés de caution mutuelle)* created by commercial professions do not provide credit but constitute guaranty funds which in turn make it possible to secure the caution of the National Fund for State Contracts, thereby facilitating the obtaining of relatively medium-term loans by businessmen from their own banks, because this caution allows these loans to be rediscounted by the Bank of France.

5. The Regional Development Companies (S.D.R.), whose function is to facilitate the financing of new investments for concerns which normally have no access to the money market, witnessed an extension of their activities to the commercial sector in 1961.

6. Real Estate Companies for Commerce and Industry (S.I.C.O.M.I.) may lease buildings and, under certain conditions, enjoy the guarantee of the National Fund for State Contracts.

7. A number of professional groups or banks have created companies or

specialized organizations for the granting of loans or for equity participations. However, as far as the retail trade is concerned, the systems listed under 5, 6, and 7 have had but little effect.

8. Since 1965, appropriations have been made directly from the Economic and Social Development Fund for the financing of small and medium-sized enterprises which have no access to the capital market. Such loans, although modest, allow greater ease of investments by groups of enterprises.

9. One should add that commerce has also benefited from many fiscal provisions introduced since 1959 to promote investments in general.

Altogether, these different methods of financing, in spite of high interest rates during the period 1968-1970, have allowed many enterprises to undertake desirable investments. Large-scale retailers, on the whole, have been able to finance with no serious difficulty the investments necessary for their modernization during the sixties; and small or medium-sized businesses did not meet very serious financing difficulties either.

Professional Development and Social Welfare

People in commerce belong to two categories: tradesmen and commercial employees. The latter have not been the object of any particular treatment from the authorities, but simply benefit from the advantages granted to employees and commerce in general. "Tradesmen" *(commerçants)* refers to the heads of firms who personally run a commercial enterprise. These tradesmen belong to the "middle classes" which gather a large variety of socio-professional groups. For a while now, the commercial middle class has presented two rather distinct "people" problems: (1) professional training, retraining, and upgrading; and (2) social protection in the matters of sickness and retirement. Besides, one must bear in mind that the growing importance of the tertiary sector (e.g., distribution) concerns economic policy makers who worry about its lower productivity, as compared to that of the secondary sector (e.g., manufacturing). The public encouragement given to modernization and competition must be remembered in this context, but state assistance in the matters of training, information, and technical assistance are very important too. On the other hand, relatively little is done to shift tradesmen and their employees toward industry although some forms of "reconversion" help is available.

Information, Training, and Assistance. Independent businessmen, too often ignorant of the direction of the evolution that is affecting commercial techniques, often yield to discouragement and adopt a purely negative attitude, refusing the indispensable changes which are a part of economic progress.

Professional organizations and Chambers of Commerce and Industry[7] have not always spontaneously fulfilled the mission of informing their adherents and members about this evolution. The public authorities have therefore provided means for better informing the businessmen in order to create the new attitudes indispensable for the participation of a sufficient number of small individual firms in the general movement of modernization.

Better information, however, is only the first stage in the adaptation to evolution. Hence, the authorities have also started a policy of developing commercial education and advanced training so as to help businessmen who wish to modernize their establishments, and assist firms of a certain size in recruiting the associates indispensable to their development.

Finally, considering that the information and instruction of businessmen necessarily passes through the channels of representative commercial organizations, especially the Chambers of Commerce and Industry, a particular effort has been made to place at their disposal a number of specialists capable of convincing businessmen of the necessity of progress, and to provide technical assistance to businessmen about to modernize their firms.

Information. The first coherent and systematic experiment in informing businessmen of the evolution of commerce and of the government's commercial policy was accomplished in 1964 with the publication of the work done by a commission which met from July 1963 to April 1964 and which was called the "National Commerce Convention" *(Assises Nationales du Commerce).* On that occasion, the representatives of the various economic sectors met with the administration to examine commercial problems comprehensively.

These meetings, as well as those of the Commerce Committee of the Fifth Development Plan, provided the first systematic inventory of the problems of commerce and the first formulation of a policy on this matter. Since that time, the perceptible improvement that has occurred in the relationship between some of the professional milieus and the administration has allowed the latter to bring to the notice of professional organizations and of businessmen themselves, the goals of the public authorities and the details of the policy followed in the principal fields concerning tradesmen.

Without actually claiming that this action prevented the appearance of purely negative attitudes in large sections of the commercial milieu, it can certainly be said to have kindled among many groups of businessmen a new awareness of the necessity and the possibility of modernization and adaptation by small businesses through the techniques of professional and continuing education.

Professional Training and Extension Programs. There is little doubt that commerce constitutes one of the economic sectors where professional qualifications have remained at a very low level and where professional competence has never been considered as a prerequisite to its practice. This conception, inherited from times of shortages and poverty, particularly during the war, remained widespread until the mid-1960s.

Higher education in commerce was, until the recent university reforms, entirely provided by business colleges under the direction of the Chambers of Commerce and Industry. Moreover, these business colleges (such as the School of Advanced Commercial Studies [H.E.C.], the School of Advanced Economic and Commercial Sciences [E.S.S.E.C.], together with seventeen other business colleges) have always produced and continue to produce students who, for the most part, prefer to go into manufacturing rather than distributing enterprises. The recently created Institutes of Business Administration and the University Institutes of Technology now provide an education oriented toward management problems, but which at this level cannot be conceived as specifically intended to train executives or managerial staff for retailing.

On the other hand, at the level of professional and continuing education, the problems are closely related to commercial policy, and they have really been dealt with only since 1960. The Commission on the Modernization of Commerce in the Fourth Plan, in 1960, insisted on the necessity of following an active policy in matters of education so as to prepare the introduction into the commercial system of a new generation of employers and employees who would be capable of putting new methods of business management into practice. After 1961, a professional training policy was defined, based on the following principles: (1) participation of tradesmen in the working out of methods and the functioning of professional training programs, either directly or through the agency of their professional organizations or the Chambers of Commerce and Industry; (2) diversification of means and methods; (3) training of instructors who would develop an awareness in the businessmen of the need for education, and carry out professional and extension training; and (4) the financial assistance of the public authorities in order to encourage private or semi-public initiative.

This policy found its expression in new appropriations to the National Budget from 2 million francs in 1961 to 10 million in 1970. In 1970, training programs comprised:

1. The Center for Studies and Training of Technical Assistants in Commerce, which operates almost entirely on government subsidies. It trains technical assistants who are mostly employed by the Chambers of Commerce and Industry, in the fields of information and training of businessmen. These technical assistants number at present more than 400, three-fourths of whom are employed by about one hundred Chambers of Commerce.

2. The Commercial Upgrading Institutes *(Instituts de Promotion Commerciale)* numbered twenty-two in 1970. Set up by the Chambers of Commerce and Industry either at local initiative or at the instigation of the administration, they provide a complementary specialized instruction at the secondary or college levels for commercial employees or heads of firms.

3. The Centers for Continued Commercial Training *(Centres de Perfectionnement Commercial),* created in 1965, provide active tradesmen with supplementary part-time training in the principal commercial techniques (accounting, inventory management, sales promotion, etc.).

Thus, by 1970 and in ten years' time, some 30,000 to 40,000 businessmen have attended either full-time or part-time training programs or courses. We must also mention the fact that the government has, since early 1970, granted to those who have stopped working in order to attend extension courses, an allowance which varies according to their previous salaries. This measure should normally bring about a further increase in the number of beneficiaries from professional training. On the whole, this action stands out as one of the most important steps in retail trade policy so far, as it allows independent tradesmen to acquire or complete training which will henceforth be indispensable to business management.

Technical Assistance. Technical assistance to small business is chiefly provided by the Chambers of Commerce and Industry and a number of professional organizations. It includes, apart from the training programs mentioned above, a number of operations directly related to business management: preliminary diagnostic of business problems, encouragement of joint advertising, sales promotion, the setting up of collective stores, etc.

Social Welfare. French tradesmen do not have any special social security system. The heads of businesses are affiliated with special organizations for "independents" in commerce and industry, which are geographical or professional in scope but are coordinated at the national level.

Health Insurance. Health insurance was made compulsory for non-salaried workers in non-agricultural professions by a law of 12 July 1966, followed by various applicatory enactments. The system is autonomous in regard to the government and to the general social security program. Within it, each professional group preserves its own identity, and professional solidarity operates within each group.

From the outset, this system has been the object of strong criticism from professional milieus which have charged it with causing an increase in the contribution rates, and with a decrease in the number of risks covered (especially small risks) for some tradesmen. It is true that the institution of a system proper to commerce saddled it with the responsibility for tradesmen who had previously been insured by agencies supplied with public funds. Consequently, as a result of numerous complaints and of long negotiations with members of professional milieus, the 1966 system was improved in the direction desired by the tradesmen. Thus, a law of 6 January 1970: (1) extended reimbursement to small risks; (2) continued until the age of sixteen, the privileged protection of children; and (3) included long and costly illnesses.

These measures were made possible financially by: (1) the government's paying for the contributions to the National Solidarity Fund, and (2) incorporating in the independents' health plans, a fraction of the financial resources obtained by a solidarity contribution imposed on all incorporated forms of enterprise (in every economic field) by a law of 3 January 1970. Therefore, after a long crisis which seriously affected businessmen, their health insurance program was finally assured thanks to government financial assistance and to "solidarity" contributions from industrial and commercial corporations.

Family Allowances. The system of family allowances for businessmen is shared by all non-salaried individuals in professions other than agriculture. It is a part of the general system, and more precisely of the National Fund for Family Allowances, and calls for no special remarks.

Old-age Insurance. Coverage is variable and partly left to the decision of the persons concerned. For old-age pensions, different categories were defined according to the level of income. In practice, since tradesmen have generally considered their business as capital and have normally worked until a very old age, they have contributed relatively little and therefore enjoyed only modest old-age pensions.

The businessmen's old-age insurance program has been deteriorating since the early sixties, because of: (1) the extremely advantageous rights of married couples (the pension is increased by 50 percent for the spouse; and in case of death, the surviving party receives a pension amounting to 75 percent of that of the insured, which is a higher rate than in any other program); and (2) the demographic structure of the system has been slowly deteriorating since 1957 (an annual decrease of 2 percent in the number of contributors, and an increase of 5 percent in the number of retired people). Independent businessmen want more benefits and are receiving them, but there are fewer of them to finance their special system. Thus, the ratio between contributors and retired persons, which was 2.59 in 1960, was only 1.65 in 1968.

To remedy this situation, the interested parties have instituted a complementary contribution to compensate for the advantages granted to the husband or wife; and the government had a provision adopted (law of 3 January 1970) by which all corporate businesses, whatever their line of activity or their size, are obliged to pay a contribution[8] designed to balance the program. It should also be emphasized that this contribution, which must bring in FF 160 million ($32 millions) in 1972, being deductible from the corporation tax, is in fact carried by the government to the extent of 35-40 percent (corresponding to the loss of taxes collected). For that matter, the General Budget has contributed FF 160 millions ($32 millions) in 1972 to the old-age pension system for tradesmen.

Finally, on 19 May 1972, the French National Assembly first approved a government bill which progressively equalizes after 1 January 1973 tradesmen's pensions with those provided to salaried workers under the general pension system. This bill also slightly reduces old-age pension taxes. These measures will require a further contribution from the General Budget to the tune of FF 1 billion ($200 millions) by the time the transition will have been completed.

Assistance to Elderly Businessmen. In spite of the real improvements brought to the businessmen's old-age pension program, the problem posed by elderly shop owners who are often victims of commercial change, cannot be considered as satisfactorily solved. Indeed, although its financial resources have been improved, the pension system cannot guarantee to elderly retailers a sufficient income after retirement. For the more modest categories, which formerly supplied the least contributions, this income is often inferior to that accruing from the application of solidarity principles to other categories in unfavorable situations. Their position is doubtlessly not much different from that of many retired persons, but in most cases small retailers had considered their businesses as capital which they could realize when they retired. However, the loss of value of their business in many instances deprives them of an important means of support on which they counted. They therefore often find themselves under the obligation of continuing to work until an advanced age without being able to adapt themselves to the new conditions of their trade.

The public authorities were thus led to consider the creation of a system of special aid to very old shopowners, those really in need of assistance. The National Assembly first approved in May 1972 a government bill setting up a bonus system for old and poor tradesmen, to be financed by a tax on the surface of large stores. This is a portentous development heralding both a reintroduction of discriminatory taxes against large stores, and the introduction of some sort of a "solidarity principle" between small and large forms of retailing.

Therefore, in less than five years' time, since the law of 12 July 1966 established a compulsory system of health insurance, social-welfare programs for independent businessmen have undergone considerable transformation. Although all the problems have not been solved, one may consider that by the end of 1970 the worst inequalities had been removed, and that as a whole, social welfare is no longer an object of dissatisfaction to businessmen.

Conclusion

The modernization of the French commercial structure is now well under way. Means to facilitate this modernization have been established, and equal opportunity under the law for all forms of commerce has been somewhat achieved. In particular, from 1960 to 1970, regulation was appreciably altered to take into account the new conditions in commercial practices.

The coming decade will be marked by very important changes in the structure of the commercial system, as a result of foreseeable progress in industrialization, urbanization, and a higher and better standard of living. These transformations will largely occur spontaneously. The role of the public authorities will be to see that they occur in an orderly fashion.

The means for professional training and extension courses not only for tradesmen but also for salaried employees in commerce must still be increased, diversified, and better adapted to the multiplicity of situations; and forms of association must be encouraged, for they often represent the only chance of development for the smaller enterprises.

The functioning of the market, in which increasingly powerful and efficient retailers face small suppliers, must be kept under increased supervision; and the organization of competition will have to be adapted constantly to the evolution of market power and commercial practices. Besides, the public authorities will have to take the necessary measures in time to avoid being forced back upon measures restricting liberty.

On another level, the situation of shopowners eliminated by competition, especially the oldest ones, will have to be considered with great attention. It is certainly unthinkable that society should take over all the risks of commercial enterprise as some would like it to be; but it is no more conceivable that it should take no interest in those who, because of an evolution which has often been beyond their understanding and to which they cannot adapt, are now excluded from a share in the fruits of economic progress. It is in this direction that the public authorities have oriented their efforts in the last few years. Hence the rhythm of modernization, to be bearable, will have to be tempered, and the individuals excluded will have to be reconverted or assisted. The extra cost which will result for society is not negligible, but it is doubtlessly lower than the social cost that would result from a stagnation of structures. For the next ten years, therefore, the objectives and strategy in matters of retail trade have been rather clearly defined.

Short-term policy will have to be conducted carefully so as to avoid brutal and prolonged halts in the modernizing process, which although pleasing to small retailers, would only bring about a still more vigorous and destructive restructuring at a later date. This obstacle was just barely avoided in the late sixties. In a country which has been accustomed to a protectionist policy for over half a century, this risk still remains serious.

May 1972

Notes

1. Until August 8, 1969, one dollar was equivalent to about 5 French francs. After that, it took 5.5 francs to equal a dollar, at the official rate.

2. The *Préfet* is the official in charge of an administrative region *(Département)*.

3. A regulation issued by an administrative body for the enforcement of a law or of a governmental or administrative decree.

4. A "chain" or "snowball" sale works on the principle of the "chain letter."

5. The French expression *fonds de commerce* is difficult to translate. The dictionary suggests "stock-in-trade" or "business" itself. It represents the monetary difference between the value of the firm's assets and its value as a going concern—a difference which is often capitalized as "good will."

6. In 1969, the French franc was worth about 18 American cents (5.5 French francs to the U.S. dollar). In late 1971, the exchange rate returned to 5 French francs to the U.S. dollar.

7. Chambers of Commerce and Industry are public institutions in France, with compulsory membership and state subsidies.

8. The proceeds of this contribution are paid in part to the health insurance program (see above), and in part to the old-age pension program.

Partial Bibliography

General Works

Gérard, M. *La rémunération de la fonction commerciale*. Paris: Centre d'Etudes du Commerce et de la Distribution, 1969.

Le commerce intérieur français; Notes et études documentaires. Paris: La Documentation Française, 1967.

Rapport général de la Commission du Commerce du IVème Plan. Paris: Commissariat Général du Plan d'Equipement et de Productivité, 1960.

Rapport général de la Commission du Commerce du Vème Plan. Paris: Commissariat Général du Plan d'Equipement et de Productivité, 1966.

Rapport de la Commission Commerce, VIème Plan, 1971-1975. Paris: La Documentation Française, 1971.

Quin, Claude. *Tableau de bord de la distribution en France.* Paris: Ecole Pratique des Hautes Etudes, 1969.

Fourcade, Jean-Pierre. "Le rôle des pouvoirs publics dans la modernisation du commerce." *Humanisme et Entreprise* (Paris), No. 39 (octobre 1966), 49-63.

Fourcade, Jean-Pierre. "Réflexions sur le commerce et la concurrence." *Concurrence – Les Cahiers de l'ILEC* (Paris), No. 27 (1968/4), 6-23.

Principal Periodicals Consulted

Concurrence – Les Cahiers de l'ILEC
CECOD – Informations
Coopération
Etudes et Conjoncture (I.N.S.E.E.)
Libre-Service Actualités
Points de Vente
Techniques Marchandes Modernes

Public Planning of Retail Location in France and Great Britain

SUSAN P. DOUGLAS

In many European countries, an important aspect of government policy toward retailing is the planning of shopping facilities by public authorities. This has expanded considerably in recent years as growing pressures on the use of urban land have encouraged more rigorous control and planning of land use. Since such planning affects the availability and desirability of alternative sites to retailers, it may have a significant impact on retail location decisions and the resultant pattern of location. The nature of this impact depends both on what planners aim to accomplish as well as their success in achieving their objectives.

Retail location planning has developed in two different planning contexts, national economic planning and local urban planning—France and Great Britain each provide an example of these two forms of planning. In both countries public authorities are actively involved in planning retail locations, but the approaches and organization of planning differ considerably.

In France the planning of retail locations has emerged as an important feature of the programs for social and economic development set up by successive national plans. The organization of planning thus tends to be highly centralized. In Britain, on the other hand, the impetus for the planning of shopping facilities came from the development of urban planning, particularly in the context of central area redevelopment and of new housing development. Retail planning there is predominantly a function of local planning authorities and hence decentralized.

The Development of Retail Location Planning in Great Britain and France

A number of trends may lead to the development of retail location planning. In the first place, problems of urban growth and traffic congestion, placing an increasing strain on central area facilities and on the transportation network, may encourage the intervention of public authorities to work out land-use patterns to coordinate demand and supply for urban land. Retailing is a major generator of traffic and an important urban land use and consequently a critical element in these plans. Furthermore the trend toward the development of shopping centers, implying a clustering of retail land uses, makes it increasingly critical to ensure that such centers are coordinated appropriately with the transportation network and other urban land uses.

145

Urban retail planning may also develop as part of national economic planning. In the case of the retail sector, the number, relative size, and location of retail establishments is related to aggregate levels of retail productivity. Where public policy aims to raise levels of retail productivity by encouraging the development of modern retail facilities in sizable shopping centers, urban plans may become an important tool of government policy.

Social objectives may also be an important factor in retail planning. Concern with providing adequate facilities in new residential areas may lead to the public planning of such facilities, particularly in the context of government-sponsored developments such as the new towns or social housing. Furthermore, political pressures to protect the independent retailer may result in measures to encourage the development of planned centers incorporating both large and small stores.

The primary aim of public planning is therefore to establish a pattern of retail location that enables a more effective coordination of competitive forces to meet the demand for retail services. Depending on the particular context and forces behind planning, various specific objectives may be emphasized: (1) establishing a pattern of retail location that will enable efficient use of the transport network; (2) regulating the volume of retail floor space to ensure high levels of retail productivity; (3) or achieving certain social ends such as integrating the small retailer into new shopping development or providing neighborhood retail facilities.

The Development of Retail Location
Planning in France

In France, the planning of retailing first started with the National Economic Plans after World War II. The primary emphasis has tended to be on the second and third objectives, though traffic problems and urban expansion are becoming increasingly important issues.

The planning of retail facilities began to develop in the late 1950s with the construction of the *grands ensembles,* major social housing complexes, in the suburbs. As these developments were often some distance from existing facilities, neighborhood shopping centers had to be planned to meet the needs of residents. Guidelines were therefore established in 1964 in the Fourth National Plan concerning the appropriate type and volume of retail facilities to be provided.[1] The provision of these facilities was, however, left to the individual developer, often a semi-public organization such as S.C.I.C. (Société Centrale Immobilière des Caisses des Dépôts) and no control mechanism was established to ensure that these standards were met.

At the same time increased effort was devoted to the development of regional planning and to the coordination of urban development plans and regional plans. Urban centers were classified into a hierarchy, and rates of growth for each urban center were planned relative to its projected position in this hierarchy.

Since retailing was an important source of employment, this also implied planning the volume of retail facilities appropriate to this position. Local plans were then to be established to work out the spatial distribution of retail facilities in the area. Administrative procedures for establishing local planning organizations to develop such plans were also envisaged.

In practice, the establishment of plans for retail location has tended to be slow. In the Paris region a detailed plan outlining the proposed development of retailing in the area for the next ten years was established in 1968.[2] The plan was based on the development of major regional shopping centers around Paris, but little attention was paid to shopping facilities at lower levels of the hierarchy, such as district or neighborhood centers.

A number of other regions and urban areas such as Aquitaine, Marseille, and Lyon have plans outlining the desired balance of retail facilities in the area. However, in many cases, planning tends to be somewhat piecemeal emphasizing individual development projects and their integration into the existing retail structure.

Still, efforts are being made to encourage comprehensive retail planning. A circular issued in 1969 requires that urban development plans should explicitly outline the proposed pattern of retail location in the area.[3] Similarly, the report of the Commission on Towns for the Sixth Plan recommends that measures should be undertaken to encourage the development of constructive planning by strengthening the powers of local planning organizations and consolidating planning functions within a given metropolitan or regional area.[4]

The Development of Retail Location
Planning in Britain

In Britain, on the other hand, urban retail planning arose primarily in response to spatial problems such as traffic congestion. The Town and Country Planning Act of 1947, after World War II, established a comprehensive system of local planning authorities and required each authority to draw up plans for its area. In general, however, little attention was paid to retail planning. Some planning of shopping facilities was undertaken in connection with new towns, established after World War II to accommodate overspill from the major urban agglomerations.[5] Since the new towns were designed as autonomous independent units, retail facilities had to be planned for the new urban population. But such plans were typically isolated examples.

By the 1960s, however, traffic congestion and pressure for central area redevelopment became critical. As a result local planning authorities, particularly in the major agglomerations, began to draw up comprehensive plans often envisaging a restructuring of the transportation network and of land use patterns in the area.[6] In many cases these involved major shopping schemes in both central and suburban areas. Since plans were drawn up independently for each urban area, problems arose with regard to coordinating such developments in neighboring towns and planning facilities on a regional basis. In particular there was no means of evaluating proposals for major shopping developments on the urban periphery that might draw trade from more than one urban planning area.[7]

Recognition of these problems that occurred not only in relation to shopping facilities but also to other aspects of urban planning and administration encouraged a reexamination of the planning structure. A system of regional planning was established and regional plans drawn up to provide direction for long-term development. In a number of areas detailed sub-regional plans for shopping facilities have been developed.[8] These indicate the proposed hierarchy as well as the approximate size and future development of each shopping center in the area. In addition a new system of long-term structure plans for local planning units has been introduced in conjunction with local government reforms.[9] These outline the long-term development of the area for a period of approximately twenty years and may be used to coordinate the short-term development plans for several local planning areas.

Despite these trends the report of the Shopping Capacity Subcommittee of the National Economic Development Office (1971) indicated the need for further coordination of planning at both regional and national levels.[10] The report emphasized the critical importance of planning shopping over wide areas due to the interdependence of shopping provisions for different planning units. The report also recommended a greater degree of participation by the central government in establishing guidelines for local planning authorities. Following this report, the government has issued various recommendations on the evaluation of planning applications, etc., but these do not always appear to have been highly successful.[11]

Thus, although the origins and emphasis of retail planning in Great Britain and France have been very different, recent developments suggest that comprehensive planning requires the development of plans at the regional as well as the national and local levels. Just as in France national objectives have to be interpreted and carried out by detailed local plans, so in Britain regional and national planning strategies have to be developed to coordinate and guide local planning.

Planning Methods and Procedures

Planning in both Britain and France is indicative, that is, it establishes general guidelines and directions for future development. Programs to implement plans can be established for the public sector, but in the private sector the implementation of plans will depend to a large extent on the cooperation of the private sector. Planners have, therefore, to establish appropriate incentives and sanctions such as credit controls, infra-structure investment or land-use controls to encourage or coerce retail location decisions in directions consistent with planning objectives.

The procedures used to draw up plans, and the general principles on which they are based, are similar in both countries. However, there are certain differences with regard to the techniques used to implement plans. These differences appear to have a significant impact on the type of location patterns planners can envisage as well as on their success in achieving their objectives and in influencing the location decisions of retailers.

Policy Formulation and Retailer Participation

Although the formulation of planning policy is primarily the responsibility of professional planning bodies staffed by civil servants, in both Britain and France reliance on implementation in the private sector typically entails some provision for retailer participation in the planning process. In general this appears to considerably greater in France than in Britain.

France. In France planning policy is formulated predominantly at the national level. A number of different bodies ranging from official planning organizations, advisory planning commissions, to ministerial committees, participate in the development of planning policy.[12] The Commissariat du Plan acts as the coordinating body for these organizations and is responsible for drawing up the National Economic Plan, based on guidelines developed in conjunction with the government.

In the case of retail location planning, government policy is prepared and coordinated by D.A.T.A.R. (*Délégation à l'Aménagement du Territoire et à l'Action Régionale*), whose head reports directly to the Prime Minister. D.A.T. A.R. also participates in the preparation of the main policy options as well as in the administration of planning policy.

The planning commissions, which are composed predominantly of representatives from the private sector and some civil servants, provide information and advice for the elaboration of the plan. The reports of these commissions are published separately from the plan and are often highly influential. In the Sixth Plan, a special committee for Urban Retail Development was formed composed of members of the Commission for Commerce and of the Commission for Towns.[13] This included a number of representatives of retail organizations as well as urban planners and developers.

Retailers also participate in regional and local planning through local advisory commissions and the local Chambers of Commerce and Industry. In contrast with their British equivalents, the French Chambers of Commerce and Industry are "consular" rather than voluntary organizations. Their officials are elected by all those paying the local *patente,* a tax for the right to conduct a business in the town. These organizations establish regulations concerning the conduct of business, and for specific trades, and are frequently of considerable importance in both local and national politics.

The importance of retailer participation in regional and local planning was increased considerably in 1969 with the establishment of advisory committees for each *département* (the regional French administrative unit).[14] These committees were intended to assist both in the development of planning policy and in the control of private retail development. Their primary function is to review shopping development proposals over 30,000 square feet (gross area) and to advise the regional administrative authority, the *Préfet,* as to whether building permission should be granted. Since the retail members of the commission often include representatives of national retail firms who may be involved in a proposed project, this can give rise to significant conflicts of interest.

Britain. In Britain, planning policy is formulated at the local level by specialized planning departments of the relevant local government authority. Some areas have urban retail advisory committees, but in general these do not appear to have played a very important role in planning. Planners do, however, take into consideration retail interests through informal channels. Particularly when there is substantial pressure for redevelopment, planners must keep abreast of projects planned by private developers and incorporate these into development plans and programs.

At the national level, the National Economic Development Council—the official planning organization—acts predominantly in an advisory capacity, providing information for the central government rather than taking an active role in policy formulation. Retail organizations, such as the Multiple Shops Federation and the Grocer's Institute, attempt to represent retail interests with the central government and are also occasionally consulted by local planning authorities.[15]

In general, the scope for retailer participation in policy formulation appears to be somewhat greater where policy is formulated at the national level, as under centralized planning. In this context, retailers may play an important role in influencing general policy directions and pointing out problems with regard to retail development, as well as in providing a valuable source of information for the development of plans.

Planning Models

Both British and French plans are based on the premise that retail locations may be organized into a hierarchy of retail centers. Derived from Christaller's principle of market areas, the concept of a retail hierarchy suggests that retail centers can be ranked in order of importance based on the range of goods sold and the size of the market area served.[16] Thus the highest order centers will sell a complete range of goods, including "first order" goods—highly specialized items that are not available in any other center. Centers at the next level in the hierarchy will supply the needs of a smaller market area for all goods except the "first order" goods, and will sell certain items ("second order" goods) that are not offered by lower levels in the hierarchy. Only the highest order centers will compete for the complete range of goods, these and the second level centers for second order goods, and so on.

Typically five or more levels in this hierarchy can be identified, depending on the classification of the upper end of the hierarchy: major regional and/or national centers; regional shopping centers of over 500,000 square feet, in either the central area or out of town; major district centers of approximately 150-250,000 square feet; district centers of 40,000-80,000 square feet; and neighborhood centers of 5,000-10,000 square feet.[17]

In developing plans for retail facilities, the planners have therefore to determine the appropriate hierarchy of retail centers for the planning area, the volume of floor space required in the area, and its allocation among different centers.

Various procedures can be used to estimate floor space requirements.[18] In general, these are based on similar premises and parameters. The volume of floor space required is calculated from estimates of expected retail expenditure in the planning area, converted to floor space by use of a factor such as sales per square foot. Similarly, models to determine the allocation of floor space are based on assumptions about the distance consumers travel to purchase a particular item, and the minimum level of expenditure required to support the supply of a particular good by a retail establishment of a given type. Specific models differ considerably, however, in comprehensiveness, sophistication, and in assumptions and techniques used to estimate and forecast each of these parameters.

Lack of adequate or reliable data, particularly with regard to sales per square feet for different trades and types of establishment considerably hampers the application of such models, especially the more sophisticated.

In France, the problem is particularly acute, since there have been few comprehensive national surveys of retail expenditure or sales performance. Input data for regional and local plans is generally obtained by a special survey.[19] In Britain, national statistics on retail performance and expenditure are more readily available and considerable progress has been made in generating required data. The Shopping Capacity Subcommittee report suggests, however, that lack of adequate data, particularly concerning existing floor space, is still a major handicap in estimating floor space requirements and evaluating proposals.[20] The establishment of a body such as the Institute for Central Planning in Denmark to coordinate and organize local studies of shopping potential was proposed.

Thus, in both countries plans are based on similar principles, namely the organization of retailing into a hierarchy of retail centers. In Britain the hierarchy is explicitly laid out and the appropriate size and location of each center is planned in detail. The notion of a hierarchy is also implicit in French planning, but since planning is less comprehensive than in Britain, plans do not generally specify the precise allocation of floor space at each level.

Implementation Techniques

In both Britain and France public participation in shopping development is limited, since this is not generally considered a suitable outlet for public funds. Planners therefore rely to a large extent on their ability to influence and control private location decision in order to implement plans.

Various means of both a constructive and restrictive nature may be used to influence private location decisions. Development in desired locations may be encouraged by various means. Public powers of expropriation may be used to make available suitable sites at reasonable cost. This is particularly important in central areas where it would be impossible or at best prohibitively expensive for private developers to acquire suitable sites otherwise.

Planning authorities may also provide financial assistance for the desired type of shopping center development. This may be accomplished in various ways: by directly providing capital for initial development costs, guaranteeing loans for commercial development, or by encouraging other organizations to provide financing. Other incentives such as favorable tax conditions for location in certain areas may also be offered.

Alternatively development may be restrained by direct controls over the availability of sites or by imposing onerous conditions on location in certain areas. Developers may for example be required to build access roads. Decisions concerning infrastructure investment, and the location of other land uses, also affect the accessibility provided by a site and thus its attractiveness for retail use.

Britain. British planning relies primarily on a comprehensive system of land use controls administered at the local level to ensure plan implementation. Planners have extensive powers both to restrict and to promote retail development. Development or change from one land use to another requires permission from the local planning authority, enabling planners at least in theory to prevent location in sites considered undesirable. Their control is not, however, always as total as it might appear at first sight.

In the first place, where a prospective developer is refused planning permission by the relevant planning authority, he has the right of appeal to the Minister of the Environment. A public inquiry is then held and the decision of the local planning authority may be reversed. This has occurred in a number of cases, particularly where the initial refusal was based on the grounds that the development was not financially viable.[21] The central authority tended to view this as the responsibility of the developer. Problems of overprovision of floor space appear, however, to be stimulating a change in this attitude.

In addition, development controls only cover changes from one category of land use to another. Since all retail establishments are classed in the same category, a high volume retailer can take over a marginal establishment without development permission. This may nonetheless substantially alter traffic patterns in the area and thus have important repercussions from a planning standpoint.

Financial considerations and political factors may also create certain pressures limiting the use of planning controls. Since retailing is an important source of local tax revenue, it is often difficult to refuse development permission for a commercial project that is expected to generate a significant increase in local revenue. Considerations of civic prestige, particularly in the case of major central areas projects, may also influence planning decisions.

In addition to extensive land use controls, British planners also have considerable powers of initiative in retail development. They can use their powers of expropriation in order to make available sites for shopping center developments. They may also undertake development themselves, although in general this seems to be relatively rare, except in the case of the new towns.

France. In France, on the other hand, the powers of public authorities to restrict or encourage retail location are considerably more limited than in Britain, particularly at the local level. The tradition of safeguarding the right of the individual dates back to the French Revolution and includes the right to locate freely embodied in the Loi Le Chapelier of 1791.

These rights are superseded in the special development zones, areas designated in the development plan for some specific public development. Three types of zones may be created, the *zone à urbaniser en priorité* (ZUP), *the zone d'aménagement concerté* (ZAC), and *the zone d'aménagement différé* (ZAD).[22] A ZUP is created when the local authority plans to undertake some immediate public development, as for example, slum clearance or new residential development. In these areas the authority has complete powers of expropriation and preemption, and over development. Once development is completed, a *taxe locale d'équipement* is levied on businesses locating in the area to pay for the installations provided, such as roads, water. The ZAC is a more flexible formula since it gives the public authority expropriation rights but is not subject to the same fiscal and administrative regulations. Development rights in these areas can be ceded to private organizations who then contribute to the initial development costs, such as road construction, rather than paying *the taxe locale.* This shifts the burden of financing from the public authority to the private sector and is considered a particularly appropriate formula for commercial development. The third type, *the zone d'aménagement différé* (ZAD), is designed to preserve areas for long-term development and provides local authorities with rights of pre-emption for a four-year period.

Outside these areas, planners have little direct control over development of any kind. One possible mechanism of control is through the building permit required for all new construction. This was, however, intended to control the technical specifications of construction such as its density, and hence is not well adapted to controlling site location. Furthermore, it is granted by the local administrative authority rather than by the planning authority. In the case of shopping development over 10,000 square feet, the building permit is granted by the *Préfet,* the regional administrative head. He acts on the advice of the departmental retail advisory committee, which consists predominantly of retailers. For proposals under 10,000 square feet, the building permit is granted by the mayor. Neither the views of the administrative authority nor of the advisory committee are necessarily the same as those of the planning authority. Fiscal considerations, civic prestige and rivalry, and political pressures play an even more important role in influencing decisions than in Britain. Thus the opinion of the planning authority is not always followed.

Use of indirect methods of control is becoming increasingly prevalent. Tax exemptions or financing facilities may be available for location in certain areas such as the ZACs or for certain types of development.[23] Conversely, developers may be required to pay for the construction of access roads if the existing or planned transportation network is inadequate to carry the traffic generated by the proposed development.

In Britain, therefore, emphasis on regulating the spatial distribution of retail activity is accompanied by reliance on direct controls over retail location, in particular land use and development controls. In France, on the other hand, centralized planning appears to be associated with emphasis on more generalized and indirect means to implement plans. Since planners have only limited control over private retail development, they rely primarily on influencing retailers by providing attractive development conditions in certain areas.

**The Effect of Public Planning on the
Pattern of Retail Location**

The impact of public planning on the pattern of retail location will depend both on what planners aim to accomplish and in particular how far they envisage major modifications in the existing pattern, as well as on their success in achieving their objectives.

In both Britain and France, whether in reaction to the American experience or for more positive reasons, local planning authorities appear primarily concerned with two issues: (1) maintaining the role of retailing in the central area, especially in shopping and specialty goods, and (2) organizing suburban facilities into planned shopping centers. This generally results in opposition to developments on the urban perimeter, such as free-standing stores or "out of town" centers, which might detract from the importance of the central area, as well as creating a dispersion of retail facilities in the suburbs.

The Type of Location Planned

Britain. Extensive central area redevelopment in many British cities has generally enabled planners to take effective measures to reorganize the balance of shopping facilities between the central and suburban areas so as to accomplish these two objectives. Many local authorities have introduced schemes to modernize and revitalize retailing in the central area. Often these involve multilevel and pedestrian shopping centers that provide attractive shopping and specialty retail facilities at points of high traffic flow, as for example, the Bull Ring Center in Birmingham and the Elephant and Castle Center in London. At the same time, shopping facilities in the suburbs are clustered into district and major district centers. The latter provide some of the more frequently purchased durables as well as convenience items and help to relieve pressure on central area facilities for such items.

The exact pattern envisaged varies from city to city, depending on its size, the nature of its transport system and urban structure. In Liverpool, for example, considerable redevelopment is taking place permitting the establishment of a three-tier hierarchy, consisting of the central area, major district centers of 250,000 square-feet minimum, and a number of large local supermarkets.[24] In other cities, a four-tier system is more typical. Glasgow, for example, has both major district centers of 150-300,000 square feet and district centers of 40-80,000 square feet.

Relatively few plans appear to envisage any major shopping developments in the outer suburbs or on the urban perimeter along the lines of the American "out of town" center. The impression that both the central government and local planning authorities are opposed to "out of town" shopping centers and also free-standing superstores is widespread. Planning permission has been granted for several projects of this type, but these are generally considered to be atypical.

In some cases, a large suburban shopping center providing some durables retailing has been planned, as at Cowley and Yate, to relieve traffic congestion in the central area. These are generally, in satellite suburbs, either in an already established center or in a new residential area, rather than in genuine out-of-town locations.[25] In addition, they are usually of major district size, i.e., of 150-400,000 square feet rather than true regional centers. Some recent developments are however considerably larger. The Brent Cross project, for example, consists of a major regional shopping center of approximately 850,000 square feet; and several applications for shopping centers over 500,000 square feet, as at Bristol, are currently being considered. A number of retail firms modeled on the American discount house, junior department store, or the French hypermarket principle have also been established.[26] The British Woolco company has opened a number of stores similar to those of the American Woolco company. Another company is planning to open a number of stores under the ensigna of Carrefours, a French hypermarket chain. Although in both cases the free-standing site policy of the parent company has been considerably modified, they represent a new venture in British retailing.

France. With the exception of the Paris region and some other major metropolitan areas, French plans do not typically envisage radical revisions in the pattern of retail location. Planners have lacked adequate planning powers to make major changes and have often experienced considerable difficulty in obtaining the cooperation of the private sector.

Opposition from central area retailers, who are often an important political force, appears to have been a critical factor inhibiting comprehensive redevelopment schemes. Small shopkeepers tend to be apprehensive that such redevelopments will result in a reallocation of floor space in favor of organized retail elements. They themselves typically lack the financial means to participate in these projects and hence have frequently attempted to block such potential threats to their prosperity.

Consequently, few cities have been able to plan a major restructuring of the central area. A number of projects have been undertaken, such as La Défense in Paris and Part Dieu in Lyons. Efforts have also been made by the private sector to renovate central area facilities as, for example, the Boulevard Haussmann project in Paris.[27] Increased interest in such schemes is also emerging in other areas with growing traffic congestion. Measures to improve development conditions in the central area through, for example, exemption from certain taxes may also facilitate further progress.

In the past concern with protecting the central area has also resulted in the provision of somewhat meager facilities in suburban area, particularly in the *grands ensembles*. At La Source, a new town outside Orléans, only 150,000 square feet was provided for approximately 18,000 families. As a result, many suburban residents went into the central area to shop, thus adding to central area traffic problems.

Private developers have often seized this type of opportunity to develop "free-standing stores" or in a few cases regional shopping centers on the urban periphery. At Orléans, for example, a number of hypermarkets have established outlets in the outer suburbs and are drawing a substantial volume of trade from the center. While such scattered development is contrary to the objectives of planners, they have generally been unable to restrain it either through negotiation or the withholding of planning permission. Arguments that such centers cause dislocation of planned traffic patterns are counteracted by participation of developers in the cost of building new roads to serve the center.

As a result, planning policy towards suburban development appears to be undergoing a change. In the Paris region, planned decentralization around major regional centers is the main thrust of the development plan. Major suburban shopping facilities of between 500,000-1,750,000 square feet are to be provided in fifteen centers either in new towns or existing centers so as to counteract scattered and haphazard development. While planning in the Paris area is considerably more advanced than in other regions, it is probably symptomatic of future trends.

Government policy favoring shopping center proposals including both independents and chain or large-scale retailers may also help to encourage the clustering of retailing in suburban areas into planned shopping centers. According to a directive of the prime minister, departmental advisory committees are to give first priority to projects including both independents and large-scale retailers.[28] In addition, efforts are to be made to encourage the coordination and integration of isolated development projects in a given area.

Thus, although planners in both countries have similar aims in developing plans for retail location, the means by which they attempt to accomplish these objectives tends to differ. In Britain the major emphasis is on altering the pattern through central area redevelopment, while in France it has primarily been concerned with organizing retail facilities in suburban areas.

Public Participation in the Implementation of
Planned Shopping Center Development

While plans envisaging changes in existing location patterns may be drawn up, their impact will also depend on how far they are carried out. This depends largely on the extent to which public authorities participate in shopping center development as well as on their ability to channel private location initiatives toward desired sites.

Britain. The British planning authorities have encountered few problems in encouraging the desired type of shopping development. In particular, they have been able to use their powers of expropriation to make available appropriate sites—frequently a major barrier to shopping center development. A common procedure is to acquire sites designated for shopping in the development plan and put the project up for tender. Since shopping centers are typically sizable projects at points of good accessibility, there is generally little difficulty in obtaining tenders.

Commercial development is viewed as highly profitable. Commercial rents are not subject to the same controls as housing, and in the past there has been a high level of demand for additional or new retail floor space due to changes in retailing technology and rising income levels. Consequently, there is substantial interest in shopping development, which is reflected in the number of active commercial developers and an ample supply of funds for shopping development, particularly, as in the U.S., from insurance companies.

Where social factors are an important consideration in planning neighborhood shopping centers and new towns, planning authorities have sometimes taken a more direct part in the construction of centers. In some neighborhoods, joint social and shopping centers are planned; and profits from the commercial development are used to finance the social facilities. In new towns, public authorities may prefer to undertake development themselves to ensure that substantial facilities are provided early in the town's development so as to attract new residents.[29]

France. French planners, however, have not always been as successful as British planners in encouraging the desired type of development. Since much of the development planned has been in neighborhood and small district centers it has not been particularly attractive to commercial developers.

In addition, interest in commercial development is limited by the restrictive conditions of shopping center development. A particularly critical factor in discouraging private investment has been the system of protected commercial leases, the *propriété commerciale.* These provide certain occupancy rights so that the landlord cannot refuse to renew a lease during the lifetime of the tenant except on payment of an indemnity. In addition, rents are controlled and can only be raised by 20 percent every three years.[30] Not all retailers have this type of lease, although the majority do. Since the owner of premises leased to a retail establishment is no longer free to dispose of this property as he wishes, and its mortgage value is thereby decreased, few developers are interested in building premises for rent. Shopping centers are frequently built and sold to occupants rather than leased as is typical in U.S. and British retail development. The introduction of other leasing formulas is growing, but retailers still often have to find financing for premises.

The lease system further compounds financing problems. Since a commercial lease comprises an intangible property right, a *pas de porte* ("door threshold") or charge for the right to lease is added to the sales price of premises. Consequently the retailer has to obtain financing not only for the premises but also for the *pas de porte.* This may pose a problem, particularly for small retailers, as the financial market is not well developed. Private sources of funds available in other countries are often lacking in France.

Public authorities have attempted to alleviate this situation by establishing semi-public companies *(sociétés d'économie mixte)* to take charge of public development projects in a given area.[31] These may either help to organize initial financing for the construction of premises, which are then sold directly to retailers, or may directly undertake development themselves. Efforts are also being made to develop more flexible financing and leasing formulas and to simplify some of the fiscal and administrative regulations for shopping development.

The Impact of Public Planning on the Retailer

Public planning affects the location decisions of retailers either through direct control over the availability of certain sites or indirectly by influencing the accessibility provided by alternative sites and their desirability to retailers. The importance of planning to the retailer depends both on the compatibility of public planning objectives with those of the retailer, and on the degree of control or influence exercised over private development. This may vary with the type of retailer.

Small-scale retailers, whether independent or chains, generally prefer locations close to other retailers with complementary assortments, either close to the consumers' homes or in areas of high traffic density.[32] Consequently, they will normally find it advantageous to participate in the types of centers envisaged by public planners.

Planned shopping centers offering good accessibility and collective parking facilities provide small retailers with attractive location opportunities and more favorable development conditions than would otherwise be available. In particular, encouragement by public authorities of shopping center projects incorporating independent retailers may facilitate location close to large retail outlets that generate a substantial volume of customer traffic. Controls over the cost or rental values of sites in planned centers as well as assistance in obtaining or guaranteeing loans offer further advantages.

For large-scale retailers, however, the advantages of participating in collective location decisions may tend to vary with the type of retailer and the type of center planned. Such retailers can to a large extent attract customers independently. Hence proximity to other retailers may be less critical than the accessibility provided by a site. This is particularly true in the case of the discount store or hypermarket with an aggressive pricing policy that can attract clientele from a wide area. For such stores, the price of a site is a critical factor resulting in a preference for sites on the extreme urban periphery, or in "out-of-town" locations.

Department stores, on the other hand, may find it advantageous to participate in regional size centers with good accessibility, whether in town centers or in suburban areas. Experience in the United States indicates that the volume of traffic generated by a store on such a site is greater than on a free-standing site.

The advantages of planning are therefore less evident for large than for small retailers. Except where regional centers are planned, the primary impact of planning on large-scale retailers is to impose constraints on the availability and use of certain sites, as for example "out-of-town" sites on the urban perimeter.

Britain. Much of the demand for new retail floor space in Britain comes from the specialist multiple stores, the clothing and shoe store chains, the druggists, the stationer-bookstores, and the grocery and superette chains. This sector of retailing is expanding rapidly. With the exception of the new hypermarket and discount stores, other sectors of retailing are stable or declining. The department store chains, for example, have mostly expanded by buying up family department stores in central areas, and have shown little interest in new sites.

Since the multiple retailers prefer sites close to other retailers in areas of high traffic density, they have found it advantageous to locate in the planned shopping centers favored by public planners and are typically an important element in such developments. Their participation and consequent expansion has however taken place at the expense of the independent retailer. While alternative locations in planned shopping centers are often made available for independent retailers affected by redevelopment, they are frequently unable to afford the higher rents and associated operating costs.[33] Even where special provisions and lower rents are allowed, the loss of traditional neighborhood clientele and reinstallation costs may prove insurmountable.

It is somewhat difficult to evaluate how far retailers might prefer other locations, since planning authorities exercise strict control over retail development. There has generally been little evidence of any widespread interest in "out-of-town" or free-standing locations. The structured pattern of urban growth and nucleated centers and of reliance on public transportation has not been conducive to this type of development. Even the hypermarket and junior department stores, such as the Woolco and G.E.M stores, are typically located in satellite suburbs rather than true "out-of-town" locations.[34] With growing reliance on private transportation for shopping, however, there may be greater interest in sites of this type.

France. By contrast to the British situation, French retailing is characterized by the dichotomy between the small independent and the large-scale retailer. Many of the independents, particularly those located in the central area, are opposed to new development. There are some dynamic independents who are willing to participate in planned shopping centers, but these are typically newcomers who do not wield the same political power as the central area establishment. The large-scale retailers, on the other hand, typically have extensive plans for development that range from the moderate expansion policies of the department stores to the dynamic aggressive policies of the discount stores. This situation does not appear particularly conducive to the attempts of planners to organize retailing into planned shopping centers.

The most active element in retail development is the discount stores or hypermarkets, which prefer isolated sites on the urban periphery on major traffic routes. Plans to develop major regional centers to counteract hypermarket expansion tend to encounter opposition from central area independents. In addition, the relatively small number and moderate expansion policies of department store chains suggest that it may be difficult to find key tenants in such developments.

Even plans to develop small district centers have not always been highly successful, due to restrictive leasing and financing conditions. The situation is, however, improving with the efforts of public authorities to encourage the cooperation of large-scale and independent retailers. The latest hypermarket developments, for example, are in centers where approximately half the space is occupied by independents, rather than on free-standing sites. These are still, however, typically in "out-of-town sites" rather than in the inner suburban locations preferred by planners.

In both countries as more comprehensive plans are developed, planners are able to influence location decisions by their control of the transportation network and the location of other activities that determine traffic patterns. In Britain, the planning of a hierarchy of centers in conjunction with the transportation network implies that selected sites will have desired levels of accessibility for shopping center development, and the availability or suitability of alternative sites may be limited. Equally in France, the special development zones create certain site opportunities, although these are generally more limited in scope than the locations envisaged in British planning. Equally, the range of alternative sites may be somewhat greater than in Britain so that the choices of developers may not be equally constrained by planning decisions.

The importance of these indirect controls is further reinforced by the trend toward the development of larger planned shopping centers since the number of sites providing the desired level of accessibility for such development is limited. With even high-volume retailers interested in such sites, planning may therefore have an increasingly important influence on the location decisions of all types of retailers.

Conclusions

The comparison of retail location planning in Great Britain and France suggests a number of conclusions concerning the aims of both forms of planning and their impact on the pattern of retail location and on retailing.

The primary aim of public plans for retail location is to provide a more effective coordination of competitive forces so as to achieve certain objectives such as more efficient use of urban land, higher levels of retail productivity, the integration of small- and large-scale retailing, or adequate provision of retail facilities to meet consumer needs. Where planning is centralized and takes place in the context of national economic planning, it appears more likely to emphasize economic and social objectives such as problems of independent retailers and consumer needs. Where planning is decentralized and takes place in the context of urban planning, preoccupation with local problems may lead to emphasis on the spatial aspects of planning.

Although there are differences in emphasis with regard to the stated objectives of planning, these stem from the level at which policy is formulated rather than from its content. Irrespective of the degree of centralization, effective retail location planning ultimately requires the development of comprehensive plans at the local level, specifying the number, size, and location of centers to be provided for the planning area.

The purpose of these plans is to organize retail locations into a structured pattern coordinated with the transportation network and traffic patterns. Where public transportation is the dominant mode, emphasis has been placed on maintaining higher-order retailing in the central area. As consumer mobility and affluence, as well as traffic congestion, increase, there is a tendency to decentralize retailing and to move toward major regional shopping developments in suburban and peripheral locations.

The means used to carry out plans appear to differ somewhat under the two forms of planning. Both centralized and decentralized planning rely to a large extent on the private sector to implement plans. Yet under decentralized planning, emphasis on spatial problems appears to result in greater reliance on direct controls over private location, while under centralized planning more importance is attached to the psychological impact of planning and the participation of the retailer in the planning process.

These differences in planning powers appear to affect the impact of planning on the pattern of retail location, and retail location decisions. In Britain, for example, extensive planning powers have enabled planners to take an active role in reshaping the pattern of retail location. By making available appropriate sites providing attractive location opportunities for the dominant sector of retailing— the multiple chains—planners have been able to encourage the development of planned shopping centeis in town centers and suburban areas. This has, however, been achieved largely at the expense of the independent retailer forced by central area redevelopment to relocate in new, more costly premises or to go out of business.

In France, on the other hand, efforts to restrict undesirable type of development and to encourage planned shopping centers in specified locations do not appear to have been as effective as in Britain. Inadequate planning powers coupled with political pressures and unfavorable development conditions have hindered extensive central area redevelopment and the development of suburban centers in the desired locations. A major exception to this is in the Paris region where plans are based on the development of major regional centers, and where planners appear to have been successful in obtaining the cooperation of the retail sector. Recent developments also suggest that the situation may be improving in other areas.

Differences in the character and impact of public planning in Great Britain and France appear to stem not so much from the degree of centralization in planning, but rather from other characteristics of the planning process such as the comprehensiveness of planning and the effectiveness of planning controls. Planners may only envisage important modifications in the urban pattern if they possess effective planning powers and can establish comprehensive plans that take into consideration the balance of facilities in central, suburban, and peripheral areas.

Insofar as centralized planning tends to imply less comprehensive planning and less direct controls, it may be less effective than decentralized planning, although this will also depend on the ability of centralized planning to obtain the cooperation of the retail sector in the development of plans and thus in ensuring their implementation.

Factors external to the planning process also appear to be crucial to the impact of planning. In particular the structure of retailing and the nature of the urban pattern affect the type of locations required by retailers and thus the compatibility of private location objectives with public planning.

Where the dominant sector in retailing is the chain stores or multiples as in Britain, private location policies are more likely to be compatible with those of planning authorities, and hence planning may be highly effective. On the other hand where discount stores, hypermarkets, or independents are an important element, the task of the planner may be considerably more difficult. These types of retailing tend to act as a diversive force encouraging a dispersion of facilities. Success in counteracting this tendency will depend on the ability of planners to encourage their integration into planned shopping centers.

The nature of the urban pattern will also affect demand for retail floor space. Where urban pattern is highly structured and based on a hierarchy of nodal points, there may be little opportunity to locate outside these points and thus on sites other than those envisaged by planning. Where urban growth is more diffuse, opportunity for major out-of-town developments close to important traffic routes may exist, although such developments are typically viewed by planners as undesirable.

In brief, although an initial comparison of planning in Great Britain and France suggests that decentralized planning provides a more effective mechanism for influencing or controlling the location decisions of retailers, a closer examination suggests that the differences in the impact of planning are primarily due to other characteristics of the planning process and of the planning environment. In particular, differences in the powers of local planning authorities and in the character of demand for new retail floor space may affect the impact of planning.

Ultimately, therefore, effective retail location planning will depend not only on the degree of centralization or mode of organization, but also on the development of a comprehensive and integrated system of planning at national, regional, and local levels. In addition adequate measures to ensure the implementation of plans and the participation of the retailer in the planning process must be provided. As public planning becomes more extensive and directive, there is a tendency to move toward a mixed form of planning and to focus on regional planning as a means of coordinating national and local plans. Greater emphasis is placed on establishing direct control over location decisions and on obtaining cooperation of organized retail elements.

March 1972

Notes

1. Commissariat Général du Plan de l'Equipement et de la Productivité. *Le IV° Plan de Développement Economique et Social* (Paris: Imprimerie Nationale, 1964).

2. "Les Commerces: Programmes des Centres Commerciaux d'Intéret Régional en Région Parisienne," *Cahiers de l'Institut de l'Aménagement et de l'Urbanisme de la Région Parisienne*, Vol. 10 (February 1968).

3. Ministère de l'Economie et des Finances, *L'Urbanisme Commercial* (Paris: Imprimerie Nationale, 1971). A marked change in government policy toward urban retail planning was made at this time as evidenced in a series of

ministerial directives and circulars between 1969-1970. These are covered in the chapter on France in this book.

4. Commissariat Général du Plan de l'Equipement et de la Productivité, *Rapport de la Commission des Villes sur les Orientations de la Politique Urbaine au Cours du VI° Plan* (Paris: Imprimerie Nationale, 1971).

5. New Towns Act 1946 (London: H.M.S.O. 1946). See also P. Ford and C. J. Thomas, *Shops and Planning* (Oxford: Basil Blackwell, 1953).

6. J. B. Cullingworth, *Town and Country Planning in England and Wales* (London: Allen and Unwin, 1964).

7. H. Cole, "Shopping Assessments at Haydock and Elsewhere," *Urban Studies* 3, 2 (June 1966); Department of Town and Country Planning University of Manchester, *Regional Shopping Centres in Northwest England* (Manchester: Manchester University, 1964); J. P. Reynolds, "Shopping in the Northwest," *Town Planning Review* 34, 4 (October, 1963).

8. For a review of four such plans, see Ian Masser "Methods of Sub-regional Analysis," *Town Planning Review,* 41, 2 (April, 1970). See also C. Cooper, B. Howell, and D. Lydden, "Regional Planning and Implementation," *Journal of the Town Planning Institute* 56, 10 (December, 1970).

9. *Town and Country Planning Act 1968 – Part I-The Town and Country Planning (Structure and Local Plans) Regulations 1971: and Memorandum* Department of Environment (Circular 44/71) (London: H.M.S.O., 1971).

10. National Economic Development Office, Distributive Trades Economic Development Committee. *The Future Pattern of Shopping* (London: H.M.S.O., 1971).

11. R. D. Manley, "Discount Trading and Hypermarkets," *Town and Country Planning* 39, 12 (December, 1971).

12. Pierre Bauchet, *La Planification Française* (Paris: Editions du Seuil, 1970).

13. Commissariat Général du Plan d'Equipement et de la Productivité; Rapport de l'Intergroupe Commerce-Villes du VI Plan, *Le Commerce et la Ville* (Paris: Imprimerie Nationale, 1971).

14. See Ministère d'Economie et Finance, op. cit.

15. G. M. Pain, *Planning and the Shopkeeper* (London: Barrie and Rockcliff, 1967) discusses various mechanisms for incorporating retail interests into planning.

16. W. Christaller, *Central Places in Southern Germany*, trans. C. Baskin (Englewood Cliffs, N. J.: Prentice-Hall, 1970). See also B. Berry and W. Garrison, "Recent Developments in Central Place Theory," *Papers and Proceedings of the Regional Science Association IV* (Philadelphia, Pa., 1958).

17. Various hierarchies of urban centers have been established in Britain and France. In Britain see R. D. P. Smith, "The Changing Urban Hierarchy," *Regional Studies,* 2, 1 (1970); W. I. Carruthers, "Major Shopping Centres in England and Wales 1961," *Journal of the Regional Studies Association* (May, 1967). For France: *Fonctions et Besoins du Commerce dans la Nouvelle Armature Urbaine*

(Paris: Centre d'Etudes du Commerce et de la Distribution, 1966); Marie-Andrée Prost, *La Hiérarchie des Villes* (Paris: Gauthier Villars, 1965).

18. National Economic Development Council, *Urban Models in Shopping Studies* (London: H.M.S.O., 1970) reviews various procedures used in the U.K. and U.S. See also Société Centrale Immobilière des Caisse des Dépôts, *Tableau Indiquant par Nature des Dépenses* (Paris: mimeographed, 1968); Service d'Urbanisme Commercial *La Méthode des Coéfficients Budgétaires* (Paris: Service Interconsulaire du Commerce et de la Distribution, 1967).

19. The Service d'Urbanisme Commercial, for example, undertakes studies of local shopping potential, and is attempting to encourage the collection of appropriate statistics for such studies.

20. National Economic Development Council, Distributive Trades E.D.C., op. cit., p. 3.

21. For example, the refusal of planning permission by the local authority for the Hampshire Centre at Bournemouth was reversed as a result of a ministerial inquiry. At Haydock, however, the position of the local authority was upheld.

22. Bertrand Meary, "Zone d'Aménagement Concerté," *Urbanisme n° 115* (1970); and Yves Nicolas, "Droit et Urbanisme," *Urbanisme* n° 117 (1970).

23. Rapport de l'Intergroupe Commerce-Villes du VIe Plan, op. cit.

24. Liverpool City Planning Department, *Liverpool Suburban Shopping Facilities* (mimeographed: undated); City Centre Planning Group, *Liverpool City Centre Plan* (Liverpool: City of Liverpool, 1965).

25. Cf. Colin S. Jones, *Regional Shopping Centres* (London: Business Books, 1970).

26. A hypermarket is a store with over 25,000 square feet sales area, selling both food and general merchandise and using a centralized checkout. The store typically has an aggressive pricing policy and is located on a free-standing site.

27. Serge Careil, *Confort Collectif, Urbanisme et Commerce* (Paris: Centre d'Etudes du Commerce, 1967).

28. Directive du Premier Ministre du 27 Mai 1970.

29. For example, the development corporation at Cumbernauld undertook development of the town center itself.

30. Christine Dérigny, "Recherchez Toutes les Possibilités du Crédit," *Urbanisme et Commerce,* n° 7 (1° trimestre 1967).

31. The *sociétés d'équipement* are semi-public organizations with part private, part public capital. There is generally one for each region or urban planning area.

32. R. L. Nelson, *The Selection of Retail Location* (New York: Dodge, 1958); Centre d'Etudes du Commerce et de Distribution, *Profils de Commerce des Nouveaux Centres* (Paris: Centre d'Etudes du Commerce et de Distribution, 1968).

33. Hadley Buck, "Town Centres," *Town and Country Planning* (June 1970).

34. C. S. Jones, op. cit., and Sam H. Chippindale, "The Role of the Developer in Shopping Development," *Town and Country Planning Summer School* (Town Planning Institute London: Mimeographed, 1970).

Ireland

R. J. CURRAN

The Background to Policy

The Irish Economy

Level of Economic Development. The structure of the distributive sector in Ireland and hence the nature of official policy towards distribution reflect the country's level of economic development, and the economic and geographic characteristics of its population. In terms of economic development Ireland is one of the middle-ranking European countries, with a level of GNP per head somewhat lower than that of Italy and Austria, and substantially higher than that of the Iberian and Mediterranean countries.[1]

The economy is in the process of industrialization; while the contribution of industry to GNP is now considerably greater than that of agriculture, almost 25 percent of the labor force is still employed in agriculture, a figure which, as in other European countries, is continuously falling. Though greatly reduced from their former levels, unemployment (over 6 percent of the labor force) and emigration continue to pose the major long-term economic problems.

Population Distribution. The population of the state is approximately 3 million and the average density of population is low by comparison with most countries in Northwest Europe. However, population distribution is uneven. Dublin, with a population of over three-quarters of a million, holds a quarter of the population of the state, and is far bigger than any other city.[2] Cork, the second city, has a population less than a fifth of that of Dublin. The other major cities, Limerick, Galway, and Waterford, have populations in the range 58,000-27,000. Below them is a fairly evenly distributed structure of twenty-eight towns with populations in the range 5,000-20,000.

Income Distribution. The distribution of income is also uneven. Average per capita personal income in Dublin in 1969 was 32 percent higher than the average for the state as a whole; the level in the poorest county was only 53 percent of that in Dublin.[3]

Development Policy. Economic growth has been fairly steady since the late fifties, the average GNP growth rate in the period 1958-70 being 4.0 percent.[4]

167

Inducements to the establishment of new industries such as tax reliefs on the profits from exports of manufacturing companies, and generous grants towards the cost of fixed assets have resulted in a diversified stream of projects, predominantly promoted by foreign entrepreneurs, but with a sizable contribution by native interests also. This policy replaced an earlier one under which the growth of industry under native control was fostered by tariff protection; tariff walls are being dismantled and major efforts have been made, involving substantial state aid, to adapt industries that grew up in these conditions to a more competitive environment.

Ireland has a "mixed" economy in that while the bulk of economic enterprises are in private hands, there are important state trading organizations in the manufacturing and transport fields, as well as state-owned utilities, such as electricity generation. This state-supported activity has not been induced by any ideological preference, but in response to particular problems (e.g., a wartime shortage of shipping) and opportunities (e.g., the manufacture of sugar). The prevailing economic philosophy could be described as liberal capitalist; the methods of economic management, and the legal framework governing commercial activity reflect this philosophy.

Foreign Trade. Ireland is heavily dependent on foreign trade, predominantly with the United Kingdom. An agreement has been reached with the United Kingdom (the Anglo-Irish Free Trade Area Agreement) whereby in return for certain concessions, mainly in relation to agricultural exports, Ireland has undertaken to progressively reduce, and abolish by 1975, tariffs on imports of British manufactured goods, with the exception of foodstuffs. Ireland has negotiated entry into the EEC. This creates the prospect of progressively more severe competition in the Irish market, coupled with greater export opportunities. The Irish price level will be of critical importance in both home and export markets. Since the price level reflects not just the efficiency of the manufacturing sector, but of the economy as a whole, an aim of policy must be to reduce inefficiency in all sectors. This is particularly so in regard to the distributive sector, whose costs make up a sizable proportion of the price to the consumer of most articles.

For a variety of reasons, economic and geographic, the task of market penetration into Ireland by British manufacturers is relatively easy. Since British newspapers and other periodicals circulate on a wide scale in Ireland, and British radio and television can be received over much of the country and is widely listened to, British manufacturers enjoy largely cost-free spillover advertising in Ireland.

Current State of Development of Retailing

These economic conditions have a decisive influence on Irish retailing. The smallness of the total Irish market, and the small number of large areas of high population density, limit the scope for mass-marketing. The relatively low level of income per head limits the market for luxury and high-cost goods. On the other hand the Dublin area, and the other major cities, are big and prosperous enough to allow the application of the most modern methods. Supermarket chains have grown rapidly in these areas in the past ten years, and their advance has, if anything, quickened recently with the extension of their stock coverage into clothing and hardware lines. Some supermarkets recently opened in Dublin are big by European standards, the largest having floor areas in excess of 20,000 square feet. Suburban shopping centers have also been a feature of recent development in the Dublin area.

Outside the major cities change has also been underway, but change of a different kind. The increasing mobility of the population, including the farming community, which wider car ownership creates has forced retailers in many smaller towns to fight for what was formerly a largely captive market.

Modern methods have been adopted on a wide scale, but because of the limitations of market size these are typified more by conversion to self-service than by the construction of new supermarkets and shops, although the number of supermarkets in provincial towns is growing. Development is particularly noticeable in those towns which are in the process of transformation into industrial centers from their traditional role of trading and service points for the agricultural hinterland.

There still remain, however, even in the biggest centers, large numbers of retail outlets that are small, obsolete in their equipment and trading methods, and with a turnover so low as to yield minute returns to their owners. Irish retailing displays to a marked degree, perhaps more than any other sector, the characteristics of economic dualism; the co-existence of enterprises that are capital-intensive, profit-oriented, and use modern managerial methods, equipment, and layout, with enterprises that are small, family-run, outdated in equipment and layout, and yield low returns to those engaged in them. Twenty-five percent of all retail outlets in the major centers of population had an annual turnover of less than £5,000 (approx. $12,000) a year in 1966, a figure that rose to 60 percent in the less-developed regions.[5]

Implications for Policy. Policy, then, has to suit a retailing system that is changing very quickly, and that shows considerable regional variation. It has to make allowance for the one-man shop in a rural area as well as for the modern city supermarket with an annual turnover of millions of pounds. It cannot be simply assumed that the small enterprises will, and ought to, disappear, or that they are necessarily inefficient in carrying out their functions. A scattered rural population can be well served by small local shops. Small shops also provide employment, a factor of importance in an economy that has yet to achieve full employment. Finally, the income of those running small shops is not always as low as the turnover of the shops might indicate, since the profit on the shop is often supplemented by farming or other activity or the incomes of those members of a family who are in wage-earning employment elsewhere. Ownership of a shop also confers a social position, which is a factor of some importance to many people, particularly in rural communities.

The Fair Trade Commission

The official body responsible for overseeing many of the aspects of retailing discussed later in this chapter is the Fair Trade Commission, and a short description of its constitution and mode of operation might be appropriate at this point.

Constitution. The Commission was constituted under the Restrictive Trade Practices Act, 1953. The Act does not prohibit any specific trading practices, but a schedule to the Act includes a list of unfair trading practices, which is not intended to be exhaustive or to limit the Commission, but is for its guidance. The list covers restrictive practices either by individuals or by persons working in combination. The members of the Commission are appointed by the Minister for Industry and Commerce; the Commission consists of a chairman and between two and four other permanent members. In addition, temporary members may be appointed by the Minister.

Modes of Procedure. The Commission may formally act in two ways to eliminate restrictive practices, by public inquiry leading, if appropriate, to the making of an Order by the Minister for Industry and Commerce, or by the publication of Fair Trading Rules.

> The Commission are empowered to hold public enquiries into the supply and distribution of any kind of goods (including ancillary services) and to furnish a report of their findings, with recommendations, to the Minister for Industry and Commerce who may make an order giving effect to the recommendations.

> Such an order requires confirmation by the Legislature before becoming law. During the Enquiry the Commission may summon witnesses to give evidence on oath and require the production of documents. Enquiries are public, but private sessions may be held to avoid disclosure of information which might injure a person's legitimate business interests. [6]

The Commission must hold an inquiry at the request of the Minister or it may take the initiative itself. It has held inquiries into the distribution of a wide range of articles from groceries to carpets, and into resale price maintenance specifically in a more limited range. Following its inquiry into the supply and distribution of medical and toilet preparations, the Minister did not accept the recommendation of the Commission that an Order be made. When the Minister rejects a recommendation of this kind by the Commission, he is required to lay a statement before Parliament giving the reasons for his decision.

The other formal method of procedure open to the Commission is to make Fair Trading Rules. These the Commission may publish "on their own initiative or following representations from a trade association."[7] Fair Trading Rules "have not got the force of law, but the Act provides that if the Rules are not being observed the Commission shall report to the Minister who may make an Order which, if confirmed by the Legislature, would give legal effect to the

Rules."[8] In practice the Commission would probably hold an inquiry in such a case before making recommendations to the Minister. The Commission has made twenty-four sets of rules, the bulk of them dealing with trade in specific commodities, but a number covering conditions for entry into trades; nineteen sets of rules are in force, five having been revoked.

Apart from these formal methods of procedure the Commission frequently proceeds informally, by giving traders advice, or by approaching organizations with a view to having practices discontinued that have been the subject of complaint.

The Commission is backed up by strong legal provisions. Failure to attend an inquiry or to give evidence can be treated in like manner as contempt of court. Investigators authorized by the Commission may enter premises, inspect and copy books and records, and require individuals to give information. Failure to cooperate is an offense (contravention of a Ministerial Order is also an offense), and the Minister, or any other person, may be granted a court injunction enforcing compliance with the terms of an Order. Severe penalties, including fines and imprisonment, may be imposed by the Court for offences. It has rarely been necessary to bring Court prosecutions for offences.

Proposed Developments

The government has decided to amend the Restrictive Trade Practices Acts to empower the Fair Trade Commission to investigate restrictive practices in a wider range of economic activity, including services. A Bill is at present before the Dáil (Parliament).[9]

Under existing legislation the Commission's powers of inquiry are limited to restrictive practices in the supply and distribution of goods, and conditions related to the rendering of services ancillary to the supply and distribution of goods, including such matters as delivery, credit, and after-sales services. The amended legislation will empower the Commission to inquire also into restrictive practices in services generally, such as building, insurance, auctioneering, and architectural services, but excluding transport, banking, and electricity supply as well as services provided under a contract of employment.

The Commission, which will be renamed the Restrictive Practices Commission, will be relieved of the task of carrying out the day-to-day investigations into restrictive practices that at present normally precede the holding of Public Inquiries. An Examiner of Restrictive Practices will be appointed to carry out this function. Depending on the circumstances, he will report to the Commission or to the Minister for Industry and Commerce on the results of his investigations. The Commission will undertake a public inquiry if this is recommended by the Examiner or requested by the Minister for Industry and Commerce.

The Minister for Industry and Commerce has announced that it proposes to introduce further legislation, which will provide for examination by the Commission of proposed or existing monopolies, take-overs, or mergers. If these were found, on grounds of competition, to be contrary to the common good, the proposed legislation would, the Minister has said, empower him to prohibit them, or, if they already existed, to dissolve them. In addition, the Minister has indicated that he is considering further legislation that would control mergers and take-overs on grounds other than competition.

Policy Toward Retail Structure

Participation in Retailing

In general there is free unsupervised entry into Irish retailing. The state does not operate retail outlets, either directly or through state-owned companies, with the minor exception of the Electricity Supply Board, which has a monopoly of the sale of electricity and which sells electrical appliances through its own retail outlets in free competition with the private domestic appliance trade. There are no commodities whose distribution is reserved for the state.

There are no legislative or administrative arrangements limiting entry into most trades, or into trading in particular areas. The practice of trade associations allowing admission to a trade to members of the association only has been largely ended. Exceptions to free entry are in the retailing of alcoholic drinks and of drugs and medicines. The former is commonly referred to as the licensed trade, because a state license must be held to sell liquor either for immediate consumption or for taking away. A new license can only be obtained in particular circumstances, and new licenses are not created in sizable numbers. In the majority of cases entry into the licensed trade can only be obtained by purchasing an existing licensed premise or an existing license. The implicit value of the license is a significant part of the market value of a licensed premises. The trading hours of licensed premises are prescribed by law, and are subject to constant police surveillance. These arrangements are justified by reference to the need for maintaining public order; similar arrangements apply in Britain.

The retailing of drugs and medicines is in a different position in that entry into the trade is subject to the professional qualifications of the retailer. To operate a retail outlet of this type a degree in pharmacy is required by law. This arrangement is justified by reference to the demands of public safety.

Entry into the motor trade is conditional. The Fair Trade Commission has made Fair Trading Rules for entry into the trade in the sale and/or repair of motor vehicles. These require that a supplier may not supply for resale motor vehicles, spare parts (with stated exceptions), and tires to other than a motor trader. A motor trader is defined as anyone engaged in, or proposing to engage in, the business of operating a public service motor garage for the sale and/or repair of motor vehicles and complying with all the conditions set out in the Schedule to the Rules. The Schedule prescribes requirements as to premises, equipment and tools, and the employment on a full-time basis of at least one skilled mechanic if the proprietor working full-time in the business is not himself a skilled mechanic. The Rules bar entry into the motor trade to anyone who does not meet these requirements, which are not onerous.

Retailing of gasoline and motor oils is in a rather unusual position in regard to freedom of entry. From the middle-fifties the major wholesalers of gasoline, which are wholly-owned subsidiaries of the international oil companies, began to acquire gasoline stations; previously these had been the exclusive preserve of independent private operators. The percentage of gasoline sales through company-owned stations increased rapidly from 1 in 1955 to 15 in 1961.[10] In the same period the total number of gasoline stations, including those owned by independents, grew very quickly. The Fair Trade Commission remarked that "apart from any adverse effect the growth of stations on this scale might have on the economic welfare of existing retailers, there is the danger that, if continued unchecked, it could increase both wholesale and retail distribution costs to such an extent as to defeat the fundamental aim of the solus system".[11] (The solus system is one of exclusive dealing arrangements.)

The Commission therefore sought the voluntary cooperation of the oil companies in reducing the rate at which they were creating new outlets. The independent station operators have claimed that the voluntary curb has not been effective. The Commission carried out a further inquiry into the retailing of gasoline in 1970, and has submitted a report on the matter to the Minister for Industry and Commerce, which was published in April, 1972.

Apart from these cases, there are no limitations on entry into retailing, either in the form of required levels of education, experience, or capital or by reference to nationality. Bodies constituted on any of the forms recognized under commercial law may enter any trade. Most Irish retail businesses are organized as private companies, partnerships, or sole proprietorships; some, but not all, of the largest businesses are public companies with a stock exchange quotation. The competition of the market is relied upon to test the ability of individuals or organizations to operate a retail business. There is no official policy favoring either the growth or the limitation of the number of outlets (with the exceptions noted above). Again the market is relied upon to determine the required number.

Policy Towards Foreign Retailers

There are no measures controlling foreign participation in Irish retailing. Foreign interests are completely free to enter retailing, either by setting up a new business or by acquiring an existing one. No distinction is drawn in this matter between foreign interests of different nationalities, all nationalities being treated in precisely the same manner. No registration procedures, rules of behavior, or administrative arrangements apply to a foreign-owned business that do not apply to native interests also.

Participation from abroad, overwhelmingly from Britain, is already significant, particularly in the supermarket business. It has been estimated that non-national interests held about 6 percent of the Irish retail market in 1966, and in local markets (e.g., in the Dublin supermarket trade) the percentage was considerably higher.[12] Expansion by these interests is no more subject to official control than is expansion by Irish interests. The proposed legislation on mergers, takeovers, and monopolies, referred to earlier, could however prove significant in the future.

Official policy could not be said to encourage further foreign penetration in

Irish retailing. Foreign investment in Ireland is welcomed, especially when, as in manufacturing, it leads to job creation that would not otherwise take place, or brings to the economy know-how and market contacts otherwise unobtainable. These advantages do not normally accompany foreign investment in retailing. The rate of change of employment in job creation depends on the rate of growth of sales and productivity; job creation cannot take place in retailing on any significant scale independently of the general level of internal demand as it can, for example, in export-oriented industry. Irish retailing has developed sufficient native innovators to make it unnecessary to rely on foreign interests to spread the latest retailing methods.

While foreign investment in retailing has few attractions, it could have some disadvantages. An externally-controlled business that is part of a larger chain may be treated managerially as an operating unit of that chain, resulting in the important decisions being taken outside the country. No country views this practice with enthusiasm; it may be tolerated if benefits accompany it, but it is not attractive in itself. It could have adverse trading effects if the local unit were to be supplied with externally manufactured goods, which home manufacturers could equally well supply, as a result of a centralized group-wide purchasing system. The practicability of such a system increases as trade becomes freer. The top managerial posts in the local unit could be reserved for foreign personnel, depriving local staff of outlets for advancement that they could otherwise legitimately hope for. External management could act in a way contrary to local preferences in labor relations and other matters, possibly inadvertently through lack of appreciation of local conditions. It cannot be said that these disadvantages have attended to any significant extent foreign participation in Irish retailing to date, but the greater the extent of external participation the greater the possibility of them arising.

These arguments were considered at length by the Distributive Trades Committee of the National Industrial Economic Council (of which more later), which concluded in 1968 that it was not advisable that official action be taken to restrict external interests in distribution, but recommended that developments be closely watched.[13]

Apart from the desirability of controlling external interests in retailing, the practicability of doing so would have to be considered. An EEC directive requires that countries grant freedom of entry into retailing to interests from other member-states of the Community. The Anglo-Irish Free Trade Area Agreement contains a provision to the effect that Britain and Ireland affirm that it is their general policy not to impose restrictions on economic enterprises that operate in such a way as to frustrate the benefits expected from the freeing of trade between them.

The general attractiveness of investment in Irish retailing to external and particularly American interests would not seem to be high. There are larger, richer markets in nearby countries, and the opportunities for reaping the benefits of the application of modern methods have been largely exploited already, to a greater extent, perhaps, than in some other countries. Furthermore, margins in many trades in Ireland have traditionally been lower than in other countries.

Policy Towards Inter-firm Relationships

Ties Between Retailers. Most retail trades in Ireland have a national trade association; the extent of support for associations differs from trade to trade, and there is considerable variation in the degree to which associations can claim to represent their trades in all regions. There is no public requirement that a retailer belong to a trade association. In general the authorities' attitude towards trade associations could be described as favorable, provided that they do not attempt to restrict competition. It is recognized that trade associations can provide many useful services for their members, and assist them to increase their efficiency, particularly in the more fragmented trades. Trade associations form a common front in the Federation of Trade Associations, to which twenty retailer and wholesaler associations belong. The federation acts as the main means of putting the views of distribution as a whole to government and other bodies.

Cartels and Competition. Public policy is firmly against cartel arrangements or any other collective means of limiting competition in retailing, and the Fair Trade Commission is responsible for implementing this policy. When the Commission was constituted in 1953 there was "creeping paralysis of price competition in large areas of distributive trading",[14] and a tendency towards the freezing of distributive arrangements without allowance for economic change. Some trade associations had been active in maintaining and extending these conditions. The variety of methods that could be employed (not all necessarily by trade associations) is evident from the following list of practices about which the Commission received complaints during its first year of existence.

> The practices in question include limitation or regulation of entry to trade, resale price maintenance by manufacturers, price fixing and margin fixing by trade associations, punitive action against traders who have not observed such fixed prices or margins, conditional sale arrangements, exclusive dealing or limited agency arrangements, the confining of channels of distribution, attempted coercion of suppliers, restrictive arrangements with external associations and agencies, and various other devices alleged by complainants to restrain or suppress competition unfairly or to the disadvantage of the public.[15]

In general these practices have ceased to apply on a wide scale. This has been due in part to the activity of the Commission and also to changed economic circumstances. The spread of these practices had been fostered by post-war shortages, and by the lack of strong economic growth, which sometimes made a captive, if stagnant market, held by strangling competition, more attractive than an attempt to acquire a growing market in conditions of free competition. The Commission's philosophy, as illustrated by its actions over eighteen years of its existence, could be said to be pragmatic. It does not appear to hold that the maximization of competition is always necessarily desirable, or that the aim should be followed without reasonable regard for the economic and social consequences for those in the trade in question, making allowance for the economic climate prevailing.

The Commission has taken action in several trades against the practice of a trade association getting the agreement of a manufacturer or wholesaler to supply goods only to members of the association. The Commission has not, however, taken the view that a vendor need necessarily supply a retailer in all cases. The Orders and Rules usually provide that a supplier may apply to the acceptance of orders for his goods such terms and conditions as are reasonable in the interests of efficiency and economy in production and distribution or are necessary in the legitimate interests of the supplier's business, provided that the terms and conditions are applied equitably to all persons seeking supplies. The Orders and Rules generally contain provisions prohibiting suppliers from refusing to sell to traders because of the prices charged or because traders are not members of a trade association.[16] Under most Orders and Rules a supplier is required to apply his terms and conditions of sale equitably to all seeking supplies. Suppliers are generally required to submit their terms and conditions of sale to the Commission, on request, or in certain cases automatically (e.g., motor cars, radios). It is open to a person seeking supplies to complain to the Commission that a supplier's terms are unduly demanding. In one case the relevant Order empowers the Commission to require the amendment of terms and conditions of sale. In other cases the Commission may make Fair Trading Rules in relation to terms and conditions. Generally the matter is rectified by the Commission, on receiving a complaint that it feels is justified, informing a supplier that in its view his terms and conditions of sale are unduly onerous. It has never been necessary for the Commission to proceed to the next step open to it if the supplier declines to change his terms, that is to hold a review of the Order relating to the trade in that commodity, leading to an amendment of the Order designed to bring about a change in the supplier's terms (e.g., an amendment that would make it obligatory for the supplier to alter his terms and conditions of sale on lines stipulated by the Commission).

In a small number of cases where the Commission received complaints of refusal to supply commodities for which Orders and Rules had not been made, and where the circumstances did not warrant an Enquiry (e.g., cosmetics), the Commission accepted that a refusal to supply could be justified where the supplier already had sufficient outlets in the area. Refusal to supply continues to be the subject of many complaints to the Commission.

Size Restrictions. So far the Irish economy has been small enough, and free entry to retailing has resulted in a sufficient degree of competition to make restrictions on store or firm size unnecessary. It is conceivable that the recent rapid growth of supermarket chains could change this situation, particularly if the number of chains were reduced further through takeover.

Vertical Integration. Vertical integration between production and retail distribution is fairly common in Ireland; trades in which it occurs are clothing (particularly men's clothing), footwear, bread and confectionery, filling stations,[17] and grocery. A noticeable difference between Ireland and Britain is the very small number of brewer-owned licensed premises ("tied houses" in English parlance) in Ireland. This difference is probably due to the long-established dominance of one firm over the Irish market for beer. Integration may be exclusive, as in parts of the mens' clothing trade, where the products of the sole manufacturer-distributor are on sale; in other trades (i.e., grocery) the proportion of all sales represented by the firm's own products may be very small. In general, vertical integration has not had undesirable effects.

Inter-type Competition. Inter-type competition, that is competition between retailers in the same trade but of different size, operating method, or original commodity allegiance, certainly exists in Ireland, and relationships are sometimes strained as a result. This is particularly the case in the grocery trade, where there have been expressions of discord between supermarkets and smaller operators, and where more than one association independent of the main association for the trade has been formed to fight for the small independent shop. Similar tensions may exist in other trades where organizations employing modern techniques and adopting aggressive pricing policies are in competition with businesses run on traditional lines. The opening of a multiple store branch in a town that was previously the preserve of local shopkeepers can provide an illustration of these tensions at their height. Such competition is not regarded as requiring special control, subject to the observance of fair trading practices. It is inevitable that competition generates friction, which can be particularly noticeable in retailing, where expressions of individual feeling have not been replaced by the more dispassionate corporate voice.

Inter-sectoral Relationships. Until recently there was little official action taken with the specific objective of influencing relationships between retailing and other sectors. The government tended more to listen to individual interest groups, retailing included, and to invite their opinions on matters of direct interest to them, than to create any machinery that would foster the formation of a common view through the interplay of the views of individual groups. The former policy of industrial promotion through tariff protection did have the effect of enforcing close links between Irish retailers and manufacturers, but this was an incidental effect.

However a government committed to a policy of economic development in a free economy can find it useful to have a forum where its views and those of the various interest groups can interact on one another as part of the process of exploring the field of practicable economic action. For this reason the National Industrial Economic Council was established in 1963. The mandate of the Council was terminated early in 1971. The question of the formation, in succession to the Council, of a more broadly-based National Economic Council is under consideration.

The members of the Council, twenty-seven in all, were nominated by the government, the Irish Congress of Trade Unions, the Federated Union of Employers, other employer organizations, State Boards, and the Federation of Irish Industries, Ltd. Four of the members of the Council in 1970 had a direct working interest in the distributive sector; Mr. John Walsh (a government nominee), who was chairman of the Fair Trade Commission; Mr. Patrick Kelly (a government nominee), who is Secretary of the Irish Agricultural Organization Society, a farmers' cooperative organization with distributive interests; Mr. W. J.

Fitzpatrick (a nominee of the Irish Congress of Trade Unions), who is general secretary of a large union for distributive workers; and Mr. Leo Keogh (a nominee of other employer organizations), who is Secretary of the Society of the Irish Motor Industry, which among other things caters to the retail motor trade, and who was formerly general secretary of RGDATA, the largest trade association in the grocery trade; Mr. Keogh is also Secretary of the Federation of Trade Associations. General economic policy was the main field of work of the Council, and the Council was well equipped to see this field from the viewpoint of the distributive sector.

In the period preceding the establishment of the Council the Irish industrial sector had been closely studied to find out how it was equipped to cope with the transition to free trade. Little attention had been paid to the position of the distributive sector, and the Council therefore established a Distributive Trades Committee consisting of a number of its members or their alternates. The considerable knowledge of the distributive sector possessed by these individuals was supplemented by that of a small number of experts who joined the Committee with observer status, but taking full part in discussions. The Committee completed two reports on the distributive sector that explored its economic characteristics and future, and discussed current developments and problems in the sector, some of which are touched on later in this chapter.

Public Influence on the Retailing Process

Location

The location of shopping facilities in Ireland is influenced by the requirements of land-use planning legislation.[18] This legislation is not directed specifically at distribution, but applies to a very wide range of building and construction works and to the use of land and structures. A planning authority is required by law to prepare a development plan for its area, with a map, designating areas for particular uses (e.g., residential, industrial, etc.). In the cities and larger towns the zoning of areas for particular uses is naturally more sophisticated than in smaller centers. In making a development plan a planning authority has to assess the future land requirements for a variety of different land uses, including retailing, and to make provision for these in its plan compatible with other objectives such as improvement of the street system, urban renewal, and preservation of amenities.

Development plans can affect retailers in two ways. First the viability of an existing trading location may be affected. Since the overriding purpose of planning is to guide change so as to create environments that are economically efficient and of an acceptable quality aesthetically and otherwise, it does not necessarily follow that it will be in the interests of the community to protect particular groups of shops or to preserve all shopping districts in their existing form. Retailers may also be affected by planning legislation when they come to construct new premises. Planning permission will have to be sought from the local planning authority, with recourse on appeal to the Minister for Local

Government. Permission can be refused outright, or can be made subject to conditions.

The zoning provisions determine where new development such as shops and warehouses may be located, but, subject to that, the general principle has been that planning control should not be used to restrict competition between commercial interests (e.g., by refusing permission for a supermarket in the interests of existing smaller shops). In a zone where shops are admissible the particular form or type of shop is of concern to the planning authority only in relation to design, layout, and similar planning considerations. Planning permission is not required for a change in the type of trading carried on in an existing shop, with the exception of changes of use to the sale of fried fish, pets, and motor cars. Not only may the use change from, say, grocery to a hardware shop, but internal alterations and those that do not materially alter the external appearance of the structure are also exempt from planning control.

Public authorities also affect shop location indirectly through the provision of housing. In Ireland, as in many other European countries, a significant proportion of the housing stock is owned by local authorities. New local authority housing developments in the cities are frequently on a major scale, and create completely new retail markets. Some of the newest shopping center developments in the Dublin area were built to cater to new housing built for the city authority. The city authority has reserved locations for shopping centers in a number of its housing developments, and has invited tenders from developers. The developer may purchase or lease the land; the corporation (the city authority) retains a portion of the equity of the project.

Plant and Facilities

Virtually the whole of the capital equipment of the distributive sector is privately owned. Even the provision of municipally-owned markets is on a smaller scale in Ireland than in some continental countries. Parking facilities present a different picture. Until relatively recently the entire community regarded the public streets as free and uncontrolled parking areas. In many towns and cities this is still the situation, but increasing traffic congestion is enforcing a change. Parking meters are now in operation in central Dublin and some control on parking on this or other lines will no doubt be necessary in other urban areas in coming years. Retailers undertaking new developments are now often required, as a condition of obtaining planning permission, to provide parking space; and even where this is not so, retailers sometimes find it advantageous to provide free parking facilities as an attraction to customers.

So far, the street plan of most older and central urban areas has remained virtually unchanged since the pre-motor car age, often since the eighteenth century or earlier. Traffic direction on these streets may have been limited or changed, with severe effects at times on particular shopping areas. Local authorities have done little to provide new parking facilities such as multi-story car parks, and congestion was not severe enough or income levels high enough in the past to make these an attractive commercial proposition. In Dublin, however, the municipality has recently decided to arrange the provision of car parks in association with private interests. Temporarily vacant sites awaiting redevelopment have provided most of the available central city off-street public parking.

Finance for Capital Investment

The Distributive Trades Committee of the National Industrial Economic Council took a particularly close interest in the availability of capital for fixed investment in distribution. The capital needs of retail outlets are continually increasing; at the same time banking practices in Ireland have changed in a way that sometimes makes it more difficult for a retailer to raise finance for expansion than in the past. Banks are less prepared to let customers carry large overdrafts for years, thus using current accounts for capital needs. They are also taking a closer look at the financial soundness of projects for which finance is sought. In a field changing as rapidly as distribution it would not be surprising if they felt that a substantial allowance should be made for risk, an allowance that some otherwise attractive propositions would be unable to bear. The banking groups have set up associated investment banks that are prepared to advance medium- and long-term finance, but these are, in general, only interested in the larger retail project. They charge somewhat higher interest rates than are charged on current account overdrafts. Some retailers feel that a financial institution that has advanced them a large sum on a medium-term basis is bound to seek a greater influence in the running of their business than would a bank granting the traditional overdraft accommodation.

The NIEC Distributive Trades Committee, with the assistance of trade associations, carried out a survey in a number of trades that aimed at finding out the experience of retailers in securing finance for capital purposes. The results of this survey have been reported.[19] The general picture revealed was not unduly disturbing, although the response rate, even after considerable promotional work by some trade associations, was so low as to raise doubts about the validity of conclusions drawn from the survey data. About half of the finance sought by respondents was raised, and finance was made available for approximately two-thirds of projects contemplated by them. The survey showed that the commercial banks were a much more important source of finance than other sources (e.g., merchant banks, hire purchase companies).

The Committee felt that while unduly easy access to finance could result in an oversupply of shopping facilities, there was the danger under existing arrangements that worthwhile projects would be denied capital, and traders otherwise capable of survival would be squeezed out of business. It therefore recommended that the possibility be considered of the Industrial Credit Company, a state-owned finance house for industry dating back to the 1930s, extending its facilities to retailing and wholesaling. The company had been thinking along the same lines, and it is now providing capital loans to the distributive sector. The funds invested by the company in services (including distribution) exceeded £2 million in 1971, and represented 8 percent of its total invested funds.

Merchandising

The choice of lines a retailer stocks is, in general, left to himself. There are no general restrictions requiring certain lines to be stocked, or prohibiting combinations of lines. Merchandise range varies widely, from the spread of the general rural store, stocking the diverse needs of a farming community, to the specialist city center shop.

Control of vendor relations. Since the Restrictive Trade Practices Act does not make any practices illegal, there is no general legal control of vendor relations. It is not necessarily illegal for a retailer to solicit discriminatory prices, nor for a vendor to terminate a dealer franchise arbitrarily. The position depends on whether or not a Restrictive Trade Practices Order is in force proscribing the action involved. The action could alternatively be contrary to a Fair Trade Rule, but since Rules have not the force of law the action would not be illegal; breaches of a Rule could, of course, lead to further action by the Fair Trade Commission and the Minister.

The Fair Trade Commission has been concerned to ensure fairness in the terms of sale by vendors, particularly, but not solely, in the grocery trade. The Commission accepts that a vendor may divide purchases into separate classes to which different terms and conditions of sale apply, but the division must be fair, and should have an economic justification, and within each class the relevant terms and conditions should apply without unfair discrimination. The Commission has often intervened to secure better terms for individual retailers who had good grounds for expecting them, and to secure full wholesaler terms from manufacturers for retailer buying groups. Sales promotion by manufacturers supplying the retail trade have also been reviewed by the Commission. Where rebates are granted to retailers during the period of a sales promotion the Commission believes that the gearing of the rebates should not be such as to be unduly favorable to large-scale customers. Where rebates are granted as part of a sales promotion involving special advertising, etc., the Commission considers that manufacturers ought to consider the desirability of relating rebates to objective criteria, such as the specific contribution that a retailer is expected to make to the promotion. A report on the grocery trade by the Fair Trade Commission is expected shortly, and the Minister for Industry and Commerce has said that he expects it to deal, inter alia, with the problem created by the concentration of purchasing power in the hands of owners of supermarket chains.

Shelf Loading. A particular supply practice in the grocery trade, which the Commission previously investigated, is shelf loading, where a manufacturer's employees load his products on to the shelves of a supermarket. This service is obviously worth something to the retailer, but it is one that for operational reasons does not appeal in small shops, whose operators nevertheless feel aggrieved at the sight of their larger competitors getting it free. The Commission's view was that where a facility such as shelf loading is provided, it should be made available to all retailers of the same class. Unfair discrimination between large and small shops would be removed "if manufacturers who provide the service were to make an appropriate charge to the retail shops which avail themselves of it."[19]

Resale Price Maintenance. There has been no general prohibition of resale price maintenance; like other restrictive trade practices R.P.M. is dealt with by means of Ministerial Orders and Fair Trading Rules. Most Orders and Fair Trading Rules prohibit resale price maintenance, whether collective or individual, and collective price fixing. Manufacturers may recommend prices under the Orders and Rules, but they may not, in general, withhold supplies for failure to abide by these. Resale price maintenance has been greatly reduced in many trades and the scope for its further abandonment is limited.

Price Control. The legal basis for price control is the Prices Acts, 1958 and 1965. These give the Minister for Industry and Commerce power to control prices by Order. Powers given by Order are for six months only, but orders may be renewed indefinitely. Price control is mainly applied at the pre-retail stages. Manufacturers may not increase the price of a product without giving three months notice to the Minister for Industry and Commerce, who may prohibit all or part of the increase. Increases in the margins of importers and wholesalers are similarly controlled. A wide range of commodities, embracing the lines sold by most retail outlets, is affected by these requirements. Price control is not normally applied at the retail level, competition being relied upon to ensure that increases in retail margins are not excessive. Under the Prices Acts, however, the Minister for Industry and Commerce can fix maximum retail prices by Order, and if competition fails to control retail prices he can use this power. In 1970 the Minister required the licensed trade to withdraw liquor price increases that had been charged; prices in this trade were earlier decontrolled after a period of control. Complaints of overcharging at the retail level are officially investigated; the possibility of having prices fixed by Order is normally sufficient inducement to cease overcharging.

In October, 1971, a National Prices Commission was established to keep commodity prices and charges for services under review, and to advise the Minister for Industry and Commerce on these matters. The main activities of the Commission, as described in their monthly published reports, concern price control, price surveillance, and exemption from detailed price control. The Commission is concerned with prices at the pre-retail stage.

A Prices (Amendment) Bill was introduced in the Dáil (Parliament) in July, 1971, with the aim of strengthening price control and extending it to areas such as professional fees.

Special Sales and Trading Stamps. Special sales are common in Ireland, particularly in department stores; and there is no official limitation on their frequency or duration. Neither is there any current limitation on trading stamps.

Customer Credit

With the exception of hire purchase, credit arrangements between retailer and customer are not controlled. The amount of deposit required in hire purchase agreements for consumer durables, and the length of time allowed to pay off the outstanding balance can, however, be controlled in accordance with the government's current demand-management policy. The growth of price-competitive trading, coupled with higher living standards, has led to a decline in the practice of retailers granting credit to customers, except by way of hire purchase.

Promotion

The interest of the Commission in promotional practices has mainly been directed at the grocery trade, because most of the friction generated by these practices has been in that trade. Trade associations complained to the Commission about the practice of dual-pricing, in which a retailer advertises a "normal" price together with the low price that he himself charges. The association claimed that the "normal" prices quoted were frequently higher than the prices actually prevailing. The Commission concluded that the practice is "in reality a form of deceptive pricing, and, as such, would be in the realm of consumer-protection measures which is outside the scope of the Commission's responsibilities."[20] The Grocery and certain other Orders and Fair Trading Rules do, however, permit a manufacturer to withhold supplies from a retailer who displays the manufacturer's recommended retail price together with a lower price charged by the retailer.

*Hours of Trading and Conditions
of Employment*

The hours of trading in shops and the conditions of employment of shop workers, including their working hours, are regulated under separate enactments, the Shops (Hours of Trading) Act, 1938, and the Shops (Conditions of Employment) Acts, 1938 and 1942.

The main provisions of the Shops (Hours of Trading) Act are:

1. Shops must close at 1 P.M. one day each week for a weekly half-holiday. Many trades are exempt from this requirement; those not exempt include drapery, hardware, furniture, jewelry, and footwear. A "mixed" business that might trade to a limited extent in one of the non-exempt lines is obliged to close for a half-holiday.
2. The Minister for Industry and Commerce may make orders regulating the opening and closing hours of any shops or classes of shop (with some exceptions) in specified areas.
3. The Act originally prohibited Sunday trading except in certain businesses

(e.g., grocery, newspapers and books, tobacco and liquor, motor supplies). The immediate dissatisfaction caused by this prohibition resulted in its revokation.

The coverage of the ministerial orders (under provision 2) regulating opening and closing hours is far from total; many areas are free of regulation in this way. The initiative for making orders lies with the traders in an area who may make representations seeking to have one made.

The principal provisions of the Shops (Conditions of Employment) Act that are now in force are:

1. restriction on the employment of juveniles. No one under 14 may be employed in a shop, and anyone less than 14 may work in a shop only parttime.
2. the maximum working day was fixed at eleven hours, and the maximum working week at forty-eight hours. Rules for mealtimes and breaks in the working day were also laid down.
3. employees must be given a weekly half-day and at least fourteen days paid holidays a year.
4. requirements on sanitation, ventilation, heating, lighting, and seats for women workers were laid down.

A prosecution for an offense under the Act may be initiated by the Minister for Labor, an employee, or a trade union official.

There have been suggestions that these acts are, to a certain extent, outdated. New patterns of trading, such as "mixed" lines in supermarkets, have emerged that were not contemplated in 1938, and which can sometimes be obstructed by the Shops (Hours of Trading) Act. The trends towards one-stop shopping in a country where the two-car family is very much the exception, and towards the employment of married women (still low by the standards of some European countries), and the urge to maximize the use of capital-intensive supermarkets and shopping centers, have combined to increase the extent of late-night trading, which is curtailed in areas where Hours of Trading Orders exist. The conditions under which unionized employees work are now considerably better than is required by law, and labor market and union pressures, not legislation, are in practice the means by which working conditions are maintained and improved. In many trades Sunday trading is rare (e.g., clothing and drapery, supermarkets, department stores) even though it is not illegal. Religious considerations, employees' preferences, and some doubt as to the strength of public demand combine to maintain this position.

The volume of demand for changes in legislation has not been great and changes would not be welcome in all quarters. It is probably that the existing controls have had no significant effect on the rate of diffusion of modern trading methods. Employees in distribution are, of course, covered by the same state health, social welfare, and redundancy payments arrangements as are workers in other sectors.

Collective bargaining is the normal method of determining wage and salary rates and conditions of employment for the retail workers who are organized into trade unions (approximately 40-50 percent of all retail workers). In cases of dispute recourse may be had to the Labor Court, a statutory body that is not a court of law in the normal sense, but one that aims at settling disputes by investigation and conciliation. Wage settlements may be made for a particular trade in a given area (e.g., the grocery trade in Cork) or for an individual firm or group of firms.

Wage increases in Ireland in the post-war period have generally proceeded by way of rounds, which have been characterized by a national pattern of increases of about the same amount, either in absolute or in percentage terms, for workers in manufacturing, distribution, and services. The level of settlements may be influenced by what are regarded as "key" agreements, sometimes arrived at after strike action, or may be settled by a national agreement between the major organizations representing employers and workers.

Government Assistance to Retailing

Financial assistance for capital investment has already been discussed. But other governmental activities, outlined below, are also helpful to the retail trades.

Training in Distribution

There is no comprehensive system for training all employed in distribution. In certain trades (e.g., butchers, licensed premises, drapery, hardware, grocery of the non-supermarket kind) entry into employment is normally by way of apprenticeship. Apprenticeship in distribution is not supervised by a statutory body as it is in certain crafts. The degree to which employment can be taken up in the distributive trades in which apprenticeship is normal by those who have not served an apprenticeship depends on the nature of the understandings reached locally between managements and workers. In particular areas and trades employment may be restricted to union members.

In Dublin apprentices are provided with out-of-the-shop training in the School of Retail Distribution, which is run under the local Vocational Education Committee, a public body. Courses, organized in cooperation with the relevant trade union and employer bodies, are provided for the drapery, footwear, grocery, meat, and fish and poultry, hardware, stationery and office equipment and licensed trades. The courses last three to four years and lead to a diploma or certificate awarded by the trade association. The school also runs other courses, including courses for managers.

Outside Dublin the situation is not as good. The Department of Education now awards a National Certificate in Distribution, and courses leading to this qualification have been organized in various centers, but have met with a mixed response. A number of Regional Technical Colleges are being established, and it is intended that provision for distributive training will be made in them.

The Irish Management Institute, which is the premier body for management education in Ireland, has a separate division responsible for the distribution sector, and has greatly expanded its activities in this area, embracing both wholesalers and retailers. Courses of varying length are run by the Institute, dealing with all aspects of distributive management. The Institute is a private, non-profit-making body managed by a Council representative of industry and commerce. Part of its income is by way of state grant. Additional state assistance is given by way of subvention towards the fees paid by those attending courses run by the Institute. The Irish National Productivity Committee, which is state financed, has also provided short courses in selling methods at many locations throughout the country.

A statutory body, AnCo (The Industrial Training Board), has been established with the aim of improving the standards of vocational training at all levels, management included. Although its ambit extends, by law, to distribution, AnCo has concentrated its initial efforts on manufacturing industry.

Market and Operational Research

Census Studies. A Census of Distribution in Ireland was first carried out by the Central Statistics Office in 1933, and subsequently in 1951, 1956, and 1966. A Census for 1971 has been held. The Census gives figures on an area basis, and by individual trade, of sales, stocks, gross margin, numbers engaged, and their employment status; commodity information was also sought in the 1966 Census. Further data on the distributive labor force, including occupational data, is available in the results of the Census of Population. An index showing monthly changes in the level of retail sales in the various trades is constructed by the Central Statistics Office on the basis of sample returns. Papers analyzing and commenting on the principal results of the 1966 Census of Distribution have been prepared.[21]

Inter-firm Comparison. The Irish National Productivity Committee, which is supported by state funds, has established a Distributive Trades Productivity Committee. This consists mainly of persons who are involved in distribution either as managers or as employee representatives. The Committee is served by a full-time staff, including consultants, and is concerned with all means of raising productivity in distribution. It has sponsored, with trade associations, inter-firm comparison schemes in a number of trades. It has also undertaken a program of research into the distributive sector, and a work on voluntary groups has been published.[22]

Projection. Three successive national programs of economic development have been adopted by the Irish Government for the period 1959-1972.[23] The Second and Third Programs involve macro-economic targets. During the preparation of the Second Program an elaborate system of projection at individual industry level was created with the dual aim of validating the targets at macro-level by examining whether they were consistent with expectations at micro-level, and also providing a quantitative background for discussions between civil servants, managers, and trade unionists about the problems of industries and the measures needed to solve them. This process was extended to distribution, and projections of retail sales and employment in 1970 were prepared in 1964 and discussed with management and union representatives. The conclusions that can be drawn so far about the accuracy of these projections has been outlined.[24] The principal differences between projection and reality appear to have been that the rate of growth of productivity, defined as sales at constant prices per person engaged, was considerably higher than anticipated, and that the share of the consumer's pound captured by retailing did not decline as projected. Less attention was given to detailed projections in the preparation of the Third Program, and more to the policies to generate economic growth; as a result separate projections for retailing were not produced, and the scope of the discussions with industry was reduced.

Consultancy Services

The state assists retailers in using the services of consultants in two ways. A technical assistance scheme is operated by the Department of Industry and Commerce under which grants can be made available towards the cost of employing consultants. Originally this scheme was confined to manufacturing, but it was later extended to distribution. In the case of distribution, grants of up to 50 percent of cost are confined to consultancy services provided through the collective efforts of distributors, whether through the Federation of Trade Associations, individual trade associations, or other approved groups; they are not available to individual distributors engaging independent consultants. Distributors may also engage the consultants employed by the Irish National Productivity Committee, the cost of whose services to the distributor is subsidized from the funds provided to the Committee by the state.

Functions of Retailing

Government Attitude

The functions that retailing carries out in Ireland are much the same as in other European countries. The main concern of the government is not to limit or change these functions, or to guide them towards objectives other than those retailers would themselves naturally follow, but to see that they are efficiently carried out. A qualification to this is that the government would prefer that, other things being equal, retailers would give preference to Irish goods, and would give at least equal promotion to Irish goods when they are equal or better in price and quality to the imported articles. The aim, as mentioned earlier, is not to avoid the obligations of freer trade. In all countries the imported article tends to have a "snob" appeal; this is particularly so in a recently industrialized country where some consumers tend to have long, and sometimes unfair, or imagined, memories of the quality of goods produced decades back when native industry was in its infancy, and to let these influence their shopping decisions long after any grounds for this discrimination have ceased to exist. Happily this attitude is virtually dead. Campaigns promoting Irish goods have been periodically mounted, and these have been directed primarily at consumers, but at distributors also.

Tax Collection

Tax collection is another function of distribution. A turnover tax is levied by the central (but not local) government at both wholesale and retail level. This tax is calculated as a percentage of the turnover of a business and is currently at the rate of 10 percent at the wholesale level (15 percent for some consumer durables such as cars and boats), and 5 percent at the retail level. The base of the retail tax is broad, covering virtually all goods and services sold at retail level, including necessities such as food and clothing. Essentials (food, drink, tobacco, medicines, clothing, fuel, and hydrocarbon oils) are exempt from the wholesale tax. A retailer has to register with the tax authorities and pay them the retail tax related to his turnover. (Retailers with a turnover below a certain low figure are not obliged to register, but are then charged the tax by those supplying them.) It is a matter for the retailer to determine how he will recover the tax he pays, whether by alterations in the prices of his goods, possibly on a selective basis, or by adding a fixed percentage to the total of all retail bills. Competition is relied upon to ensure that retailers do not use the tax as a reason for unduly raising their prices. The retail turnover tax was introduced in 1963 and the wholesale tax in 1966; both will be withdrawn and a value-added tax on the lines adopted in EEC countries will be introduced.

Social Functions in Rural Areas

Retailing has important socioeconomic function in Ireland, particularly in rural areas. Its importance as a source of employment and income in an economy yet to achieve full employment is obvious. Less obvious is its role in providing a social focus in rural areas; the rural shop is a center of local information and gossip that is not without value in a country where farmhouses are normally situated on the land-holding, sometimes in very remote locations, instead of being grouped together in villages on the model common in continental Europe. The act of purchasing goods in a rural shop may last only a fraction of the time taken by an involved social ritual. The value of this social function is not confined to the customers; it may also be shared by the proprietor and his family, particularly if the proprietor is an old person, possibly living alone, who might otherwise tend to drift out of the social life of the area. The importance of the social fabric in rural areas, in which shops are an important feature, is well recognized in Ireland, since there have been many cases where it has been grievously damaged by emigration and late marriage. The social and economic role of shops in the life of a small Irish town has been described in a revealing sociological analysis. [25]

Retailing and the Exporting Manufacturer

Finally, retailing has an important function as a testing ground for Irish manufacturers. The size of the Irish market often dictates that the growth of a firm beyond a certain size must be through exports; this also applies to the Irish economy as a whole. Irish manufacturers have been increasingly successful in foreign markets. The job of penetrating a foreign market is made easier if the distribution channels and marketing systems there are familiar. Since distribution in the EEC and Britain is changing rapidly, with modern techniques being applied on an ever-increasing scale, it is important to the manufacturer that these techniques are being adopted in Ireland also, thus relieving him of the problems of having to cope with two markedly different marketing systems. Irish retailers can help export growth also by drawing up and insisting on standards of quality and design from Irish manufacturers that are set up to internationally acceptable levels.

May 1972

Notes

1. *OECD Observer,* February, 1970.

2. The combined populations of Dublin City and County was 849,542 in 1971.

3. Michael Ross, *Further Data on County Incomes in the Sixties* (Dublin: Economic and Social Research Institute, 1972).

4. *National Income and Expenditure, 1970* (Dublin: Stationery Office, 1972).

5. J. Sexton, "Retail Trade in Ireland. A study of its structure and an analysis of trends over the period 1956-66," paper delivered to the Statistical and Social Inquiry Society of Ireland, 1970.

6. Fair Trade Commission, *Appendix to Annual Report for the Year Ended 1.12.1960* (Dublin: Stationery Office, 1961).

7. Ibid.

8. Ibid.

9. Restrictive Trade Practices Bill, 1971.

10. Fair Trade Commission, *Report for the Year Ended 31.12.1962* (Dublin: Stationery Office, 1963).

11. See note 9.

12. National Industrial Economic Council, *Report on Change in Distribution* (Dublin: Stationery Office, 1968).

13. Ibid.

14. Fair Trade Commission, *Report for the Period Ended 31.12.1953* (Dublin: Stationery Office, 1954).

15. Ibid.

16. Fair Trade Commission, *Annual Report for the Year Ended 31.12.1968* (Dublin: Stationery Office, 1969).

17. Vertical integration is indirect in the case of filling stations. A fairly common (though not typical) arrangement is where a filling station is owned by an Irish-registered company, which is a subsidiary of a British Company, which may be, in turn, a subsidiary of one of the major international oil companies, with production interests.

18. The principal planning law is the Local Government (Planning and Development) Act, 1963.

19. Fair Trade Commission, *Report of a Review of the Operation of the Grocery Orders* (Dublin: Stationery Office, 1966).

20. Ibid.

21. C. Lyons, The Census of Distribution 1966 (Dublin: Irish National Productivity Committee, 1970). Also see Sexton, "Retail Trade in Ireland."

22. Irith National Productivity Committee, *Voluntary Groups – A Study of the Development of Voluntary Groups in the Non-food Trades* (Dublin, 1969).

23. These were the First and Second Programmes for Economic Development and the Third Programme for Economic and Social Development. All were published by the Stationery Office, Dublin.

24. R. J. Curran, Contribution to the discussion of J. Sexton's paper. See note 5. To be published in proceedings of the Statistical and Social Enquiry Society of Ireland.

25. John A. Jackson, *The Skibbereen Social Survey* (Dublin: Human Sciences Committee, Irish National Productivity Committee, 1967).

10 Israel

DOV IZRAELI

Introduction

Observers of the Israeli scene and visitors to the country are frequently impressed by the progress achieved in certain sectors of the economy. At the same time, they are puzzled by the relative backwardness in other sectors. In fact, considerable differences in the levels of economic development do exist side by side. This is one of the reasons why it is difficult to make a comparative study between Israel and other countries, or to place it along the continuum between highly developed and underdeveloped countries.[1]

A striking example of the inconsistency in sectorial development is the contrast between the sophisticated advances made in agriculture and the low standard of retailing. This situation seems ironic when one considers the popular stereotype of the Jew and his traditional occupational roles in exile. For generations, Jews were prohibited from owning land and were consequently prevented from farming. Yet in Israel, Jews have proved to be excellent farmers using methods and achieving results comparing favorably with those of the most advanced countries. On the other hand, while Jews were reputed to be good traders and, where given the opportunity, became successful entrepreneurs and innovators, particularly in retailing, this sector in Israel was, and to a large extent still is, at a very low level. Even the small progress achieved in retailing during the last decade was initiated mainly by the government,[2] which also got foreign investors and the consumer cooperatives interested. The explanation for the inconsistency and apparent contradition is rooted in the historical development and socioeconomic structure of the country.

Here, two major orientations in the historical development of Israel's socio-economic structure may be considered as having influenced the development of retailing and the emergent public policy towards it: (1) the ideology, values, and activities of the Zionist movement, particularly those of its pioneering socialist sector; and (2) the policy, values, and activities of industrialization, modernization or westernization in the Israeli economy and society.

These two orientations often have had contradictory effects on the development of retailing and on the public policy towards it. The two have operated concurrently and with varying relative strength from the beginning of Zionist settlement in Palestine in the 1880s. Still, it is convenient to analyze the evolution of public policy towards retailing in terms of three eras, each featuring a different emphasis: the "Zionist Era" (1882-1947) during which ideological considerations were dominant; the "Transition Era" (1948-1959), which began with an emphasis on the first orientation, but gradually shifted towards the second, which became more dominant during the "Industrialization Era" of the 1960s.

The Zionist Era: 1882-1947

It was always the dream and aspiration of Jews to return to the Holy Land. In fact, this country was never empty of Jewish population as some Jews always stayed, and others joined them as individuals or in small groups. When the first wave of modern Zionist immigration started in 1882, there were 24,000 people in the Yishuv, a term used to refer to the Jewish community of Palestine, prior to the establishment of Israel.[3] As a result of five major waves of immigration, the Jewish population grew to 646,600 by 1948 when the State of Israel was established. By 1968, the population of Israel was 2,841,100, out of which 2,434,800 were Jews.

Immigration to Palestine (and later to Israel) was the cornerstone of Zionist ideology and the manifestation of active Zionism. Another aspect of the Zionist ideology was the creation of a "New Society" of Jews through the establishment of new settlements and a break with many of the traditional occupations of Jews in the diaspora, that is, the countries to which they had been dispersed:

Unlike the general run of modern Jewish immigrants, the attainment of economic goals or personal security was not of prime importance for the immigrants to Palestine. These goals were largely subordinated to social and cultural aspirations—to the establishment of a new type of wholly Jewish society, modern, mainly secular, autonomous, and economically independent. The objective of the new community was not economic betterment and a rise in the standard of living, but rather the normalization of the community's economic and social structure and the complete reversal of the usual Jewish economic structure in the diaspora. Hence the great emphasis on the "return to the soil" as an essential agricultural basis for the community, as its primary occupational foundation. Hand in hand with these attempts went a strong emphasis on social justice and security, especially among the various socialist sectors of the movement. These sectors also tended to subordinate economic considerations to certain basic premises of social solidarity and to weaken the individualist and competitive aspects of modern economic activity. Thus, although the establishment of a modern, economically adequate community was strongly stressed, this was not envisaged in purely economic or technical terms but was rather set within the framework of a new national entity.[4]

Certainly, not all the immigrants arrived as "idealists" who left behind them comfortable homes to create this "new national entity." Many Jews were forced to leave their countries in Europe because of pogroms, persecutions, and wars. Yet, even those usually had the choice between emigrating to American and other more promising countries or to Palestine where the promise of personal security and the attainment of economic goals were much less. It was not that these people did not want to improve their economic situation but rather that they were willing to sacrifice a measure of opportunity in following the idealist groups—if not to "return to the soil," then at least to undertake some "productive" work in town. Within the context of an ideological community that stressed productivity, it was no wonder that retailing was regarded in the original Jewish community as an inferior occupation suited only for people who could not be productive (e.g., the old and disabled), or even more serious, for people who excluded themselves from the general norms of the society.

The most negative attitudes towards retailing and retailers stem from the ideology of the socialist sector of the Yishuv, particularly the "pioneer" groups. These groups, disappointed with the outcome of the social reform movement and the October Revolution in Russia, constituted the second wave of immigration (1905-1914). They came with a radical ideology and determination to create a new society. Their spirit was of self-sacrifice for the sake of the community, with great emphasis put on the future needs of such a new society. They created social, economic, cultural, and political institutions which greatly influenced the structure of the Yishuv and even the State of Israel up to this time.

The "Halutz" (the Hebrew word for pioneer, meaning *avant-garde*) was the ideal type of the Yishuv. A large proportion of the population either came with the Halutz groups, joined their collective settlements *(Moshavim)* or communes *(Kibbutzim),* or at least supported them by affiliating with their political parties within the Labor-Zionist movement in town. The education in most schools and youth movements was in the spirit of the Halutz according to which trade and commerce were anathema; and to call a person a middleman *(Metavech)* was an insult.

However, since retailing services were needed for the population and as outlets for the producers, the labor movement encouraged the establishment of consumer cooperative societies by its members in town. Dozens of small cooperative societies established shops in workers' neighborhoods. These shops *(Tzorchaniot)* were usually a little bigger than the privately-owned shops, and they handled mostly food. All the consumer cooperatives were loosely integrated members of the Consumer Cooperative Federation. The elected directors of the cooperatives were usually politicians in the Labor Movement who had neither much training, experience, or interest in retailing, nor did they have the financial incentive to devote more time and effort to improve their performance.

The most important exception to this trend in retailing during the Zionist Era came about with the arrival of the German Jews in the early 1930s. Among them there were experienced retailers who knew modern methods and who saw retailing as a respectable occupation even in the Holy Land. At that time, they could still take out some of their capital, which they invested in the development of modern retail institutions such as chain stores and variety stores. Even their small shops were on a higher level than what had existed before them. One could speculate that a new trend would have started, but the outbreak of conflict with the Arabs and the British in the years 1936-1939 and later, the

Second World War, stultified retail development. Only a small number of these German retail stores were opened, mostly in the three large urban centers of Tel Aviv, Haifa, and Jerusalem.

Public policy toward retailing under the British Mandatory Government (1917-1948), as in other spheres of commercial life, was to institute law and order on the one hand, while minimizing its intervention on the other. Consequently few laws were passed. The Israel government inherited all mandatory laws (except for those officially declared null and void), and these served as the basis of the legal framework of retailing after 1948. The relevant British legislation was as follows:

The Product Labels Ordinance (1927) proclaims that the customer must be advised on the quality and quantity of the product, and it enables the authorities to control or to supervise these matters. Manufacturers have to mark all their products, and deceiving descriptions constitute a criminal offense.[5]

The Trade Mark Ordinance (1937) protects manufacturers and merchants from imitations of their trade marks, and it regulates the registration of trade marks, including those which are registered abroad.[6]

The Weights and Measures Ordinance (1947) fixes the standards for weights and measures and requires compliance with these standards.[7]

The Food Control Ordinance (1942) empowered the authorities to control the distribution of food.[8]

Local Authorities Ordinance (Business Tax) (1945) permits local authorities to pass by-laws levying a municipal business tax. It is interesting that local authorities used the authority granted them by this ordinance mostly in respect to retailing. Retailers claimed that it is a discriminatory law, and the Merchants' Association is still engaged in trying to have it repealed.[9]

The Transition Era: 1948-1959

With the establishment of the State of Israel in 1948, the national efforts of the Yishuv sharply intensified. They were concentrated in four major areas: the War of Liberation, absorption of mass immigration, new settlements, and production of food and other basic necessities. Each of these areas of intensified efforts brought changes unfavorable to the development of retailing and to the public attitude and policy towards retailers.

The War

While the war for survival went on, many retailers took advantage of the shortages and rationing of consumer products, by selling in the black market. This further strengthened the negative image of retailers in the eyes of both the general public and government bodies. Ironically, the government's administration of product distribution strengthened the economic and political position of retailers and of their trade association because: (1) retailers enjoyed the benefits of a sellers' market coupled by rationing and rapid inflation; and (2) their trade association gained power vis-à-vis its members as well as vis-à-vis the government by serving as a channel through which the government administered its controls and rationing policies. At the same time, this situation of noncompetition offered no motivation for retailers to improve their shops and services.

Absorption of Mass Immigration

Within the first two and a half years of statehood, the Jewish populations of Israel more than doubled. Most of the immigrants were refugees from European and from Arab countries who came with practically no capital means. The absorption had to be done rapidly, and mostly by public bodies such as the government and the Jewish Agency.[10] The major tasks were to provide housing and jobs. All the buildings in the absorption centers were built and/or owned by public bodies. The retail shops in these neighborhoods were used to solve the welfare problems of old and disabled immigrants.

A survey conducted in nine towns[11] revealed that 52 percent of the retail outlets were given to social welfare cases as a source of income. Table 10.1 shows that about two-thirds were food shops. The survey, however, did not cover other types of outlets such as market stalls, newsstands and various types of kiosks that were almost exclusively reserved for welfare cases.

Table 10-1

Distribution of Shops According to Trade

Trade	Rehabilitated		Non-Rehabilitated	
	No.	*%*	*No.*	*%*
Food	249	66	137	39
Textiles and Clothing	43	11	74	21
Houseware and Furniture	19	5	43	12
Other Shops	67	18	97	28
Total	378	100	351	100

Source: Berler and Yavin, p. 18. "Rehabilitated" refers to welfare cases that were given stores by government agencies, in contrast to "non-rehabilitated" persons who acquired stores by other means.

This survey also showed that in addition to being old or disabled, the rehabilitated retailers were on the average less educated and less experienced than the other retailers in those towns; and Table 10.2 reveals that the rehabilitated retailers had a much lower rate of success.

This policy of the public authorities was obviously a reflection of the attitude of the ruling labor movement that looked down upon retailing and considered it as an occupation suitable only for those who could not do anything more productive. This attitude, as can be seen in Table 10.3, prevailed well into the 1960s and to some extent still persists.

The same attitude prevailed among the general public as well. In fact, most of

Table 10-2
Distribution of Retailers According to Degree of Success

Degree of Success	Rehabilitated		Non-Rehabilitated	
	No.	%	No.	%
Success	38	10	106	30
Medium	217	57	205	59
Failure	123	33	40	11
Total	378	100	351	100

Source: Berler and Yavin, p. 23.

Table 10-3
Distribution of Shops According to the Years Received

The years in which the shops were given to disabled people	Rehabilitated		Non-Rehabilitated	
	No.	%	No.	%
Until 1952	11	3	30	8
1953–1956	31	8	9	3
1957–1961	237	63	121	35
1962–1963	99	26	191	54
Total	378	100	351	100

Source: Berler and Yavin, p. 19

the non-rehabilitated retailers did not have a much higher level of education, training, experience, or entrepreneurship. They opened shops for very similar reasons as those classified as rehabilitated, except that the investment was made by their own family and/or by other charitable, social, or political organizations.

New Settlements

Hundreds of cooperative or collective agricultural villages *(Moshavim)* and dozens of towns and urban centers were developed during the first few years of Israel. The requirements of these new places for retail outlets were resolved in three different ways:

1. Each new *Moshav* received a *Tzorchania* (a cooperative shop) which sold food and some other necessities for households and farms. It was owned by the members of the *Moshav* and managed by a hired manager. In most cases, the manager was of low calibre and the service provided was unsatisfactory. In recent years there has been a trend towards improvement by the introduction of self-service and/or by leasing the *Tzorchania* to private individuals.
2. The Labor Movement was interested in developing consumer cooperatives in

all the new immigrant urban centers. Since most of the post-1948 immigrants, however, were not educated or indoctrinated with the Zionist Socialist ideology, the Federation of Consumer Societies was required to develop a cooperative shop without consumers being members of cooperative societies. Later, the private sector in Israel raised the issue of the Tzorchania as an example of how the Histadrut (the Federation of Israeli Workers) was pushing away private enterprise in the attempt to take over the whole economy. Although there is an element of truth in this claim, there were two other major reasons for this development. First, retail outlets were needed in every settlement even before there were enough customers to support them. Only a retail organization which was willing and able to give the service without expecting immediate profits could open such stores. Second, many of these settlements were far from the established urban centers and their inhabitants poor. It was proven that in places where a cooperative store was not opened, private retailers increased prices unreasonably and exploited their poor customers in many other ways. Hence, even today, the existence of consumer cooperatives is considered to be a safeguard against increase in prices wherever the competition mechanism is not enough to provide for it.

3. The absorption authorities[12] did build small shopping centers with the development of every urban center. The shops were given to welfare cases or rented very cheaply to people who had, or could mobilize, some means of their own. These people were not of the types that could play the role of merchants in community building as in the American West, nor was the socioeconomic environment supportive in this direction.

Production and Trading Controls

As long as basic consumer goods were in short supply and some of them rationed, there was little sense in devoting much public effort to improve marketing or retailing methods. Most of the economic development efforts went into agriculture which could provide the necessary food. Agriculture could also accomplish other national goals such as the absorption of immigrants at relatively lower cost, the settlement of certain areas for security and political reasons, as well as the realization of the ideology of returning to work the land. While there was some development of manufacturing prior to and during this era, it was not an area of economic priority. Since there existed a sellers' market, the retailers themselves did not find it necessary to improve their own methods even when and where they were able to do so.

Typical of government policy during the Transition Era is the *Commodities and Services (Control) Law (1957).*[13] This law gives authority to the Minister to declare any commodity or service to be a controlled one (Article 4). For such controlled commodities and services, a minister may prescribe:

(1) a maximum price for controlled commodity; (2) a maximum profit which

may be derived from the sale of a controlled commodity if a maximum price has not been prescribed for it; and (3) a maximum remuneration for a controlled service or a class of controlled services . . . (Article 6).

Besides, a Minister may direct by order (such an order being referred to as an "acquisition order") the acquisition of any controlled commodities if he is of the opinion that it is necessary to do so in order to prevent the hoarding, concealment, unreasonable withholding from the market or from use, or the illegal use, thereof . . . (Articles 6 and 7).

All basic foods and many other products were declared controlled commodities, as were certain services such as barbering and car rentals. The law also specified that prices must be displayed on all controlled products and services, and that the sale of a controlled product must not be conditional on the buyer's purchase of another product.

Hitherto, the government had exerted its control by implementing the laws, and the orders and regulations which had been enacted by the British Mandatory Government during World War II. To these, the Israeli government had added specific orders which were found to be necessary.[14] Toward the end of the 1950s, the trend was to free the economy from many of the wartime controls. However, the country was still in a state of semi-war with the Arab states and one could not be certain when a new open war would break out (as indeed happened in 1956 and 1967). The problem was resolved by enacting the Commodities and Services (Control) Law (1957) which contains a provision limiting its use to times when a state of emergency is officially proclaimed. Such an official state of emergency has in fact existed from the first day of the establishment of Israel. The authority of the Minister to issue such orders is limited to cases for which "he has good reasonable grounds for believing that it is necessary to do so for the maintenance of an essential activity or the prevention of profiteering and speculation."[15] The last word, "speculation," is of particular interest because it reflects what was the dominant image of retailers and retailing in the labor movement. The Hebrew word in the text of the Law is *Safsarroot,* which the dictionary translates as "brokerage," and the person who does it is a *Safsar,* translated as "middleman." In the colloquialism of the Labor Movement, however, it became synonymous with "speculation" or "speculator," and the terms were heavily charged with negative meanings.

Although the processes of change were gradual, 1959 may be taken as the last year of the Transition Era in the economic development of Israel and of its retail trade. The transition was from a market of scarcity and rationing to surplus and competition, and from a sellers' market to buyers' market, in many consumer goods. Between 1954 and 1959 rationing of food and other basic consumer goods was gradually abolished and never reintroduced despite the persistence of a state of war. Government control over prices was reduced to a few products such as bread, milk, and gasoline.[16] The population enjoyed a continuous rise in the standard of living (the average annual rate of increase between 1956-1959/60 was 5.6 percent), and demand increased for more variety and better quality of food and clothing as well as for electrical and other household appliances. The end of the Transition Era marked a major change in government policy towards both production and marketing. Until then (1959), the main efforts had been concentrated on supplying the needs of the population and reducing imports by replacing them by locally produced commodities. The emphasis had been on developing physical and technical capacity for production, while costs and quality were treated as issues of secondary importance. However, towards the end of this period the government expressed the change in its views and outlook concerning economic development as follows:

Our industry is now going over to a new way of thinking. Henceforth efforts will be directed to a large increase in exports, the lowering of costs, the improvement of quality, the "deepening" of production, and greater efficiency and better organization in marketing . . .

If our industry is to be adapted for exports, we will need certain organizational instruments and will have to develop marketing channels at home and abroad. "Individualism in production—Cooperation in Marketing" is a watchword that will demand a change in our thinking and a psychological preparedness that have hitherto been alien to Israeli manufacturers.[17]

This statement of policy was articulated through two laws. The first was the revised Encouragement of Capital Investments Law (1959) whose object was to attract capital to Israel and to encourage initiative and investments of foreign and local capital.[18] The benefits stemming from this law are granted to enterprises and investments that are approved by the Investment Center, which is the Government Office responsible for administering it. An investment is approved under this law if it is made in a foreign currency by a non-resident. In addition there are benefits for "approved enterprises," which are granted to export industries or those built in "development areas." At about the same time, the government realized that the current state of retailing in the country was inadequate for a modern economy. By the year 1958, the Ministry of Commerce and Industry had started to shift its main interest in retailing from that of supply, rationing and price control to the improvement of the system.[19]

The government did not see much hope in improvements coming from the then existing retailers or retail structure. The decision was, therefore, to offer the benefits of the new investment law to foreign retail organizations that would introduce modern retailing methods into the country. While the law attracted a limited number of foreign investors, such as Supersol Supermarkets and the Shalom Department Store, their entry into the market stimulated a process of modernization in Israeli retailing.

The second law was the Restrictive Trade Practices Law (1959).[20] The explicit purpose of this law was to prevent the formation of cartels and monopolies, but there were many exceptions stated in the law itself. Furthermore, the law does not *forbid* restrictive arrangements, but allows anybody who considers himself to be hurt by such arrangement to complain before the Supervisory Council, which is a special public body for the administration of the Restrictive Trade Practices Law. The parties to the arrangement must file their agreement with the Supervisory Council, which is authorized to decide whether to approve, disapprove, or restrict the agreement. The criteria for such decisions are stated in Article 28 of the law, which specifies when a restrictive business arrangement can be considered in the interest of the general public. The law was used to prevent resale price maintenance practices by manufacturers and retailers. Article 28 has also often been used to encourage manufacturers, wholesalers, and retailers to form buying and/or marketing organizations. The underlying assumption was that small business firms operating in a small country would not be able to compete effectively in world markets unless they united to do it.

The change in attitudes of the Labor Government and its official policy towards the distributive trades were gradually developed during the last few years of the Transition Era. However, they were finally explicated only in the second plan for industrial development:[21]

The advancement and development of commerce in Israel must be approached with great care. For many years, retailing was used for the absorption of immigration and to resolve welfare problems. This fact makes it difficult to take stringent actions about retailing structures. It is clear that in dealing with organizational and structural changes, we must take into consideration the outstanding individualism in retailing, the old age, and the background of retailers, all of which make it difficult for them to adjust to new concepts and changes in methods of operation.

The Ministry will encourage . . . chain stores in branches such as clothing, footware, furnitures and electrical household appliances. In these branches, the direct contact between manufacturers and retailers is important and we find that wholesalers did not develop in these branches either in Israel or in other countries. Through such chain stores it is possible to achieve concentration of purchase from manufacturers to enable them to produce in large batches. The Ministry's assistance to chain stores will be given provided that the following factors are secured:

(a) For the chain to be able to guide production and to enable industry to organize its production, it must concentrate a considerable purchasing power. The required minimal size of chain stores from the point of view of their ability to guide and direct production, is currently being investigated. The size of the chain store has ramifications regarding its ability to fulfill other functions in the areas of advertising and quality.

(b) Chain stores should release the manufacturer from problems of financing marketing. Therefore they will have to secure working capital that will enable them to buy with cash as well as to finance inventories and to warehouse them.

(c) Chain stores will assume responsibility for the products they sell. They will test the products received from manufacturers in their own or in other laboratories. It is desirable that the stores which are closer to the consumer and his problems, guide the producer on quality and design. To this end, they should establish technical departments which will plan specifications of quality and design and then control the production accordingly. Since this is feasible only when the volume is large, it has implications for the size of the chain.

(d) It is desirable that chain stores acquire consumer acceptance. This will be achieved by quality control as well as by creating a brand name and by advertising.

(e) The required know-how for the management of these stores should be secured so that the unexpected achievement may be secured . . . In Israel there was an unsuccessful experiment to organize such stores in *Sharsherret* (voluntary chain). Industry will encourage and give its assistance for the establishment of voluntary chains, provided that it will be possible to secure the satisfaction of the above conditions. At the same time, the Ministry will also encourage the establishment of corporate chains while attempting to bring into the country some of the chain companies which already operate successfully in Europe.

The case in the following section will demonstrate how the above statement of government policy was carried out in practice. This case also illustrates some features regarding the state of retailing at the end of the Transition Era and at the beginning of the Industrialization Era.

The Case of the Voluntary Chains[22]

In the autumn of 1958, Israel's first modern supermarket was opened in the heart of Tel Aviv on a major residential and commercial street already lined with grocery stores. This Supersol supermarket was owned primarily by a Canadian group of investors, including the owners of Loeb supermarkets in Ottawa, who brought modern know-how to their enterprise, and declared their intention to build a network of chain stores in Israel within the near future. The owners received government support in the form of financial assistance, economic privileges, and moral encouragement.

The opening of the first supermarket was a turning point of Israel's food retailing. The consumer cooperative movement assessed the situation and decided to follow in the steps of the Supersol stores. It forged ahead with a countrywide program for building modern supermarkets carrying an ever-increasing variety of products, while improving or closing down existing stores as necessary. The first line of attack by the independent grocers, working through the General Merchants' Association, was to try to prevent the opening of the first Supersol branch in the autumn of 1958. At the opening ceremony, hundreds of grocers gathered outside in a protest demonstration, demanding that the government avert this threat to their existence by closing the store. They appealed to various public bodies, including the Prime Minister's Office, and the Ministry of Commerce and Industry to stifle Supersol's expansion plans. The government's answer was that the General Merchants' Association should take more constructive and positive measures in assisting its members to enhance their competitive advantages. It also promised financial assistance to those bodies which would take the initiative and organize voluntary chains.

In April 1958, before the opening of the first supermarket, but while it was being constructed, the General Merchants' Association evolved a plan to establish "The Supplying Company for the Grocers' Chain in Israel." During the same period the Khen-Paldag wholesale company laid down plans for the creation of a wholesale-sponsored voluntary chain of grocers which would be under its management.[23]

The Ministry of Commerce and Industry welcomed the plans of both the General Merchants' Association and those of Khen-Paldag, recognizing these as important efforts to advance food retailing. This welcome received practical expression when the Ministry declared that a special fund would be established to extend loans to retailers for the purpose of modernizing their stores.

The two chains—M.A.H. of the General Merchants' Association and the Chain Company *(Ha'Sharsherret)* of Khen-Paldag—were finally inaugurated in the autumn of 1958 to coincide with the opening of the first Supersol store. Later on, they combined, but then they collapsed for a number of reasons that can be summed up as follows:

1. Negotiations with government bodies were prolonged and fraught with conflict over matters such as source of finances, terms, and conditions of the loans, eligibility criteria, and the like. Unfortunately, the fumbling and procrastination at the implementation stage of this program stifled a great deal of initial enthusiasm and optimism that existed among both the organizers and pioneer retail members.

2. The expert hired to transform the grocery shops into self-service stores concentrated on getting merchants to buy appropriate shop equipment. He had, however, no appreciation of self-service as involving fundamentally different mode of operation to which all aspects of store activity have to be functionally related.

3. The grocers, on the other hand, were not pleased with the conversion and most concluded that self-service was an inappropriate method for them. The small increase in turnover did not justify the relatively large investment and was mitigated by a corresponding increase in leakage. Since the grocers were not trained to comprehend their changed role in the self-service store, and since the stores were not planned with their needs in mind, they gradually reverted to their former pattern of operation, despite the gondolas in the middle of the shop.

4. Wholesalers and manufacturers not associated with the chain struggled to win the buying potential of the chain members. These competing manufacturers and wholesalers tempted member grocers with identical products at below market price in an attempt to undermine their competitors who were affiliated with the chain, and thus ultimately to undermine the chain itself, even if this involved a short-term loss to themselves. The small merchant member failed to realize that, indirectly, it was his membership in the chain that resulted in these sudden cut prices. They myopic perspective of the grocer led him to prefer a 5 percent immediate tangible reduction from some wholesaler to perhaps a 10 percent rebate on the same item, several months later, as a member of the chain. Generally the individualistic merchants believed their years of experience left them with little to learn and feared that chain membership would open them to tax inspection and suspicion.

5. The small turnover for the wholesaler did not really provide the advantages of big-volume buying. Both chains had no recourse to low-interest finance and thus were unable to get advantageous cash discounts. On the whole, the

chains received the regular wholesale discount which was hardly enough to cover the extra expenses of operating such an organization. Furthermore, the organization was top heavy with personnel and inefficient. And as business faltered, delivery ceased to be prompt, and the orders were delivered, at times, not in accordance with those actually placed.

After a year of operation the chain was still too small, its members too scattered geographically, and their respective stores too limited in their turnover to justify the investments made by Khen-Paldag and its services to the members. Shortly after the amalgamation of the two chains, Khen-Paldag was sold to a subsidiary of Supersol. When they found that the chain's volume did not justify even the expenses involved in selling to the stores, Supersol curtailed its activities and officially disbanded the Chain Company in November, 1961.

The Industrialization Era: 1960-1969

Public policy toward retailing in the 1960s must be examined within the context of other environmental factors. The most important of these was the fast rate of industrialization. Between 1960 and 1964, the real investment in industry increased at an average annual rate of 21.6 percent. The rate of investment decreased during the recession and war years of 1965-67 and then increased again by 87.6 percent in 1968 and by 36 percent in 1969. The industrial production tripled during this period from 128.7 index points to 355.6.[24] Although industrialization started in the 1950s, there are some basic differences between the two eras in the nature of industrialization as well as in the effects it had on the country. In the 1950s, industry was almost completely protected from competing imports; and little competition in the local market did not induce industry to be more efficient. During the 1960s, government policy was to encourage only those industries that could show business efficiency under conditions closer to free world trade. The goal was to improve the country's balance of payment by exports and by the replacement of imports according to economic criteria. To this end, the government gradually liberalized imports and started to reduce import duties, thereby exposing local manufacturers to import competition.

Business efficiency thus gradually gained prominence as one of the national goals. Since business efficiency is usually measured in terms of profits, the desirability of profits, and consequently the pursuit of profit, became more acceptable values even within the Labor Movement. This development was in contrast to the values of economic self-sacrifice, self-imposed austerity, and even asceticism which prevailed before, but even the new values were couched in the traditionally ideological terms of the priority of national needs. In addition, the need for marketing and improved marketing channels was gradually recognized as imperative for business efficiency in industry. Public attitude shifted from being negative about private retailing and retailers in general, to a denunciation of their inefficiency and inadequate services for producers and customers. This change in attitude was reflected in the following three areas of public policy which come under the jurisdiction of the Ministry of Commerce and Industry: (1) studies of the distributive trades; (2) advancement of modern retailing; and (3) protection of public interests.

Studies of the Distributive Trades

The first statistical survey of the distributive trades was conducted in Israel in 1962/63.[25] The importance of this survey was explained in the introduction to it:

The purpose of this publication is to assist all those who are involved in directing the trade and services in the country (government offices, trade associations, etc.) who need statistical data in their work. This publication may also be useful for the owners of businesses, for potential investors . . . and for all those who are interested in the structure of the Israeli economy.

Despite this convincing statement, this is the only survey to date that has covered all establishments. In this respect, it supplies the only comprehensive data on the situation of retailing in Israel since the Israeli Central Bureau of Statistics (ICBS), which is the major source of comprehensive data, limited its later surveys (1965/66 and 1967/68) to those establishments with employees.[26] These comprise only approximately 4,000 out of 28,000 (or approximately 14 percent) of the total store population and 30 percent of the total number of people working in retailing.

The ICBS has on occasions been commissioned by government to do other studies of more limited scope. Various government offices such as the Ministries of Housing, Interior, and Commerce and Industry have, in addition, used other public and private research institutions. While each of the studies produced is helpful and important, unfortunately there is no systematic procedure for making them available or their findings accessible to interested parties.[27]

Israel lacks and requires a current comprehensive census of distribution of the British type. Even the 1962 survey is less of a census than estimates derived mainly from data collected for other purposes such as the Population Census of 1961 and the Manpower Survey of 1962.

According to the 1962/63 statistical survey, the estimated number of retail and wholesale establishments in 1962 was 31,150 (peddlers excluded[28]), and the number of people employed (including owners) was estimated at 75,500 or 79,000 (peddlers included), which was 10 percent of the total number of people employed in Israel. Of these, 80 percent or 64,000 were in retailing. The average number of people employed per retail establishment was 2.2 (peddlers excluded), vs. 2.7 in Western Europe (1955) and 5.7 in the United States (1954). Since 1962, the gap between Israel and other developed countries has increased, but exact comparisons are difficult because recent figures on Israel are not available.[29] Normally we associate a high percentage of people employed in services with more advanced economies. In this case it reveals the relative inefficiency of the structure of retailing, particularly its high proportion of small stores. While the 1967/68 survey was more limited in the size of population covered, it collected more extensive data than the 1962/63 survey. The figures on the growth of "organized retailing" are particularly interesting.[30] The survey population included chain stores (three stores or more, and including gasoline station chains), cooperative stores, and department stores. These included, at the end of 1968, a total of 1,133 shops of which 703 were chain stores owned by 26 firms (including 278 commercial stations for the retail sale of petrol and related products); 384 cooperative stores incorporated in 28 cooperative unions and 7 regional and organizational buying groups; and 46 department stores owned by 8 firms. Of the 1,133 shops,[31] about 400 are food shops (220 of which are self-service, including the food departments in department stores).

The predominance of very small stores led the government to try to improve the existing structure by encouraging them to organize into chains. The Israeli government's interest in the distributive trades was restricted to its contribution to the development of industry. The small stores could not supply market information or order large quantities—all services required by industry. The survey of Marketing Channels of Internal Industrial Products 1963/64[32] revealed that: (1) independent retailers bought direct from manufacturers 10 percent of their output while the organized retailers[33] bought 2 percent; (2) independent retailers bought direct mostly from very small manufacturers and workshops while organized retailers bought mostly from the bigger manufacturers; and (3) only 60 percent of the products were sold through distributors in the channel while 40 percent were sold direct to customers or to export.

A comprehensive study was conducted in 1963/64 of six branches of consumer's products. Its conclusions supported the current government policy toward retailing (see above), and were publicized as such.[34] There was another study of Business Establishment in Settlements of 5,000-65,000 Inhabitants for the Ministry of the Interior (1965). Several municipalities have ordered general monographs that include retailing, or special studies about their needs for commercial establishments, and/or feasability studies for planning shopping streets and shopping centers. Of particular interest are the findings of the study on the open markets in Tel Aviv,[35] which revealed that approximately half of the produce consumed in Tel Aviv is purchased in two major open markets, and that about 60 percent of the families in Tel Aviv and many in neighboring towns see the open markets of Tel Aviv as their major supplier of fresh produce. These findings may indicate that there is a need and an opportunity for the development of modern, out-of-town, discount houses and shopping centers, two institutions that do not exist yet in Israel.

A source of difficulty in comparing retailing in the beginning of the 1960s and the end of the era stem from the changes that followed the Six-Day War, as the 1967/68 survey includes the population of East Jerusalem but not the population of other occupied territories. Yet, retailing in the Arab sector is quite different from that of the Jewish sector, and a thorough study should be conducted on this subject as well as on related subjects, such as the effects of the unification of Jerusalem on the two sectors; public policy towards retailing in the occupied territories; effects of the "open border" policy with Jordan, and so forth. All these seem to have had, and may have further, repercussions on retailing in both sectors.

Advancement of Modern Retailing

The official government policy during the 1960s was to encourage the development of more modern and efficient retailing methods and institutions such as self-service stores, supermarkets, department stores, corporate chains, and voluntary chains. Following this policy, the government encouraged and gave financial incentives to foreign investors to start the Supersol supermarket chain. At the same time, it assisted the consumer cooperative societies to develop and modernize their stores, and groups of independent retailers to organize in voluntary chains. While the latter failed, the first two made some progress: Supersol has developed a chain of fifteen supermarkets, with several more planned for each of the next few years. The Consumer Cooperative Societies have converted most of their cooperative stores and have approximately 200 supermarkets and big self-service food stores.

With government incentives such as low-interest loans and tax allowances, foreign investors, together with Israeli investors, opened the first big department store (Shalom) in Tel Aviv. The cooperative movement followed by modernizing its junior department-store chain of fifteen stores, and developed two big department stores (in Tel Aviv and Jerusalem) with several more planned for the near future. Another chain of junior department stores (Shekem) was developed by the Ministry of Defense to provide reduced prices for the families of people who serve in the armed forces. Because of Israel's security problems, a high proportion of Israeli families have somebody in the armed forces (including the police) and can, therefore, buy in these Shekem stores. Other retailers have complained about the unfair competition created by subsidized stores and particularly about the 12½ percent discount given on most products in these stores. The management of Shekem claims that its stores are no longer subsidized, but can extend the discount because they are the most efficient mass merchandising retailers in Israel. Possibly for the sake of better public atmosphere (as well as for increased volume and profits), however, it might be advisable to open these stores to the general public and run the organization on a strictly commercial basis as a public corporation. Such a move may increase the influence of the Shekem stores on their competitors, which is in line with the government's policy of raising the efficiency of retailing.

In addition to encouraging large-scale retailing, the government is trying to advance independent retailers in two ways: (1) by providing low-interest loans for renovations and working capital: 3,200 retailers had, between them, loans aggregating I.L. 500,000 from funds run jointly by the Ministry of Commerce and Industry and four commercial banks;[36] and (2) by financing and encouraging activities such as training courses, seminars, and lectures throughout the country, publications, surveys, and direct consulting services. Most of the latter activities are carried out by the Institute of Productivity, but directed by the Department of Internal Trade in the Ministry of Commerce and Industry.

Protection of Public Interests

Legislation. Only one law with direct relevance to retailing was legislated during the 1960s, the Standard Contracts Law (1964).[37] The purpose of this law was to protect buyers from sellers who make standard contracts in which they take advantage of their respective customers by including unfair conditions, particularly in fine print. In addition, several orders and regulations were issued by ministries regarding standards and markings for certain products, and the control of weights and measures (1963), but the most important development is probably the preparation of the draft for the Fair Trade Law. This law is about to be suggested to the Israeli Parliament *(Knesset)* and is the most comprehensive piece of legislation in Israel, regarding trade, so far. The major purpose of the suggested law is to protect the public from untruthful or misleading information about products, services and their sellers.

Enforcement of the Law. The Ministry of Commerce and Industry sends its inspectors to check the shops' compliance with the law on the display of prices (controllable products). During the budget year 1968/69, the Ministry examined 1,085 complaints by consumers concerning irregular supply, refusal to sell, quality, excessive prices, false weights and measures, and the like. During the same year, 104,539 scales or measuring instruments were calibrated, and 12,100 inspections of shops took place.[38] However, not all the laws are enforced by government. Limitation of manpower on the one hand and the dilemma of how much control and regulation is desirable for the economy, on the other, leave the consumers open to unfair practices by the trade. In addition, there are many borderline cases that must be treated differently than by strict enforcement of the law.

Consumer Protection. The Israel Consumers' Council was established by the Ministry of Commerce and Industry to provide the Israeli consumer with the tools required to protect his interest. The head of the council is appointed by the ministry, which also provide its budget; while the members of the council consist of representatives of various public bodies such as consumers' organizations, merchants' associations, and the like. The Council deals with customers' complaints, makes special inquiries and surveys on products and services, and publishes the quarterly magazine *Da-Ma* which is similar to the American *Consumers' Report.*

The Role of Local Authorities

Entry into retailing is freely open to private enterprise. There are no barriers of entry in terms of nationality, professional training, character references, and the like. This freedom is unlimited geographically with the exception of the *Kibbutzim,* where there are no shops, and the *Moshavim* (cooperative agricultural settlements) where the shops are owned and run by members or leased by them to others. These two comprise approximately 9 percent of the Jewish population.

Most matters related to this subject come within the jurisdiction of local authorities (municipalities and regional councils) who supervise the granting of retail licenses to those incumbents who comply with the prescribed national regulations and local by-laws. These vary with the type of merchandise sold, but usually concern guaranteeing hygienic and safe conditions and setting the minimum limits for store size.[39]

The jurisdiction of local authorities in addition covers zoning ordinances and the provision of such retail facilities as stores and parking space. Unfortunately, some local authorities are more preoccupied with collecting revenues from retailers than with assisting them to improve their services to the community. Some authorities, however, have recently undertaken the redevelopment of municipal areas and have included modern shopping facilities as part of their general plan. Small shopping centers are normally provided when new planned neighborhoods are developed.

By national law, all retail outlets must remain closed on Saturdays and Jewish Holy Days, with the exception of non-Jewish shops in non-Jewish areas and public services such as gasoline stations, eating places, and a limited number of pharmacies. The local authorities have jurisdiction over the opening and closing hours of retail establishments. Opposing pressures are exerted on them by those who prefer to remain open all day and those who demand a regulated mid-afternoon break. Local authorities have enforced a standard evening closing time, but no regulations exist with regard to mid-afternoon breaks in most local areas. The big majority of merchants, however, close their shops between 1-4 P.M. and then reopen until 7 P.M.

Concluding Remarks

A current trend in Israeli retailing is the increasing concern for satisfying the consumer's wants and expectations. Greater attention is being given to creating a pleasant and clean shopping environment, and to giving service to both the public and industry. Many improvements have also been made in response to the requirements of a growing tourist industry. Here, the Ministry of Tourism plays an active role in encouraging the development of better shops, particularly in tourist centers.

It is understandable that a country which on the one hand is industrializing and struggling to improve its trade balance and on the other is at war with its neighbors would be unlikely to give high priority to retail development. Yet, the Israeli government in recent years has encouraged modernization and large-scale retailing. The realization of these policies, however, is hampered by insufficient capital and lack of professional know-how and management skills among retailers. While the government can contribute to the resolution of these impediments, recent developments indicate that the big impetus will come from American and other Western retailers who penetrate the Israeli market.

American retail organizations with international orientation can profitably penetrate the field by contributing capital and expertise while using local manpower as well as some capital resources. A promising organizational structure in this direction is the franchising system, which shows signs of rapidly gaining importance in the world at large. A start in this direction has been made in the fields of services, catering, and industry as international organizations have established local franchised operations. This form of vertical integration is in line with the government's policy and will probably gain public support.

May 1972

Notes

1. See Yoram Wind, *Marketing in Israel,* (Palo Alto, Cal.: International Center for the Advancement of Management Education, Stanford University, 1968), 1-4.
2. "Government" refers to the national authorities. The role of municipalities is discussed towards the end of this chapter.
3. *Statistical Abstract of Israel, 1969.* Israel Central Bureau of Statistics, September, 1969, Table B/3, 20.
4. S. N. Eisenstadt, *Israeli Society* (London: Weidenfeld & Nicolson, 1967), 4.
5. *Laws of Palestine,* Vol. B, 889.
6. *Official Gazette,* No. 742 (9, XII, 37).
7. *Official Gazette,* No. 1563, 1947.
8. *Official Gazette,* No. 1178 (19, III, 42).
9. *Laws of Israel,* ch. 223, 3977.
10. The Jewish Agency is an arm of the World Zionist movement. Its major functions relate to immigration and immigrant settlement. It operates in collaboration with the government.
11. A. Berler and S. Yavin, *Rehabilitation of Welfare Cases by Providing Retail Shops* (Tel Aviv: Ministry of Housing, 1964).
12. There are organizations such as the Jewish Agency and the Ministry of Absorption whose specific function is immigrant absorption, but other government and public bodies play a role in this process as well, such as the Ministries of Housing and Labor.
13. *Laws of Israel,* Vol. 12, 1957/58, "Commodities and Services (Control) Law, 5718-1957", 24-40.
14. For example, the Control on Products and Services (Product Labeling) Order (1950) forbids stocking and distributing products unless they are labeled according to the specification of the law. Yet, it permits private labels by merchants on the condition that the head of the Chemistry and Food Division of the Commerce and Industry Ministry gives his permission to do so.

15. *Commodities and Services (Control) Law (1957),* op. cit., Article 3. The high Court of Appeal may abolish an order if issued for reasons other than those specified by the Law.

16. Following the devaluation of the Israeli Lira in 1971, the government attempted to impose temporary price control measures on manufacturers. The intention was to curb inflationary pressures undermining the benefits of devaluation. The measures, however, proved rather ineffective.

17. *Israel's Future Industrial Outlook 1960-65,* (Jerusalem: Ministry of Commerce and Industry, 1960), pp. 11-12. The slogan "Individualism in Production—Cooperation in Marketing" means that production facilities may be owned and managed by individual persons or concerns, but coordinated through central marketing organizations.

18. *Laws of Israel,* Vol. 13, 1958/59, No. 77, 258.

19. *Israel Government Year Book,* Jerusalem, 1958, 238.

20. *Laws of Israel,* Vol. 13, 1958/59, No. 54, 159.

21. *Plan for the Industrial Development of Israel, 1965-70* (Jerusalem: [Hebrew] Ministry of Commerce and Industry, 1960, 157-58 (translation).

22. Dov Izraeli and Z. Seltzer, *Voluntary Chains in Israel,* (Hebrew), Ministry of Commerce and Industry.

23. Khen-Paldag was the biggest and practically the only big grocery wholesale organization in Israel outside the cooperative movement.

24. Source: *Bank of Israel Report 1969,* Jerusalem, 1970, Table K-1; and *Monthly Bulletin of Statistics,* Vol. XXI, No. 4, Israel Central Bureau of Statistics, Jerusalem, April 1970, 65.

25. *National Survey of Trade and Personal Services, 1962,* Israel Central Bureau of Statistics, Special Publication No. 164, Jerusalem, 1964.

26. *Trade Survey 1965/66,* Special Publication No. 275, ICBS, 1967, and *Trade Survey 1967/68*, Special Publication No. 229, ICBS, 1969. The data on persons employed include employees, working owners as well as unpaid members belonging to their respective families. The reason given for limiting the survey to establishments with employees was the difficulty in collecting data on those without employees. These figures exclude peddlers.

27. The list of surveys gathered for this study is the only compilation of its kind in Israel, although it is probably still incomplete.

28. There is no clear or consistent policy toward peddlers. They are generally considered to be a public nuisance, but little is done to restrict their activities although they are required to obtain a license—a requirement not always enforced.

29. From my personal experience as marketing manager and marketing consultant, many of the estimates seem to be inaccurate. For example, while the figure for the electrical shops is only 750, I at that time supplied some 1,000 stores and this did not include all electrical shops. While the figure for grocery shops is only 7,150, I know manufacturers who supplied 8,000 grocery shops and this, too, did not include all of them.

30. Source: ICBS 1969, 464.

31. This number includes franchised shops.

32. ICBS Special Publication, No. 198.

33. The expression "organized retailer" is used by the ICBS to refer to chains and large retail establishments such as supermarkets, department stores, and consumer cooperatives.

34. A. Niri and Z. Seltzer, *Survey of Distribution Channels 1962/64* (Jerusalem: Ministry of Commerce and Industry, 1965).

35. Y. Cohen, *Size and Location of Retail Markets in Tel Aviv* (Tel Aviv: The Municipality of Tel Aviv-Yaffo and the Ministry of Agriculture, 1967).

36. Israel Government Year Book 5730 (1969-70), Central Office of Information, Prime Minister's Office, Jerusalem, 1970, p. 108. In 1958, $1 = I.L. 1.80; since 1968, $1 = I.L. 3.50.

37. *Sefer Ha-Chukkim*, No. 418, (20/II/64).

38. *Israel Government Year Book,* op. cit.

39. Regulations covering pharmacies require that a certified pharmacist be present at all times.

11 Japan: Rationalizing the Retail Structure

MICHAEL Y. YOSHINO

Introduction

Throughout Japan's modern history, the government has consistently exercised strong influence on the nation's business community. In the early days of Japanese industrialization, the state was, in fact, the promoter, owner and administrator of all the strategic industries. While the government turned over the ownership of all but a few of these industries to a handful of family groups, which became known as Zaibatsu, it continued to have a dominant voice in the strategic industries and financial complexes. In the aftermath of World War II, Japan was subjected to a most thoroughgoing reform by the Allied Occupation. Although the political and economic systems that have emerged subsequently are substantially different from those that existed prior to World War II, nevertheless, the government in contemporary Japan still exerts strong influence over Japanese industries.

William Lockwood, a noted authority on the Japanese economy, succinctly described the close relationship between the government and business in the following manner:

The hand of government is everywhere in evidence, despite its limited statutory powers. The Ministries engage in an extraordinary amount of consultation, advice, persuasion, and threat. The industrial bureaus of MITI proliferate sectoral targets and plans; they confer, they tinker, they exhort. This is the "economics by admonition" to a degree inconceivable in Washington or London. Business makes few major decisions without consulting the appropriate governmental authority; the same is true in reverse.[1]

It should be noted, however, that from the early Meiji era, the government's interest in the conduct of business primarily focused on large business enterprises, particularly strategic mining and manufacturing industries and large financial institutions. Until very recently, it took little interest in the welfare of the myriads of small businesses that have remained extremely important to the economy to this day. This was understandable, given the very circumstances under which Japan's industrialization was initiated and carried out.[2] This close government guidance has been credited with being largely instrumental in promoting Japan's rapid industrialization in the early Meiji era as well as in her phenomenal economic growth in the post-World War II era.

213

Another characteristic of the government's historical industrial policy has been its strong emphasis on production. This too is understandable in view of the fact that in the early days of the country's industrialization, as well as in the postwar economic recovery, production loomed as the key economic necessity. Both the public and private sectors were preoccupied with improving production know-how and increasing productive capacity. The needs of the distribution sector hardly entered into their consideration.

This situation is, however, rapidly changing. Dynamic developments have been taking place in the Japanese distribution sector, particularly the retail sector, in recent years. It has become increasingly apparent to government officials that distribution—especially retailing—has become a major national problem, and systematic programs are needed to help develop viable solutions. This is indeed an opportune time to examine the government's policy toward the retailing sector. The main emphasis of this chapter is on government policy toward retailing, but it is viewed in the broader context of the government's policy toward the entire distribution sector.

It should be noted at the outset that this chapter will not discuss government regulations affecting pricing, promotion, consumer protection, and entry. Reasons for excluding consideration of these topics are two-fold. One is that the Japanese government has thus far taken only a limited interest in this general area; and, furthermore, the existing regulations are highly fragmented under different jurisdictions.[3] Secondly, the government policy emphasis has been almost exclusively on sectoral rationalization, and this is the area in which dynamic developments have been taking place in recent years.

A meaningful way in which to analyze recent developments in governmental policy for the distribution sector is to examine how this policy has evolved historically. During the past two decades, government policies have gone through three clearly identifiable evolutionary stages.

The First Stage: Protecting Small Retail Stores

Covering the period roughly between 1948 and 1962, the first period may be called the protection stage. During this stage, the government's main concern was to protect small independent retail establishments from large-scale competitors, particularly department stores, as well as from special types of retail outlets such as cooperatives.

Restricting Department Stores

Until recently, the department store has dominated the Japanese retail scene as the only large-scale retail establishment. Two hundred or so department stores have been responsible for roughly 10 percent of the total retail sales. The origin of the Japanese department stores, at least in the present form, goes back to shortly after the turn of the century, and by the 1920s they had become well established. The rapid growth of department stores invited organized resistance from small retail stores, and by the early 1930s this resistance had gained momentum. In 1938, such protest culminated in passage of the Department Store Act, designed to restrict the activities of department stores. This act, however, soon became dormant under Japan's wartime economy, and it was abolished during the Occupation in 1947.

By the early 1950s, as the Japanese economy, having recovered from war damages, began its rapid growth, department stores with enormous resources and tremendous prestige at their command soon regained their dominant position in the Japanese retailing scene. With their reemergence to the leadership position, the organized resistance from small retailers once again began to manifest itself. This ultimately led to reenactment of the Department Store Law in 1956.

This law is designed to prevent powerful department stores from unduly repressing small independent retail establishments, which is viewed as being detrimental to the public welfare. The law is designed, at least ostensibly, to protect the consumer's interest by assuring the owners of small- to medium-size enterprises the opportunity to compete. Consequently, it imposes the following major restrictions on the operations of department stores:

1. The approval of the Ministry of International Trade and Industry is necessary to open a new store, to expand the existing ones, or to acquire or merge with another department store.
2. The number of days that department stores can operate in a month, as well as the store hours, are stipulated.
3. The department stores are prohibited from providing certain types of special customer services that are deemed harmful to small retailers. This includes such activities as provision of free transportation for customers to and from stores.

The law also stipulates penalties for violation of these requirements. To advise the Ministry of International Trade and Industry, it established the Council on Department Stores, consisting of business leaders, academic experts, and prominent citizens.

Closely related to the Department Store Law was a stipulation in the Anti-Monopoly Act of 1954 restraining department stores from engaging in unfair dealings with their suppliers. The department stores, traditionally the dominant element in the retailing sector, commanded an enormous advantage in dealing with their suppliers, particularly small wholesalers. They have often capitalized on this power to the wholesaler's serious detriment. Specifically, department stores are barred from engaging in eight specific types of activities, including unfair retaliatory actions against their suppliers, and unfair demands for delivery of goods on consignment. Although these restraining orders were not designed to protect small retailers, to the extent that they curtailed the competitive advantage enjoyed by department stores, they have been a side benefit to the small retailer.

The third legal action to protect small retailers was taken in 1959 in the form of the Special Act for Retailers. The Act placed certain restrictions on the operation of company stores. Large Japanese firms customarily maintain company stores for employees where they can purchase a variety of merchandise at a substantial discount. This service is considered as part of the rather extensive fringe benefits that large Japanese companies offer to their employees. Some of these company stores are of substantial size and pose serious competitive threats to small independent retailers in the area. To minimize this adverse effect, the Act restricts shopping in these stores to employees and their families.

Another important provision of this Act is to require manufacturers and wholesalers to obtain specific approval if they wish to enter into retailing. Finally, the Act authorizes the prefectural governors to serve as arbitrators, upon the request of parties involved in conflicts, between manufacturers and wholesalers, between wholesalers and retailers, and among retailers themselves.

Another legal protection for small retail establishments is found in the Consumer Cooperative Act, which prohibits consumer cooperatives from selling merchandise to nonmembers, unless specific permission is obtained.

How effective have these measures been in protecting small retail stores? The common view is that they have not met the goals for which they were established. This has been particularly true of the Department Store Law, by far the most important of the protective measures. In the opinion of the average small merchant, the law is of marginal value in protecting him from the competition of large department stores. This evaluation is in part substantiated by the fact that between 1956 when the law was enacted and 1969, the number of department stores has increased by some 80 percent, the total floor space has more than doubled, and department store sales have increased 5.6 times. Moreover, through legal loopholes, the rapidly growing mass merchandising firms are virtually unaffected by this law, and this alone has all but negated its effectiveness. Likewise, enforcement of the restrictions on the operation of department stores has been rather lax, as evidenced by the fact that there is only one full-time enforcement official.

One notable characteristic of this stage is that these programs were formulated as part of the government policy toward small- to medium-size enterprises. In other words, it was felt that small marketing intermediaries would deserve protection and assistance, not because they were engaged in distribution activities, but because they were small.

The Retail Structure

In recent years, however, some dynamic developments have been taking place in the Japanese distribution system, resulting in fundamental changes in what used to be a highly tradition-bound field. As background to an understanding of the evolving pattern of public policy toward retailing in Japan, let us review the highlights of these changes.

Despite the fact that Japan has achieved an advanced stage of industrialization, until very recently the distribution sector had remained virtually unchanged for centuries, having retained many of the features commonly associated with the marketing system of premodern societies. For one thing, the Japanese distribution sector has traditionally consisted of a large number of very small establishments. According to the latest Commercial Census in 1968, there were some 1,390,000 retail establishments, or roughly one retail store for every 75 people. These stores had an average of three employees and averaged in annual sales no more than ¥ 9.8 million or approximately $27,000. Over 88 percent of them had fewer than five employees and nearly half were no larger than 200 square feet. As high as 77 percent of all retail stores relied exclusively on family members as the source of labor. Typically, the owners of these very small stores have been barely eking out their daily existence, and some in fact have found it necessary to seek other employment to supplement their meager income from operation of their stores. A recent government survey revealed that some 15 percent of the owners of stores with four employees or less had other sources of income.

Another striking feature of the Japanese distribution sector is that it is highly complex and circuitous. Merchandise, particularly consumer goods, must pass through multiple levels of marketing intermediaries. Particularly complicated is the wholesaling structure. It is not uncommon for merchandise to pass through several different types of wholesalers: primary, secondary, and local. This is evidenced by the fact that in 1968, the wholesale volume was nearly 5 times that of total retail sales (in contrast to roughly 1.4 times in the United States). Less than 20 percent of wholesale establishments (accounting for 15 percent of the wholesale volume) buy from manufacturers and sell directly to retailers.

Further complicating the Japanese distribution system are complex trade customs that have evolved over the centuries. The small size of most retail firms and their limited financial capacities, coupled with strong competitive pressure, force wholesalers to sell to retailers in small quantities at very frequent intervals. In a number of industries, rather elaborate discount and rebate structures have evolved. These are often manipulated according to prevailing competitive conditions and personal relationships between the seller and the buyer.

Another widely-shared characteristic of the Japanese distribution system is that the Japanese merchant class has traditionally been conservative. A partial explanation for this can be found in the historical evolution of the merchant class in Japan. But it is also in part due to the fact that the great majority of the merchants simply have been eking out their daily existence and have had little opportunity or resources to innovate.

The highly-fragmented traditional distribution sector was quite adequate until recently in meeting the needs of the Japanese consumers. Several recent developments are, however, creating considerable strain on the system, making it rapidly obsolete and incapable of meeting the new demands created by these environmental changes. Let us briefly examine these changes.

A Changing Market

Most significant has been Japan's rapid postwar economic growth. Thanks largely to extensive socioeconomic and political reforms undertaken in the immediate aftermath of World War II, the benefits of this economic growth have been widely diffused among the masses. This has led to the emergence of a viable middle class for the first time in the nation's history.

Closely related to the emergence of a mass consumer market is the development of full-fledged consumer industries in postwar Japan. Prior to World War II, large manufacturing firms dominated by the Zaibatsu had confined their activities largely to heavy strategic products and had paid virtually no attention to the limited domestic consumer market. Totally deprived of the military market in the immediate aftermath of the war, however, these large firms were compelled to shift to peacetime production. With characteristic zeal, they sought out new opportunities in consumer-related industries. Significantly, it was these large manufacturing firms that first recognized potential opportunities in the emerging mass consumer market. Out of this dynamic process emerged, for the first time, well-developed consumer industries designed to serve the needs of the domestic market.

Within a short period of time, Japan has become first in world production of cameras, motorcycles, color television sets, and transistor radios, and second only to the United States in the production of cosmetics, pharmaceuticals, home appliances, automobiles, and synthetic fibres. In their aggressive search for rapidly expanding opportunities in the consumer market, large manufacturers have: (1) introduced the mass production system in consumer industries; (2) undertaken a series of active expansion programs which has resulted in a steady increase of their productive capacities; and (3) introduced a wide range of new products, ranging from breakfast cereals and home appliances to synthetic fibres.

With active entry into consumer fields, large manufacturers of consumer goods have begun to place greater emphasis on marketing. In the process, they have departed from the traditional production orientation and have become increasingly marketing oriented. These changes cannot help but have a major impact on the nation's distribution sector.

There are yet two other forces that are now impinging on Japan's distribution system. One is the increasingly serious labor shortage, a by-product of the rapid postwar economic growth. The distribution sector in Japan, as in many other countries, has traditionally served as a haven for those who would otherwise have been unemployed. This, however, is no longer true. For the first time in the nation's history, Japan has begun to experience a rather serious labor shortage, resulting in a steady rise in wages. Between 1967 and 1969, the wage level has tripled and the rate of increase has been rapidly accelerating. No longer can the distribution sector depend on "cheap" labor or family workers. Thus, the traditional modus operandi has been seriously questioned, creating a need for basic reassessment of the distribution structure.

The other important source of pressure is potential foreign competition. The very impressive record of Japan's postwar economic growth has invited increasing demands for liberalization of her stringent restrictions on direct foreign investment. The Japanese government has committed itself to a step-by-step liberalization to be consummated by 1972. Two rounds have been completed at the time of this writing and the third is due soon. As we shall see later, there is a strong possibility that in the third round, there will be substantial relaxation of restrictions against entry of large foreign retail firms into Japan.

In light of these significant environmental changes, the traditional Japanese marketing system has been under considerable strain. Indeed, it is being confronted for the first time with the challenge of having to evolve a system appropriate to a modern mass consumption society. It should be noted that the marketing system, particularly retailing, although dominated by conservatively oriented small establishments, has not been totally unresponsive to these dynamic environmental changes. In fact, though small in number, some very significant developments, spearheaded by highly innovative managers, are taking place. Particularly noteworthy has been the sudden emergence of large-scale mass merchandising retail firms.

There has been a growing awareness among government policy planners that the traditional distribution system in Japan is inadequate to meet the new demands placed upon it by a rapidly changing environment, and that if left alone it would not be entirely capable of responding effectively to these changes. As a result, in recent years there has been, albeit gradual, a rather perceptible change in the government's attitude toward the distribution sector.

In the mid-1950s, in view of the changes examined earlier, it became increasingly apparent to government officials that the past programs designed merely to protect small independent merchants was neither sufficient nor even appropriate in view of the rapidly changing conditions.

The Second Stage: Rationalizing Small Retail Stores

It was against this background that the Committee on Distribution was formed in 1967 within the Council on Industrial Structure, a prestigious advisory committee to the Minister of International Trade and Industry (MITI). This committee consisted of marketing experts drawn from the academic and business communities, as well as other prominent citizens. The organization of this committee indeed marked an important milestone in the evolution of government policy toward the distribution sector. With the naming of this committee, the policy emphasis shifted from attempted protection and maintenance of status quo to positive assistance to small wholesale and retail stores for modernization. Upon the recommendation of the Committee on Distribution, the Ministry of International Trade and Industry developed several specific programs to assist small retailers in their rationalization efforts.

Encouraging Cooperative Stores

The first to be proposed was a measure to encourage establishment of cooperative department stores and supermarkets. The program called for small independent neighborhood stores selling a narrow range of products to pool their resources and jointly construct a large store in a strategic location, and physically move into this central establishment. Under this system, participating stores may remain independent as to ownership and management, or they may merge into one corporation under a unified management. Whenever feasible, MITI encouraged the latter course. The basic objective of this program is to improve and strengthen their competitive ability through reducing duplication of efforts, enabling them to attain greater economy of scale, and increasing customer convenience.

To be eligible for this program, the participating stores must meet the following conditions:

1. There must be more than five participating retail stores.
2. At least 70 percent of the participants must be retail stores with 50 or fewer employees.
3. The proposed stores must have at least 200 square meters or 2,140 square feet of floor space.
4. The proposed building must be designed to meet minimum standards of durability and safety.

To those who qualify under this plan, MITI in cooperation with the prefectural government can extend a loan up to 65 percent of the cost of construction of the store and equipment at 2.2 percent annual interest. The maximum repayment period is fifteen years, which starts within three years after the loan is made. Since its inception, over 100 loans for cooperative department stores and about 60 loans for cooperative supermarkets have been approved.

Modernizing Shopping Districts

Another program designed to assist small retailers is for the modernization of shopping districts. This program is designed to encourage a group of stores located in the same area to cooperatively renovate and modernize the entire shopping district to enhance its appeal to customers. This program grew out of recognition that the modernization of a single store often was not sufficient: in order to attain the maximum impact, it is far more desirable to seek the modernization of an entire neighborhood shopping district. This program calls for renovation of existing facilities as well as for addition of some common facilities such as parking accommodations. To be eligible for government assistance under this program, participating stores must satisfy the following conditions:

1. At least 80 percent of the participating stores have to maintain a store in a proposed shopping district.
2. There must be at least thirty participants, and at least 75 percent of them must be small- to medium-size retail establishments.[4]
3. The proposed center must have some common facilities such as parking, storage, and housing facilities for employees to be used by participating establishments.

Government assistance is made on the same basis as for the program previously described. Since its inauguration in 1964, five such centers have been approved.

Results

While in theory these cooperative approaches are sound, neither program is considered successful. The majority of cooperative stores established thus far have fallen far short of original expectations. Some have been almost total failures. According to one estimate, only a dozen or so out of more than one hundred projects can be considered successful. Several factors may be cited to explain this generally disappointing result. First, the success of such a cooperative venture depends, to an important degree, on the willingness of each member to give up a certain amount of independence and autonomy for the common good. For independent-minded small retailers, this has not been always easy. Another common reason for failure is that competition between participating stores frequently destroyed their unity and cooperation. The absence of effective leadership and capable management has plagued a large number of these projects, and some have suffered from internal power struggles. Finally, in a number of cases, participating stores have found their new financial obligations too burdensome as anticipated cost reduction and greater operating efficiency proved illusionary. The second program, that is, the modernization of entire shopping neighborhoods, has had only limited impact.

Encouraging Voluntary and Cooperative Groups

Recognizing the limitations of these earlier programs, MITI, beginning around 1966, shifted its policy emphasis to encouraging the formation of voluntary and cooperative buying groups. A major strength of this approach is that, unlike the earlier methods, it does not involve drastic actions on the part of participants such as having to move their stores physically, or to give up their independence. The possibility of conflict of interest among member stores also appears to be considerably less than that of the cooperative department stores and supermarkets. MITI began intensive campaigns to promote the concept of voluntary and cooperative chains among small retail and wholesale establishments.

To encourage the formation of cooperative buying groups, MITI has made considerably greater commitments than it did to the earlier programs. It has developed programs to extend both financial and managerial assistance. Low interest loans are made available for the construction of headquarters facilities and warehouses as well as for working capital of chains in their formative stage. In addition, extensive management assistance is offered, including seminars given by experienced American and European authorities on cooperative buying groups as well as intensive training programs for those who will engage in cooperative buying arrangements. Another benefit is the provision of accelerated depreciation on warehouses and other installations. This program is considerably more successful than either of the previous programs. By early 1970, forty cooperative chains with nearly 6,000 participating stores had been organized in a variety of fields including food, apparel, drugs, cosmetics, furniture, and home appliances.

The Third Stage: Concerns for the Total System

While the programs in the second stage were much more positive than those in the first stage, they still focused their attention on the rationalization of traditional practices among very small retail establishments. But they did have the serious drawback of being piecemeal, affecting only a very small segment of the retail sector. By the late 1960s, this limitation became increasingly apparent.

Against this background, the Committee on Distribution and MITI officials began to recognize that a basic assessment of the past approach was in order. No longer did it seem adequate to promote rationalization of only a very limited number of small retailers. The view gradually emerged that the government program must be more comprehensive in scope, and systematic in design. It was concluded that the overriding goal of the government policy should be the development of a viable and effective distribution system on a national basis. This change in outlook is understandable. Rapidly growing mass merchandising institutions were gaining strength and concrete steps had been proposed for capital liberalization. Reflecting these dynamic changes, the Committee on Distribution was given the responsibility of developing well-coordinated and viable programs to modernize the entire distribution sector.

Toward Modernization of Distribution

The Committee, working closely with MITI policymakers, called public hearings, consulted with a large number of experts, and held a series of careful deliberations of its own. In the summer of 1968, it submitted an interim report to the Council on Industrial Structure. The report was appropriately entitled *Perspectives and Challenges of the Modernization of the Distribution Sector*. This was the very first attempt to examine the problems of the distribution sector from the point of view of the entire national economy, and as such it heralded a new era. Since this report is likely to have profound influence in shaping MITI's future policies and programs in this field, it is worthwhile to review the major points and recommendations it proposed.

The report begins with a brief examination of the dynamic changes that have been taking place in the environment in which the Japanese distribution system must now function. It then identifies four major challenges that lie ahead in achieving modernization of Japan's distribution system: (1) thorough examination of the role and function of key marketing institutions, including, of course, a variety of retail institutions; (2) development of proper market conditions and a sound competitive atmosphere; (3) creation of an effective and efficient physical distribution system; and (4) development of the infrastructures and institutional framework to promote modernization of the distribution sector.

Having identified the four major challenges, the report then sets forth the following criteria to be applied in formulating the national policy on modernization of the distribution sector:

1. The policy must seek maximum impact and must contribute to the improve-

ment of significant segments of the nation's distribution sector. Given the number and diversity of establishments engaged in distribution activities, the first step should consist of educational programs designed to create awareness of the implications of relevant environmental changes and the changing role and functions of distribution institutions in a dynamically envolving environment.

2. The policy must be designed to encourage small retailers and wholesalers to take the initiative in attempting their own rationalization and modernization rather than complacently depending on government assistance.

3. The policy should encourage development of model projects with the maximum demonstration effect.

4. Each program should be designed from the point of view of the total distribution system and must be carefully coordinated with other programs. Utmost attention should be given to the protection of consumer interests.

5. Policy should be formulated with close consultation between the government and the private sector.

6. Specific programs would be implemented by seeking maximum cooperations from trade associations, and regional and local voluntary associations of commercial establishments.

Against the foregoing criteria, the report recommends that specific programs be developed in the following areas:

1. *To encourage cooperative actions among small independent wholesalers and retailers.* This is a reaffirmation of the previous programs discussed earlier.

2. *To improve operating efficiency and managerial practices.* The report recognizes that modernization of the distribution sector must begin with rationalization of individual firms. Areas singled out as needing rationalization include improvement of merchandising techniques and of information processing, adoption of self-service techniques, and establishment of central warehouses.

3. *To reorganize labor policy in consideration of the acute labor shortage.* In view of the increasingly tightening labor market, the report recommends programs to promote the introduction of labor-saving management concepts and techniques in the distribution sector. The report also recognizes the importance of training middle management personnel because of the rapidly growing demand for it.

4. *To rationalize trade customs and relationships.* The report notes that the presence of complicated trade practices tends to increase the cost of distribution and it urges that these practices be rationalized and streamlined.

5. *To rationalize physical distribution.* The report recognizes important functions of physical distribution. Particularly critical is the development of an efficient integrated national network of physical distribution through standardization and mechanization.

6. *To promote coordinated development of large-scale distribution facilities.* The report stresses the importance of coordination in the development of large-scale distribution facilities such as shopping centers, wholesale centers,

and warehouses and distribution centers. The report suggests that individual firms give appropriate consideration to selecting sites for these large-scale distribution facilities to achieve the optimum allocation of resources for the benefit of the entire national economy.

7. *To improve collection of commercial statistics.* Recognizing the importance of ready access to detailed commercial statistics to serve as a basis for better planning by individual firms as well as by the entire economy, the report stresses the need for improvement in the collection, tabulation, and presentation of comprehensive commercial statistics, and it recommends the establishment of a computer-based information storage and retrieval system.

8. *To provide needed capital.* The report takes the position that to the maximum extent possible, modernization programs should be financed by private capital. However, given the enormous amount of capital required, it urges the government to channel public funds to finance large-scale projects, thus encouraging the flow of private capital to this area.

These policy recommendations are now being translated into specific actions. Although still in a rather preliminary stage, a number of steps are already being taken. First, a program has been initiated to improve physical distribution facilities. Plans are now being formulated for construction of wholesale centers, trucking terminals, and purchasing facilities. As a step toward rationalization of trade practices, the prevailing trade customs of six major merchandisers were investigated, and, as a result, more efficient trade practices have been recommended. At the time of this writing, a similar study has been undertaken to cover a number of other product categories.

A small budget has been provided for preliminary work on standardization and mechanization of the physical distribution process. Likewise, a modest budget has been approved to explore the establishment of central computer facilities to be used by a number of wholesalers and retailers. A program is also underway to promote rationalization of the distribution sector on a regional basis. This program is expected to be implemented in conjunction with regional development programs. Other measures are under consideration, including the establishment of a specialized educational institution to train future managers for the distribution industry.

In the summer of 1969, the Committee on Distribution made public another important report that was prepared by the Subcommittee on Distribution Policy. Central to this report is application of the systems concept in improving the efficiency of the distribution sector. It stresses that the systems concept can only be successfully implemented through cooperative efforts between the public and private sectors. The report recommended that the government establish a central coordinating administrative body, a series of guidelines for the private sector, and provide loans and special tax incentives to encourage the adoption of the systems concept.

Remaining Problems

The concepts and recommendations embodied in these two reports are radical departures from the rather piecemeal approaches of the previous stage. They are designed to deal with fundamental problems confronting the Japanese distribution system in which retailing occupies a central role. For effective implementation, however, several major problems must be resolved. We shall now consider these problems.

First, recommendations of the Committee are stated in rather vague terms. This is by no means inconsistent with the Japanese bureaucratic tradition under which such a report typically sets the basic tone and direction, while the formulation of specific programs and their implementation are left to bureaucratic functionaries. The real test of success then depends on how effectively MITI can translate these recommendations into viable action programs.

Closely related is the fact that the statutory power of the government to deal with the private sector is quite limited. For a variety of reasons, this has not been a serious handicap in its relationship with large oligopolistic firms; but in dealing with small shopkeepers, bureaucrats face an entirely different situation. The sheer number of shops presents a formidable problem of communication. More basically, however, there is an almost unbridgeable gap in orientation and outlook between the elite bureaucrats and independent-minded small merchants. In dealing with these merchants, short of outright control, the government lacks absolutely effective means to enforce their guidelines. The power of MITI is essentially limited to providing various forms of incentives and moral persuasion.

Another major impediment is sheer indifference on the part of a large number of small retail store owners. They are not responsive to government guidelines. Some are preoccupied in attempting to make a meager daily living, while others, assured of a reasonably satisfactory standard of living, lack proper motivation for innovative changes.

Finally, essential to the successful implementation of these programs is the degree to which MITI can obtain cooperation from other Ministries. While MITI has been largely responsible for promoting rationalization of the distribution sector, jurisdiction over the distribution sector is widely diffused among a number of government agencies. For example, food distribution comes under the jurisdiction of the Ministry of Agriculture. Programs relating to transportation and physical distribution fall under the Ministry of Transportation; whereas road construction, urban and regional planning, and related activities are under the Ministry of Construction. Above all, the Finance Ministry controls the allocation of the national budget. Typical of government agencies elsewhere, interministry rivalry is intense. How to coordinate their activities to the common goal remains a very serious problem.

Policy Toward Foreign Retailers

Let us now turn our attention to examination of the government's attitude toward entry of foreign retailing firms. We have noted earlier that one of the major forces prompting the Japanese government to take greater interest in rationalization of the distribution sector is the mounting pressure for liberalization of the tight restrictions that Japan had imposed on the entry of foreign capital. The Japanese government in the mid-1960s has committed itself to step-by-step liberalization of restrictions of foreign direct investment to be completed by 1972.[5] As of late 1970, the first three rounds have been completed. Thus far, the impact on the distribution sector has been limited. The approach that the Japanese government has been taking in capital liberalization is to designate those industries for which automatic approval will be given without individual government action, provided that certain predetermined conditions are met. In the first round that took place in 1967, some 50 product categories were selected, and in the second round 155 product categories were so designated. In the summer of 1970, the third stage was implemented affecting 332 product categories. Up to this point, however, liberalization has had only limited impact, inasmuch as the industries selected so far have been those in which Japan has clear competitive advantage.

No actions which affected the distribution sector were taken in the first round. In the second and third rounds, only a token liberalization was made in this industry. Only single-store establishments are allowed to enter, and so far chains have been excluded. Despite much prior speculation to the contrary, department stores and supermarkets were excluded from the second stage. Clearly, the government was anxious to exclude large-scale chains from entering Japan until more progress is made toward rationalization.

Conclusion

We have examined the evolution of government policy toward the distribution sector, in which retailing occupies a central role. Clearly, the government programs, though laudable, mark only a beginning. Thus far they have made only limited impact. Of course, in judging the government's progress, it is only fair to recognize its relative inexperience in dealing with these matters as well as the inherent difficulties involved in formulating effective programs in this area. Given these conditions, it is quite likely that viable policies and programs will be formed through a series of groping experiments rather than through a well-thought-out and systematic approach.

It is highly significant, however, to note that when the need for modernization of the distribution sector became apparent, the government stepped in to assume an active role in this field to encourage, supplement, and coordinate the efforts that are made by the private sector. The characteristically programatic and close cooperative approach between the public and private sectors has again emerged in the solution of one of the most critical national problems in contemporary Japan.

June 1971

Notes

1. W. W. Lockwood, "Japan's New Capitalism" in W. W. Lockwood, ed., *The State and Economic Enterprise in Japan* (Princeton, N. J.: Princeton University Press, 1965), 503.

2. For details, see William W. Lockwood, *The Economic Development of Japan: Growth and Structural Change, 1868-1936* (Princeton, N. J.: Princeton University Press, 1954), 3-18.

3. For example, food distribution comes under the jurisdiction of the Ministry of Agriculture. Programs relating to logistics and physical distribution are under the jurisdiction of the Transportation Ministry; whereas road construction, urban and regional planning, and related other activities so vital to the distribution system, are under the Ministry of Construction. The Economic Planning Agency, the Ministry of International Trade and Industry, the Fair Trade Commission, and the Ministry of Welfare share responsibilities in the area of consumer protection. It is noteworthy, however, that virtually all the regulatory power over key marketing activities such as price regulations are in the hands of the central government; and the statutory powers of the local governments in these matters are extremely limited.

4. Small-medium retail establishments are those with less than fifty employees.

5. M. Y. Yoshino, "Japan as Host to the International Corporation" in Charles Kindleberger, ed., *The International Corporation* (Cambridge, Mass.: The M.I.T. Press, 1970), 345-372.

12 Mexico

Douglas F. Lamont

Two fundamental political decisions, which were made by the Mexican government during the era since the 1910-1920 revolution, have had a critical impact upon Mexican retailing. First, in the government's desire to promote effective Mexican control over market decision making, it has created new market institutions, and has given them the economic power to prosper against foreign competition. Some of these marketers supply products and services to retailers either through traditional channel contacts or through government-sponsored forward integration of wholesalers and retailers. Other new marketers are retailers whose reason for being is to service new market segments among Mexico's economically active population. Both types of market structural change have profoundly altered the quantitative and qualitative performance of Mexican retailing.

Second, in the government's desire to promote economic growth, it has encouraged market institutions to modernize their employment opportunities and assortment offerings to both the growing middle class and the burgeoning urban poor. For the middle class, a substantial improvement in its standard of living has come about because retailing, along with other sectors in the economy, has modernized the way in which it carries out its functional activities. However, even though retailing has been upgraded in a similar manner for the urban poor too, they have not shown an equal amount of improvement in their standard of living. For them, growth through domestic control, the hallmark of the Mexican government's involvement in the economy, has been a failure.

The formation of Mexican public policy towards the economy in general and retailing in particular will be discussed below. Emphasis will be given to the differing conditions under which middle class retailing and retailing for the urban poor developed.

The Formation of Mexican Public Policy

Economic planning as practiced by the Mexican government is an abomination to most traditional economic planners. A formal comprehensive plan, which directs investment and predicts output by sectors, is not promulgated officially. What passes for a planning document is a series of public announcements by the Mexican president and by a limited number of high-level subordinates who have planning authority within his government. During each president's one and only

229

six-year term, the governmental bureaucracy implements what the president says about carrying the economy towards the extreme political left; the extreme political right; or, as is the current situation, towards a more central position that will minimize the violent swings in traditional political relationships among competing groups within Mexico. Mexican economic planning, then, is in the hands of the man judged to be the most skillful pragmatist in the country. His success or failure depends upon how good he is at giving just enough government support to the middle class (the white-collar employees of government and business), the military, the urban poor (the unskilled industrial and retail workers), the peasants, or to whichever group needs to be bought off at the moment, without undermining the fundamental political and economic strengths of the interests groups that put him into power in the first place.

For example, Lázaro Cárdenas, president from 1934 to 1940, gained the historic loyalty of the peasants by promulgating "Land for the landless" as the main program of his administration. He turned expropriated hacienda lands into *ejidos,* or small plots of land, that were to be solely for the benefit of the rural poor. Only one of his successors, Adolfo López Mateos, president from 1958 to 1964, followed Cárdenas' land redistribution policy with the same intensity to aid the peasants.

The other presidents paid lip service to this peasant-oriented policy for they were convinced that these *ejidos*—which, in many cases, lacked sufficient water, machinery, and the requisite arable soil—were less efficient than the haciendas as means to increase agricultural productivity. These *alemanistas* (or followers of President Miguel Alemán) wanted the agricultural sector to become capital intensive so that it would create a surplus of exportable products that would earn critically needed foreign exchange to finance their industrialization projects. Along with this, they established state-owned enterprises that partially or wholly monopolized the production and distribution of products and services in the following industries: petroleum, electricity, public storage, retailing to the urban poor, and others. Moreover, they shielded Mexican private industry from some of the rigors of foreign competition through import-substitution programs and other devices. All in all, the *alemanistas* were eminently successful in increasing the productivity of export-oriented agriculture and using the gains from this sector to promote increasing industrialization under close Mexican control.

What were the results of this developmental program? Although only 75 million acres of the total land surface of Mexico are arable, *cardenistas* (or followers of President Cárdenas) forced successive presidents to turn 140 million acres of land over to the peasants. *Alemanistas,* however, won the day by keeping one-half of the arable land out of the hands of the peasants and under the control of their supporters, the hacienda owners. Thus two-thirds of the land that was redistributed to the peasants was non-arable land. At the same time, the annual rate of population was increasing between 3.2 percent and 3.6 percent each year. Thus more and more peasants were finding that they were unable to support themselves, let alone sustain themselves on the land allocated to them.

By necessity, they migrated to the cities. Although manufacturing jobs were being created under the industrialization program, the supply of these jobs was kept dear by restricting the number of foreign competitors who could compete with Mexican firms. This policy drove the peasants to seek work in the distributive sector. Thus, as a consequence of the rapid increase in population, the inability of the land made available to the peasants to sustain them, and the lack of industrial employment opportunities in the cities, disguised unemployment in the retail trades—i.e., a surplus of labor—became endemic within the urban areas of Mexico.

One final note. The creation of disguised unemployment in certain retail trades was a cause of developmental policies followed in other sectors of the economy. Mexican planners thought that the service sector in general played only a passive role in the development of an economy. This did not prove to be true.[1] This surplus labor force was in fact being trained in more modern skills to support the growing number of retail institutions that were coming into existence to service the new middle class and the urban poor. By indirection, government policy had used retailing (and its sister marketing activities) to modernize the skills of the work force. Therefore, this policy, in effect, helped to create the proper groundwork for the well-reported Mexican economic takeoff.

Middle Class Retailing

What passes for market analysis of Mexico's great economic strides since the Second World War is invariably a study drawing attention to the showcase growth that has occured in the standard of living of the urban middle class. The consumption needs of this politically important class forced immediate changes in retailing. The model that was chosen to provide the framework for these changes was the existing one in the United States. There was a conscious effort to copy structure, strategy, and function from the north so as to quickly renovate Mexican middle-class retailing. Moreover, the goods in these retail establishments soon reflected the rapid Americanization of Mexican middle-class tastes with only a very few specialty items catering to the real cultural differences that exist between the two peoples. The feeling that you can get almost everything in Mexico that you could get in the States only a few years back, for just a higher price, dazzles the researcher and has lead him down the road towards false conclusions about the general state of economic health in Mexico.[2] More of this in a moment.

Mexico City's middle class, or 34 percent of the capital's urban population, has family monthly incomes ranging from $231 to $578.[3] Add to this the 4 percent with incomes greater than $578,[4] and the market for most middle-class retailers is complete. Thus 38 percent of the population in the Federal District and the adjacent State of Mexico—about two and one-half million—are consumers with sufficient income to live above the poverty line as drawn by standard of living formulas applicable to Mexico. Who are these people?

Information retrieved from credit card applications made at the department stores in the capital provide a clue to employment background of the middle class.[5] Merchants who own their own retail businesses—the beauticians, the corn millers, the street vendors, and the taxicab drivers—plus their employees, make up about one-third of credit card customers in the department stores. Professional people (from doctors and teachers to bullfighters and jai-alai players) make up 20 percent. Another 15 percent are the government bureaucrats, and another 12 percent work for service companies (banks, insurance firms, and the telephone company). Factory workers and their employers make up 9 percent; and mechanics, plumbers, electricians, and other craftsmen make up 8 percent. The remainder of credit card customers are landlords and other wealthier customers. Few wealthy Mexicans would show up on credit card applications because there is a disdain towards asking for credit among the A/B income group. However, an on-the-spot investigation tracing the purchasing habits of the owners of new cars parked in the lots of department stores and specialty shops suggests that "the carriage trade" is a major segment in the customer market of the capital's retail stores. What volume of retail sales do these market segments generate?

This is an impossible figure to develop with any degree of accuracy at all. The A/B income group plus the merchants, the professional people, the bureaucrats, and the white-collar employees of service and industrial companies buy also from the retail distributor of U. S.-made contraband goods. Many white-line, big-ticket items (refrigerators, washing machines, etc.) and some smaller appliances wind their way through the long supply lines of the smuggler's wholesale-retail distributive network until they are delivered to the homes of their middle-class customers. Other products with high margins, such as the newest synthetic fabrics, the newest household detergents, and the newest home or office stereo-dictation equipment, form a part of the merchandise offered for home delivery through this illegal distribution network.

The middle-class customers themselves make semiannual trips to San Antonio, Los Angeles, and other large U. S. cities to purchase goods they feel are not available in the quality desired within Mexico. It is estimated that one-half of the new cars that are being driven in the streets of Mexico City were not made in Mexico, but were smuggled in across the long frontier with the United States and driven to the capital. Since many Mexican-made automobile parts do not fit U. S.-made cars anymore, there is a large market for automotive replacement parts that also have to be smuggled in from the United States. This also holds true for large and small appliances. Thus the shopping list that middle-class Mexicans take with them on their trips to the United States includes spare parts as well as the typical soft goods merchandise reported in the press. These shopping habits are confirmed whenever an unlucky Mexican shopper is stopped by a contraband roadblock whose police officials cannot be bribed. Usually, the proper bribe sends the returning shopper on his way with his U. S. purchases. For these reasons, then, retail sales in the urban centers of Mexico are a statistic without merit.

A second phenomenon, which usually escapes the U. S. researcher, is that the Mexican military has its own Post Exchange system for retail distribution of goods. The PX system was established as one of the benefits given by the government to the military so that the military would stay out of politics and remain loyal to civilian authorities. Some of these benefits for the military were curtailed as a result of the large cash drain imposed on Mexican governmental agencies by the 1968 Olympics. This change in policy resulted in an increase in retail sales for urban middle-class retail institutions.

Thus the volume of sales generated by the Mexican middle class, as shown by retail sales statistics for urban retail establishments, is understated by a lack of knowledge of contraband sales and by the military using its own distribution system. The urban middle class in Mexico is better off than statistics show it to be through analysis of its historical ability to buy merchandise at retail. Government policy implementing its import-substitution developmental program has altered the locus of retail trade rather than curbing the propensity of the Mexican middle class for quality produced, lower-priced U. S.-made goods. This policy has slowed down the rate at which retail institutional changes could have yielded real short-term, high-payout productivity increases to the Mexican economy.

Government Influence Upon Structure:
The Department Stores

In 1947, the government gave Sears permission to open a department store using the successful merchandising innovations it had introduced in the United States. Its policies included two-page newspaper display ads, modern window displays, and goods on open counters at fixed prices and always returnable. Sears' success has been noteworthy. Now Sears de México is a multiple-branch department store chain with A, B, and C stores whose merchandise assortments reflect neighborhood shopping patterns. It has generated over 1,300 Mexican suppliers so that over 90 percent of the goods it sells are from Mexican manufacturers.[6] Moreover, it has pushed the two traditional, French-style department stores, El Palacio de Hierro and El Puerto de Liverpool, into adopting most of its merchandising innovations. The irony of it all is that in recent years they have earned higher profits on sales than Sears, and thus they have been beating Sears at its own game.

Government Influence Upon Structure:
The Discount Stores

No foreign retail company was asked by the government to introduce the discount store to the lower middle class in Mexico City. This was now the late 1950s and early 1960s and Mexican businessmen had grown up with the government's resolve to rebuild the economy (and its middle-class retail structure) based upon the best examples that were available throughout the world. Mexican discounters copied from the United States model the concepts of fixed low prices and the one-transaction, L-shaped checkout counter. These operations were extremely popular with those middle-class Mexicans seeking lower prices on food and clothing. One traditional retail store, Viaña y Cía, rebuilt its stores to cater to this lower middle class market that was rapidly being captured by the newly established discounters, Aurrera and Gigante.

Over the years, the discounters have had a penchant for going into the prepackaging of land deals for the creation of shopping centers with their discount store as the chief store within the complex. Since the government limits by law the number of stores any chain can operate, one discounter, Aurrera, has set up the Superama supermarkets as the chief store within some of its shopping center complexes so as to, by subterfuge, increase the volume of its non-food merchandise sales in clothing, toys, drugs, and notions. And as this volume has increased, Aurrera has been able to gain significant economies of scale for purchasing more of these items. In this way, discounters have strengthened themselves in their supply markets, and have passed on many of the economies gained to their middle-class customers. Recently, the department stores have followed the discounters in this and have begun to set up shopping centers with their own branch department stores as the main attraction among a host of captive specialty shops. It is too soon to say whether or not the department stores can block the continued outflow of sales to the discounters.

Government Influence Upon Supermarket Operations

Supermarkets that did not have the power of the discounter behind them were unable to expand their numbers rapidly. One of the determining factors in slowing the rate at which supermarkets were established in Mexico was the withholding of the all-important license to sell liquors.[7] These were retained by the traditional food stores; and when they became available, the more affluent discounters cornered the market on many of these licenses.

These licenses are important to the initial profitability of the supermarkets, because the government sets the prices on many of the food items sold by the supermarkets. However, over time, prices begin to creep above the maximum prices set as government surveillance slackens and supermarkets learn how to play the game of bribing price inspection officials. Then the inevitable government crackdown comes again. Prices are controlled at new maximum levels that are somewhat higher than the previous official levels, but not as high as the "free market" rates previously used by the supermarkets. For a time, therefore, profits must be made on liquor and other items that are not price-controlled.

Food prices in supermarkets are affected also by government taxation policy. The government places a higher tax on food as it becomes more and more processed. For example, corn meal sold by weight in the streets by vendors or sold in the public markets incurs a very low tax; however, corn meal that is processed, packaged, and sold under a brand name incurs a higher tax. Naturally, the increased costs due to marketing and taxation are passed along to the middle-class customer.

Finally, middle-class Mexicans are culturally unable to shop for price savings when to do so would reduce the prestige their class gives them in their own eyes.

Comparison shopping shows that chains have one set of higher prices for their supermarkets in the wealthiest sections of the city and another lower set of prices for their supermarkets in the more modest sections of town. Yet customer movement between these two groups of supermarkets, whose trade names are the same, is virtually non-existent. Moreover, the same prepackaged food items that are sold in the middle-class supermarkets all are sold in government-owned supermarkets catering to the urban poor.[8] Prices are a great deal lower in these outlets. The government insists that manufacturers of prepackaged food items sell these goods at cost to the government-owned supermarkets, and permits these same manufacturers to absorb their losses by charging higher prices to the middle-class supermarkets. In terms of price, therefore, the government has a strong influence upon supermarket operations.

Government Influence Upon the Retailing of Gasoline

Middle-class retailing in hard goods, soft goods, and food is affected by public policies initiated by the Mexican government to regulate imports, to restrict the supply of licenses, and to control prices. Important functions usually carried out by businessmen are circumscribed by government decisions affecting suppliers as well as retailers. In one instance, the retailing of gasoline, the Mexican government has delineated a specific national policy that designates how the retail sector will be structured.

Cárdenas' expropriation of the foreign petroleum companies in 1938 led to the creation of a state enterprise with monopoly on the production and distribution of petroleum. For many years, Petroleos Mexicanos (PEMEX) concentrated on the search for oil within Mexico and the fractionation of oil for sale overseas. The domestic market for gasoline was very small.

With the emergence of the urban middle class as a strong force in the Mexican economy, the demand for gasoline to fuel the increasing number of cars on the road became a burden to PEMEX. It was not prepared psychologically nor organizationally to meet the demands for better retail service at its gasoline stations. This caused a significant shift in the thinking of the government on the retailing of gasoline.

Now PEMEX brand gasoline is being sold in gasoline stations operated by private-sector companies. One of the first to do this was the Ezukadi-Goodrich tire company. Naturally, only PEMEX brand gasoline may be sold. However, oil, tires, and other accessories produced by competitors of PEMEX can be sold whenever the state monopoly fails to give a better margin on these products. Profit is to be made retailing gasoline for the first time in many years by providing better service.

These gasoline stations are found in the wealthier sections of Mexico City where those with political power demand a greater return for the money they are spending. This change in the strategy of retailing gasoline suggests that even the most sacred of public policies—i.e., national government control over petroleum—cannot stand in the face of the need to provide a very strong consumer group with better retail service. Further adaptations of government policy to meet the needs of modern retailing could be implied from this one instance of the Mexican government's shift in its statist economic philosophy.

Other Government Influences Upon
Middle-Class Retailing

There are few if any restrictions on who might engage in retailing in Mexico. Retailers consist of native-born persons, naturalized Mexicans, and foreigners. In fact, foreign ownership of retailing has not been challenged, but has been permitted to gain in strength. For example, Sanborns, a variety-store chain that caters to both American tourists and the Mexican middle class, was bought by an American drug and variety-store chain, Walgreens.

One restriction applies both to foreign retail firms as well as to foreign industrial firms. That is, over 90 percent of the workforce must be made up of Mexican nationals. And for those foreigners the foreign firm does want to bring in to work in its Mexican outlets, the firm must prove to the satisfaction of the government that there are no Mexicans of equal competence available for the same job. Sears, with its long experience in Mexico, now has only one foreigner—the local subsidiary's president—working in all of its stores throughout the country.

All businessmen, whether they work for domestic firms or for foreign firms, are encouraged by the government to take part in government-sponsored businessmen's organizations. These are not voluntary organizations similar to the Chamber of Commerce. They are instead a means by which the government attempts to read the collective mind of its businessmen, and, at the same time, a device through which the government gathers support for its developmental policies. Similar organizations exist for the other interest groups (labor, the peasants, etc.) that support the current government. Although membership in these businessmen's organizations is not a requirement for entry into retailing, they are the collective voice of private-sector business firms to the Mexican government and thus important to the firms' continued economic well-being.

In terms of control over the process of retailing, the Federal District (or Mexico City proper) has laws requiring mandatory evening closing hours for retail institutions selling liquor. However, these laws are frequently disregarded. Also the State of Mexico, which includes many of the new suburban towns surrounding Mexico City, uses its zoning power to pull new shopping centers and other retail groupings onto its side of the state line. There are examples of easements and right-of-ways being refused to property within the Federal District from contiguous property located in the State of Mexico, all for the purpose of securing new taxable revenue for the state. Finally, door-to-door selling is free of local municipal restrictions that ban such type of selling under the so-called "Green River" ordinances common within the United States. This freedom to engage in door-to-door selling permits Avon Products to be a major competitor of retail stores selling cosmetics.

Except for the price controls mentioned above, there is little desire on the part of the national government to involve itself in pricing decisions generally.

Resale price maintenance does not exist as a concept in Mexican law. There is no attempt outside the Federal District and the federally administered territories to date products and control their freshness; and even where the national government does have jurisdiction, milk and its by-products are generally the only products controlled by dating them. All premiums and trading stamps are forbidden by the national government for it is felt that these giveaways would be undue competition for the national lottery.

All in all, both the Mexican national government and its subordinate state governments place very few restrictions on the process of retailing. Competition is left to play out its course as is true in the United States.

Summary

The middle class is an economic and political force to be reckoned with today in Mexico. It has become use to the Americanization of its shopping and consumption habits. The changes that have occured in the retail structure supporting this class suggest that the Mexican government went along with the desires of this class, to a great extent, rather than face political trouble in the wealthier sections of its cities. The one thing the government has refused to do is to permit the wholesale importation of U. S.-made consumer goods. In this issue, the urban middle class has lost the battle to forces with greater strength within the Mexican government. The government is committed to creating more manufacturing jobs for the urban poor. Periodic crackdowns on contraband goods give the urban poor the illusion that the government is protecting its livelihood. Since the urban middle class is part and parcel of the government bureaucracy making and administering the rules and regulations on the importation of goods, there is serious doubt as to whether or not the Mexican government can be effective in implementing any policy that adversely affects the interests of the middle class and by extension middle-class retailing. The high incidence of smuggling in goods highly desired by the Mexican middle class suggests that Mexican public policy will bear only lightly upon the urban middle class.

Retailing and the Urban Poor

As was noted earlier, the government's inability to resolve the land redistribution question coupled with the great surge in population forced many peasants to move to the cities. These urban poor established themselves in *colonias* or neighborhoods with relatives and friends from their own villages so that over time it has become less and less difficult for more and more peasants to wrench themselves away from their ancestral homes and join the flood of migrants to the cities.

The standard of living of the urban poor is directly related to the kind of work available. Some are trained for the limited industrial jobs open in the city, and these lucky few begin the long climb towards a middle-class standard of living. Many more peasants make this climb by taking jobs in retailing. They new-found prosperity in the middle class. Sixty-two percent of Mexico City's population has a monthly family income of less than $231,[9] and makes up the market for retailing catering to the urban poor.

Government Influence Upon the
Public Markets

Almost all *colonias* within Mexico City have access to one of the 235 public markets there. Each merchant has his own traditional space within the market, and pays rent on this space based upon size and volume of sales. Offerings are more limited and customers must spend a greater time searching for the goods that will properly meet their demands. Although some bargaining takes place, there is an understood upper and lower limit of prices that both the merchant and his daily customers understand. Strangers will be charged higher prices until the merchant gets to know them as being among his regular customers. Some markets are only open at special hours, and in the provincial cities are only open on special days. During the last ten years, the Mexican government has had a policy of renewing the public markets. Buildings were built with proper sanitation for draining blood from newly dressed poultry and beef, and carrying the run-off water from freshly washed produce and fruit. Moreover, refrigeration was installed to give longer life to food products. Scales with accurate measurements were required of all merchants. And the government strictly enforced its maximum prices for necessities within these public markets.

Both the urban poor and many of the middle class shop here. They do not expect to find produce sized and graded or put into gaily decorated protective packages. They shop here because they feel they are getting a better quality in their fresh produce. Quality is defined by the ability to handle the food, smell it, and thus choose the best in the lot. Moreover, many of these shoppers feel that with the government's careful watching over the public markets there are sufficient safeguards over the problems of public health and price.

It is believed by shoppers in the public markets that prices fluctuate less here than in the supermarkets. That is, there is more of a swing in prices in the supermarkets, because the government is less careful about controlling prices in retail institutions dealing with the middle class. Yet in terms of length of the channel and how prices are determined based upon distributive cost, the supermarkets have the advantage of lower costs. All fresh produce in Mexico City is bought from two central agricultural markets: El Rastro or La Merced. Small wholesale companies buy in these markets and sell the produce to merchants in the public markets; whereas, supermarket chains buy direct from these central markets and do without these intermediate wholesalers. The latter have the advantage of mass buying power. To counter this advantage, the small wholesalers have had to arrange for guaranteed sales *(ventas solas)* so that they too would have some economic power as a large buyer in the central markets. It would seem that the higher prices found in the chain supermarkets reflect the willingness of the bulk of their customers to select stores for convenience rather than price. Smaller supermarkets located near public markets, and hence in channel and how prices are determined based upon distributive cost, the supermarkets have the advantage of lower costs. All fresh produce in Mexico City is bought from two central agricultural markets: El Rastro or La Merced. Small wholesale companies buy in these markets and sell the produce to merchants in the public markets; whereas, supermarket chains buy direct from these central markets and do without these intermediate wholesalers. The latter have the advantage of mass buying power. To counter this advantage, the small wholesalers have had to arrange for guaranteed sales *(ventas solas)* so that they too would have some economic power as a large buyer in the central markets. It would seem that the higher prices found in the chain supermarkets reflect the willingness of the bulk of their customers to select stores for convenience rather than price. Smaller supermarkets located near public markets, and hence in neighborhoods housing the lower middle class and urban poor, have prices that are more competitive with the public markets. Their customers do not rate convenience as highly and thus these stores must compete with other retail institutions in the area.

CONASUPO: A Government Retail Institution

This acronym designates the Mexican government's state-owned wholesale-retail food enterprise, Compañía Nacional de Subsistencias Populares. CONASUPO is an attempt on the part of government to dictate the form that retail structure will take in servicing the urban poor. Its wholesale operations were designed to minimize the middleman's profit in the transportation, storage, and handling of commodities from the haciendas and *ejidos* to the public markets; and thereby prevent food prices from rising. In this effort, CONASUPO has not been a success. Today, prices on staples have risen to levels higher than pre-revolution days. These inflationary trends have not been brought under control. Unfortunately for the poor, incomes have risen very slowly if at all. Thus part of the unrest that is now current in Mexico is the awareness on the part of urban and rural peasants alike that their standard of living, as measured by their ability to buy corn and beans with their incomes, has declined as prices have risen. In effect, the promises of the revolution as carried out through the public policy of state enterprises have not been forthcoming to the poor in the one vital area of their lives. Their basic food supply is dearer today than ever before.

CONASUPO's retail operations have reduced the extent to which the urban poor feel unhappy about their current state of affairs. These operations include small-scale retail supermarkets built in the poor *colonias* of Mexico City and the provincial cities to provide the urban poor with some of the benefits from the advances in modern marketing. Since the wholesale part of the organization provided commodities, prices on the basic necessities could be rigidly controlled. Moreover, prepackaged foods of all kinds were purchased from private-sector foreign and domestic firms at cost. Those firms that balked at selling to CONASUPO at prices lower than they charged the middle-class supermarkets were quickly disciplined by more frequent public health and sanitary inspections and greater fault finding (in the case of Mexican firms) or by the prohibition of foreign labor import permits or by the raising of duties on basic supplies (in the case of foreign firms).[10] Thus CONASUPO was able to offer the urban poor a limited selection of packaged foods and dry goods for a lower cost than the urban poor could find in the small urban *tiendas* (or small-scale "Mom and Pop" groceries), the public markets, or the middle-class supermarkets. By permitting the firms selling to CONASUPO to raise the prices they charged the middle-class supermarkets, the government was in effect using the pricing policies of private-sector firms as a welfare transfer mechanism. A few cents more per can or box was not even noticed by middle-class consumers, but substantially higher income taxes would have been noticed and avoided at all costs by the same group. As a means for transfering wealth, without the usual refusals on the part of those that have money in Latin America, the CONASUPO device worked very well. Unfortunately, it only affected very few of the urban poor and it only affected a minority of the goods they purchased.

CONASUPO has been noteworthy in another respect. Modern retail services have come quicker to the urban poor, because CONASUPO was able to copy the practices of the middle-class supermarkets. Brand selection and packaging are now a part of the life of the urban poor; and if some of them climb to the middle class, they will be better prepared to utilize the retail institutions serving that class. For many, CONASUPO together with newly constructed public markets have provided the urban poor with their only means of pure food. Both retail institutions maintain higher sanitation requirements than had been possible or thought necessary under the old rat-infested, dilapidated public markets of the past and the continuing hole-in-the-wall *tiendas*. For many, CONASUPO has increased the assortment of goods available to be purchased. Only those urban poor who work as servants for the other classes are exposed to the better assortments in middle-class retail institutions because, in many cases, the maids do the shopping for their employers. Only on rare occasion does one run into Indians who are dressed in a serapé, dilapidated dress, and sandals, and who cannot read the printing on the packages, shopping in a middle-class retail outlet. Prices and custom force them to shop elsewhere.

Summary

The urban poor are an emerging political force in today's Mexico. They recognize that their life is worse off today than it was in the past. While the middle class has prospered greatly during the last decade, the urban poor have not had their standard of living rise along with the general prosperity, but have been subject to an absolute decline in the bundle of goods their incomes could buy for them. Most recently, these feelings have been publically articulated by rebelling university students. Peasants and students joining together to make common cause is a new phenomenon in the history of the continuing Mexican revolution. Unless defused it could end the current government's overwhelming dominance of Mexican life. Rebuilding the public markets and establishing a chain of small-scale government supermarkets should be viewed in this context. These were moves on the part of an essentially middle-class bureaucracy, who see themselves as the creators of change that would trickle down to the peasants in the long run, to provide the benefits of its technical successes to peasants crying only for bread, a little corn, and some beans. Technicians, or *tecnicos*[11] were again, as in the days of Díaz, in control. Only this time what they did was wrapped in the symbols of the revolution. Scandals in the administration of CONASUPO are hushed up; and the peasants must pay for the ensuing inefficiencies because prices are higher than they should be.

However, all of these marketing short-term, high-payout developmental projects will be to no avail if the great gains accruing to the middle class are not more widely distributed. Almost all of the increases in agricultural and industrial productivity have been translated into consumer benefits for the middle class alone. Newer foods—American foods—and better quality foods are feeding mouths no longer hungry. What is needed are low-cost, high-protein food supplements. Newer machines—American-designed gadgets—are creating an affluent class among a majority of economically destitute people. The Mexican economy, rather than spreading its gains among all classes, has favored those who were already on the bottom rungs of the ladder reaching towards success. Those who had not taken the first step by themselves were cast aside in an ever-growing and ever-deepening pit. Middle-class retailing is the success story of the decade. Retailing for the urban poor is a failure. In a government that believes in state socialism—at least to keep the foreigner at bay—the current government has used its powers very lightly indeed to force changes necessary to the betterment of the poor. It was easy to expropriate petroleum, the railroads, and electricity, and force foreign firms to sell their interests in the telephones and the sulphur mines. And once it was learned how to run these businesses, a creditable job was done in providing the required services. It is much more difficult to expropriate businesses owned by nationals so as to convert them into agencies for uplifting the urban poor. It is in fact an impossible task given the political conditions current in Mexico.

Conclusions

The Mexican government intrudes upon retailing in many unseen ways. It reduces the volume of retail sales by placing unreasonably high duties on American-made products that are both higher in quality and cheaper in price. Through its use of infant industry policies, it has limited the range of products that could be made available through middle-class retailing. And it has virtually eliminated top-of-the-line products from the product lines of Mexican manufacturers. Today, there is a second wholesale-retail structure that exists beyond the reach of the law.

The government intrudes upon retailing by setting prices for many food items. Although these controlled prices do not halt the rise in prices generally, they are generally too high for the poorest of the urban poor and are wonderfully low for everyone else. Thus the middle class receives an extra bargain from this practice of the government. Prices are controlled for non-food items and services as well. Again this is a boon to those who already have a steady income, and is of no great help to those who do not have a share in Mexico's slowly increasing prosperity.

The government intrudes upon retailing in terms of the quality of food that can be sold in the market. Through a curious quirk in Mexican thinking, this highly unitary state (the Mexican states have very little authority) permits the states to administer their own food and drug laws. Thus one can only be sure of the safety of one's food and milk in the Federal District and the two territories that the federal government administers. These federal laws are strict. All laws and regulations announced by the United States' Pure Food and Drug Administration immediately become the official policy of the Mexican government. The rationale behind this is not so much to protect the Mexican consumer, but to insure that Mexican food items are not stopped at the border but are immediately granted access to the American market.

The government intrudes upon retailing by limiting the number of stores that any chain can operate. This is one of the reasons why Aurrera went into the subterfuge of opening supermarkets. It had already reached its limit in discount stores.

The government intrudes upon retailing in insisting that suppliers provide its CONASUPO stores with merchandise at cost. These manufacturers in turn charge middle-class supermarkets higher prices. In this way the government is forcing the retailing system to perform part of the welfare function. This is an easier way than trying to get higher taxes out of those who are earning the bulk of the money in Mexico.

The government intrudes upon retailing by setting up its own state-enterprises to do certain tasks at retail. CONASUPO is one example of this. Some pundits suggests that once CONASUPO learns the mechanics of operating at retail, state socialism will be carried to other retail market groups as well. There is evidence to the contrary. PEMEX, the petroleum monopoly, has been unsuccessful in operating all the retail operations necessary for the growing consumer market for cars. It has licensed private-sector firms, such as Ezukadi-Goodrich, to sell PEMEX gasoline. These private firms tend to operate a more efficient retail service station than PEMEX did in the past.

In all of the examples given above, these intrusions by the government on retailing are for the most part indirect and without revolutionary impact. Why? Government-supported interest groups found greater gains to be made in the industrial sector or the export-oriented agricultural sector. Once the traditional wholesale middlemen in commodities were supplanted by CONASUPO, little profits were expected from wholesale-retail operations in Mexico. These interest groups disdained the small retailer because of his proclivity for low volume and high prices.

Now Americans have shown Mexicans how to make money at mass retailing. At first, these interest groups acted in concert to protect the established retail margins. Later, traditional suppliers and long-established merchants whose contacts with the current government ran very deep found that the retailing revolution overtook them long before they could get all the interest groups to decide upon a course of action. In fact, non-retail interest groups within the government allied themselves with the new retailers in hopes of getting on the profit bandwagon.

This example points out a facet about the Mexican environment surrounding the creation of public policy that one would not gain by studying land reform or industrialization. Namely, Mexican public policy adjusts itself to the strongest economic realities of the market. Even though there is bias for industrialization through state control of decision making, the public preference for consumption wants today vis--à-vis industrial success tomorrow has had a telling effect upon Mexican public policy towards retailing. Even in days of extreme public xenophobia, foreigners were permitted to enter retailing and transform it into a modern sector of the economy that could fulfill the demands of the growing middle class. Meeting these demands without disturbing too many of the entrenched interests of the groups supporting the government has been the key to the success of Mexican public policy towards retailing.

The Mexican government has paid little attention towards retailing for the rural poor. Little profit was seen by the interest groups supporting the government to try to educate owners of very small-scale *tiendas* in ways to reform rural retailing. Rather, each rural grocer continues to monopolize what little retail trade exists at his village crossroads store. The story of Mexican retailing is in the cities. Its success came in its ability to provide new goods, services, assortments, and stores for the urban middle class. Its failure came in its inability to do the same for the urban poor.

May 1971

Notes

1.   For a recent article on the idea that the service sector did make a positive contribution to the economic development of Mexico, see Donald B. Kessing, "Structural Change Early in Development: Mexico's Changing Industrial and Occupational Structure from 1895 to 1950," *The Journal of Economic History* 24, 4 (December, 1969): 716-738.

2.   "South of the Border: A Jumping Market," *Business Week*, 2080 (July 12, 1969), pp. 120-121, 124, 126, 128, 130.

3.   All figures quoted in U. S. dollars. The equivalent amount in local currency is 2,000 to 5,000 Mexican pesos or the C income group reported by the *Secretaría de Hacienda y Crédito Público*.

4.   Family income of over 5,000 Mexican pesos per month makes up the A/B income group.

5.   Richardson Wood and Virginia Keyser, *United States Business Performance Abroad: The Case Study of Sears, Roebuck de Mexico, S. A.* (Washington, D. C.: National Planning Association, May 1953), pp. 18, 31. A private study by the author confirms this pattern in Sears today and in the other department stores in Mexico City.

6.   Department Stores (11) *Review of the Economic Situation of Mexico* 39, 456 (November, 1963): 456.

7. Jane McCabe, "The Supers' Invade Mexico," *Mexican-American Review* 29, 5 (May, 1961): 18.

8. The CONASUPO case will be discussed below under "Retailing and the Urban Poor."

9. Family income of less than 2,000 Mexican pesos per month makes up the D income group. *Secretaría de Hacienda y Crédito Público.*

10. For the CONASUPO story, see the following article by this author, "Opportunities for Marketing Growth in the Mexican Market," *Southern Journal of Business* 4, 2 (April, 1969): 272-280.

11. Raymond Vernon, *The Dilemma of Mexico's Development: The Roles of Private and Public Sectors* (Cambridge, Mass.: Harvard University Press, 1963).

13 The Netherlands

J. F. Haccoû AND P. J. M. Lübbers

The authors wish to thank Mr. L. A. H. M. van Goch for his assistance in assembling the necessary data for this article.

Introduction

Before World War II, public policy in the Netherlands was only occasionally concerned with the problems of retail trade. In accordance with the general political philosophy, those public measures that were directed toward the trade were primarily of a social, rather than an economic, nature and dealt with such matters as hours, working conditions, and the (attempted) exclusion of incompetent entrants. Since 1945, however, policy objectives have included a desire to influence both the structure and the future growth of the national economy.

This new policy resulted from several considerations, the most important of which were the explosive population growth and the urge to stimulate economic growth and prevent severe depressions such as that of the 1930s. Internal development, increases in international trade, and the Netherland's international economic cooperation—both with Belgium and Luxemburg in the Benelux, and later with the other Common Market countries—led to economic changes that forced the national government and the relevant regional authorities to develop structural policies for some parts of the country. At first these policies were especially directed towards agriculture and some sectors of manufacturing, and later on also towards mining. More and more, the government sought to extend its policies to retail trade and other sectors of economic life in which medium- and small-sized business plays an important role.

The accelerated growth of population together with increasing urbanization, especially in the western part of the country, made it increasingly necessary to extend spatial planning to the retail trade in order to obtain optimal use of the scarce factor, land.

Definitions

For a good understanding of the context of this chapter it is necessary to start with a few explanatory remarks regarding retail trade and government.

Retail Trade. In the Netherlands, the term "retail trade" refers to the sale of

245

finished goods (and items such as clothing that only require small individual adaptations) to ultimate consumers. The catering industries, handicraft trades and agents are not considered as belonging to the retail trade, although they also supply goods and services to ultimate consumers.

Public Business Organization (P.B.O.). The term "government" in the Netherlands includes the central government, the provincial and municipal authorities, and the public organization of trade and industry (P.B.O.) described below.

These industrial and trade organizations, which were first authorized by a 1938 change in the Netherlands' Constitution, were introduced during the German occupation and have since been continued in a form that is more acceptable to Dutch attitudes. The considerations that led to the postwar continuance of the P.B.O.'s are beyond the scope of this chapter, but the essence of the system is the organization of trade and industry into appropriate boards. These boards may be formed on a vertical basis, comprising two or more successive levels such as primary production, manufacturing, wholesale trade, and retail trade in a product category, or on a horizontal basis such as certain branches of manufacturing, wholesaling, or retailing. The hotel and catering industry is organized in a board. In addition to the organizations for special lines, there is a Central Board for Retail Trade[1] (C.B.R.T.) and a Central Board for Handicrafts.

Each board has a bipartite executive committee consisting of members nominated respectively by the entrepreneurs' and the employees' organizations. The committee's functions are: (1) to assume the tasks of government, including the promulgation of regulations concerning the industry or trade, under final approval of the government; and (2) to create advisory boards on several levels in behalf of public policy. The entire system of boards is headed by a tripartite Social and Economic Council. One-third of the Council's members are appointed by the entrepreneurs' organizations; the three central trade union organizations which are considered to represent the workers appoint another third; and the final third, consisting of independent professionals and others who are considered as public representatives, is appointed by Royal Decree. The public representatives are selected entirely from among individuals in the private sector rather than in government service. The Social and Economic Council, with the assistance of its secretary's office, acts as the managing institution for the entire organization. Its role as an advisory committee to the government is, however, even more important. The government authorities are required to ask its advice concerning all measures to be taken in the social and economic field and the Council has the right to give unsolicited advice when this is felt desirable. Thus, the Council is the most important economic and social advisory organ in the Netherlands.

The activities of the P.B.O.'s may be illustrated by the work of the Central Board Retail Trade (C.B.R.T.). This work can be divided into four categories. The first category is the granting of advice to government, e.g., as to changing the Shop Closure (store hours) Act. As already mentioned, the board may also do this on its own initiative; examples are recommendations concerning gift (premium) systems, orderly economic activity, settlement (entry into business) legislation, and the turnover tax. Second, the C.B.R.T. can draw up regulations controlling retail establishments: an example is the regulation of secondary labor conditions (fringe benefits and working hours) in the retail trade. Third, the C.B.R.T. is charged with the execution of certain regulations, for example, the legislation concerning settlement (entry) and bargain and clearance sales. And finally, the C.B.R.T. may initiate other activities, such as its study of the possibilities of automation in the retail trades.

Other Institutions. Other institutions under public law in the Netherlands include the semi-official Chambers of Commerce and Industry organized regionally to further economic interests by giving advice to the relevant central and local authorities. In addition to their advisory function, these chambers (which include representatives selected by the trade) influence retail trade through their administration of the regional trade registries. Each firm is obliged to furnish information about its financial and organizational structure for inclusion in the regional registry before engaging in retail trade, and the Chamber can check for conformity to such things as the financial requirements of the Settlement Act. The Chamber, in conjunction with local authorities, also administers the choice of options under national shop closure (store hours) legislation and has responsibilities in the control of the installment credit system.

The retail trade, moreover, participates in various consultative committees established by the central government and by local authorities. It is represented, for example, in the Price Consultation Committee established by the Ministry for Economic Affairs in connection with the 1969 general price administration plans.

Government-owned Retailing

With relatively few and conceptually minor exceptions, government does not practice retailing and there are no state shops. The only exceptions are electric- and gas-appliance showrooms maintained by provincial or municipal public utility authorities, and canteens and shops in governmental establishments such as military bases, camps, prisons, and ministries.

Entry into Trade

In principle, freedom of settlement (entry) exists in the whole field of retailing in the Netherlands. The official point of view is that government should be very reluctant to restrict freedom of settlement: such restrictions should be used only when there is strong evidence of emergency in either a region or a trade.[2]

This does not mean that everybody has completely free entry to any branch of retailing, but rather that accessibility is only restricted by requirements designed to stimulate good business operations. The existing requirements for entry to retail trade, handicrafts, or some other trades must be considered in the light of that objective. There are no restrictions with respect to birth, race, or nationality. This means that freedom of settlement for foreign firms, one of the aims of the Common Market, does not cause any difficulty in the Netherlands where discrimination against foreign entry is unknown.[3]

The whole legislation concerning entry into retail trade must be considered as a threshold that has been intentionally placed at a somewhat raised level, not as an impregnable obstacle, but as a means of increasing the deliberateness of a decision to open a business. The would-be entrepreneur is required to meet certain minimum qualifications concerning practical business knowledge, professional skill, and solvency. This legislation goes back to the 1930s. The depression caused ruinous competition because many inexperienced, mostly unemployed, persons started retail shops with insufficient knowledge and financial means, often at the encouragement of local authorities who tried in this way to reduce the idleness relief they had to pay. In 1937, at the instigation of the retail trade organizations, an act was passed providing the framework for regulation of entry of new small firms in retail trade and handicrafts. Its essentials were: (1) freedom of entry for everybody who had the required abilities; (2) the initiative for application of the act to a particular trade was placed in the hands of the relevant trade organization; (3) the regulations established under the act could only specify minimum requirements. The government believed that this legislation would promote better business operation among the small firms and thus strengthen their competitive force and protect the interests of consumers as well.

It appeared to have shortcomings, however, and a new act regulating the establishment of new business firms was passed by Parliament in 1954. The new act had considerably wider scope in that it could be applied to other sectors as well as to retail trade and handicrafts. The basic principle of requiring knowledge, skill, and solvency remained the same, but the new legislation placed more emphasis upon promotion of good business operations through training and the development of more appropriate tests of knowledge and ability.[4] The government took the position that entry requirements must be different and somewhat more varied in a growth period—such as the 1950s—than during depression so as to avoid such unfavorable consequences as the restriction of competition.

The enlargement of scale in retail trade started about 1950. This resulted in a decline in the number of firms and a somewhat smaller decrease in the number of selling points (establishments). Although consumer spending at retail increased greatly since the end of World War II, the large increase in operating costs forced a number of retail trade firms out of business. The entry of new entrepreneurs was slowed down because of the constantly growing investment required for new establishments. Besides, general economic development made many employee positions more attractive financially than entrepreneurship in small business.

Since 1960, the government policy concerning entry into trade has been characterized by a gradually growing flexibility, especially in view of the clear need in many cases to broaden the assortments carried in the individual shops. Production and distribution are developing strongly in ways that are changing the structure of retailing. The government has noted, in a 1969 memorandum to Parliament, that the investment required to open a modern shop is now likely to serve as an effective screening device and will almost automatically eliminate the unqualified or insolvent entrant.[5]

Public policy now also favors the simplification of entry requirements. The number of specialized certificates of technical capacity had multiplied over the years as a result of trade-association pressures in practically every line of retailing. Consequently, almost every important enlargement of a shopkeeper's assortment required one or more supplementary certificates. Recently, however, the government has favored reduction or elimination of technical (product) knowledge requirements on the grounds that such knowledge was not necessary for good entrepreneurship. This policy has culminated in a law, probably effective in October 1972, under which only one certificate is required for participation in the whole field of retailing. The one-license system means the withdrawal of line- or product-bound regulations, and gives the retail trader complete freedom to fix both the volume and the assortment of his business.

This simplification of legislation is important not only for small- and medium-size businesses, but also for larger enterprises, such as chains and department stores. It permits the improvement of organizational and (to a lesser degree) cost structures in the large firms, because in the future the required abilities can be centralized instead of being decentralized throughout the stores or departments. This results from the abolishment, by the new act, of the old requirement for having fully licensed persons in each selling point. In the future, one license will be sufficient for a firm, regardless of the number of stores. Finally, the solvency requirement has also been abrogated.

Finance

One of the most difficult problems for medium- and small-size businesses is obtaining the necessary financial resources for equipment and inventory acquisition and for working capital. The Netherlands are no exception to this generalization, and in 1927, when the financing of small- and medium-size business was in a deplorable condition, measures were taken to improve the situation. A new banking institution, in which the older middle-class (small- and medium-size business) financing banks were incorporated, was established in that year through the close cooperation of the government and the organizations of middle-class entrepreneurs. This Nederlandsche Middenstandsbank has become one of the large banks in the Netherlands and remains the only bank handling loans to medium- and small-size business under government guarantee. In most other countries, a great number of banks and other institutions participate in financing retail trade and handicraft, but the Netherlands are one of the few countries where the majority of government loans are provided through only one resource, the Nederlandsche Middenstandsbank.

Government influence is very strong in the financing of medium- and small-size business and thus in financing retailing. The loan arrangements under government guarantee have developed very strongly, especially since 1950, and there are currently eight different forms of long-term loans:

1. Special business loan: for financing of capital equipment or to enlarge working capital if this is necessary for the firm's continuity.

2. Loan for economic cooperation: for stimulating economic cooperation such as voluntary chains or buying groups that may produce better retail operating results.
3. Loan for equipment purposes: for setting up a new business building (shop, etc.) in an efficient modern way.
4. Settlement loan: a participation loan having the character of equity resources, and which may be provided to entrepreneurs who are entering business through either acquisition of an existing firm or establishment of a new one.
5. Mortgage loan: for financing the purchase or construction of a new building and site.
6. Development loan: for financing development of an existing business with good prospects.
7. Adaptation loan: for retailers who wish to take over a business.
8. Guarantee fund loan: may be given to an entrepreneur who has been active in business for more than two years to help him overcome financial difficulties connected with his business.

Government is now considering whether the number of types of loans may be reduced to three: mortgage loans, loans with an equity character, and all others.

The greatly increased need for long-term financial resources for small- and medium-size businesses in retail trade and other fields can only be satisfied to a considerable extent through government assistance. At the end of 1969, the total of outstanding loans given under governmental guarantee to middle-class enterprises amounted, according to the annual report of the Nederlandsche Middenstandsbank, to 534 million guilders (approximately $150 million).

Competition, Economic Activity, and Cooperation

The government's cartel policy is based on the principle that competitive abuses should be prevented in favor of sound competition. This is contrary to the prohibition of restrictions on competition in the legislation of the important other Common Market countries. The law of 1935, the Netherlands' earliest law on the subject, gave the government authority to declare agreements reached by a majority of the firms concerned, binding (or not binding) on an entire economic sector. This act was replaced by the Cartel Order in 1941 which in turn was replaced by the 1956 act on economic competition.

Except in a few cases mentioned in the current law, every agreement dealing with restriction of competition between firms has to be submitted to the Minister for Economic Affairs. The Minister can check the agreements and, after following the required procedures, use his powers under the law to curb or prohibit any abuses of competition. The 1956 legislation has a much wider scope than previous laws and deals with the whole set of problems of competition and its restrictions. One of the important ways in which it differs from former legislation is that now various *types* of agreements can be collectively declared not binding whereas formerly the government had to proceed on a case-by-case basis and test each individual agreement for its consequences for general welfare. Agreements can be prohibited for periods varying from three to five years, with the possibility of appeal for the parties concerned.

The act can also be used in support of other aims, such as a public price policy for the establishment of minimum prices. Before the Second World War, competition often had a disastrous effect on some categories of business. It was especially difficult to establish and maintain economic agreements in the retail trades; and exclusive dealing arrangements were the only ones that sometimes had some success. After 1945, tradespeople in general—having learned from bitter experience—seemed to understand more clearly the significance of mutual agreements. As a consequence, the public authorities are now obliged to spend more effort in maintaining sufficient competition rather than in trying to obtain participation of entire branches of trade in orderly competition agreements.[6]

Resale Price Maintenance

The most important topic for retailing in connection with this legislation is resale price maintenance (RPM). Before 1940 and in the first years after World War II, resale price maintenance existed but did not attract much attention, although a number of successful suits were brought against retailers who sold below the prices set by manufacturers. After 1945, the authorities introduced a great many measures that restricted competition in order to start trade and industry again, but better opportunities for free enterprise developed after their abolition. Discounting practices in some sectors of retailing on the one hand and measures to strengthen resale price maintenance on the other hand attracted the attention of the authorities. Resale price maintenance was often strengthened by agreements between organizations at successive stages of trading—viz., manufacturing, wholesaling, and retailing—and by forms of exclusive dealing or fining, and eventually refusal of delivery in case of transgression.[7]

The Act on Economic Competition of 1956 gave the authorities instruments for maintaining sufficient competition. In 1964, the government issued a Royal Decree under Article 10 of the act prohibiting, as of the first of January of that year, all forms of collective resale price maintenance (where all of the sellers in a particular industry agree to refuse deliveries to a dealer who sells any item supplied by any firm in the agreement for less than the established price). Individual resale price maintenance (under which each individual supplier enforces the maintenance of his own prices) was also forbidden for a number of household and luxury articles as of 1 November 1964. Suggested pricing remained permissible for those items, and individual RPM continued to be valid for such things as foods, pharmaceuticals, drugs, cosmetics, and books. There were possibilities of dispensation from the prohibition. The decree remained in force for five years and then was extended by legislation for an additional three years. In 1968, the Economic and Social Council was asked for advice with regard to the desirability of resale price maintenance and for recommendations as to definite legal principles. The Council created an expert committee which, by a small majority, recommended continuance of RPM; and the Council itself also recommended, by a small majority, the continuance of RPM. Such continuance will lead to difficulties with the Common Market rules, but as of May 1972 government had not reached any decision as to future policy in this matter.

Orderly Economic Activity

As mentioned above, cartel policy aims at the maintenance of sound competition, defined as active inter-firm rivalry that serves economic expansion and prevents economic stagnation. Competition of this sort is believed to lead to a reduction in the cost of production, the promotion of a satisfactory relationship between costs and profits, and in general a reasonable distribution of the fruits of economic expansion. Given this point of view, orderly economic activity *(orderlijk economische verkeer)* is defined as the behavior of economic units that promotes, rather than hinders, sound competition. The government's main instruments for promoting orderly economic activity are the two acts already mentioned, the Settlement Act 1954 and the Act on Economic Competition 1956, as well as a number of other legislative measures such as the Act on Restriction of Gift Systems (to be dealt with immediately below), the Act on Selling-Off (clearance sales) in retail shops, the Shop Closure (hours) Act and the Food and Drugs Act (discussed later in this chapter).

In this regard it should be noted that the authorities do not, in principle, oppose intertype competition. This position has been of considerable importance since, in spite of the commodity line boundaries that existed in the entry legislation, the different branches of retail trade have increasingly encroached upon each other's assortments. This trend towards "scrambled merchandising" has intensified competition among the different branches of trade.

Gift Systems

The purpose of the Act on Restriction of Gift Systems (premiums) is to set rules and limits on the use of presents as a means of competition. The legislation was not intended to prevent the normal use of gift or premium systems as a competitive device, but was designed to combat excrescences which had gradually arisen and which were contrary to orderly exchange and sound competition. The basic provision of the law prohibits the gift of goods that are outside the seller's normal assortment; that is to say, a retailer cannot offer as gifts or premiums items that he does not normally sell in his store.[8] The prohibition does not apply to gifts of money, coupons, checks, or to price reductions on items in the assortment. Other exceptions are provided for so-called complementary goods that are intended to be used with items sold in the store and that bear some indelible type of advertising material, and for small items of little absolute economic value.

In principle, the authorities of the public business organizations have the power to issue supplementary regulations concerning gifts, for example, by imposing rules on the use of gifts selected from within the branch's customary assortment. In practice, the PBOs have made little use of this power, in part because of the increasing vagueness of line boundaries and in part because each PBO can only bind its own members and not those participating in other boards. This argument has also been decisive for the Central Board Retail Trade which could issue a regulation that would control or prohibit gift systems in all types of retailing but has not done so because it cannot control gift plans that originate at the manufacturing level.

Changes may be expected, however, in the current regulations affecting gift systems. The prohibition of "gifts not belonging to the branch assortment" has become less usable as a result of the increasing vagueness of line-boundaries and the consequent overlapping of assortments. The new entry regulation, which establishes the single license system for all retailing, makes this prohibition almost meaningless. The government is now seeking a formula that will not prohibit gift plans but will impose two conditions: (1) the buyer must have a choice between the gift commodity and an appropriate amount of money; and (2) customers must also be able to buy the gift item directly if they so desire at a price no higher than the monetary amount indicated in condition (1) plus a stipulated percentage markup. The second condition is intended to solve the problem of determining the appropriate alternative monetary amount or "comparable shop value of the gift" under condition (1). The Social and Economic Council has rendered its advice on this proposal, but the government has not acted as yet.

Price Reductions and Stamp Systems

Price reductions and saving stamp systems are also frequently used to stimulate sales. The price reduction plans offer either a direct reduction in the price of the goods or, in some cases, coupons that are redeemable for money. These plans encounter no legal regulations except in those instances where resale price maintenance applies. The saving stamps may be offered gratis or, more commonly, are sold at their face value and are usually supplied at the rate of one 10-cent stamp for every guilder of purchases. Upon accumulation of sufficient amounts, these stamps can be exchanged for various goods and services,[9] although in some plans a partial cash payment is also required. In those plans where the stamps are sold rather than offered gratis, or where a cash payment is also required, the total cost of the gift item to the customer is still (at least ostensibly) substantially less than the prevailing "comparable shop value" of the same item in its normal trade channels. In principle, these last practices fall under the Act Restricting Gift Systems, and the retailers who use these plans must proceed very cautiously to avoid obvious violations.

Lotteries and similar schemes cannot be used to stimulate sales, although attempts are often made to do so, since the Act on Games of Chance forbids all lotteries that have not been approved by the Ministry of Justice. This act is rigidly and rigorously enforced, and the Ministry will not approve lotteries or other similar games that are used for commercial purposes.

Growth and Cooperation of Firms

Public policy does not interfere in any way with the growth of retail firms, and legally no bounds are set to growth.

Economic cooperation in the forms of wholesaler-sponsored voluntary chains and of retailers' buying cooperatives has developed very strongly among medium- and small-sized businesses in Dutch retailing. Economic cooperation among these retailers, practiced to some extent from the beginning of the century, was stimulated again during the 1930s by the growth of large retail enterprises with their economies of scale. The major growth of both the retailers' buying cooperative and the wholesaler-sponsored voluntary chains has come since World War II, as a result of the great economic expansion and the general enlargement of scale of operations in retailing. Moreover, the Netherlands provides a congenial environment for commercial cooperation among small- and medium-size retail businesses. The government favors such cooperation and feels that sufficient competition will exist, and will even be enhanced, with the development of coordinating organizations among small retailers so that there is no fear of monopolization. The government takes the position that the development of such organizations will make public policy in the retail sector more effective.[10]

Historically the grocery line shows the strongest development of the collaborative idea, both in the form of buying groups of independents and of consumer cooperative associations, and later on in the form of the wholesaler-sponsored voluntary chains. The grocery line is now almost entirely in the hands of large chains, groups of affiliated retailers, and the consumer cooperative societies. It is remarkable that although the wholesaler-sponsored voluntary chain form of organization started in the United States and was introduced into the Netherlands at the beginning of the 1930s as an imitation of the American development, in other European countries those chains were organized according to the Dutch example, often in consequence of the internationally-directed dynamic character of the Dutch organizations concerned.[11]

Commercial organizations have also developed in other retailing lines, particularly in the form of retail buying groups. This is especially so in textiles, and to a lesser degree, in the drugstore (household chemicals) field, household lines, and fruits and vegetables.

The government has contributed to the growth of these organizations through the special loans mentioned earlier. Loans for economic cooperation are intended to support the pursuit of better financial results through cooperative action in buying, selling, production, bookkeeping, and advertising. This is the only type of government-guaranteed loan that has no mandatory ceiling, because of the many and varied possible activities and organizational plans that may need assistance.

Rationalization of Milk Delivery

The program for reorganization of milk delivery to households provides a good illustration of the government's permissive attitude towards close cooperation among vendors if the cooperation contributes to the national welfare. It also is an example of the promotion of orderly economic intercourse by the P.B.O. form of administration. The Board for Milk and Dairy Products Retailing developed a rationalization plan through reorganization of delivery routes, exchange of customers between vendors, and consolidation of vendors. The plan maintained competition, a requisite for government approval, but also tended to guarantee the sellers sufficient sales volume to permit profitable operations. The scheme has been successful, thanks also to the close cooperation of the milk-handling industry; and the charges for home distribution of milk in the Netherlands are among the lowest in Europe.

New Forms of Business

The emergence of so-called "consumers markets" (low priced, partly self-service establishments) and other new forms of discounting also illustrates the government's neutral attitude toward new initiatives in business. But it also shows that neutrality does not mean losing sight of the interests of already established firms. The national government has notified the local authorities (who may sometimes be hostile to the new entrants) that these newer retailing institutions must be accepted insofar as their success is the result of sound entrepreneurship. Nevertheless, the authorities must consider regional land-use plans in connection with the establishment of these firms, many of which locate outside normal shopping districts, so that they do not benefit from artificially low occupancy costs to the detriment of existing forms of retailing.

Pricing

Another area of public interference with retailing is pricing. Right after 1945, Dutch price legislation had a very temporary character, and government only intervened in occasional cases. At first, the base for public measures was the supposedly short-lived Price Increase and Hoarding Act of 1939 which was extended time and time again. Government intervention under this legislation occurred in such extraordinary circumstances as during and immediately after the Second World War, after the devaluation of the guilder in 1949, and at the time of the Korean conflict in 1951.

But there has since been a fundamental change in this field. Price legislation has grown from being a matter of emergency control and now provides the government with a tool for the implementation of general economic policy. The current Prices Act of 1961 gives the government substantial power to intervene in economic life. The act applies to all goods other than buildings and other fixed real property and to all services except those labor-intensive activities that come under comparable wage legislation and policy. The government considers this Prices Act as primarily a management tool for the maintenance of economic equilibrium. Presently, the difficulty with the use of this tool is that the increase of both wages and prices has not come to rest; it will still take a couple of years before a new equilibrium will be attained. While this Prices Act of 1961 tends to affect all phases of economic life, our discussion here will be confined to the most important points of contact with retailing.

In general, the price policy rests on the voluntary cooperation of industry and trade; and direct governmental intervention is strictly restricted to the essentials. Trade and industry must, however, observe certain rules of behavior. For retail trade, the first one is the so-called rule of external costs. This rule states that prices of goods manufactured in the Netherlands may be raised only if, and only so far as, the prices of raw and auxiliary materials have increased; on the other hand a fall in those prices must be followed as soon as possible by a decline in the price of the finished product. In order to stimulate compliance with this requirement, price increases that result from subsequent cost increases may be denied in the case of any prices that were not adjusted down to earlier cost decreases.

The rule of the money margin is of particular interest to the retail trade, too. This rule stipulates that the monetary (absolute) amount of the margin may not be increased in case of a price increase; this is intended to prevent the cumulative effects of applying prevailing percentage margins at successive trade levels to an increased cost base; and it thus dampens price increases. The authorities must be notified of all price increases so that the Ministry for Economic Affairs can check for conformity to the rules. The Ministry investigates any changes whose appropriateness is in doubt, and any cases of change without proper notification. Moreover, preconsultation and prior approval are required before raising the prices of certain specified necessities, including bread, milk, margarine, and heating fuels.

The Prices Act gives the public authorities power to prescribe maximum prices, bookkeeping practices used in justifying price changes, and price posting methods.[12] The price posting requirement is particularly important for retailing. Anyone who, as part of his business, sells food and allied products or textile or leather articles to consumers must provide a conspicuous indication of their price; and the same rule applies to any other goods that are displayed where they can be seen from the street. A bill now under consideration provides additional control over price marking and display techniques by permitting regulations to curb fictitious discount or reduction claims. The new bill will also allow the authorities to require "unit pricing" in some instances, that is, indication of the price per some standard unit of weight, measure, or quantity. The government believes that these regulations will greatly help eliminate deceit or confusion of the consumer.

The government also favors the establishment of minimum prices when necessary to prevent ruinous competition. According to this point of view, minimum price regulation should only be undertaken to prevent disastrous consequences and should not be used to suppress sound economic competition. The government has declared that the use of specific guilder minimum prices applying to entire branches of trade are more likely to eliminate justifiable competition than are minimum prices based upon each individual seller's own costs. For this reason, it prefers regulation in the form of price calculation schemes rather than specification of uniform prices.

In this connection, the government has asked the Social and Economic

Council for advice concerning the desirability of legal regulations that will establish minimum prices to curtail excessive competition. The Council has been asked to give special attention to the problems of determining the appropriate levels for such minimum prices.

Another situation for public intervention arises when severe price cuts are followed by price increases after competitors have been driven out of the market or after the price-cutting competitors reach an agreement or a new equilibrium. The Act on Economic Competition allows the authorities to take action in certain circumstances, particularly after local or regional price wars among bakers, butchers, or other merchants.

Location

It will be readily understood that in a country as densely populated as the Netherlands, space is more and more becoming a very scarce resource. In the western part of the country, particularly, recreational and agricultural areas are being sacrificed to housing, industry, roads, and port equipment. Distributing land between various possible end-uses has become a serious problem for central and local authorities. The municipal authorities are increasingly specifying retail locations as well as zones for other purposes.

The modern idea is to cluster various lines of retailing, often together with other activities, in both neighborhood and regional centers. In principle, the composition of the center is planned and approved before construction. The representatives of medium- and small-scale retailing and large-scale retailers participate in preparing these plans. There exists a certain belief in an orderly relationship among the stores within a center, and in limits on the overlapping of assortments. Otherwise, the center will have too much competition to permit profitable operations, and the lack of attention to specialized lines will limit the center's ability to attract customers. Although the agreements are not enforced with excessive rigidity, the center participants must accept stipulations as to the products and services they can offer in the space at their disposal. The retailer is not only obliged to observe this agreement, but is usually also bound to oblige any legal successor to the same restrictions. These agreements often have a long term of life (thirty to fifty years or even unlimited) and tend to diminish, or if possible, to eliminate competition in the center, district, or street concerned.

The government is alert to this development and holds that such restrictions can contravene entry policy and can interfere with the consumer's freedom of selection. In the one specific case decided to date, an agreement fixing the structure of competition within a particular shopping center for a period of fifty years was held invalid and contrary to the public interest. The government has announced that in general it will not object to similar plans for the regulation of intra-center competition that do not exceed a certain fixed period of time, typically five years from the date the center is opened. This decision was contrary to advice received from the Central Board Retail Trade, which held that there were no compelling reasons for a general ruling at this time, and that government should merely watch developments closely.

Location Policy

As the discussion to this point indicates, town and country planning in the Netherlands is increasingly considering the economic and commercial aspects of location in addition to the technical factors that were predominant during the early years after 1945. This changed view is illustrated not only in the location planning for commercial structures in new communities, but also in the reconstruction of existing cities. The aim is to foster as harmonious a growth of retailing as possible. The government defines this policy as an attempt to balance the following considerations: (1) intensifying the reconstruction of downtown areas; (2) locating new shopping centers in such manner as to avoid siphoning off downtown business; and, generally speaking (3) avoiding excessive competition between the various clusterings.

This increased interest in planning is the logical consequence of a population growth that enforces a careful use of available space. New views in the field of town construction have created new methods of both regional and local space planning, typically including the establishment of space limitations and complete or partial architectural and aesthetic requirements as well as locational controls. This has led to more and more attention to planning research. The government is strongly convinced of the need for developing better indices for planning the location and structure of the distributive and service trades. The Ministry for Economic Affairs has instructed the Economic Institute for Medium and Small Size Business to investigate the data needs for improved planning in the service, retail, and other small- and medium-size business sectors.

The Institute has also been assigned the task of considering whether, and to what extent, planning data can be differentiated on a regional or local basis. This assignment has important implications for retailing since the government particularly wants to place more emphasis upon regional (inter-provincial) factors in its spatial planning. Accomplishing this will require, first, special investigations of regional economic development, and then improved communications between central government, regional and local authorities, and industry and trade. Steps have already been taken in this direction by a group of government officials who act as consultants for medium- and small-size business and tourism, by the Chambers of Commerce and Industry, and by the so-called structure committees. The government, however, expects to go further by establishing regional central offices to coordinate all planning and related activities in each region.

Another step in the improvement of planning research and information has been the creation of a special advisory agency under the joint sponsorship of the government and the organizations of medium- and small-size entrepreneurs. In spite of the governmental assistance, this agency is regarded as a private institute supported by organized trade; and all of the organizations and institutions affiliated with the Central Board for Retail Trade (C.B.R.T.) cooperate in its work. It has a two-fold function of research and information. It advises the local authorities about the correct planning of shopping centers in new housing quarters; it promotes technical research; it investigates desirable types of buildings and efficiency of construction; and it does market research for site selection. Since 1966, the institute has operated as a department for regional planning within the C.B.R.T.

The government's actual intervention into shopping center planning has, among other things, aimed at preventing inexpedient and unremediable investments on the part of the local authorities and private participants. In general, neither the central government nor the local officials interfere with the actual design and construction of commercial properties (except, of course, through enforcement of building codes that deal primarily with safety and sanitation), and usually the control is limited to approval of the location and extent of the shopping center. However, there is a certain amount of informal cooperation between government and industry and trade; and in several instances since 1945 the construction of commercial properties was slowed down by agreement to release resources for housing construction.

On principle, moreover, the government is not willing to subsidize the building of shops. Nevertheless, it has facilitated the financing of new shop construction through the government guaranteed mortgage loans mentioned above.

Shopping Centers

Real estate companies, building concerns, and subsidiaries of the general banks undertake most of the shopping center projects, working, as already indicated, in close cooperation with representatives of big, medium, and small retail businesses, the Central Institute for Medium and Small Size Business, and the local authorities. Two subsidiaries of the Nederlandsche Middenstandsbank—the Foundation Development Office Shopping Centers, and the Finance Society for Industrial Objectives—were established as the pioneers in this field with a two-fold task: (1) to plan and erect shopping centers, and other retail and service establishments; and (2) to provide long-term financial resources for these new entrants, and for new factories for medium- and small-size manufacturing concerns. The actual financing often comes from the pension funds of the big manufacturing concerns and life insurance concerns. Foundations or limited liability companies are usually created for the operation of these new shopping centers, with equal representation on the controlling board for medium- and small-size business and for the large retail enterprises. The local authorities concerned and the Central Board Retail Trade are also represented.

Parking

The parking problem is becoming an ever more serious part of the space problem, and is receiving governmental attention. Local authorities are now being required to incorporate traffic and transportation schemes, including the provision of short-time parking facilities, in their space utilization plans. Several municipalities have amended their building codes to require the provision of parking accommodations in connection with any new traffic-attracting construction. This requirement usually does not create any serious problems when the space is available, but when it is not—the much more frequent situation—some of the municipalities have required a substantial contribution to the municipal parking fund. In this way, the authorities have tried to couple the issuance of construction or rebuilding licenses with support for the parking fund. One community even set the mandatory contribution at 50 percent of the cost of creating the stipulated number of parking spaces.

This practice has, however, encountered resistance. The Crown (State Council) annulled one local regulation that required a contribution to the parking fund; and the Minister for Housing and Spatial Planning has ruled that building permits may not be made conditional upon such contributions. The government has also pointed out that overly-rigorous parking requirements may increase costs to a point that will threaten the profits of the center participants. Its statement notes that a shopping center's viability depends upon the profitability of its occupants, and that excessive costs will interfere with functions for which the center is planned.

Building, Layout, and Related Controls

A number of state regulations, some general in character and some related to specific lines of trade, affect the layout and design of commercial properties. Important specific line regulations exist for, among others, the fish, poultry, butchery, milk, and alcoholic liquor trades. The most significant general regulations affecting the retail trade as well as other businesses are: (1) the Nuisances Act with rules to prevent people from inflicting environmental or other dangers, damages, or nuisances upon each other; (2) the Gauges Act regulating the use of weights and measures and related devices; (3) the Food and Drugs Act with regulations concerning the storage, preservation, and preparation of the goods that fall within its jurisdiction; and (4) the Meat Inspection Act which establishes a system of local authority inspection of meat and meat products.

In addition to these general regulations, the retail trader is also confronted with municipal rules such as the local restrictions on objects and structures placed on, above, or beneath public ground (e.g., signs and vending machines); local rules concerning the shape and external layout of buildings; and local zoning plans that determine the possibilities of location.

Finally, there is a state (national) regulation that requires businesses to have shelters available within one week after the proclamation of a state of preparedness. The regulation only affects the larger shops that may contain thirty or more persons at one time. The firms do not have to install these facilities now, but they are supposed to plan or consider whatever steps are necessary to provide this protection within the mandatory period if a state of preparedness should be declared. Several large firms have installed shelters in new or reconstructed buildings, and in many cases they can be combined with warehousing facilities. However, in practice the government has not enforced this requirement. But there are also some possibilities of a rather important subsidy from the government if the shelter will serve public use, with the size of the allowance of course depending upon the shelter's location and capacity.

Protection against Rent Increases

Although it is not an aspect of public policy concerning land use, protection against rent increases will be discussed here since it is an aspect of location and occupancy problems.

A recent law provides new protection in this respect for retail, handicrafts, small-transport, hotel, catering, and camping businesses. According to the regulations issued under this law, a tenant who completes a rental contract after 1 May 1971 has reasonable certainty that he will be able to use the premises for a period of ten years. The rental may be made dependent upon a price index, but otherwise cannot be raised for a period of five years, and the tenancy contract is valid for the same period. At the end of that period, the rent can only be changed by order of a justice of the peace if the parties cannot reach a private agreement. Moreover, the tenant can insist upon the right to remain on the premises for another five years if he so desires unless the landlord or the landlord's immediate family want to occupy the property themselves or unless the lessor can convince the justice that the tenant has not run his business properly. This latter claim is difficult to maintain in court in view of the vagueness of the relevant rules.

Either party can terminate the contract at the end of the ten-year period, upon at least one year's notice. If the lessor does so, however, the tenant has six weeks in which to apply to the justice of the peace for a further continuance of his lease. The law also contains other benefits for the tenants. Under previous regulations, the tenant had to obtain the lessor's approval for transfer of the tenancy contract if he sold his business. Now the tenant can appeal to the courts if the lessor denies that approval without valid grounds. Under certain circumstances, the tenant also has a claim for indemnification of lost goodwill in case the lessor terminates the rental contract.

Education, Research, and Information

Education

The new developments in entry policy discussed earlier will affect retail trade education. Currently this education is organized in two ways. On the one hand, it is provided during the day in lower-level retail trade schools (age 12-15 years), followed by secondary retail trade schools (16-20 years). These schools are not part of the compulsory education system but they are supervised by the government, and the teachers are paid by the state. On the other hand, retail instruction is also provided in private courses that cover both general commercial knowledge and the technical skills previously required for admission to various lines of trade. The sponsors of these courses may apply for a government subsidy, in which case they also become subject to government supervision. Moreover, the course examinations must be submitted for state approval, and a representative of the government must attend the examinations or the certificates of capacity issued at the end of the program will be valueless for use in obtaining the license to start a new business. In accordance with the changed requirements for entry into business, the general policy now is to try to integrate general commercial knowledge and the technical aspects of training for the separate lines of retailing. The general commercial and entrepreneurial aspects of the education are receiving growing emphasis.

The forms of education mentioned above are intended to prepare young people for entrepreneurship in retailing. However, not all of the certified pupils are in a position to start their own firms, either immediately or in the near future. In such case, they usually can obtain a middle or high level job in retailing.

Besides this entrepreneurial education, there are several forms of basic education that include full-time training for lower level employees in retailing. Nevertheless, it has become clear in recent years that much more attention needs to be paid to the training and education of younger employees as a result of the enlargement of scale in retailing and the new entry legislation. The authorities and organizations concerned are considering, among others, the possibilities of creating apprenticeship programs for the retail trade that would be adapted to the several existing instruction levels. In principle, such programs would give the young workers a chance to reach higher, or even the highest, levels in business. As a first step, they are considering a primary apprentice training program for salespeople, to be organized by a national institution in order to improve both their commercial and general knowledge. Another program is administered by the Foundation for Foreign Contacts in Retailing whose governing board includes representatives of the Ministries for Economic and for Social Affairs, the Central Board for Retail Trade, and organizations and institutions in the field of retail trade education. This foundation promotes temporary traineeships abroad for promising young people, and it maintains foreign contacts for retail trade education. The results of sending young people to England, Germany, Switzerland, and Belgium have been very favorable, and the number of participants in the program is increasing steadily.

Research and Information

The importance that government attaches to general and market research and statistics is illustrated by the Ministry for Economic Affairs' memoranda to Parliament on small- and medium-size business and entrepreneurship in 1954, 1959, and 1969. These documents contain, besides a survey of past proposed future policy, a wealth of data and figures concerning medium- and small-size business in general and retail trade in particular. The Central Bureau of Statistics, a government office, plays an important role here through the publication of data and figures concerning retail trade and handicrafts. As to retailing, it publishes the general census of the trade and statistics on turnover, employment, income, operating costs, retail prices, balance sheets, etc. At present, it is also preparing a central business registry to combine the data now collected in regional registries.

The Central Registration Office for Retail Trade and Handicrafts handles the registration of all retail firms for the Central Board for Retail Trade. This office compiles statistics on the number of establishments, and registers all changes, in cooperation with the Chambers of Commerce and Industry. Its statistics on changes, subdivided according to merchandise lines, are a valuable tool for understanding the structural development of retail trade. They not only contain information about entry into, and withdrawal from, business but also about changes in merchandise lines, transfers of ownership, and other details. The registry is a very useful source of research data in studying such matters as the causes of business liquidation. The Central Registration Office's investigations have concluded that on the average in the retail trade, approximately 60 percent of the business terminations are due to death, age, or illness of the proprietor, 8 percent to a preference for wage earning instead of entrepreneurship; and 32 percent to different causes such as town reconstruction, bankruptcy, merger, discontinuance of the retailing activities in a multi-function business, and emigration.

The Central Board for Retail Trade and the Central Board for Handicrafts have also established a joint institute, the Council for Medium and Small Size Business, as a scientific advisory organ to study the macro-socioeconomic problems of middle-class business. The Council is not concerned with detailed, individual-firm managerial problems but instead deals with the phenomenon of small- and medium-size business as a part of the overall economic structure.

The government holds the very pronounced view that rapid economic, social, and technical developments have made scientific research increasingly important to medium- and small-size business. Its significance is considered to be three-fold: (1) as a necessary basis for public policy and for trade organization policy; (2) to help shape training and instruction in retailing; and (3) as a guide and management tool for the individual entrepreneur. Consequently, the public authorities try to promote collaboration among the existing research institutions, including the universities and high schools. The objectives are to prevent unnecessary duplication of effort and to divide the research work in accordance with the special abilities and facilities of the different institutions. In order to further these objectives, and in view of the resource limitations that the research institutions face, the government plans to draft a priority scheme for retail trade research in the coming years, and it has created a committee to advise on such a scheme.

The most complete information is furnished to the retail trade, both collectively and individually, by two institutes financed by government and the public business organizations, namely, the Economic Institute for Medium and Small Size Business, already mentioned, and the Central Institute for Medium and Small Size Business.

The Economic Institute for Medium and Small Size Business, founded in 1930, is an independent institution with a board of directors consisting of representatives of public and semi-public authorities. It does research in the fields of retailing, handicrafts, hotel and catering, and transportation, with the greater part of its activities concentrated on the sectors first mentioned. Its research includes investigations in the fields of business economics, socioeconomics, sociology, and social psychology; and among other subjects it includes structural research, business cycle research, branch research, interfirm comparisons, productivity studies, and management research, predominantly on behalf of medium- and small-size business.

The Central Institute for Medium and Small Size Business (especially its Department of Location Planning) also engages in fundamental research to further the scientific and practical planning of shop location. In this connection, reliable data are collected on structural developments in certain lines; and studies are made of consumer behavior, consumer preferences, and of business-economic problems such as minimum and optimum space productivity.

Many of the research activities result in direct or indirect information to the trade. This information is provided by the two institutes mentioned and by the following public offices: Central Bureau of Statistics, Economic Information Service, Central Organization for Applied Technological Research, and the Industrial Information Service. Other public or semi-public institutions providing information are: Central Board for Retail Trade, and P.B.O.s of the respective branches of trade, the Chambers of Commerce and Industry, and the Economic Technological Institutes.

Operations and Merchandising

Shop Closure (Store Hours)

Public intervention into the operations of business can have both a restrictive and a protective or stimulating character. One of the most important and radical regulations was, and still is, that of shop closure. Originally, closing hours were regulated by the municipal authorities, but in 1932 the first state (national) regulation was instituted. This national regulation withdrew this matter from the jurisdiction of the local authorities, although the latter retained a certain very restricted autonomy. The introduction at that time of a decree regulating the working hours of shop employees was an important stimulus to the national Shop Closure Act. In the opinion of the government, the control of employee working hours would have given merchants without paid personnel an unfair advantage in the absence of store-hours limits.

The shop closure regulation was changed during World War II, in 1952, and in 1959. The general principle of the regulation now in force is that shops must be closed all day Sunday, and on other days from 6:00 P.M. (18:00 hours) until 5:00 A.M. (5:00 hours). the closing hour may be delayed, by legislation, until 7:00 P.M. (19:00 hours) for special groups of shops, and the municipal authorities have the power, subject to Crown approbation, to grant exemptions from the closing rules when local circumstances make this desirable. This is mainly done to permit one late closing per week.

Furthermore, the local authorities can permit Sunday openings for the benefit of tourism and recreation, and they can also restrict opening hours even more rigorously than is required under the national regulation. They can, for example, insist on a half-day weekly closure for all shops or for special groups by prohibiting store openings before 1:00 P.M. (13:00 hours) on Mondays or after 1:00 P.M. on Mondays, Tuesdays, or Wednesdays. Although there is pressure from several sides to change the closure regulations, the parties concerned cannot agree about the way in which this should be done. Government is of the opinion that, within certain boundaries, the individual retailer should have more freedom in fixing the opening and closing hours of his shop. On the other hand, a recent official statement says that the present regulation has created a social pattern that cannot be easily changed.[13] The Central Board for Retail Trade has made a report on this matter, and the possibilities for changes are now being studied.

The local authorities have still another restrictive power in that they can force groups of shops to close for a twelve-day yearly vacation or for two six-day vacation periods. However, they cannot exercise this power without the agreement of the local Chamber of Commerce and Industry. The Chambers have a similar right to veto weekly half-day closing plans in order to prevent unreasonable closure rules.

Assortment

An indirect effect of the older entry legislation was government intervention in merchandise assortment decisions. The 1954 Settlement Act established separate entry decrees for each line of trade, and it required the determination of the assortment that each line or branch of retail trade was entitled to handle. However, the general tendency in retail trade, in the Netherlands as well as elsewhere, has been to expand the merchandise assortment beyond the traditional boundaries, and the old restrictions have been an obstacle to sound growth in this direction. In part this problem was dealt with through a system of exemptions, in consultation with the retail trade boards, when warranted by the nature of the business or by regional or local circumstances. As noted earlier, the new settlement legislation provides much more inherent flexibility without use of the cumbersome exemption process.

Relations to Suppliers

There is no public control or regulating function in the Netherlands with regard to the relations between a retailer and his suppliers. Some exceptions to this generalization exist in the emergency food supply and rationing laws, but those laws only become operative under extraordinary circumstances such as war or the threat of war.

Sales Promotion

Special public regulations affect retail advertising and sales promotion. One of the most important is the Selling-Off Act that controls clearance sales and their advertising, and is designed to prevent misleading use of the words "clearance," "selling-off," and "selling-out." Under this act, the term "selling off" (clearance) can only be used for bona-fide after-season price reductions, limited to two nineteen-day periods per year established by the Central Board for Retail Trade. A "selling out" (liquidation) sale can be conducted at any time of the year in order to liquidate a business, but can only be held under the circumstances of a genuine liquidation, and it requires the approval of the appropriate Chamber of Commerce and Industry. Before this legislation was adopted, the terms "selling-off" and "selling-out" were often used simply as advertising to increase ordinary turnover; and by the turn of the century some retailers were "selling-off" throughout the year, even in the peak selling season. This is now considered an improper and unacceptable method of competition.

Several other laws affect retail sales promotion. The gift systems restrictions already mentioned control one type of sales promotion. The Food and Drugs Act, mentioned above also, contains some specifications as to the labeling and advertising of the products under its jurisdiction. The recent Act on the Supply of Medicines establishes an Inspection Committee to check recommendations and advertised claims for packaged (patent or proprietary) medicines. This work has been handled by a privately-composed Inspection Committee for Public Recommendation of Medicines, containing representatives of the press, advertising agencies, importers, traders, physicians, and pharmacists.

The Committee for Maintenance of the Dutch Advertising Code is also a private organization, although strongly encouraged by the government. The rules of conduct in this code are intended to promote: (1) protection of the public against misleading representations; (2) development of good taste in advertising expressions; and (3) advertising's social values. This Code has been approved and accepted by the most important advertising organizations, by the press and cinema operators (advertising films are part of cinema presentations in the Netherlands), and by the Dutch Advisory Board on Housekeeping and the Dutch Consumers Association.

Voluntary private regulation of this sort does not exclude the possibility of governmental intervention. A recent governmental committee report comments that there is little cause for public intervention if private regulation satisfactorily prevents misleading or improper advertising. However, the government should take action if the private rules are unable to prevent consumer deception concerning such matters as price and delivery, or if the misleading advertising interferes with orderly economic activity to the detriment of the general welfare.[14] It should be mentioned that the Committee has the impression that relatively few abuses occur in advertising in the Netherlands. The Committee also encourages as much reliance as possible on voluntary regulation and on cooperation between industry and trade and consumers. Nevertheless, the government is now studying the possibility and desirability of a law against misleading advertising.

Finally, the boards of the Public Business Organizations can issue regulations that prohibit certain forms of advertising that interfere with orderly competition in their branches of trade.

Installment Credit

All installment and hire-purchase sales, except those with a term of less than three months, come under the Act concerning Installment Payments Systems as well as under the Civil Code. The act also deals with rental and service agreements that involve installment credit. The rules affect suppliers and door-to-door salesmen and finance companies, and they include specification of an obligatory down-payment.

Other Legal Obligations

The Commercial Code requires every businessman to keep books of account, to prepare an annual financial balance sheet, and to preserve certain records for a specified period of years. As noted, the Act concerning the Registry of Commerce obliges every firm to inscribe itself on the registries that are maintained by the Chambers of Commerce and Industry. Both domestic companies and foreign firms having subsidiaries, branch offices, or commercial agents with proxy in Holland are required to place certain information about themselves on the registry. This information is open to inspection by any interested party, and its availability provides a measure of protection to anyone who deals with the listed companies. This Act on Trade Names and the Merchandising Marks Act protect the public against misleading names and marks, and also protect property rights in brands and trade marks.

The Significance of Retail Trade in the Netherlands

Medium- and small-size business, which includes the greater part of the retail trade, occupies an important position in the Netherlands. This is not only a matter of numbers, but is also illustrated by the attention that the public authorities give to this sector. A recent government statement notes the benefits to society and the economy that result from good opportunities for the establishment and expansion of small businesses. Moreover, the statement continues, the importance of small business is not confined to its social and economic impact. Small business entrepreneurship tends to promote well-rounded personal development and evokes a variety of abilities in contrast to the specialized and limited nature of many positions in large organizations. It is this "human" side of medium and small business, according to the government memorandum, that justifies and inspires an active policy in support of such business.

The work of the retail trades in supplying private consumption is indicated by the fact that they accounted for slightly over 60 percent of 1968 private consumption expenditures.[15] Even this figure is somewhat understated, although the sales of firms that engage in retailing as a sideline to other activities are included as well as those primarily in the retail business. However, the business done by automobile dealers and some of the other types of merchants who are outside the jurisdiction of the Central Board for Retail Trade are classified as nonretail in the source from which the 60 percent figure was derived.

Retail trade employment is also of great importance. Figures for the year 1968 show that there were 188,000 selling points (establishments) resulting in 451,000 man-years of employment (a man-year equals 300 working days). Subdivided according to size of firm, the figures are:[16]

	Establishments	Employment (man-years)
Medium- and small-size businesses	182,600	197,000 employees 169,000 proprietors 336,000 (total)
Large businesses	4,800	
Consumer cooperatives	600	85,000

During the period 1960-68, employment in medium- and small-size business increased by 9 percent and the average number of active persons in retail stores with employees (111,000 stores as of 1968) grew from 1.7 to 2.1. Growth has not been universal or uniform, however, throughout medium- and small-size business. For example, a remarkably different employment situation exists in the groceries and allied products sector. This sector suffered about a 5 percent decline in employment during the 1960-68 period; the number of proprietors decreased by about 22,000, while employee man-years increased by about 16,000. In contrast, employment in the durable and other consumer goods sector increased by about 18 percent during the same period, mainly with regard to the number of employees (plus 42,000).

The share of retail trade in the national income can be set at 5-6 percent for medium- and small-size business and at 8-9 percent for the entire retail trade.

Final Remarks and Conclusion

We have refrained from critical remarks in the chapter, since we believe that the purpose of this volume is not to discuss what should be, but rather to provide a survey of existing policy in various countries, both as a source of information and as a means of comparison.

This survey shows that public policy in the Netherlands influences retail trade in many directions and in some respects very drastically. This is partly the consequence of general public policy developments after the Second World War. Society in general and economic matters in particular have become more complex in the postwar period. Consequently, the majority of people have favored intensification of the public grip on economic life, and the retail trade has had no privileged position in this respect. Some aspects of retailing, such as pricing and location, have been especially likely to be subjected to control. Many of the measures have been intended to serve consumer interests and to provide protection as to both the quality the consumer receives and the price he pays.

The policy with regard to medium- and small-size business also has another character. On the one hand, it serves to protect young people against the risks of ill-conceived entrepreneurship; on the other side, it offers them a helping hand towards overcoming the many difficulties of retail business ownership. Examples of this assistance are found in education, research, and business finance.

The Foreign Entrepreneur

Finally, we will recapitulate the possibilities and position of the foreign entrepreneur in retailing in the Netherlands. As was seen before, there is no form of discrimination with respect to birth, race, or nationality concerning entry into trade. In other words, foreigners and Dutch nationals alike must conform to the same requirements, and both will receive the same license of capacity to start a business if they meet those conditions. The current change in the licensing system, to a single license for all types of retail trade, should make it even easier for foreigners to obtain the certificate of capacity. Moreover, it is not necessary for the manager or the entrepreneur himself to have such a certificate, since the law only stipulates that one of the active persons involved in the business must have it. Consequently, employment of a qualified person solves any difficulty in this connection.

There are no distinctions between nationalities with regard to other legal obligations as foreigners and nationals must comply with these obligations in the same way. This does not alter the fact that it may be more difficult for foreigners to obtain government-guaranteed loans. These loans are only issued after an investigation of the profit possibilities, and it is always possible that the office making the decision will give the foreign request a low priority or will conclude that the prospects are poorer if a foreigner establishes the business. There are, however, no restrictions on the importation of capital resources or on their repatriation if the firm is liquidated. Similarly, profits and cash flows from the business may be freely transferred without any restriction.

May 1972

Notes

1. According to the Foundation Decree the following lines do not fall under this central board: pharmacies, ship chandlers, dealers in cars and gasoline, and dealers in agricultural and horticultural seeds and potatoes for planting.

2. "Middenstandsnota 1959" (Memorandum to Parliament of the Ministry for Economic Affairs concerning the problems of middle class entrepreneurs).

3. "Nota Midden- en Kleinbedrijf 1969" (Memorandum to Parliament of the Ministry for Economic Affairs concerning medium- and small-size business).

4. The Establishment Act (Staatsblad No. 99), 25 February 1954.

5. "Nota Midden- en Kleinbedrijf 1969."

6. This possibility is described in the following way: when in our opinion

public interest makes it necessary, stipulations in agreements with regard to competition can be declared not binding on account of the nature or tendency mentioned in the agreement concerned. In this way certain forms of cartels can be declared not binding regardless of the branch in which they appear.

7. "Nota inzake de verticale prijsbinding" (Memorandum to Parliament of the Ministry for Economic Affairs re resale price maintenance).

8. Whether an article is considered as belonging or not belonging to the branch is decided by the circumscription of the trade line in the Settlement Decree for that line in accordance with the Settlement Act 1954.

9. In 1955, the largest grocery chain introduced the opportunity to exchange stamps with a total value of f79. for an income bond with a nominal value of f100. This was a very great success and had to be stopped in 1961. In 1971, this same chain offered a new possibility for coupon-collecting consumers who are now given the opportunity to purchase bonds issued by a subsidiary company with interest rates increasing during the term (1971/1997) from 8½ percent to 13 percent a year. Approximately f25,000,000 of these bonds are issued. (f1.00 = U.S. $.31)

10. "Middenstandsnota 1954" (Memorandum to Parliament of the Ministry for Economic Affairs concerning the problems of middle class entrepreneurs).

11. "Middenstandsnota 1959."

12. The Prices Act (Staatsblad No. 135), 24 March 1961.

13. "Nota Midden- en Kleinbedrijf 1969."

14. "Rapport van de Commissie Orderlijk Economisch Verkeer 1967" (Report of the Committee on Orderly Economic Activity).

15. Annual Report 1969, Central Board for Retail Trade.

16. Council for Medium and Small Size Business

14 Poland

J. Hart Walters, Jr.

Introduction

The very idea of a public policy towards retailing, as it is usually understood in the West, has limited application in a centrally planned, socialist economy. Differences in policy postures and regulatory practices among capitalist and "mixed" economies are amply documented elsewhere in this volume. However, all such economies have in common an important private sector of retailing that interacts with one or another form of public authority.

The major feature that differentiates the public policy of capitalist from that of socialist nations is neither central planning, by itself, nor the institution of socialized or state ownership. Rather, the congruence of *both* socialized ownership *and* central planning results in the incorporation of retailing as an integral part of the state apparatus—structurally, within the network of state-owned or -controlled industries, and functionally, in the flow of planning directives and administrative orders. Under these conditions—and in marked contrast with the West—retail institutions cannot operate as *independent* loci of power, interacting with the state and playing important and even dominant roles in formulating the legislative and other enactments that regulate their behavior.[1]

This conception of the retailing structure as an integral component of the state economic and political apparatus is not meant to suggest a monolithic organization; nor does it assume away significant areas of conflict. It *does* mean that any model of countervailing power, i.e., of some entity called "retailing" acting in relation to some other entity entitled "the state," has limited applicability because the retailing organizations are neither independent of the state, nor possess separate constituencies or political bases of their own. Consideration of state policies towards Polish retailing is therefore mainly: (1) a study of state policies and attitudes towards consumer goods and personal consumption, in general, and the role that retail trade is supposed to play, in particular; (2) a description and analysis of the organizational structure of retailing and its relevance to socialist objectives; and (3) a study of planning and the effects of planning directives on the operation of retail enterprises.

The Private Sector

As was the case with prerevolutionary Russia, Poland had no meaningful legacy of private retailing that could serve as a nucleus for building a modern system,

271

regardless of form of ownership. Before World War II, small-scale petty retail trade predominated. The number of establishments was large, and many could hardly be classified as "permanent, localized establishments," i.e., stores. Retail trade establishments were, moreover, undergoing a process of "fragmentation" into yet smaller units, a trend that was halted only by the onset of the war.[2] Small establishments not really in the category of shops in fixed locations comprised over 70 percent of total retail outlets, but accounted for less than 25 percent of retail sales volume on the eve of the Second World War.[3]

Much of what had been fragmented by economic forces was physically destroyed during the war, occupation, and resistance. While the private sector controlled, in 1946, about 90 percent of Polish retail establishments, the subsequent shift to socialized retailing was rapid. By 1949, the socialized sector had achieved dominance (60 percent) of total national retail sales; by 1950, there were more socialized than private establishments.[4]

Since the advent of socialist power in Poland, the decline of the private sector has been continuous, except for a brief resurgence in the two years immediately following the liberalizations of 1956. By the end of 1968, the private sector accounted for less than 9 percent of Polish retail establishments, with less than 1.5 percent of the nation's retail sales volume.[5]

While this very small private sector in retailing is not an important subject of state policy, its decline from its preeminent pre-war status *was* the direct result of a conscious policy of the new regime: the establishment of social ownership or control over most means of production. In contrast with agricultural production, Polish retailing, along with other elements of goods distribution and industrial production, was to be socialized. The role for private trade is thus a residual, and disappearing one.

While farming in Poland, unlike most of the rest of Eastern Europe, is overwhelmingly private, there is no direct equivalent to the *kolkhoz* marketing network of the Soviet Union. Outside of a very few "farmers' markets," the bulk of farm produce is purchased by state and cooperative wholesaling or processing enterprises, and eventually finds its way into the socialized retail trade network.

Entry into private trade is effectively discouraged by rigorous licensing procedures, high taxes, and difficulties in obtaining goods or supplies, the major or sole sources for which are socially controlled. Presently, private establishments seem to have their greatest strengths in services such as tailoring, shoe repair, automobile repair, and the like. As the socialized sector continues to expand and modernize its facilities, one would expect the private sector to become even more marginal.

General Policies Towards Consumption and Trade

The coming to power of the Polish United Workers' Party (PZPR) followed by more than twenty-five years the establishment of the Soviet Union. The PZPR thus had not only the large body of Marxist thought, but also the experience of the USSR to rely on. Although the Soviet Union served as the general planning and policy model, the Western exposure of many of its leading planners and academic economists, as well as differences in its own condition produced important modifications of attitude in Poland.

Polish Marxists, as did their Soviet counterparts, were quick to polemicize on the exploitative character of *capitalist* trade. But trade, itself, the functions attendant to it, and the network of intermediary agencies necessary to carry it out were all recognized as essential economic activities. The social and economic purpose of trade under socialist conditions was to effect the distribution (literally, "turnover" or circulation) of goods to the working population.[6]

The stated goals of Polish socialism were by no means ascetic, and consumers' satisfaction, along with efficiency in the use of resources, was one of the major criteria in judging performance of the trade network. The correct function of socialist trade was viewed as helping to maximize "the satisfaction of social needs in given economic conditions."[7] While consumers have had little direct influence in defining the precise nature of those "given economic conditions," the very broad objective of consumers' satisfaction was defined as meaning: "... not only the quantity, assortment, and quality of products delivered to their recipients, but equally the quality of service and the convenience of the consumer, the saving of his effort and time."[8]

The translation of these goal and policy statements into action has been variable. Few in Poland would contend that the level of consumer service and convenience is, by Western standards, high. Yet, there are positive elements that are at least indicative of a "pro-consumer" attitude on the part of the authorities: (1) virtually all state and many cooperative stores display the legend "the customer is always right," which has meant quite liberal "return" policies for defective or unsatisfactory merchandise; (2) a very wide spectrum of consumer goods, including processed foods and a number of fresh items, are grade-labeled; (3) all packagings are in even divisions or multiples of the metric system; (4) virtually all manufactured consumer goods are guaranteed, and the language of the warranty is clear, simple, and unambiguous.

In some contrast with the Soviet Union, there has been a quite substantial growth in self-service stores, concomitant with which has been prepackaging. The development of self-service was occasioned, in part, by the incentive structure given retail trade enterprises, which tended to *discourage* additions to the labor force. The latter employment policy, however, often left clerk-service stores with insufficient personnel to provide customers with rapid service. While the *kassa* system so typical in the Soviet Union exists in Poland, it is by no means prevalent. (This is a system whereby two or three separate transactions with so many clerks are necessary before completing a purchase.)

Consumer convenience suffers from some of the same physical space problems characteristic of the Soviet Union. The ground level space of apartment houses and office buildings are set aside for retail and other consumer and public service facilities. Thus the total retail space is broken up into physically small units that are locationally convenient, but which are limited in their assortments. Moreover, because of the high employment rate of women in Poland, there is a very heavy peak-hour concentration in urban retail trade, and the small establishments become quite crowded. The crowding and queues so characteristic of the peak hours reflect these inadequacies in space rather than shortages of goods.

The need for more modern forms was amply demonstrated by the instant .success of the first true supermarket, replete with parking lot, that was opened in Warsaw in the spring of 1962. However, the cost of such projects is high for a poor country with other pressing priorities, and the large and expensive (and architecturally quite stunning) "Supersam" (literally, "super self-service") was criticized.

In planning the growth of an economy that had, in the first place, been underdeveloped by European standards, and that had, secondly, been virtually destroyed during World War II, the new Polish regime perceived the necessity of making a basic choice between a rapid growth of current consumption at the expense of investment, vs. a high rate of capital accumulation at the expense of current consumption. In making the choice, the Polish authorities relied heavily on the Soviet experience:

The basis for industrialization is always heavy industry, although in the second stage of the industrialization process, movement in the direction of building up light industry can occur, along with development of nonproductive investment and services.[9]

And some of the problems created by this choice were understood:

... a socialist society attempts two basic objectives: first, the growth of well-being, i.e., the increase of satisfaction of material and cultural needs of the members of society; and secondly, the development of industrial power. Between these two objectives there exists to a certain degree a contradiction. But [it] is only relative, occurring mainly in the short run, because the development of industrial power guarantees the increasing of material well-being and the cultural level.[10]

The effects of this type of choice have provided a growth rate for total industrial production considerably above that for goods intended for personal consumption.[11] The results of Polish planning also include: (1) essentially full employment involving the urbanization and industrial employment of large numbers of peasants; (2) a large backlog of consumers' needs that have not been fully satisfied; (3) a broad distribution of purchasing power—including increases in "discretionary" buying power—through an egalitarian wages policy. As a consequence, the pressures upon consumers' goods industries and on the trade network have been considerable. While the concept of total "planners' sovereignty" has long since been abandoned, the basic investment decisions required to respond to those pressures in terms of more consumers' goods and more and different kinds of marketing facilities are still mainly subject to planners' choice rather than consumers' sovereignty.

Organizational Policies and Structures

In Poland, a rather large number of types of retail enterprise exist under a variety of control centers. Leaving aside the small private sector, the socialized sector of Polish retailing can be divided, broadly, into two types of enterprise: cooperative and state. The distinction is made, not only because the cooperatives are organizationally discrete from state firms, but because they figure differently in the flow of planning directives.

It was a deliberate policy decision, following the incorporation of the cooperatives into the socialized sector, to take steps to foster and develop them. Besides being given the principal role in supplying rural ration-card holders in the years following World War II, the *rural cooperatives* were given, for all practical purposes, a monopoly position in all villages and towns of less than 10,000 population. The basic rural cooperative unit was typically a multi-purpose society formed at the village or township level. Most, if not all, of the retail establishments in a locality, regardless of type, would "belong" to the local society. The society, in turn, would be affiliated to a federation or union of cooperatives at the county *(powiat)* and/or provincial *(województwo)* level, and eventually to the national union of farm cooperatives. The local societies maintained liaison with the trade division of the appropriate peoples' council (local government body), although the directives affecting state enterprises were not directly binding on them. Rural cooperatives account for about 25 percent of Polish retail trade in the socialized sector.[12]

Producers' cooperatives, in some instances, maintain retail outlets, especially in the cities. They operate within the frame of directives binding the particular industry, rather than those operative through the provincial councils. *Consumer cooperatives* operate a full range of different types of retail establishment in the cities and larger towns. Typically, the cooperative functions under the aegis of the local government body. They, too, are affiliated with a national union of consumer cooperatives. Unlike the state enterprises, the cooperatives retain their profits and pay taxes to the state.

The cooperatives are only indirectly subject to the planning indicators that bind state enterprises. Consequently, they have had somewhat more flexibility in operation, being able to utilize after-tax profits more freely and to fix the size of their labor forces in a somewhat less rigid manner than the state enterprises. However, this freedom is considerably circumscribed by their being bound, as are *all* components of the socialized sector of retailing, by such centrally-set controls as retail prices and margins on goods.

State stores, which account for about half of the socialized sector's retail sales,[13] can be divided broadly into three categories: (1) manufacturer's branch outlets, which are governed by the directives controlling the particular industry and, in turn, the particular firm; (2) manufacturer's association outlets, which are governed similarly; and (3) "MHD" (Urban Retail Trade), which are state retail trading enterprises. The latter, which constitute the single largest group, are controlled regionally by the trade division of the appropriate political division (province or county). Within each such control center, the enterprises are then organized by typical retail specializations, such as general groceries, household articles, department stores, and the like.

With the exception of the near-monopoly position of the rural cooperatives, a concept of competition was implicit in the organizational policies concomitant with Polish planning. This competition, however, was only nominal, in that the

Polish consumer's area of choice lay largely in the decision of which store under what control center was to be patronized. The consumer had no choice insofar as price was concerned since the price of a given item of merchandise was fixed—and was the same—regardless of the type of store through which it was sold.

Since prices were fixed, there was not any meaningful competition in services. The state stores were under pressure to keep costs low, and the directive indicators under which they operated acted as a factor against additions to the labor force. Further, given the general context of a "sellers' market," i.e., inadequacies in the supply of many consumers' goods as well as a shortage in the total "supply" of retail shops and service personnel, there was little compelling reason for retail enterprises to improve their services.[14]

The organizational structure of retailing also inhibited yet another element of consumer service, namely, assortment variation. Those outlets that were branches of a particular manufacturing enterprise tended to stock only that factory's output. The retail outlets of manufacturers' associations would typically carry a wide range of the output of the particular industry, which often would not constitute a convenient consumption assortment. The retail stores under *MHD* were, to be sure, organized into the more usual retail branches, but establishments were typically small-scale with narrow, highly-specialized assortments, not unlike the traditional specializations of France and Great Britain.

A further result of regional and local control of much of retailing, especially the *MHD* stores, was a fragmentation of the retail structure into a large number of small-scale enterprises and establishments. Thus, one or more retail grocery firms would be controlled together with, say, a household goods enterprise, by the trade division of the county government body. Such enterprises would then have no direct connection with counterpart firms in the same branch of retailing in the neighboring locality or region. This policy effectively nullified the possibility of large-scale operations with their attendant potentialities of both vertical and horizontal integration.

What were the consequences of this policy of organizational fragmentation regarding efficiency? By American standards, retail gross margins in Poland are low.[15] However, percentage margins are somewhat deceptive. In Poland, manufacturing costs are relatively high, so that an absolutely high marketing cost could appear as a relatively low proportion of the total social cost of delivered goods. The truth of this elementary proposition is suggested by data on rates of inventory turnover, one of the most important measures of retail productivity. On the whole, the number of stock-turns per year is low in comparison with U.S. standards.[16] This phenomenon is at once a consequence of the small size of the *establishment* (as opposed to the firm) and of the institution of fixed prices, which could not be adjusted by management to take into account changes in the balance between supply and demand.

Planning: Pre-1956

Prior to the October reforms of 1956, the Polish planning system was highly centralized. It relied mainly on a system of administrative orders that defined specified tasks for each branch of the economy and included the setting of sales targets for retail enterprises.[17] This pattern of centrally setting goals and then allocating resources directly in relation to them was viewed as necessary, because: "The difficult economic situation . . ., the unsatisfactory supply of industrial materials, (and) the lack of basic consumption articles necessitated the allocation of goods and a guaranteed form of supplying the working population with essential articles."[18]

A system of ration cards was employed for foods and certain other consumers' goods, and the cooperatives were given the chief role in supplying cardholders.[19] The latter reflected a conscious state policy of strengthening the cooperatives, which had been a relatively important feature of prewar Polish retailing.

Given the immediate postwar context of a low level of economic development, widespread destruction of marketing facilities, short supplies, and the goals of *"socialist* reconstruction." the centralized, highly directive modes of planning were undoubtedly necessary to insure the basic integrity of the plans themselves, as well as to ration extremely scarce resources in the direction of their intended uses. Pre-1956 state policy could be characterized as: (1) insuring the socialization of retail trade; and (2) "running" the socialized enterprises by directives and administrative orders that were binding on the managers as well as on the administrative bodies to which they were responsible.

Post-1956 Planning Patterns

The policy of highly centralized planning generated its own, internal contradictions. The planning system created growth, not only in industrial production, but also in the volume of retail sales and the numbers of retail establishments. In short, the growth process substantially increased the numbers and scope of available, alternative choices, including the placing of a larger proportion of the population in total reliance upon the organized marketing structure. These new conditions made it difficult, if not altogether impossible, to maintain highly centralized modes of direction and control. Besides, given the pressures then existent for social and political liberalization, the move towards more decentralized modes of planning and control were virtually inevitable.

The post-1956 decentralization signified no abandonment of the concept of central planning through directive indicators. Rather, it meant more of a "flow" of planning in which higher bodies would set certain basic tasks and impose certain broad limitations upon organizations at each succeeding stage. Working in relation to these defined goals and limits, a given organization would develop its own plans, which in turn could involve setting goals and limits for units at yet lower levels.

There was thus a dual system consisting of: (1) a decentralized flow of planning including a stepped series of directive as well as "orientational-analytical" indicators; and (2) centrally-determined administrative controls that affected all segments of a particular industry or sector of the economy. Prices, in particular, were an important subject of direct central control.

The flow of decentralized planning begins, in effect, with the "long-term" (three- to five-year) plans. Enacted nationally by the *Sejm* (Parliament), it is imperative (obligatory) for Ministries on the national level and for the Praesidia of the *Województwo* (Provincial) Peoples Councils *(WRN)*, regionally. Eventually, the retail trade enterprise develops, within the frame of directives coming to it, its own long-term plan. This includes: (1) establishing the rate of growth of turnover (sales); (2) planning for changes in the structure or composition of turnover; (3) establishing policies in relation to inventory levels; (4) setting goals and defining methods for increasing labor productivity; (5) defining other steps towards the lowering of costs; (6) setting investment goals; and (7) planning for development of the network of establishments under its control.

The National Economic Plan, enacted annually with the State Budget by the *Sejm,* is the direct, operational means for putting the long-term plan into effect. This Plan is imperative for the government, for sectors of the economy and for *Województwo* and *Powiat* (County) Peoples Councils *(PRN),* and through them eventually for all state enterprises. Like the long-term plan, the annual plan is complex, covering in its subject matter all major aspects of economic activity— first in the form of goals and programs, and second in the form of balances, norms, and the construction of specific methods of achieving goals.

Speaking more concretely of retail trade, the annual plan of internal trade is set out in its final form by the Planning Commission of the Council of Ministers and enacted by the *Sejm* as part of the National Economic Plan. Since the various Ministries in the *national* government are bound by this plan, each Ministry affected develops a trade plan for enterprises under its control. At the same time, at the provincial level, the plenary sessions of the *WRN,* acting on the basis of imperative indicators in the National Economic Plan, develop plans for the functioning of all retail trade enterprises that are under *województwo* or provincial control. The objective of the provincial trade plan is to coordinate the plans and activities of the socialized trade network with the needs of the local population, and in addition to set proportions in the supplies to the various counties within the province. In turn, the plenary sessions of the *PRN* establish the plan of trade turnover for the county; these are governed by the imperative indicators of the provincial trade plan.

Finally, the trade-financial plans are the working plans for retail trade enterprises. They encompass all tasks for the enterprise, the means by which they are to be realized, as well as the planned financial results for the enterprise. These are worked out on a five-year basis, as well as annually.

The annual national plan for trade is broken down even further into quarterly-monthly trade plans. These are established by the Economic Committee of the Council of Ministers, and they bind the Ministries and *WRN.* Quarterly-monthly plans for enterprises are worked out independently by the enterprises themselves, on the basis of imperative indicators embodied in the annual plan.

The three major imperative indices of the National Economic Plan that directly affect the functioning of trade as a division or sector of the national economy are: (1) the value of retail sales in general; (2) the value of *goods* intended for retail sales, and (3) the quantity and value of certain important goods that are allocated centrally between city and country. These indices are imperative only in the sense of treating trade as a branch of the national economy. Responsibility for their observance is vested nationally in the Minister of Internal Trade, and in the trade division of the Praesidium of the *WRN* at the provincial level. For other sectors of the economy, these indices have only an indicative character, and can be changed by the Minister of Internal Trade or the Praesidium of a *WRN* to correspond to changes in the actual market situation. These national and provincial indices do not directly bind particular enterprises.

The next five imperative indicators of the National Economic Plan are: (1) the number of employees in trade, (2) the size of the fund of payments, both as wages and non-wage payments to persons, (3) the financial limit on centralized investment, (4) the amount of investment for trade enterprises, and (5) the amount of payment from profits of trade enterprises to the state budget. These five indicators are imperative, not only in the sense of being binding on trade as a branch of the national economy, but in an organizational sense through their "division" among enterprises that are centrally and regionally planned. Since these indices are in the nature of limitations on the operation of the trade system as a whole, eventually they must be "allocated" as limitations on the operation of particular organizations, even though they are not *directly* binding on trading enterprises. In turn, the Ministries and Praesidia of the *WRN* set out, for the enterprises under *their* control, the following imperative indicators, which in effect are a "concretizing" statement of the previous indicators: (1) percentage relationship of the fund of payments to sales, (2) numbers of workers employed in trade enterprises, (3) the size of the fund of payments for those workers whose wages are not directly connected with the volume of sales, (4) payments from profits to the budget, stated as a proportion of profit, and (5) limit of investments to be received from centrally-allocated investment funds.

The real sense of decentralization is realized when it is taken into account that the number of indices binding Ministries and Praesidia is considerably more than those binding trade enterprises. Thus, even so basic an indicator as the value of retail sales is *worked out independently by the enterprise itself.* It is therefore possible that the sum of sales volumes planned by retail enterprises will not be consistent with those established in the regional or national plan.

In the above connection, it is pointed out, that a one-for-one correspondence in the indicators governing enterprises and Praesidia would only be a formal guarantee of consistency.[26] The basic reason for the inability to establish more than a formal consistency between a broad, provincial, or national goal of sales with the plan of distribution for the particular trading enterprise lies in the impossibility of establishing really objective criteria for the sales an enterprise can actually achieve. While it is possible, on a national and provincial scale, to plan the gross value of goods that will go into retail sales as well as the gross buying power that is available to consumers, it is not equally possible to project *realistically* precisely how consumers will allocate that buying power among various retail enterprises, and among various goods sold at retail.

In planning, the retail trade enterprise is given incentive to attempt to maximize its sales volume. This is the case, because the *percentage* relationship of the wages fund to sales is fixed. The ability of the enterprise vastly to exceed sales goals is, however, limited both by the buying power of the population it serves (set broadly by the planned fund of payments to personal income accounts), and by the quantity and variety of goods that the production sector of the economy can make available to it. Secondly, there are institutional rigidities that inhibit the trading enterprise in manipulating certain market variables (such as price at retail), which act as a brake on autonomous expansion of sales volume. Thirdly, the *degree* of autonomous sales maximization that is desirable is questionable, both from the standpoint of maintaining balance in the execution of the National Economic Plan and from the standpoint of consumer welfare and convenience.

Post-1956 Planning: Conclusions

Despite some of its undesirable consequences, the twin policies of regionally-controlled planning of retail trade and regionally-centered organizational structures were not at all inconsistent with prevailing conditions. Given, first, the pattern of regional decentralization of *all* major elements of planning consumption, it was only natural that retail trade be planned similarly. Secondly, since planning was to be regional, it was logical that the relevant planning *units* be regional. Given the regional aspect of planning directives, it would have been extremely difficult to use larger-scale and higher-level organizations and still preserve the regional control of trade planning, without developing an additional bureaucracy for interregional coordination. Thirdly, Poland was still operating under conditions of a "sellers' market," so that concentration of retail trade was viewed as being inimical to consumer welfare—very much on the anti-monopoly grounds that are familiar in the West.

Emerging Patterns[21]

By the late 1960s, conditions of production and consumption had changed sufficiently, so that the fragmented pattern of regionally controlled, small-scale retail trade was perceived as inefficient and a bottleneck. The policy that is currently, and still very tentatively, evolving has two major elements: (1) further reduction in the number of imperative indicators binding enterprises; and (2) the creation of horizontally and vertically integrated retail trading organizations on a national and interregional scale.

In 1970, responsibility of the MHD stores to the trade division of the *WRN* was largely nominal. Only two directives bound most enterprises: (1) the amount of investment funds available to them, and (2) profitability as a return on investment *(rentowność)*. There is still, however, price control, although the pressures to ease it are considerable.

Organizationally, there is a tendency towards creating what are tantamount to true retail chains controlled from a central, parent organization. Thus, one of the cooperative organizations *(Społem)* has all of its stores affiliated directly to it on a national basis. By the same token, one can expect state enterprises in the same retail branch, but currently operating under different county and provincial control centers, to merge into "chains." A direct consequence of such mergers should be vertical integration towards supply sources, in that the new "chain" would operate its own wholesale-level facilities, rather than be supplied from an "independent," centrally-controlled wholesaler as is still largely the case.

Conclusions

It can be seen that policies of retail planning and organization in Poland are in a state of evolution. Narrow retail specialization and small-scale organization were, to a considerable degree, based on the traditional European patterns. While these patterns had some short-term relevance to conditions prevailing in the mid-1950s to the mid-1960s, there was no "small-business" rationale for their retention, as might be the case in a capitalist country. The current, if still tentative, shift to larger-scale retailing structures illustrates well the real meaning of socialist power—the ability not only to change policies by conscious choice, but to effect those changes through the appropriate organizational measures. It still remains to be seen whether the apparent move towards greater organizational autonomy on the part of the new, larger-scale enterprises will be accompanied by appropriate operational freedom, particularly in the realm of flexible pricing formulae.

March 1971

Notes

1. J. Palamountain, *The Politics of Distribution* (Cambridge, Mass.: Harvard University Press, 1955).

2. A. Hodoly and W. Jastrzębowski, *Handel Wiejski w Polsce Międzywojennej* (Warsaw: PWG, 1957), 13-15.

3. *Mały Rocznik Statystyczny: 1938* (Warsaw: GUS, 1938), 93.

4. *Rocznik Statystyczny: 1947* (Warsaw: GUS, 1947), 84; *Rocznik Statystyczny: 1950* (Warsaw: GUS, 1950), 69.

5. *Rocznik Statystyczny: 1969* (Warsaw: GUS, 1969), 324 ff.

6. W. Jastrzębowski, "Handel i pojęcia pokrewne," *Handel Wewnętrzny*, No. 5 (1960), 12.

7. E. Garbacik, *Ekonomika Obrotu Towarowego* (Kraków: Polskie Towarzystwo Eknomiczne, 1961), 207.

8. Ibid.

9. J. Rutkowski, "Z zagadnień industrializacji socjalistycznej," in O. Lange, ed., *Zagadnienia Ekonomii Politycznej Socjalizmu* (Warsaw: Książka i Wiedza, 1959), 70.

10. B. Minc, "Zagadnienia wyboru ekonomicznego w planowaniu oraz problem cen," in Lange, op. cit., 356.

11. *Rocznik Statystyczny: 1969,* op. cit., 32 ff.

12. *Rocznik Statystyczny: 1969,* op. cit., 324 ff.

13. Ibid.

14. W. Jastrzębowski, "Rynek nabywcy," *Handel Wewnętrzny,* No. 6 (1959), 3-4.

15. Z. Krasiński, "Marża handlowa," *Handel Wewnętrzny,* No. 7 (1967), 22; *Wyniki Ekonomiczne Przedsiebiorstw Państwowych,* Vol. 7/1, 352 ff; and Vol. 7/2 (1968), 344 ff.

16. See note No. 12.

17. M. Górny, *Ekonomika Handlu,* Part IV (Warsaw: PWG, 1960), 7.

18. T. Sztucki, *Dyrektywne Wskaźniki Planowania Handlu* (Warsaw: IHW, 1961), 25.

19. Ibid.

20. Górny, op. cit., 25.

21. This material is drawn from personal discussion.

15 Sweden

SVEN LINDBLAD AND INGRID HALLENCREUTZ

Introduction

Swedish policy toward trade and commerce has varied greatly during the course of the country's history. There was a geographical restriction on trade and craftsmanship during the Middle Ages. The regulation confined the buying and selling of products to the towns. Over the years this prohibition against provincial or rural trade certainly lost much of whatever effectiveness it once had, but it remained national law until 1864. Then, by means of a Decree for Freedom of Commerce, the state removed the existing limitations on the rights of Swedish citizens to conduct trade, and at the same time abolished regulations concerned with unfair pricing, quality control, and improper methods of competition. This decree, in turn, was not repealed until 1968, although it gradually lost its importance as new legislation was introduced during the years following World War II.

In line with the Decree for Freedom of Commerce, there was considerably less legislation affecting trade in Sweden than in some other western European countries during the first half of the twentieth century. Similarly, there was little administrative or special regulation of commerce. Freedom of entry, freedom of competition, and freedom to agree concerning purchase and sale were regarded as fundamental principles. In comparison to other countries, Sweden had few market laws or controls even in the years after the First World War.[1]

Temporary regulations were put into effect during the war, but the 1920s were characterized by decontrol. The depression of the 1930s was not as severe in Sweden as in some other countries, and consequently it evoked fewer regulations. The 1940s saw the introduction of rationing and of new controls, some of which tended to remain in effect after the end of the wartime emergency. The turning point, towards increased freedom of movement for retail trade, came in 1953 with the introduction of the law on restrictions on competition. The 1950s and 1960s have therefore been dynamic periods, characterized by greater competition, more rapid changes in economic structure, and more consumer-directed policy. This has led, at the end of the period, to greater government intervention.

283

Policy on Competition During the 1930s and 1940s

Before World War II

Cartels and other attempts by businessmen to limit competition increased greatly in some countries by the end of the nineteenth and the beginning of the twentieth centuries. In the U.S.A. these efforts at concentration were attacked through the Sherman Act in 1890. But in western Europe, where the formation of cartels began somewhat later, the reaction was different. Agreements in restraint of trade were accepted as long as they did not conflict with the civil law, although in the 1920s some countries introduced some rules against restrictions on competition. In Sweden, various governmental investigations were conducted, parliamentary motions were proposed, and an anti-cartel bill was presented. However, all of this activity produced few results.

The harsh economic climate of the 1930s induced changes in attitudes towards competition. Keen competition was now considered to be destructive. But, in contrast to some countries where the government could force firms into cartels established for their branches of trade, the Swedish government applied its principle of "non-interference" with obvious consequences.

During this period, various groups sought limitations on the then-prevailing freedom of entry. Merchant groups also urged measures to curb certain types of competition, such as direct selling (house-to-house selling and other peripetetic trade). The government, however, failed to respond to these requests. The retail trade then took care of the matter itself, and arranged extensive controls over the entry of new firms. Retail trade organizations made agreements with suppliers, who promised to confine their sales to stores that had been approved by the organizations. These agreements were enforced by the threat of boycott; a threat that was implemented, for example, when Epa and Tempo (two specially-low priced department and variety store firms) entered the market.

Resale price maintenance (fixed gross prices) also began to receive wider use during this period. The manufacturers, who established the fixed prices, cited them in their advertising and marked them on their packages. Fixed prices were also set, in some instances, by agreement among retailers.

The controls over entry plus the extension of price maintenance gave the existing retail firms a certain safety and reduced the risk of competition. The effect, on the whole, was a relatively static condition with little change in structure. Thus even though the government refrained from limiting freedom of entry (the 1864 decree for freedom of commerce was still in effect), the retail trade itself imposed rather extensive restrictions on entry and competition. The situation in Sweden in the thirties was therefore actually more or less the same as in many other countries—a return to more extensive regulation—but in this case the regulation was initiated and maintained by the trade rather than by the government.

Retail Trade Participation in Emergency Regulations

Like the preceding war, the extraordinary conditions of World War II necessitated extensive regulation and rationing. The shortages of consumer goods were extremely severe from time to time, and required control plans. In order to improve the situation as much as possible, the retail trade participated, through its organizations, in the formation of the various types of regulations and coordinated their administration.

Postwar Restraints on Competition

The return to peacetime conditions was rather slow in many parts of western Europe. The new capital introduced through the Marshall Plan provided a much-needed stimulus for economic growth in the various countries, including Sweden. But the government's economic and social policies seemed to blunt, rather than stimulate, the will to compete.[2] The Swedish retail trade itself also developed a favorable attitude towards regulation arising out of its experiences in the 1930s and 1940s. The controls that it exercised over commerce, cited above, are an example of this attitude. A law for "supervision of restrictions on competition" was passed in 1946, but this merely provided for the registration of the restrictive agreements and for special investigations in some instances.

Stimulation of Competition

The Law to Counteract Certain Restrictive Practices in Trade and Commerce

The law prohibiting restraints on competition was passed in 1953. In the discussions that preceded the law, many businessmen raised the objection that the proposed bill would interfere with the traditional freedom to enter into agreements concerning purchases and sales. The consumer cooperative association, however, emphasized in its comments that commerce and industry had used that freedom to reduce competitive forces and to enhance profits, rather than to promote efficiency. The association also pointed out that the manufacturing and processing units it had acquired in some cartelized industries (overshoes, electric light bulbs, flour, etc.) had introduced price competition that proved beneficial to the consumer. It recommended that new legislation against competitive restraints should not consist of affirmative regulations and controls, but rather should prohibit trade-imposed restrictions on business activity.[3]

The 1953 law against restraints on competition, and its subsequent amendments, aimed to further a generally desirable competition. It contains specific prohibitions against certain types of restraints, notably price maintenance and tender-cartels (agreements on offering prices), but also provides for the possibility of eliminating any other restrictions found to be prejudicial to society. The law emphasizes the importance of negotiations between the relevant authority and business for purposes of eliminating any undesirable effects of competitive controls. This is characteristic of Swedish legislation, which places great reliance on negotiation and publicity to prevent and manage any lack of compliance with public policy.

Administrative and Enforcement Agencies

Several institutions are responsible for administration of the law. The Antitrust Ombudsman (Näringsfrihetombudsmannen, abbreviated NO) receives and investigates complaints from businessmen, consumers, and the mass media about restraints on competition, and also receives information from the Swedish Price and Cartel Board. The Market Court (Marknadsrådet) deals with matters passed from the Antitrust Ombudsman and negotiates with the party who has caused the restraints on competition. (Before 1971 this responsibility was handled by the Freedom of Commerce Board.) The Swedish Price and Cartel Board (Statens pris-och kartellnämnd, abbreviated SPK) conducts investigations of various branches of trade and maintains the register of cartels and agreements. This office, moreover, collects and publishes information concerning the prices of various goods and services. The Council for Fair Competition within Industrial and Commercial Life (Näringslivets konkurrensnämnd) is a body for self-regulation of business, composed of representatives of the different commercial organizations including the Sveriges Köpmannaforbund (the Swedish Retail Association). Its function is to work in conjunction with the public authorities in obtaining compliance with the law.

Price Maintenance and Suggested Prices

After the prohibition of resale price maintenance (gross prices), a term that might be translated as "guiding price" or "standard price" was introduced to indicate that the retail price stated by the manufacturer was only a recommendation and could be lowered. Later a government investigation studying this practice of price suggestion concluded that some consumers regarded the recommended price as the right price, which had led to some price rigidity. The investigation recommended a change to the term "approximate (circa) price." This proposal was accepted by the major commercial and industrial organizations in 1966.

Refusal to Sell

Among other forms of restrictions on competition prejudicial to society are control of store location, refusal to sell, and price discrimination. Refusal to sell has been one of the most frequent problems in the enforcement of competition, and has particularly occured in instances where vendors have refused to supply mail order companies, discounters, and membership stores because of fear of reprisals from traditional outlets. In most instances of this sort, the authorities' (after 1971, the Market Court's) decision favors the price-competing firm that has been denied merchandise.[4] In one well-publicized case involving government action against a manufacturer in 1966, the law was sharpened by a ruling that the Court had the right to impose a fine on a vendor refusing to sell.

Price Discrimination can be Allowed

The law encourages suppliers to differentiate prices to various buyers through quantity, seasonal, and cash discounts that reflect the cost savings resulting from different types of purchases. Moreover, through negotiation buyers may obtain "power discounts." Whether these are larger than the cost savings that the suppliers enjoy is difficult to prove. These power discounts have become more frequent as a result of the continuous concentration of retail trade in bigger chains and groups. Even here the law is relatively permissive. On the other hand, trade and functional discounts are always subject to comprehensive scrutiny. The granting of lower prices to dealers who promise to give full service or to maintain a complete assortment discriminates against the dealers who compete on the basis of price rather than service.

Exemptions from the Law Against
Restraints on Competition

Special regulations can provide exemptions from the law against restraints on competition, and this is the case in such areas as postal and telecommunications, gas and electricity, medicines, and the rights to patents and trademarks. The four Scandinavian countries—Denmark, Finland, Norway, and Sweden—have recognized the international nature of patent and trademark problems and have been working for a long time to develop uniform laws in these fields. The new Scandinavian legislation is considered to be generally compatible with the relevant laws in other European countries.[5]

Importance of Negotiations

In spite of the strengthening amendments of 1956 and 1966, the Swedish law against restraints on competition does not appear to be very thorough-going or comprehensive as compared to similar laws in other countries. Nevertheless it has been much more significant than its provisions might indicate. The law's effectiveness is due, in good part, to the success of the negotiatory relationship between the authorities and business. The Freedom of Commerce Board (and its successor, the Market Court) have had considerable implicit authority, and the commercial and industrial trade organizations have been anxious to avoid increased legislation; both factors have facilitated negotiations. Consequently the discussion between the authorities and business in a case where the authorities have found a competitive restraint to be undesirable is usually not concerned with the question of whether that restraint will be removed. Rather, the question normally is: how shall it be eliminated?

The Investigation of the Distribution of Goods

At about the same time that the law against restraints on competition was adopted, the government also authorized a general investigation of distribution. The investigating committee's responsibility was to consider ways of accelerating the pace of rationalization within trade with the objectives of reducing costs and increasing productivity. In this connection manpower was to be considered as a scarce resource.[6] It was noted that from 1931 to 1951 the number of employees in retail business had increased by about 50 percent while the figure within manufacturing industry was 30 percent. The sales volume per employee within retail business had increased by 1 percent per year, as compared to 3 percent per year in industry.[7]

The investigators concluded that complete competition could seldom be achieved, but that much could be done. The controls on store location should be removed and the sources of loan financing for business should be improved. Long-range town planning should be flexible and should encourage the establishment of new types of distributive institutions. Consumer information was considered important to support rational buying decisions. Continuous surveillance of price levels was also considered important, and the investigators recommended the creation of a permanent agency that could watch and report on price developments. This function was assigned to the National Price and Cartel Office.

Freedom of Entry and Entry Controls

The principle of freedom of entry (establishment) has been and still is characteristic of Swedish legislation. There are few exceptions, such as the 1966 Radio Law which reserves radio and television broadcasting as a state function and which prohibits radio and TV advertising. Two additional exceptions arise in the case of alcoholic beverages and pharmaceuticals. A special company, Nya Systembolaget, handles all sales of alcoholic liquors under state control, and retail stores are only allowed to sell beer with a maximum 3.6 percent of alcohol by volume. All drugs, including both those that do and those that do not require a physician's prescription, are sold in special stores, pharmacies, which were taken over by the government in 1971. Articles that can be regarded as food supplements (e.g., vitamin pills), cosmetics, and hygiene and bandage articles are sold through ordinary retail channels.

This basic principle of freedom of commerce of Swedish citizens was stated, as has been mentioned, in the Law for Freedom of Commerce (1864). When the law was repealed in the 1968 legislative changes, it was replaced by a similar enactment dealing with foreigners' right to conduct business in Sweden. The

Minister of Commerce, at that time Gumar Lange, stated that: "the right of Swedish citizens to conduct business is self-evident."[8] Although it seemed that legislation was unnecessary, the Government Commission on Constitutional Matters later proposed that the principle should be written into the constitution.

Swedish policy has also been neutral to various types of retail organization. While Denmark and Norway have had prohibitions against chain organizations to protect privately-owned single store enterprises, Sweden has never had similar rules. The private controls over entry that the retail trade had exercised during the 1930s received a great deal of attention from the government during the preparation of the law against restraints on competition. No actions were taken, however, because the trade controls had lost much of their effect.

The major restrictions on entry now come from new sources. The changes in structure in the retail business, which resulted in larger and more rationally managed stores, substantially increased the investment needed to establish a new business and this has served as an effective barrier against excessive entry. Town planning legislation gave the municipal governments of the new residential areas very considerable power over the allocation of retail space. The position of the stores, their size, and the number and lines of trade were fixed and proportioned according to the current and planned growth of the community. In this way a real entry control developed in spite of the efforts of the state authorities to maintain freedom of entry. The stores in these new residential areas were relatively sheltered from competition, which made those locations very desirable. In some instances the local authorities had planned for two competing retail stores, one private and one cooperative. In reality, it became a question of distributing those locations; and the principles for this distribution seem to favor units of the larger organizations in the retail business. Elsewhere the municipal and planning authorities can also prevent the entry of new stores through reference to the risk of over-establishment. The expansion of out-of-town discount stores has been partially delayed in this way.

Changes in Structure

The developments noted above result in a greatly changed situation from that which prevailed immediately after World War II. The wartime price regulations were removed and did not reappear until 1970. Other emergency controls were liquidated. The opportunities for competition increased substantially as a result of the law against restraints on competition. The investigation of distribution called for necessary improvement in productivity and rationalization. These forces lead to extensive changes in Swedish retail trade structure along lines very similar to developments in the United States.

Within the food sector about 10,000 stores, or 30 percent of the total, disappeared between 1951 and 1963.[9] The development followed a well-known pattern, going from the predominant importance of small specialty stores with meat or bread or milk, to the growth of large supermarkets and discount stores. This concentration was really necessary, especially to improve marketing conditions at the wholesale and supplying levels. The self-service system of retailing, which had been tested at the end of the 1940s, also spread rapidly. It resulted in decreased salary costs and increased sales volume. With the growth of self-service, service became less important; and price along with completeness of assortment and availability of parking space became more important as competitive factors. Advertising also received more attention along with various types of promotional gimmicks and special offers.

These structural changes resulted in considerably increased productivity. The increase was estimated at about 50 percent (in constant prices) between the years 1950 and 1963.[10] But the changes in retailing alone would not have had as much effect on productivity if manufacturers, other suppliers, and especially, consumers had not also adjusted to those changes.

Question of Welfare

Reduction in Social Welfare

A governmental investigation of business concentration, which reported in 1968, noted that the change in retail structure had exerted favorable downward pressure on retail prices. Retail margins had not increased, and consequently had transmitted improvements in productivity to the consumer.[11] But the changed store structure had also forced the consumers into new buying habits that tended to involve increased planning of purchases, access to an automobile, and the need for increased storage space within the home. During the later part of the 1960s it became more and more obvious that many people, especially the elderly, the handicapped, and the residents of thinly populated districts, could not change their buying behavior to adjust to the new structure. Demands for increased retail service in residential areas have become more intense, while the number of stores has declined severely. Handelns Utrednings Institut—the research institute of commerce—estimates that 20,000 stores disappeared in six years, with the total number of retail outlets dropping from 71,000 in 1963 to 51,000 in 1969.

New Investigations

The government has noted the inconvenience that many consumers face in buying. The Concentration Investigation mentioned above outlined the general situation, but many investigative bodies are looking at particular aspects of the problem. The Service Committee studies the question of retail facilities in the plans for new residential areas and this matter is also receiving attention from investigating committees established to examine building laws and problems of store location. A special investigation of sparsely populated areas is testing various plans for subsidization of distribution costs by either providing taxi transportation between the stores and the consumers' residences or by providing delivery service for the goods. A consumer investigation recommended a

"Consumer Office" to guard the consumers' interests, and a newly-adopted law creates such an office that will begin functioning in 1973.

Is Development Detrimental to the Consumer?

A new major investigation into the distribution of goods was started in 1970. The new investigative body recognizes that the productivity improvements sought in the earlier study have been realized, but now the question is: Are the disadvantages of a fewer number of shops with longer walking distances from the consumer balanced by the advantages of the larger assortment in the super-market? Or have the developments been detrimental to the consumer? The investigating commission's mandate recognizes the importance of distribution and points out that usually more than half of total consumption value is compensation for various forms of distributive and marketing activities.[12] Retail sales in 1968 were about 36 billion SW. crowns out of a gross national product of 141 billion. The commission will try to map out the economic and social consequences that consumers will experience as a result of retail concentration. It will also consider other factors that will affect retailing and consumption in the future, such as increased leisure time, growing urbanization, and increased number of automobiles.

The Government's Grip Strengthens

Consumerism

The investigations mentioned above are likely to result in new statutes, regulations, and controls over retail trade. This growing body of regulation will be consistent with new concepts of consumption and the position of the consumer. The growing tide of consumerism and the reaction against excessive emphasis on consumption is an international phenomenon. It has been expressed in many ways, including demonstrations, attempts at boycotting department stores, and the campaign for a "different Christmas" that would omit the traditional splurge of purchasing. These manifestations have come from the more extreme groups in society, but they have been accompanied by a more widespread critical attitude towards those, such as retailers, who in the end are considered responsible for the overemphasis on consumption. A total freeze, or ceiling on prices, imposed in the autumn of 1970 and retained until 1972, has also focused attention on retailing. The Swedish Price and Cartel Board has sharpened its controls over weights and measures. Newspapers and radio programs discuss prices more critically. All of these factors, such as the increasing state regulation of commerce, the growing consciousness of consumers, and increased critical attitudes in certain public sectors, have resulted in a rather cold climate for the retail business.

New Social Goals

The long-run aims of public economic policy have, since World War II, included monetary stability, full employment, high growth rates, and control of the balance of international payments. At the end of the sixties, new and more specific goals are assuming increased significance. As we have already noted, questions of consumer welfare are occupying an increasingly central position in policy discussions. Other major objectives now receiving attention include: increased investment, increased allocation of resources to the public sector, reduction in income disparities, greater regional balance in employment and growth, improvements in the physical and social environment, and greater aid to the developing countries.

Long-Period Investigation

The government undertakes a "long-period" or "long-run" investigation of the country every five years. These investigations examine the way the country's resources have been allocated during the preceding years and prepare recommendations for the forthcoming period. The 1970 recommendation included, among other things, that during the forthcoming decade the growth in actual consumer expenditures should be limited to 2.1 percent per capita exclusive of changes in the value of the currency. (The proposed growth rates would be 1.85 percent for daily necessities such as food, and 2.3 percent for other items sold at retail). The corresponding increase during the first part of the 1960s was 4.6 percent.

Government Actions

The "long-run" investigating report is purely advisory and is not binding upon either government or the private sector. Nevertheless the state has the ability, through general and selective measures, to manage development in the desired direction. The refocusing of objectives has induced a variety of measures, regulations, and controls (discussed below) and can be expected to produce still others in the near future. Government actions to control the economy, in addition to general fiscal and monetary decisions, have included building regulations, investment taxes, employment taxes, credit regulations, subsidies for re-education and relocation of redundant or obsolete workers, and financial assistance to businesses which choose to locate in sparsely populated areas.

Other Legislation

Price Control

The price control law that was issued during World War II was replaced by similar legislation in 1947. This contained provisions concerning fixed maximum prices. The commercial and industrial trade associations voluntarily cooperated with the government in the administration of price control, and negotiated many pricing questions with the government. This process had a somewhat anti-competitive effect.

After extended debates on the question, it was decided that price control should be abolished in 1956 and replaced by a preparedness law that is still in effect. It comes into force when there is a war or risk of war, or when "for some other reason considerable risks have emerged which can lead to a serious increase in the general price situation within the country." As we have previously noted, the law against restraints on competition was sharpened when price control was removed in 1956. It was believed that the stimulation of competition and the wider distribution of consumer information would help prevent unwarranted price increases. Nevertheless, proposals for the reintroduction of price control were voiced on several occasions during the 1960s. The government, however, considered that the benefits would be outweighed by possible negative effects, such as decreased competition, risks of quality deterioration, distortion of price relationships, and the possibility of price explosions when the ceilings were removed.

Moreover, in order to make the price ceilings economically (rather than only politically) effective, they would have to be combined with wage controls. Also a study made in 1965 pointed out that a price control law would only affect about 35 percent of private consumption expenditures. The rest would consist of prices that were not affected, such as those for agricultural goods and rents (which are covered in special regulations), public services, imported goods, and indirect taxes.[13]

Nevertheless, the economic situation within the country became such that the government was forced to proclaim price control in August 1970 for certain food items, and somewhat later for almost all types of merchandise. At the beginning of 1972 price control was eliminated. Already before that (in 1971), the Swedish Price and Cartel Board had started a campaign to "compare prices" in the retail shops. But as yet, there is no law about this.

The New Marketing Law

Following an investigation of unfair competitive methods, Parliament adopted a new Marketing Law that came into effect in 1971. This law is designed to protect consumers against improper marketing activities. A simple rule of thumb in interpreting the law holds that "defects in sincerity and honesty towards the consumer are not acceptable." The Act specifically prohibits:

a. Misleading or false advertising or advertising contrary to "fair business customs."
b. Trading stamp offers except for stamps that are redeemable in money rather than goods. A further minor exception to this prohibition permits the issuance of stamps or coupons that can be exchanged for repair and maintenance service on the product being purchased.

c. Combined offers of two articles that have no connection with each other at a common price (or a tied offer of an additional unrelated item at an extra price). It is believed that this type of offer makes it difficult for the consumer to judge value.[14]

The guidelines for interpretation of the law are based upon the "basic rules for advertising" of the International Chamber of Commerce and standards developed by the Swedish Council on Business Practice. That council, which was composed of representatives of the commercial and industrial organizations and of consumers, was replaced by the previously-mentioned Market Court as of 1 January 1971. The Market Court acts as the judicial body in cases brought under the law, while the new Consumer Ombudsman acts as prosecutor and is generally responsible for enforcement of the Act. Besides the new Marketing Law, a bill adopted on 25 May 1972 imposes an advertising tax of 10 percent. Government hopes that it will reduce the volume of advertising.

Repeal of Hour Legislation

The Business Hours Law of 1967, which allowed stores to be open between 8:00 A.M. (8:00 hours) and 8:00 P.M. (20:00 hours), was abolished at the end of 1971. Earlier exemptions were permitted for extended business hours if consumers have a real need for such service. Generally, however, most stores still close at 6:00 P.M. (18:00 hours) even though they are not required to do so. Comparatively few take advantage of the permission to be open beyond that time, as wage costs rise by 50 percent during the extended working time. On the other hand, some of the larger and more capital-intensive retailing units obtain a better utilization of capacity through prolonged hours of business, and the delayed closing can also be an effective competitive device.

Social Constraints

A decree issued under the Labour Welfare Act, effective July 1, 1972, establishes minimum physical requirements for cashiers' stations in retail shops, including provision of a chair for each cashier and mandatory minimum distances between desks. The same act has also been invoked to require various employee facilities in stores, such as rest and washrooms and dining areas.

In addition to legislation, social pressure is also being exerted to shape retail behavior. Much of this pressure is focused on the food processing and food retailing sectors. For example, the law prohibits retail shops from selling beer to persons under age 18. There is also an agreement in the industry not to advertise beer in such a way as to stimulate consumption on the part of young people. There is no legislation preventing the sale or advertising of candy (sweets) to young children, but consumer groups and the mass media are urging the stores to curb their candy-selling efforts. The merchants are expected to refrain from displaying sweets at the checkout counters and are supposed to place them where they will be less visible to children.

The sale of beverages in throw-away bottles has been labeled as environmental pollution, although there is, as yet, no prohibition against such bottles. Other such social and environmental concerns are likely to influence future legislation and future public concepts of appropriate retail behavior.

June 1972

Notes

1. Ulf Bernitz, *Marknadsrätt* (Market Law: A Comparative Study). (Stockholm: Jurist-och Samhällsvatarförbundets Forlags AB, 1969), p. 422.

2. Kungl, Maj:ts proposition 1953:103 (Bill Proposing a Law to Counteract Restraint of Competition in Business, 13 March 1953), p. 65.

3. Kungl, Maj:ts proposition 1953:103, p. 40.

4. Holst Malmstrom, *Marknadsföring* (Marketing). (Stockholm: Laromedelsförlaget, 1969), p. 111.

5. Ulf Bernitz, *Marknadsrätt*, p. 174.

6. SOU 1955:16 Varudistributionsutredning (1955 National Public Investigation No. 16—Distribution of Goods), p. 14.

7. SOU 1956:53 1955 Langtidsutredning (1956 National Public Investigation No. 53—Long-run Investigation).

8. Ulf Bernitz, *Marknadsrätt*, p. 170.

9. SOU 1968:6 Koncentrationsutredning (1968 National Public Investigation No. 6—Concentration Investigation), p. 17.

10. SOU 1968:6, p. 23.

11. SOU 1968:6, p. 36.

12. The directive from the Ministry of Commerce for the investigation of distribution.

13. Ulf Bernitz, *Marknadsrätt*, p. 166.

14. Sten Tengelin, "Marknadsforaren och konsumenten" (The Marketing Man and the Consumer), pamphlet.

16 Thailand

DOLE A. ANDERSON

Thailand cannot be said to have as yet a national policy toward retailing, in the sense of a program of government action that pursues national objectives or responds to national problems concerning the retailing sector. It does have a recent Western-sounding statement of national objectives for the commercial sector of the economy. And it has a history of a variety of acts and restraints on retailing that manifest economic nationalism against the Chinese, who dominate distribution. Beyond that, no study of distribution efficiency in the kingdom or comprehensive examination of the problems and points of view of the interest groups involved in retailing has been undertaken. Other national problems have been considered more urgent or offered greater payoff.

For the Western reader, a summary of the broader frame of national economic policy, and broader still, of national political policy is essential to understand this example of an incipient policy toward retailing.[1]

National Political and Economic Policy

A sovereign state's primary objective of survival has not been easily won by Thailand and economic policy, including that toward retailing, reflects this struggle.

Thailand has been a country caught in the middle. In the thrust of Western imperialism of the last century, it found itself a buffer state between British and French interests in Southeast Asia and thus remained the only country in the Indochina peninsula not subjected to colonialism. More recently, and with the passing of the old imperialism, such modern forms of Western influence as financial and technical assistance programs, planned social and economic development, democratic government, and a modern life style have been urged or thrust upon it. The Thai response has been artful accommodation. From 1850, free trade was accepted and the population concentrated on growing and exporting rice and other primary products of lesser importance, such as tin, teak, and rubber, while importing finished goods from the West.

Modernization of the government was also essential for survival; the absolute monarchy was eliminated in 1932, bureaucratic machinery developed, a series of eight constitutions was written over a period of thirty-six years, elections were held and parliaments convened. By the 1950s economic and social development became an objective and the government embarked upon a program of promotion of industrialization to reduce the heavy dependence on agriculture, which still provides nearly four-fifths of the employment and two-fifths of the gross domestic product. Scarcity of foreign exchange was not a problem, thanks to a long tradition of fiscal conservatism that served as insurance against external threats.

The second challenge to Thai sovereignty comes from the threat of exploitation by fellow orientals. The problem of the overseas Chinese that has colored the history and set the tone of economic nationalism today through Southeast Asia has been handled with admirable restraint by the Thai. From the earliest days of the kingdom, Chinese traders have been predominant in commerce. Later, when Thailand needed non-agricultural labor to build the railroad and irrigation systems, Chinese immigration was encouraged. The Thai had neither the inclinations nor the competencies for commerce, but the Chinese provided their perfect complement. Chinese industriousness and frugality, the extended family, and the close economic ties between immigrants coming from the same province and united by the bond of a common dialect—all contributed to the formation of a commercial web extending from Bangkok to the farthest corners of the kingdom. This network controlled the collection, milling, and exportation of the country's products and, in the reverse flow, the distribution of imported consumers goods. The coup group of military and civil servants that ended the absolute monarchy in 1932 introduced a philosophy of economic nationalism or Thaification. Since then, restrictions on the economic activities of aliens have been alternately tightened and relaxed, depending on the political group in power, the perceived threat to Thai sovereignty of wars in the Indochina peninsula, and developments in mainland China. The periods of greatest concern over the Chinese problem and hence of government attention to retailing have been in the late 1930s when the nationalist Prime Minister Pibun was in control, in the period of readjustment after the end of the Second World War and Japanese occupation, in 1952-1953 at the close of the Korean War, and in the late 1960s. Thai reaction to the Chinese threat is manifest in three developments: (1) imposition of immigration quotas after the Second World War, so that the proportion of China-born Chinese, which peaked at over 5 percent of the total population in the late 1920s, is steadily declining; (2) assimilation of the Chinese through intermarriage, although at present some 37 percent of Bangkok households are still classified as ethnic Chinese (defined as those in which Chinese is spoken at home by two or more members of the household)[2]; and (3) symbiotic business relationships whereby Thai officials are invited to participate as directors of Chinese firms, thus providing protection against government harassment.

Although the Chinese have constituted the principal threat to Thaification, Japanese imperialism, which culminated in the occupation during the Second World War and has been replaced in the postwar years by a powerful industrial and trade presence, deserves mention. Finally, minor threats to national integration come from the Lao war refugees of the 1950s who have settled in the least-developed Northeast, the Malays who dominate the Southern provinces, and the primitive hill tribes of the North, all of whom drain government resources in efforts to accommodate these alien bodies.

During this century, national economic policy has been ambivalently poised between support of public and of private enterprise, but tending increasingly in recent years toward the latter. The most recent constitution, promulgated in mid-1968, announces the government position in these terms:

> The State is to encourage private economic initiative. The State is to take measures to coordinate the enterprises of a public utility nature with private economic activities so as to benefit the people as a whole. Private enterprise of a public utility nature or monopolistic enterprises may be permitted only by virtue of law. (Section 64)

> The State is to encourage private trade and production, both in agriculture and industry. (Section 66)[3]

In fact, however, the list of state enterprises is substantial. There are, of course, the public utility enterprises—the state-owned railways, electricity, telecommunications including radio and television, water supply, port facilities, etc. Secondly, there are the government monopolies, the most important being the Tobacco Monopoly that produces, imports, and distributes all tobacco products. The Tobacco Monopoly was formed by nationalizing the highly successful British-American Tobacco Company in 1948 and today contributes significantly to the revenues of the government. Finally there are a variety of state-owned industrial and commercial undertakings that compete with the private sector in the production of glass, storage batteries, canned foods, textiles, plywood, sugar, and in services such as motor bus and trucking, hotels, and in retailing consumer goods and petroleum products. Generally, these competitive undertakings have a minor share of the market, are relatively inefficient, and provide little or no profit to the government. Many had their origins as sources of supplies for the armed forces or in efforts to achieve Thaification of the economy. Their continued support by the government, however, has undermined the confidence of the private sector in government economic policy and been widely criticized, especially by Western advisors on development policy who have recommended immediate divestiture of most state enterprises except the public utilities and monopolies.

Even the following recent government statement of policy toward public ownership has not quieted the fears, however, since it leaves the government substantial room to move:

> The Government will operate only those state enterprises which are considered public utilities, which contribute to Government revenue, or which are essential to the security of the nation. The Government will not establish new state enterprises, except those which will be of unquestionable benefit to the public and will not conflict with the policy of promoting private enterprises.[4]

It is important to note that the ideology of socialism plays no part in Thai policy.[5] The government's need for revenue has been important, however. From 1855 to 1926, treaty provisions with the West restricted the use of duties on foreign trade and the government came to depend on profits from the provision of commercial services such as the state railway system.

In addition to the needs of the government for revenue, members of the

ruling elite and the bureaucrats have personally benefited from the state enterprises. Much more important to the bureaucracy, however, is direct participation
in the private sector. With no constraint such as the Western concept of conflict
of interest, some public officials have developed substantial business interests
that are coming under increasing criticism.[6]

Government policy regarding the commercial sector has been enunciated in
the *Second National Economic and Social Development Plan,* covering the
period 1967-1971. The elements of this policy that have relevance to retailing
are:

1. the recognition of the importance of efficient distribution to the economic
    development of the nation,
2. the importance of a strong and healthy free enterprise system where the
    governmental role is not regulation but assistance to the private sector,
3. the promotion of healthy competition and the discouragement of monopo-
    listic trade practices and cartels, and
4. the encouragement to Thai nationals to participate more effectively in
    commerce.[7]

Of these four elements, implementation is evident only on the latter two;
Chinese domination of the commercial sector has given rise to a series of
measures over the years against cartels and in favor of the ethnic Thai.

In addition to the statements of policy, the Second Plan announced the
budget of governmental appropriations for development during the five-year
period. Only about 9 million U.S. dollars, one-third of 1 percent of the total
planned expenditures, was budgeted to the commerce sector; of this minute
allocation to commerce, about 59 percent was for export promotion, 22 percent
for price support of the rice crop, 15 percent to promote the participation of
Thai nationals in commerce, and 4 percent to support market research on
domestic products by the government.

The Formulation of Public Policy

It should be clear, from what has been said above, that public policy toward
retailing is not a matter of the government mediating the conflicting interests of
groups in the society. Power rests with a small clique of military and government
officials who are still often isolated from feedback from the governed and who
have continued to rule much in the tradition of the absolute monarchy that
preceded them.

The distributive sector is characterized by a large number of small firms,
mostly family-operated and predominantly Chinese. The first census of commerce, made in 1966, disclosed nearly 16,000 establishments operating exclusively in retail trade in the municipality of Bangkok. Of these, nearly 43 percent
were reported as owned by persons of Chinese nationality. Of the remainder
(except for 63 establishments owned by other aliens, principally Indian) which
were owned by Thai nationals, the proportion who were ethnically Chinese is

not known although it was probably the large majority. In the other relatively minor urban areas and in the rural areas, the concentration of Chinese was lower; of the more than 126,000 exclusively retail establishments elsewhere in the kingdom, nearly one-fifth were owned by individuals of Chinese nationality.[8]

From early times, the ethnic Thai have shown little interest in business; their preferred activity has been rice farming in the rural areas and government service in Bangkok, the only city of significance. In recent years, the prestige of government employment appears to have diminished as the higher salaries paid by the growing private sector became apparent. It is possible that the few Thai who are interested in entering retailing have exerted pressure on the government. The main body of small Chinese retailers is without a voice or the government's ear, however. On the consumer side, the story is similar. Some 80 percent of the population is still in the agricultural sector and only recently has begun to move from self-sufficiency and barter into a money economy. Outside of Bangkok, the feeling that the central government neither knows nor cares is only slowly dying and an onerous regulation is simply disregarded, largely with impunity. The urban consumer and particularly the civil servant class has had some influence on policy making, particularly regarding the rising cost of living. But in the main, public policy toward retailing reflects the ruling elite's perception of the threat to the society of a distribution system largely in the hands of aliens or subject to their control.

For a number of reasons, it is difficult to evaluate the effectiveness of public policy, or even to discover it. In the first place, although the intent during periods of Thaification has been to restrict the Chinese merchant, whether alien or merely ethnic, the Chinese has seldom been specifically mentioned in formal policy measures. Regulations may have been deliberately ambiguous, out of fear of international complications.[9]

Secondly, the government strategy has often been to intimidate the merchant or to achieve by suasion what it could not hope to enforce by police power. Thus, it is possible that the successive steps involved in legislating formal policy merely narrow down to manageable proportions much broader statements of objectives. Typically, an *enabling act* sets the objectives and general scope of the policy. Subsequently, *royal decrees* may be issued, making the act applicable to certain activities or in specified regions. Finally, *ministerial regulations,* which have the full force of law, may spell out details of implementation. For example, the *Act in Control of Consumable Goods of 1952* provided that "whenever required by circumstances in order to ensure public welfare or in the interests of national economy and stability, the Government [by Royal Decree] may place control over consumable goods." This enabling act specified that future royal decrees might limit the quantity of consumable goods in an individual or firm's possession, fix the quantities to be bought, lay down rules for dealing in such goods including fixing the times, places, and circumstances of sale, forbidding the sale or use of goods, and enforcing rationing. Subsequently, royal decrees were in fact issued which: (a) declared the act in force for the two provinces comprising the Bangkok Metropolitan Area (out of the 71 provinces in the kingdom), (b) listed specific foodstuffs, all kinds of clothing, toilet accessories, construction material, etc., as within the scope of the act, and (c) required price tags on or near the articles, in Thai or Arabic figures not less than 2 centimeters (¾ inch) high, and specified that the prices shown should not be open for bargaining.[10]

It is impossible to say to what extent these regulations were enforced; within two years of their promulgation, intensive repression of the Chinese waned. Another government tactic used then and on other occasions has been to circulate rumors of impending restrictions against aliens; in 1952, Chinese merchants were warned that the government might soon nationalize the retail trade. With respect to all such repressive regulations and threats, the government has not attempted implementation where the result would have been paralysis of commerce and this caution is not lost on the commercial class. Of the 1952 threat to nationalize, a local newspaper observed at the time that while the threat might not frighten the merchants, it certainly cast terror into the hearts of the consumers.[11]

Finally, evaluation of implementation is difficult where the policy is directed against a minority that must suffer in silence, fully aware of the fragility of its position in the society. Administrative action may exceed the written or explicit legal authorization or even occur without authorization. Laws in Thailand are administered by men; and men, as in so many societies, developed or developing, can often be bought.[12] The following newspaper report from the mid-1950s describes the situation then; while now much improved, it would be naive to suppose it is completely eradicated today:

> Any person hearing merchants relate the actions of some groups of policemen, who use the influence and authority they possess to bleed these Chinese in a barefaced and shameless manner, would be simply aghast . . . It is the easiest thing in the world to bleed Chinese in our country. Merely preferring a charge of being a communist or having communist tendencies is more than sufficient for members of the police to obtain huge sums of money from them as they please. But the police are not able to use such tactics with Indian or western merchants, because [their] governments are capable of protecting the rights and property of their citizens . . .[13]

The Actors in Retailing

There are no restrictions at the present time on entry into retailing by either nationals or aliens, although legislation is being considered that would require work permits of aliens and reserve certain occupations to nationals. The former type of restriction has not been used before, but there is a long history of reserving to Thai nationals those occupations that are felt to be either sensitive to national security or appropriate to the Thai. The first such restriction dates from 1939 when taxi driving was limited to Thai nationals; since then, dozens of other occupations have been added to the list when the government felt threatened, or removed as the government felt more secure or as the perceived external threat diminished. Similarly, percentages of Thai employees to total employment by firms in particular activities have been stipulated and relaxed as the situation demanded. With a few exceptions, however, retailing has not been restricted to Thai nationals nor have minimum percentages of national employees been stipulated.[14] In the latest example of restrictions on foreigners in business the Cabinet announced in late 1970 that the regulations then being drafted would apply only to specific businesses and occupations and not generally to all, and that aliens already employed would be permitted to continue.[15]

The current constitution, promulgated in 1968, assures full liberty in the choice of occupation and residence to every person (Section 39). However, this guarantee is followed by the statement that restrictions on such liberty may be imposed by laws specifically enacted "for the safety of the country, national economy, or public welfare." Similarly, while the Constitution assures that "every person enjoys full liberty to form an association, provided that the object thereof is not contrary to law," all associations of persons and firms engaged in business are subject to detailed control, as described below.

All business operations in Thailand, whether industrial or commercial (but excluding peddling and street-stall selling) are required to register with the government. The primary purpose of this requirement is identification of elements in the business sector rather than control or regulation. However, the nationalities of officers, directors, partners, and shareholders must be divulged in the registration application and a provision of the law provides for revocation of registration of those "who defraud the public through the adulteration or falsification of goods or commit other gross misconduct in the conduct of business."[16] An important source of government revenue is the business tax—a gross-receipts tax levied on the manufacturer or importer, but not on the retailer; the government has in this way avoided the difficulties of trying to use the small-scale retailer for revenue collection. Retailing thus is subject only to the normal income tax as any person, partnership, or corporation.

While retailing is not subjected to restrictions on entry, encouragement has been given to Thai to enter the field. In 1952, the government created a group of state industrial enterprises (covering products such as prepared foods, storage batteries, and glass) that were empowered to market their products in such a way as to assist and promote Thai merchants. Similarly, the creation of state-owned trading companies (actually retail stores selling food, appliances, hardware, etc.) in each of the seventy-one provinces after the Second World War was intended to provide competition to the private sector, to assure supplies of essential goods not capable of interdiction by aliens in a national emergency, and to provide employment opportunities for Thai nationals. By the mid-1960s, about two dozen of these companies were still active; they were not, however, a significant factor in retailing, accounting for only about 1.4 percent of the sales of retail-only stores reporting to the 1966 Census of Business Trade and yielding the government a miniscule profit.[17]

A recent program of the government in Thaification of the retailing sector provides another example of encouragement of entry along ethnic lines. The Second Economic Development Plan observed that lack of capital and the inability to obtain prime locations for retail activities have hindered the entry of Thai nationals into commerce and the Plan budgeted 22 million baht (or 1.1 million dollars) for loans to retail shopowners. The Department of Internal Trade has two efforts presently under way: a loan office in the Retail Shops

Promotion Division and the Small-Sized Trade Service Project. The former lends up to 30,000 baht (or $1500) at a favorable 9 percent interest rate to shop-owners of Thai nationality "under the patronage of the Internal Trade Department." The latter project has the objective of conducting research on the problems of Thai traders in general, but it may also stimulate their activities by appointing shopowners who are under department patronage as agents or distributors of state industrial enterprises or of those private industrial firms that are enjoying promotion privileges from the government. Since firms holding promotion certificates account for much of the recent foreign and local investment, implementation of this provision might make this stimulation quite significant.

The Structure of Retailing

The distribution system of Thailand resembles that of so many developing nations in the low level of specialization achieved. Peasant marketing, involving the adjustment of household stocks by barter, may require only a few hours a week for the women of the family and the itinerant trader may both collect the small rice surpluses and retail a narrow line of consumer goods to the rural household. Even in urban areas, the distinctions between wholesale and retail may be blurred among full-time merchants who may engage in both or either regularly or sporadically. There are no restrictions, cultural or legal, on the extent of a firm's vertical integration. Not surprisingly, however, there is a long history of policies to control associations of business firms. With an alien ethnic group dominating a large part of the economy, the opportunities for conspiracy are large and the suspicions of both government and the people justifiably aroused.

As early as the seventeenth century, Chinese secret societies joined immigrants with a common regional origin and speech dialect, for social and economic benefits and protection. The combined effect of the extended family that was a part of the Chinese culture and these secret societies was to develop speech-group dominance over particular occupations, guild-type control over entry, and the forging of vertical chains in the distribution process. For example, Chinese control over the very important rice trade was based on tying the upcountry Chinese collectors of the small surpluses of the Thai peasant with the Chinese rice millers who in turn were tied with the Chinese exporters who sold to their compatriots overseas in Singapore, Hong Kong, and elsewhere in Southeast Asia. By the end of the last century, government recognition of the threat to the economy of foreign control was manifest in the required registration of such societies. However, their importance declined and they were superceded by associations emphasizing common economic interests rather than speech and regional origins. Trade associations of Chinese in the same line or trade developed to exchange information, formulate defensive programs against government regulation, reduce excessive competition, and on occasion restrict the entry of newcomers into the trade. At the turn of the century, chambers of commerce came into prominence—first a chamber founded in Bangkok by European businessmen with membership restricted to western firms, followed in 1908 by the Chinese Chamber of Commerce. This latter organization admitted only respected and legitimate business firms and soon came to represent the entire Chinese community vis à vis the Thai government and society. After the 1932 coup, another chamber was formed in Bangkok, open only to Thai firms and perhaps under the aegis of the nationalists in the new government.

The current posture of the government regarding cartels is reflected in the *Chambers of Commerce Act* and the *Trade Associations Act,* which were passed the same day in 1966 and contain many identically-worded provisions.[18] Both laws require the registration of organizations with the government, proscribe in identical terms monopolistic practices and other acts contrary to the public interest, and prohibit persons engaged in business from joining together except as registered associations. Trade associations and chambers are defined in similar terms as institutions of persons joined to promote business or trade interests without seeking profit or income for distribution among members by the institution. Trade associations consist of persons operating in a particular line of business specified in the charter.[19] If more than half of its members are aliens, the association must be created and operate within the Bangkok metropolitan area (where it can be more easily watched by the government).

The following categories are provided for chambers: provincial chambers, of which there may be only one in each province, the Thai Chamber of Commerce, serving the Bnagkok metropolitan area, and foreign chambers, of which there may be one only for each nationality and which must be located in Bangkok.

The objectives of the Acts are revealed in the reiteration in a variety of contexts of the aim of preventing actions "causing damage to the economy or security of the country or to public peace, order and good morals." Other specific prohibitions applicable equally to trade associations and chambers include:

- any actions whatsoever which unreasonably depress or increase the price of merchandise or service charges, or upset prices of merchandise or service charges, or upset prices of merchandise or service charges. (Sec. 22 (2) of both Acts.)
- any action whatsoever to increase, reduce or restrict the volume of production, volume of merchandise distributed or other service resulting in damage to the domestic or foreign commercial market or finance or the economy of the country. (Sec. 22 (4).)
- any action whatsoever destroying normal business competition unless pursuant to government policy or regulations. (Sec. 22 (5).)
- obstruct or interfere with the admission as a member of any person qualified, ... compel a person engaged in business to become a member involuntarily, or, in bad faith, ... remove a member from the association. (Sec. 22 (7).)

Finally, provisions of the Acts attempt to insure visibility of associations (as requiring the additional use of Thai lettering if the name is in foreign lettering and the prominent display of a sign at the front of the office) and accountability to members and to the government (as requiring filing of by-laws and an annual financial statement and report of activities, and even the right of the government to have a representative present at association meetings when there is a suspicion of unlawful activity).

The Process of Retailing

Except for attempts at price control, government action with respect to the process of retailing has been limited. Although there have been a few instances of zoning that limit small areas in the city of Bangkok to residential use only, in general retailing is free to go anywhere and is found everywhere. Public markets provided by the municipality are found in all urban areas and may contain hundreds of small rented stalls offering a wide variety of food, housewares, and clothing. The vast majority of retailing establishments, however, operate from rented or owned stores, with no public control except for the requirement that they be registered as business establishments.

No labor regulations are imposed specifically on retailing and because of the small size (an average of 2.5 engaged persons) and family nature of most establishments, many regulations do not apply. For example, legislation on working hours that limits employees in commerce to not more than fifty-four hours per week applies only to firms with ten or more employees.[20] Except for gasoline service stations that have been required to stay open twenty-four hours a day in certain areas, mandatory opening or closing regulations have apparently not been used. Similarly, there have been no regulations regarding merchandising or promotional methods. Signboards have been taxed for some time and with higher rates for foreign lettering. For example, since 1967, a business sign containing only Thai lettering is taxed annually at the equivalent of approximately 10 cents per square foot, but with Thai and foreign lettering, at $1.00, and with foreign lettering only, at $2.00 a square foot.[21] The sale of drugs has been subject to special regulations such as the mandatory use of Thai letters on drug store signs, and the prohibition of promotions that make exaggerated claims, that offer premiums on lottery, prizes, etc.

Price control at the retail level has been attempted on various occasions as part of the movement in repression of the Chinese merchant; most recently, there were reports in 1967 of anti-profiteering legislation in preparation to supersede legislation dating from the period of shortages at the end of the Second World War.[22]

The Functions of Retailing

Finally, we may summarize by noting the manifestations of public policy toward the functions performed by marketing in general and retailing in particular. Traditionally, the middleman has been viewed as an exploiter of the upcountry rice farmer and the urban civil servant. Since the middleman is typically Chinese with cultural and speech, if not family, ties to other channel members, his economic power is feared. The historical record, (especially regarding agricultural marketing) is replete with references to the need to eliminate the unnecessary middleman and transfer his profits into higher prices to the farmer or lower prices to the urban consumer. But it is the bureaucrat in Bangkok who brings these charges, not the supposedly aggrieved peasant. Since the government is not yet truly representative, public policy frequently scratches where the people do not itch.

The statement of objectives for the commercial sector in the current economic development plan have a Western tone, suggesting that they came from the West or were made for the benefit of the West, or both. For a century, Western advisors resident in Thailand have been giving advice, which has not always been easy to accept when the power elite was trying to maintain the nation's identity and unique society. However, the Thai have initiated reforms that they sensed were expected of them by the community of modern nations. Whatever the source of the statements of policy, it is doubtful if the government has any deep interest in attempting such reforms, or the capacity as yet to carry them out. But rapid change is occurring; increased mobility resulting from a greatly expanded road system is developing a national market for consumer goods and the evolution of a more comprehensive public policy than the mere repression of aliens as in the past seems likely for the future.

January 1971

Notes

1. A Westerner's distillation into a few pages of aspects of a complex oriental culture is dangerously superficial. In the author's *Marketing and Development: The Thailand Experience* (Division of Research, Graduate School of Business Administration, Michigan State University, 1970), more details are available as well as bibliographic references to the work of the many Western social scientists who have been intrigued by the unique Thai society.

2. Business Research Ltd., *Bangkok Profile: Selected Characteristics of Households in Bangkok and Thonburi,* 1966.

3. *Royal Thai Government Gazette,* June 20, 1968, Bangkok, International Translations Co.

4. National Economic Development Board, *The Second National Economic and Social Development Plan, 1967-1971,* Bangkok, mimeo [1968], p. 110.

5. A radical economic plan for complete state socialism was proposed in 1933 by Pridi, one of the leaders of the coup group that had eliminated the absolute monarchy the year before. The Pridi Plan was roundly criticized as bolshevist by most of his colleagues. Pridi ultimately went into exile in Communist China, and socialism has not since been seriously discussed.

6. The *Monthly Review* of the Bangkok Bank, the largest and perhaps most influential commercial bank, has noted the government has time and again failed to adhere to its stated policy of not competing with the private sector and observed: "In banking, industry, and other commercial activities, the Government or government officials have, either directly or through some deceptive screen, come into competition with private enterprises. . . . it would be wise for the Government to make no further attempt to interfere with private enterprises through either competition or partnership." August, 1967, p. 260.

7. The phraseology of the relevant sections of the Plan are as follows:

Sec. 1. The development of commerce in Thailand is an important factor in raising the standard of living of the people, in generating revenue for the government, and in accelerating the growth of the economy as a whole. Since Thailand is still basically an agricultural economy, domestic consumption and the export of agricultural products are important to the economic welfare of the country. In this respect, an efficient and freely functioning commercial system, with equitable treatment for those who are engaged in the production and distribution of goods and services, is necessarily a primary force in the economic development of the country.

Sec. 2. At present there are approximately 20,300 registered business firms in the country. The rate of increase in number has been on the average about 9% per annum. In addition to the registered firms, there are numerous unregistered business establishments in the Bangkok-Thon Buri area and the provinces. Most of these are small retailers, and research is being conducted to obtain reliable data and information on them. The rate of growth in the number of firms is expected to continue. The government intends actively to promote the development of an efficient commercial system, so as to facilitate the flow and the exchange of goods within the domestic market and as exports to overseas markets. Encouragement will also be given to greater participation by Thai nationals in commercial and service activities.

Sec. 5. The Government will seek to create an orderly and efficient commercial system and to promote healthy competition so as to enable the commercial sector to serve the public interest more fully. Subsidiary objectives are to promote exports and to encourage wider participation by Thai nationals in commercial and service activities. To achieve these objectives, the government will:

(i) Promote healthy and orderly competition in private commercial activities, so as to secure equitable treatment for the producers, the distributors and the consumers.

(ii) Discourage monopolistic trade practices and cartels which are contrary to the best interest of producers or consumers.

(iii) Develop and promote export trade so as to achieve growth in terms of export volume and value, as well as diversification of export products.

(iv) Maintain price stability for both industrial and consumer goods, so as to prevent harmful increases in the cost of living.

(v) Support and stabilize the domestic price level of important export commodities, such as rice, and other agricultural and industrial products, in order to provide equitable treatment for the producers, the distributors, and the consumers of the country.

(vi) Encourage Thai nationals to participate more fully in commercial and service activities by designing new and more effective measures than in the past . . .

Sec. 31. Policies and measures for the development of Thailand's commerce and services are based on the desire to encourage the growth of a strong and healthy free enterprise system. The Government's role is not one of regulation, but of assistance to the private sector, particularly in the provision of technical assistance and the solution of critical problems and the bottlenecks in commerce and services." (Same source as note 4.)

8. National Statistical Office, *Census of Business Trade or Services,* 1966, Bangkok.

9. Frank H. Golay, Ralph Anspach, M. Ruth Pfanner and Eliezer B. Ayal. *Underdevelopment and Economic Nationalism in Southeast Asia,* (Ithaca, N.Y.: Cornell University Press, 1969), p. 268.

10. *International Translations Law Directory, 1952.* Bangkok, International Translations Co.

11. Virginia Thompson and Richard Adloff, "The State's Role in Thai Economy," *Far Eastern Survey,* July 30, 1952, p. 127.

12. Cf. the discussion of the relation between the reliance on discretionary controls, by which Myrdal characterizes Asian societies, and corruption. Gunnar Myrdal, *Asian Drama, An Inquiry into the Poverty of Nations* (New York: Pantheon Books, 1968), pp. 905, 951.

13. Quoted in G. William Skinner, *Chinese Society in Thailand: An Analytical History* (Ithaca, N.Y.: Cornell University Press, 1957), p. 360.

14. In 1952 the government took steps to deny aliens the right to hold wholesale agencies for government-produced tobacco and liquor and ". . . plans were also made ... to eliminate aliens from the retailing of cigarets, refined sugar, oils, matches, umbrellas, cloth, cotton yarn, hats, shoes, and so on. Not all of these proposals, however, were effectively implemented." Skinner, op. cit., p. 356.

15. *Bangkok Post,* November 18, 1970.

16. Business Registration Act, 1956, Sec. 16. *International Translations Law Directory, 1956,* p. 141.

17. In the *Second National Economic and Social Development Plan, 1967-1971,* the government observed that the need for these commercial or trading companies had declined significantly during the First Plan period (1961-1966) but that they still constituted an effective tool in government regulation of the nation's commerce (pp. 114-15).

18. *International Translations Law Directory, 1966,* pp. 159-69 and 445-54.

19. Some typical examples of trade associations registered under the Act are: Photographic Equipment Merchants Association, Home Products Association, Druggists Association, Liquor Dealers Association, Southern Chinese Merchants of Thailand and the Petchaboon Merchants Association (a provincial city) whose stated objectives are "to unify members and promote commercial business, etc."

20. Charles Kirkwood and Associates, *Thailand Business – Legal Handbook,* Bangkok (1968) p. 45.

21. Sign Tax Act, 1967 in *International Translations Law Directory, 1967,* p. 450.

22. In the Act for Control of Profiteering, 1947, profiteering was defined as selling above the ceiling price as fixed by five-man committees in each province and a central committee for the entire kingdom. The committees were empowered to specify the kinds of merchandise for which profiteering was prohibited, to fix maximum prices at wholesale and retail, to administer rationing, to control the movement of goods in and out of a district, and to order the sale of goods to the committee or any designated person at such prices and quantities as

the committee should fix. Violations were punishable by a fine of not more than the equivalent of $250 or five years imprisonment or both, and alien violators were to be deported. The extent of implementation of this act is unknown but it was probably very limited. Act for Control of Profiteering, 1947 in *International Translations Law Directory, 1952*, pp. 675-678.

17 Tunisia: Reforming the Commercial Structure

ALAIN-GÉRARD COHEN*

Commercial reform became a key objective of public policy in Tunisia because of the exceptional importance it gradually acquired economically and politically.

On the economic level, commerce has come to be regarded both as the symbol of under-development and as the best remedy for it. The traditional trade that is carried on in the characteristic *souk* markets and the miserable handicraft workshops is exotic and colorful only to the tourist. For most Tunisians, it is, on the contrary, an object of shame, the sign of a deplorable archaism, and a way of perpetuating such unwholesome psychological habits of the past as laziness, palavering, and usury. The wholesale and foreign trades, on the other hand, with exactly the opposite features, recall and perpetuate the practices of colonialism: speculation, exploitation of the consumer, plundering of the national resources, and undue profit.

From this came a double objective: the modernizing of the retail and wholesale trades. These were supplemented in Tunisia by a "grand design," economically much more ambitious and original. Since commerce appeared to be the only field in the nation's economy which, on the one hand, grouped capable and dynamic men apt to become "entrepreneurs," and on the other, where important but unproductive capital was available, it was felt that two goals could be simultaneously reached. While reorganizing and modernizing commerce, men and capital might be persuaded to turn to new fields so as to advance the country's industrialization. In short, on the economic level, commerce could be turned into a real industry, and at the same time an industry would be born of commerce.

On the political level, the starting point may seem to be much the same. Under-development is mainly caused by social and political conservatism deeply rooted in the commercial middle class, whether it be its upper stratum (the wholesale merchants and the export-import dealers), or its lower part (the retail shopkeepers in the *souks*). For some, therefore, the setting up of a veritable socialism in the country requires not only agrarian reform but commercial reform as well. The commercial middle class must be eliminated as such, insofar as it supports conservatism, while the state must stimulate the other two sectors characteristic of socialism: the public and the cooperative sectors. Commercial functions can then be carried out by new men: in the state-run commercial enterprises, by civil servants; and in the commercial cooperatives, by members of

*Translated by Mrs. Sylvia Ullmo (Paris).

311

the party. Nowhere do private business or individual small businessmen seem indispensable.

This is where we find the fundamental disagreement between President Bourguiba and his former Minister of Economy and Finance, Ahmed Ben Salah, whose political views on the matter we have roughly summarized. The latter seemed to consider that the commercial middle class must be *entirely* replaced by the cooperative system, if socialism is to be established. But Bourguiba, the founder of the Neo-Destour Party,[1] on the other hand, asserted that the doctrine expressed in 1964 at the Congress of Bizerte was founded on a competition between three parallel sectors: the public, the cooperative, *and* the private. For him, there is no class struggle, and national unity must be preserved, together with the socio-political bases of the party, of which the commercial middle class is an essential component.

These contradictory views account for the gradual transition from an essentially economic "reform" to an essentially political "revolution" under Mr. Ben Salah's leadership—a situation which was to reveal a double contradiction: one between political and economic considerations, and the other, between two conceptions of socialism, which in turn led to President Bourguiba's intervention. The following sections analyze the evolution of the commercial reform in Tunisia, with particular emphasis on the structural aspects of trade. Other dimensions of public policy toward retailing have largely been left out.

The Commercial Reform from 1962 to 1967: Priority of Economic Goals

During this first period, economic considerations predominated over such political ones as the elimination of the "profiteers" connected with the former colonial regime, and the creation of a system of cooperatives in conformity with the original ideas of Destourian socialism.

Two phases can be distinguished. The first was in 1962 when the import trade was given over to national companies, while the wholesale trade was to be carried out by Regional Commercial Companies. The latter have private status, bring together nearly all the wholesale dealers of a "governorate" (province), and deal only in food products (grocery) and textiles (fabrics).

All the wholesale dealers in these lines have certainly not entirely disappeared, but their number and liberty of action have considerably diminished as the Regional Commercial Companies have been rapidly extended. In 1967, the Regional Commercial Companies carried from 70 to 80 percent of the country's business in food and textiles, excepting the Governorate of Tunis.

The second phase began in 1966, when a reform of the retail trade structure was started for food products and textiles. The reform consisted, on the one hand, of obliging the retailers to form private associations with a minimum of three members, called Commercial Units. In 1967, from 80 to 100 percent of the retailers of the governorates were already actually regrouped, with the exception of Tunis. On the other hand, the reform created "commercial cooperatives" at the wholesale level (in each governorate), retail-wholesale level (in each "delegation" (or district), and retail level in each township. In short, in 1967 the

Tunisian commercial structure looked as follows in the reformed sectors (the others are still independent):

Level	Private Sector	Cooperatives	Public Sector
Wholesale	Regional Commercial Companies	Purchase Centers Regional Cooperative Unions	Import-export of basic commodities (tea, sugar, coffee, oranges, dates, phosphates, etc.) through national companies and the Tunisian Bureau of Trade.
Retail - Wholesale	—0—	One central cooperative per delegation (district) for stocking goods.	—0—
Retail	Commercial Unit	Consumer cooperatives (sales areas)	—0—

The results achieved hitherto by these reforms can only be appreciated by relating them to the two economic objectives they were to serve: that is, (1) the modernization of commerce; and (2) the redirection of men and capital towards other fields of economic development. The reform has been partly successful on the first point but a total failure on the second.

The Modernization of Commerce

Modernization of commerce covers two things: (1) the modernization of commercial activity (i.e., men, methods, and investments), and (2) the modernization of channels through an improvement of practices, and greater concentration and organization along the lines of the above diagram. Here too, the first goal seems to have been reached to a much greater degree than the second.

The Modernization of Commercial Activity

1. **Investments.** The regrouping of small businessmen made it possible to achieve greater, sanitation which had hitherto been almost utterly disregarded. This was done not only by the strict enforcement of rules, but also by the

introduction of new sanitary facilities and various other equipment (refrigerators, modern larders, automatic scales, etc.). Moreover, consumers came to be better supplied with a higher quality and a greater variety of goods. These beneficial effects were mainly noticeable in rural and suburban areas.

2. **Personnel.** Working conditions, before the structural reforms were enforced, were exceptionally difficult. There was no limit to the work day and almost no provision in the work week for days off, especially in the retail trade. Child labor was widespread, in spite of regulations to the contrary, under the dubious title of "apprenticeship training," which in fact meant a kind of human exploitation that left no hope for promotion. Tradesmen nowadays enjoy the same kind of conditions as any other worker employed in the "modern" sector.

3. **Methods.** Although accounting was introduced mainly for tax purposes, it nonetheless represented an economic advance and even an improvement in human relations, insofar as it transformed the mentality and behavior of the merchants.

Modernization of Channels

1. **Wholesale Trade.** "Intermediaries" disappeared (not only the large-scale wholesale dealers, but also many of the retail-wholesalers), and their removal had a favorable, two-fold effect on prices: speculative movements tended to disappear while the general level of prices was lowered, thanks to the reduction of margins on wholesale goods. Thus, the gross margin realized by the Regional Commercial Companies has varied between 3 percent and 6 percent, and the net margin between 1 percent and 3 percent, decreasing as their business turnover increased.

2. **Retail Trade.** An economic improvement resulted from the elimination of the impoverished or incompetent merchants who were really nothing more than unemployed workers, or were employed in several activities at the same time. Yet, the number of persons thus eliminated should not be overestimated—for example, of the 1,720 retailers in Sfax in 1967, only 80 were eliminated.

3. **Concentration.** At the wholesale level, as early as 1967, there was only one Regional Commercial Company in each governorate, handling a much larger turnover (from 2 to more than 5 million dinars).[2] At the retail level, the number of individual licensees has been considerably reduced. Although the authorized minimum number of merchants obliged to form such a unit is three, there has often been a heavier concentration (the governorate of Sfax had an average of eight merchants per unit in 1967; and Kef, an average of 28). Besides, the smallest shops and those poorly located have sometimes been closed down. The larger companies, on the other hand, are run like chain stores, and are thriving.

4. **Reorganization of Channels.** The reform had more original ambitions going

far beyond mere technical modernization. It also aimed at new forms of organization, either from a "technocratic" point of view—as was the case with the Regional Commercial Companies—or from a more political desire to comply with the principles of Destourian Socialism, as was the case when a complete network of commercial cooperatives was created. The technocratic project was to fail, however, while the cooperative, because of its very success, was to result in economic waste which would ultimately constitute a political danger.

The Failure of the Regional Commercial Companies. The idea of creating in each governorate a single wholesale company regrouping the former wholesale dealers who became its employees and stockholders did not lead to any appreciable stimulation nor, therefore, to the reorganization expected. While this new system was able to get rid of some of the worst abuses associated with the capitalist system, and even more so with a colonial-type economy, it fostered others, owing to a lack of incentive and to a "bureaucratization" of management. The following weak points are particularly noticeable:

1. *Generally insufficient capital in the Regional Commercial Companies.* Their capital is from 25 to 70 times smaller than their turnover (an acceptable standard would be about 20 times smaller). This results from the reluctance of the former wholesale dealers to risk their money on an enterprise which they no longer run and which is no longer entirely governed by the rules of capitalistic profit.
2. *Excessive indebtedness.* Following the preceding condition, bank credit since 1967 has been often run to several times the capital outlay. Besides, supplier credit has financed the bulk of goods on hand and is several times greater than the credit to clients.
3. *Poor technical management.* Stock turnover is very low (7 to 19 times yearly, as opposed to 20 to 25 for comparable stores in France). The problem is that the personnel, paid according to the Civil Service rate, is not of very high quality, even, and especially, at the upper echelons.
4. *Temptation to speculate.* Paradoxically, the lure of profit still plays a part at times, but only as speculation since a profitable operation may cover countless management errors. Such operations are often performed at the expense of the public interest as when the differential between the price paid to producers and the price charged consumers is sharply increased at harvest time.
5. *Insufficient integration.* One of the major ambitions of the reform of commercial channels was to integrate agricultural production and distribution to the benefit of the farmer, but this was only partially achieved.
6. *Increase in government intervention.* Government intervention has occasionally been detrimental to good management on account of compulsory price-cutting, stocking requirements, credit-granting to local collectives, etc.

Waste Within the Cooperative Network. The reform made a point of setting up a whole cooperative sector. The economic reasons given were to create competition in order to regulate and stimulate the private sector, and to collect consumer savings according to the principle of cooperation. In fact, a political apriorism was present here, namely, to conform to the pattern of Destourian Socialism that extols competition between the three sectors—public, private, and cooperative. The economic results of the creation of a cooperative sector in the commercial field have not, however, been at all conclusive.

1. *The creation of a cooperative network has fostered unnecessary competition.* Price cuts have generally been limited, especially as far as the most common consumer products are concerned. When larger, it may result in larger consumption of less essential commodities and of imported goods—which may not be desirable.

2. *The accumulation of new savings is a delusion.* In 1967 there were 100 cooperatives in operation with an average paid-up capital of 3,500 dinars, which is a ridiculously small amount, especially in the case of a cooperative serving an entire district, particularly since these figures include, besides the consumers' savings, often larger contributions from the former merchants now integrated into the cooperative system.

3. *Cooperatives contribute to the altering of conditions of normal competition, the depletion of capital, and the waste of human resources.* The weakness of the spontaneous cooperative movement led the government to assist it in various artificial ways, which have distorted competition with the private sector. Thus, cooperatives have been exempted from the license fee and from taxation on profits; membership in consumer cooperatives has been strongly urged; there have been compulsory transfers of capital from the Regional Commercial Companies to the new cooperatives; and town and governorate councils have provided cheap buildings and facilities; cooperatives have been favored in the supplying of scarce goods and credit; and greater freedom has been allowed in paying employees, thereby permitting the recruitment of a higher quality of staff than the private companies can afford.

    As for investments, waste resulted from the duplication of commercial premises at the wholesale and retail levels as there are now private and cooperative stores.

    The waste of human resources is at least as serious, since again the number of employees and cadres was needlessly increased in a sector that was supposed to be "deflated."

It is, therefore, already noticeable to what extent the other series of objectives sought by the reform, namely, the transfer of men and capital to other sectors of the economy, might also fail to be achieved.

The Transformation of Commerce

In the Wholesale Field.

Capital. The number of wholesale dealers concerned by the reform has been estimated at about 150. The capital controlled by each of them varying from

10,000 to 50,000 dinars, the funds made available by the collectivization of these individual enterprises amounted to about 5 to 7 million dinars, after selling their inventories and reinvesting only part of their funds in the new Regional Commercial Companies. Such extra funds permitted the implementation of a few industrial programs, especially in Sfax (shoes, glue, mattresses, brakes, etc.), Kef, and Kairouan. A frequent use of these financial resources has been the construction and equipping of hotels, which made possible the recent development of the tourist trade in Tunisia.

However, the capital that the wholesale-trade reform made available was far from being completely re-invested in other sectors. Instead, the former wholesalers have tended to increase their spending on luxury items (cars, refrigerators, carpets, etc.) with the capital thus released. Therefore, it would seem that only one out of the 5 to 7 million dinars made available by the wholesale trade reform was re-invested by 1967.

The men involved. Statistics concerning the former wholesale dealers in Sfax, which can be considered as representative of the rest of the wholesalers in the country, indicate a three-fold changeover: (1) a good third of the wholesalers went into industry or the tourist trade; (2) another third took up such individual commercial activities as are still permitted (export or retail trade); and (3) the final third are participating in the management of the Regional Commercial Companies, as salaried employees or stockholders.

In the Retail Field. Here, the reorientation of personnel has been even more limited in scope. Most of the merchants have remained employed in commerce, but children and apprentices have moved into occupations with a more promising future, such as the tourist trade or industry.

Direct diversion of capital toward other sectors of the economy seems to have been still more limited, although it has affected a small number of farmers who were also engaged in small commercial ventures, and who have decided to give up trade and place their capital solely in agricultural activities. Besides, there was some indirect redirecting of financial resources through: (1) state taxes, which take an important part of the profits and redistribute them to other sectors of the economy; (2) the spread of commercial accounting that made it possible for merchants to become familiar with the use of bank accounts, which in turn brought about the appearance of new liquid savings; and (3) the retailers' contribution to the capital of the Regional Commercial Companies, which constitutes a new source of financing for the wholesale trade.

Still, the lack of sufficient capital in the new Commercial Units reveals an important diversion of capital from the normal economic channels of distribution. Thus, by the end of the 1962-1967 period, marked incidently by a relative calm, it is estimated that a third or, at the most, half of the capital formerly invested in commerce can now be found in the commercial units. The rest has been hoarded up. However, since the sector has not actually shrunk in size, this means that the depletion of supplies and working capital has been partly compensated by an unsound credit structure. At best, the associates prefer to put their capital at the disposal of the new units in the form of loans—a formula that reveals the extent of the lack of confidence.

Thus, little by little, a contradiction became apparent between commendable economic objectives—even though some of them are more or less utopic and the means of enforcing others are inadequate—and a more clearly political intent. The latter turned out to be coercive and partisan against the private sector in favor of cooperation, in order to enforce by means of the commercial reform, a socialism which was no longer in keeping with Destourian concepts, since it did not tolerate the private sector.

The Commercial Reform after 1968:
Political and Technocratic Excesses;
Failure and Reaction

The economic and political tendencies continued to develop, but after 1967 each was to take its own particular direction. Economically inclined reformers, in their haste to achieve their objectives and certain that they were valid, yielded to the temptation to become "technocratic," that is, they tried, on the one hand, to regulate everything down to the minutest detail and, on the other hand, to impose their views without taking into account either the law of the market or the principles of human psychology.

The political forces' decision to create a third, cooperative sector was, little by little, to take a different direction, which consisted of replacing the private sector with cooperatives, leaving only *two* sectors, one public and the other cooperative—a pattern which obviously represented a departure from Destourian Socialism, which draws its originality from the fact that it preserves a sphere of action for private initiative.

Still, the technocratic and political tendencies, in spite of their obviously different sources of inspiration, may at times agree on a number of objectives, although they disagree on the final results. For the first group, economic success is essential, while the second group views it with indifference. In this context, three periods are distinguishable in the evolution of the commercial reform after 1968: (1) the first year, when the two tendencies coincided completely; (2) a period when the political purpose openly prevailed, from the law on commerce of January 1969 to Ben Salah's removal in September of the same year; and (3) the present reaction.

The Growth of Technocratic and Political
Excesses (1968)

In 1968, the reform was extended and applied systematically. Thus, Tunis and Sfax, which because of their already appreciably modernized trade had been spared up to this point, were now forced to comply with the reform (i.e., to create commercial units and cooperatives). Besides, governors received guidelines that clearly accentuated both the technocratic character of the reform and the preference for the cooperative movement. For instance, on 1 January 1968, Mr. Ben Salah signed a "Note on the general orientation of the commercial reform," in which the technocratic and political tendencies run side by side.

Technocratic excess is marked by the intention to put into effect as soon as possible an ideal pattern for commerce, described in detail and characterized by four main features:

1. Adoption of high minimal standards of capital and size (minimum capital outlay, sales, and employment) in order to achieve modernization through increased dimensions, as well as the elimination of superfluous merchants. These two objectives are noticeable in the fact that individual concerns (proprietorships) henceforth eliminated, since all commercial concerns had to be partnerships or cooperatives.
2. Fixing of gross and net margins for each sector, the profit being supposed to be distributed among the contributors of capital, the employees, and the consumers, while what is left over is used to finance other sectors of the economy through an investment fund for the economy.
3. Reorganization of the channels of distribution so as to eliminate middlemen, to promote production, to serve and whenever possible direct consumption, and to control prices.
4. Creation of a rational geographic structure, with a limited number of retailers and only one retail-wholesale and one wholesale concern per unit (geographic monopolies) in order to avoid unnecessary waste.

Political excess, characterized by the preference for the cooperative system, is evident in Ben Salah's Orientation Note, but still more so in the way in which the reform was actually put into practice. This Note first declared the coexistence of two parallel channels, private and cooperative, at the levels of wholesale (governorate) and retail-wholesale trade (district), but then announced a decision in favor of a single channel, the cooperative one. Furthermore, it considered consumer cooperatives as better adapted to the requirements of the retail food business.

In fact, cooperatives were systematically favored. Since they are difficult to setup, governors pushed the formation of cooperatives to which former retail dealers are induced to contribute capital, experience, and labor, while the consumers gain, theoretically, the right to be represented. However, a few politically oriented "consumers" dominate the cooperative's General Assembly, leading to profits being largely diverted to the investment fund for the economy.

Thus, although pursuing very different objectives, the technocratic and political trends converged on a number of points:

1. *The elimination of small business in the shortest possible time.* The objective sought by the "politically-oriented" is the elimination of the extremely conservative lower middle class, while the technocrats like to get rid of all seats of economic abuse and low productivity. Both groups nevertheless make a fundamental error, even within their own system of logic:

   a. The politicians forget that Tunisia does not really want a revolution which will replace the present regime with one further to the Left. Hence, although a change of regime may be effected at "the top" and by force, it is hardly conceivable to start it at the bottom with socioeconomic changes.

b.   The technocrats, equating modernization and productivity with size, have come to believe that these things are necessarily the opposite of small business and synonymous with regrouping and concentration at any price. What is more, the privately-owned concerns, whether large or small, appear to them as an archaic form.

2.   *A restrictive interpretation of commercial functions.* Both technocrats and socialists agree that commerce is not really an economic sector, but is at best a *function,* at the service of producers on the one hand, and consumers on the other. There is also the old idea that commerce makes no contribution to society although men and profits are unduly attracted to it. Here again experience and theory do not confirm such an opinion, for trade must exist as a separate sector if it is to render the services expected of it. It is economically unsound to reduce it to a function of production—or worse still, of consumption—that can be performed by either side without the assistance of the tradesmen.

3.   *Distrust of commercial profit.* The "politically-oriented" are obviously hostile to capitalist profit on principle, but commercial profit is also a matter of suspicion to the technocrats, for two reasons: (1) because of its supposed origins in price increases, exploitation of the consumer and the producer, speculation, etc.; and (2) because of its possible uses in hoarding or unproductive investment, as opposed to investments along lines that serve the national interest. Thus the technocrats have either appropriated private profits or favored the cooperative system over the capitalistic one, or else have shifted profits out of the commercial field.

Here again, however, it can be said that the technocrats—to say nothing of the political elites, with whom discussion on this point is impossible— make mistakes in relation to their own reasoning. A controlled appropriation of profits, no matter how just their utilization, nullifies all incentive in the exercise of an activity. The cooperative system, because it lacks incentives, has not led to the high level of productivity hoped for. Besides, by taking profit away from the commercial field through restrictive regulation, in order to induce entrepreneurs to turn to other fields of activity, one leaves little credibility to the guarantee that these activities in turn will not be regulated too.

Thus, failure was unavoidable as much in the sphere of commercial modernization, for lack of any incentive, as in that of the reorientation of men and capital toward other sectors, for lack of confidence. The growing predominance of a cooperative system imposed by force was an object of fear to small and large owners alike, and money disappeared as if by magic.

Pre-eminence of the Political Aspect
(January - September, 1969)

On 20 January 1969 a law was passed which brought about regulation of the distribution of commercial goods. It was followed in the same month by three decrees dealing with food supplies in general, textiles, and fruits and vegetables; and it was followed in June by a fourth one, relative to building materials. This set of measures constituted the official ratification and re-enforcement of the "political" tendency.

The Law of 20 January 1969. The first article of this very general law established that the practice of all commercial activity is henceforth subject to the preliminary authorization of the State Secretary for the National Economy and Planning, after consultation with the regional trade commissions which one may suppose to be in the hands of the governors and controlled by persons appointed by the secretary. The same article provides that each distribution sub-sector will be individually regulated by a government decree defining the legal status of the concerns within each sector, the minimum capital required, as well as the repartition of the net surpluses generated. Four of these decrees were issued.

The Decree of 21 January 1969 on Foods. Three very important points reveal the predominance of a political intention to officially eliminate private business and replace it with cooperatives:

1. "At the retail level, all concerns permitted to trade in food supplies must be organized into commercial cooperatives; such concerns may be allowed, exceptionally, to assume the form of distributing companies. In this case, the decision rests with the Secretary . . . (Art. 2) "At the wholesale level, handling of food supplies is to be carried out by cooperatives . . ."
2. "The working capital for any cooperative . . . must not be less than 25,000 dinars." This figure is obviously very high (food stores operated on an average capital of only 1,500 dinars in 1968); and even a technocratic determination to regroup small businessmen could not have imposed such a high figure. There seems, then, to be an obvious political design to set the limit so high that the majority of merchants, even though grouped, could not or would not try to reach it, as no merchant would care to risk a large sum in a venture with no guarantee of being in control of its management.
3. The remuneration allowed contributors of capital (in cooperatives or in companies) is fixed at 20 percent of the net profit after taxes. The rest is given out in rebates, employees' profit-sharing plans, and especially, for a "savings fund, the use of which is to be defined by decision of the Secretary." Profits thus shrink and no longer serve as incentives.

The Decree of 21 January 1969 on Textile Trade. The purpose of this decree is similar to the above apart from an apparent choice at the retail trade level, between the cooperative and the privately-owned company. But the minimum capital being set at 50,000 dinars, the deterrent effect on private enterprise is simultaneously increased. Moreover, a commentary circulated at the time declared that the objective sought was to get "ten times fewer merchants in that field than before."

The Decree of 21 January 1969 on Fruits and Vegetables. This decree is concerned with the poorest part of Tunisian commerce—the *souk* markets and the itinerant fruit and vegetable sellers. The minimum capital required is therefore apparently much smaller (1,500 dinars for a cooperative, 4,000 dinars for a private venture), but these figures once more establish a major distinction between the cooperatives and the private venture. What is more, considering the fact that individual salesmen have practically no capital at all (the itinerant seller usually buys on credit, lays out his wares on the ground or on a wooden stand, and afterwards pays for the goods he has just sold), it becomes obvious that the capital required is actually exorbitant and unbearable, and that in practice only the "supported" cooperatives can satisfy such requirements overnight.

The Decree of 20 June 1969 on Building Materials. This decree introduces, at the retail level, a reform that does not differ much from the previous ones, and which is rather moderate. The minimum capital is 400 dinars, but this decree aims at eliminating foreign dealers from import channels (the major part of building materials are imported). The decree sets up a mixed company with a monopoly on all imports, and where foreigners are in the minority and their profits are reduced to one-fifth of the net surplus (as with foods).

Failures and Current Reaction

It is easily understandable that these decress that were carried out rapidly and forcibly should have fostered a number of abuses and produced rather poor results. Altogether, the reform failed *economically* on three points: (1) exodus of capital and merchants; (2) disorganization of channels and threat of shortages; and (3) constitution of underground channels and of a black market. In the *political* field, the reform shattered the confidence of the merchants—who are fervent Destourians—in the regime's sense of justice.

However, it was the still faster and more aberrant evolution of the *agricultural reform,* conducted according to the same principles of forced collectivization, that brought about Minister of Economy and Finance Ben Salah's downfall, trial, and condemnation. Hence, the law of 21 September 1969 re-established the *three* sectors in agriculture.

The commercial field, however, had to wait until 16 April 1970 for the promulgation of a new law, although the reform had obviously been suspended de facto, from the moment Ben Salah was imprisoned. Yet, while the law indicates a reaction, it does not represent a return to free trade. Some of the goals of the reform are still considered valid by the government, and a mood of "wait-and-see" prevailed at the end of 1970.

The Law of 16 April 1970. This law "regulating marketing activity, ascertaining the principle of the co-existence of three sectors, and repealing the law of 20 January 1969," emphasizes two fundamental points for public opinion: the repeal of a disgraceful regulation and the acknowledgment of the right to existence of the *private* sector in commerce, in conformity with the principles of Destourian Socialism. The new law establishes precisely, though at times timidly, three important principles:

1. *Recognition of a private sector.* Equality between the various legal forms, and freedom for the tradesman to choose the form that suits him, is asserted in Article 2: the cooperative, the private company (instead of the distributing company with reduced rights provided by the law of 1968), or even a total absence of legal form (individuals actually engaged in the operation of private retail concerns are authorized to continue their operation).

2. *Rehabilitation of small business.* The possibility of individual development of a business is henceforth ascertained although minimum capital requirements have been retained, even if they have been lowered to a uniform 10,000 dinars (instead of the former 25,000 and 50,000 dinars). On the other hand, it is possible to depart from the norms "whenever the conditions particular to any field of activity or to any part of the country should require it," which introduces an appreciable albeit discretionary amount of flexibility.

3. *The revival of competition.* The free choice between different forms of commerce already introduces a certain amount of competition among them. Above all, the geographically based monopoly of marketing cooperatives is abolished, with all its abuses and economic mistakes. However, the failure of the cooperative reform now suggests the creation of a number of state-owned retail stores (whereas previously there were none) to be run by the Tunisian Bureau of Trade. The public sector would thus be represented at this level, in conformity with the doctrine of the three sectors. This confirms that it was not a question of a return to economic liberalism but to Destourian orthodoxy. Several objectives should really be emphasized in this respect.

The Goals that Have Been Retained

"Should this reform miscarry, we shall have to reconsider it as a whole. But in any case, we shall not return to the practices of the past . . . Such backtracking would necessitate a complete absence of price-controls which would foster an anarchy we do not want to face again." This statement by Prime Minister Bahi Ladgham on 16 January 1970 reveals that nothing is in fact further from Destourian principles and the psychology of the present government than economic laissez-faire, even though the preference for a government-directed economy is happily tempered by considerable pragmatism and good will. As far as the commercial reform is concerned, there remain quite a few of the ideas that inspired its establishment:

1. *Modernization of trade, and the technocratic ideal.* The establishment of a business is still subordinated to an approval following the fulfillment of all the requirements. (Articles 1, 4, and 6) The "technocratic" intent of regulating every field of commercial venture in order to impose modern standards has not, therefore, been abandoned; and these standards still vary in direct proportion to the size of the enterprise.

The Prime Minister thus declared, on the passage of the new law: "We consider that trade must be carried out on modern premises with an extensive clientele . . . This does not mean that there should be no small tradesmen in *souks,* or craftsmen whose workshops constitute tourist attractions, but their quality can be improved . . . The regrouping of commercial as well as other activities remains a valid goal."[3]

Build-up of savings, and industrialization. The new text provides in Article 5 that 20 percent of the net profits after taxes shall be apportioned not only to employee profit-sharing plans, but also to an investment fund. This proportion is smaller than before, but this fund can be used to self-finance, at least in part, the investments of the firm itself. The idea of using commerce to finance industrialization or the tourist trade, therefore, has not been abandoned.

3. *Maintenance of a cooperative sector.* Although discredited in the eyes of the public, the cooperatives have remained in favor with the leaders, as constituting the fundamental originality of the Destourian doctrine. This is why Article 3 maintains the taxation privileges they have enjoyed; and why the cooperatives created by Ben Salah were not dissolved. Indeed, private initiative has not regained its prominent place in the affections of the Tunisian leaders, since they still fear, as in the past, the extremes to which it might lead.

4. *Distrust of private commerce.* "There is no question of returning to the anarchy of the past . . . Commerce should not be the privilege of a handful of people . . . The consumers' interests must be preserved and the country assured of a supply of goods, whatever the circumstances," the Prime Minister declared to the National Assembly when the law was voted. He added that the new law "formulates a middle-course solution which assigns a social function to trade."

Do the abuses of trade in the colonial period still seem to be strongly felt, or is there a fear that they are likely to be repeated? Still mixed in with the more political than economic reflex that sustains it, one finds that idea—more socialistic than technocratic—that commerce must be a "function" that consequently needs to be regulated and controlled, and which can never truly justify profits.

There is undoubtedly a contradiction between such ideas and the intention of making Tunisia commerce modern "like the Galeries Lafayette," something which could only be achieved through the logic of the profit system and by restoring the tradesman's full rights and his entrepreneurial role. The Tunisians think otherwise: this is the originality, the interest, and, one might add, the "courage," of their experiment.

June 1971

Notes

This analysis used the legal texts quoted in the chapter, but also data collected during a field trip in 1967-1968, and others found in the French and Tunisian presses.

1. The Néo-Destour Party was created by (now President) Bourguiba in 1934. This party led the nationalistic fight against the French protectorate, and finally obtained Tunisia's independence on 20 March 1956. Its focus explains why the Néo-Destour Party united all classes against French domination. On the other hand, it lacked any economic and political philosophy. Only at the 7th Congress (Bizerte, 1964) was "Destourian Socialism" defined. Its originality lies in its acceptance of the co-existence of the three sectors—private, public, and cooperative—precisely in order to retain the support of all classes. Since this congress, the official name of this single party is "Destourian Socialist Party."

2. The official exchange rate is: $1 = 0.538 dinar; 1 dinar = $1.859. While the dinar is not a strong currency, this official exchange rate is adequate for our analysis.

3. Foreigners can still own and operate stores, as do the French Galeries Lafayette.

18 Uganda

HELMUT LAUMER

Introduction

The government of Uganda has laid down its economic policy program in the Second Five Year Plan.[1] In this document the government clearly indicated its awareness that the functions of trade will materially increase in the coming years, as the monetary sector becomes more important, and that retail trade in its present structure will not be capable of performing the functions required sufficiently. Since publication of the Plan in 1966 the ideas of the government on her policy towards retailing have been worked out in more detail in some principle declarations and "White Papers" (Government's White Paper on Africanisation in Commerce and Industry; Common Man's Charter; Proposals for Document Nr. 1 on the Move to the Left). From these documents the following emerge as the government's most important guiding principles in the matter of trade:

a. Africanisation of trade;
b. promoting the efficiency of African traders;
c. increasing of government influence through the transfer of trading functions to newly founded organizations; and
d. building up the cooperative system.

A brief review of the present structure of Ugandan retail trade will indicate the background in which the government policies must operate.

Structure of Retail Trade[2]

Organized institutional trade began in Uganda about the turn of the century. One of the pioneers was the Indian Allidina Visram, who started to trade in Uganda about 1900. In 1916, when he died, he left 240 shops in Kenya, Uganda, Tanganyike, and the Congo. About that time Kampala was already becoming the main trading center in Uganda. The successful exporting of cotton, which was cultivated on a major scale from about 1910 onwards, strengthened Kampala's hold on that position.

According to the Statistics Division's findings in connection with the Census of Distribution there were in Uganda, at the end of 1966, not quite 14,000 firms. Of these firms 10,500, or 75 percent, were operating in rural and just under 3,300, or 25 percent, in urban areas. Retail sales in 1966 were found to

Table 18-1.
Number of Retail Firms, Persons Employed and Receipts, 1966

Location	No. of firms[b]	Persons employed[b]	Tot. rec. in mills. in shillings
Kampala	796	5,350	474.2
Jinja	505	1,685	138.2
All other towns	1,945	7,800	565.0
Rural areas[a]	(10,500)	(47,300)	(653.9)
Uganda, total	13,745	62,135	1,831.3

[a]These and all subsequent data for the rural areas are statistically less certain than the data for the urban areas.
[b]End of year.
Source: Uganda Government, Statistics Division—Ministry of Planning and Economic Development: *Census of Distribution, Part II*. Entebbe, Government Printer, 1969 (quoted hereafter as Uganda Government: *Census, Part II*).

Table 18-2.
Percentage Proportion of Firms and Sales in Urban and Rural Retail Trade, According to Categories, in 1966

Category	Towns		Rural areas	
	Firms	Sales	Firms	Sales
Grocers	26.6	13.2	30.2	6.0
General Trading Stores	22.4	21.8	49.4	80.4
Clothing, textiles, footwear	21.1	17.9	15.7	10.9
All other groups	29.9	47.0	4.7	2.7
Total	100.0	100.0	100.0	100.0

Source: Uganda Government: *Census, Part II*.

total Shs 1,800 million (one East African shilling equals USA $.14). Of this amount one-third was effected in the country's two largest and most highly industrialized towns, Kampala and Jinja (see Table 18.1).

The average firm's annual sales in 1966 was Shs 133,000, but more than 10 percent of all urban retailers, and 61 percent of all rural retailers, had a turnover less than Shs 10,000. Some 20 percent of the retail firms in the towns, with sales in excess of Shs 500,000, accounted for 70 percent of the total sales volume.

Uganda's retail trade, especially in the rural areas, is still very little specialized. Of all the firms about one-half, accounting for four-fifths of all sales, are general trading stores that normally cover many categories such as food, textiles, household articles, tools, and medicines. In each of these they carry only a few articles, which moreover are the same in all neighboring shops. In the towns and the larger trading centers, on the other hand, specialization has made perceptible progress during recent years.

Table 18-3.
Urban Retailers' Purchases, Operating Costs and Stocks Classified by Size of
Sales, in 1966

Sales per firm in shill.	Purchases as % of total sales	Operating costs as % of tot. operating receipts[a]	Stock of gds. (yr. end)	
			as % of annual sales	per emp. (in shill.)
Less than 10,000	87.4	30.6	29.5	940
10,000 to less than 100,000	77.8	18.4	24.0	4,650
100,000 to less than 500,000	86.5	12.6	20.4	10,610
500,000 to less than 1 million	89.2	8.2	14.2	16,370
1 million or more	92.1	9.0	12.0	18,300
Total	89.4	10.2	15.2	11,900

[a]Sales and other income.
Source: Uganda Government: *Census, Part II*.

The average wage or salary paid per employee in 1966 was Shs 7,020 at
Kampala, Shs 4,970 at Jinja, Shs 4,290 on the average for the other towns, and
Shs 1,210 at the rural trading centers. Expenditure on wages and salaries materially affects operating costs; it accounts in the towns for about 49 percent, and in
rural areas for some 43 percent of these. In proportion to sales the operating
costs of retail trade amount, in the towns, to 10.2 percent and in rural areas to
9.6 percent. The costs are relatively highest in the case of the smaller firms; as
the size increases, the ratio of operating costs to sales greatly declines.

The effective trading profit margin for retail traders is greater than the
difference of 10.6 percent between the ratio for goods purchased in percent of
sales (89.4 percent) and 100 percent, because there is no doubt that stocks
greatly increased between the beginning and the end of 1967, but no definite
data are available concerning this growth in inventories. The frequency with
which the stock turns over increases as the size of the firm rises; the small firms
have a good deal of dead stock, which merely burdens the cost structure.

The Government's Directives

Africanisation of Trade

During the thirties nearly the whole of Uganda's trade was still in Asiatic hands.
The first European trading companies at Kampala included the "Mengo Plan-
ters," a retail trading enterprise that was managed by a former missionary, selling
a wide range of simple consumer goods and foodstuffs. Even at that time,
however, the government already began trying to interest natives in trade, and
making it easier for them to penetrate that sphere. The *Trading Centres Ordinance,* issued in 1933, imposed some relatively minor local limitations on the

activity on non-native traders. During the subsequent period, however, only a few Africans set up retail shops.

Not until just after the Second World War did the first major *Africanisation* of trade begin. It started because in that period of shortage the government began to import some necessary goods under its own arrangements, selling these goods through traders on the basis of fixed prices and profits. Many Africans took the opportunity to establish a footing in trade through conducting such business, which entailed no risk. At that time, moreover, many returning soldiers invested their pay or their gratuities in small retail *dukas,* i.e., general stores. In 1952 there were already nearly 12,000 African traders, so that almost 70 percent of all the trading firms in Uganda were African.

In 1952 the great majority of the African traders were widely spread in the bush, or operated in rural trading centers outside the towns. Town trading, however, remained almost exclusively in the hands of Asians. There were no African wholesalers at all. The average volume of sales in African trading firms was extremely small. It is estimated that in 1952 the African firms, numbering little short of 12,000, accounted for not more than between 10 percent and 12 percent of the total sales.

During the next decade the African traders greatly strengthened their position. They increasingly managed to establish a footing in the larger towns. The two largest towns in Uganda are Kampala and Jinja. The number of African firms there was of course at the outset very low, but it has risen by many times as much as that of the Asiatic and European firms.

In 1966, of the 62,000 persons who were employed in retail trade (including active proprietors and assisting family members), not quite 85 percent were Africans and 13.5 percent Asians. The proportion of Asians is of course a good deal higher in urban retail trade than in the rural areas (see Table 18.4).

Uganda's Africanisation Policy became highly relevant in 1970, when the new Trade (Licensing) Act was set into action. It is being used to limit dealings in a range of thirty-four categories of goods, which include beer, cigarettes, soft drinks, corrugated iron sheets, soap, motor cars, to Uganda citizens, and to non-citizens who are licensed by the Minister of Commerce and Industry to trade in these items.

Table 18–4.
Number of Traders in Uganda, Classified by Race, 1952

Race	Number	%
Africans	11,634	68.8
Asians	4,809	28.4
Arabs	319	1.9
Europeans	99	0.6
Others	47	0.3
Total	16,908	100.0

Source: Uganda Government, Department of Commerce: *The Advancement of Africans in Trade.* Entebbe, Government Printer 1955, p. 14.

Table 18–5.

Number of Trading Licenses, Classified According to the Licensee's Race, Issued at Kampala and Jinja, 1952 and 1966

	Kampala			Jinja		
	1952	*1966*	*Percentage change*	*1952*	*1966*	*Percentage change*
Africans	27	101	+274	22	64	+190
Asians	1,014	1,127	+ 11	351	333	− 5
Europeans	50	77	+ 54	22	14	− 36

Source: Licensing statistics of the Kampala and Jinja Town Councils.

The Trade (Licensing) Act empowers the Minister to divide the country into "general business areas" and to bar non-citizens from trading in such specified areas. In a first step he has declared 38 small towns and 150 rural trading centers as such areas. But this prohibition will not apply to companies or firms that are composed partly of citizens and partly of non-citizens, if they were registered by January 1, 1969. In the bigger towns, as Kampala, Jinja, and Mbale, there are general business areas, where non-citizen trading is not restricted.

Promoting the Efficiency of African Traders

Since independence was gained in 1962 the increased introduction of Africans into wholesale and retail trade, both at the outset dominated almost exclusively by Asians, has been one of the Uganda government's declared aims. On appraisal of all the measures since executed it must be admitted that the government, in prosecuting this aim, has acted with reason and skill. Despite many radical demands it attached prime importance less to making it harder for Asian traders (so far as they are Ugandan citizens) to pursue their calling, and more to active government assistance towards raising the African traders' standard of performance, thereby enabling them to compete. It must be appreciated that this is a lengthy process. Although during recent years significant results have already been achieved (the number of successful African traders with flourishing businesses is clearly rising), the experience and business relations of the Asian traders, who have done so much for the economic development of the country, will remain indispensable for many years if serious difficulties of supply are not to be risked. The view is sometimes expressed that the effect of trade, especially of such trade in Asian hands, is to make goods unduly dear through excessive profit margins. After thorough study of the facts, so far as the bulk of the firms are concerned, this view cannot be confirmed. In most trades there is extremely keen competition between the individual firms, so that the danger of monopolistic price-fixing is on the whole very slight. By international standards the trading expenses and profits of trading firms in Uganda cannot be described as excessive.

Among the government measures for promotion of African trading firms the following are prominent.

Educating towards economic thinking, and training of traders in all matters connected with the conduct of retail and wholesale business. Most African traders have a non-economic attitude, many of them still regarding conduct of the business as a part-time job; they also have little business skill. These are no doubt the chief reasons why they find it hard to compete with Asian traders. Given the traditionally established social structure of most African tribes it is, for example, hardly possible to form capital resources for financing a business. If any African's business does begin to yield a profit, all his relatives—often quite distant relatives—will feel themselves entitled to share in his prosperity. If the owner of the business refused to distribute the earnings or capital gains to his relatives, the result would be his social ostracism, or even his expulsion from the family community. On the other hand the mentality of Asian families is such that they tend to join forces in accumulating capital, even at the cost of personal privations, so as to promote the success of a business belonging to one of their members.

Opening up sources of credit, and help in capital formation. These special difficulties, which beset the formation of capital resources for African traders, make the problem of finding capital for investment in fixed and current assets particularly urgent. Since most applicants can offer no sufficient material security, the African traders depend on help from the government.

Creation of better facilities for supplying rural retailers through establishment of wholesale stores in remote areas. Many parts of the country are thinly settled, and communications are in some cases inadequate. These fact prevent wholesalers from regularly or frequently supplying the retailers in certain areas. The retailer is therefore forced to hold disproportionately large stocks. Apart from the fact that in most cases he is short of the capital required for this purpose, any holding of large stocks entails a correspondingly great risk of perishing. Advantage is taken of this situation by so-called traveling wholesalers; these are small intermediaries who often supply retail dukas at distant places with poor goods at a high price.

Greater concentration of rural retail trade in trading centers, and promoting of specialization in particular trades. Nearly all rural African retailers carry an extremely mixed general-shop range of goods, among which low-profit bread-and-butter lines like sugar, kerosene, cigarettes, matches, and soap predominate. Some tools and cloths eke out the range, which hardly differs as between all the traders in a wide surrounding area. Greater specialization in particular goods would considerably increase the shops' attraction for purchasers, since they could then offer a fuller selection of cloths, tools, or other goods. It is also certain that greater specialization would favorably affect the retailer's profit. A prerequisite for specialization is, however, even greater concentration of shops in trading centers. These centers must not be too small, and customers must be able to find in them the various specialized shops nearby. The trading center should resemble a department store with various special departments, each conducted by a different shopkeeper.

The task of implementing the measures required for encouragement of African traders was first entrusted to the *African Trade Development Section* in the Ministry of Commerce and Industry, as well as to *African Business Promotion, Ltd.*, a subsidiary of the Uganda Development Corporation. The two organizations have cooperated closely with each other. The emphasis in the Trade Development Section's activity was on advising and training traders in the individual districts. African Business Promotion, besides importing goods and arranging agencies for African traders, chiefly concentrated on helping in the provision of capital; it also assumed credit guarantees, discounted bills, confirmed credits, and provided for the sale of trucks (lorries) on hire purchase terms. In the years 1962 to 1966 African Business Promotion instigated the formation of numerous buying groups for minor African traders, and supported them by providing loans. However, only a few of these organizations were successful. Internal disputes and jealousies in many cases quickly led to their collapse, and to financial losses for African Business Promotion.

A better way to improve the terms on which the smaller African traders can procure goods has been found to be the formation of wholesale companies, in which the retailers hold a financial interest. Some of these companies, newly formed during recent years with help from African Business Promotion and from the Trade Development Department, are now operating with great success, and are fully a match for the Asian traders.

On objective assessment it can be said that the work done by both organizations has been very fruitful, and has materially contributed to the advancement of African traders. With effect from 1 January 1967 both African Business Promotion and the African Trade Development Section were merged into the newly formed *National Trading Corporation*. Apart from trade in goods this corporation engages in the following activities connected with the promotion of African trading firms:

· Assuming credit guarantees;
· Confirming for the import trade;
· Hire purchase credit to finance procurement of trucks;
· Granting of loans;
· Auditing the books of African traders;
· Conducting courses in business organization, accounting, financing, marketing and the like.

The National Trading Corporation established wholesale depots in remote areas so as to ensure a constant supply of goods to rural African traders at reasonable prices, the arrangement for such supply having previously been poor.

Government Influence on Trade

There is no mistaking the fact that the government is trying to obtain greater control than hitherto of the goods flows, both from and to foreign countries, as well as inside Uganda. It believes that by doing so it can effect the distribution of goods more cheaply and more smoothly, can avert difficulties of supply, and can speed up the Africanisation of trade.

The government's increasing activity is apparent not only in the marketing of agricultural products, but also in the procurement and sale of industrially manufactured consumer goods for the home market. As regards agricultural produce marketing, attention may be drawn to the newly established Produce Marketing Board, to the marketing boards that exist for coffee and cotton, to the Dairy Board, and to the Tea Authority and the Meat Marketing Board. For the sale of consumer goods on the home market, the *National Trading Corporation* was formed with effect from 1 January 1967. Its functions are described as follows in the National Trading Act:

- to engage in commerce and trade

- to organise and effect exports and imports of all such goods and commodities as the Board may, with prior approval of the Minister, from time to time determine, and the purchase, sale, and transport of the general trade in such goods and commodities in Uganda or elsewhere;

- to promote or aid in promotion of, subject to proper and adequate safeguards to be determined by the Board, any person being a citizen of Uganda in trade and business;

- to do all such other things as are incidental or conducive to the attainment of the above objects or any of them.

During the first years of its existence the National Trading Corporation was already appointed to be the sole importer of onions, rice, salt and ghee, wines and spirits, and some other items. These are sold to the retail trade through a total of thirty-six appointed wholesale sub-distributors.

The National Trading Corporation's policy is directed to obtaining the monopoly of trade in more and more goods: "Nevertheless we shall become involved, sooner or later, in the supply of all consumer goods. We may in some cases become main distributive agents for local manufacturers, and still allow their present agents to buy through us. In the case of imported goods we shall try to secure direct appointments for the import, export, and sale of the goods we need to handle. We do not wish to work through agents, although we appreciate that current contracts could be allowed to run out, except in cases where the Government has appointed or will appoint us to be the sole importer."[3] The Africanisation Committee, appointed by the Minister for Trade and Industry, also recommends considerable strengthening of the NTC's position through legal and administrative measures.

These ambitions, which aim at far-reaching or even complete elimination of private wholesale trade, and hence of all competition, appear extremely dangerous. In the light of the experience gained in other developing countries there is reason to doubt whether the effect, which results from the streamlining of distribution channels through assumption of trade functions by a state trading company, can make up for the consequent loss of the flexible effect exerted on supply and prices by competition between many private enterprises. Even with the best possible managers the conduct of a gigantic organization, like a state trading company that holds a monopoly, is bound to be ponderous. This entails considerable risks, which may produce far-reaching effects.[4]

Although the government may prefer, for political or other reasons, to exert its influence directly in trade, it should not overlook, however, that a distribution of risks between numerous private enterprises may be of advantage; it is also cheaper, even if these enterprises earn a reasonable profit. The government can prevent profits from rising unreasonably high by taking steps to ensure efficient competition. The National Trading Corporation ought to confine its activity in trade to categories of goods in connection with which private trade does not yet ensure proper supply of the population or smooth marketing.

The recent developments confirm these fundamental reservations. The military government that took office at the beginning of 1971 held the National Trading Corp. partly responsible for the price increases and distribution difficulties that had appeared in recent years and as a result relieved this organization of some of its distribution functions. Although the National Trading Corp. is to be retained, it will be totally reorganized with a view towards restoring a competitive market situation.

Building up the Co-operative System

An efficient cooperative system can materially contribute towards solving the problems, some of them very difficult, that marketing in Uganda entails. The basic cooperative idea of mutual self-help is especially suited to developing countries with an agricultural production structure based on small units. The government of Uganda is therefore much interested in building up the cooperative system, and strongly encourages that process.

The consumer cooperatives are as yet hardly significant in Uganda so far as the supply of consumer goods is concerned. It is true that the first experiments with this form of marketing were already carried out during the fifties, but they all failed with only one exception, namely that of the Lugazi Consumer Co-operative Society. Not until very recently was a new start made, with strong support from the government and foreign experts. But by the end of the sixties apart from the Lugazi Consumer Co-operative Society, only the Kilembe Consumer Co-operative Society (with about 1,000 members) had begun to operate. In addition three further consumer cooperatives were registered at Mbale, Masaka, and Hoima, and some of these were on the point of starting operations.

The existing consumer cooperatives have formed their own wholesale purchasing company (this is named the Uganda Consumer Co-operative Wholesale Society), but up until now it has been able to operate only on a very small scale. The Ugandan consumer cooperative movement is indeed still in its first initial stage.

September 1971

Notes

1. Uganda Government, *Work for Progress, Uganda's Second Five Year Plan, 1966-1971*, Entebbe 1966.

2. H. Laumer, "Channels of Distribution in Uganda," in *Studies in Production and Trade in East Africa* (Weltforum Verlag Munchen, 1970).

3. See S. Y. Nyeko, "Implementation of Policy," in *National Trading Corporation,* No. 9 (September), 1967.

4. The example of Guinea may serve to make this clear:

The state trading venture was an unmitigated disaster, afflicting the whole economy. An inexperienced Guinean management found itself in charge of what was, in effect, the largest trading firm in Africa. Despite some gallant efforts the distribution system rapidly fell victim to a massive administrative muddle ... Fundamental reappraisals were hindered by the need to maintain socialist purity, and by an unwillingness to look coolly at all alternatives. Official economic discussion, in fact, became increasingly divorced from reality ... The costs of Guinea's false starts cannot be calculated only in terms of wasted resources and forgone growth. Much of the popular enthusiasm for the regime, and for the dynamism of its leadership, has been dissipated. Cynicism and corruption have spread, and signs of disaffection appeared. The moral and political cement binding the state together has been weakened, as respect for law, and for the regime, has diminished."

See Elliot J. Berg, "Socialism and Economic Development in Tropical Africa," in *The Quarterly Journal of Economics,* No. 78 (November, 1964), pp. 558-560.

EDITORS' NOTE: The moderate pace of the Ugandan Africanization policy, as described by Dr. Laumer, was drastically altered in the summer of 1972 with the expulsion of all Asians holding British and other non-Ugandan passports and with announcement of other measures to be taken against non-African individuals and interests.

19 USSR

MARSHALL I. GOLDMAN

Introduction

A discussion of the government's role in Soviet retailing involves consideration of almost the whole Soviet retailing process. The Soviet government owns not only all the means of production, but virtually all the means of distribution as well. A corollary of this is that until the Soviet citizen buys the good for his own use, the state also owns almost all of commodities and goods that are moving through the various stages of production and distribution. The one exception to all of this is the limited amount of trade carried out by the peasants on the kolkhoz (collective farm) market. ,

Because its system is so different from those studied by most western marketing specialists, considerable effort has been expended to determine whether or not the Soviet system is more effective than those in the West. Such studies almost always show that Soviet retailing has suffered because of lack of efficiency and innovation. All too often this is attributed to the effect of communist ideology and the consequent banning of private enterprise and private competition. Undoubtedly, ideology does play a major role in explaining why Soviet retailing lags behind the rest of the developed world, but it is often forgotten that Russia's historical inheritance has also had a major effect. In a study of the Soviet Union, it is important to stress that a country may have a poor marketing system partly due to historical neglect. In other words, you don't have to be a communist retailer to be inefficient.

The Historical Lag

Once the bolsheviks turned from being revolutionaries and attackers to being functionaries and managers, those placed in charge of retailing found there was not much in Russia's prerevolutionary tradition to draw upon. Except for St. Petersburg and Moscow, there were few cities with stores equivalent to those in the more advanced retailing centers of Europe, and even in St. Petersburg and Moscow the best facilities were generally imitative. A group of resident English merchants, Miur and Merrilees, operated a western-type department store in Moscow. (It was subsequently renamed the Central Department Store (TsUM) after the revolution.) Similarly Singer Sewing Machine had a network of twenty-one stores in St. Petersburg and its salesmen spread throughout the country.

Singer managed to sell over a million sewing machines before it was nationalized in 1917.[1] Foreign activity of this sort, however, was fairly limited.

Most members of the Russian aristocracy bought their clothing and other nonfood items directly from stores in Western Europe. Some styles and products were imported and sold in locally-owned shops or salons in the large cities, but these items seldom penetrated into the generally impoverished and unsophisticated countryside. Moreover, most Russian-owned stores were small and not particularly innovative. With the exception of a few stores like the elaborate grocery chain run by the Eliseyev Brothers, renamed Gastronomi by the communists, most Russian merchants were accustomed to combining together into separate shops within a common building. This arrangement evolved from the practice of earlier days when the merchants clustered their stands together in outdoor markets. In Moscow, as many as 240 shops were housed together in the Verkhnie Torgovlie Riad. Under communist control, this eventually became the GUM Department Store. In Leningrad, a similar complex called Gostyni Dvor was built on Nevski Prospect. The building itself dates from the 1760s and at its peak contained 288 separate firms. Today the building and the name have been preserved and it is Leningrad's main department store.

Stores and shops of this sort were out of the reach of most Russians for both monetary and geographical reasons. The overwhelming majority of the population were peasants who were largely self-sufficient. On occasion they bought or sold something at the provincial outdoor markets or dealt with itinerant peddlers, but most of what they consumed they either grew or produced themselves. It is not an exaggeration to say that most Russians were unaffected by the absence of sophisticated retailing operations. Even if retailing had been more advanced, the majority of the people would have been too poor to benefit from it. Rudimentary efforts at providing cheaper prices and better service for the poor were attempted through the formation of village cooperative societies. The cooperatives date back as early as 1861. However, even at their peak, when there were 10,000 societies, the success of the cooperative movement was limited.[2]

An Ideological Lag

Faced with such a meager retailing network, the communists realized that it would be difficult to produce any marked improvement in retailing practices in the near future. Unfortunately for the consumers, this attitude coincided with that of state officials who generally assigned a very low priority to consumers and almost anything associated with consumption. The prevailing axiom of Soviet economic growth has been that heavy industry must come first. This has been the theme of the five-year plans since late 1928 when they were first introduced. The whole development strategy of Soviet economic growth has stressed that the heavy-industrial sector would grow at a faster rate than light industry. With few exceptions this was true until 1968 when the government began to assign slightly higher growth priorities to light industry. This new decision seems to herald at least a minor change in priorities, but it comes fifty years after the revolution. The prior emphasis on heavy industry has left indelible effects on the marketing structure that will be difficult to erase.

The emphasis on heavy industry is based on a combination of political and economic factors. It is a fundamental tenet of Soviet policy that heavy industry is necessary to assure a strong military posture. More than that, Russian theoreticians have embraced the concept that long-run growth of the economy and consumer goods production would be more readily attained by initial concentration on heavy industry. Once the heavy industrial structure has been established, it could then be diverted to the production of machine tools for light industry. In the long run, this presumably would make possible a higher output of consumer goods than if initial stress were placed on light industry. In essence the communist theoreticians asserted that the basic challenge in any economy was the establishment of a solid industrial base and efficient production. Once this had been accomplished, the industrial floodgates could be opened and the consumer goods would flow forth. It would be a simple matter, they thought, to direct such merchandise to an eagerly awaiting population. This had not happened in other capitalist societies such as prerevolutionary Russia because of the intrigues of the capitalists. Soviet theoreticians readily accepted the Marxist view that capitalist businessmen were generally more intent on creating scarcity than distributing abundance. It was bourgeois businessmen, they argued, that had prevented the full utilization of Russian resources before. With the bourgeoisie overthrown, the communists fully expected that they could easily expand industrial production and eliminate artificial scarcity. Then distribution would take care of itself and the Soviet citizen as promised would be able to consume according to his need. Communist industry would have no trouble determining these needs. Unfortunately, it has not worked out this way.[3]

The Structure of Soviet Retailing

Reflecting both the low priority and skimpy endowment from the prerevolutionary years, the basic pattern of retail distribution in the USSR has been fairly unsophisticated. There were some initial experiments during the period of the New Economic Policy (NEP) from 1921-28 when private enterprise in trade was tolerated if not actually encouraged. But the NEP period was short-lived as was private enterprise in the USSR. Today, with only minor exceptions, there is no private enterprise. Instead the state owns and controls virtually the whole marketing operation in the Soviet Union through the All Union Ministry of Trade of the USSR. This ministry coordinates the activities of the Ministries of Trade in each of the fifteen Soviet republics. In turn, the All Union Ministry serves as an intermediary between Gosplan, which plans economic activity for the whole economy, and the Republic Ministries. The All Union Ministry of Trade also works with the All Union Ministry of Foreign Trade to distribute consumer goods that have been imported into the country.

The retailing function itself is broken down into three seemingly independent networks: (1) the state store system, (2) the cooperative store system, and (3) the *kolkhoz* markets. The Minister of Trade of the USSR is ultimately responsible for all retail trade, but he exercises day-to-day control over only two of the three—the state stores and the *kolkhoz* markets. The state store network is the largest operation. As of January 1969, it operated over 337,000 retail outlets and 155,700 places to eat.[4]

The *koklhoz* markets are farmers' markets where the peasants and city gardeners can bring their own produce to sell to the public. The Ministry of Trade provides and supervises the 7,500 markets that operated in 1969, but the goods that are sold and the receipts obtained belong to the sellers.[5] Occasionally nonfood goods, especially flowers and handicrafts, are also sold in this last vestige of the private market.

The third retail network consists of 323,000 cooperative stores and stalls and 221,000 eating places.[6] They are operated and supervised by Tsentrosoiuz, the All Union Central Cooperative Society, but it in turn is subject to the overall guidance of the All Union Ministry of Trade. Theoretically the present cooperative stores are the direct descendant of the original cooperative movement that began in the nineteenth century. Immediately after the revolution most urban residents were forced to become members. Eventually this situation was reversed and the cooperative network was moved into the rural areas to serve the peasants. By the mid-1930s, the cooperative stores were assigned a virtual monopoly in the countryside and they in turn were generally excluded from the urban area where the state stores, supplemented by the *kolkhoz* markets, provided the only official outlets. In 1953, some cooperative stores were reopened in the city, but they were few in number.

Despite their geographical separation, there is not much difference between the two trade systems. It is entirely possible that someday the whole cooperative system may be merged into the state store network. Although the sales volume in state stores is double that of the cooperative stores (see Table 19.1), essentially both systems sell the same products in the same way. Moreover, the prices of almost all commodities are set or at least coordinated by the same central government organ. The cooperative stores, as far as I have been able to determine, pay no patronage dividends and extend no rebates. In fact, until January 1966, the cooperatives charged a 7 percent premium on most goods. Since this surcharge was not related to extra transportation costs, it had the effect of a

Table 19–1.
Retail and Restaurant Sales Volume (in billion rubles)

	State Store Network	Cooperative Network
1940	12.8	4.7
1950	26.	9.9
1960	54.9	23.7
1965	73.8	31.
1968	94.	40.

Sources: TsSU, *op. cit.*, p. 613.

negative dividend imposed on the peasants. The higher prices of rural stores combined with the wider assortment and usually more advanced styles found in the state stores in the cities attracted the peasants to the state stores whenever possible.

Prices throughout the Soviet Union are subject to control by the State Committee on Prices of the Council of Ministers of the USSR. The Committee's jurisdiction covers both wholesale and retail prices. The only exceptions are the prices formed on the *kolkhoz* market that are set by the peasants themselves. At one time retail prices were regulated by the Ministry of Trade, but now the Chief Administration of Prices in the Ministry of Trade is subordinated to the State Committee on Prices. In an effort to provide for the movement of shopworn or out-of-season merchandise, each retail manager is authorized a certain ruble fund by which he can mark down particularly needy items. At last report, this markdown fund was to total no more than .5 percent of the store's retail sales volume. This meant that a particular store with yearly sales volume of 100,000 rubles could mark down various products so that the total difference between the official and markdown sale price totaled no more than 500 rubles. Otherwise all other seasonal price fluctuations were ultimately under the control of the State Committee on Prices or its subordinate agencies.

In both the state and cooperative store networks, the stores are usually linked together horizontally. All the clothing shops in a city, oblast, or republic are supervised by chief administrations (glavks) in the city or oblast (province) or administrations of trade or the Republic Ministry of Trade. The same is true of food and department stores. Occasionally a factory will open a branch store, so that there are some instances of vertical organization, but most stores are administered on the basis of horizontal associations. The glavks are organized according to lines of trade, so that there is one for each major product category or type of store. Their responsibilities include control of merchandise and expense budgets, subject to direction from both the next higher level of glavk (province or republic) and the municipal (provincial or republic) trade administrators.

In an effort to stimulate better service, the state fosters what it calls socialist competition. In effect this involves competition between sectors within a store and stores within the same administrative framework. Consequently, GUM often finds itself competing with TsUM to attract buyers, merchandise, and government funds. But even though GUM doesn't always tell TsUM, socialist competition has not stimulated the effort evoked by private competition.

The competition that does exist may take many forms including the efforts of the merchandisers to obtain more attractive goods, the development of a more courteous (or less discourteous) salesforce, the creation of better store arrangements, or the provision of better delivery or repair service. Store hours are usually centrally determined and are not a subject of competition.

The importance of the *kolkhoz* market has been reduced sharply since World War II, but as Table 19.2 indicates, the *kolkhoz* market still performs an important function. The main source of supply for the *kolkhoz* market is the private plots of the peasants. In 1968, these plots produced 62 percent of all the potatoes, 41 percent of all the other vegetables, and 60 percent of the eggs sold

Table 19-2.
Share of Sales by State Stores, Cooperative Stores and Kolkhoz Markets (in percentages)

	1940	1960	1965	1968
A. All Goods				
State stores	62.7%	66.7%	68.1%	68.3%
Cooperative stores	23	28.8	28.5	28.9
Kolkhoz markets	14.3	4.5	3.4	2.8
B. Only Those Goods Sold on *Kolkhoz* Markets				
State stores and Cooperative stores	69.8	86.1	89.7	91.4
Kolkhoz markets	30.2	13.9	10.3	8.6

Source: TsSU, *op. cit.*, p. 612–613; TsSU, *Narodnoe Khoziastvo SSSR v 1961 q.* (Moscow, Gosstatizdat, 1962), p. 632.

in the country.[7] Most but not all of this produce finds its way to the ultimate consumer through the *kolkhoz* market. Officially the *kolkhoz* market is regarded as a relic of the petty-bourgeois past, and many Russians are sensitive about their continued reliance on this nonsocialist form of activity. This helps explain why periodically efforts are made by the government to discourage patronage of these markets by both customers and sellers. The fact that such markets seem to be indispensable for maintaining the flow of fresh fruit, vegetables, and meat to the market makes it all the more frustrating for those who ardently await the day when the *kolkhoz* market will wither away. Many Russian trade officials feel this will be possible when the state and cooperative stores become more competitive and are able to attract the Soviet consumer away from the *kolkhoz* markets. This will be difficult to do since prices in the state stores are already lower than those in the *kolkhoz* markets. Anyone familiar with farmers' markets in the noncommunist world will recognize the uniqueness of the present Soviet situation. In the capitalist world, prices in the regular food shops are normally *higher* than prices in the farmers' markets. The only way that the farmers outside the communist countries can hope to compete and attract customers is to charge lower prices. Presumably the customer is willing to pay for the extra cost of maintaining a store's premises in order to avail himself of the privilege of buying from an established and modern store operation. In the USSR, exactly the reverse situation now exists. The reason is that quality and variety are usually better and seasonal products appear earlier in the *kolkhoz* markets. Nonetheless, when and if conditions improve in the state stores, the peasants should still be able to attract customers by offering lower prices, just as their counterparts in the noncommunist world do. The peasant traders will simply earn lower profits, but probably they will still be able to earn enough to make the *kolkhoz* trade profitable for them.

Processes

The upside-down world of prices on the *kolkhoz* market illustrates how the typical retailing operation in the USSR may sometimes differ from that in most other societies. The myopic emphasis of the Soviet government on production and heavy industry has a decidedly negative impact on retailing. Inevitably the whole process, from the type to the quality of the service rendered, is affected. This is reflected in how the Ministry of Trade treats such questions as store location, operations, personnel training, merchandising, and promotion.

Because of the emphasis on heavy industry, for many years there were few if any resources to spare for the construction of new stores. Thus nothing was done to supplement the primitive network of stores inherited from the czarist government. Moreover, during the massive crunch caused by the collectivization of agriculture and the beginning of the five-year plans in the early 1930s, goods were in such short supply that it was necessary to impose rationing. Since there was often nothing to put in the stores, instead of opening new stores, it was often decided to close down existing facilities. Thus Moscow's Verkhnie Torgovli Riad was converted into an office building until 1953 when it was reopened as GUM.

As the country recovered from World War II and a heavy industrial base was indeed established, more resources were finally made available for consumption and housing. Still complaints have continued about the failure of the trade authorities to keep pace with the new housing construction that has spread over the face of the USSR. Soviet policy is to set aside the first floor of every tenth or so apartment building for some type of store. This is intended to provide neighborhood shopping facilities. Architecturally, however, this imposes severe restraints on the type of store designs that can be used. Whatever is done must first of all conform with the higher priorities of arranging for the cheap construction of apartment units. Reflecting this frustration, more trade officials are asking for unipurpose and separate buildings designed to their particular specifications. Unfortunately construction funds are still in short supply so that such buildings are not yet readily available.

Because of outmoded planning guides, even stores that are designated purely as retail buildings are often poorly designed with little provision for future needs. For example, officials in the Ministry of Trade continue to ignore the impact of the automobile on future shopping habits. Under Khrushchev, Russian planners were told that there would never be many private automobiles in the USSR. Instead emphasis was to remain on public transportation. Consequently planners in the Ministry of Trade saw no need to provide for parking space at their stores nor for easy automobile access to store sites. After Khrushchev's outster, Kosygin decided that the failure to provide private automobiles was a poor policy both politically (it was unpopular) and economically (automobiles up to a certain point do facilitate movement). With the completion of the Fiat plant in 1970, annual automobile production has risen rapidly. From 200,000 units in 1965, the Russians hope to produce 1,200,000 automobiles by 1975. Unfortunately, Ministry of Trade officials have not reflected this change in their building plans. As yet there is no indication that adequate parking facilities are being provided and no indication that stores are being located near major road junctions. The consequences for the future will be expensive.

A second planning error is the use of the concept of *rabochii mest* or the "number of salesclerks" in determining the size of a store. That is to say, the space allocation for a projected store is based upon the estimated size of the salesforce, through the use of a norm of traditional "work space" provided for each worker, rather than being planned directly from estimated sales volume or inventory-holding requirements. This may have been an appropriate guide several decades ago before the growth of self-service, but today the number of sales-clerks in a store is not necessarily a measure of anything. Nonetheless the Russians have retained this concept, which naturally leads them to put the stress on salesclerks rather than on self-service or available sales space.

The use of the concept of *rabochii mest* is not the only reason for the hesitant spread of self-service in the USSR. The seriousness of this lag is indicated by the fact that as of mid-1970, only 10 percent of all food stores and 7 percent of all nonfood stores had self-service.[8] Virtually all the rest maintained some form of the cumbersome *kassa* system, which involves standing in one line to find the price of a good, standing in a second line to pay for it and obtain a receipt, and finally standing in a third line to exchange the receipt for the good itself. This inefficient and much condemned system persists not only because emphasis is placed on the number of salesclerks employed in a particular store, but for two other reasons as well—the unwillingness of the salesclerks to be responsible for merchandise shortages under such a system and the paucity of prepackaging.

The salesclerks fight the spread of self-service because under Soviet law, each salesclerk is held "materially responsible" for any shortages that result among the goods he has under his control. The state must take such measures to assure the taxpayers of the country that trade personnel are not stealing at the expense of the state. Whenever losses are discovered, the clerks must pay for them out of their own pockets. That explains the popularity of the *kassa* system among the salesclerks. It provides a system of double checking against theft by both customers and fellow employees. In effect each salesclerk is responsible for only one aspect of the sales process and his accounts must match those of the cashiers. Moreover, the customer is denied access to the good until he has paid for it. With self-service the salesclerk not only has to guard against shoplifting by the customers, but the salesclerk also finds himself at the mercy of fellow employees who may be tempted to steal something from the area under his jurisdiction.

Because of the understandable resistance of the salesclerks to self-service, when self-service is finally introduced, it often takes unique forms. Initially some stores adopted the practice of admitting on the sales floor only as many customers as there were salesclerks to watch them.[9] A more lasting practice has been the decision to station two cashiers at every checkout position. The second cashier recalculates the amount of the purchase and insures that the customer has paid the proper amount to the first cashier. This is to prevent collusion between the customer and the first cashier.[10] Such checks are necessary because of the prevalent attitude that there is nothing wrong with stealing in the stores. The reasoning seems to be that since what is being stolen "only" belongs to the state, a little bit taken here and there will never be missed. (As corporate units grow larger and larger in capitalist societies, a similar attitude may be developing.)

The absence of prepackaging by the manufacturer or processor is an equal obstacle to the spread of self-service. In the USSR, only 32 percent of the food goods are sold in prepackaged form.[11] If a salesclerk has to find, wrap, weigh, and price the products for the consumer on the sales floor, there is not much service left for the customer to provide for himself. Although the retail store may decide to supplement the process of packaging, this is a less efficient system than if the factories do it themselves on a mass-production basis. Despite these arguments, most processors continue to resist the retailers requests for the prepackaging of goods.

Such resistance by manufacturers and processors provides an insight into the general question of competition and its net effect on retailing. While competition undoubtedly has its negative by-products, the absence of some of the more vigorous forms of competition in the USSR has also proven to be costly, especially in the sphere of retailing services. One of the main reasons why manufacturers and processors in the USSR resist the prepackaging of merchandise is that if they do provide such a service, they stand to gain nothing, but they stand to lose some of their present operating profit. This undesired result is due to the need to obtain state permission if prices are raised even when extra services are provided. Moreover, it is not always easy to obtain such permission. In addition, failure to provide such services usually involves no risk to the Soviet food processor. Because there are no alternative sources of supply for the customer, there is no danger that the customer will take his business elsewhere. The obstacles faced by the retailer in such circumstances is illustrated by a discussion I heard in the office of the officials in charge of meatpacking in Leningrad. An American meatpacker was trying to explain why he undertook to bear the expense of prepacking his meat for his supermarket customers in his plant. The retailers did not have to convince him of the need for such a move. It was obvious to him that if he did not buy the equipment for prepackaging his output, he would lose all his business to other meatpackers. At this point, a Russian from the Ministry of Trade who had been listening interrupted, "See, that's just our problem. We have been trying to get the state meatpacker to package meat for us but he won't listen and there is no way we can threaten him by taking our business elsewhere."[12]

The need for competition seems to be particularly crucial in stimulating the provision of personal services. It is not only suppliers who need to be stimulated, but sales personnel too. In effect each salesclerk is guaranteed his job by the state, which is the owner of the store. This is equivalent to giving the salesclerk the status of a low-grade civil servant. Civil servants all over the world are not especially noted for their warmth and desire to please, especially since it is difficult to fire or transfer such employees. This helps to explain the disinterest and rudeness of Soviet service personnel.

To compensate for the absence of private competition and the motivation it generates, the Russians have tried to provide a variety of substitutes. For the individual salesclerk, this often takes the form of nonmaterial rewards. Trade personnel are encouraged to vie for such forms of recognition as the worker of the month award or the best young communist. Another method of stimulating improved service is to offer extensive training in retailing and general marketing practices. These courses also include a study of the physical properties of various consumer goods so that the salesclerks will be better informed about what they are selling. Such training is provided in high schools and technical institutes. The hope of the Soviet government generally is that if it can raise the professional qualifications of the labor force through schooling, the increase in employee work skills will offset the lack of motivation resulting from the absence of private competition. It would be as if every production worker in the United States were a trained engineer and every salesclerk a graduate of Dale Carnegie Institute and the Wharton School.

State trade officials have often introduced other measures in an effort to provide central guidance and support for efforts that would otherwise originate within private firms. One such measure was the decision to open a series of advertising agencies operated by the Ministry of Trade to prepare advertising for print and broadcast media. In addition to facilitating the dispersion of information about new products, the need for such activity was also motivated by the sudden discovery that a surplus of certain goods had accumulated on the store and warehouse shelves. At one point in 1963, excess stocks of consumer goods were estimated to have amounted to $4.3 billion.[13] By means of a program of advertising, installment credit, selective price, production adjustments, and export promotion, inventory stocks have been reduced somewhat so that by 1970, the size of excess stocks had fallen to $2.7 billion. It should not be assumed, however, that the reduction of inventory is necessarily evidence that the merchandising policy of the Ministry of Trade has been a complete success. During this same period, consumer savings in the state savings banks have risen from $12 billion in 1960 to $36 billion in 1968.[14] In other words, savings rose by 200 percent while sales only increased by 70 percent. Many Russian economists see this as evidence that the Russian consumer does not like a good portion of what he sees in the stores and, therefore, he simply refuses to buy merchandise that he feels is not worth the money.

In order to make decisions more accurately the Russians have also authorized the expansion of marketing research. Affiliates of both Gosplan and the Ministry of Trade are engaged in collecting budget studies and drawing up models of consumption. They hope to be able to anticipate future demand in order to prevent the future build-up of inventory. Such efforts are necessary because the present planning system does not provide adequate feedback between the customer and the manufacturer. The economic reforms of 1965, often associated in this country with the ideas of Professor E. Liberman, attempted to facilitate the flow of signals between the ultimate consumer and the manufacturer, but considerable static remains. The main problem is that the manufacturers still find themselves accountable more to their superiors in the various ministries of production, such as the Ministry of General Machine Building and the Ministry of Industry, than to the outlets of the Ministry of Trade. As a result, goods are often produced whether or not they are wanted by the retailer and, in turn, goods are sometimes offered for sale whether or not they are wanted by the consumer. Unfortunately market research in itself is unlikely to repair completely this gap in the flow of information and response. Unless the incentive system and chain of command are changed, the provision of better information will not in itself cause managers to act differently than they presently do.

Function of the Retailer

As in any society, the function of the retailer in the USSR has been to serve as a middleman between the producer and the consumer. As we have seen, however, until recently the Soviet retail organization has been regarded more as a passive than an active force in this process. It was always assumed that the improvement in consumer well-being would come from above from either Gosplan or industry itself. All the retail organization would have to do is then distribute the goods.

With time has come the realization that the retail organization must assume a more active role if the consumer's well-being is to be significantly improved. If the retailer begins to act as a spokesman for the consumer, then the likelihood is considerably greater that the quality and variety of goods being offered for sale will improve. Rather than wait for the manufacturer to act as a lever on the retailer, many marketing officials are beginning to acknowledge that the retailer must begin to assume more initiative and act as the lever on the manufacturer.

The well-being of the consumer is affected by the process of shopping. If the goods he seeks are unavailable or in bad repair or sold with an unpleasant attitude, the utility of consumption is diminished. If it is necessary to stand in line or search in several stores for a product, this too negatively affects the consumer. In turn, if the worker finds it difficult to shop for the necessities of life, his productivity at the factory will be adversely affected. This is especially important in the USSR where housewives almost always have a full-time job in addition to their job of running the household.

As part of the effort to accelerate the improvement of marketing services in the USSR, the Russians have apparently decided to expose themselves to foreign products and processes. In recent years, large quantities of foreign goods have been imported and offered for sale to Russian consumers. Not only does this appeal to a large segment of the Soviet public, but the appearance of such goods in official distribution channels stimulates product improvement by Russian manufacturers who are thereby provided with a continuing look at foreign quality and style. With somewhat the same purpose in mind, the Russians have also arranged for the Italian firm of SIRCE to build fourteen complete western-type supermarkets.[15] Once erected and equipped, these stores are to be operated by the Ministry of Trade. It is intended that these new stores should serve as demonstration models to be duplicated by other Russian trade organizations throughout the country.

The contract with SIRCE and the importation of foreign goods is as far as the Russians seem prepared to go in permitting foreign retailing activity in the USSR itself. At present and for the foreseeable future, the Russians do not appear ready to allow foreign retail ventures to operate on Soviet territory. The only exceptions are firms such as Pan American Airlines, American Express, Hertz and Avis. But even here these companies are normally permitted to deal only with tourists and other foreigners temporarily living in the USSR. The Russians are not prepared to give up their retailing monopoly.

While the importance of marketing is gradually being accepted in the Soviet Union, much more remains to be done before the planners consider it important enough to introduce necessary improvements. As indicated earlier, this is a result of both historical and ideological factors. In many societies, especially those that were underdeveloped until relatively recently, the merchant is still viewed with scorn and treated as a parasite. He is frequently regarded as a necessary evil. In the USSR, this tradition of hostility is augmented by the Marxist ethic that production is the most important economic and creative activity. Consequently, even in a communist society, where the state is the retailer, the sales clerk (although he is a state civil servant) is still regarded with suspicion. It is automatically assumed that marketing personnel are crooked or unable to do anything better in life. If they were more able, the presumption is that they would never have gravitated to marketing. Such attitudes, which are widely reflected in Soviet literature, and do find some basis in fact, inevitably have an effect on the type of people who *are* recruited into marketing. Naturally if the personnel are of low caliber, marketing activities will not be innovative and service will suffer.

Fortunately Soviet officials are coming to recognize the dangers of such a situation, and they are trying to upgrade the role of sales employees. Novelists are being urged to write more positive novels about marketing and a national holiday for all marketing personnel has been declared. The fourth Sunday of July each year has been set aside as Salesclerks Day. All stores are closed (most of them are closed on Sunday anyway) and lauditory legends are printed about the rigors of being a salesclerk. Unfortunately considerably more will probably have to be done before there is any measurable change in attitudes.

Conclusions

The Russians have discovered there is something more to consumption than production. Even more unsettling, they have also discovered that production itself may suffer if inadequate attention is paid to consumption. For one thing, whether communists like it or not, shopping amidst the lights and colors of advertising can bring a form of excitement to one's ordinary routine. Russian officials have even acknowledged that attractive stores and advertising can provide a form of vibrancy even for nonshoppers.[16]

Overvigilant control of marketing operations and a downgrading of retailing and light industry may not only bring monotony, it may also create a cumbersome impediment to sensible change and improvement in consumer well-being. Whenever bureaucratic controls proliferate, there is always the likelihood that the means of control will become ends in themselves. The Soviet Union finds itself in this position. All too often in the past the Soviet retailing process has responded more to satisfy the rules of the regulating authorities than the consumer. Given the existing framework of Soviet retailing, this will become a difficult set of priorities to reverse.

January 1972

Notes

1. A. I. Sobolev, *Torgovlia v Leningrade* (Moscow, Gostorgizdat, 1958), pp. 5-18. When the Singer offices were confiscated, the authorities found the credit files of the thousands who had bought their machines on credit and were convinced they had uncovered an American espionage plot.

2. A. P. Polovnikov, *Torgovlia v Staroi Rossi* (Moscow, Gostorgizdat, 1958), p. 81.

3. Marshall I. Goldman, "Trade and the Consumer," *Survey,* July 1967, p. 129.

4. Tsentral'noe Statisticheskoe Upravlenie (hereafter abbreviated TsSU) *Narodnoe Khoziaistvo SSSR v 1968 g.* (Moscow, Statistika, 1969), p. 641.

5. *Ekonomicheskaia Gazeta,* No. 25, June 1970, p. 17.

6. TsSU, op cit.

7. TsSU, op. cit., p. 321.

8. *Sovetskaia Torgovlia,* June 18, 1970, p. 1.

9. *Sovetskaia Torgovlia,* July 1959, p. 7.

10. *Sovetskaia Torgovlia,* December 16, 1969, p. 3.

11. *Sovetskaia Torgovlia,* January 13, 1970, p. 3.

12. Goldman, op. cit., p. 134.

13. *Dengi i Kredit,* December 1963, p. 22.

14. TsSU, op. cit., pp. 597, 609.

15. *Business Week,* September 20, 1969, p. 79.

16. *Sovetskaia Torgovlia,* September 1961, p. 47.

20   The United Kingdom

W. G. McClelland

Great Britain (England, Scotland, and Wales) and Northern Ireland form the United Kingdom. There are legislative and administrative differences between these component parts of the U. K. but they are relatively minor. The partially-autonomous Channel Islands and Isle of Man are also part of the U. K., but involve a total population of only approximately 160,000. Some official figures exclude Northern Ireland and some are published separately for Scotland. [1]

The structure of local government in Britain is complex and currently undergoing reorganization.[2] Subject to appeal to the Minister of the Environment, and subject to general guidance from him, local authorities are responsible for land-use planning. The local authorities are also involved in administering those laws, such as hygienic codes, weights and measures regulations, and working-conditions rules that require inspection of premises. They have limited discretion in respect of shop opening hours. In the main, however, the governmental system is unitary and highly centralized. Consequently, the discussion that follows will emphasize national policy and national legislation.

Actors

Britain is a mixed economy. About a quarter of industry and commerce, including most of such basic industries as fuel and power, transport and iron and steel, is in public ownership. Retailing, however, is primarily in private hands. As an experiment in encouraging sobriety, the liquor trade has been conducted under state management since the First World War in three (Carlisle, Gretna, and Cromarty Firth) of the approximately 1,000 districts (i.e., subcounty units) in Britain.[3] More important, the nationalized electricity and gas industries sell associated consumer durables (fuel-using household appliances) through their own retail showrooms in competition with private enterprise; they thus accounted in 1966 for 1.67 percent of total retail trade. (The government now intends to dispose of some of these showrooms and other peripheral activities of the nationalized industries, as well as its own limited interest in the liquor trade.) Local authorities went into catering (through "British Restaurants") in the Second World War, but little of this remains. Welfare distributions, such as school milk and meals, might also be mentioned. Moreover, though pharmaceutical retailing is in private hands, the National Health Service has a dominating influence on the medical prescriptions side of it. All this is however negligible.

It should not be concluded that all that is not in public hands is in the hands of private enterprise as normally understood. The consumers' cooperative movement,[4] founded in Rochdale, Lancashire, in 1844, is extremely strong, accounting in 1966 for 11 percent of all retail trade. It is particularly strong in food retailing and in milk and coal distribution. After some decades of stagnation it began a major reorganization in the later nineteen-sixties and may be a force to be reckoned with once more in the seventies and eighties. It has strong ties with the Labour party and its views on questions of public policy towards retailing are therefore capable of being influential.

One interesting mutation from private capitalism, moreover, has occurred in the case of the John Lewis Partnership. By virtue of two irrevocable Settlements in Trust made in 1929 and 1950 by the owner, son of the founder, a family firm became in essence a workers' cooperative.[5] It has flourished, with annual sales in 1970 of some $250 million in department stores and food shops.

The existence of public, consumer, and employee ownership in the retail trades does not mean that any particular areas of retailing are reserved to them. In fact, any private would-be capitalist can start to retail almost anything. There are personal requirements for entry only in respect of pharmaceuticals, where each establishment must have a professionally qualified pharmacist,[6] and for alcoholic beverages, licenses to retail which are issued only to individuals regarded as of good character. Restrictions on the number of news agencies (news dealers) were imposed by agreement between the Newspaper Proprietors' Association and the association of distributors, but the Restrictive Practices Act of 1956 contained a general prohibition against such arrangements. The Restrictive Practices Court refused, in 1961, to grant an exemption for the news agency agreement. Unlike many European countries, Britain has never had legislation discriminating against the chain, though there were attempts to introduce it in the nineteen-thirties.[7] As a result chain store trading is exceptionally strong.[8] There are no restrictions on foreign-owned retail companies either. The most prominent are F. W. Woolworth (American), C. & A. Modes (Dutch), and Associated British Foods (Canadian). Safeway (American) encountered operating and marketing difficulties in attempting to break into British food retailing in the early 1960s, but at the end of 1970 operated approximately twenty-five stores in Britain.

Nor are there restrictions on size of establishment. Again in contrast to some countries on the European continent, any combination of trades can be housed in the same establishment, at least in principle, with any relevant decisions by those charged with enforcing hygiene regulations being taken on the merits of the case and in respect of those regulations themselves. Private and local-authority landlords have, however, imposed restrictions on tenants in shopping centers as to the class of goods they may sell. This has been done in order to maintain a balance of specialist trades and to attract tenants through the assurance that their neighbors would not poach into their own lines of business. Such restrictive covenants probably apply to less than 5 percent of all retail floor space at present in use. The power of shopping-center developers, whether expressed formally or not, remains, however, considerable. Nor are political pressures or ideologies in favor of one type of retailer, whether the cooperative society or the "small man," entirely absent when local authorities come to make or to influence decisions about the allocation of retail premises.

The picture in general remains however one of unrestricted entry into retailing. On the other hand, there is not much in the way of positive and particular encouragement of entry. Vocational education and training subsidized from public funds exists, but so it does for most other trades and occupations. Fiscal provisions generally discriminate against rather than in favor of retailing (see the discussion of taxation later in this chapter), though the treatment of the surplus of cooperative societies, by comparison with that of corporation profits, perhaps cuts the other way. Any special financing or other assistance that is, or may be, given to small business may help the retail sector more than other sectors, but this does not arise out of any conscious plan to help retailing per se. A similar view might be taken of the fact that mail order, which has grown dramatically in the last twenty years, is doubtless helped by the general efficiency of the postal service.

Finally, there are no specific restrictions on growth as such. A Monopolies Commission was, however, set up in 1947. It operates by quasi-judicial investigation into cases or matters referred to it by the Department of Trade and Industry (formerly the Board of Trade). It reports to the department, which can then take action in the light of the Commission's recommendations. Since 1947, the board (and now the department) has been empowered to refer cases of a dominant (over one-third) share of the market to the Commission and in 1965 it was also authorized to refer cases of proposed mergers, if they would lead to or strengthen a monopoly, or if the assets taken over would exceed $12 million. The only monopoly or merger cases significantly affecting the retailing scene have been the prohibition in 1967 of a proposed merger between the two major men's tailoring companies (both of whom operate large numbers of stores) and perhaps the abandonment, through the delay imposed by the government's decision to authorize an inquiry, of the proposed merger between Unilever and Allied Breweries announced in 1968.[9]

Structure

Absence of restrictions—with the exceptions noted—on entry, size, or growth are accompanied, since the Restrictive Practices Act of 1956 and the Resale Prices Act of 1964, by attempts to enforce competition. This means in general that trusts, cartels, and similar relationships, whether horizontal or vertical, governing trade between units under different ownership are prohibited unless they can be shown in court to be in certain specified ways in the public interest. The only alternatives are arm's-length commercial and competitive relationships, or outright merger.

At the same time it has been the government's policy, in particular through the Economic Development Committees of which there has been since 1964 one for the Distributive Trades, to encourage industrial and commercial enterprises to collaborate in national economic planning and the promotion of efficiency.[10] This policy came into headlong conflict with the Act of 1956, which, for example, rendered any trade association that urged its members to adopt certain practices liable to being brought before the Restrictive Practices Court, as a result of action which the Department of Trade and Industry and its predecessor the Board of Trade (as well as the Registrar of Restrictive Trading Agreements) were under a statutory duty to take. The problem was particularly acute in the case of voluntary chains, which were generally agreed to have promoted efficiency in the small-merchant sector of the grocery trade (and the development of which it was thought should therefore be encouraged in other trades), but which in their recommendations to their members, in particular in respect of resale prices, were in danger of the law.[11] The situation was, however, remedied in 1968 by an Act empowering the Board of Trade to approve agreements of "importance to the national economy" and fulfilling certain conditions or holding down prices.[12]

There are no statutory trade associations in British retailing. Trade associations do have an important role in dealings with the government, however, and this is recognized both by the government and the trades. The Chairman of the Distributive Trades Economic Development Committee therefore made particular attempts to encourage mergers between some of the excessive number of associations in this sector,[13] and major consolidations took place in 1967 and 1970. The Confederation of British Industry, which was formed in 1965 from three predecessor bodies, occupies a well accepted semi-official role in British government-business relations generally, but the Retail Consortium and the Retail Trades Alliance, the two major groups of retail trade associations in Britain, have not affiliated with it.

Despite the political pressures that can be brought to bear by particular types of retailer, exemplified by that of the cooperative movement on the Labour party and of the small retailers on the Conservative party, government has interfered little in protecting them or controlling or modifying their relationships. The Resale Prices Bill of 1964, in particular, which led to the final demise of resale price maintenance in most trades, was steered through the House of Commons by Mr. Edward Heath as President of the Board of Trade with little change, despite fierce opposition from numbers of his fellow members of the Conservative party. The question of the granting of liquor licenses to supermarkets, although it has aroused some fierce discussion, has remained ultimately a matter for the local licensing authorities.[14]

The picture is different when we consider retailing vis-à-vis other sectors. Nationalized industries have variously statutorily required forms of consumer consultation and representation. There are no similar requirements for the private sector, but the consumer movement has partly stimulated, and partly been stimulated and supported by, the government.[15] The government in particular established and financed the Consumer Council in 1964 (and wound it up in 1971) and provides grants for the Citizens Advice Bureaux and the British Standards Institution.

Retailing has generally been regarded as a sector with low productivity relatively to manufacturing and in particular with a low contribution to make to the balance of payments problem that persisted through the quarter-century after the Second World War.[16] There have therefore been sustained attempts to squeeze resources out of retailing and into other sectors. Retail premises, for example, unlike industrial premises, were never removed from any liability for local taxes and have never qualified for depreciation allowances for (national) tax purposes.

The most widely debated measure of this sort was, however, the Selective Employment Tax, introduced in 1966. This tax, which was imposed upon the employer, was designed to discourage employment in some industries, and consequently to shift workers to other industries, such as manufacturing, that were deemed more advantageous to the national interest. For administrative convenience the tax was levied on all payrolls, but was refunded with, in some instances, a premium in the case of employees in manufacturing establishments. The government justified this discriminatory treatment on several grounds, including the claim that services were otherwise lightly taxed, as well as the desirability of shifting manpower into manufacturing.

The Selective Employment Tax proved intensely controversial. One problem was that the tax was originally levied at a flat rate per employee per week with no differentiation between full-time and part-time employees, and thus as a percentage of wage-cost the tax bore more heavily in respect of part-timers. This seemed likely to cause retail employers to replace part-timers—who could not be used elsewhere and who would have consequently been squeezed out of the labor force—with full-timers, who could have otherwise been used in manufacturing: a result exactly opposite to that intended. After the first year of operation, therefore, the rate became related to hours worked. A second point of interest to distributors was that the same wholesale distribution operations if carried out by a manufacturer from predominantly manufacturing premises qualified for rebate whereas if carried out by a wholesaler or chain attracted the full tax; this is one of those borderline anomalies that always crop up in taxation matters and remained as long as the tax did.

The Treasury commissioned the Department of Applied Economics at Cambridge University to study the tax in its operation and the first report covered retail distribution.[17] The findings were in general favorable to the tax. It raised considerable revenue at low administrative cost and with relatively slight harmful side effects. It appeared to have resulted in a substantial improvement in retail productivity, though this might have been due to the contemporaneous crumbling of resale price maintenance or to a decline in standards of service. The Conservative government, however, halved the rate of tax in 1971, prior to its complete elimination and replacement by a tax on value added.

Retailing has also been substantially affected by other aspects of central government taxation. High indirect taxes, for example on liquor and alcohol, have led to retail interests protesting that they were "unpaid tax-gatherers," particularly when in circumstances of price control the tax rates were raised without an increase in the *unit* retail margin, leading thus to a reduction in the *percentage* retail margin. There is no sales tax in the U.K., but there is a "purchase" tax levied at the wholesale stage on selected commodities at a small number of different but relatively high rates. Changes in these rates, and particularly the expectation of such changes, can lead to difficulties in the distributive chain.[18] Purchase tax also is to be abolished in favor of a tax on value added.[19] This tax too would cause difficulties in the retail sector, since an exemption for small traders would be desirable on administrative grounds.

Perhaps both as cause and effect of being seen as one of the less important and "worthy" sectors of the economy, retailers have probably been under-represented on statutory bodies. They are of course present in such obvious cases as the Consumer Council or the statutory advisory committees on censuses of distribution, but have had some difficulty in ensuring adequate representation in respect of such matters as town planning, small business, decimalization of the currency, or adoption of the metric system. The Union of Shop, Distributive and Allied Workers is the sixth largest in the country and its General Secretary therefore plays a leading role in the Trades Union Congress and sits on such bodies as the National Economic Development Council.[20] But on the employers' side the dominance of the small firm and possibly the fragmentation until recently into many trade associations has meant that any retailers on bodies dealing with general economic matters have been there primarily as outstanding individual personalities. At the local authority level, however, particularly in relation to town planning, there has probably been substantially greater influence, either on the part of leading local stores or enterprises, or through the local Chamber of Trade, a voluntary association of traders.

Process

Retailers in Britain operate within a framework of statutory constraints of enormous variety and complexity. They have evolved over centuries and will go on doing so, current trends being in most respects towards greater control.

There are comprehensive provisions to control land use,[21] which may be in large measure responsible for the continuing strength of the retail patterns laid down in the landscape before the car made a substantial impact on local circulation.[22] All planning authorities have drawn up plans that allocate areas to a particular category of use, shopping being designated "commercial." Any change of existing premises from one category to another, such as from commercial to residential, requires permission. Any new building or substantial alteration or extension of an existing building requires "planning permission" which covers such matters as use, access, appearance and later "bye-law permission" which covers detailed requirements as to hygiene, employee facilities, and so on. At the earlier stage, special attention will certainly be paid to provision for loading and unloading. The retailer is, however, not wholly at the mercy of the local authority as to where he puts his shop and what sort of premises it shall be; there are provisions for appeal to the Minister of Housing and Local Government (now a part of the new Ministry of the Environment).

Since 1946 twenty-two comprehensively planned new towns have been designated in Britain, with an ultimate population of 1,625,000, an estimated capital expenditure of £459m. (approximately $1 billion), and 2,562 new shops.[23] This venture has been outstandingly successful and has received worldwide attention. A large proportion of all new retail premises are part either of new towns, or of the comprehensive redevelopment of the centers of existing towns, and are therefore initiated by new town corporations, or by established local authorities or their agents. Retailers or developers may however apply for planning permission for any proposed development anywhere. Planning permission is granted in most cases and indeed it was officially estimated in 1966 that existing shops, plus those for which planning permission had at that time been granted, would cater for a population of 164,000,000 or some three times the current population![24] There were 20,833 planning decisions in respect to shops and restaurants in 1968, or 4.9 percent of all such decisions. Only 13.0 percent of the planning applications for shops and restaurants were denied, compared with a 15.7 percent refusal rate for all applications.[25] In the three years 1964-67, additions to shopping floor space in England and Wales amounted to 40 million square feet, and reductions to 16 million, a net increase of 24 million in respect of an unknown total and a population of 48 million. The net increase was unevenly spread in relation to existing population. Greater London, for example, a highly congested area, accounted for 16.5 percent of the population but only 11.0 percent of the floor space increase. Expressing the latter figure as a percentage of the former gives a figure of 67. The corresponding figure for the expanding Outer Metropolitan (London suburban) Area, by contrast, was 133. Similarly, the prosperous West Midlands showed a ratio of floor space increase to population of 128, whereas the figure for the North West was 63 and for Wales 73.

So far, permission for out-of-town centers has been rare. Authorities have been conscious of the dereliction of the centers of many American towns and cities and anxious to preserve their own (and the consequent taxable values), with the modifications necessary to carry them into the era of a car-borne population. They have been anxious also to preserve green belts around urban areas. Following the success of "hypermarkets" in France, they were however in 1971 facing increasing pressure from retailers to permit this form of development.

An important case was the proposal to establish a regional shopping center in the northwest, halfway between the two principal centers of population (Manchester and Liverpool), adjacent to the intersection of the road between them and a major north-south motorway, the M6. A study by the University of Manchester established that in commercial terms, the success of the center was likely to be even greater than the estimates that had led the developers to put forward the proposal.[26] The outcome of a public inquiry was negative, however, on the grounds that the road system had not been designed to cope with the additional traffic that would have been generated and which (in the absence of tolls on public highways in Britain) would have used it without charge.

Local authorities vary in their practices as to whether they own and rent store buildings, or for example, having exercised powers of compulsory purchase to make comprehensive redevelopment possible, then sell the land on terms to a developer; from the retailer-tenant's standpoint, the result is similar. They also differ in the provision of, and requirements as to, parking facilities. Whilst in some cases planning permission for retail developments has depended on the provision of a certain quota of parking spaces in each individual case, it is generally recognized that the result is uneconomic and that the advantage to retailers of good parking provision nearby, whether privately or publicly provided and whether or not partly or fully financed by parking charges, should be reflected in the local property taxes (called rates in Britain), or in a capital contribution.

Once he begins trading the retailer has other provisions to comply with. Banks and publicans alone have mandatory hours, but all retailers face complicated requirements as to maximum permitted opening hours, enshrined in the Shops Act, 1950, and the Shops (Early Closing Days) Act, 1965. The requirements cover Sunday openings (generally prohibited except for a limited number of selected trades, such as pharmacists), evening hours of business (generally not permitted past 9 P.M. on one day a week and past 8 P.M. on all other days) and the observance of a weekly early closing day. Any change would be likely to be in the direction of relaxation of these requirements, but none is immediately in prospect.

Most of the provisions in Britain relating to employment are common to all sectors. Retailing is, however, one of the few sectors with minimum remuneration statutorily enforced. Proposals by Wages Councils representing both employers and workers in particular trades are, under an Act of 1945, embodied in ministerial orders giving them statutory effect.[27] The need for and effectiveness of this provision is however not fully established.[28] There have been occasional references of retail wage questions to the Prices and Incomes Board, a body set up by the Labour government in 1965 as part of its machinery for a prices and incomes policy, and abolished by the Conservative government in 1971.[29] The Shops Act of 1950, already mentioned, covers conditions and hours of work as well as hours of trading. The Offices, Shops and Railway Premises Act of 1963 in part replaced and extended it.[30]

The Industrial Training Act of 1964 applies to the whole of industry and commerce, but depends on the establishment of an Industry Training Board for each industry, with wide discretion in implementing the intentions of the Act. The Distributive Industry Training Board was set up in 1968 and set about its duty of developing a levy/grant scheme in the circumstances of a sector where this was bound to be unusually difficult. Principles have had to be established as to which training activities by firms would qualify for grant and on what basis a levy to finance grants would be raised. In 1970-71 the Board was operating on a levy of 0.5 percent of firms' wagebills, with exemption for small traders.

There are regulations also with regard to merchandising. It has not been necessary since 1954 for the government to operate any rationing schemes (except briefly for gasoline in 1956/57 after the closure of the Suez Canal), nor are there requirements as to the stocking of particular lines or prohibitions of particular combinations of lines. There are however important other requirements. The Sale of Goods Act of 1893 protected the consumer by making it an implied condition of a transaction that the goods should correspond with their description, be reasonably fit for a particular purpose, and be of merchantable quality. The Merchandise Marks Acts of 1887 to 1953 made it a criminal offense to apply false or misleading trade descriptions to goods. The Trade Descriptions Act of 1968, *inter alia,* extended misdescription to oral communication and rendered illegal unjustified "double pricing"—the practice of indicating a price reduction by quoting a fictitious higher price.

The Weights and Measures Act of 1963, replacing all previous legislation on this matter, took account of the great increase in prepackaging in recent years, and covers the inspection of equipment, the labeling of quantity on packages, and the penalties for giving short weight or measure. There is also special legislation to protect the customer in cases of hire-purchase. A campaign by the Consumer Council in 1964 for compulsory licensing of door-to-door salesmen was opposed by the Retail Credit Federation and did not lead to legislation.[31] The Hire-Purchase Act of 1964, however—largely consolidated in the 1965 Act—introduced the "cooling-off" period of four days, during which time a householder was at liberty to repudiate a doorstep hire-purchase contract for any sum of £30 or over. The 1965 Act also covers conditional sale agreements.

Subject to provisions about misrepresentation (including an Act of 1967 about hire-purchase advertising), there are no public-body restrictions on advertising except those imposed by the Independent Television Authority equally on all television advertisers, retailer and non-retailer alike. Most newspapers, however, take steps to satisfy themselves about advertisements placed with them for mail order.

Retailers are, of course, much affected by promotional activity on the part of manufacturers of consumer goods, such as the incorporation of coupons into packets and the supply of goods at temporarily reduced prices. The Monopolies Commission Report on detergents (1966) is of interest in this context.[32] By subsequent agreement with the Board of Trade, the two leading manufacturers undertook each to market a brand at a permanently lower "straight" price, without heavy advertising and promotional cost. The arrangement was allowed to expire.

The post-1964 Labour Government's Productivity, Prices and Incomes Policy led to pressure to contain price rises, but retail prices were never subject to the "early warning" system of notification of pending increases. That government did however call for reports on several distributive trades from the National Prices and Incomes Board, though the consequent reports have not led to specific new controls.[33]

There are no controls of sale dates, price posting, or price discrimination at retail. Legislation in 1964 on stamp trading, however, enforced the offer of redemption for cash and the printing on each stamp of the corresponding cash value, though it did nothing to ensure the solvency of trading stamp promoters.[34] The Small Lotteries and Gaming Act, 1956, requires an element of skill in any promotion that offers prizes.

The background to resale price maintenance in Britain has been summarized elsewhere.[35] The 1956 Restrictive Practices Act contained a general proscription, subject to some exceptions, against collective r.p.m. enforcement plans. Under those plans *all* of the suppliers participating in a program agreed to refuse merchandise to any dealer who cut the prices set by any *one* of the participating suppliers. In 1962, the Restrictive Practices Court ruled that the Net Book Agreement, a collective price maintenance plan for the book trade, qualified for an exemption from the Act's provisions as an agreement that provided "substantial benefit to the public." The Net Book Agreement has also been exempted from the 1964 Resale Prices Act that prohibited individual manufactuers' price maintenance plans unless reprieved by the Court. The 1964 Act lead to wide-spread abandonment of individually-enforced r.p.m., both before and after the first case under the Act, that on Chocolate and Sugar Confectionery,[36] and few other cases have been brought.

Suppliers are still, however, at liberty to recommend prices or to set maximum resale prices. The Monopolies Commission recommended powers to ban the recommendation of resale prices "only in selected cases after investigation."[37]

Retailers are of course subject to the same laws in relation to company accounts and finance as other businesses, but have been particularly affected by successive governments' use of the control of retail credit, and in particular hire-purchase credit, to assist in their general management of the economy.[38] Restrictions have concerned not the rate of interest but the proportion of the purchase financed in this way and the length of credit given. A committee under Lord Crowther was set up in 1968 to examine the whole matter of consumer credit and its report was published early in 1971.[39]

Retailers are required to complete many statistical returns, and Censuses of Distribution have been taken in 1950, 1957 (a sample census), and five-yearly from 1961.[40] Annual sample figures cover stocks and capital expenditure, and monthly figures show sales by region, trade, and form of organization. There are also yearly estimates of labor engaged. A useful guide to the official figures has been prepared by the E.D.C.[41] Government itself publishes some explanation and interpretation of these figures, but no detailed operating statistics. Its Manpower Research Unit has attempted manpower forecasts[42] and as mentioned above, the Treasury commissioned the Reddaway inquiry into the effects of the Selective Employment Tax. It has also indirectly financed much valuable work commissioned by the Economic Development Committee. It has not provided any management consultancy services specifically for retailers, though the experimental provision of state-subsidised consultancy for small firms in Bristol and Glasgow in 1968 was highly successful, and the E.D.C. has recommended a scheme for the support of such services for retailers through individual trade associations.[43]

Functions

The functions of retailing are perhaps little different in Britain from what they are in other countries, though there may be differences in degree. It would certainly be wrong to take too narrow a view of retailing's contribution to economic and social life.[44] A further preliminary point is that its functions are changing as its environment changes. Finally, it is worth considering how its various functions are viewed, particularly by those in authority.

Most obviously, retailing satisfies consumer demands by having a choice of goods readily available and, through replenishing its inventories, communicating consumer preferences directly to manufacturers in the most forceful way possible. Through introducing new lines and varieties retailers may also lead and develop consumption patterns. Conversely, many large retailers in Britain, through careful buying and in particular by the design and specification of goods to be marketed under their own label, have had a profound influence on whole manufacturing industries, in some cases with valuable effects on exporting. Marks and Spencer in the clothing field is the best-known example, but is by no means unique. Government purchasing officers have thought sufficiently highly of this retailing achievement to seek to apply its lessons to their own operations. With regard to the balance of payments effect, it is of course unusual for retailers to contribute to exports—it is rather their function to seek those imports that will best satisfy their customers' preferences—but it has been possible through the agency of government for the expertise of retailing buyers to be used to convey to home manufacturers certain possibilities of import substitution.

Retailing employs many persons, at times and places convenient to them, who would not otherwise be part of the labor force. The lack of understanding of this point on the government's part was shown by the absence of provision for reduced rates for part-time workers during the first year of the Selective Employment Tax; that lesson, however, has since been learned. In the years of mass unemployment between the wars, and more briefly after the Second World War with the aid of ex-servicemen's gratuities (veteran's bonuses), retailing provided an easy entry for many into independent entrepreneurship. With the sector latterly under squeeze, partly as a result of the fiscal and consumeristic policies cited above, and partly through technological advance, this role has not been prominent in the traditional trades, except to the extent that some lively new supermarket and electrical-goods groups have sprung up; it has been more noticeable in such fields as fashion boutiques and new forms of catering.

The contribution of retailing to the character and liveliness of town and suburban centers is generally appreciated. The interaction between retailers' drive and planning authorities' control is producing land-use patterns and community centers that seem generally satisfactory; there have been failures, due to overestimation of demand in a particular place, but the dreary straggle of shops along main radial routes to city centers is not being repeated.

In the context of a prices and incomes policy, retailing may have had a substantial part to play. Increased competition in the High Street (the major shopping locations), for a variety of reasons, has reduced retail margins, and brought downwards pressure on suppliers' prices, at a time when this was nationally critical. Some major retail groups with a sense of national responsibility have initiated price cuts or refrained from price increases with probably significant consequences.

To sum up, it may be said that a framework of legislation, expanded and modified step by step over the years to match changing circumstances and ideas, regulates the retailer in his relations with his competitors, customers, employees, suppliers, and other parties. Within and alongside this legislative structure, he is further affected directly and indirectly by the discretionary actions and even attitudes of central and local government, of governmental and quasi-governmental agencies, and of the courts. Retailers in their turn, through their efficiency or inefficiency, their enterprise or stagnation, as individual firms or through their trade associations, affect attitudes towards them and thus the provisions made to influence or control the sector in the public interest or in that of other interest groups. Governments may change, leaning now towards intervention and now towards "disengagement"; but the differences are merely of degree.[45] In the long term, with increasing emphasis on the quality of individual and communal life and on preserving and developing a satisfactory physical environment in a predominantly urban and high-technology society, retailing will be seen more and more as one important element in a complex economic and social system; public policy towards it will reflect this perspective in new ways, seeking to influence retail activity to make its optimum contribution to common goals as then understood.

December 1970, with subsequent minor amendments

Notes

1.   In writing about this subject for a laregely non-British but English-speaking academic readership, the opportunity has been taken, at the risk of over-loading the text with notes, to provide some guide to source material, particularly from official sources. The volume of such material relating to public policy towards distribution has greatly increased in recent years. Grateful acknowledgement is made to Mr. Keith Read of the National Economic Development Office and to Mr. Charles Thompson of the Manchester Business School.

2.   See: *Report of the Royal Commission on Local Government in England,* Chairman, The Rt. Hon. Lord Redcliffe-Maud. (London: Her Majesty's Stationery Office, 1969), Cmnd. 4040.

3.   Home Office: Annual Report, *State Management Districts* (H.M.S.O.)

4.   A. M. Carr-Saunders, P. S. Florence, and H. Peers, *Consumers Cooperation in Great Britain.* (London: G. Allen & Unwin, 1938); Co-operative Union, *Co-operative Independent Commission Report* (Manchester: the Union, 1958).

5.   A. Flanders, R. Pomeranz, and J. Woodward. *Experiment in Industrial Democracy.* (London: Faber, 1968); see also: J. Spedan Lewis. *Partnership for All* (London: Kerr-Cros Publishing Co. for the John Lewis Partnership, 1948); *Fairer Shares* (London: Staples Press, 1954).

6.   This refers only to medicines that require a doctor's prescription. A former agreement among the members of the Chemists' Federation, to restrict the sale of proprietary (nonprescription) medicines to qualified pharmacists, has been terminated as a result of the 1956 Restrictive Practices Act. An attempt was made to obtain an exemption under *(inter alia)* a clause of the Act relating to agreements that protect the public against injury, but was unsuccessful.

7.   F. G. Pennance and B. S. Yamey, "Competition in the Retail Grocery Trade," *Economica* 22 (November, 1955), 303-317. See esp. p. 313, n. 3, concerning the unsuccessful Shops (Retail Trading Safeguards) Bill.

8.   International comparisons are given in M. Hall, J. Knapp, and C. D.

Winsten, *Distribution in Great Britain and North America* (London: Oxford University Press, 1961), and in J. B. Jefferys and D. Knee, *Retailing in Europe* (London: Macmillan, 1962).

9. Monopolies Commission, *United Drapery Stores, Ltd. and Montague Burton Ltd.: A Report on the Proposed Merger* (London: H.M.S.O., 1967); *Unilever Ltd. and Allied Breweries Ltd.: A Report on the Proposed Merger and General Observations on Mergers* (Ibid., 1969).

10. T. C. Fraser, "The Economic Development Committees," *Journal of Management Studies,* 4 (May 1967), 154-167; Economic Development Committee for the Distributive Trades, Newsletters and Reports, (London: National Economic Development Office).

11. C. Fulop, *Buying by Voluntary Chains* (London: G. Allen & Unwin, 1962); D. Izraeli, *Aspects of Integration in Marketing Channels; Dependence of the Optimal Arrangements on Environmental Factors and Implications of this for Food Distribution Organisations,* Ph.D. thesis, University of Manchester, 1969.

12. Restrictive Trade Practices Act 1968.

13. *Trade Associations in the Distributive Trades* (London: N.E.D.O., 1967).

14. The position is governed by the Licencing Acts. The case for the granting of licences to supermarkets is presented in *Licences for Supermarkets?* (Supermarket Association of Great Britain Ltd., 1965).

15. The consumer movement in Britain, virtually non-existent in the 1950s, gathered considerable strength in the following decade. The Consumers' Association, concentrating particularly on comparative testing, was established in 1957, and publishes *Which?* It later spawned the Research Institute for Consumer Affairs, which has published a series of "Essays and Enquiries." The British Standards Institution published *Shoppers Guide* from 1957 to 1963, under the aegis of its Consumer Advisory Council. Both the main political parties published pamphlets in 1961 supporting consumer protection. The *Final Report of the Committee on Consumer Protection* (London: H.M.S.O., Cmnd. 1781) published in 1962 led to the establishment of the Consumer Council, which published *Annual Reports* (H.M.S.O., 1964 to 1971) and a monthly magazine, *Focus;* see also its *The Consumer Council: the First Seven Years 1963-1970* (June 1970). It relied on an already-existing national network of Citizens Advice Bureaux to deal with individual consumer complaints. At the local level, also, the Consumers' Association has fostered consumer groups.

The development is reflected in hardbacks. Eirlys Roberts, author of *Consumers* (Watts, 1966) is editor of *Which?* Elizabeth Gundrey (see note 31) was editor of *Shoppers Guide.* J. Martin and G. W. Smith, who wrote *The Consumer Interest* (Pall Mall, 1968), were on the Consumer Council staff. F. Knox, *Consumers and the Economy,* (Harrap, 1969) is an economics textbook with a consumer orientation. R. Millar, *The Affluent Sheep* (Longmans Green, 1963) echoes Nader, Packard, and Galbraith. J. T. Graham, *Buyer Beware* (Wheaton, Exeter, 1967) is a straight guide for shoppers. G. Barrie and A. L. Diamond—the latter one of the original members of the Consumer Council—wrote *The Consumer, Society and the Law* (Penguin, 1964; revised ed., MacGibbon and Kee, 1966), one of several books on legal aspects of consumer protection, this one with a useful annotated bibliography and lists of relevant cases and statutes.

16. Margaret Hall, "Are Goods and Services Different?", *Westminster Bank Review* (August, 1968).

17. W. B. Reddaway, *Effects of the Selective Employment Tax. First Report, on the Distributive Trades* (H.M.S.O., 1970).

18. See the *Report of the Committee on Tax-paid Stocks* (London: H.M.S.O., 1953, Cmd. 8784).

19. *Value Added Tax. A Report* (London: N.E.D.O., 1969); *Value-added Tax* (London: H.M.S.O., 1971, Cmnd. 4621).

20. The National Economic Development Council, which meets monthly, brings together the leaders of the trade union movement and of the employers' confederation, with the principal Economic Ministers under the chairmanship of the Prime Minister or Chancellor of the Exchequer. It is serviced by the National Economic Development Office. The various development committees for particular industries (often called "Little Neddies") are subordinate to it.

21. J. J. Clarke, *The Gist of Planning Law* second edition (London: Macmillan, 1968).

22. See Charles Thompson, *Land use planning and control in Great Britain: its effects on retail distribution patterns* (forthcoming).

23. *Annual Abstract of Statistics*, 1969. See *The New Towns* (London: H.M.S.O., 1965) or *The New Towns of Britain* (Central Office of Information Reference Pamphlet No. 44, H.M.S.O., 1969).

24. R. K. Cox, *Retail Site Assessment,* (London: Business Books, 1968).

25. It is important to note however that a formal refusal recorded in the statistics is the final stage of a long process. A significant proportion of applications that would be refused are probably withdrawn or amended after informal discussions with planning officers.

26. University of Manchester Department of Town and Country Planning, *Regional Shopping Centres in North West England, 1964.*

27. T. W. Cynog-Jones, *The Regulation of Wages in the Retail Trades, 1936-57* (Manchester: Union of Shop, Distributive and Allied Workers, undated).

28. E. G. A. Armstrong, "Birmingham and Some of Its Low-Paid Workers," *The Manchester School* 36 (December, 1968), 365-87.

29. See, for example, the Board's Report No. 27, *Pay of Workers in Retail Drapery, Outfitting and Footwear Trades,* (Cmnd. 3224, H.M.S.O., 1967). Other Board reports on retailing are cited in a subsequent footnote, *infra*. The Board's last report, No. 170, (*Fifth and Final General Report*) appeared in April, 1971.

30. This is one of many acts of Parliament about whose operation the

relevant government department—in this case, the Department of Employment —publishes an annual report.

31. For a self-styled "exposé" of high-pressure door-to-door selling, see E. Gundry, *A foot in the door* (London: Frederick Muller, 1965).

32. Monopolies Commission, *Household Detergents,* (H.M.S.O., 1966).

33. Between 1967 and 1969 these reports covered fresh fruit and vegetables (Report No. 31), milk (Cmnd. 3294 and 3477), a selection of consumable non-foods (Reports No. 80 and 97) and of durables (No. 97); the Board also investigated London's principal wholesale meat market, Smithfield (No. 126). In 1970/71 it investigated costs of food distribution generally; see *Prices, Profits and Costs in Food Distribution* (Report No. 165, Cmnd. 4645, H.M.S.O., 1971).

34. See C. Jameson, *Stamp Trading,* (London: Consumer Council, 1964).

35. W. G. McClelland, *Costs and Competition in Retailing* (London: Macmillan, 1966), pp. 274-77 and references there given. Also: J. F. Pickering, *Resale Price Maintenance in Practice* (London: G. Allen & Unwin, 1966).

36. Harold Crane, *Sweet Encounter* (Macmillan, 1969). The book, though sponsored by the Respondents (i.e. the manufacturers) and written from their point of view, is acknowledged by the Registrar's economist witness to be scrupulously fair.

37. Monopolies Commission Report on *Recommended Resale Prices* (H.M.S.O., 1969) para. 78. See also the N.P.B.I. Report on *Distributors' Margins in relation to Manufacturers' Recommended Prices* (Cmnd. 3546, 1968).

38. F. R. Oliver, *The Control of Hire-Purchase,* (London: G. Allen & Unwin, 1961).

39. Consumer Credit: Report of the Committee, Cmnd. 4596 (H.M.S.O., 1971).

40. The background is provided by the *Report of the Census of Distribution Committee,* 1946 (Cmd. 6764); the consequent Statistics of Trade Act, 1947, and the *Report of the Committee on the Census of Production and Distribution, 1954* (Cmd. 9276). The Report on the *Census of Distribution and other services, 1966* (H.M.S.O., 1970) gives also some of the figures for earlier years. See McClelland, op. cit., p. 328.

41. National Economic Development Office, E.D.C. for the Distributive Trades, *Distributive Trade Statistics: A Guide to Official Sources* (H.M.S.O., 1970), 45 pp.

42. Department of Employment and Productivity, *Food Retailing* (Manpower Studies No. 8) (H.M.S.O., 1969).

43. *Evidence to the Bolton Committee of Inquiry on Small Firms,* (N.E.D.O., 1970). See also the Committee's Report *(Report of the Committee of Enquiry on Small Firms)* (Cmnd. 4811, H.M.S.O., November 1971).

44. W. G. McClelland, *Studies in Retailing* (Oxford: Basil Blackwell, 1964), ch. IV.

45. A General Election in June 1970 returned a Conservative government, and by the end of the year a number of changes had been made or were in prospect; it was clear that the new government's actions were going to be far more consistent with its basic philosophy (or you may, according to taste, say: doctrinaire) than had been expected. By the spring of 1972, however, ineluctable circumstances had compelled it to backtrack to a considerable degree.

21 United States of America

STANLEY C. HOLLANDER

Foundation

Four key and somewhat inconsistent concepts have strongly influenced American governmental policy towards retailing. None of these concepts has been observed uniformly and unflinchingly; in fact this chapter is as much concerned with the deviations as with the observances. Moreover, at least two or three and perhaps all four concepts are becoming less representative of American policy as time goes on. But the deviations have usually been treated, both in the relevant legislative bodies and in their public justifications, as special cases and necessary exceptions to the general rules. The four ideas that have been at the root of most governmental action and inaction in the distributive trades are: Federalism, laissez-faire, competition, and the concept of retailing as a residual.

Federalism

The U.S.A. consists of fifty states, each of which is supposed to possess considerable autonomy over its internal affairs; it also includes the District of Columbia (city of Washington) for which the federal Congress acts as local legislature, a few overseas territories, and the commonwealth affiliate of Puerto Rico. The national Constitution gives the federal Congress prime authority over interstate and foreign commerce, while the individual states have prime control over purely internal trade. The concept of state autonomy, which clearly becomes anachronistic if pushed too far in an increasingly complex and interdependent economy, has been subject to constant erosion at least since the New Deal economic legislation of the 1930s. But retailing has often been thought of as a relatively local activity subject primarily to state and local jurisdiction. The states themselves are divided into an enormous number of municipalities, townships, counties, and special-purpose districts which often overlap and which may have various taxing, zoning, licensing, public health regulation, and other capabilities. Consequently American policy towards the retail trades must be discussed in terms of patterns of federal, state, and local action.

Government-retailing relationships are further complicated by the fact that many of the American trade regulations provide not only for civil and/or criminal prosecution by the public authorities, but also for private civil suits in which the aggrieved parties may seek redress ranging from one to three times the

367

amount of the damages they have allegedly suffered. A portion of the relevent case law arises out of the decisions on these private claims. Many advocates of increased consumer protection have recently been urging expansion of the "class action rule" so that one or a few consumers might bring suit on behalf of all consumers, treated as a legal class or category. Such a change would remove the principal barrier to private suit in many instances of alleged misrepresentation or consumer mistreatment; the fact that the small dollar amount involved in a single purchase usually does not warrant the legal costs involved in suit.

Laissez-faire

In spite of the vast number of laws, ordinances, and regulations produced by the various public bodies, the basic philosophy has been one of laissez-faire. Subject to the exceptions noted below, anyone who wishes to enter a retail trade and can obtain the necessary financing for himself is free to do so. He will normally receive little overt special assistance from the public authorities, but subject again to the exceptions noted below he will enjoy considerable discretion concerning the operations of his business.

Competition

The American espousal of a laissez-faire philosophy has been accompanied by a belief in the merits of competition. However, it is easier to obtain agreement upon the desirability of competition than upon any specific definition. Some of the partisans in public policy debates will define competition in terms of the number of firms operating in a market, others will define it in terms of the vigor of the rivalry between the firms. Consequently, highly inconsistent retailing regulations will often be all labeled procompetitive or, more commonly, anti-monopolistic.

Retailing as a Residual

Public policy planners and high-level economic strategists in the United States, as in most other countries, have not regarded retailing as a key area. The general feeling in top policy circles seems to have been that if the agricultural, manufacturing, transportation, and financial industries functioned properly, retailing and the other distributive trades would more or less automatically fall into place. Consequently merchandising has never received either the support that agriculture has enjoyed or the supervision that has been imposed upon the financial sector.

Much of the more significant retailing-oriented legislation of the past has been intended to curb what Palamountain calls inter-type competition,[1] and particularly to protect small merchants against competition from larger and more aggressive rivals. This legislation has probably hindered, but certainly has not prevented, chain store growth. In 1963, 191 large retail chains, each of which operated more than 100 establishments, accounted for 15.8 percent of all retail sales. There were 204 chains with 101 or more establishments in 1967 and they did 18.6 percent of all retail business.[2]

Currently a new wave of law-making seems to be on the way, this time in response to the demands of a suddenly-burgeoning and vigorous consumer movement. The exact shape and impact of all the new and forthcoming rules cannot be predicted at this time, but retailers are likely to have to provide more information to their customers (e.g., price per standard unit of weight for foodstuffs, acquisition date and expected period of satisfactory quality for perishables), may have to curb some promotional practices (e.g., use of lotteries, "drawings," and games of chance), and may have to provide extended warranty and other services. Consumer decision making probably will not improve as much as the proponents of these laws hope, and similarly most merchants probably will not find the laws as vexatious in operation as they now anticipate. But it is safe to predict that a revision of this chapter a few years from now would have to include a good many rules not currently on the statute books.

Actors

Government-owned Retailing

Retailing in the United States is almost entirely a private sector activity. The armed forces do maintain a system of post exchanges and commissaries that furnish military personnel and their families, both within this country and abroad, with groceries and food purchases, gasoline, off-duty clothing, sporting goods, and miscellaneous items at substantially reduced prices. The military establishments within the fifty states and the District of Columbia had 1967 sales of almost $3 billion, or slightly less than 1 percent of the country's total retail trade.[3] Eighteen so-called "control" or "monopoly" states confine sales of alcoholic beverages for off-premise consumption to special state-owned stores, presumably in hopes that distribution through non-promotional, depot-like public facilities will encourage sobriety and morality.[4]

Aside from these two exceptions, government-owned retailing institutions are of little significance in the national distribution system, although individual facilities are sometimes important to their customers and possibly to their competitors. Many public universities operate their own bookstores; art, craft, and gift shops are located in some public museums; public hospitals make pharmaceutical and prosthetic sales to both in- and out-patients. But all of these add up to only a small fraction of total retail business. Even the retail shops that are located in many publicly-owned establishments, such as municipal airport terminals and federal national parks, are usually leased to private concessionaries.

Consumer cooperatives have always played a very minor role in American distribution. Some agricultural or farmers' supply cooperatives offer their members some consumer goods in addition to farming equipment, fertilizers, and the like. But most retail trade is conducted by private individuals, partnerships, and corporations.

Few Closed Fields

Moreover, few groups of private firms are statutorily excluded from any major retail field. Some states have laws prohibiting or controlling employer sales of general merchandise to their employees. Historically most of this legislation was designed to prevent exploitation of industrial, mining, and agricultural workers who might be forced to spend their wages in employer-owned commissaries or "company stores." A few such statutes, adopted mainly in the 1930s, attacked exactly the opposite problem; conventional retailers resented what they called "trade diversion" on the part of employers who used their purchasing facilities to acquire household goods, electrical appliances, and other consumer products for their employees at "wholesale" or discount prices.[5] A number of states prohibit corporations from practicing optometry, a profession that has often been combined with the sale of corrective eyeglasses in department and chain stores.[6] However, optometric sections are sometimes maintained under individual ownership as leased departments or concessions within large stores. Six states have used statutes or administrative regulations to bar physician ownership of retail drugstores (pharmacies), but the constitutional validity of some of this regulation is subject to controversy. Approximately the same number of states now require various degrees of pharmacist ownership or participation in the ownership of any newly licensed pharmacies.[7] Seventeen of the thirty-five "license" states will not issue retail liquor store licenses to establishments that sell other types of merchandise,[8] but this does not necessarily preclude ownership of liquor stores by merchants who also own other types of businesses. But again these restricted fields are only a small part of all retail distribution.

Licensure

Although almost all types of retailing are thus potentially open to all aspirants, local and state license requirements do affect entry into a number of retail trades and retail-related service occupations and professions. License requirements may be imposed upon both businesses (e.g., pharmacies) and occupations (e.g., pharmacist). A chain store operator's guide, published in 1971, showed that one or more states required specific licenses for the retail sale of the following non-food items: air conditioning equipment, automotive antifreeze solutions, automobile accessories, automobile tires, bedding and upholstered furniture, bicycles, building materials, Christmas trees, cigars and tobacco products, coal and coke, commercial fertilizers, contraceptives, dice, drugs and medicines, eyeglasses, fireworks, flowers and wreaths, gasoline, guns and pistols, heaters and stoves, locks and safes, magazines and periodicals, musical instruments, nursery stock (trees and bushes), office equipment, photographic film, playing cards, psitticine birds, radios and television sets, refrigerators, seeds, sewing machines, and small animals. Food licenses were broken down into numerous conventional categories, such as eggs, meat, bakery products, and milk and dairy products. Licensing is also required in a wide variety of service trades, such as restaurants, barber shops, furniture repair, carpet and linoleum installation, and the like.[9] A recent federal study indicates no withering away of these state requirements.[10] Moreover, many municipalities also impose their own licensing systems.

Licenses for some trades in some jurisdictions are issued to all applicants without restriction in return for fees that vary from nominal to substantial; in other cases they are subject to various educational, experience, examination and/or other qualifications, and may also be limited in number. Licensure may be intended primarily as a source of revenue, as a device to help insure compliance with health and police regulations, as a means of controlling practitioner qualifications, or as a device to restrain entrants and competition.

The sheer nuisance aspect of even the most nominal licensing requirement is likely to bar some competition. Florists, for example, who complain about supermarket operators' temporary entry into the floral business at the peak of Christmas, Easter, and Mothers' Day seasons, often urge licensing for their trade. They feel that the bother of securing a permit, the hazard of violating some part of the licensure requirement, and the cost involved will deter at least some casual competition. But some licensing systems have a more direct and more powerful anticompetitive effect. License issuance and renewal is sometimes controlled, particularly in the service trades, by administrative boards that are composed almost entirely of practitioners within the trade. And such boards are often tempted to use their powers to enforce compliance with norms of "orderly" or restrained competition.[11] Nevertheless, the importance of most American licensing requirements should not be exaggerated. The number of would-be entrants who are excluded from most retail trades purely because of licensure is undoubtedly much smaller than the number who do manage to enter.

Financial Support

Although government thus does relatively little to deter entry into the retail trades, it also provides relatively little direct support for either would-be entrants or for on-going firms. Aside from some special programs, such as the Veteran's Administration business loan guarantees for World War II and Korean conflict veterans, the U. S. Small Business Administration has been the primary public source for financial assistance to new or operating small businesses. In fiscal 1970, SBA participated in, provided, or guaranteed approximately $1.1 billion worth of loans at moderate interest rates. Some of this support was funneled through autonomous private entities such as Small Business Investment Corporations and Local Development Companies; some came from special programs for the relief of businesses in catastrophe or disaster-struck areas and for assistance to disadvantaged minority ethnic groups. The SBA aid was provided to all types of businesses and not merely to the retail trades. Unfortunately, the agency's annual reports do not provide an analysis of the loan recipients' industrial or trade classifications. But since small firms still occupy a large share of retail trade, small business loan plans are of obvious interest to retailing. A relatively new SBA program helps provide guarantees of rental payments for local merchants who seek space in planned shopping centers and is intended to help overcome the developers' usual preference with large chains.[12]

In spite of many worthwhile programs, the Small Business Administration's history has not been one of outstanding success and accomplishment. The agency has suffered from internal chaos, it has faced conflict or reluctant cooperation from other branches of government, it has experienced a very high rate of administrative turnover, and it has frequently lacked substantial budgetary support. Moreover, its definition of "small business" has been quite elastic, so that firms with several millions of dollars in sales or assets have qualified for assistance under some programs. Consequently SBA's impact has been quite modest when compared to the total size of the business population or to the needs of truly small businessmen.[13]

A new administrator, appointed at the beginning of 1971, has received considerable praise from congressional committees on small business (the fact that he is a former congressman has not been harmful in this connection) and from small business trade organizations. He has announced a number of changes in agency organization and methods and has also reported considerably increased loan activity for the fiscal year ending June 30, 1971.[14] Nevertheless, the total SBA program is not of sufficient magnitude to alter fundamental trends in a $1,000 billion economy.

The SBA and other government agencies have announced a number of special programs for encouraging independent business entrepreneurship, including retail store ownership, among blacks and other ethnic minorities. These Black Capitalism programs have been subject to all the difficulties inherent in any small business promotion activity. They have also been criticized on the grounds that small-scale retailing, regardless of ownership, is inefficient and thus dysfunctional for the ghetto consumer. The limited benefits for black economic development, in this view, would come at the expense of the black consumer.[15]

Other Direct Support

The other limited types of direct governmental support for retailing may be conveniently examined at this point, although they deal more with operations (process) rather than with the encouragement of selected firms (actors). The Small Business Administration provides some free consulting services, but has only a tiny staff available for this activity. For example, in 1964 its fifteen regional offices had only eighteen consultants to serve all possible advisees.[16] SBA, the Department of Commerce, and other government agencies publish a very considerable number of research reports, handbooks, manuals, and bibliographies for small merchants and other businessmen. Some of these publications are excellent sources of advice, but they may not always be utilized by the people who need the instruction. SBA and some public educational institutions have sponsored a number of management training courses for merchants.

The federal, state, and local educational systems also support a moderate amount of secondary-school and post-secondary school training for the distributive trades. The term "distributive education" is defined very broadly at some points in the decentralized educational system and has included such things as training for transportation industries, insurance sales and real estate brokerage, garage operations and condominium residence management. However, much of the emphasis is on retail sales and operations. Some courses for potential distributive workers include scheduled store employment, although this is being deemphasized in current curricula development. Other courses are intended as part-time or spare-time "refreshers" and upgrading services for store staff and owners. In 1969 expenditures for federally-assisted vocational distributive education came to approximately $58 million, of which the federal government provided about $10 million, and served approximately 480,000 enrollees.[17] These figures do not include the bulk of university, college, and proprietary business school offerings relating to the distributive trades.

Numerous other public services are advantageous to retailers. The $3 billion mail-order sales industry, of course, places considerable reliance on parcel post service for distribution of both catalogs and merchandise. Municipal parking facilities have been created or extended in numerous cities to help downtown merchants retain trade. Large chain organizations make considerable use of census reports, particularly in location studies. Department of Agriculture research on food processing and handling has been useful to the supermarket industry. But the retail trades in the American context probably stand to gain much more from overall macroscopic government policies designed to provide a reasonably prosperous and orderly economy than from any past or likely future policy designed to be of specific aid to retailing. In fact, given the currently prevailing high rates of pilferage and other forms of theft, some retailers probably feel that government's greatest potential specific contribution might be stricter anti-shoplifting laws. (Actually many states have modified their false arrest laws so that merchants may temporarily detain suspected shoplifters without fear of excessive liability for claims of improper detention.)

Structure

Horizontal Linkages

A firm belief in the undesirability of horizontal agreements between same-level competitors is a fundamental tenet of the American antitrust credo. This principle applies, in concept if not always in practice, to retailers as well as to most other types of businesses, and it plays a central role in many of the policies toward horizontal linkages discussed below.

Trade associations are permitted, but so far as government is concerned membership is purely voluntary; and there are many retailers who do not belong to the relevant associations. Aside from the short-lived National Recovery Administration experiment of the 1930s, retail associations have had few special privileges under the law. Retail trade associations do, of course, frequently act as lobbyists (i.e., unofficial petitioners and proponents) before state and federal legislative and administrative bodies.

Some state retail groups have formal or informal power over nominations to some state boards of licensure or trade practice control. And some services trade organizations, particularly those in trades where the shop proprietors normally work at the same tasks as their employees, have been classified as labor unions and thus enjoy relative freedom in setting wages (prices) and working conditions (e.g., shop hours). The master barber associations fall in this category in many states. But merchants who are concerned with the resale of goods, and their associations, are not supposed to agree on prices, market shares, locational strategy, or most other aspects of competition. Such agreements, if reached in interstate commerce, are per se violations of the federal antitrust laws.

Between 1945 and 1969, the Department of Justice and the Federal Trade Commission, the two federal antitrust agencies, obtained about eighty consent decrees and court decisions against retail groups who were considered to be restraining competition, mainly through price and service agreements. Some of these cases involved rather trivial matters, such as a uniform charge imposed by San Diego, California, grocers for cashing customers' checks; others were more significant, such as a uniform prescription compounding fee schedule established by several pharmaceutical associations in the western states. As these cases suggest, American retailing actually deviates in many instances from the pure competitive state that some writers attribute to it.

Local retail agreements are, in spite of the case roster cited above, considered low priority topics in the federal antitrust agencies. State authorities, who have primary jurisdiction with regard to such local matters, are generally notoriously weak in antitrust enforcement and often favor so-called "soft" or restrained competition. Many examples of horizontal collusion, and of a sort of "live and let live" oligopolistic interdependence can be cited in the retail trades.[18] Nevertheless, on the whole, retailing should be characterized as competitive rather than collusive. The federal antitrust cases have had some direct and some cautionary effects. But the prime procompetitive forces are ease of entry, the difficulties of organizing large numbers of sellers who have various sets of interests, customer mobility, and the absence of viable cartelization institutions and techniques.

One significant type of horizontal linkage, the affiliation of independent merchants into quasi-integrated voluntary or cooperative chains for joint procurement, promotion, and other activities, has encountered little legal difficulty. Even though the joint, or commonly-enforced decision making inherent in such arrangements may occasionally skirt the technical limits of antitrust, government authorities usually regard the voluntary-cooperative chain system as an ideal mechanism for preserving small retailers' competitive viability. The normal spatial separation between the members of any given chain, and the intensity of their competition with nonmembers are generally considered sufficient to offset whatever competitive restraint intra-chain agreement may involve.

Size Limitations

The federal government has imposed no per se limits on the size of retail firms or, for that matter, on the size of most other types of business. Size, or market share, often becomes a consideration when behavior is questioned under various provisions of the antitrust laws, but the major structural sanctions are concentrated in Section 2 of the Sherman Act and Section 7 of the Clayton Act, (Celler-Kefauver Amendment, 1950), neither of which at least technically makes size itself illegal. Section 2 prohibits monopolization and attempts to monopolize; the Celler-Kefauver Act strengthens the Clayton Act provisions against anticompetitive mergers and acquisitions. As Massel points out, monopolization cases call "first, for a finding of a high degree of concentration among the sellers in a market and, second, for behavior that indicates intent to monopolize."[19] The merger cases are obviously concerned not with growth itself but with the route to growth.

Section 2 charges have seldom been invoked against retail firms; and when they have been raised, as in the 1946 A & P and the 1957 Safeway grocery chain cases, they have dealt more with conduct, such as pricing or procurement practices, than with mere size alone.[20] Of course, the conduct charges probably would not have arisen if these firms had not been among the giants of the food retailing industry.[21] But the paucity of Section 2 retail cases seems to reflect the long-standing view of both government and academic economists and attorneys that monopoly power and the returns to monopoly are small in distribution when compared with major manufacturing industries. The legislatures have often had to be responsive to the political power of small retailing. But most economists have tended to agree with J. K. Galbraith's view that the economy needed more, not fewer, A & P's to exercise more countervailing power against the manufacturing sector.[22]

This view now seems to be changing somewhat. The antitrust agencies have recently become concerned with merger movements on the part of large chain-store organizations, and have used their antimerger authority, particularly under Section 7, to block several retail amalgamations and acquisitions. The Federal Trade Commission has announced that retail food chain mergers and acquisitions that result in over $500 million food store sales per annum will "warrant attention and consideration," (i.e., probably will be prohibited); while food chain mergers, etc. that result in combined food store sales between $100 and $500 million will "warrant investigation."[23] Several FTC orders and concent agreements now limit or restrict merger activity on the part of such grocery chains as Grand Union Co., National Tea Co., and Winn Dixie Stores.[24] The Department of Justice won a Supreme Court decision in 1966 that required divestitute of Shopping Bag (before merger the sixth largest grocery chain in the Los Angeles area) from Von's (premerger, the second largest).[25] Merger controls have also been applied to several department and discount store organizations, and the government has also intervened in horizontal and horizontal-vertical mergers in the shoe store, drugstore, and candy store industries.

The antimerger strictures, which so far have only been applied to amalgamations between firms in the same line of business, have probably accentuated the recent tendency of large retail firms to unite different types of retail establishment under one ownership. Thus a number of the larger retail organizations now own a variety of retail entities including, for example, separate supermarket, drugstore, and discount store chains. In this sense many American firms are now coming to resemble some of the larger, more conglomerate European retail enterprises. A 1970 case, concerning the merger of a Cleveland department store with a local bookstore chain, might have had some implications for this conglomeration trend, although the government's allegations centered primarily on the overlap between book departments in the two types of stores. The case was settled, however, without litigation or adjudication of the issues involved since the department store agreed to a pretrial "consent decree" that required divestiture (sale) of the bookstores.[26] Another result of the domestic strictures has been to stimulate American retailers' interest in foreign expansion.

A number of the states, particularly those in the southern and western parts of the country, have used their tax and license power to impose more explicit size handicaps on chain store growth. Twenty-eight states adopted chain store tax or license fee schedules during a wave of anti-chain store agitation in the 1920s and 1930s; eleven of these tax systems remained in effect at the end of 1970.[27] Most of the schedules increase the per store fee progressively according to the number of stores operated by the same firm within the state. Thus Texas charges only $4.00 to license the first store under a given ownership, but all stores beyond the fiftieth are charged $825 per store per year. Louisiana and Mississippi base the in-state store license classification on the total number of stores that the chain has anywhere in the country, so that a large national organization has to pay the maximum fee for even its first unit within the state.

The chains were originally quite sluggish in their response to the anti-chain movement. However, they were finally able to blunt the wave of hostile taxation, primarily by engaging the political and legislative support of significant agricultural and consumer organizations. The rates are not prohibitive in most states that still have these taxes, although they might easily have been increased to prohibitive levels if the chain organizations had not ultimately developed some political and public relations expertise.[28]

Vertical Integration

The major controls that affect vertical linkages occur at the federal level, since the significant manufacturer-retailer ties usually involve interstate commerce.[29] Again, there are no per se limits on vertical integration. Some small business groups have sought laws that would prohibit firms from engaging in both manufacturing and retailing, with some exceptions for small craft shops, but Congress has shown little interest in such legislation.

However, vertical growth can, under the appropriate circumstances, be construed as part of an attempt at monopolization. Even as early as 1920, an antitrust case against the "Big 5" meat slaughtering and processing firms was settled by a consent decree that, among other things, required the meatpackers to refrain from retailing. A petition to set that provision aside was denied in 1960.[30] Recently, the government used the antimerger rules (section 7) to obtain a consent order that requires Hart, Schaffner & Marx, the largest manufacturer of better-grade men's clothing, to divest itself of a considerable number of retail outlets that it had purchased during the last several years.[31] In an important 1962 case, the Supreme Court cited both horizontal and vertical considerations in condemning a merger between Brown Shoe, a large manufacturer and retailer, and Kinney Shoe, another large retailer with some manufacturing interests. The court pointed out, however, that the only vertical mergers that were illegal were those that had substantial anticompetitive effects:

> The primary vice of a vertical merger or other arrangement tying a customer to a supplier is that, by foreclosing the competitors of either party from a segment of the market otherwise open to them, the arrangement may act as a "clog on competition" ... However, the Clayton Act does not render unlawful all such vertical arrangements, but forbids only those whose effect "may be substantially to lessen competition or to tend to create a monopoly in any line of commerce in any section of the country."[32]

Franchising and other Vertical Linkages. Manufacturers and suppliers, on one hand, and dealers, on the other, are often united in contractual or quasi-contractual relationships that fall short of outright ownership, but are considerably closer than total independence. The growing number of supplier-dominated relationships of this sort, and particularly the more closely-knit ones, are more and more frequently being referred to as "franchising."[33] Thus both the term and the practices it implies are receiving increased usage.

But it is extremely difficult to be very precise about the legal aspects of franchising. Franchise relationships vary significantly among themselves. One expert distinguishes two basic types (as well as many subtypes) of franchise: (a) product franchises or rights to sell specific products, often on some sort of exclusive basis, and (b) trademark licenses based upon the right to use the licensors' names and operating systems.[34] Product franchising has long been used in automobile, gasoline, and major electrical appliance distribution, a combination of the two is widely used in soft drink bottling, and trademark licensing is increasingly being applied to quick-service restaurant, hotel and motel, and other service trade applications.

Moreover, franchising firms differ greatly in size, market share, degree of power, and planned stringency of control over their franchisees. The franchise industry is also changing, and some of the important newer franchisors are now using their profits to recapture a substantial portion of their licenses for wholly-owned or integrated operation.[35] Government policy, law, and judicial interpretation and application of the law with regard to franchising are in a state of flux. The Small Business Administration and the Department of Commerce tend to consider franchise systems as healthy vehicles for the salvation of independent merchants; the Department of Justice and the Federal Trade Commission tend to suspect them as sets of restrictive business practices.

Nevertheless, vague and imprecise as they may be, the implicit rules on franchise relationships include, with some exceptions, all of the government policies on vertical relationships discussed below. Two special aspects of franchising should be noted, however.

1. Dealers often have to make considerable investments to join and participate in franchise systems. Government policy seems to be moving toward giving the dealers greater protection against any misrepresentation of costs and benefits, against coercive operation of the system, and against any arbitrary revocation of the relationship. The Federal Trade Commission has proposed trade practice rules that would force franchisors in general to provide prospective franchisees with very detailed and reliable information about their offers.[36]

    The Supreme Court recently ruled that a group of automotive muffler dealers could bring a private antitrust action against their franchisor and its parent corporation for alleged conspiracy to impose restrictive rules on the system, even though they, the dealers, were in a sense part of the conspiracy.[37] Motor car dealers are already given special consideration under the so-called Auto Dealer's Day in Court Act, which permits an automobile franchisee to sue for damages if a manufacturer acts in bad faith in revoking or failing to comply with a dealership agreement.

2. But the courts also tend to recognize the way in which a franchisee's acts can affect the franchisor's name and reputation, especially in trademark licensing. In fact the licensing firm may be held responsible for what the licensee does in situations where the consuming public relies upon the franchisor's reputation. In such situations, the courts are inclined to accept whatever *minimum* controls and obligations are necessary to protect the licensor's goodwill and to insure the maintenance of satisfactory service standards.[38]

In general, whether a franchising system is used or not, any central or group control of resale prices is usually illegal. The only significant exceptions are for resale price maintenance where permitted by state law, as discussed later on in this chapter, and for bona-fide consignment arrangements where the supplier retains ownership of the product until final sale and the dealer acts purely as an agent. However, the Supreme Court has said that "a 'consignment' device . . . used to cover a vast gasoline distribution system, fixing prices through many outlets . . . " is unacceptable.[39]

The Schwinn case (1967) indicates that territorial restrictions upon the dealer's selling area are also generally illegal, except again for bona-fide consignment sales. However, earlier decisions suggest that territorial controls might sometimes be acceptable when imposed as part of a necessary marketing strategy on the part of a weak or nondominant firm.[40]

A product franchise obviously exists to sell the franchisor's goods and merchandise, and consequently may involve reasonable purchase requirements. But attempts to force unwanted goods upon the dealer, or to unreasonably restrict his purchasing freedom, may be restrained. Any restriction upon a non-franchisee dealer or upon a trademark licensee's purchasing practices, over and above what is absolutely needed to insure quality standards, may involve conflict with the antitrust laws.

Yet most experts believe that, in spite of these conditions and limitations, vertically organized marketing systems will become more, not less, prevalent and predominant in the future. There is a paradox, as Thompson notes, in that the "conspiracy to restrain" orientation of the antitrust laws prohibits quasi-integrated organizations from doing some of the things totally integrated firms may do.[41] Nevertheless, the laws and the actual enforcement practices, which tend to give some consideration to the total web of conduct within any given marketing organization, seem to provide considerable latitude for viable semi-integrated and integrated marketing systems.

Other Structural Relationships

The limited American governmental interest in retail structure, per se, is almost entirely confined to questions of size and to the sets of relationships, between competitors and between merchants and suppliers, discussed above. Statutory consultative and planning bodies normally play a very small role in American politico-economic life and there are very few such semi-official agencies on which retailers, qua retailers, might demand the right of representation. The emergency economic control systems of the 1930 depression, World War II, and the Korean conflict did involve elaborate systems of industrial representation, but those were exceptions to the normal state of affairs. In general, the retail trades are not structured as participants along with other commercial or con-suming sectors in official or quasi-official corporative and syndicalist agencies, since such agencies are not a feature of the American political system.

Process

Retail operations are also relatively unfettered, although the total volume of federal, state, county, city, and other retail-related legislation would seem to contradict this statement. If all of these laws applied universally throughout the country and were rigorously enforced, distribution would indeed be a highly controlled activity. But many of these rules have restricted, in some cases very limited, geographical applicability. Both the pattern of legislation and the degree of enforcement may vary considerably from place to place.

Location

Land-use, or zoning, ordinances can have some obvious implications for control of retail competition. These ordinances are typically local matters and usually apply only to new, rather than existing, uses of controlled sites. Consequently they can and have at times been used to shelter established firms and sites against the emergence of new competition and particularly against new shopping centers.[42] This sort of anticompetitive zoning, however, is usually not feasible in large cities where much of the land is necessarily open to industrial and commercial use. And the consumer mobility of an automotive-based society largely offsets restrictive zoning in smaller communities, since prohibitions on new centers simply push the trade outside the zoning authorities' jurisdiction, to the suburbs or to the next town.

The automobile has also influenced many other aspects of government intervention in retail locational matters. One special type of location control problem concerns the placement of eating, automotive service, and other facilities along limited-access expressways and superhighways. Some of the state authorities who are primarily responsible for the design and control of these roads have created regulated monopoly facilities at planned intervals for rental to approved concessionaires. Other states, yielding to pressure from the bypassed communities, permit no public service facilities on the controlled highways, thus forcing the motorists to leave the expressways to refuel themselves and their cars.

Many retail problems, however, center around stationary rather than moving vehicles. Parking difficulties have been an especial handicap to downtown city center merchants in their competition with suburban shopping centers. Many municipalities have provided various degrees of financial and other assistance for the creation of downtown parking lots and garages that might partially offset the suburban advantage. Some of the larger municipalities have also encouraged experiments in developing special mass transit services for shoppers. An increasing number of cities are now experimenting with total or peak hour exclusion of vehicular traffic from selected shopping streets and with the development of landscaped, pedestrian-only downtown shopping malls.

Although many of these efforts have had significant palliative effects, none have as yet really solved the city center problems. The right of access to planned suburban shopping centers becomes increasingly important as those centers absorb larger shares of total retail trade. Some small retailers complain that the center developers prefer to rent space to nationally-known chain organizations. They claim that well-established small, local firms have been refused leases in many new centers. The major stores in some shopping malls have reportedly obtained veto power over the admission of various competitors and center development policies sometimes exclude cut-price or discount firms. (This policy is not always detrimental to the discount retailers, who, in many cases, now prefer less-expensive independent locations near, but outside, the organized centers.) The government has responded to these complaints in two ways. One program, noted above, provides some rental payment guarantees for selected small merchants who want to lease center space. The Federal Trade Commission has undertaken an investigation of restrictive leasing policies and has entered complaints (not yet litigated) against the developers of one center and against a department store firm that participates in numerous other shopping centers because of alleged exclusion of competition.[43]

Store Hours

The suburban shopping center and the automobile are also partially responsible for the only significant current controversy concerning legislated store hours. Evening selling hours are not regulated in the United States, except for some instances of liquor trade control, and stores may be open twenty-four hours a day if the proprietors so desire. (Such lengthy hours are unusual, but by no means unknown; and many supermarkets and discount stores are open until nine or ten P.M. five or six nights a week.) There are no mandatory early closing days, such as are the practice in many European countries. But most of the states and many individual communities have always had so-called "Blue" or Sunday-closing laws. These laws are typically quite complex, with numerous exceptions for specified recreational services, exempted commodities, specified sales in resort areas, and in some cases, for small, family-operated businesses.

The growth of the suburban shopping centers and the free-standing general merchandise roadside discount houses have rekindled interest in the Sunday selling issue, since those outlets naturally gain from the American tendency to drive and shop as a family unit on the weekend. Urban central business district merchants, in contrast, normally find themselves unable to attract substantial Sunday trade, and thus find their economic interests allied with those who advocate Sunday closing on religious or social grounds.

A long history of litigation seems to have culminated in the 1961 Sunday Closing Cases, where the Supreme Court held that the laws had become secular and economic in nature in spite of their religious origins and consequently did not violate the constitutionally-required separation of church and state.[44] Although the laws were thus validated, they have proven increasingly ineffective in the face of an apparent popular desire for retailing services throughout the weekend. Many of the laws are subject to technical and procedural enforcement difficulties, the local prosecuting authorities are often loath to require closing (perhaps especially so if the open stores drain trade away from adjacent communities), and in some cases the penalties are small enough to be treated as minor operating expenses. Sunday selling is now becoming more and more prevalent throughout the country.[45]

One other temporally-related aspect of retailing-government interaction concerns employee compensation rather than store hours. The Federal Fair Labor Standards Act of 1938, which created national minimum wage and over-time payment standards for workers in businesses involved in interstate commerce, contained substantial exemptions for the retail and service trades. These exemptions have been successively reduced by 1949, 1961, and 1969 amendments that also increased the specified minima. Since February 1, 1969, employees of retail establishments that have gross sales in excess of $250,000 per annum and two or more paid, non-family workers are subject to essentially the same statutory wage and overtime payment minima as the workers in any manufacturing or other industrial establishment.[46] Retail automobile salesmen, however, are excluded from the mandatory overtime pay provisions of the law. Moreover, recent anti-discrimination legislation requires employers to pay women the same salaries they pay men for performing relatively similar work. This requirement will affect many department store retailers who have traditionally paid the female staff in the women's clothing departments less than their male counterparts in the men's clothing departments.

Merchandising

Public policies affecting retail pricing, promotional, and operating practices may often indirectly influence retailers' purchasing decisions. But the more direct forms of governmental intervention in the merchandising process (the selection and purchase of goods for resale) focus almost entirely on vendor relations. There are normally no mandatory lines or required inventories, and merchandise combinations are subject to little regulation. Some state codes impose various degrees of separation between alcoholic beverages, including in some jurisdictions wines and beer, and other commodities, with some states permitting distribution only through specialized liquor stores. Pharmacies are almost always required to set up special, controlled access, sections to hold their stocks of prescription medicines, but are free to sell almost any nonprescription item in the remainder of the store. Other health and fire regulations may affect the juxtaposition of goods within the store, e.g., the items that may be placed within a single cabinet, but do not normally affect retail competition in any significant way. (Local fire and health regulations have sometimes been used to harass retailing innovations, such as the introduction of self-service gasoline filling stations, but truly determined innovators often manage to ultimately overcome this sort of harassment.)

Retail-supplier relationships, partially discussed above under the heading of franchise and other vertical linkages, are subject to the same statutory and common law rules as all other commercial transactions. The courts apply the same tests that they would use in any other situation (e.g., sanity and maturity of the contracting parties, legal subject matter, valuable consideration offered by both parties) to determine whether agreements between vendor and merchant are enforceable at law.

The antitrust laws prohibit trade-restraining agreements and conspiracies among buyers as well as among sellers. Numerous cases have held that groups of retailers may not unite in setting up lists of vendors who are to be denied orders because of some marketing practice to which the retailers object. Some informal boycotts and threats of boycott undoubtedly do occur, but formal organized refusal to buy is proscribed.

In contrast, an individual merchant is free to select his suppliers. He may refuse to buy from a vendor who, for example, sells to lower-priced competitive dealers. Within limits he may, if he so desires and if his vendor agrees, condition his purchases upon exclusive selling rights for the items in question in his community, a not uncommon practice in the fashion goods and some other trades.[47] But these freedoms end at the vague and indistinct point where the courts may infer plans to monopolize, to compete unfairly, or to impose unlawful price controls. In the *Klor's* case, a private antitrust case ultimately settled out of court, the Supreme Court held that a department store would be violating the antitrust laws if it obtained an agreement from a group of electric appliance manufacturers to refrain from selling to a competitive furniture retailer.[48] A U. S. District Court (the lowest level of federal court) awarded a Dayton, Ohio, department store a treble-damage judgment of approximately $4 million against its larger competitor, because the larger firm had allegedly used exclusive dealing contracts in a consistent pattern to cut off the plaintiff's supply of desirable merchandise. The verdict, however, has been reversed on appeal. The appellate court held that neither the existence of an illegal conspiracy to restrain trade nor the amount of the damages was adequately proven, and has remanded the case back to the lower court for retrial.[49]

But the most important legislated influences on retail merchandising are embodied in the federal Robinson Patman Act (a 1963 amendment to the Clayton Antitrust Act). This law has often been applied to industrial purchasing as well as to retail procurement; it was instrumental, for example, in leading to the abolition of the basing point pricing system commonly used in steel, cement, and basic chemicals marketing. Nevertheless, the Act was part of the anti-chain store movement of the 1930s; Congress' primary motive in passing it was an attempt to curb the buying advantages of the large grocery chains; and many of the Act's provisions have a strong retail flavor. Reasonably simple in concept, the law is extremely vague and imprecise in application. Fairly haphazard enforcement and three decades of litigation (very little of which has been fought through to final resolution at the appellate court level) have only served to compound the confusion. Many experts believe that most large sellers are probably in constant technical violation of the law, but no one knows precisely where the boundaries of legality fall.[50]

Section 2(a), the basic portion of the law, forbids discrimination (difference) in the prices at which a firm engaged in interstate commerce sells goods of like grade and quality to different customers, when the effect of such discrimination may be harmful to competition. The Federal Trade Commission, the primary prosecuting agency for this Act, and the courts have interpreted many of the terms of this, and other sections, in an inclusive although imprecise fashion. Thus "harm to competition" includes the possibility of injury to the sellers' competitors, the buyer's competitors, or the buyer's customer's competitors. A special discount given to one wholesaler or buying agency that allowed it to resell at low prices to retailers who could then undersell the customers of another wholesaler could easily run afoul of the Act. Similar items produced by the same firm under national (manufacturer's) and private (retailer's) brand have been held to be goods of like grade and quality, although a complicated series of Circuit and Supreme Court decisions in the *Borden* case suggest that some differential in a supplier's prices for his branded and unbranded output may be acceptable as lacking "anticompetitive effects."[51]

Sections 2(a) and (b) provide two major defenses that may be set up to support price differentials that otherwise violate the above provisions. The seller may show that his price differentials are due to "differences in the cost of manufacture, sale, or delivery resulting from the differing methods or quantities in which such commodities are . . . sold and delivered," or that they were used to meet prices charged by the seller's competitors. In practice, the cost defense has proven much less useful than anticipated. The FTC rejects many conventional cost accounting classifications and allocation methods, and its standards of proof for cost data go beyond normal internal accounting practice.[52] Many accountants and pricing executives therefore believe that they cannot afford to prepare anticipatory "cost justification" studies in support of every price differential for possible use in case of a possible governmental objection to the differential. Yet the FTC and the courts have also proven highly suspicious of retrospective cost studies conducted after a complaint has been issued. The "meeting competition" defense has also been restricted, since systematic price matching plans do not qualify, and the differentiating seller also cannot match any prices that he knows or should know are illegal.

A dormant provision of the law, the Quantity Limit Rule, authorizes the Federal Trade Commission to restrict the discounts given on very large purchases, regardless of cost savings, when the Commission finds that such restriction is needed to curb the oligopsonistic and oligopolistic power of a few very large buyers. In essence, after holding hearings and evaluating economic evidence, the Commission may decree that cost savings notwithstanding, no purchaser of a specified commodity may receive a quantity discount in excess of the allowance granted to those who buy some specified smaller amount. This power was invoked only once, in 1952, when a Quantity Limit Rule was prepared for replacement automobile tires and tubes. The order was intended to curb the alleged anticompetitive advantages of the large mail order and automobile supply retail chains. The courts, however, found serious inadequacies in the FTC hearing procedures and remanded the rule back to the Commission for further study.[53] Meanwhile a change in the national administration resulted in appointments that altered the Commission's political and philosophical composition, and the proposed rule was allowed to lapse. Thus to date there has been no substantive implementation or test of the quantity limit provision.

Sections 2(c), (d), and (e), which were essentially designed to prevent evasions and avoidance of 2(a), have many retail implications. 2(c) flatly prohibits any payment or price reduction to a direct-buying customer in lieu of the fee the seller would otherwise have to pay to an agent or broker. This provision was aimed squarely at the large food chains which felt that their direct purchases from canners, packers, and food processors entitled them to the commission those firms normally pay the agents (so-called food brokers) who sell the smaller accounts. It has also been held that a voluntary or cooperative chain headquarters may not collect a brokerage fee from suppliers on purchases made for members of the chain.[54] Sections 2(d) and (e) require that advertising allowances, payments for retail display space, merchandising services, and the like be proferred to all customers on "proportionately equal" terms. "Proportionately equal" is difficult to define, but has tended to mean that a smaller customer must be effectively offered usable services and allowances having a dollar value, in relation to the services given any larger customer, roughly proportional to the ratio of their dollar purchases. In the *Fred Meyer* case, the Supreme Court held that a supplier who gives an advertising allowance to direct-buying large retailers must make certain that proportionately equal allowances are offered to the smaller retailers who purchase his products from wholesalers.[55] The Trade Practice Rules for the Cosmetic and Toilet Preparations Industry in effect provide that manufacturers who furnish demonstrators (highly paid professional retail salespeople) to department stores must offer display fixtures or other services of the appropriate dollar value to druggists who also sell their products and who cannot qualify for or use demonstrator services.[56] Section 2(f) applies directly to customers, in that it prohibits "knowingly" and willfully inducing or receiving a discriminatory price. Although 2(f), which has been invoked rather seldom, only applies to the beneficiaries of 2(a) violations, the FTC has used Section 5 of the Federal Trade Commission Act (unfair methods of competition) against purchasers who have induced allowances in violation of the other sections.[57] Private suits, brought by disadvantaged competitors, are also coming to play a somewhat increasing role in Robinson-Patman enforcement.[58]

The Robinson-Patman Act has been subject to varying appraisals, although general agreement exists concerning its importance, complexity, awkwardness, and lucrativeness to the legal profession. The Attorney General's National Committee to Study the Antitrust Laws (1955) criticized many aspects of the law's provisions, enforcement, and judicial interpretation. One member of the Committee, in turn, criticized the panel's failure to consider the question of whether the law should be completely repealed.[59] The National Commission on Food Marketing, another ad hoc study group established by Congress in 1964, concluded the act was "desirable and essential." "Discriminatory practices in the industry have not been eliminated, but they have been kept in check. Clearly the act has had special significance to the small and medium-sized operator."[60]

The 1969 "President's Task Force Report on Productivity and Competition" strongly criticized the act's rigidities and deterrents to price competition. The report commended the FTC's recent relaxation of RP Act enforcement, but held this to be an "inadequate reform" so long as the Act also permitted enforcement through private treble damage suits.[61] Dickinson concluded that the law has forced large vendors to be more rigid in their pricing than they otherwise would be; has reduced the price concessions that large retailers obtain; consequently has reduced tendencies towards centralized purchasing within large non-food chains; has probably somewhat encouraged private branding on the part of large chains; has also encouraged the natural tendency of large retailers to rely as much as possible on small vendors; and has encouraged the large vendors' use of national advertising to obtain consumer acceptance that will offset the large retailers' desire to purchase from more controllable small sources. Nevertheless, he believes that the Act, as administered, contains enough evasive and avoidance opportunities to preserve market flexibility.[62]

Promotion

The postal service, which handles an enormous volume of catalogs and advertising materials at rather low rates, provides the only significant government assistance to retail promotion. At the same time, relatively few limits are imposed upon promotional practices, as discussed below, although control over promotional statements and information seems certain to increase.

Many states, as well as several industry codes of self-regulation, severely restrict some or all aspects of advertising in liquor trades. Almost all other retailers have the right of access to all advertising media, both print and broadcast, that they can afford. Exterior signs and billboards are sometimes restricted or controlled on esthetic grounds, but the signmaker's general freedom is readily visible to the naked eye.

Almost all of the fifty states prohibit advertisement of the retail prices for prescription drugs or compounded prescriptions.[63] Some states also ban price advertising in selected service trades and semi-professions, including in various instances barbering and optical services. However, some self-imposed agreements and codes to refrain from price advertising have been held to be illegal restraints.[64] Gasoline dealer groups often seek municipal ordinances that will prohibit the use of large price signs at gasoline stations, in hopes of limiting competition for transient trade, but these ordinances are almost always nullified under judicial review as improper exercises of the municipal police power. Price information, on the other hand, must normally be displayed at the gasoline pump.

The automobile dealers' association lobbied for, and apparently pleased its members, with a federal law requiring a manufacturer-supplied statement of the list price for the car and its accessories to be attached to every new car available for sale. The dealers believe the requirement restrained the growing practice of some automotive retailers of over-inflating the asking price for a new car so as to offer a seemingly attractive excessive trade-in allowance for the customer's old vehicle.[65] But since these "sticker prices," as they are called, are still usually only the starting point for bargaining with the customer, they tend to be in conflict with another FTC rule that prohibits prelabeling of goods at any point above the usual selling price.[66] In general any manufacturer who prelabels his goods with a retail selling price faces a dilemma: if he lets the retailers cut that price he can be accused of false labeling; if he tries to stop them from cutting he may be violating the antitrust laws.

"Unit pricing laws," which require posting or marking the retail price per standard unit of size, weight, or quantity (that is: per pound, quart, gallon, etc.–the standard measures of this nonmetric country) for foodstuffs packed in odd-sized containers have been adopted in Maryland, Massachusetts, and New York City, and have been widely urged elsewhere. Some of the major chains, after first complaining that unit pricing would be prohibitively complex and expensive, have now voluntarily instituted the practice on a national or regional basis; and this has reduced the pressure for legislation.[67] A somewhat similar situation has developed with regard to "open code dating," which would require food retailers to reveal the symbols they use to indicate the arrival date and anticipated shelf-life of packaged perishables. The State of New Jersey has negotiated an agreement with the local food retailers' association and with the large chains for disclosure of this information.[68] Elsewhere, other more or less voluntary steps on the part of the larger organizations seem to have forestalled possible legislation. These disclosure practices, of course, involve a paradox in that the information is mainly used by the educated, well-informed, and rational consumers who probably least need such help.

Many other federal, state, and local laws and regulations, besides these mandates for and strictures against price posting, affect the messages that retailers may or must use in their advertising, display, and labels. The Federal Trade Commission, for example, administers a group of laws, including the Wool Products Labeling Law, the Fur Products Labeling Act, and the Textile Fibre Products Identification Act, that set up very rigid and detailed labeling requirements for the specified products when sold at retail. These laws impose the primary responsibility for label accuracy on the product manufacturers, except for private (retailer's) brand items, but the retailers must see that the labels remain affixed until final sale, and in some instances are also responsible for checking the suppliers' statements about their products. Ostensibly passed as consumer protection legislation, some of these laws such as the Wool Products Act have been most ardently advocated by raw material and ingredients producers who felt the required identification of imitation, alternative, or imported components would safeguard their own interests. The FTC and the Federal Food and Drug Administration jointly administer the Fair Packaging and Labeling Act, which requires identification of package contents by count, weight, or volume in easily understandable terms and prohibits the use of such terms as "jumbo quart" or "giant pound." These two agencies also share responsibility over the labeling and promotion of foods, drugs, and cosmetics. The Department of Health, Education and Welfare, acting under the 1968 X-Radiation Act, has placed special information recording requirements on television set retailers so as to facilitate prompt identification of the purchasers of any potentially hazardous model.[69]

The Wheeler-Lea Act (1938), which added "unfair acts and practices in commerce" to the previously-proscribed "unfair methods of competition," gave the FTC more general authority to move against false and misleading promotion whenever consumers, as well as the competitors, were likely to suffer. The Supreme Court has given considerable support to this broadened view of the Commission's responsibilities through a ruling that the FTC's power to curb "unfair competition" includes the ability to forbid practices that injure consumers as well as those that injure competitors or otherwise violate the antitrust laws.[70] The FTC has invoked its authority against retail sellers who misrepresented their trade status, i.e., described themselves as manufacturers, importers, or wholesalers when they were not; who made misleading or false claims for their products, guarantees, or services; who attempted to sell merchandise through lottery schemes; who advertised very low-priced merchandise they did not intend to sell in hopes of switching the customers to more lucrative items; or who indulged in other types of deceptive or fraudulent activity. For example, a new Federal Trade Commission rule requires grocery stores to carry "sufficient quantities" to satisfy a reasonable anticipated demand for any item advertised as a "price special" or bargain.[71] The quasi-official guidelines that the FTC has issued for many industries often set promotional standards for retailers as well as suppliers.[72]

Nevertheless, many critics feel that the Commission has not been active enough in prosecuting undesirable retail practices. These critics believe the Commission has exaggerated the "interstate commerce" limitation on its general powers and could actually handle any retail promotion that circulates in an interstate medium or that "affects" interstate commerce. An American Bar Association committee is unofficially reported to have concluded:

> At the same time, the FTC has exercised little leadership in the prevention of retail marketing frauds. . . . Unjustified doubts within the FTC as to its power or effectiveness in dealing with local frauds has caused it to remain largely passive in this area of enforcement.[73]

The Commission seems to agree, and has announced plans for increased local involvement. These plans include more autonomy for its eleven major city field offices and the establishment of local Consumer Protection Advisory Committees composed of federal, state, and local officials, and representatives of private consumer groups. Yet it is not clear how far the FTC can go in local matters without lending weight to the other frequent criticism that it is overly embroiled in such details and trivia as the mechanical minutiae of product labeling. Even now, *Business Week* magazine comments: ". . . it seems that the commission's major activity is enjoining infractions of the fur labeling act in Bent Spoon, Nebraska."[74]

The state and local governments have, however, exerted only limited control over retail promotion. Approximately seventeen states, the District of Columbia, and numerous municipalities require licenses for the conduct of "store closing" or "going out of business" sales and prohibit misleading use of these terms.[75] Each of the states has also adopted numerous very narrow and specific statutes dealing with particular promotional practices in various individual lines of business. One such New York statute, for example, cited in a recent law review article, makes it a misdemeanor to use false statements to lure a prospective guest from one hotel or boarding house to another. As the article points out, "these laws have seldom been judicially construed," and "only underscore the episodic manner in which the legislature has attacked the problem" of misrepresentation.[76]

More basically, practically all of the states have adopted some version of the *Printer's Ink Model Act,* which bars "untrue, deceptive, or misleading" advertisements. All of the states also have various fraud statutes that might be used against serious misrepresentation in both advertising and personal selling. Nevertheless, these laws have been described as "confusing, disjointed, and incomplete," administered through "procedures that are cumbersome and inefficient," and suffering from grossly inadequate enforcement.[77]

But, as already noted in this chapter, a rising volume of consumeristic sentiment is inducing changes in the laws and, quite possibly, in the vigor of enforcement. The Federal Trade Commission and two prestigious semi-official organizations, The Council of State Governments and the National Conference of Commissioners on Uniform State Laws, have proposed model consumer protection acts that have already been enacted in some states. These laws vest broad enforcement powers and an array of remedial devices in one official, usually the state attorney-general.[78]

Trading stamps, which stand at the borderline between pricing and promotion, have been the subject of extensive studies, debate, and discussion in congressional committees and in the trade-related federal agencies. The investigations have so far produced conflicting opinions and evidence concerning the value and impact of stamps and no significant federal legislation or regulation has emerged. A few states prohibit, or prohibitively tax, either all stamps or all stamps that are redeemable in merchandise (the usual form) instead of cash. A number of other states require cash redemption at the customer's option, and several other minor state laws have some slight influence on stamp distribution.[79] The relative ineffectiveness of most of this legislation is demonstrated by the phenomenal growth in stamp usage in most parts of the country during the 1950s and early 1960s. By 1963, 47 percent of all food stores, including most chain supermarkets, were distributing stamps and, as a consequence, stamps lost some of their earlier power in differentiating one supermarket from another.[80]

During the late 1960s, a number of major grocery chains and gasoline distributing firms tried to replace or supplement stamps with new and different types of promotion based upon lotteries and other games of chance. The FTC and a congressional investigation uncovered serious abuses in the administration of these prize contests, such as misrepresentation of the total number and value of the prizes actually or likely to be awarded and secret manipulation of the geographic distribution of prizes to serve the using firm's marketing strategy. Consequently the FTC has issued trade regulation rules for games of chance in the food retailing and gasoline industries.[81] The new rules, the unfavorable publicity generated during the various investigations and, probably most important, the normal ebb and flow in the marketing effectiveness of such devices seem to have lead to a considerable diminution in the current use of these lottery games.

Government policy concerned with retail operations and promotion also exercises some special influence on direct (door-to-door) and installment selling, discussed below.

Door-to-door Selling (Canvassing)

Numerous communities have ordinances affecting or prohibiting house-to-house selling and sales solicitation activity. (Exceptions usually exist, either in the ordinance or its enforcement, for regularly operated wagon delivery services of perishables, such as milk and newspapers.) Many of these ordinances, adopted often at the behest of local storekeepers, are unenforced and others have been struck down when the affected sellers have been willing to contest the law through state and federal courts. However, the Supreme Court has validated the so-called Green River type of ordinance, which makes uninvited entrance on private residential property for sales purposes a misdemeanor. Green River laws, plus discriminatory enforcement of other acts, have curtailed direct selling activities in some smaller communities, but not generally throughout the nation. (Direct selling, including route vending, amounted to approximately $2.5 billion in 1967, or about ¾ of 1 percent of all retail sales, and about one-third of all nonstore retail sales. Mail order and automatic vending accounted for the rest of the nonstore business.) A shortage of willing and skilled sales solicitors is undoubtedly the most stringent limitation on canvassing operations.

Recently considerable concern has been expressed over unscrupulous and "high pressure" methods used by some of these solicitors, particularly in selling to poor and disadvantaged consumers. A mandatory "cooling off" period, in which purchasers could cancel any orders given to direct salesmen for expensive items or for installment (hire purchase) sales, has been strongly urged as an antidote to high-pressure selling and may soon be legislated in some states. More than a dozen American states have established such optional recision periods for various types of installment sales.[82]

A number of "multi-level plan" direct selling companies have entered the market in recent years. These plans contain an element of franchising in that the sales agents are allowed (or encouraged) to appoint various levels of subagents of their own and are entitled to a commission or compensation on their subagents' sales. Some of these arrangements may be quite legitimate, but abuses have appeared in others. The number of subagents that a solicitor is allowed to franchise may be made dependent upon the size of the initial inventory order, and credulous people may be duped into buying outrageously excessive inventories. Unfortunately it is difficult to frame legislation that would stop these abuses without also inhibiting perfectly proper franchising and agency systems. Some state governments have initiated actions against the more spectacular plans, but these actions have been brought under rather stretched interpretations of the anti-lottery, chain letter, deceptive advertising, and consumer fraud laws and have not always succeeded. The Federal Trade Commission has started proceedings against a few firms and the federal Securities and Exchanges Commission is investigating the question of whether the sale of solicitation rights violates the securities law.[83]

Credit

The government's most basic intervention in the retail credit process is the provision of an elaborate legal and judicial system for the enforcement of debt obligations. Even though only a minute percentage of all credit transactions ever result in litigation, American retailers could never have developed their extensive and pervasive credit system without the ultimate protection of legal enforceability.

Many states have established limits on the service charges and other fees that can be charged in various types of installment and credit transactions. Of course, a retailer who sells entirely or almost entirely on credit can usually avoid the provisions of these statutes by simply raising his prices to include whatever interest premium he considers commercially feasible. The federal Consumer Credit Protection Act of 1968, primarily a disclosure act, requires the seller in most consumer credit transactions to provide information as to the dollar amount of all credit and finance charges, the true annual rate of interest involved, the payment requirements, and the delinquency penalties. Special disclosure rules are provided for open-end or continuous credit plans, and a three business day optional cancellation period is required whenever the buyer's home is used as a security for the purchase of goods or services. At least twenty states and the District of Columbia had adopted consonant legislation by the end of 1969.[84]

Many American retailers who sell on credit rely on reports from central credit rating bureaus (private or cooperative organizations) and from other retailers to evaluate the acceptability of credit applicants. These reports were normally kept highly confidential, and individuals who were being harmed by adversely erroneous or incomplete statements had little practical recourse under the supposedly relevent laws of libel and slander. The Fair Credit Reporting Act of 1970 has changed this situation by placing limits on the types of information that may be collected and disseminated, by requiring frequent verification of adverse information, by making the files open to the applicant's inspection upon demand, and by giving him opportunity to rebut adverse statements.[85]

Other aspects of credit business are also being placed under new controls. Federal regulations now affect the use of credit card systems, prohibit unsolicited distribution of such cards, and limit the cardholders' liability for any misuse of lost cards. The creditors' remedies against defaulting debtors, which once included a stringent combination of possible actions (private suit, repossession of the goods, and levy against wages, depending upon the situation), are now being curtailed through changes in federal and state law. Several states have reduced maximum permissible rates for interest charges on installment contracts, in some instances to a point where merchants claim that sales to marginal credit risks have become unprofitable.

The next probable change is elimination, or reduction, of the "holder in due course" privilege. Under prevailing law, a third party who has obtained a negotiable instrument, such as a promissory note, in due course and in good faith is not vulnerable to some of the defenses that might be invoked against the original payee. A consumer who signs a note or other negotiable promise as payment for merchandise that subsequently proves defective may be able to assert the inadequacy of the goods as a defense against the original seller's demand for payment. But he cannot offer that defense against a demand from any outside party, such as a bank, to whom the dealer may have transferred or discounted that note. Instead, the consumer is now obliged to pay his debt and then undertake private suit, an expensive and cumbersome process, against the vendor for recovery of the merchandise defects. Considerable pressure is now developing for legislation that will require the seller's warranty liabilities to accompany any negotiable instrument received in payment for the sale of consumer goods.

Pricing

Governmental policy towards retail pricing resembles its policy towards all other aspects of retailing: general freedom subject to some more or less particular exceptions. Prices in general have been controlled only during periods of great stress, such as World War II and the Korean conflict.

In August 1971 President Nixon declared an emergency ninety-day price, rent, wage, and profit freeze to curb some of the effects of a rapidly growing price inflation. This was subsequently extended as "Phase II" of the economic controls. Sales of unprocessed agricultural commodities and some other commodities were exempted from all of these controls and exemptions were later created for small retailers and then for all firms with less than sixty employees. Controlled retailers are prohibited from increasing percentage markups beyond those prevailing during the pre-freeze base period, and in addition (subject to some exceptions) may not earn annual profits that exceed an average of the best two out of the three preceding years. A few chains have been ordered to reduce prices because of excessive profits. Retailers subject to control are supposed to display signs indicating the base prices for the forty best-selling items in each department and are also required to give consumers other price information on request. The freeze supposedly also controls the retailers' labor, occupancy, and merchandise costs.

However, the regulations are complicated and vague, and the government is trying to achieve its objectives without developing a large administrative bureaucracy. Enforcement, and many interpretive, responsibilities have been assigned to the already overburdened Internal Revunue (federal tax) Service. Consequently it is unlikely that the stabilization program can be continued effectively for an extended period without substantial changes, and some critics believe that it has been relatively unsuccessful even in the short run.

In more normal times few price controls are applied to retail (or other) transactions. Retail prices for fluid milk are regulated in a few localities under milk marketing orders designed primarily to protect dairy farmers' interests, but this is a rare exception to the general rule. Price posting requirements and prohibitions have already been discussed above. State and local authorities maintain weight and measure inspection systems, and in some jurisdictions set the physical units in which bulk items such as raw foods and coal may be retailed. (Fundamental physical units, such as the precise gravitational force of the pound and the length of the inch, are of course set by federal standard and are uniform throughout the country.) These controls, however, impose little restriction on retail price determination. Somewhat more conscious price policy is enunciated in the state unfair practices and resale price maintenance acts.

Considerable attention in both unofficial and official circles has recently focused on retail prices charged in poorer urban districts, particularly those areas where ethnic minorities live, and on the consequent prices these consumers pay. Some analysts argue that the two questions are identical but other researchers report that 80 to 90 percent of the black consumers (the principal group studied) shop outside their immediate residential neighborhoods and thus are not bound by ghetto prices.[86] The situation undoubtedly varies from area to area and may differ between food, clothing, and electric appliance and furniture marketing, but at least some segments of the poorer population are disadvantaged in their shopping. Three possible causes have been cited: (1) For several reasons, including lack of information, greater need for credit, poorer transportation, and less time for shopping, the poor tend to be relatively ineffective shoppers. (2) The poor, and especially again the ethnic minorities, are served by poorer, less efficient and more expensive retail institutions than the middle class. (3) Those retail institutions, i.e., large chains, that serve both depressed and more affluent neighborhoods tend to charge higher prices in the ghetto area. The chains vigorously deny this allegation; and appear to be supported in that position by most governmental and academic surveys.[87] The chains, however, do have only a relatively limited number of units, and those mostly their poorer and older outlets, in the ghetto neighborhoods.[88]

Finding a remedy is even more difficult than diagnosing the causes of the problem. Several quasi-official attempts at launching consumer cooperatives have had unsatisfactory results.[89] As noted earlier, attempts to establish more small-scale retailing in the ghetto areas, even under the rubric of Black Capitalism, will not initially provide much consumer advantage. Tax incentives and other inducements to encourage large-scale chain store expansion in disadvantaged neighborhoods were widely discussed a few years ago, but the charges of discriminatory pricing and other considerations have considerably diluted any governmental or chain store management enthusiasm for the proposal. Nevertheless, this, along with improved public transit facilities and improved credit services, may be the most helpful solution for the disadvantaged consumer.

State Price Control Legislation. Approximately thirty states have general applicability unfair practices acts that prohibit retail sales of goods, and in a few instances services, at less than cost. Several others have similar laws concerning specific products such as cigarettes. Some of the states ban below-cost sales only when made with intent to harm or destroy competition, but all permit sale of damaged and obsolete merchandise at less than cost. Cost is variously defined as acquisition cost or acquisition cost plus actual or some specified "cost of doing business." Competitive pricing is often allowed as a defense to charges of violation.

Although the unfair practices acts are often at least technically enforceable by both public and private action, the main burden normally devolves on the public authorities. And few public prosecutors have been seriously interested in enforcing the laws, either because violations seem trivial or actually in the public interest or because of the difficulties of prosecution. In order to win a relatively insignificant restraining order, the complainant in some instances may have to prove (a) the fact of sale, (b) cost (which may be difficult to ascertain), (c) willful intent, (d) injury, and (e) the sequence of competitive price cuts. One writer reports that the Minnesota attorney-general brought 200 actions under that state's law in 1957-59, but was unable to obtain effective relief because of inability to prove intent to injure competition.[90]

However, the laws can and sometimes do place resilient but nevertheless fairly effective floors under retail price competition. They sometimes serve as a vehicle for informal public intervention when government officials think a retail price war has gone too far. And they also sometimes serve, perhaps illegally, as a nucleus for retail trade association programs designed to discourage price cutting.[91]

In addition to these state laws, the federal antitrust acts have occasionally been invoked against large national chains that have been accused of selling at a loss in some particular area or region in order to drive out local competition. Several such cases have arisen in the grocery trade.[92]

Resale price maintenance in the United States, which has attracted much more attention than the unfair practices acts, is enormously complicated by its own history. The basic antitrust law prohibition against agreements in restraint of interstate commerce outlawed resale price maintenance when, as was usually the case, the manufacturer and the retailer were located in different states. Congress was unwilling to legalize r.p.m. agreements per se, and to this day has not authorized price maintenance in the District of Columbia, for which it acts as a local legislature. In 1936, however, a vigorous lobbying campaign led by the National Association of Retail Druggists in conjunction with growing congressional sentiments for decentralization in economic matters brought passage of a "states' rights" rule on price maintenance. The federal Miller-Tydings Enabling Act passed that year created an antitrust exception for interstate price control agreements if and when the retailers' state authorized such agreements, a privilege more or less promptly claimed by forty-five of the then forty-eight states. Ostensibly this came to almost the same thing as direct federal authorization. But over the years the existence of a variety of state laws and state judicial interpretations along with the growing competition of an increasing number of non-resale price maintenance territories has tended to cripple r.p.m. implementation. There has also been considerable question as to whether price maintenance can be applied legally to interstate *retail* transactions, say between a mail order customer and a retailer in different states, and the rule seems fairly firmly established that it cannot apply when the mail order firm itself is in non-price maintenance territory.[93]

The price maintenance laws began their erosion after the first *Schwegmann* decision (1951),[94] when the U. S. Supreme Court said that the Miller-Tydings Act could not be interpreted to legalize the "non-signer's clause" that was an essential element in the state legislation. This clause, basic to price maintenance for widely distributed commodities such as drugs and cosmetics, bound all retailers in the state if a price-fixing manufacturer concluded a maintenance agreement with one retailer and then gave notice to the rest of the trade. Congress remedied the *Schwegmann* defect through passage of the McGuire Act (1952), but the issuance of even one adverse Supreme Court opinion apparently induced second thought on the part of many state judiciaries and some legislatures. Many of the courts began to find state constitutional flaws in the laws, and as of early 1972, only about one-third of the states had court-validated non-signer's clauses. Thirty-six states, including many of the most important market areas, had laws permitting control of signatory retailers' prices. However, the appropriate state courts had affirmed the local constitutionality of only about twenty-eight of these laws.[95] A great growth in the number and market importance of many types of discount sellers also contributed much to weakening price maintenance.

Manufacturers do have a few means for controlling resale prices even in non-r.p.m. states. They can select their own customers and thus may avoid those dealers who are likely to cut prices. But they may not set up an elaborate price surveillance system or enter into any explicit or implicit agreements with either retailers or wholesalers. Consequently, the right of choice loses its price maintenance effects when the manufacturer sells through intermediaries. Prices may also be controlled in a bona fide consignment system, where the manufacturer retains title to the goods until final sale, and the dealer acts as an agent. However, in view of its many costs and other legal disadvantages, consignment selling is a viable alternative in only a limited number of instances. Finally, the manufacturer may use a variety of extra-legal and illegal tactics to obtain adherence to his suggested resale prices. At least one senator expressed concern during 1962 price maintenance hearings, over the high degree of adherence to suggested prices in Washington, D. C. (non-r.p.m. territory) and thirty-eight out of fifty-seven retailers queried in one Texas town (also non-r.p.m.) reported that they never sold below suggested prices.[96] But from time to time the FTC has proceeded against manufacturers who have been overly active in seeking observance of their "suggested" resale prices.[97] Some increase in the use of formal r.p.m., where available, also seems to have occured in the electrical appliance trade during the last two or three years, in part because some of the maturing discount sellers now need increased margins, and along with the traditional department stores, have sought increased price protection from their suppliers.[98] But the r.p.m. renaissance seems to have been very limited in scope, and the great bulk of merchandise passing through American retail stores is not subject to resale price control.

Summary

The preceding pages have indicated a number of points of governmental intervention into American retailing. At times individual merchants are likely to find this intervention vexatious and, less frequently, it may seem helpful. But essentially the system is a libertarian one. Checked by the pluralistic play of interests, by the division of authority, and by the tradition of the free open market, government has foreclosed few of the alternatives that responsible merchants might want to pursue. Public policy and regulation modify and influence some retail decision making, but the basic choices on entry, location, merchandising, promotion, operations, and pricing remain within the business community. The customers retain the final vote.

The retailing industry that has emerged in this context is characterized by convenience, competition, innovativeness, and expense. Although inattentive salespeople or long lines at the supermarket checkout counter may evoke some degree of customer irritation, American retailing really delivers a very high degree of convenience. Most consumers have access to very large assortments of goods that can be purchased with little bother and effort at nearby locations during a good many hours of the day. Parking facilities, credit, and most other types of service that do not require a high degree of personalization are readily available. The amount of meaningful information that flows to the consumer certainly could be increased, and public policy is likely to induce some such improvement. Nevertheless, the informational shortcomings of present operations appear primarily in comparison with what might be rather than in comparison to consumer data standards throughout the world. Part of the consumer problem also arises from the very variety and complexity of the goods passing through retail channels.

The industry is also a competitive one, although much competition takes forms, such as rivalry in service and promotion, that would not delight a classical economist. The average consumer is free to choose among many different sellers, some of whom will be using very different methods of operation. Some analysts believe that concentration in distribution is increasing to an undesirable extent, and government policy is beginning to show signs of adjusting to this belief. But most American retailing still seems, in the economist's terms, imperfectly competitive rather than oligopolistic or monopolistic.

The system is also highly innovistic. Many of the newer types of retail institution have emerged or developed in this country. Much retail-oriented legislation has been handicap legislation, designed to thwart the growth of new types of outlets. Fortunately most of that legislation has never been very far-reaching or effective.

But the American system is not an inexpensive one. Wholesale and retail trade account for an exceptionally high percentage of the American labor force.[99] American retail margins tend to be very high by world standards, although this partially reflects the absorption of wholesale functions in many vertically integrated retail firms. The things and services that consumers want do come at a price. But government has fundamentally left the merchants and the consumers free to work out that relationship through fairly independent, often even atomistic, decision making.

May, 1972

Notes

1. See Joseph Cornwall Palamountain, Jr., *The Politics of Distribution* (Cambridge: Harvard University Press, 1955), pp. 38-47.

2. U. S. Department of Commerce, *1967 Census of Business, Advance Report Retail Trade: Single Units and Multiunits* (Washington. Department of Commerce, October, 1970), p. 1.

3. U. S. Bureau of the Census, Census of Business 1967, *Retail Trade: United States Summary BC67-RA1* (Washington, D. C.: Government Printing Office, 1970), Tables 17, 1. This figure includes approximately $300 million sales of food and beverages for on-premise consumption at post snack bars and similar facilities.

4. Michigan, one of the eighteen, also franchises private liquor stores and departments. Some municipalities in Minnesota, South Dakota, and Wisconsin, and the Montgomery Country government in Maryland, among the "license" or

private-trade states, operate government-owned stores. Distilled Spirits Institute, *Summary of State Laws & Regulations Relating to Distilled Spirits,* 19th ed. (Washington: the Institute, 1969). The 21st Amendment, which repealed national alcoholic beverage prohibition, gives the states extraordinary power over the liquor trade within their borders.

5. See Ole S. Johnson, *The Industrial Store* (Atlanta: School of Business Administration, Atlanta Division, University of Georgia, 1952), pp. 22-79, for a discussion of the first type of legislation; see *Michigan Compiled Laws Annotated,* par. 445.106 (Public Act #271, 1941) for an example of the second type.

6. Monroe J. Hirsch and Ralph E. Wick, *The Optometric Profession* (Philadelphia: Chilton Book Company, 1968), p. 175. Doctors of optometry (who deal exclusively with structural defects of the eye and who frequently dispense glasses) should be distinguished from both opthalmologists (medical doctors who treat both structural and functional defects and who are less likely to dispense eyeglasses) and opticians (who are primarily lens-preparation and fitting technicians). Seventeen states license dispensing opticians, who both recommend and fit glasses but have neither the O.D. or M.D. degree. (ibid., p. 302).

7. F. Marion Fletcher, *Market Restraints in the Retail Drug Industry* (Philadelphia: University of Pennsylvania Press, 1967), pp. 141-44.

8. Distilled Spirits Institute, *Summary of State Laws.*

9. Gladys M. Kiernan, ed., *Retailers Manual of Laws and Regulations,* 18th ed. (New York: Research Company of America 1971), pp. 61-98; Juvenal L. Angel, *Directory of Professional and Occupational Licensing in the United States* (New York: World Trade Academy Press, 1970).

10. Karen Greene, *Occupational Licensing and the Supply of Nonprofessional Manpower,* U. S. Department of Labor, Manpower Administration, Manpower Research Monograph No. 11 (Washington, D. C.: Government Printing Office, 1969).

11. The journals contain many discussions of the problem. See, for example, William F. Brown and Ralph Cassady, Jr., "Guild Pricing in the Service Trades," *Quarterly Journal of Economics* 61 (February, 1947), pp. 311-18; J. F. Barron, "Business and Professional Licensing," *Stanford Law Review* 18 (February, 1966) pp. 640-45.

12. U. S. Small Business Administration, *Annual Report 1970* (Washington, D. C.: Government Printing Office, 1971), pp. 23, 28.

13. See, for example, "Sandovel Stands Siege at the SBA," *Business Week,* 18 July 1970, pp. 60-64; "ARF [American Retail Federation] Charging Weak, Ineffective SBA Loan Policy," *Women's Wear Daily,* 24 July 1970; "A New Day at the SBA," *Dun's,* June 1971, pp. 42-44.

14. "A New Day at the SBA; A Bigger Help to Small Business?" *Nation's Business,* May 1971, pp. 26-30; U. S. Senate, Select Committee on Small Business, *Review of Small Business Administration's Programs and Policies– 1971* (Hearings, 5, 6, 7, and 20 October 1971) (Washington, D. C.: Government Printing Office, 1972).

15. Andrew F. Brimmer and Henry S. Terrel, "The Economic Potential of Black Capitalism," (paper presented at the 82nd Meeting of the American Economic Association, December 29, 1969); Richard S. Rosenbloom and John K. Shank, "Let's Write off Mesbic," *Harvard Business Review* 70 (September-October, 1970), p. 95; "Shaky Times for Aid to Black Capitalism," *Business Week,* 13 May 1972, pp. 56-58.

16. William Proxmire, *Can Small Business Survive?* (Chicago: Henry Regnery Company, 1964), pp. 95-96.

17. U. S. Department of Health, Education and Welfare, Office of Education, *Vocational and Technical Education: Annual Report – Fiscal Year 1969* (Washington, D. C.: Government Printing Office, 1971), table 12, 44.

18. Stanley C. Hollander, *Restraints Upon Retail Competition* (East Lansing: Bureau of Business and Economic Research, Michigan State University, 1965), pp. 48-70.

19. Mark S. Massel, *Competition and Monopoly* (Washington, D. C.: The Brookings Institution, 1962), p. 230.

20. *U. S.* v. *New York Great Atlantic & Pacific Tea Co., 67* F. Supp 626 (D. Ill., 1946), 173 F2d 79 (CA-7, 1949, affirming DC); *U. S.* v. *Safeway Stores,* (1957 Trade Cas. par. 68,770), *nolo contendere;* (1957) Trade Cas. par. 68,871) *Consent Decree.*

21. See Richard Holton, "Competition and Monopoly in Distribution," in *Competition, Cartels and Their Regulation,* ed. J. P. Miller (Amsterdam: North Holland Publishing Co., 1962), p. 293.

22. See his *American Capitalism* (Boston: Houghton Mifflin Co., 1952), pp. 123-33, 147-50. See also Holton, "Competition and Monopoly," pp. 302-304.

23. U. S. Federal Trade Commission, statement, "Commission Enforcement Policy with Regard to Mergers in the Food Distribution Industry," January 17, 1967, *(Commerce Clearing House Trade Regulation Reporter,* hereafter cited as *CCH Trade Reg. Rep.),* par. 4520.

24. Ibid., at p. 6805.

25. *U. S.* v. *Von's Grocery Company and Shopping Bag Food Stores,* 384 U.S. 270, 86 S.Ct. 1478 (1966).

26. *U. S.* v. *Higbee Company,* consent decree 4 October 1971, *CCH Trade Regulation Cases* Par. 73,685; U. S. antitrust case no. 2079.

27. Gladys M. Kiernan, ed., *Retailers Manual of Laws and Regulations* 18th ed. (New York: Research Company of America, Inc., 1972), pp. 111-16.

28. For discussions of the chain store tax movement, see Godfrey M. Lebhar, *Chain Stores in America, 1859-1962,* 3rd edition (New York: Chain Store Publishing Co., 1963); pp. 125-54, 239-55; Palamountain, *Politics of Distribution,* pp. 159-87.

29. Firms that establish vertical linkages (as well as those with horizontal ties) will have many points of contact with general state business law in the states where their outlets are located; for example they may at times be susceptible to private suit in state (rather than federal) courts. See Walter D.

Wekstein, "Interstate Problems," in *Franchising Today: 1966-1967*, eds. Charles L. Vaughn and David B. Slater (Albany, N. Y.: Matthew Bender, 1967), pp. 359-64. But the question of federal vs. state jurisdiction, in this respect, is merely an operating problem for the firm, rather than a major determinant of channel structure.

30. *U. S.* v. *Swift & Co., Armour & Co., The Cudahy Packing Co., 1960 CCH Trade Cas.,* par. 69,871 (N.D., Ill., 1960).

31. *U. S.* v. *Hart, Schaffner & Marx, 1970 CCH Trade Cas.,* par. 73,153 (N.D., Ill.: 1970).

32. *Brown Shoe Co.* v. *U. S.,* 370 U. S. 323-24, 82 S.Ct. 1502 (1962).

33. No quick catch-phrase exists for the less common situation of retailer dominance of quasi-affiliated suppliers, although the term "specification buying" is sometimes used for the Sears Roebuck type of relationship with contractually-tied vendors. The term "franchise" is also used at times to designate the right of membership in an horizontal organization, e.g., a voluntary or cooperative chain.

34. Donald N. Thompson, "Franchise Operations and Antitrust Law," *Journal of Retailing* 44 (Winter, 1968-69), p. 40. This article has been used extensively in the preparation of this section. See also, Jerrold G. Van Cise, "Guiding Principles of Antitrust Law," in *Franchising Today: 1966-1967*, eds. Charles L. Vaugh and David B. Slater (Albany, N.Y.: Matthew Bender, 1967), pp. 321-34.

35. See Alfred R. Oxenfeldt and Anthony O. Kelly, "Will Successful Franchise Systems Become Wholly-Owned Chains?" *Journal of Retailing* 44 (Winter, 1968-69), pp. 69-83.

36. 36 *Federal Register* 21608, 22187; *CCH Trade Regulation Reporter,* par. 38,029.

37. *Perma Life Mufflers Inc.* v. *International Parts Corp.,* 392 U. S. 134, 88 S.Ct. 1981 (1968).

38. See Philip F. Zeidman, "Are Your Controls Necessary?" and Matthew L. Lifflander, "Enforcement of the Franchise Agreement," in *Franchising Today: 1966-1967*, pp. 335-58.

39. *Simpson* v. *Union Oil Company of California,* 377 U. S. 21, 84 S.Ct. 1051 (1964).

40. *U. S.* v. *Arnold Schwinn & Co.;* but see *White Motor Co.* v. *U. S.,* 372 U. S. 253 (1963); *Snap-on Tools Corp.* v. *FTC,* 321 F.(2d) 825 (CA-7, 1963).

41. "Franchise Operations and Antitrust Law," p. 42.

42. Gordon H. Steadman, "Shopping Centers and Local Government — Collision or Cooperation?" *Journal of Retailing* 31 (Summer 1955): 80-81; Louis F. Bartelt, "Shopping Centers and Land Controls," *Notre Dame Lawyer* 35 (March 1960): 184-209; Richard L. Nelson, *The Selection of Retail Locations* (New York: F. W. Dodge Co., 1958), p. 316; "Zoners Play Hard to Get With Sites," *Supermarket News,* 8 September 1969, p. 34.

43. Samuel Feinberg, "FTC's 'Silent Presence' Will Guide Center Leases,"

Women's Wear Daily, 19 November 1971, p. 17; *CCH Trade Regulation Reporter,* par. 19,720; 19,834.

44. *McGowan* v. *State of Maryland,* 366 U. S. 420, 81 S.Ct. 1101; *Gallagher* v. *Crown Kosher Super Market of Mass.,* 366 U. S. 617, 81 S.Ct. 1122; *Two Guys from Harrison-Allentown* v. *McGinley,* 366 U. S. 582, 81 S.Ct. 1135; *Braunfeld* v. *Brown,* 366 U. S. 599, 81 S.Ct. 1144 (1969).

45. See, for example, "When Sunday Selling Comes. . ." *Chain Store Age* (Variety and General Merchandise Executives Edition), July 1970, pp. 24-27; James R. Lowry, *The Retailing Revolution Revisited* (Muncie, Ind.: Ball State University, 1969), pp. 18-19.

46. See "The Fair Labor Standards Act Amendments of 1966," *White Collar Report* (Bureau of National Affairs, Inc.), November 17, 1966.

47. Irving Sher, *Manual of Federal Trade Regulations Affecting Retailers,* new ed. (New York: National Retail Merchants Association, 1969), pp. 55-62.

48. Klor's Inc. v. *Broadway-Hale Stores, Inc.,* 359 U. S. 207 (1959).

49. "Antitrust Verdict Rocks the Stores," *Business Week,* 26 July 1969, p. 29; "Edler-Beerman Ruling Reversed," *Women's Wear Daily,* 12 April 1972, p. 2.

50. See Corwin Edwards, *The Price Discrimination Law* (Washington: The Brookings Institution, 1959); Roger Dickinson, "The Retail Buyer and the Robinson-Patman Act," *California Management Review* 9 (Spring, 1967): 47-54; Sher, *Manual of Federal Trade Regulations,* pp. 10-43.

51. *Borden Co.* v. *FTC,* 339 F.2d 133 (CA-5, 1964); 383 U. S. 637, 85 S.Ct. 1092 (1966); 381 F.2d 175 (CA-5, 1967).

52. See Herbert F. Taggart, *Cost Justification* and *Cost Justification – Thomasville Chair Company* (Michigan Business Studies, Vol. 14, No. 3, and Vol. 14, No. 3, Supplement 1) (Ann Arbor, Michigan: University of Michigan Bureau of Business Research, 1959, 1964). Professor Taggart does hold that cost studies prepared prior to the granting of price differentials may be useful in pre-litigation negotiation, partially as evidence of management's good faith, and that the general unavailability of other defenses provides a "lack of anything better" argument for attempting cost justification during litigation.

53. *B. F. Goodrich Co.* v. *FTC,* 134 F. Supp. 39 (1955); 242 F.2d 31 (1957).

54. See *Independent Grocers Alliance Distributing Co.* v. *FTC* 203 F.2d 941 (CA-7, 1953).

55. *FTC* v. *Fred Meyer, Inc.,* 390 U. S. 341 (1968).

56. 31 *Federal Register* 9058, 9267; *CCH Trade Reg. Rep.,* par. 41,221; (Sec. 221.1, par. f). The Trade Practice Rules, which are a form of official FTC-adopted guidelines, are not as specific in language as the above statement, but the guideline requirements for "equivalency" of allowances have this result.

57. Sher, *Manual of Federal Trade Regulations,* pp. 21-23, 39-41.

58. Edward William Gass, "Private Enforcement of the Robinson-Patman Act: The Damage Controversy," *The Antitrust Bulletin* 15 (Summer 1970); 153.

59. Attorney General's National Committee to Study the Antitrust Laws, *Final Report* (Washington: Government Printing Office, 1955), p. 218.

60. *Food From Farmer to Consumer: Report of the National Commission on Food Marketing* (Washington: Government Printing Office, 1966), p. 86.

61. *CCH Trade Reg. Rep.,* par. 50,250.

62. "The Retail Buyer and the Robinson-Patman Act," pp. 52-54.

63. "Drug Makers Recant and Support Pharmacists in Opposing Ads," *New York Times,* 23 December 1968, p. 18; "Drug Pricing and the Rx Police State," *Consumer Reports,* March 1972, pp. 136-140.

64. *U. S.* v. *Gasoline Retailers Ass'n.,* 285 F.2d 688 (CA-7, 1961); *U. S.* v. *National Funeral Directors Ass'n of the U. S., 1968 Trade Cas.,* par. 72,529 (E.D., Wis., 1968) *consent decree.*

65. "Everybody Loves Posted Prices," *Business Week,* 20 December 1958, pp. 24-25.

66. "Do Auto Prices Mean What They Say?" *Business Week,* 6 September 1969, pp. 60-65.

67. "Unit Pricing in Stores Spreading Rapidly Across U. S.," *New York Times,* 8 June 1971, p. 2.

68. "Clearer Dating Set on Food in New Jersey," *New York Times,* 28 January 1972, p. 1.

69. "HEW Record Ruling Costly to TV Stores," *Home Furnishings Daily,* 7 July 1970, p. 1.

70. 92 S.Ct. 898 (1972).

71. "Retail Food Store Advertising and Marketing Practices," 16 CFR (Code of Federal Regulations) 424, 36 *Federal Register* 8781, *CCH Trade Reg. Rep.,* par. 38,026, effective 12 July 1971.

72. Sher, *Manual of Federal Trade Regulations,* pp. 97-107, 139-49.

73. "Report of the ABA Commission to Study the Federal Trade Commission," *CCH Trade Reg. Rep.,* par. 50,255 (1970). Also see George J. Alexander, *Honesty and Competition* (Syracuse: Syracuse University Press, 1967), p. 3.

74. "Business Responds to Consumerism," *Business Week,* 6 September 1969, p. 106.

75. Kiernan, *Retailer's Manual of Laws and Regulations,* pp. 419-423.

76. Richard F. Dole, Jr., "Merchant and Consumer Protection," *Cornell Law Review* 53 (May 1968), p. 754, n.24.

77. "Consumer Protection in Michigan: Current Methods and Some Proposals for Reform," *Michigan Law Review* 68 (April 1970), pp. 927-28. Also see "New York Leads the Consumer Crusade," *Business Week,* 31 January 1970, pp. 50-53.

78. "Consumer Protection in Michigan," p. 971.

79. Federal Trade Commission, *Economic Report on the Use and Economic Significance of Trading Stamps* (Washington: Government Printing Office, 1966), pp. 10-12.

80. Fred C. Allvine, "The Future for Trading Stamps and Games," *Journal of Marketing* 33 (January 1969), p. 48.

81. 16 CFR Part 419; *CCH Trade Reg. Rep.,* par. 7,975 (August 4, 1970); "Prices Upstage Stamps and Games," *Supermarket News* 22 September 1969, p. 5.

82. Robert D. Goodwin, Lester Nelson, and Ernest A. Rovelstad, eds., *Credit Manual of Commercial Laws,* 1971 (New York: National Association of Credit Management, 1970), pp. 180, 184-85.

83. See "Cracking Down on Pyramid Plans," *Business Week,* 11 December 1971, pp. 104-106; "Glenn Turner: Franchiser With Flamboyance," *New York Times* 13 January 1972, p. 59; Federal Trade Commission proposed complaints, No. 692-3102 and 671-0190, *CCH Trade Regulation Reporter,* par. 19,291 and 19,576. Also see "Enter the Pyramid Protective Association," *Sales Management* 7 February 1972, pp. 16-17.

84. Goodwin, Nelson, and Rovelstad, *Credit Manual,* 1971, p. 176. For a review of earlier legislation see Edgar R. McAlister, *Retail Installment Credit: Growth and Legislation* (Columbus, Ohio: The Ohio State University Bureau of Business Research, 1964).

85. Public Law 91-508, 26 October 1970.

86. The seminal study in this area is David Caplovitz, *The Poor Pay More* (New York: Free Press, 1963; rev. ed. 1967). Mobility evidence is presented in Charles S. Goodman, "Do the Poor Pay More?" *Journal of Marketing* 32 (January, 1968), pp. 18-24; W. Leonard Evans, Jr., "Ghetto Marketing: What Now?" in *Marketing and the New Science of Planning* (Proceedings of the A.M.A. 1968 Fall Conference), ed. Robert King (Chicago: American Marketing Association, 1969), pp. 528-31; George H. Haines, Jr., Leonard S. Simon, and Marcus Alexis, "Maximum Likelihood Estimation of Central City Neighborhood Food Trading Areas," (paper presented at the Fall, 1970 Conference of the American Marketing Association). Many aspects of the problem are considered in Frederick D. Sturdivant, ed., *The Ghetto Marketplace* (New York: Free Press, 1969).

87. See Sturdivant, *Ghetto Marketplace,* pp. 5-6; Dennis Gensch and Richard Staeline, "Consumer Attitudes and Purchase Behavior in a Ghetto Neighborhood," (paper presented at the Fall, 1970 Conference of the American Marketing Association); "City Poor Pay No More in Columbus, Poll Shows," *Supermarket News,* 27 October 1969, p. 14; "Federal Bureau Aid Doubts Chains Gouge," *Supermarket News,* 11 August 1969, p. 10; William T. Bonwich and Edward B. Conway, "Pricing in Food Chains: Poverty Area Versus Nonpoverty Area Stores," *Journal of Retailing* 46 (Summer, 1970) pp. 60-63.

88. Margaret Hall, John Knapp, and Christopher Winsten have reported that middle income neighborhoods, rather than very poor or very affluent sections, seem to nurture chains in Britain and Canada as well as in the U. S. *Distribution in Great Britain and North America* (London: Oxford University Press, 1961), p. 96.

89. William E. Cox, Jr., and Sue R. Seidman, "Cooperatives in the Ghetto,"

in *Marketing Involvement in Society and the Economy* (Proceedings of the A.M.A. Fall 1969 Conference), ed. Philip R. McDonald (Chicago: American Marketing Association, 1970), pp. 40-46.

90. Vernon A. Mund, *Government and Business,* 3rd ed. (New York: Harper & Brothers, 1960), p. 426. Also see Robert L. Knox, "Competition and the Concept of Sales Below Cost," *Arizona Business Bulletin* 16 (November 1969), pp. 227-32.

91. See Donald Gene Halper, *Public Policy in Marketing: Sales Below Cost Prohibitions in the California Grocery Trade* (Ann Arbor, Mich.: University Microfilms, 1958), Chap. 7.

92. R. Duffy Lewis and J. Norman Lewis, *What Every Retailer Should Know About the Law,* 2d ed. (New York: Fairchild Publications, Inc., 1963), p. 68.

93. *Sunbeam Corp.* v. *Wentling,* 185 F.2d 903 (CA-3, 1950); *Bissell Carpet Sweeper Co.* v. *Masters Mail Order Co. of Washington,* 240 F.2d 684 (CA-4, 1957); *General Electric Co.* v. *Masters Mail Order Co. of Washington,* 244 F.2d 681 (CA-2, 1957).

94. *Schwegmann Brothers* v. *Calvert Corp.,* 341 US 384.

95. *CCH Trade Reg. Rep.,* par. 6,041.

96. U. S. Senate, Committee on Commerce, *Quality Stabilization* (subcommittee hearings, Washington, 1962), p. 169; H. N. Lackshin, "Refusal to Sell," *Texas Law Review* 36 (1958), pp. 808-11.

97. For example, "FTC Warns Producers," *Home Furnishings Daily,* 18 February 1970, p. 1.

98. See "Price Protection Is Snowballing," *Home Furnishings Daily* 17 July 1968; "G. E. Adopting Fair Trade in California," *Home Furnishings Daily* 25 June 1970; "Fair Trade for Philco Products Expected in Connecticut Soon," *Home Furnishings Daily* 6 October 1969. But see E. B. Weiss, "Will Fair Trade Stage A Comeback?" *Advertising Age* 19 August 1968, p. 70 for a discussion of the limits on r.p.m.'s revival.

99. Cf. Lee E. Preston, "The Commercial Sector and Economic Development" in *Markets and Marketing in the American Economy,* eds., Reed Moyer and Stanley C. Hollander (Homewood, Ill.: Richard D. Irwin, Inc., 1968), pp. 9-23.

22 West Germany

HELMUT SOLDNER

This chapter is a condensation of part of a study still in process on trends in mass distribution in Germany, with the collaboration of William Applebaum, Lecturer Emeritus, Harvard University, Graduate School of Business Administration. Appreciation is recorded for partial financial support from Harvard Business School toward the full study.

In 1948, the Western part of the former German Reich, split and truncated by World War II, adopted a rather free and competitive market system. Still, various restrictions and inhibitions inherited from earlier times and reflecting old issues and conflicts are embodied in current public policy toward retailing, which is being adapted to new concerns and pressures.

Principles

In the late forties, the system of a controlled and centrally planned economy introduced by the Nazis in 1933 was replaced by a much freer one. The new "Social Market Economy" was to combine the advantages of a competitive market system with the demands for social justice and harmony. This meant that free enterprise was to be tempered by considerations of protecting, and possibly improving, the social standing of citizens and the interests of consumers. Ideally, competition was to forestall positions of extreme economic power, and to strike a balance between the economic freedom of manufacturers and consumers.

From these principles followed two basic goals of public policy toward retailing: (1) the principle of social justice calls for protecting the social standing of the very large group of small retailers; and (2) the principle of a consumer-oriented economy calls for a retail structure geared to the life styles and shopping preferences of consumers. These two goals have been conflicting in quite a few instances.

The idea of a market economy did call for a minimum of protective restraints. However, the great number of small retailers accustomed to a great deal of protection stepped up after 1933 could not be exposed to free competition without risking serious social unrest. Just born and living next-door to communist governments, the new Federal Republic had to make sure that socioeconomic changes took place gradually. Therefore, the business and professional middle classes were attributed a "value of their own," to be protected

405

for the sake of social and political stability.[1] For this purpose, one school of thought deemed it appropriate to slow down the overdue structural changes in retailing. The majority of experts, however, favored a policy of supporting the small retailers' own efforts towards modernization and higher efficiency, and of putting them on an equal footing with their larger competitors, by eliminating all statutes favoring the latter.

To arrive at a consumer-oriented retail system, public policy should promote the evolution of retailing to the extent that consumers enjoy unlimited choice of *what* (e.g., categories of demand), *where* (e.g., suburban or downtown), *when* (e.g., store hours), *how much* (e.g., in "one-stop" diversified stores, or in narrow-line specialty stores), and *how expensively* (extent and quality of services) to shop. With regard to the postulate of social justice, this freedom of choice should be guaranteed to all consumers, and not only to some privileged groups (for example, the rich or the smart ones).

More specifically, the most important vantage points for a public policy in pursuit of freedom of choice for all consumers would appear to lie in the area of services. Recent innovations in retailing are widely characterized by a reduction of services (self-service, discounting). In other instances, consumers' needs call for a regrouping of services (e.g., when problem-free merchandise is not yet sold in self-service, whereas expert advice provided by highly specialized sales clerks is lacking in the distribution of technically complicated or socially problematic items). Such an improvement in the allocation of productive factors (via the interrelationships between personnel and space) would also result in a more economical distribution of goods, particularly if prices charged reflect precisely the costs of allotted factors.

Inasmuch as this can be achieved best under a minimum of competitive restraints, public policy would strive for an optimum of competition in retailing, and the authorities would:

1. Refrain from imposing restraints on competition (e.g., statutes hampering price-active innovators).
2. Promote competition by:
   – fighting all attempts by participants in the market to restrain competition (e.g., collusion, cartels, price maintenance agreements)
   – improving all retailers' capability to compete actively (e.g., training and credit programs for small business)
   – enabling consumers to shop more circumspectly (e.g., informative labeling and pricing, testing, etc.)
3. Eliminate statutes not neutral in the area of competition (e.g., the old sales-tax system).

Actual Policies

Practice was bound to depart from these principles on account of conflicting views and interests, tradition, and plain inaction on the part of the authorities.

The following sections analyze the new postwar laws and regulations, but also surviving statutes of earlier periods, and gaps in public policy toward retailing.[2]

Actors

Licensure. Officially, the restrictive Law for the Protection of Retailing (1933) was not set aside until 1957. In practice, however, its requirement of proving "local need" for new retail establishments was completely ignored, and the enforcement of the proof-of-competence and honorability requirements was so lax that there were no restrictions on entry worth mentioning. The new Law on Trading Permits in Retailing (1957) did not change this situation very much. Applicants had again to demonstrate competence and honorability, but the protective function of the law was practically limited to keeping out untrained fringe operators. However, the Federal Constitutional Court, at the close of 1965, declared unconstitutional the part of the law requiring proof of competence (except for grocery, pharmacy, and medical supply outlets).

Financial Support. The federal and state governments provide financial assistance to new or operating retailers under a number of programs. Loans at moderate interest rates are available for junior entrepreneurs who plan to establish or take over a retail store. Similar credit programs exist for the establishment of smaller stores in new housing or urban renewal areas, new shopping centers adjacent to such areas, and any new retail facilities in specific areas included in a federal plan for regional development (e.g., areas along the East German border). For small retailers who do not qualify for any of these programs, loan guarantees are available. The government also sponsors loan-guarantee associations organized by trade associations, chambers of commerce, and associations of private banks. However, the amount of credit per applicant is relatively low for most of these programs, and their impact on the modernization of retailing must not be overestimated.

Other Direct Support. Thanks to a very active Federal Bureau of Statistics, retail management can obtain comprehensive data about the latest trends in distribution. Retailing also benefits from a highly developed educational system, including good public vocational schools. Attendance of these schools is mandatory for all trainees in retailing during their apprenticeship, which in turn is governed by official guidelines and controlled by the semi-official Chambers of Commerce. A new Training Encouragement Law (1970) allocates considerable public funds for continuing education by giving financial support both to the educational institutions and to the employee who is willing to improve his skills.

Besides, public funds go to the schools and training centers run by regional and national retail associations. Seminars with stronger emphasis on retail management problems are also conducted by the Agency for Retail Consulting (BBE), an affiliate of the Central Association of German Retailers. For retailers with annual sales below DM 2 million,[3] consulting by the BBE is subsidized to a considerable extent by the government. Other BBE services, primarily geared to small retailers, include data processing, publications and business forms, and the sponsoring of small-business statistical-exchange groups.

Comprehensive and detailed data covering essentially small and medium-sized specialty stores are published monthly by the Institute for Distribution Research (Cologne). This institute receives considerable public support, just like the special Institute for Small Business Research (Cologne/Bonn), which has produced a number of studies on the competitive situation of small business. The federal government also finances distribution research projects executed by the Association for Rationalization in Distribution (RGH, Cologne) and the Research Institute for Trade (FfH, Berlin).

Size Limitations. The list of statutes that contain explicit size handicaps is a very short one. Until its repeal in 1954, Section 6 of the Rebate Law prohibited consumer cooperatives from selling to non-members and from granting a membership refund. Also in 1954, Section 5 of the Rebate Law, repealed after World War II, was reinstituted, stipulating that the membership refund may not exceed the 3 percent cash discount customary in retailing. The consumer cooperatives were thereby denied a major attraction of membership in their organization. The part of Section 6 prohibiting department stores and limited-price variety stores ("five-and-tens") from granting the 3 percent cash discount was declared unconstitutional by the Federal Constitutional Court in 1967. As these large enterprises had, for a long time, been offering net prices to the consumer, this decision was merely of academic significance.

More important, a discriminatory tax was levied on multi-store retailers until 1965, as municipalities were empowered to tax the outlets of chains and department stores headquartered elsewhere at a rate up to 30 percent higher. In 1965, this special taxation was declared unconstitutional by the Federal Constitutional Court, and large retailers were refunded for the amount of taxes paid.

Restrictions on Growth. By far the most interesting and significant aspect of public policy concerning restrictions on growth cannot be found in the statute books. Although the topic of chain store and particularly department store expansion has always been a sensitive one, there has been hardly any explicit governmental action in this regard after World War II. The key to an explanation of this phenomenon lies in the extremely circumspect and moderate expansion policy adopted by the major department store concerns.

Department-store expansion policy after 1945 was determined by their experience for more than half a century of political attacks by their (small-business) rivals, culminating in the ruinous anti-department-store rallies in the mid-thirties. From the very beginning, department store managers were extremely anxious not to create new or revive old resentments on the part of the middle classes, which might again lead to political pressures and election deals likely to result in new discriminatory legislation. Consequently, accommodation has been achieved by keeping in close contacts with the public authorities and the retail associations. In this way, department stores have learned about the deliberations and plans of small business and government early enough to exert at least some mitigating influence and to adjust their own plans so as to avoid serious conflicts with small business and/or the state.

Besides, department stores have refrained from rapidly expanding their market shares through aggressive price policies. Instead, they have chosen a "soft pedaled" yet progressive, self-financed expansion by means of relatively high unit margins on comparatively low volumes. For the same reason, they have opted for one of the "sacred cows" of small business retailers, i.e., resale price maintenance. Thus, they have earned conveniently the funds for their moderate expansion, instead of the massive protests of small business and the ensuing political trouble.

Another unwritten rule carefully observed by department stores concerns the thwarting of new suburban shopping facilities, particularly regional shopping centers, that would siphon business away from established retailers at conventional locations. Instead, until recently, most of their expansion has taken place in traditional business centers—mainly, the downtown areas. Thanks to this "peace in retailing," carefully nurtured by means of tactful maneuvering and astute public relations work, and by respecting the "unwritten rules" on expansion, the department stores have been able to forestall stronger restrictions on growth on the part of the authorities, and to build up their market shares considerably (between 1962 and 1970, the proportion of total retail sales accounted for by department stores increased from 8.4 percent to 10.4 percent).

The few expansion curbs of large retailing initiated by the small-business-oriented Central Association of German Retailers in "cooperation" with the Federal Ministry of Economy, were of little practical significance. In more or less voluntary "self-limitation declarations," large retail enterprises promised in 1965 not to open new stores in towns with less than 200,000 inhabitants until the end of 1967, after a similar earlier agreement (1952-54) for towns with less than 50,000 inhabitants. Prior to the 1961 parliamentary elections, a similar assurance had been given by the four leading department stores for the next four to five years. These expansion limitations were intended to give small business retailers a breathing spell, enabling them to improve their efficiency. It would appear, however, that the large stores used this time at least as well as their small competitors, by preparing expansion plans for the next years and by enlarging or renovating their existing facilities; and investments by department stores probably did not decline during these years.

Foreign Retailers. There are no differences in public policy toward domestic and foreign retail enterprises, shopping center developers, and other investors in distribution (the foreign capital working in this country being primarily of Dutch, British, Canadian, and Swiss origin). Along these lines, the Federal Supreme Court ruled in a recent case (dealing with the discrimination of a foreign retail tenant by a landlord) that foreign entrepreneurs may not be treated any differently from domestic retailers.

Structure

Permitted Cartels. Since 1957, there is a special Cartel Act designed to stimulate competition and at the same time to promote the maintenance of an optimal degree of economic freedom.[4] As a rule, agreements between enterprises on horizontal restraints (Section 1) and vertical restraints of competition (with regard to prices and trade terms, Section 15) are prohibited. However, there are exemptions to these two sections that, in practice, permit very serious and basic restraints in retailing.

While there are no formal cartels between retailers, price conspiracies among small local competitors are difficult to control by higher-level authorities. Depending to a certain extent on the objectives of public-policymakers, the affiliation of independent retailers into horizontal buying and marketing organizations such as voluntary or cooperative chains may be considered as a cartel. After prolonged investigations and negotiations with these chains, the Federal Cartel Authority (FCA) passed the following resolution: "The collective purchases of a group of independent enterprises are not prohibited by the Cartel Act as long as there is no legal obligation to cover requirements, either entirely, in a certain percentage, or in certain specified items, by means of collective purchases." Because the statutes, resolutions, or guidelines of the voluntary or cooperative chains do not contain such legal obligations, they were not considered to be subject to Section 1 of the Cartel Law. However, in practice there often are purchase obligations on the part of retailers toward their group wholesalers. Therefore, these organizations may be considered as tolerated small-business cartels.

Section 3 of the Cartel Act permits rebate cartels[5] "insofar as rebates represent a genuine compensation for services and do not lead to an unjustified differential treatment of other distributors or their customers who render the same service to the suppliers in the distribution of goods." Manufacturers' rebate cartels tend to limit price competition by strengthening the maintenance of manufacturers' list prices, as well as of suggested and fixed retail prices. Inasmuch as the introduction of resale price maintenance has been frequently demanded or at least supported by retailers, it can be looked upon as a sort of price cartel between retailers.

When a rebate cartel, as often happens, is coupled with resale price maintenance, the injuries to competition that are produced by the combined effect of vertical fixed-price agreements and rebate cartels may be even greater than those produced by the individual restraints. Section 3 (2) of the Cartel Act gives the distributive trade a voice in establishing the conditions of a rebate cartel. The nationwide trade associations of the wholesale and retail trades negotiate with industry, primarily as the representatives of small business. In setting the size of the rebate, the reference point is the marginal enterprise. Regardless of its size or efficiency, a firm will always receive the same rebate from the cartel. It is in this way that rebate cartels, regardless of their combination with vertical fixed-price agreements, tend to preserve the traditional distribution system.

Vertical Integration. So far, vertical integration has not reached dimensions that would make it a central issue of public policy toward retailing. There are no cases where large enterprises had to divest themselves of companies acquired through vertical merger, because of the latter's substantial anti-competitive effects. A simple rule prohibiting or controlling vertical integration does not exist. Rather, the interest of the lawmaker has centered around contractual arrangements resulting in various forms of semi-integraton.

This does not mean that there is not any public policy dealing with the competitive position of vertically integrated enterprises. Lately, the authorities have pushed for the revision of regulations putting vertically integrated enterprises and independent firms on an unequal competitive footing in such matters as taxation, exclusive dealerships, and franchising.

Value-added Tax. Preceding the 9 February 1967 decision of the EEC Council of Ministers to change the tax system in the member countries to a value-added basis, the Federal Constitutional Court in a 1966 decision expressed grave misgivings about the constitutionality of the old tax system. The Court felt that the old sales-tax system was not neutral in the area of competition because it favored vertically integrated enterprises over the small- and medium-sized firms. To stop this encouragement of vertical integration was the major reason given by the authorities to introduce the new value-added tax in early 1968.

Until the end of 1967, a 4 percent tax was levied on each purchase as merchandise flowed from the original producer to the ultimate consumer.[6] Because the tax liability depended on the number of transactions, the old tax system favored large, vertically integrated enterprises combining multi-level distribution operations; and it discriminated against small- and medium-size firms that had to bear taxes accumulated separately at many distribution levels. In the new, so-called value-added tax system, a (currently) 11 percent tax is levied on the value added to a product as it passes from its original producer to the consumer, while the number of intermediate institutions and agencies in a channel is not considered. Because the tax liability is now on the total value added instead of depending directly on the number of transactions, the tax is no longer an incentive for vertical integration.

Since the value-added tax is applied to the gross margin, which is identical with the value added, it has cleared the way for more active and aggressive pricing because the lower the margin, the lower the tax burden. Whereas under the old tax system, there was a 4 percent tax liability on the selling price regardless of whether the retailer had made a profit, today there is no tax due when a retailer sells merchandise at cost, and there is even a tax credit if he sells below cost.

Exclusive Dealerships, Franchising, and other Vertical Linkages. The renewed emphasis on channel of distribution management from a systems standpoint is reflected in a great variety of exclusive and selective contractual or semi-contractual arrangements and franchising systems. These forms of semi-integration raise a growing number of important public-policy issues particularly in the matters of exclusive dealing arrangements and controlled sales agreements.

The Cartel Act does not provide a simple per se rule for these contracts. Generally, enterprises are free to agree upon both exclusive dealing arrangements [Section 19 (2)] and controlled sales agreements [Section 18 (3)]. Unlike resale price maintenance pacts, they need not be registered with the FCA. However, all such agreements are subject to "control of misuse." These contracts can be declared void by the FCA if they unfairly restrict access to a market for other enterprises (third parties), or result in a substantial lessening of competition in the market for these and other goods or commercial services.

Whether such unfair restraint in access to a market is present must be judged separately in each case. Similarly, the question of whether there is a substantial lessening of competition can be answered only after an analysis of the special circumstances—particularly the economic interest of the parties involved, and the delimitation of the relevant market. Experience tells that in most cases it is very difficult, if not impractical, to prove that such competitive injury exists. According to the FCA, the law presents serious enforcement difficulties, particularly with regard to market-dominating or influential enterprises building up their market shares by means of exclusive dealing arrangements.

Most exclusive dealing arrangements and controlled sales agreements are used for the purpose of enforcing the pricing policy of the "channel captain" (usually a strong manufacturer) by excluding marketing channels or intermediaries that are not considered safe for maintaining fixed or suggested prices. This particularly holds true for controlled sales agreements since, in combination with a suggested price agreement, they may be equal, or sometimes even superior to, a resale price maintenance pact.

Controlled sales agreements restricting resale to certain types of stores have been enforced as a device for relieving traditional retailers (mainly, specialty stores) from the rigors of competition by other retail outlets. Thus, primarily price-fixed national brands have been withheld from department stores, mail-order houses, consumer markets,[7] variety stores, consumer cooperatives, food stores in general, newsstands, mobile stores, etc.—mostly in the radio/TV, electrical appliances, prestige photographic and optical supplies, jewelry and watches, sporting goods, and drug trades. As long as those excluded types of retailers do not provide the same standard of service (store fittings, personnel training, etc.) as specialty stores, there is no legal recourse against manufacturers unwilling to supply them—even not against price-fixing manufacturers, cartels, and market-dominating enterprises, for which Section 26 (2) otherwise restricts the right of "refusals to deal."

In these ways, and more generally by strengthening the effects of resale price maintenance pacts, these contractual arrangements have supported the "status quo" in distribution. As long as dominant manufacturers believed that their marketing interests were best served by barring innovative and price-aggressive dealers, progress toward a consumer-oriented distribution system was hampered, and specialty stores were able to concentrate on service rather than on price competition.

More recently, under the pressure of rapidly changing market conditions, the manufacturers of prominent national brands have adopted a more realistic policy. Switching increasingly to "dual branding," they have reserved one brand-name line to specialty stores, another for the food trade, a third for department stores, and perhaps a fourth as a private label for discount operators.

Consequently, the growing competition between established national brands and private labels has led to a renewed importance of exclusive dealing arrangements and controlled sales agreements pursuant to Sections 18 (2) and 18 (3) of the Cartel Act. Frequently, however, the character of these contractual arrangements has more or less changed from "exclusive" (in the sense of "restrictive") to "selective." This means that there is trend for brand-name manufacturers to build up their own network of contract dealers (e.g., for hi-fi equipment, high-class furniture, shoes, designer dresses). Inasmuch as the controlling party usually reserves itself some voice in the selection of the assortment, store fittings, etc., certain elements of franchising are added. But even if these contracts more strongly accentuate the partnership between the manufacturer (franchisor) and the dealer (franchisee), they are basically still combinations of exclusive dealerships and controlled sales agreements pursuant to Section 18 (2) and 18 (3).

Franchising contracts (in the sense of franchising a complete system or operations program) are now beginning to appear side-by-side with the more conventional vertical arrangements. Although materially quite similar, they differ legally from exclusive dealing arrangements and controlled sales agreements in that they are mostly agency contracts, subject to the regulations governing manufacturers' representatives. The restraints on competition contained therein are, in contrast to the contractual vertical arrangements pursuant to Section 18, not subject to supervision by the FCA.[8]

Miscellaneous Ordinances Affecting Intertype Competition. These ordinances impose restrictions on the assortments of certain forms of retailing, but their impact upon the relationships between retail types is rather limited. Section 66 of the *Trade Ordinance* empowers municipalities to restrict the assortment of merchandise offered on the weekly open-air markets. Local merchants frequently exert pressure upon the local authorities to apply such restrictions in such a way as to discriminate against ambulant traders:

1. *The Drug Ordinance* gives pharmacies a virtual monopoly in the sale of drugs and medical supplies.
2. The *Working Hours Ordinance for the Bakery Trade* stipulates that baking between 10 P.M. and 4 A.M. as well as deliveries before 5:45 A.M. (until 1969, 6:30 A.M.) are forbidden. This favors small craft enterprises over grocery retailers (especially the food chains) that cannot get fresh baked goods delivered to all their stores before opening since few have their own production and delivery facilities.
3. According to the *Minced Meat Ordinance,* this product and fresh sausages made from it must be inspected daily by a master butcher (generally, fresh meat may be sold only in separate butcher shops). This ordinance favors the butcher shops and prevents grocers from selling such products without employing a master butcher (something done by the food chains).
4. The *Law Governing the Fees of Cattle Markets, Slaughter Houses, and Meat Markets* also favors butcher stores over other food retailers, because it empowers the municipalities to levy a meat tax on all meat slaughtered elsewhere, i.e., not in the municipal abattoir, thereby increasing the price of fresh meat in non-butcher shops. By charging higher fees for the inspection of "imported" meat, the price level for fresh meat sold in retail food stores is further increased. According to a recent change of this regulation, the meat tax will be gradually reduced until its final abolition in 1976.

Process

Location. A pending Town Planning law is expected to provide the framework of clearly defined guidelines for urban development, urban renewal, and regional planning, that have been missing so far. On the other hand, existing building and town-planning ordinances can be somewhat flexibly interpreted by regional and local authorities. Their decisions vary, depending upon the influence of the interested parties (local small business and department stores) in city councils and regional parliaments.

Another important location factor is taxes—particularly the business taxes levied on larger enterprises, which are of major importance to municipalities. For example, the regular maximum ratio of floor space to building lot for downtown areas until recently was 2.0.[9] However, for tax revenue reasons, ratios of up to 4.0 have been permitted in order to attract a department store. With regard to the location of large new shopping facilities in suburban areas, similar reasons frequently play a strong role.

As yet, public policy has not answered the question to what extent automobile shopping can be allowed to shift important retailing facilities from downtown areas to suburban locations. This lack of answers is reflected in the existing zoning regulations. Until recently, the establishment of large shopping centers, consumer markets and cash-and-carry stores, was permitted in areas zoned for business or light industry. Consumer markets were also allowed in villages, urban core areas, and areas of mixed uses.

Since 1968, however, the location of regional shopping centers and self-service department stores (consumer markets) is subject to "special area" legislation, instituted to control and even to hamper the establishment of such shopping facilities. Most local authorities, however, interpret the new regulation in a way that leaves them ample freedom of decision; and things actually have not changed too much.

On the other hand, public thoroughfare ordinances continue to impede the development of highway retailing. Besides, in the older business and residential areas, the establishment of new retailing facilities and the replacement or modernization of existing stores has frequently been hampered by the lack of modern building and expropriation regulations, although the rebuilding of structures to cover adjacent lots as well as the construction of underground delivery areas, has been facilitated since 1968. Expropriation was the last recourse when owners of relatively small lots or old buildings were jeopardizing larger urban renewal programs or larger projects (e.g., shopping precincts in CBDs) by not selling their property or asking "moon prices" for it.

Plant and Facilities. According to the Garage Ordinance (1939), each retailer must provide one car parking space for a certain number of square meters of selling space. As a rule, the retailer pays the town to provide the parking space, at the rate of up to DM 8,000 for each space.

In rebuilding the destroyed cities, many municipalities took only limited advantage of the opportunity to improve traffic conditions in the downtown areas. Later on, there were efforts to tackle the city-center problem by building (or helping to finance) parking facilities and by converting major shopping streets into pedestrian malls. Besides encouraging experiments with park-and-ride systems, the large cities have made costly efforts to improve their convenient mass transportation systems that regularly operate in the red. In practically all major cities, extensive construction of new subways is under way or at an advanced planning stage. The federal and state governments provide the larger part of funds needed for these ambitious programs.

Requirements concerning facilities and equipment are particularly strict for large stores. Safety requirements, like sprinkler systems and a second exit for basements, now apply also to the new self-service department stores.

Store Hours. The regulations governing store hours are among the most restrictive in the world. Section 3 of the Store Closing Law (1956, amended in 1957 and 1960) stipulates that sales outlets must be closed for business with customers during the following times: (1) on Sundays and holidays; (2) Monday to Friday until 7 A.M. and after 6:30 P.M.; and (3) Saturdays until 7 A.M. and after 2 P.M. (on the first Saturday of the month, and on four consecutive Saturdays before December 24, after 6 P.M.).

Over time, this law has changed its character from an instrument for the protection of employees to one for allegedly restricting competition in favor of small retailers who do not want other retailers to do business after a certain hour. While large enterprises could stagger employee working hours after 6:30 P.M., the small retailer and his family would have to put in their free time. These arguments were influenced by the fact that in 1968 some 40 percent of German retailers were still part-time operators who also pursued other occupations.

Strangely enough, department stores support the present regulation even though the Store Closing Law is supposed to discriminate against them for the protection of small business. Originally opposed to this law, department stores soon realized its advantage. Since store hours and working hours (including the trip from and to work) are nearly identical, employees do not have much time to shop around. Therefore, working people prefer large stores that carry a wide selection under one roof (department stores, supermarkets, consumer markets) over the small, conventional, full-service, specialty stores.

The Store Closing Law benefits particularly the large stores in downtown areas that are still the almost exclusive stronghold of department stores and the hub of efficient public transportation systems. Many working housewives as well as other downtown or "in-transit" employees, tend to shop downtown, because stores in their (suburban) living quarters are about to close when they return from work. This holds true even for convenience goods, since department stores operate excellent food departments (which, in 1969, accounted for about 22 percent of total department-store sales).

Generally, the present restrictive regulation acted as a strong deterrent to a more rapid development of suburban shopping facilities geared to the automobile trade. The establishment of regional shopping centers, which were boycotted by the strictly downtown-oriented department stores, could not have been thwarted so successfully had it not been for their tacit support of the Store Closing Law.

Consumer markets, including large self-service department stores, would have appeared on the scene earlier if evening hours had been permitted. Instead, cash-and-carry stores, the forerunners of the consumer markets, enjoyed a boom in the mid-sixties. Operating officially as wholesale outlets that are not subject to the Store Closing Law, they do the major part of their business in the evening. Quite a few cash-and-carries took on a mixed nature by selling more or less readily to customers other than bona fide retailers, tradesmen, and other institutional users.

Since this legislation restricts leisurely evening shopping by automobile, especially for major purchases, many a family has decided to do part of its shopping in the pages of the voluminous catalogues offered by the large mail-order houses. The restrictive hour legislation has thus enabled these enterprises to achieve spectacular growth in the sales of major items.

Merchandising

While there are no regulations calling for mandatory merchandise lines, some questions of prohibited merchandise combinations have been touched above under the topic of inter-type competition.

Sections 25-26 of the Cartel Act regulate retailer-supplier relationships between enterprises that are not semi-integrated within vertical marketing systems (as discussed above). Section 25 (1) prohibits forced compliance, inasmuch as suppliers may not coerce price-active dealers to follow their price "suggestions." Such coercion is usually achieved by refusal to sell or by blocking deliveries, but refusal to supply a nonconforming dealer is legal only if the retailer has violated a price-maintenance contract. At the same time, with the exception of market-dominating, price-fixing, or cartelized enterprises, every manufacturer is free to choose his customers. However, he may not organize his marketing channels in such a way that only price-loyal purchasers are supplied.

Section 16 (1) stipulates that "enterprises or associations of enterprises shall not induce another enterprise or associations of enterprises to block deliveries or purchases with the intent of unfairly harming certain competitors." Thus, suppliers may not be forced to boycott low-price sellers or other innovative retailers in order to retain established retailers (particularly, specialty stores) as customers.

Voluntary chains and retail cooperatives, in their efforts to grow from relatively loosely organized forms of cooperation into marketing organizations with a higher degree of control over their members, have to proceed somewhat carefully in order not to get in conflict with the law. Section 25 (2) stipulates that members of cooperative groups may not be pressured to charge specific prices and/or to act uniformly in the market, by threatening them with withdrawal of supplies, suspension of membership in the group, or other disadvantages. This applies also to cases where retailers would be obliged, not legally but de facto, to concentrate their purchases exclusively with their group wholesaler, or take any other collective action in purchasing, with intent to influence competition.

Still, these cooperative groups enjoy certain privileges in determining resale prices. Section 38 (2) entitles "associations of enterprises" (meaning small retailers) to suggest prices to their members, provided that: (1) these "small-business price suggestions" are intended to create conditions promoting competition with large enterprises or with similar types of enterprises; and (2) they are explicitly stated not to be binding; and no economic, social, or other pressure is exerted toward their observation. However, a 1958 decision of the Federal Supreme Court legalized suggested prices for branded products, if filed with the FCA. Still, cooperative groups objected to the requirement that their suggested prices be nonbinding on retailers, although these prices are generally followed anyway.

Discrimination. The Cartel Act does not contain a general ruling against discrimination. The right of individual sellers to discriminate in the choice of customers has already been mentioned; and price discrimination is also permitted. In reaction against the corresponding legislative experience in the United States (Robinson-Patman Act), German lawmakers held that price discrimination should not be eliminated because it provides an important stimulus to competition.

On the other hand, the Cartel Act does not provide unrestricted license to discriminate. For one thing, the freedom to decide whether and under what conditions a firm will deal with one another has been rescinded to a certain extent for specific parties. According to Section 26 (2), cartels, market-dominating, and price-fixing enterprises "shall not unfairly hinder ... another enterprise in business activities that are usually open to similar enterprises, and shall not ... treat them in a manner different from the treatment accorded to a similar enterprise in the absence of facts justifying such differentiation." This compromise between a general prohibition of discriminatory practices and absolute freedom of action is based on the idea that monopolistic power may lead to excessive discrimination against a dealer that would not have been achieved if substantial competition between suppliers had been present.

Even for enterprises with a monopolistic type of market position, there is no general, but only a limited, prohibition against discrimination. Basically, only "similar enterprises" may not be subjected to discriminatory treatment. The marketing function of a dealer has been used as the criterion in deciding whether he should be considered as "similar" or not. For example, courts have ruled that wholesalers and retailers, or specialty stores and itinerant traders, are not similar in contrast to specialty stores and the specialty departments of department stores which are.

The issues of "unfair hindering" and "unjustified discrimination" raised mostly when deliveries were blocked have not sparked very much excitement. Over time, discounters have been able to get most of the merchandise they wanted, and the department stores even more so. Section 26 (2) has also enabled supermarkets to add new merchandise lines such as nonprescription drugs and cosmetics. In principle, the more an item is of significance for the dealer (as in the case of a leading national brand), the less the manufacturer may refuse to deal.

Action by a supplier, including pricing, does not constitute unjustified discrimination when it is based on organizational or marketing considerations. Actually, his autonomy in pricing remains largely untouched since nearly all quantity rebate scales and the resulting differential treatment can be factually justified. The same liberal guidelines apply with regard to advertising allowances, merchandising services, premiums and the like, and deviations in the quality or quantity of the merchandise. There are also no restraints preventing individual dealers, buying organizations, and voluntary-chain headquarters from soliciting such discriminatory prices, allowances, and other differentials.

In order to eliminate some of the unwelcome consequences of not prohibiting discriminatory practices in general, the Cartel Act contains a framework for trade-practice rules, in Sections 28-30. In principle, these rules must be registered with the FCA and should be directed against unfair (or otherwise illegal) competitive behavior. However, according to a 1966 ruling of the Federal Supreme Court, trade-practice rules must be directed only against unfair practices that *actually* exist (e.g., a dominant enterprise starts a permanent weeding-out process among its customers), but may not include, a priori, any prohibition of discriminatory practices that *might* arise. Since trade-practice rules on non-discrimination were declared eligible for registration only in 1966, they have been only of marginal influence upon structural changes in distribution.

Promotion. Besides the severely restricted use of outdoor signs and the strict prohibition of highway advertising for esthetic reasons, the legal attitude toward retail promotion is considerably more stringent than in the United States. This attitude reflects the fact that: "The understanding of the nature and advantages of competition has always, and to a marked extent, been dimmed by a certain guild and chamber-of-commerce mentality."[10] This philosophy clearly marked the Law Against Unfair Competition (1909). Its Section 1 states that anyone using competitive practices that are contrary to good business ethics can be ordered to cease and desist and to pay damages. The interpretation of the term "good business ethics" was left to the courts which, over the years, curbed not only unfair competition, but also, in a number of instances, effective competition itself.

A striking example is the prohibition of comparative advertising. Based exclusively on repeated high-level court interpretations of Section 1, it is illegal to advertise one's own performance by comparing it with that of a competitor. Except for a few insignificant exceptions, a dealer may, therefore, advertise only his own good values and services, but may not mention the prices and services offered by competing retailers. This applies even if the comparison is based on facts and is presented objectively. The beneficiaries of this restrictive attitude are the conventional retailers, because innovative or low-price dealers are denied any honest comparison of their own price-service mix with that of their established competitors.

Section 3 of the Law Against Unfair Competition is directed against misrepresentation, deception, and misleading statements. This principle of "truth in advertising and promotion" requires that dealers must not misrepresent their trade status by offering "wholesale" or "factory" prices (Section 6a). Advertisements which imply that an article is offered for sale because of alleged special circumstances are also prohibited, as well as untruthful statements about business practices as well as the origin, method of manufacturing, procurement, and quality of a merchandise or service. There is no special prohibition of loss-leader promotion in the sense of "selling below cost" (however this may be defined). Still, according to court rulings, quoting a bargain price without having an adequate inventory to support the sale (bait-pricing) is clearly in conflict with Section 3. This holds true also for deceptive lottery schemes, games, and similar promotional devices.

With the exception of anniversary sales, individual retailers are not allowed to hold any special sales. According to Sections 7-9a, the entire retail trade may conduct special sales only twice a year "around the end of the season." These "End of Winter Sales" and "End of Summer Sales" start the last Monday in January and July, and they are limited to twelve business days. Remnant sales are permitted only during the last three days of the end-of-season sales.

Besides these price-promotional laws, a growing body of regulations touching the promotional aspects of packaging and labeling has gained in importance for retailer-consumer communication. Thus, advertising for foods and cosmetics may not promise results that cannot be proven scientifically; food labels as well as manuals have to disclose any preservatives or other additives used; and the durability must be shown on all canned goods. Among other statutes improving consumer information and protection, the Textiles Identification Act (1970) calling for clear material and take-care information has added a new element to manufacturer-retailer relations.

Pricing. Price information has been improved by a new Price Posting Ordinance enacted in 1970. Quoting prices that do not include taxes (gross prices) or the necessary accessories of a product is no longer permitted for dealers selling to consumers, even if other customers account for the major part of their business. Consequently, cash-and-carry wholesalers have had to switch over to gross prices. Drugs, expensive jewelry and watches, high-class apparel and Oriental rugs are no longer exempt from the requirement to show prices; while only objects d'art, collector's items and antiques may still be displayed or advertised without indicating prices. Gas stations in residential areas have to display prices on signs identifiable from the street; and on highways, drivers must be able to read prices immediately after entering a gas station.

The new law on Weights and Measures will further improve the consumer's ability to compare prices and see which brand gives the best value. Since January 1972, packaged items must clearly show the price per standard unit of weight or volume (kilograms, liters). Exempt are foods, cosmetics, detergents, and other products sold in standardized packages containing specified fractions (e.g., 50, 100, or 250 grams) of the basic units (e.g., quarter of a kilo, half-liter). This means that the consumer will have the choice between such standardized packages or packages that state clearly the basic price per kilo. Thus shoppers are no longer faced with a plethora of confusing sizes and weights and prices.

A 1969 amendment to the Installment Sales Law has increased consumer information about credit-service charges and other conditions of installment-sales contracts. Another currently pending amendment will grant buyers the right to back out of a credit plan several days after the contract was entered into.

Trading Stamps and Premiums. The offering of premiums, stamps, coupons, and similar promotional devices is governed by the Premium Ordinance and the Rebate Act. The Premium Ordinance only allows premiums of trifling value. Offers such as "six eggs free with every . . ." or "free mug with fill-up" are therefore not permitted. For the same reason, no stamps redeemable in merchandise can be issued by retailers and other businessmen, but dealers may give rebate stamps redeemable in cash.

According to the Rebate Act, businessmen may grant consumers a 3 percent discount for cash payment on their posted or customarily charged prices, either as a 3 percent price reduction or in the form of rebate stamps. Besides, stamps may only be redeemed by the issuing retailer or by an association of such retailers. This precludes the establishment of profit-making independent stamp companies.

Resale Price Maintenance. Section 16 of the Cartel Act confers the right of resale prices fixing upon the owners (manufacturers and distributors) of trademarked or branded goods, provided these products compete in price with similar goods of other sellers. Price maintenance agreements in the form of written individual contracts have to be filed with the FCA. Complete data on all sales prices charged by the manufacturer or distributor to the subsequent dealer, as well as on trade margins, have to be entered into the Price Agreement Register kept by the FCA.

Even though a "non-signer's clause" does not exist, there are ways to proceed against price slashers. According to the established interpretation of Section 1 of the Law Against Unfair Competition by the courts, the undercutting of fixed prices is against good business ethics, and therefore constitutes unfair competition. This applies to all price cutters, whether or not they have signed a contract to maintain fixed prices. A price-cutting signer's only recourse is by proving that fixed prices were already undersold so widely that further adherence to the contract would have been unreasonable. Price-cutting non-signers are considered to violate good business ethics when they obtain their merchandise "under the counter," induce a wholesaler to break his contract with the manufacturer, or just take advantage of a breach of contract on the part of a dealer.

Thanks to this important prop for resale price maintenance, manufacturers have for a long time been able to keep price-aggressive dealers from creating conditions under which the FCA may (upon its own motion) or must (upon request from a purchaser bound by such a contract) rescind resale price maintenance contracts. Pursuant to Section 17 of the Cartel Act, such action by the FCA can be expected particularly if retail price maintenance is being improperly used or apt to raise prices or to prevent their lowering. Improper use is presumed if the seller cannot prevent gaps in his price maintenance system; while fixed prices are considered to cause higher prices when items are sold openly below fixed prices by a considerable number of retailers.

Most discussions about retail price maintenance in West Germany include the topic of suggested prices. This is so because the issue with pre-pricing is not so much fictitious pricing but rather the extent to which widespread adherence to suggested prices results in de facto resale price maintenance. Aware of the fact that suggested prices may serve to bypass the general prohibition of vertical sales restraints (regarding prices and trade terms) as stipulated in Section 15, the architects of the Cartel Act included a prohibition of suggested prices [Section 38 (2)]. However, the Federal Supreme Court, in a 1958 decision, ruled on the analogous application of Section 16 (4) to pre-pricing: suggested prices for branded or trademarked items, which are communicated to the consumer, are valid if filed with the FCA.

High-ranking officials of the Federal Ministry of Economy agree with the FCA that the suggested-price system severely restrains price competition. To illustrate the unusually strong effect of suggested prices on the actual price structure, the FCA revealed that 75 to 90 percent of preticketed items are actually sold at the indicated prices.[11] This confirms that especially in oligopolistic markets—the market situation prevailing in West Germany—the difference between suggested and fixed prices tends to blur.

Among the reasons for these severe constraints on pricing produced by the suggested-price system, is the difficulty of detecting the application of pressure by manufacturers to secure compliance with suggested prices. That such tactics are considered as abuses and subject to the "control of misuse" by the FCA (analogous application of Section 17), is of little practical value as long as the FCA, according to its own statements, is faced with almost unsurmountable difficulties in controlling such abuses. For example, the number of secret boycotts in connection with suggested prices is supposed to be fairly high. There are also tacit agreements among local merchants not to undersell suggested prices, while the Rebate Act provides another "price-stabilizing" effect since retailers are required to obliterate the preprinted price if they intend to undersell it by more than the 3 percent cash discount.

Function

Consumer vs. Small-Business Orientation. As was seen at the outset of this chapter, the welfare of small business (which, to a certain extent, automatically means the preservation of the traditional retail structure) and the promotion of a consumer-oriented distribution system are among the fundamental goals of public economic and social policy. In contrasting "theory" with "reality," it is therefore important to consider which of the statutes presented above as the embodiments of public policy toward retailing are actually oriented to, or at least work primarily in the direction of, one or the other of these two basic goals, or are in harmony with them. Table 22.1 classifies these measures and ranks them accordingly if tentatively.

Table 22.1 corroborates the general impression that there is a considerably larger body of statutes providing an umbrella for established retailers—particularly small ones—than of statutes fostering a competitive, consumer-

Table 22-1

Classification of Statutes With Regard to the Basic Principles
of the Social Market Economy

Statutes Favoring Small Business (or the Traditional Distribution System)	Statutes in Harmony With Both Goals	Statutes Favoring a Consumer Oriented Distribution System
Restrictions on the growth of department stores	Permitted "small business cartels"	Cartel Act (general prohibition of horizontal and vertical restraints
Resale price maintenance	Value-added tax	Price discrimination (no prohibition of)
Suggested prices	Prohibition of forced compliance (members of cooperative groups)	Prohibition of boycotts and blocked deliveries
Store closing ordinance		Price Posting Ordinance
Zoning regulations	Management consulting, data processing, and figure-exchange services	Regulations on weights, measures, packaging, and labeling
Exclusive dealerships and controlled sales agreements	Small-business price suggestions	Installment Sales Law
Rebate cartels		
Prohibition of comparative advertising		
Prohibition of price cutting		
Prohibition of special sales		
Restrictions on entry		
Rebate Act		
"Inter-type" assortment restrictions		

oriented distribution system. Besides, the first group not only outnumbers the second one, but is also much weightier since it comprises more than half a dozen statutes to which a really strong influence upon retail competition may be attributed, compared with about three for the second group (the statutes are tentatively ranked within each group along these lines, i.e., their weight decreases from top to bottom).

Therefore, the total effect of these statutes is more in the direction of fulfilling *established* consumption patterns. Most laws and regulations do not favor a distribution system responsive to basic socioeconomic changes and the resulting new trends in consumer life-styles and shopping preferences, or one designed to show consumers new ways of fulfilling their needs.

Instead, most regulations remain oriented toward the interests of manufacturers and dealers, and quite frequently restrict competition at the consumer's expense. While some of the newer statutes (such as the Price Posting Ordinance or the Installment Sales Law) show greater regard for consumers' interests, older regulations that also benefit them were not initiated primarily for that purpose. As a case in point, the Rebate Act ostensibly was to protect consumers from dishonest rebate manipulations. Actually, it was primarily a move to stop the 3 percent cash discount practice of consumer cooperatives, limited-price variety stores, and department stores.

Likewise, the Law Against Unfair Competition forbids special sales, except at fixed periods twice a year, in order to protect consumers. But still stronger was the motive to put small retailers on a more equal footing with department stores that had frequently offered special sales. Officially, the restrictions on entry required proof of competence in order to protect consumers against unqualified fringe operators, but it actually was intended to prevent unwelcome new competition.

More generally, public policy has tended to favor a predominantly static distribution system that is incompatible with the demands of a wealthier and more mobile society for more convenient shopping facilities.[12] Besides, it has not sufficiently fostered efficiency in distribution since it has encouraged service- rather than price-competition. Here, proponents of severe restraints on price competition in retailing have lately argued that fixed prices would contribute to stabilize the prices of important consumer goods in times of rapidly rising inflation. The FCA, however, after conducting a survey, disclosed in 1971 that it could not find any evidence supporting the validity of this argument.

For a distribution system primarily oriented toward the interests of manufacturers and trade, consumers not only have to pay higher prices but must put up with a number of other disadvantages. Time and traffic convenience, for example, remain low when regulations tend to support the monopoly of established retailers clinging to traditional locations and limited selling hours. If shopping has to be done in a rush in congested, older business districts, there is also little room left for circumspection in shopping, let alone truly informative sales discussions. Recently, the government has been striving to increase consumer information by organizing and supporting the Consumer Goods Test Institute (Berlin). Although the results of this research are widely published, they cannot substitute for the time necessary to compare the offers of different stores, and for the advisory services retailers are not able to render to consumers.

Retail Modernization. Structurally, public policy has resulted in blocking or slowing down the modernization of the retail system—at least in the short run. Its modest evolution has implied some internal changes, primarily growing market shares of the "big fellows" (department stores, chains, and particularly mail-order houses), and a rapid organization of retailing into vertically integrated groups with great aggregate purchasing power (voluntary chains, retailer cooperatives, and other buying organizations). Otherwise, the established retailers have succeeded in remaining among themselves and in running a kind of department-stores/speciality-stores cartel, protected by an umbrella of restrictive statutes. Thus retailing has continued to be geared to satisfy some sort of an average demand, while new types of stores aiming at specific market segments by offering a different price-service mix have not been able to develop.

However, under rapidly changing socioeconomic conditions, the "wheel of retailing" could not be halted for long even by an elaborate network of legal restraints. Since the traditional retailers did not respond sufficiently to the changes in consumer income, location, education, leisure, and both social and physical mobility, various forms of closed-door discounting and "gray" marketing developed. Supported by the efforts of the FCA and the EEC Commission to rescind price maintenance agreements,[13] closed-door discount operations could switch to open discounting. This is the history of the consumer markets, which started another evolutionary cycle in retailing around 1966, to equal within three years the selling area of the four dominating department store concerns.[14]

This has also paved the way for other modern shopping facilities like large planned shopping centers.

Thus, in the long run seldom contemplated by lawmakers, a public policy favoring the status quo has proved ineffective. However, in considering the interdependence between the short-run and long-run impacts of public policy, the mainly restrictive legislation did accomplish something, in the sense of forcing a vigorous reaction. The longer innovators were hindered from moving to new locations, from instituting efficiencies in distribution, and from passing on (part of) the savings to consumers, the more countervailing forces gained momentum. The longer consumers were deprived of possibilities to shop more cheaply, by saving time, from larger assortments, more leisurely and casually and at easily accessible locations, the greater the buildup of the demand for an adequate system of retail distribution. When the dam finally broke, the breakthrough may well have been more vigorous than would have been the case under legislation less hostile to modernization of the retailing system.

Forces

Such a period of innovation in retailing implies the relaxation or (partial) rendering obsolete of major competitive restraints, after they had been gradually undermined by powerful new trends in distribution. It is particularly under these conditions that public policy toward retailing appears not as a monolithic phenomenon but rather as the result of many conflicting interests. Promoted by the various trade associations, the lobby of small business, manufacturers, and other pressure groups, these special interests underwent numerous modifications in the complexities and subtleties of the policymaking process. The final transformation into existing legislation was conditioned by various governmental institutions with goals of their own. Eventually, the application of given laws depended, within limits, on the basic philosophy of the bodies that enforced them, and of the courts that ruled over infractions.

Developments in distribution have changed the position of these parties over the last twenty years. The latest trends in retailing and pending legislation would indicate that future public policy will be determined to an even higher degree by the interactions between the parties participating in the policymaking process and the retailing system itself, as well as by the feedback between "designers" and "subjects."

The *Central Association of German Retailers,* representing the entire retail trade, has played a very active role in the policymaking process. It has largely pursued a determined and energetic policy rather than a militant radicalism and has been primarily small-business-oriented. Today, the Association is on a course of "mild" restraints on competition instead of asking for rigorous state protection for retailers regardless of their qualification. Besides operating very intelligently within the Association, large retailers maintain excellent relations with the public authorities. This direct representation of their interests is through the "Work Group of Medium-Sized and Large Retailers" (BAG),[15] run by an extremely clever and versatile management.

As a consequence of the consumer market boom, there has been a fundamental readjustment of the power groups in retailing. The rivalry is no longer simply between large and small but also between conventional retailers and the price-aggressive newcomers. The department stores—previously the bogeyman in retailing—are now fully a recognized integral part of the classic retail system and enjoy a completely new political freedom of movement.

The influence of *manufacturers* upon the legislative process must not be underestimated, particularly with regard to the issues of resale price maintenance, rebate cartels, exclusive dealerships, and controlled sales agreements. However, developments in the market have led to a considerable erosion of restraints that suppliers had been able to secure in earlier years.

The attitude of the *federal government* has been largely favorable to competition and the interests of the consumer even though some earlier tendencies have remained evident: (1) the authorities give in to powerful pressure groups such as small business whose problems cannot really be solved through protectionism; and (2) some of their data and assumptions are incorrect, as when restraints on the expansion of department stores turned out to be in the interest of the latter who acquired a quasi-monopoly position thereby. Besides, in accordance with the two basic principles of the Social Market Economy, concessions in the form of competitive restraints have had to be made to less competition-minded interest groups in industry and trade, although in many instances the authorities were able to prevent more severe ones. In particular, the Federal Ministry of the Economy has followed an elastic policy of skillfully forestalling or watering-down more radical demands, and of softening up or relaxing existing restraints. For example, through discussions with the representatives of retailing, this Ministry has frequently been able to deflate restrictive demands raised by conventional merchants.

Cases in point are the attempts to arrive at more severe restrictions on entry (particularly throughout the fifties), promotions and store location (mid-sixties). Additional efforts were aiming at a general prohibition of price discrimination, retail transactions in factories or offices between employees or employer and employees (mid-sixties), or at preventing the abolition of the prohibition for consumer cooperatives to sell to non-members (in the early 1950s).

In the struggles of structuring the Cartel Act, the administration also acted as a defender of free enterprise. Where powerful pressure groups managed to have legislators include severe restraints on competition, there were successful efforts to save some freedom of action for a liberal interpretation or application of these statutes. Besides, there were provisions to guarantee a certain amount of control over these restraints by the authroities, or conditions under which administrators could lessen or rescind restrictive statutes (e.g., the "control of misuse" of price maintenance and controlled sales agreements by the FCA). When developments in the market (e.g., the widespread undercutting of fixed prices) supplied the ammunition to attack these restraints, the authorities could and did eagerly make use of these "built-in" possibilities to abolish them.

As another case in point, the federal government has tried repeatedly to abolish resale price maintenance. When efforts to achieve this failed again in 1968 (as in 1962 and 1965) due to the opposition of the manufacturers' and small retailers' lobbies, the Ministry of the Economy advised the FCA to be particularly severe on misuse of price-maintenance pacts. In the same way, i.e., "by administrative practice," the Ministry tried to implement other improvements of the Cartel Act contained in an amendment that failed to win parliamentary support in 1968.

The Federal Cartel Authority (FCA) works under the supervision of the Ministry of the Economy. Combining administrative and judiciary functions, it must act in accordance with the orders given by the Ministry, but there is close cooperation and exchanges of ideas between the two. The FCA has definitely attempted to create and maintain a climate favorable to free enterprise, the development of an efficient distribution system, and the best interests of the consumer.

In most of their recent decisions, the *courts* have shown an increasingly progressive attitude, especially compared to their previous decisions bearing on the Law Against Unfair Competition. Thus, the Federal Constitutional Court has declared unconstitutional such restrictive provisions as the proof of competence requirement for entry in retailing, the special tax levied on multi-store retailers (1965), and Section 6 of the Rebate Act prohibiting the granting of rebates by department stores and limited-price variety stores (1967). In the case of the new value-added tax, the government was, in fact, under pressure from this Court to introduce a tax system that gives all distributors an equal chance (1966). The Federal Supreme Court confirmed the legality of direct sales by wholesalers to consumers (1958) and showed a more liberal attitude with regard to comparative advertising (1968). In the case of trade practice rules, the Federal Supreme Court has been somewhat more restrictive. The intensified FCA-control of price fixing mentioned above is based on decisions handed down by the Federal Supreme Court that has set more restrictive conditions on legal price maintenance agreements.

This new initiative concerning fixed prices has been encouraged by the *EEC Commission,* which has held that prohibition of re-exports is illegal [Section 85 (I) of the Rome Treaty]. The same holds true for controlled sales agreements determined to support re-export prohibitions. Without such prohibitions, price maintenance systems cannot be rigidly enforced and are therefore void. Generally speaking, the European Economic Community has been influential in liberalizing regulations. The EEC Commission has already announced that some of the extremely restrictive German regulations on competition will not be adopted as a guide for future EEC legislation. Thus, resale price maintenance is among the prospective victims of further EEC integration.

In harmony with the EEC policy on competition, the concept of "workable" competition is being substituted for that of "pure" competition in a pending amendment to the Cartel Act. As a consequence, the proposed Section 5b will allow a close cooperation of small- and medium-size enterprises, in order to enable them to compete more successfully with their larger competitors. The authorities also plan to keep a close eye on anti-competitive mergers and acquisitions. In the future, mergers between enterprises of more than DM 1 billion annual sales will have to be recorded with the FCA, and will be permitted by the Ministry of Economy only under specific conditions (at present there are about ten retail enterprises with such sales).

These developments and the basic trends in retailing can be expected to improve the power of the authorities to reduce restraints on competition in retailing. As the number of small retailers declines, the middle classes will become a less important social and political issue. The innovators (particularly consumer markets) will increasingly make demands on traditional retailers for a competitive response. Thus, when department stores get more involved in suburban retailing, their interest in restrictive store hours or zoning regulations will probably decrease.

Besides, the *unions* increasingly recognize the interest of their members as consumers. Whereas the unions catering to individual trades (such as the union of employees in distribution, banking, and transportation) still oppose a liberalization in specific areas (e.g., store hours), the overall policy of the influential Federation of German Labor Unions is pro-competition. Thus the unions immediately asked for new attempts to abolish resale price maintenance when the last efforts by the government failed. Finally, the influence of the *consumer,* both organized and as an individual, is increasing in times of a rising consumerism. In this climate, it will be easier for the government and the FCA to foster competition in distribution even more, for the sake of a retailing system of greater diversity and efficiency.

March 1972

Notes

1.   The term "middle classes" comes closer to the German *Mittelstand* to which small- and medium-size retailers usually belong. This expression applies to the "independents" carrying the full risk of personally run businesses, with no or rather limited access to the capital market. Due to their large number (70 percent of retail firms), small businessmen yield considerable political weight.

2.   Today, state and local jurisdiction is of very little importance. Practically all important laws and other statutes are "federal," i.e., valid throughout the Federal Republic of Germany where the various states (Laender) enjoy a good deal of autonomy in the regulation, taxation, and promotion of economic activities. The highest-level courts are also "federal." The Federal Constitutional Court *(Bundesverfassungsgericht)* is dealing with all matters of constitutional relevance, while the Federal Supreme Court *(Bundesgerichtshof)* is the last instance for all other decisions.

3.   The value of the German mark was $0.250 in 1961, $0.273 in 1969, and $0.312 in 1972.

4.   Law Against Restraints of Competition (usually called "Cartel Act").

5.   Rebate cartels are primarily found in trade sectors where merchandise is sold on the basis of manufacturers' list prices and contain agreements between suppliers to grant uniform functional, quantity or functional rebates to their customers.

6.   The literal translation "turnover tax" for the German *"Umsatzsteuer"*

would indicate more clearly that this tax applied to transactions at all levels rather than to purely retail sales.

7. The "consumer market" name was coined for the retail establishments representing the second discount wave in Germany that began to swell in 1967. Thus it stands not for a specific store type but rather for a wide range of shopping facilities operating more or less on a discount basis with food discounters of approximately 4,000 square feet as the smallest units, and self-service department stores of 200,000-250,000 square feet as the largest consumer markets. The latter, selling food, general merchandise, gasoline, and a variety of services, frequently incorporate characteristics of regional shopping centers, and operate under names like XY Center or YZ Self-Service Department Store rather than *Verbrauchermarkt* (consumer market).

8. That agency agreements of franchising contracts are not subject to Section 18 is a view widely held by legal writers but not shared by the FCA.

9. In a building of 1,000 square meters, the maximum total floor area for a building with four floors or more may not exceed 2,000 square meters.

10. According to accepted legal practice, the innate morality of the average sensible and decent tradesman and of the general public is decisive.

11. According to a 1970 survey of the Ifo-Institute, suggested prices are actually observed by about 75 percent of retailers.

12. Total retail sales rose from DM 40.1 billion in 1952 to DM 91.5 billion in 1961, and to DM 184.5 billion in 1970.

13. According to a 1970 survey of the Ifo-Institute, between 1961 and 1969 the percentage (of total retail sales) of price-fixed items declined from 30 to 17 percent.

14. By the end of 1970, in less than four years, the selling area of consumer markets exceeded 25 million square feet.

15. Members of the BAG are department stores, limited-price variety stores, and large specialty stores (particularly textile stores) with more than DM 2 million annual sales.

Bibliography

Batzer, Erich; Greipl, E.; Laumer, H.; Meyerhoefer, W. *Marktstrukturen und Wettbewerbsverhaeltnisse im Einzelhandel.* Schriftenreihe Struktur und Wachstum, Reihe Absatzwirtschaft, Vol. III. Edited by Ifo-Institut fuer Wirtschaftsforschung. Berlin-Muenchen: Duncker und Humblot, 1971.

Britsch, Walter. "Wirtschafts und Strukturpolitik — Vorstellungen des Bundeswirtschaftsministeriums/Absatwirtschaftliche Gesichtspunkte." *Strukturwandel im Einzelhandel.* Edited by Hauptgemeinschaft des Deutschen Einzelhandels. Koeln: Betriebswirtschaftliche Beratungsstelle fuer den Einzelhandel, 1970.

Bundeskartellamt, ed. *Zehn Jahre Bundeskartellamt — Beitraege zu Fragen und*

Entwicklungen auf dem Gebiet des Kartellrechts. Koeln-Berlin-Bonn-Muenchen: Carl Heymanns Verlag, 1968.

Hauptgemeinschaft des Deutschen Einzelhandels. *23. Arbeitsbericht.* Koeln: Hauptgemeinschaft des Deutschen Einzelhandels, 1971.

Klein-Blenkers, Fritz. *Die Oekonomisierung der Distribution.* Schriften zur Handelsforschung, Vol. XXVII. Koeln-Opladen: Wesdeutscher Verlag, 1964.

Marzen, Walter. *Wettbewerb und Verbraucherpolitik.* Saarbruecken: Malstatt-Burbacher Handelsdruckerei, 1964.

Mueller, Heinz, and Giessler, Peter. *Kommentar zum Gesetz gegen Wettbewerbsbeschraenkungen (Kartellgesetz).* Frankfurt/Main: Lorch-Verlag, 1967.

Schueller, Alfred. "Vermachtungserscheinungen im tertiaeren Sektor." *ORDO, Jahrbuch fuer die Ordnung von Wirtschaft und Gesellschaft.* Vol. XIX, 1968.

Soldner, Helmut. *Die City als Einkaufszentrum im Wandel von Wirtschaft und Gesellschaft.* Betriebswirtschaftliche Schriften, Vol. XXVII. Berlin: Duncker und Humblot, 1968.

Wein, Josef. *Die Verbandsbildung im Einzelhandel.* Untersuchungen ueber Gruppen und Verbaende, Vol. VIII. Berlin: Duncker und Humblot, 1968.

Woll, Artur. *Der Wettbewerb im Einzelhandel.* Quaestiones Oeconomicae, Vol. II. Berlin: Duncker und Humblot, 1964.

Periodicals

Blick durch die Wirtschaft

Frankfurter Allgemeine Zeitung

Handelsblatt

Lebensmittel Zeitung

Mitteilungen der Forschungsstelle fuer den Handel

moderner markt

verbrauchermarkt information

Wettbewerb in Recht und Praxis

Wirtschaft und Wettbewerb

23 Conclusions

J. J. BODDEWYN AND STANLEY C. HOLLANDER

This final chapter attempts to generalize about the analyses contained in this volume, but these generalizations are subject to several caveats.

First, the lesser developed third-world countries are under-represented in the previous chapters, which tend to emphasize Europe and North America. This certainly limits the scope of the general comments that follow.

Second, the necessarily condensed character of the chapters probably makes certain complex aspects of policy look simpler or more varied than they really are.

Finally, the authors of this concluding section have their own prejudices and limited vision that make them see (and want to see) certain things, and leave them blind to other matters of similar or even greater importance. Still, an attempt was made to be as objective as possible in outlining the major trends in the development and application of public policies toward retailing.

Is There a Policy At All?

The introduction to this volume started by pointing to a paradoxical situation. Few, if any, countries have *a* public policy toward retailing, de facto or de jure, but they usually have a *set* of policies that deal with retailing more or less (mainly less) explicitly, coherently, and consistently. How can this situation be explained?

Laissez-faire as Policy

The simplest explanation would be to say that there is an underlying policy, namely laissez-faire. Most of the chapters included in this volume deal with more or less capitalistic systems, and laissez-faire policies toward retailing would be consonant with the fundamental philosophical orientation of such systems. But two factors indicate that it is overly simplistic to ascribe the lack of a retail policy to nothing more than a belief in relatively unfettered free enterprise.

First, most of the countries described herein have tended to intervene in other sectors, such as agriculture and even manufacturing, to a greater extent than in retail distribution. Laissez-faire, of course, is never applied in a pure and unadulterated fashion, but the departures have been more striking in the non-retailing sectors.

Second, even the fully planned economies usually do not have a policy toward retailing. For that matter, the various plans increasingly prepared all over the world appear to pay relatively little attention to domestic commerce in general and to retailing in particular. The increasing importance of the "tertiary" (non-agricultural and non-industrial) sector is likely to alter this situation, but again retailing may be somewhat ignored in the process of planning for the entire tertiary sector. Obviously, then, factors other than laissez-faire must be taken into consideration in explaining why there is little in the way of general public policy toward retailing.

Benevolent and Malevolent Neglect

Other priorities have certainly played a role in leaving retailing without an overall policy as the policymaker's first love seems to have been production and the related infrastructures. This infatuation has been variously explained but everywhere observed.

Galbraith has drawn attention to the paramount position of production in the U.S. economy on account of full employment goals and of the American obsession with work and goods. In Communist countries, it has been justified by the need to provide the new leaders with the political support of the new industrial class, as well as by the necessity to become strong in an environment of hostile and economically advanced capitalist nations. Developing countries, on their part, tend to equate growth and development with industry if only to reduce their neocolonialist dependence on trade with foreign countries.

This view of the relatively greater importance of production is largely shared by technocrats everywhere. They tend to visualize exchange as intermediate between high-priority production and lesser-priority consumption, as the ducts or channels through which productive outputs pass, with particular emphasis being put on the physical and rational facets of distribution (transporting, storing, displaying, informing, etc.). They also believe that many social and economic problems can be alleviated through larger industrial outputs, and that the rate of progress in industry largely determines the possible rate of transition away from agriculture, and strongly affects the possibilities of raising the efficiency of the commercial sector through increases in the volume handled by each outlet.

There is even a tendency in highly centralized economies of the Russian type and in countries going "Socialist" not to recognize retailing (or commerce for that matter) as a separate sector but to view it simply as a function that either manufacturers and consumers can assume (the Russian and Tunisian chapters are illuminating in this respect).

In these perspectives, retailing receives only marginal or even negative attention, since it is either believed that taking care of production and/or of the consumer will automatically "shape-up" retailing, or that the latter should even be made to minimize its use of resources (labor, capital, technology, land) needed elsewhere.

In other countries and regions (Latin America is a good example), public interest centers on the fate of small business in general rather than on commerce or retailing per se. In such a case again, retailing is treated marginally in the context of something else.

This phase of neglect—benevolent or malevolent—is being modified, however, as new policies toward retailing are beginning to emerge.

Emerging Policies Toward Retailing

A variety of factors internal and external to retailing have been stimulating the emergence of a public policy toward that sector, even though the process has been grudging, slow, and piecemeal.

External Factors

Economic Factors. Governments are paying greater attention to retailing because it is an important and growing economic sector in terms of value added, as well as a very substantial and apparently increasing source of employment. Moreover, in many countries, it has been plagued with relatively low rates of productivity increase and with faster-growing labor costs. Although retailers' pricing practices may sometimes dampen the short-run impact of factor cost fluctuations on the final price-indices, those fluctuations are ultimately, and sometimes very quickly, reflected in retail prices. These considerations help explain governmental interest in retailing during an era very much concerned with economic growth as well as price stability.

Furthermore, there is a growing recognition that distribution is not a simple process that demands little in the way of talent and capital. Thus, because retailing is acquiring some priority, and because the necessary change in mentalities, structures, and practices may be considered too slow or too small in coming on their own, governments feel increasingly inclined to step in through regulation, promotion, state enterprises, removal of barriers to competition, etc.

The secular and cyclical stages of the economy have, however, been the most potent economic forces determining public policy toward retailing. As discussed subsequently in this chapter, affluent nations have tended to act differently than depressed ones, and nations at a high stage of economic development differently from less developed ones.

Moral Factors. Retailing is closely related to consumption, an activity of interest to government not only because of consumption's impact on the size of investment in growth-conscious economies, but also because "private wants" are often seen as morally competing against "public needs." The "quality of life" is being stressed more and more. This encourages government efforts to control private expenditures in favor of collective ones, to educate the consuming public against sales persuasion, and to protect the consumer against fraud, deception, monopoly power, and even his own desires. Moral considerations also enter into store-opening and working-hours regulations, into controls over the distribution of some commodities (notably alcoholic beverages), into credit-sales legislation, and into other matters. Collective moral pressures are evident in recent reactions against the "consumption society" and certain products such as plastics and throw-away bottles (see the Swedish chapter).

Social Factors. Retailing matters for social reasons too as, historically, it has provided an important avenue for social mobility in many countries. Governments here are interested in avoiding social conflict among various classes of retailers, and with other segments of the population such as farmers, manufacturers, and consumers. They also want sometimes to protect the small independent businessman's way of life in a world increasingly polarized between "big business" and "big labor." Finally, retailing often fits into welfare schemes as when it is used to employ deserving or difficult-to-absorb groups such as immigrants (see the Israeli chapter), veterans, and handicapped people (newspaper stands, tobacco stores, etc.). Concerns about the cost of retailing for certain underprivileged groups (e.g., poor people) are also increasing (see the United States chapter).

This desire on the part of the authorities parallels the more general reversal of the nineteenth-century trend from "status to contract." Contemporary man increasingly wants to protect his standing in society, and to avoid the social uncertainties inherent in the capitalistic system. With employees, farmers, and even large employers increasingly guaranteed a living, independent businessmen also want some cushioning against the impact of continuous economic change. One readily recognizes here the resulting "protection of competitors rather than of competition."

Physical Factors. Another element is the spread of urbanization and suburbanization. The first introduces many rural people to a market economy from whose excesses they must be protected after leaving communities resting much more on self-sufficiency, reciprocity, and redistribution.[1] Suburbanization, on the other hand, threatens downtown shopping areas and raises questions about land use, thus leading to greater physical planning of retail facilities (see the Dutch chapter). Conversely, the disappearance of many neighborhood stores raises problems about serving poor and handicapped people (see the Swedish chapter).

In another vein, environmental control measures such as restrictions on plastics and non-returnable containers are becoming an important aspect of public policy toward retailing.

Political Factors. The political weight of the "middle classes" to which tradesmen usually belong in capitalistic nations has led them to look to their governments for political solutions to some of their socioeconomic problems. Thus, the retailers themselves often resort to political action for resolution of their internal conflicts and their struggles with suppliers and customers (see the Belgian chapter).

Although the atomistic nature of trade and the varying degrees of cohesiveness found among retailers may either enhance or diminish the effectiveness of such action, retailer-induced legislation is a fact of economic life in many parts of the world. Governments have often listened to other interest groups as well in this connection, since the retailer's position as middleman leaves him vulnerable to consumers' and suppliers' conflicting demands. Besides, the inherent conspicuousness of retailing makes it an arena for the demands of many other advocates such as sabbatarians and ethnocentric nationalists.

The exclusion of foreign influence is a major socio-policitcal issue in those developing countries where alien minorities (Indian, Middle-Eastern, Chinese, etc.) or colonial powers have dominated the field (see the Thailand and Uganda chapters).

More generally, there is some built-in mechanism in government intervention whereby once regulation starts somewhere in the economic system, it has to be progressively expanded to the rest in order to plug various loopholes. Consequently, retailing is getting more attention because, in a way, its turn has come.

International Influences. Public attention to retailing also spreads because of international influence and the "demonstration effect." Foreign examples reveal new problem areas, suggest possible solutions, and help justify new measures since precedents have been created. Here some countries serve as reference points for others—for example, Great Britain for Australia, France for Belgium, and the U.S.S.R. for satellite countries. Economic integration in the context of common markets and free-trade zones also makes for more measures in the process of harmonizing laws and regulations. Although not covered very much in this volume, the growth of international institutions (e.g., the OECD, FAO, WHO) and the spread of international agreements (e.g., on trademarks) also contribute to greater foreign influence (see the Belgian and Swedish chapters).

More generally, public policy spreads because of the growing international economic interdependence of nations that often discover the same problems at the same time (e.g., the large increase of modern consumer credit in the post-World War II period) or want to avoid catching somebody else's problems. A good example is Belgium's adoption of licensing measures in order to prevent Dutchmen from selling freely in other Benelux countries, since the Netherlands had stricter requirements for starting a retail business. Yet, there are lags, gaps, and contradictions in this process as situations are never completely alike.

Internal Factors

The major retailing development conductive to the growth of public policy has certainly been the continuous appearance of new, aggressive forms of retailing and the concomitant growth of intertype competition. "New" has often meant "large," thus contributing to the socio-political tensions and responses mentioned earlier. However, the new competition has also taken place between full-time and part-time (marginal) retailers, between sedentary and itinerant traders (including, in a way, mail-order houses and automatic vendors), and between traditional and innovative merchants. Foreign retailers have also challenged domestic ones, adding a "foreign" vs. "domestic" dimension to the rivalry. Each time, vested rights have been threatened, leading to charges of unfair competitive practices or advantages of one kind or another, and to demands (often successful) for regulatory restrictions or compensating public assistance.

Where innovation and competition have not been present, the "laggardness" of the retailing system has increasingly been challenged by the authorities who have seen it fit to develop parallel state or cooperative networks, or to displace certain groups such as foreign merchants (see the Tunisian chapter).

The growth of large-scale retailing has also introduced "countervailing power" in the marketing system, thereby challenging the position of manufacturers and wholesalers, with the government again either supporting such a challenge or trying to check it. More recently, the authorities have definitely sided with the consumers who remain by and large the only unorganized group in the marketing channel.

Objectives

Governments everywhere are in the process of expliciting goals instead of letting the market system set them implicitly. In the socioeconomic field, these goals center on: (1) full employment; (2) price stability; (3) expansion of production; (4) improvement in the allocation of the factors of production; (5) improvement in the distribution of income and wealth; (6) protection of certain regions, industries, and social groups; (7) improvement in the pattern of private consumption; (8) reduction of working hours and days; (9) improvement in the balance of payments; (10) satisfaction of collective needs (education, defense, proper land-use, ecology, infrastructure development, etc.); (11) security of supply; and (12) improvement in the size and structure of the population.[2] Such socioeconomic goals are themselves linked to other political and cultural objectives such as protecting (and possibly spreading) the nation's sovereignty, ideology, and way of life.

The earlier discussion of the various factors making for the emergence of public policies made it clear that retailing is increasingly viewed—both positively and negatively—in the context of these objectives. In particular, four goals have received special attention in policies toward retailing: (1) protecting smaller retailers; (2) achieving price stability in retailing; (3) improving the efficiency of retailing; and (4) insuring consumer protection. A fifth goal, protecting the environment, is now emerging in a number of countries.

Protecting Small Retailers. This goal appears and reappears in most chapters and the various periods they cover, outside of the Communist countries where at best small retailers are tolerated. Such a goal centers on achieving "social equilibrium" in order to: (1) integrate various social strata (such as the commercial middle class) into society, and avoid conflict among them; (2) provide opportunities to move up in the social order to various lower-lever groups such as farmers, craftsmen, and employees; (3) preserve certain values and ways of life considered desirable in a pluralistic society; (4) create and maintain a reservoir of entrepreneurial talent for later stages of economic development and for other sectors; and, last but not least, (5) retain and reward an important political group.

In developed countries, the drive for protection has been strongest during periods of depression such as the 1930s in Europe and North America, when the retailing middle classes felt threatened and saw no avenues of escape into other employment. On the other hand, the pressure for such protection diminishes during periods of business expansion and manpower shortages: the post-World War II relaxation of trade-restrictive legislation in Western Europe and North America exemplifies this phenomenon. To some extent, the desire for "nativization" of retail trade in many of the developing countries is another illustration of efforts to protect small traders, but it flows from other motivations, primarily ethnic and nationalistic, as well.

To protect small tradesmen, governments have: (1) restricted the expansion of large and marginal stores (e.g., through discriminatory taxes, limited opening hours, and anti-price-discrimination legislation); and (2) helped smaller stores survive and/or expand (for instance, through educational programs, low-cost credit, and the encouragement of voluntary chains). In the new countries of Africa and Asia, this protection has often taken the form of expelling foreign retail minorities that have traditionally dominated the field.

Improving Retailing's Efficiency. As we saw before, retailing is often pushed toward greater efficiency in order to remove obstacles to the growth of other sectors such as agriculture and manufacturing. Still, it is also increasingly being considered as a sector whose own efficiency is worthy of special attention on account of the fast-rising cost of distribution. In the words used in the Tunisian chapter, the goal thus becomes "to transform commerce into an industry, while at the same time an industry can be born out of commerce" as resources are released for use elsewhere. Communist countries have been particularly anxious to increase the efficiency of retailing through input minimization rather than output maximization even though they are not always willing to make the investments necessary to do it intelligently (see the Russian and Polish chapters).

Governments use one or both of the following approaches: (1) they encourage new, more efficient and competitive retail forms, often of a larger size; but also (2) they raise the productivity of existing organizations through better people, methods, and structures (e.g., better qualified employees and owner-managers, self-service, voluntary chains). Governments are particularly and increasingly willing to bear the expenses involved in the second approach since the latter can be fairly readily reconciled with the goal of protecting small retailers. Hence, follows the growth of subsidized credit and educational programs, licensure, and the encouragement of associational endeavors.

Stabilizing Retail Prices. Price stabilization objectives vary in importance in direct relationship to the severity of economic changes. This objective normally becomes paramount when prices are unusually depressed or unusually inflated. Inflation has long been rampant in underdeveloped countries, but it is a recurrent problem in more advanced economies although Communist countries have been much better able to prevent it through their comprehensive management of the economy. Price controls are thus becoming more prevalent, although competition is also being encouraged to acheive price stability (witness the decreasing public support of resale price maintenance and other forms of collusion).

Consumer Protection. Commercial codes generally include provisions against fraud and deception, but an increasing demand is being voiced for expanded consumer protection. In some instances, public policy has singled out certain types of retailers as being particularly prone to untoward practices—at least this is often the avowed rationale for measures aimed at auctions, itinerant vendors, house-to-house canvassers, and other marginal dealers. More often, however, consumeristic measures are directed against practices considered inimical to consumer welfare. Hence the development of regulations concerned with labeling, weights and measures, consumer credit, price posting, "truth in advertising," liquidations, special sales, etc. In the light of current experience, it is tempting to associate such consumer protection with prosperity, since consumeristic issues seem to come to the fore when prosperity-induced expectations outrun the benefits that the system actually delivers.

Protecting the Environment. The ecological-environmental considerations that are just beginning to influence retailing regulation (land-use planning, waste disposal rules, product limitations, etc.) in the more prosperous countries are, at least so far, clearly correlated with affluence. On the other hand, the less developed countries have generally felt that ecological problems are primarily artifacts of overabundance and should rank low on the scale of national priorities.

Instruments and Measures

One witnesses major changes not only in the nature and number of instruments and measures, but also in the very principle of using them in the first place.

From Contract to Regulation and Status. Law in the nineteenth century was mainly concerned with protecting the freedom of individual wills as expressed in contracts and as interpreted in the light of customs. Hence, the bulk of litigations were private and centered on breaches of contracts and on harm done to other persons. This private and contractual emphasis has been progressively superseded by imperative rules that limit the wills of individuals and do even upset business customs.

Such an emphasis started generally with various measures that *forbade* fraudulent and unhealthy practices, and obliged the guilty party to repair or compensate for the harm done. Now, the tendency is toward *preventing* such harm by requiring the advance testing of products and validation of advertising claims; and toward *extending control beyond the transaction* (e.g., by allowing the consumer to change his mind) *and over the life of the product* in such matters as warranties.

One observes also a certain historic tendency to restrict the practice of retailing to certain people and groups, and to recognize certain rights to particular categories, instead of letting individuals or parties decide freely. Of course, minors, criminals, bankrupts, mental incompetents, and even women have usually been restricted; while natives, invalids, and veterans have often received preferential access to certain occupations. Licensure, where it exists, stresses the right "inputs" (such as minimum education, experience, credit and equipment, but also one's parents' occupation) rather than "output." While licensure is not spreading, special credit assistance (e.g., low-interest loans) is often limited to certain types of retailers considered worthy of protection or promotion.

Such measures affect particularly entry and growth, but also process and structure as the law now tends to favor buyers (particularly the ultimate customers) over sellers, tenants over landlords, licensees over licensors, and debtors over creditors. The trends are both toward protecting vested rights, and those of the party considered weaker. There is also a tendency toward defining certain practices as "unfair" to the interest of *particular* categories of suppliers, competitors, and customers, rather than focusing on a broader concern for the *general* interest.

Greater Variety and Pervasiveness. Everywhere, governmental powers to *directly* regulate, hamper, and/or promote retailing have increased. Besides, more general tools have also affected retailing *indirectly* through monetary, fiscal, commercial (international), regional, industrial, agricultural, environmental, and social policies—to mention the major ones.

Governments no longer limit themselves to setting the *general rules* of the game, but have developed many measures of control over most marketing activities—from relations with suppliers, landlords, and licensors to pricing, product, and promotion practices. Land-use planning promises to further these instruments. While control is associated with prohibitions and restrictions, governments are also increasingly in a position to promote a certain sector (or part of it) and to encourage certain practices through various *monetary* measures where the granting of cheaper (or more abundant) credit figures prominently, although its refusal or withdrawal has also been used to affect retailing (e.g., in the matter of consumer credit). Besides, *fiscal* measures have been used against itinerant traders and chain stores; while the tax-on-value-added system is beginning to have some *structural* effect on retailing. Furthermore, *public expenditures* on commercial education, research, and statistics, and on the administration of these programs, are also more evident. Finally, there are now more *public and semi-public institutions* to group and represent retailers.

Such instruments have been translated into numerous measures of regulation, promotion, intervention, suasion, consultation, self-regulation, and contractual agreements with private parties. However, lack of action, threats of regulation, and delays in making or applying policy have also been used to further government objectives.

This growing pervasiveness of regulation and institutionalization is almost a perfect illustration of the principle that all the facets of marketing (price, product, promotion, and place-time) are interrelated and can be substituted for one another. Similarly, public policy has to progressively blanket all retailing operations because otherwise an alternative approach can be used around the regulation found bothersome. Installment-credit legislation illustrates this point because, to be effective, it has to deal with interest rates (price), goods and services covered (product), truth-in-lending (promotion), and—in some countries—the registration and/or limitation of lenders (place).

Yet, it would be erroneous to visualize the trend as being only away from laissez-faire and toward state interventionism—all the way to the Russian type. Governments are also delegating some regulatory powers to professional associations, chambers of commerce, and businessmen's tribunals considered better equipped to determine what is "fair" and "unfair." This trend reveals the growing complexity of economic life that sets limits to what the state can achieve. It also demonstrates the increasing demand for participation in the making and application of policies. Corporativist tendencies are thus more evident nowadays—particularly outside of the United States and the socialist countries. Self-resolution of conflicts by retailing actors among themselves and/or with other groups are also present although the chapters in this volume did not shed too much light on the topic.[3]

Besides, programs of consumer education and small-business credit reveal that state intervention is not exclusively couched in restrictive terms. Moreover, regulation helps retailing when it clarifies the status of certain types and practices (e.g., supermarkets in Brazil and franchising in Belgium) in statutory-law countries where these types and practices would otherwise remain unused for lack of clear legal standing.

Finally, it would be erroneous to visualize public policy as progressively engulfing the retailing process. After all, some laws and regulations are occasionally removed from the books; others become obsolete; and a third group is seldom or never enforced. Moreover some restrictions are only imposed temporarily to slow down the process of economic change and to allow a better balance among retail types so that the weaker party can again engage in competition.

Greater Flexibility and Discretion. The growth of regulation can easily be interpreted as meaning greater rigidity in public policy. However, this trend is not as obvious as it may appear. For one thing, measures get changed and adapted as when "weekly closing" replaces "Sunday closing." Besides, the authorities are aware of the growing need for flexibility on account of the constancy of change in retailing. Moreover, policy now extends its reach to more complex problems (e.g., land-use planning) without any easy or permanent solution in sight. This situation demands more flexible legislation that can be applied through decrees according to the current situation and without resorting to the lengthier legislative process.

This development leads to more discretionary powers for the executive and judiciary bodies who apply laws through decrees and court decisions but also through administrative rulings and "bargained solutions" with private firms or trade associations. The outcome is of course much more indeterminate, as it depends on the judgment and respective powers of the parties—not to mention venality. The fact that obtaining permission for rezoning an area for commercial purposes, for a retail sign, or for a low-interest loan is not a function of clear-cut rules only, certainly introduces a greater flavor of "a government of men rather than a government of law," but change and complexity seem to dictate this course which can and should be guarded with more appeal procedures.

Flexibility is also fostered by the pervasiveness of regulation as governments now dispose of many powers that can be alternatively used to achieve a certain purpose. For example, if a country lacks authority to penalize a retailer who short-weighs his customers, its regulators may be able to catch him for over-pricing his merchandise.

Forces

Economic Interest Groups. While most chapters did not address themselves directly or consistently to this topic, one can see in the background various interest groups battling for government support against actual and potential competitors, and against those with more power. Hence, horizontal, vertical, and intertype competitions have their rough counterparts in the political arena as small stores battle large ones, as retailers face wholesalers and manufacturers, as domestic traders try to expel or keep out foreign ones, as traditional stores try to fend off innovators, as established and sedentary merchants fight marginal ones, and so on.

Retailers, of various stripes, however, remain largely divided among themselves, and as such do not carry much weight against better organized groups such as farmers, manufacturers, and labor unions when such issues as price controls, land-use planning, credit, and overall economic and social planning are being debated and resolved. This very frustration, as well as the increasing recognition that governments wield a lot of regulatory power and dispense many benefits, is bringing about a slow build-up of collective political action.

Until now, consumers have not been very well organized either, but the consumer movement or at least a pro-consumer ideology are becoming more important, and retailing will thus increasingly face another powerful claimant and influencer of public policy. While the aims of the consumer movement are most praiseworthy, they may result in too much emphasis on the regulation of retailing rather than on its promotion.

The Pull of Ideologies. However, the contest for government support and favorable policies does not reflect only economic interests. There are also various ideologies at stake, as when small retailers defend their type of enterprise. They see themselves as bearers of certain values such as independence (personal and national), creativity, individualism, and responsibility in a world grown organized, mechanized, and anonymous; and they view commerce and the middle classes to which they belong as a channel for achieving social mobility in stratified societies, and as a political buffer group (together with other members of the middle classes) between "capital" and "labor." The consumers' ambivalent attitude toward large stores reflects in part the attraction of this ideology which clashes with that of economic efficiency and progress, and prevents them from lining up squarely with one group or another.

Another ideology is that of cooperation that many find appealing because it promises greater social and economic solidarity, and offers a substitute to competition and regulation as a way of organizing economic and social life. However, the consumer cooperative movement is weak in most countries or has become a caricature of its ideal. It is now controlled by autonomous cliques or bureaucracies rather than by consumers. In some instances, it has been imposed by government as a needed countervailing economic force or as the embodiment of "socialist" principles.

In contrast, cooperation among retailers is growing in various legal (e.g., voluntary chains, mutual-credit unions) and illegal (e.g., explicit or implicit collusion) forms. Governments usually support and encourage this movement that is becoming a force of its own.

Besides, as their planning and regulations tasks increase, and as they come to recognize the importance of the retailing sector or function, governments are encouraging the representation of interest groups through professional associations and the creation of consultative and self-regulatory bodies—either with voluntary or compulsory membership.

Other Forces. One should observe that retailers of all sizes have been quite ingenious in circumventing many laws—whether legally through loopholes or illegally for lack of enough government inspectors. This in itself represents a "force", too—oftentimes the only form of power available to marginal retailers (e.g., peddlers) who have been weak in the political arena.

In another vein, foreign influence is often noticeable all the way from the imitation of foreign initiatives, or the imposition of certain philosophies and practices on satellite countries, and to the impact of supranational bodies such as the European Economic Community on national regulations.

In a way, labor unions also represent a growing regulatory power, as in the more capitalistic nations they provide some de facto regulations of closing hours and staffing, and can even prevent new types of retail stores from appearing on account of the excessive labor costs they impose.

Governments, of course, are not simply the passive recipients and translators of all these external forces and demands for public action. Legislators, ministers, and bureaucrats have their own interest to consider (see the section below on public policymaking and application); public stores have been created as a "third force" besides the private and cooperative sectors; and in centralized economies, the authorities are largely sheltered from the immediate pressures of interest groups.

Effects

The results of public policy toward retailing must be related to its objectives, as outlined above. However, such an appraisal should also consider broader questions regarding the desirability of these objectives in the first place, the possibility of achieving them, as well as their unintended consequences.

The Consumer Interest. Before appraising the achievement of the objectives of retail policy, one must remember once more that the interests of the consumer have received rather scant attention although in principle consumption is the main end of economic activity. For that matter, developing and Communist nations have not been interested in encouraging consumption. This situation is not foreign to a certain elitist view of consumers as being unable to judge their own needs and organize their own consumption. A good deal of credit-sales regulation in terms of minimum down-payments and maximum number of installments reflects this view; while the high-rate taxation of "luxury" goods provides another manifestation of this elitist or puritanical view.

Things are changing now because humanitarian goals, democratic pressures, and the growth of consumer movements in the more advanced countries have led to further attention to the consumer in terms of increased protection but also of information and education. In a more positive vein, also related to the consumer's welfare, rationing has been abolished in many places; and governments are encouraging the development of convenient distribution facilities.

Protecting Small Retailers. In the short or medium run, this policy has usually succeeded in slowing down retail innovations; but in the long run, economic and other types of considerations have usually nullified or greatly limited the effectiveness of such measures. Public policy can thus only slow down or postpone the evolution of retailing. Still, several remarks are in order.

First, a public-policy answer designed to prohibit or restrict an innovation is usually slow in coming. Hence, many years do elapse before novel retail forms and practices are regulated, thereby providing some respite for the innovator.

Second, public policy is usually unable to provide for all contingencies so that loopholes subsist in the protectionist regulation, besides the fact that applying it to a very large number of retailers is bound to be sporadic and selective.

Third, while protectionist legislation tends to prove inacceptable or inoperative in the long run, the situation never ends up being exactly that of the status quo ante. Meanwhile, the competitive situation has changed, and the innovators have aged and become more "disciplined"—a factor which in fact facilitates the removal of protection.

Fourth, protection is not always for the small retailer, but does often in fact protect de jure or de facto any established retailer, whatever his size (see the West German chapter). In fact, many innovators start small, and the protectionist regulation is frequently directed against the operator (e.g., peddler, moonlighter, company store) who operates on marginal principles, with a minimum of assets and overhead burdens.

Finally, protection also has its positive side, as when governments help support the weaker party through subsidies, educational programs, cooperative action, and collective representation. Here, of course, the observation that "one can bring a horse to the water but cannot make it drink" often applies. Hence, the results of such promotional policies are slow and seldom dramatic although usually real.

Achieving Price Stability in Retailing. This is an easy task for the socialist economies since they largely control all prices. Elsewhere, price stabilization takes two forms. On the one hand, it is concerned with slowing down recurrent rates of inflation through price controls that are usually fairly effective in the short run but that cannot fundamentally alter demand and supply conditions over the long term.

On the other hand, in periods of stagnation and/or of rapid innovations, the ultimate aim of price stabilization is usually one of protecting small and traditional retailers from price competition under the guise of "fair-trade" regulations. The latter are also used to enhance the power of the weaker parties when some price-aggressive distributive group acquires too much power. These remarks indicate that price stabilization in retailing is usually a subsidiary policy subordinated to other retail-policy goals or to the general policy of price stability throughout the economy.

Protecting Consumers. In many ways, consumer protection is the oldest goal of public policy toward retailing and it finds applications both in periods of stagnation and turmoil. However, the achievement of this goal is frequently related to that of the other ones since: (1) "fair competition" is connected with protectionism; (2) dishonest practices increase in periods of intense competition; and (3) consumer protection frequently applies to prices. Recently, there has been a resurgence of public interest in the consumer's welfare that is multiplying regulatory measures, but their enforcement and effectiveness is likely to wax and wane as much as those designed to protect competitors, to increase competition, and to stabilize prices.

Improving Retailing's Efficiency. This goal tends to be much less explicit and frequent because: (1) governments see other sectors such as manufacturing and agriculture as being more important or more amenable to control and/or reform; (2) competition is generative of social conflict or simply anathema to socialist and communist ideologies; (3) there are recurrent oppositions to economic efficiency and progress as being contrary to certain human values; and (4) improving the efficiency of retailing is usually considered only in the context of sporadic efforts to combat inflation or general stagnation, rather than as a constant goal by itself. Besides, what constitutes efficiency is not easy to determine because low costs and prices represent only one benchmark that has to be complemented by considerations of convenience and service to the consumer.

While all of the chapters reveal measures that run counter to this goal, one also witnesses increasing attempts to increase competition via various antitrust regulations, and several attempts to make retailing a more specific goal as other more favored sectors have received their due, and as the importance of the growing tertiary sector becomes more evident.

However, modernizing fragmented and numerous retailers is complex and slow, even under central-planning conditions; and modernization increasingly requires social programs to retrain, relocate, or retire those "condemned to progress." Thus, the goal of furthering economic development must be constantly reconciled with that of achieving social equilibrium, and this slows down the process while raising its cost.

Protecting the Environment. It is too early to evaluate the achievement of this new goal. However, environmental protection is likely to reduce some aspects of consumer convenience and/or to increase the costs of retailing.

Intangible and Dysfunctional Results. Still, public policy can be deemed successful from some points of view even when its explicit goals are not completely achieved. Here, many of the chapters corroborate what has been called the "symbolic uses of politics" whereby *intent* and *form* matter as much as, or even more than, *content,* since public action can become an end in itself, irrespective of its effectiveness.[4] Thus, the passage and maintenance of various laws offer tangible evidence of the government's interest in certain groups, even if these laws' intrinsic shortcomings, the evasive tactics of various types of retailers, as well as fluctuating interest on the part of the state, prove frustrating.

Conversely, the threat of regulation can effectively curtail objectionable practices, as when department stores in several countries (e.g., West Germany) slowed down their expansion in fear of a worse fate. In such cases, the evaluation of public policy has to reckon with this "invisible hand" of regulation that must be distinguished, however, from those cases where the lack of regulation amounts to a policy by itself which indicates that the government favors the status quo ante or even laissez-faire.

On the dysfunctional side, one can observe that many policies work at cross-purposes, and remain more or less operative long past their period of relevance. In particular, measures designed to place a moratorium on innovation seldom result in encouraging traditional retailers to catch up with progress. Instead, protection fosters complacency and creates monopoly positions for the early innovators (see the Japanese chapter).

Furthermore, the anticipation of regulation sometimes precipitates the very behavior to be curbed, as retailers try to get under the wire; while the regulated often devise ways of circumventing the law, so that regulation generates the need for further regulation in order to catch up with new loopholes.

Finally, one should not overemphasize the role of public policy: most changes in retail actors, processes, structures, and functions have succeeded or failed in the absence of any policy addressed to them, or irrespective of it (e.g., discount houses in Brazil and trading stamps in the United States). Similarly, general policies designed to insure a reasonably prosperous and orderly economy have probably achieved more for retailing than any specific public policy toward it, since many problems take care of themselves when business is good.

Policy Making and Application

The preceeding chapters suggest additional comments about the "who, where, when, what, and how" of public policy whose "why" has already been examined.

Agents and Arenas (Who and Where). Outside of federal systems such as those of the United States, Canada, and Australia, the national level definitely predominates. Still, regions and municipalities have their waxing-and-waning roles within the national scheme in order to reflect local problems, capabilities, and powers as well as the current demands for greater participation by the parties concerned. This latter phenomenon mirrors the level of overall development—not only economic, but also political, social, and cultural—of the countries, as younger nations tend to centralize in the process of nation building, while more mature nations alternate between decentralization and recentralization according to the current situation.

In socialist regimes and parliamentary democracies, the executive government tends to dominate over the legislative, as the former initiates most laws, translates them into decrees, and applies both—sometimes through administrative tribunals or powers to negotiate out-of-court settlements. These procedures short-circuit the regular courts, but the latter do not necessarily play a minor role, especially when certain matters are left to commercial courts that apply the law in the light of business customs and interests.

The role of the courts and the legislature(s) are greater, of course, in common-law countries and where there is a stronger separation of powers among the branches of government (e.g., the United States). Even here, however, the executive government is very strong because of the tendency to give it broad powers in emergency situations that tend to endure or to reappear frequently, or in order to cope with changing conditions.

Executive power is frequently distributed over many ministries, subministries, bureaus, and even independent agencies, as far as retailing is concerned or, for that matter, the whole of trade or commerce. Other ministries such as Public Health, Labor, and Justice are also involved, besides whatever public organizations plan, organize, direct, and control the whole economy. Consequently, the diffusion, overlapping, and poor integration of policymaking and application are rather common, with a resulting lack of effectiveness.

We have already mentioned the growing if still small role of international agencies such as the European Economic Community and the Food and Agriculture Organization, and of multinational agreements in developing standards, harmonizing regulations, and eliminating barriers to trade.

Self-regulation presents dangers, but may also have value where customs, professional ethics, trade associations, certain segments of the marketing channels, and/or public opinion are strong. For that matter, several governments have definitely encouraged self-regulation on account of the complexity of certain matters whose ordering is better left to the parties closer to the problem, and because of the growing demand for "participation." The consultative function is also being developed for the same reasons. This development is both facilitating government tasks but also restricting the authorities' independence in decision making as more people have to be consulted and more interests have to be considered.

Timing (When). Public-policymaking and application is typically not a steady process. There are periods marked by great outbursts of regulation and/or enforcement that reflect parallel developments in retailing innovations and/or more general problems in the economy and society. These outbursts are often fairly simultaneous in a number of countries that share common problems. They find it easier to go ahead or harder to resist demands for public action, once a precedent has been set in another nation and some experience is available abroad.

However, there are usually lags between the appearance of a problem and its regulation, particularly as retail systems become more complex and as interest groups become better organized and balanced. Public policy here usually reacts and follows rather than anticipates or brings about deliberate changes in the system, outside of the Socialist and/or new nations that set deliberately on a new course of action such as planning, nationalization, and the expelling of foreigners. Furthermore, "temporary" regulation tends to become "permanent" as legislators are often too busy to review and amend old measures, but mainly because policy (or its absence) always creates vested interests that object to its removal.

Finally, there is some chronology in the development of regulation and policy. In the West, for example, weights and measures and peddling were first regulated, while price regulation is a much later phenomenon, and consumer protection is presently going through another round. The newer nations, on the other hand, are able to telescope this process by borrowing whole systems from former colonial rulers or from model nations of their choice.

Content (What). Some matters are harder to regulate or promote than others because of their intrinsic complexity or because the nature of the problem is not clear. Hence, the imperfect translation of an objective into a measure may result not only from external obstacles (e.g., political pressures, administrative and legislative inadequacies, personalities), but also from the nature of the problem itself.

On the other hand, a new policy becomes almost inevitable when a variety of factors happen to converge. Thus, the regulation of trading stamps (redeemable only in merchandise) and of premiums results from the many criticisms directed against them as they are (rightly or wrongly) accused of confusing consumers, of diverting attention from prices, and of taking business away from established retailers.

Process (How). Public policy is not usually a very deliberate, explicit, and rational process. Because problems are multiple, fluid, complex, and interrelated, there is rarely if ever the opportunity, ability, and willingness to handle them completely and permanently. Instead, as Lindblom and Braybrooke have pointed out,[5] a policy of sorts usually emerges from a series of measures that are repeatedly expanded and/or refined in familiar ways (e.g., *more* credit, *more* price controls), or on the basis of foreign examples. Only very grave circumstances and/or the presence of a charismatic leader permit breaks from this incremental routine in policymaking and application.

While good policymaking demands ample time and resources, lawmakers often lack time and staff to study problems; they are suspicious of other branches of government and unwilling to use the latter's advice (including that of consultative bodies); and they are prone to assume that a way can always be found to apply or amend an imperfectly drafted law.

Administrators face serious problems in enforcing vaguely worded laws, especially when lawmakers fail to provide them with the necessary resources and powers. Furthermore, conflicting public policies have to be resolved "politically" at higher levels; internal coordination among departments and bureaus cannot be taken for granted; and communication and collaboration are even harder to achieve with other ministries. Hence, the government's internal structures and processes exercise their own conditioning effects on public policy. Additionally, the lack of personnel—researchers, planners, inspectors, prosecutors, judges, etc.—sufficiently knowledgeable about business practices and convinced of the appropriateness of economic regulations can create additional difficulties in the enforcement of policy, particularly in less-developed countries.

Unfortunately, interest groups and public bodies have not yet completely learned these lessons as the temptation is strong to assume that a new law or amendment, that another outburst of enforcement activity, that moral exhortation to behave within the law, or that a few more subsidies will cure the problems considered fit for government intervention. This tendency is supported by the "symbolic" evidence of government interest that regulation provides for the demanding parties, apart from their tangible effects. Besides, economic administrators have a vested interest as well as a moral (if selective) commitment in intervention. The practical problem is thus one of improving the public policy process that remains an intellectual choice process embedded in a social process of influences, which in turn has to be understood in the context of past, present, and future events and issues.[6]

Prospects and Recommendations

Increasing attention to retailing on the part of the authorities has not yet resulted in any full-fledged public policy toward retailing, although the components have been developed either to cope with retailing itself or in the context of some other policy such as the protection of the small businessman and the consumer, or the increase of production and competition. Such direct and indirect approaches appear likely to continue until some "critical mass" is reached and a policy *sui generis* is felt needed and possible (e.g., in Belgium, France, and West Germany).

The authors of this chapter (the editors of this volume) find themselves in remarkably complete agreement concerning many of the elements of an "ideal" public policy toward retailing. They differ somewhat, however, (more in emphasis than in substance) in their views of the most promising approach to the closest achievable approximation of that ideal.

First, public policy should recognize the positive aspects of retailing's contribution, rather than simply stress such negative concepts as "too many intermediaries," "parasitism," and "hidden persuasion." Policymakers have tended to regard retailing as, at best, a necessary evil and have often overlooked many of the functions it performs for the total social and economic system. A number of the contributors to this symposium have reported at least some current modifications of such attitudes, but there is still room for substantial improvement.

Second, positive contributions should be expected from all retailing, and not just a part of it. Hence, policy should encourage the firms most likely to make such contributions, whether small or large, old or new, foreign or domestic, existing or potential. Encouragement should be available to viable existing firms as well as to prospective or potential future entrants. Public-policy instruments affecting entry, behavior, and exit should, therefore, be as non-discriminatory as possible. Moreover, government should extend whatever assistance is compatible with the economic deployment of available resources to help the less productive retail firms improve their efficiency.

Third, policy should be flexible so as to accommodate innovations in distribution, changes in economic pressures, new consumer needs, and modifications of existing value scales. In the face of such constant change and of demands for considering special situations (e.g., of a regional nature), one is likely to witness grants of flexible regulatory power to the exectuive and administrative branches of government, in lieu of fairly rigid laws in need of regular but difficult amendments. Discretionary powers are thus likely to increase and will therefore require the development of better consultative review and appeal procedures at the executive level. Building in some phasing-out procedures into a regulation will be another way of obtaining flexibility, even though removal always butts against vested interests for whom it represents an all-or-nothing proposition.

Finally, the principle of subsidiarity dictates that the state limit its intervention to "as little as possible, as much as necessary." In the case of retailing, where changing conditions are not very amenable to rigid regulation, this principle dictates that the state should establish the framework within which private rataling initiative will operate; and for the rest, inspire the development of retailing in the light of the public interest. Essentially this means three things: (1) banning or restricting practices that are clearly harmful and/or fraudulent; (2) leaving the main regulatory role to competition and self-regulation; and (3) providing positive social measures to alleviate the human costs of economic evolution.

The question then becomes one of whether such a policy is likely to emerge and if so, what are the recommendable measures for its achievement. The view advocated by J. Boddewyn points out that, generally speaking, governments have been increasingly framing particularistic policies for other socioeconomic sectors such as agriculture, research, energy, and transportation. These policies often contain explicit or (even more frequently) implicit implications for the distributive trades, although the input of information from those trades and the consideration of the distribution implications of these other policies is often fragmentary and haphazard. Besides, given the disorganized state of the retail trades in many countries, informal lobbying may fail in adequate representation of the interests of all (or even any) affected merchants.

Since no full-fledged return to laissez-faire is in sight, since disorganized lobbying is inadequate, and since better coordination of governmental initiatives and actions affecting retailing is required, *some organizational and conceptual modifications will then have to be introduced into the government-retailing interface.* This may involve new, or strengthened, consultative mechanisms such as the creation of new or reinforced statutory advisory bodies or commissions. It will also require stronger ministries or executive departments for commerce or possibly even for the distributive trades and services. Progress along these lines is evident but slow.

Additionally, self-regulation is advisable because some matters are better left to those more knowledgeable about retailing's problems and because of the growing demand for participation in the political process. Clearly, this approach demands great surveillance from the state lest some segment of retail self-interest take over against the common weal. The problem, however, is no harder to manage than that of the alternative, the use of regulatory commissions, which frequently become the captives of their industry. Besides, supervised self-regulation is clearly preferable to hidden collusion.

In those matters not susceptible to organized self-regulation, the administrative and executive branches of the government should possess flexible regulatory power, so as to permit adjustment to regional variations or to changing conditions. These powers should rest primarily on civil (rather than penal) sanctions to insure increased acceptance and support from the administrative and judicial branches. Some regulations may well contain preplanned programs for their own elimination, so as to avoid the ossification of archaic rules; and improved review and appellate procedures will be needed. In any case, all of these trade and governmental actions should rest upon an improved base of information concerning the distributive trades.

Hence, according to J. Boddewyn, there is a need for a separate public policy toward retailing in order to give greater attention and visibility to this sector, and in order to better insure coherence and articulation with other policies and sectors.

The modified view of this position, held by S. C. Hollander, holds that increased information and research are clearly necessary. To some extent it is the duty of the trade; and new and imaginative analytical programs are needed for trade progress. All of the country reviews included in this volume, moreover, demonstrate deficiencies in the input of retailing-oriented data in the policy-making process. (The gaps arise in part from the orientation of the policymakers, and in part from the rudimentary state of distribution research). The creation of new, and the strengthening of older, public and private research institutions seems highly desirable. *However, it is questionable whether this requires the framing of a "retail policy" per se.* Such a policy may, in fact, be dysfunctional for two reasons.

Philosophically, retailing is an instrument rather than an end. It exists to serve a variety of socioeconomic functions, as outlined in the Introduction to this volume. Consequently, optimal policy should be framed in terms of those primary functions, rather than in terms of any particular agency that exists for their achievement. Thus, models recently developed by the Michigan State University's Latin American Planning Project suggest that changes in retail structure will do little to improve food distribution efficiency in the developing countries unless accompanied by appropriate corresponding adjustments at the other levels of the marketing channel.[7] The practical problem, not easily resolved, is in insuring adequate attention to distribution problems when framing these function-oriented policies. A consumer policy, for example, that does not consider the practicalities of the distribution system may easily disadvantage, rather than help, its supposed beneficiaries.

A formalized public policy toward retailing also suggests some operational dangers. The chapters presented here indicate that government often treads with a heavy foot. Public policy toward trade frequently fails in accomplishing its objectives or pursues the wrong objectives; and the history of regulation in retail trade often seems to be a recital of barriers against progress. Those barriers do tend to whither away or to be overthrown when they become sufficiently unsuitable to the needs of a dynamic society, but the process is wasteful and time-consuming.

Government obviously should intervene when there are substantial externalities, that is, when the costs or benefits that trade in general or society suffers or receives because of some retailing development differ significantly from what the individual firm's cost-revenue calculus would recommend. Public action may be necessary at times to stimulate marketing and economic improvements in a stagnant society. *But the record indicates, according to this view of S. C. Hollander, that a policy of "no policy" can be preferable to what might develop under excessive or ill-advised planning.*

In spite of this divergence, the authors are again united in urging attention to the interrelationships between public policy and retailing on the part of retailers, governments, and marketing students. They are also united in believing that the chapters included herein will contribute to the process of discussing the relevance and proper contents of public policies toward retailing.

Notes

1. For an explanation of these concepts, see J. Boddewyn, "Marketing in Economy and Society," in George Fisk, ed., *New Essays in Marketing Theory* (Boston, Mass.: Allyn and Bacon, 1971), 409-21.

2. This list is adapted from E. S. Kirschen et al., *Economic Policy in Our Time,* Vol. I, *General Theory* (Chicago, Ill.: Rand McNally, 1964), 5-6.

3. See Henry Assael, "The Political Role of Trade Associations in Distributive Conflict Resolution," *Journal of Marketing* 32 (April 1968), 21-28.

4. Murray Edelman, *The Symbolic Use of Politics* (Urbana, Ill.: University of Illinois Press, 1964).

5. Ch. E. Lindblom and David Braybrooke, *A Strategy of Decision* (New York: The Free Press, 1963).

6. R. A. Bauer and K. J. Gergen, eds., *The Study of Policy Formation* (New York: The Free Press, 1968).

7. See H. N. Riley et al., *Market Coordination in the Development of the*

Cauca Valley Region – Colombia (East Lansing, Mich.: Michigan State University; Research Report No. 5, Latin American Planning Project, 1970); and Colin Guthrie, "Food Distribution in a Latin American City," Ph.D. dissertation, Graduate School of Business Administration, Michigan State University, 1972.

About the Contributors

Dole A. Anderson is Professor of Business Administration and Director of Research in the Graduate School of Business Administration, Michigan State University. He holds a Ph.D. degree from New York University where he taught for a number of years. During 1966-1968 he headed a foreign advisory team at the National Institute of Development Administration in Bangkok, where he wrote *Marketing and Development–The Thailand Experience.* He spent seven years in Brazil with the Michigan State University projects to establish schools of business in that country.

J. J. Boddewyn, Professor of Management and International Business, Graduate School of Business Administration, New York University, holds a Ph.D. degree from the University of Washington (Seattle), and a Commercial Engineer degree from Louvain University (Belgium). His publications include: *Comparative Management and Marketing, Belgian Public Policy Toward Retailing Since 1789, World Business Systems & Environments* (co-author), and *International Business-Government Relations* (with A. Kapoor).

Alain-Gérard Cohen is an *Inspecteur des Finances* seconded to the Director General for Domestic Trade and Prices, in the French Ministry of Economy and Finances. He graduated from the National Administration School (ENA), and holds a Doctorate in Economic Sciences from Paris' Faculté de Droit et Sciences Economiques. He assisted the Tunisian government in 1967-1968.

Pierre F. Cortesse is a graduate of the National Administration School (ENA, Paris). Presently he is a Civil Administrator within the French Ministry of Economy and Finance, and Chief of the Control Bureau for Petroleum Firms (Mission de Contrôle des Entreprises de Recherches, d'Exploitation, et de Transport de Produits Pétroliers). He is the former Director of the Commerce Section within the Domestic Trade and Prices Bureau (D.G.C.I.P.) of that Ministry, where he has served in several other high-level capacities since 1962.

Robert Curran is an Assistant Principal Officer in the Development Division of the Irish government Department of Finance, Dublin. He obtained a Bachelor of Engineering degree from the National University of Ireland (University College, Dublin) in 1959, and he received the Master of Arts degree in 1971. After spending two years with a major British synthetic fibers manufacturer, he joined the Department of Finance in 1961. Most of his subsequent career has been spent in the Development Division of the Department, concentrating on aspects of economic development and planning at national and regional levels, and assisting the work of the Distributive Trades Committee of the National Industrial Economic Council.

Donald F. Dixon, Professor of Marketing at Temple University, holds a Ph.D. degree from the University of London. He has taught at the University of Pennsylvania and Villanova University, and has been a visiting faculty member at the University of New South Wales. His publications in the fields of retailing and public policy have been concerned with the petroleum industry in Britain and the United States, and the food industry in the United States.

Susan Douglas is currently Visiting Professor of Marketing at the Centre d'Enseignement Supérieur des Affaires, Jouy-en-Josas—France. She has a Ph.D. degree in Business and Applied Economics from the University of Pennsylvania, and has taught at Temple University, Philadelphia. She has published various articles in the area of international marketing and consumer behavior in both American and European journals.

Marshall I. Goldman is a Professor of Economics at Wellesley College and an Associate of the Russian Research Center, Harvard University, the university from which he received the Ph.D. degree. His publications include *Soviet Marketing: Distribution in a Controlled Economy* (1963), *Soviet Foreign Aid* (1967), and *The Soviet Economy: Myth and Reality* (1968). Among other places, his articles have also appeared in the *Harvard Business Review, The Journal of Marketing, Foreign Affairs*, and *The Journal of Political Economy*.

J. F. Haccoû, the late Professor of Economics with special reference to Business Economics (the chair of organization of business life and marketing) at the University of Amsterdam, holds a doctoral degree from the Faculty of Economic Science of the same university. He previously held a chair in the University of Indonesia. He has received the International Award for Scientific Activities in the field of Commerce. His principal publications are: (in Dutch) *Futures Dealing in Commodities* (1947), *Commerce and Commodity Markets* (1957), *The Essentials of the Top-Manager's Function* (1951), *The Entrepreneur and His Function in Modern Economic Life* (1952), *Wholesaling: Dynamics and Prospects* (1970); and (in English) *Management of Direct Investments in Less Developed Countries* (1957), *Some Fundamental Problems of Policy Formation and Organization in the Commercial Field* (1957), "Wholesaling in the Netherlands," in Robert Bartels, ed., *Comparative Marketing: Wholesaling in Fifteen Countries* (1963).

Ingrid Hallencreutz works as a free-lance editor. After studies at the Universities of Uppsala and Stockholm she received the Master of Arts degree with economics as her main subject. She has especially studied and written about changes in private consumption and for some years has been a contributor to the Swedish trade magazine *Supermarket*. As a member of the city council of Västerås, she has been particularly interested in city planning, including among other things, the changes and development of retailing systems.

Polia Lerner Hamburger is Associate Professor of Marketing at the Escola de Administração de Emprêsas de S. Paulo da Fundação Getúlio Vargas, São Paulo, Brazil. She received her B.A. degree from the College of Philosophy, Sciences, and Arts, University of S. Paulo in 1955, the M.A. from Michigan State University in 1958, and will receive a Ph.D. from Michigan State in 1972. She is the author of several articles in the *Revista de Administração de Emprêsas de S. Paulo–RAE,* and is co-author of a textbook, *Marketing Management–Principles and Methods,* and of a monograph *Marketing in Small and Medium-Size Industries,* as well as co-editor of a casebook, *Cases in Marketing.*

Stanley C. Hollander, Professor of Marketing in the Graduate School of Business Administration, Michigan State University, received the Ph.D. degree from the University of Pennsylvania, where he also taught for a number of years. His books and monographs on retailing and related fields include: *Explorations in Retailing* (editor, 1959), *Restraints on Retail Competition* (1965), *Markets and Marketing in Developing Economies* (co-editor, 1969), *Multinational Retailing* (1970), and *Modern Retailing Management* (co-author, 1972). He is a member of the editorial boards of *The Journal of Marketing, The Journal of Retailing,* and *MSU Business Topics,* and he prepared the article on retailing in the *Encyclopaedia Britannica.*

Dov Izraeli is Professor of Marketing at the Tel-Aviv University Graduate School of Business Administration, and acts as a marketing consultant in Israel and Europe. He holds a B.A. degree from the Hebrew University, Jerusalem; a M.B.A. degree from New York University, and a Ph.D. from the Manchester Business School. His publications in the field of marketing include *Franchising and Total Distribution Systems, Israeli Cases in Marketing and Business Management* (Hebrew, co-author), *Readings in Marketing* (Hebrew, co-editor), *The Dictionary of Marketing Terms* (English-Hebrew and Hebrew-English, co-author), *The Cyclical Evolution of Marketing Channels, Voluntary Chains in Israel* (Hebrew, co-author), and various articles on marketing published in Israel (Hebrew).

Douglas F. Lamont, Professor of International Business at the University of Alabama, holds a Ph.D. degree from the University of Alabama. He previously taught at the University of Notre Dame, has been a Fulbright professor at Universidad Católica del Ecuador, and has been a Visiting Professor at Universidad de las Americas. He has lectured at the Helsinki School of Economics, Université de Nancy, and the University of North Carolina. His numerous publications in the fields of marketing and international business include: "Opportunities for Marketing Growth in the Mexican Market" and "Marketing Policy Decisions Facing International Marketers in the Less-developed Countries" (co-author). He is a member of the MILA Committee of the American Marketing Association, and of the Association for Education in International Business.

Helmut M. J. Laumer, a graduate in Business Economics, who received his doctor's degree from Munich University, is a research economist in the Trade Department of the Ifo-Institute for Economic Research at Munich, West Germany. He has carried out numerous investigations of structural and cyclical trends in wholesale and retail trade, both in the Federal Republic of Germany and in other countries. During 1966 and 1967, he served as an adviser in the Statistics Division of the Ministry of Planning and Economic Development at Entebbe, Uganda. His publications include *Labor Situation in Wholesale Trade, Macro and Microeconomic Aspects of Stockholding in Retail and Wholesale Trade, Distribution of Branded Articles in EEC Countries and Their Effects on Competition, Channels of Distribution in Industry and Trade* (co-author), *Structural Change and Progressive Strategy in Wholesaling* (co-author), *Mail Order Trading* (co-author), and *Market Structure and Competition in Retail Trade* (co-author)—all published in German. He contributed the chapter on "retailing" in the *Management Encyclopaedia,* and is editor of the business magazines *Wirtschaftskonjunktur* and *Ifo-Schnelldienst.*

Claude Lebédel heads the Economic, Financial, and Forecasting Division of the Research and Documentation Direction of the French National Assembly in Paris. He has published in several French and foreign journals.

Sven Lindblad is head of the Retail Information Section of the ICA Publishing Company in Sweden, a subsidiary of the ICA retailer-owned cooperative food chain. A graduate of the Filip Holmquist Business College in Gothenburg, Mr. Lindblad had several years' experience as a retailer before joining the ICA organization. He has been an editorial consultant to *Detaljhandelsboken* (a comprehensive dictionary for the retailer), and was responsible for the Swedish edition of *Self-Service: A New Way to the Customer.* He serves on various committees of the Swedish food trade and has lectured at numerous international conventions in Europe.

P. J. M. Lübbers is General Secretary of the Central Board of Retail Trade, The

Netherlands. In this function, Dr. Lübbers sits on several committees advising the Dutch government with regard to problems relating to the retail trade.

W. G. McClelland, M.B.A. (Manchester), M.A. (Oxford), is Director of the Manchester Business School and Professor of Business Administration in the University of Manchester. He has been a Senior Research Fellow at Balliol College, Oxford, a member of the Economic Development Committee for the Distributive Trades, and a member of the Consumer Council. He is chairman of Laws Stores Ltd., a chain of supermarkets in the north of England. His publications include: *Studies in Retailing* and *Costs and Competition in Retailing*, and he was founding editor of the *Journal of Management Studies*. He is a member of the National Economic Development Council and of the Social Science Research Council.

Helmut Soldner, Assistant Professor of Marketing at San Diego State University, holds a Ph.D. degree from the University of Erlangen-Nuernberg (Germany). He previously worked as a research fellow at Harvard University, Graduate School of Business Administration. He is the author of *The Downtown Area (CBD) as Shopping Center Under Changing Socio-Economic Conditions* (in German).

Max D. Stewart, Professor of Economics at The University of Alberta, holds the degrees: B.A. and B.Com., University of Alberta; M.A., University of Toronto; and Ph.D., Michigan State University. He has taught at the Royal Military College of Canada and at Waterloo Lutheran University. He has carried out economic research as a staff member at various times of The Value Line Investment Survey, New York; United Nations, Economic and Social Council; Combines Branch, Department of Justice, Ottawa; the Dominion Bureau of Statistics, Ottawa; and the Economic Council of Canada. His publications in the field of industrial organization include: *Concentration in Canadian Manufacturing and Mining Industries,* and an essay, "Industrial Organization" in L. H. Officer and L. B. Smith, eds., *Canadian Economic Problems and Policies.*

J. Hart Walters, Jr., Professor of Marketing at Temple University, holds A.B. and M.A. degrees from the University of California at Berkeley, and the Ph.D. degree from the University of Pennsylvania. He was chairman of the Marketing Department at Temple and Director of its Program in International Business. Previously he held faculty positions at Cornell University and at the George Washington University. His publications have been principally in the area of marketing and economic planning, and he has been a contributor to such journals as the *Journal of Marketing,* the *Indian Economic Journal,* and the Temple University *Bulletin of Economics and Business.* He has been the recipient of Ford Foundation fellowships for research in Poland and India.

Robert G. Wyckham is Associate Professor, Department of Economics and Commerce, Simon Fraser University, Burnaby, British Columbia, Canada. Publications in the retailing area include "Consumer Images of Retail Institutions" for the *Handbook of Marketing Research,* and "Perceptual Segmentation of Department Store Markets," *Journal of Retailing* with William Lazer. Marketing publications include: "American Marketing: Environment, Practice and Theory" *World Marketing* (co-author), and *Attitude and Image Research in Marketing: A Selected and Annotated Bibliography* (co-editor). He acts as academic consultant to the Institute of Canadian Bankers.

M. Y. Yoshino, Associate Professor of Management, Graduate School of Management, University of California (Los Angeles), received the M.B.A. degree from Columbia University and a Ph.D. from Stanford University. His major publications include *Japan's Managerial System: Tradition and Innovation* and *The Japanese Marketing System: Adaptations and Innovations.* His current research is concerned with the international expansion of major Japanese corporations and is sponsored in part by the Harvard Business School's Comparative Study of Multinational Corporations.

Index

460

Hire-Purchase, installment, transactions, 19
  conditional bills of sale, 19
  registration of, 19
  definition of, 19
  purchaser difficulties, 19–20

Industrial Commission, 27
Industrial Disputes (Amendment) Act of
    1909 (N.S.W.), 26
  subsequently Industrial Arbitration Act of
    1912, 26
Inudstries, Australian, Preservation Act of
    1906 (for public benefit), 25–26
  problems with application of, 26
  prosecution of, failures, 25
  repeal of, 1967, 28
Industries Act, N.S.W. Factories, Shops and,
    1962, 17
Industry, Board of, 27

Labor movement, development of, 24
Labor (reform) Party, 26
Liberal and Country Parties, 26
Liberal Country Party Coalition (replaced
    Act of the Trade Association Registra-
    tion Act of 1959), 28
Licensing,
  in Victoria, 1958, consolidation of, 13
  of fish retailers, 13
  of gasoline (in bulk), 13
  of milk, 13
  restrictive requirements, 12–13
    lack of, 32–33
Linkages, horizontal and vertical, 29, 31
Liquor Act of 1912 (N.S.W.), 12
Literature Board of Review, The, 13
  Literature, Questionable, Act, 1954
    (Queensland), 13
  "Playboy" Magazine case, 13

Marketing Court of Appeal, 30
Marketing and Packaging Codes, 1967, 16
  bylaws of Port Adelaide, 16
  Municipal Corporations Amendment Act,
    1903 (South Australia), 16
  Trade Marks Act, 1892 (South Australia),
    16
Marketing of Primary Products Act,
    1953–1956 (Victoria), 21
McEwen, J., Country Party Leader, 23
Melbourne, City Council of, 13
Menzies, Sir Robert, 23
Merchandising, 14, 15
  "scrambled merchandising," amendment,
    1900, 14
Milk Board of Western Australia, 1932, 21
  N.S.W., 1929, 21
  Victoria, 1933, 21
Milk Boards, legislation of, 13

Palmolive Company, 30
Parliament, Federal vs. state, 11, 31
Parliament of South Australia, 28
Personnel practices,
  "sitting accommodation," 14

Victorian Act, 1890, and amendment,
    1896, 14
Petrol, Uniform Price of, Western Australia
    Parliamentary Select Committee on,
    1957, 23
Petroleum products,
  Inflammable Liquids Acts, 1915 (N.S.W.),
    13
  Standard Oil (USA), 1901, 29
  subsidy scheme for, 1965, 23–24
Pharmacy Act, 1876 (Victoria), 12
Pharmacy, Board of, 12
Police Act, 1833 (N.S.W.), 14
Police Offences Act, 1900 (Victoria), 12
Police Offences Act, 1901 (N.S.W.), 14
Price controls, 21–23
  and price competition, 29
  end of, 21–22
  exception (petroleum products), 22
  importance of, 23
Price-fixing, retail ("refusal to deal"), 30
Price, Resale, Maintenance (RPM), 29–30
Prices Act Amendment, 1963, 28
Prices Commission, South Australia, deter-
    minant group, 22
Prices, Commonwealth, Adjustment Board,
    1916, 27
  Federal War Precautions Act, 27
Prices, Commonwealth, Commissioner, 25
Prices, control of "necessary" commodities,
    27
Prices, Fair, Act, 1924 (South Australia), 27
Profiteering Prevention Act of 1948, 22
Profiteering Prevention Act, 1920 (Queens-
    land), 30
Profiteering Prevention Acts, 1920 (N.S.W.
    and Queensland), 27
  example of (Queensland), 27
  replaced by Monopolies Act, 1923
    (N.S.W.), 27
Profits, Fair, Commission, 1920 (Victoria),
    27
Privy Council, 15, 21, 25
Public interest,
  concept, 32
  workers' and producers' interests favored
    vs. commercial, 25–26, 28
Public policy,
  on monopoly growth vs. small business
    protection, 24
  toward competition, 32
  underdevelopment of secondary indus-
    tries until 1900s, 24

Railroads, state ownership of, 24
Retail and trade associations, 14, 28
  N.S.W. Traders Protective Association, 15
Retailers, non-store,
  controls, 12
  Hawkers Act of 1904, Tasmania (liquor
    sales), 12
  Hawkers and Pedlars Acts, 1849, 12
  social attitudes toward, 12
  Victorian Hawkers and Pedlars Act, 1958,
    12